PARIS
ACCESS®

Paris

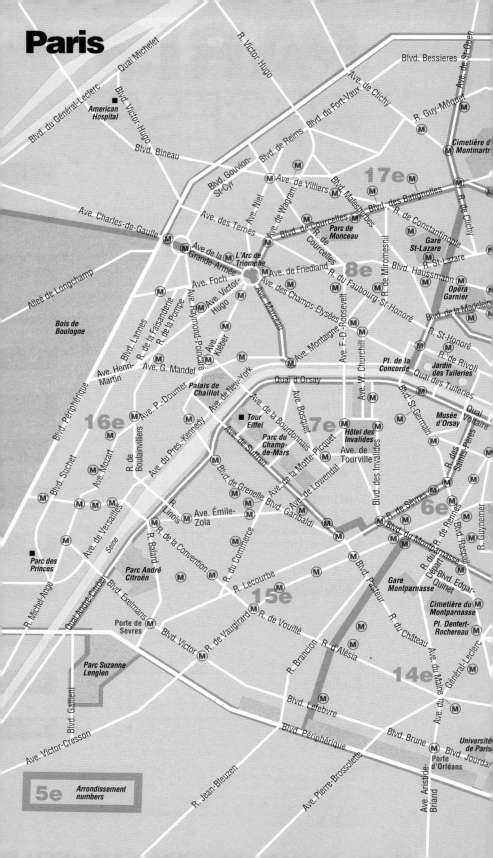

Quai Michelet
Blvd. du Général-Leclerc
American Hospital
Blvd. Victor-Hugo
Blvd. Bineau
R. Victor-Hugo
Ave. de Clichy
Blvd. Bessieres
Ave. de St-Ouen
Blvd. du Fort-Vaux
R. Guy-Môquet
Cimetière d Montmartr
Blvd. Gouvion-St-Cyr
Blvd. de Reims
Ave. de Villiers
Blvd. Malesherbes
17e
R. de Constantinople
R. de Clichy
Ave. de Wagram
Ave. Niel
Ave. des Ternes
Blvd. des Batignolles
Ave. Charles-de-Gaulle
Blvd. de Courcelles
R. de Courcelles
Parc de Monceau
R. de Miromesnil
Gare St-Lazare
R. St-Lazare
Ave. de la Grande-Armée
L'Arc de Triomphe
Ave. de Friedland
R. du Faubourg-St-Honoré
Blvd. Haussmann
8e
Opéra Garnier
Allée de Longchamp
Ave. Foch
Ave. des Champs-Elysées
Blvd. de la Madelein
R. St-Honoré
Bois de Boulogne
Ave. Raymond-Poincaré
R. de la Faisanderie
R. de la Pompe
Ave. Victor-Hugo
Ave. Kléber
Ave. Marceau
Ave. Montaigne
Ave. F.-D.-Roosevelt
R. de Rivoli
Blvd. Lannes
Ave. Henri-Martin
Ave. G. Mandel
Ave. W. Churchill
Pl. de la Concorde
Jardin des Tuileries
Quai des Tuileries
Blvd. Périphérique
Ave. P.-Doumer
Palais de Chaillot
Ave. de New-York
Quai d'Orsay
Blvd. St-Germain
Musée d'Orsay
Quai Voltaire
16e
R. de Boulainvilliers
Ave. du Pres.-Kennedy
Tour Eiffel
Ave. de la Bourdonnais
Ave. de Suffren
Ave. Bosquet
7e
Hôtel des Invalides
Ave. de Tourville
R. des Sts-Pères
R. Mozart
R. de Seine
Parc du Champ-de-Mars
Ave. de la Motte-Picquet
Ave. des Invalides
Blvd. Suchet
Blvd. de Grenelle
Ave. de Lowendal
R. de Sèvres
6e
Ave. Émile-Zola
Blvd. Garibaldi
Blvd. du Montparnasse
R. des
Départ.
Blvd. Raspa
Ave. Guynemer
R. Linois
R. de la Convention
Ave. de Versailles
R. Balard
R. du Commerce
R. Lecourbe
Gare Montparnasse
Blvd. Pasteur
R. de Rennes
Blvd. Edgar-Quinet
Parc des Princes
Parc André Citroën
15e
Cimetière du Montparnasse
R. Michel-Ange
Quai André-Citroën
Blvd. Exelmans
Porte de Sevres
Blvd. Victor
R. de Vaugirard
R. de Vouillé
R. Brancion
R. d'Alésia
R. du Château
Pl. Denfert-Rochereau
14e
Ave. du Maine
Ave. du Général-Leclerc
Parc Suzanne Lenglen
Blvd. Gallieni
Blvd. Lefebvre
Blvd. Périphérique
Blvd. Brune
Université de Paris
Blvd. Jourdan
Porte d'Orléans
Ave. Victor-Cresson
R. Jean-Bleuzen
Ave. Pierre-Brossolette
Ave. Aristide-Briand

5e Arrondissement numbers

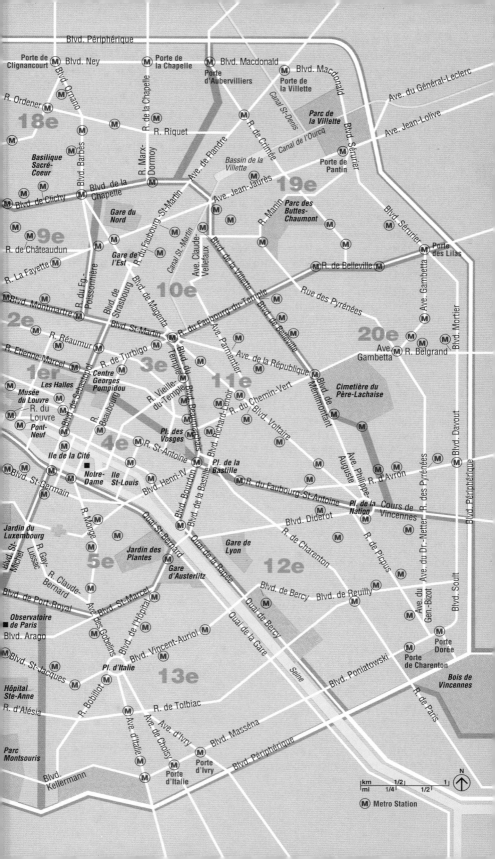

Orientation

"Paris is the greatest temple ever built to material joys and the lust of the eyes," wrote novelist Henry James. Indeed, the richness and variety of France's capital elevates even the necessities of life to works of art. Parisians seem to perform such everyday routines as eating and dressing with vitality and flair. The streets themselves are museums lined with splendid architecture and historic monuments, making even the simple act of walking through the city one of life's greatest pleasures.

Paris is located in the north-central part of France in the **Ile-de-France** region, in the **Seine** river valley. Covering only 40 square miles (105 square kilometers) and populated by over two million people, it is France's largest city and the densest of all European metropolises. It is roughly circular in shape and bounded by the **Boulevard Périphérique,** a ring road on the site of mid–19th-century fortifications that once defined the city limits.

Cutting across the whole map is a seven-mile stretch of the Seine river that separates Paris into two distinct areas, the northern **Rive Droite (Right Bank)** and southern **Rive Gauche (Left Bank).** The Seine unites rather than divides the city; Paris is linked by no fewer than 26 bridges in the city center alone. The quays are lined with fine apartment and town houses, *bouquinistes* (book sellers) and street artists, world-class museums such as the **Musée du Louvre** and the **Musée d'Orsay**, and dazzling monuments such as the **Tour Eiffel** and the **Cathédrale de Notre-Dame.** The Seine is alive with commercial barges and *bateaux mouches* (tour boats) taking sightseers up- and downriver to enjoy the panoramas, and the riverbanks are animated with people promenading along their course.

Each of the city's 20 arrondissements (quarters) boasts its own distinct character, so Paris feels less like a monstrous metropolis and more like a score of small towns. This book divides Paris into eight promenades throughout the city center, each covering a range of sights that convey some of the city's history and character. You may travel from the villagelike atmosphere of **Montmartre,** the **Latin Quarter,** or the **Marais** to the grandeur of the **Avenue des Champs-Elysées** and the **Hôtel des Invalides;** from the haute-couture shopping areas along the **Rue du Faubourg-St-Honoré** and the **Boulevard St-Germain** to the trendy areas around the **Bastille** and **Les Halles;** and to the two islands that form the physical and spiritual heart of the city, the **Ile de la Cité** and the **Ile St-Louis.** In Paris the past is ever present, and a stroll through the city of today is also a journey back in time.

Paris is an ancient city, more than 2,000 years old. Begun as a fishing village named Lutetia inhabited by a tribe called the Parisii, it was subsequently settled by the Romans and then became the capital city of the kingdom of the Franks. Under

Charlemagne the capital of France was moved to Aix-la-Chapelle, but Paris regained its capital status in 987 under Hugh Capet, the first of the Capetian line of kings. During the Middle Ages the city was an intellectual and religious center, but it lapsed into chaos during the Hundred Years' War with England (1337-1453), a period that also saw outbreaks of the bubonic plague.

The city again flourished during the Renaissance and saw significant expansion and development under the Bourbon kings of the 17th and 18th centuries. Although Louis XIV moved the court to **Versailles** in the late 17th century, Paris enjoyed great wealth and power during his reign, which was known as *Le Grand Siècle* (the Great Century). Under Louis XV Paris emerged as a center for culture and ideas, the arts flourished, and intellectuals such as Voltaire, Rousseau, Diderot, and Montesquieu were renowned throughout Europe. At the end of the 18th century, however, the extravagances of Louis XVI and his court led to the French Revolution and the bloodbath known as the Reign of Terror.

The instability following the Revolution allowed General Napoléon Bonaparte to seize control of the French government, and by 1804 he had proclaimed himself Emperor of France and set about making Paris the most magnificent city in the world. After Napoléon's defeat at Waterloo and subsequent exile, the Bourbon monarchy took one last gasp; then Napoléon's nephew assumed power, declaring himself Napoléon III in 1851. Like his uncle, he undertook a vast urbanization program. Unfortunately, however, he also embroiled the country in a succession of wars, culminating in the 1870 Franco-Prussian War, during which Paris suffered under siege and famine. The insurrection that followed France's capitulation to Prussia in 1871 saw violent massacres in Paris.

Ile de la Cité

By the end of the 19th century, Paris had recovered and was once again a driving force in Western culture. This optimistic period, known as the Belle Epoque (Beautiful Age), was captured in the work of the Impressionist painters. In the early part of this century, Paris became a mecca for intellectuals, artists, and philosophers, including Pablo Picasso, Georges Braque, Man Ray, Marcel Duchamp, Ernest Hemingway, Gertrude Stein, James Joyce, F. Scott Fitzgerald, Simone de Beauvoir, and Jean-Paul Sartre. After being occupied by the Germans, the city emerged from World War II with relatively little damage to its buildings and monuments. The 1950s, 1960s, and 1970s saw the construction of numerous modern buildings in Paris; more recently, the face of Paris has changed with the *grands projets* of the late Socialist president François Mitterrand.

Paris continues to evolve into the 21st century as one of Europe's most modern cities; yet it is at the same time an ancient city, with reminders of its remarkable history evident at every turn. The artistic and cultural capital of a unified Europe, the Paris of today offers a wealth of beauty and experiences. Few visitors fail to succumb to the splendor of this city, made even more appealing by the Parisian's love of grace, beauty, and fine living.

How To Read This Guide

PARIS ACCESS® is arranged so you can see at a glance where you are and what is around you. The numbers next to the entries in the following chapters correspond to the numbers on the maps.

The text is color-coded according to the kind of place described:

Restaurants/Clubs: Red   **Hotels:** Blue
Shops/ Outdoors: Green   **Sights/Culture:** Black

Rating the Restaurants and Hotels

The restaurant star ratings take into account the quality, service, atmosphere, and uniqueness of the restaurant. An expensive restaurant doesn't necessarily ensure an enjoyable evening; however, a small, relatively unknown spot could have good food, professional service, and a lovely atmosphere. Therefore, on a purely subjective basis, stars are used to judge the overall dining value (see the star ratings at right). Keep in mind that chefs and owners often change, which sometimes drastically affects the quality of a restaurant. The ratings in this guidebook are based on information available at press time.

The price ratings, as categorized at right, apply to restaurants and hotels. These figures describe general price-range relationships among other restaurants and hotels in the area. The restaurant price ratings are based on the average cost of a three-course meal for one person, excluding tax and tip. Hotel price ratings reflect the base price of a standard room for two people for one night during the peak season.

Restaurants

★	Good
★★	Very Good
★★★	Excellent
★★★★	An Extraordinary Experience
$	The Price Is Right (less than $25)
$$	Reasonable ($25-$70)
$$$	Expensive ($70-$120)
$$$$	Big Bucks ($120 and up)

Hotels

$	The Price Is Right (less than $75)
$$	Reasonable ($75-$150)
$$$	Expensive ($150-$300)
$$$$	Big Bucks ($300 and up)

At press time, the exchange rate was about 5.72 francs to $1 US.

Map Key

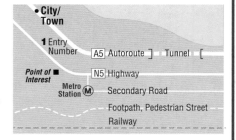

- City/Town
- 1 Entry Number
- A5 Autoroute] Tunnel [
- Point of Interest ■
- N5 Highway
- Metro Station Ⓜ
- Secondary Road
- Footpath, Pedestrian Street
- Railway

Getting to Paris

Airports

Roissy–Charles-de-Gaulle Airport

Twenty kilometers (12 miles) north of Paris, **Roissy–Charles-de-Gaulle Airport** is the busier of Paris's two airfields. It consists of two separate terminals: **Roissy I** handles all foreign carriers, and **Roissy II** services **Air France** only. Both have tourist information and money-exchange facilities, and a shuttle bus connects the two terminals.

Airport Services

Airport Emergencies/Security 01.48.62.31.22

Business Service Center 01.48.62.33.06

Currency Exchange 01.48.62.84.67

Customs and Immigration 01.48.62.35.35

Damaged Baggage 01.48.62.52.89

Information 01.48.62.22.80

Lost and Found

    Roissy I 01.48.64.51.92

    Roissy II 01.48.62.65.73

Medical Emergencies

    Roissy I 01.48.62.28.00

    Roissy II 01.48.62.53.32

Parking...01.48.62.12.83

Traveler's Aid 01.48.62.28.24, 01.48.62.59.00

Airlines

Air France 01.44.08.22.22, 800/237.2747

Lufthansa 01.42.65.37.35, 800/645.3880

Northwest 01.42.66.90.00, 800/225.2525

TWA ....01.49.19.20.00, 01.40.69.70.00, ... 800/221.2000

United 01.41.40.30.30, 800/241.6522

Getting to and from Roissy–Charles-de-Gaulle Airport

Barring any major traffic snarls, the trip to **Roissy–Charles-de-Gaulle Airport** from the center of Paris by bus, car, or taxi should take about 45 minutes. The **RER (Réseau Express Régional)** trains also provide 45-minute service, except during peak commuting hours when there may be significant delays. Play it safe by allowing about an hour and a half to reach your destination.

By Bus

The **Air France** bus (01.41.56.89.00) travels between the airport and the **Place Charles-de-Gaulle** (the **Arc de Triomphe**) and the **Place de la Porte Maillot** (both on the métro line **Grande Arche de La Défense/Château de Vincennes**). Buses leave every 15 minutes from 6:15AM to 9PM; the fare is 55 francs. The **Roissybus** (01.45.65.60.00) runs between the airport and the **Place de l'Opéra.** Buses leave every 15 minutes between 5.45AM and 11PM; the fare is 40 francs.

By Car

From the airport, take **Highway A1** south to the **Porte de la Chapelle** in the north of Paris, or **Highway N17** south straight to **Porte de la Villette** in the north of Paris. From Paris, take Highway A1 north from Porte de la Chapelle or Highway N17 north from Porte de la Villette to the airport. Shuttle service is offered from the parking lots to the terminals every eight minutes from 4:30AM to 1AM.

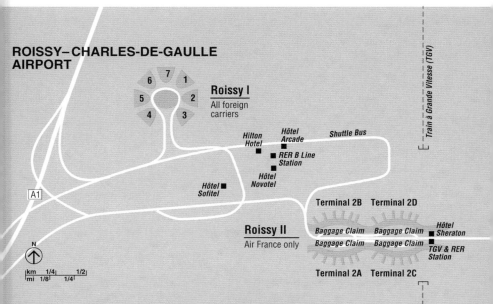

ROISSY–CHARLES-DE-GAULLE AIRPORT

Rental Cars

The following rental car companies have counters at **Roissy–Charles-de-Gaulle Airport;** all are open Monday through Friday from 6AM to midnight.

Avis..
    Roissy I.......................................01.48.62.34.34
    Roissy II...............01.48.62.59.59, 800/331.1084
Europcar ....
    Roissy I.......................................01.48.62.33.33
    Roissy II 01.48.62.56.47, 800/CAR.EUROPE
Hertz ....
    Roissy I.......................................01.48.64.29.00
    Roissy II...............01.48.62.58.58, 800/654.3001

By Limousine

To arrive in (or depart from) Paris in style, hire a chauffeur-driven private car, minibus, or stretch limousine. The trip from the airport into town (or vice versa) costs 700 to 900 francs for a private car, 1,100 to 1,200 francs for a limo (rates are slightly higher for night service).

The following limousine companies offer airport service 24 hours a day, seven days a week:

A Prestige Limousines 01.42.50.81.81
Avis Chauffeurs................................01.45.54.33.65
....800/331.1084
Biribin et Guarniéri 01.43.48.65.65
Martin Didier 01.45.54.71.07
Massey...01.43.80.04.37

By Taxi

There are a number of taxi stands at the airport (look for the signs) and there are usually plenty of cabs. A ride downtown will cost between 200 and 350 francs depending on traffic and your exact destination. Rates increase by 30 percent between 7PM and 6AM.

By Train

The **RER B** train runs between **Roissy–Charles-de-Gaulle Airport** and the **Gare du Nord, Châtelet–Les Halles,** and **Luxembourg** stations. One-way tickets, sold at all **RER** stations, cost 43.50 francs. Trains leave about every 15 minutes from 5:30AM to 11PM. Call 08.36.68.77.14 for **RER** information.

Orly Airport

Orly Airport, located 14 kilometers (9 miles) south of Paris, consists of two terminals: **Orly Sud** (south) handles both trans-Atlantic and European flights, and **Orly Ouest** (west) handles mostly domestic flights. Both terminals have tourist information and money-exchange facilities, and there is frequent transportation service into the city. A complimentary shuttle bus connects both terminals.

Airport Services

Airport Emergencies/Security...........01.49.75.43.04
Business Service Center...................01.49.75.12.33
Currency Exchange 01.49.75.78.40
Customs...01.49.75.78.50
Immigration/Border Police 01.49.75.43.04
Information ....
    Orly Sud.......................................01.49.75.77.48
    Orly Ouest....................................01.49.75.78.48
Lost and Found.......01.49.75.34.10, 01.49.75.42.34
Medical Emergencies 01.19.75.45.12
Parking...01.49.75.56.50

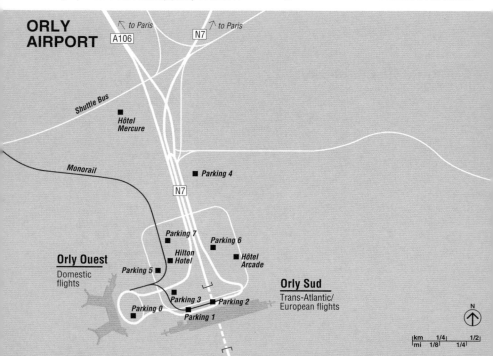

Airlines

American.................01.69.32.73.07, 800/433.7300

Continental..............01.42.99.09.09, 800/525.0280

Delta.......................01.47.68.92.92, 800/221.1212

USAirways 01.49.10.29.00, 800/428.4322

Getting to and from Orly Airport

Like **Roissy–Charles-de-Gaulle Airport, Orly** is about a 45-minute trip from the center of Paris by bus, car, taxi, or train. But allow an hour and a half just in case there are traffic tie-ups or other delays, which are common during weekday rush hours.

By Bus

The **Air France** bus (01.41.56.78.00) provides transportation between **Orly** and the **Air France** offices in the **Montparnasse** (25 Blvd de Vaugirard, between Pl Raoul-Dautry and Blvd Pasteur) or **Invalides** (Esplanade des Invalides, 2 Rue Robert-Esnault-Pelterie, between Rue de l'Université and Quai d'Orsay) sections of Paris. Departures are every 12 minutes from 5:50AM to 11PM; the one-way fare is 34 francs. The **Orlybus** (01.43.46.14.14) travels between the airport and the **Place Denfert-Rochereau**, also in the center of Paris. Buses leave about every 15 minutes from 6AM until 11PM. A one-way ticket costs 30 francs.

By Car

From the airport, take the **Highway N7** north to the **Porte d'Italie** in the south of Paris. From the Porte d'Italie, take the N7 south to **Orly.** The **P1** parking lot is closest to the **Orly Sud** terminal and the **P0** lot is closest to **Orly Ouest.** Free shuttle service operates every seven minutes between 5AM and 12:15AM from the **P4** through **P7** parking lots, which are farther away from the terminals.

Rental Cars

The following rental car companies have counters at **Orly Airport;** they usually are open Monday through Friday from 6AM to midnight.

Avis 01.49.75.44.92, 800/331.1084

Budget 01.49.75.76.00, 800/472.3325

Europcar............01.49.75.47.47, 800/CAR.EUROPE

Hertz 01.49.75.84.92, 800/654.3131

By Limousine

See the **Roissy–Charles-de-Gaulle Airport** entry (on page 8) for a list of companies that offer chauffeur-driven private car, minibus, or stretch limousine service to and from both airports. The trip from **Orly** into town (or vice versa) will cost 600 to 800 francs for a private car, 900 to 1,200 francs for a limo (rates are slightly higher for night service).

By Taxi

There are a number of taxi stands at **Orly;** look for signs. A ride into Paris will cost between 100 and 150 francs. Rates increase by 30 percent between 7PM and 6AM.

By Train

The **RER Orly Rail (C Line)** is linked to **Orly Airport** by shuttle bus; it connects with the **Gare d'Austerlitz, St-Michel/Notre-Dame,** and **Invalides** stations. Trains leave approximately every 15 minutes from 5:30AM to 11PM. Tickets are available at **RER** stations; the one-way fare is 28 francs.

Orly also is connected to the **RER B Line,** the métro, and train stations by the **Orlyval** monorail service from **Antony** station; the combined monorail/train trip takes about 30 to 45 minutes. The monorail operates from 6:30AM to 9:15PM Monday through Saturday, and 7AM to 10:55PM on Sunday. One-way fare is 54 francs, 25 francs for children under 12. Call 08.36.68.77.14 for **RER** information.

Bus Station (Long-Distance)

Buses arriving from other European cities disembark at the **Gare Routière Internationale** (Ave Général-de-Gaulle) in the eastern suburb of **Bagnolet.** The métro connection to the city center is via the **Galliéni** station. For bus information call **Eurolines** at 01.49.72.51.51.

Train Station (Long-Distance)

In Paris you can't simply jump into a taxi and cry *"A la gare!"* (To the station!). Paris has six train stations, each one offering service to different regions of France and Europe: **Gare d'Austerlitz** (53 Quai d'Austerlitz, between Pont de Bercy and Pl Valhubert), for southwest France, Spain, and Portugal; **Gare de l'Est** (Pl du 11-Novembre 1918, at Rue du 8-Mai 1945) for eastern France, Luxembourg, Switzerland, southern Germany, Austria, and Hungary; **Gare de Lyon** (Cour Diderot, off Blvd Diderot) for south and southeastern France, Switzerland, Italy, and Greece; **Gare Montparnasse** (17 Blvd de Vaugirard, between Pl Raoul-Dautry and Blvd Pasteur) for western France (including Versailles), Chartres, and Brittany; **Gare du Nord** (15 Rue de Dunkerque, between Rue du Faubourg-St-Denis and Pl de Roubaix) for northern France, Belgium, the Netherlands, Scandinavia, the former Soviet Union, northern Germany, and Britain; and **Gare St-Lazare** (20 Rue de Rome, between Pl Gabriel-Péri and Rue de Vienne) for north-western France, Normandy, and Le Havre, a port city where ships depart for Britain and the Americas.

Two types of train serve each station: *banlieue,* for riding to the suburbs, and *grandes lignes* for long-distance travel. Before boarding either type of train, you must *composter* (punch) your ticket in one of the orange machines in the station; if you fail to do this, the conductor might charge you the price of another ticket.

When reserving a ticket be sure to request either a *fumeur* or *non-fumeur* (smoking or nonsmoking) car. Reserved seats are available in both first and second class. First-class tickets are approximately

40 percent more expensive; the extra bucks buy you a slightly more comfortable seat, a less crowded car, and a fancier dining car. For reservations and general train information for all stations, call 08.36.35.35.35.

Getting Around Paris

The quickest and easiest ways of getting around Paris are by métro, taxi, and your own two feet.

Bicycle

Two wheels can be more fun—not to mention more hazardous—than four. Bicycle lanes are now a permanent fixture on most major routes in central Paris. Energetic and adventurous visitors can rent bicycles from **Paris Vélo** (2 Rue du Fer-à-Moulin, at Rue Geoffroy-St-Hilaire, 01.43.37.59.22) or **La Maison du Vélo** (11 Rue Fénelon, between Rue d'Abbeville and Rue de Belzunce, 01.42.81.24.72).

Paris is surrounded with beautiful, flat countryside that's perfect for bicycling. If you're planning day trips outside Paris—to **Chantilly, Fontainebleau,** or **Versailles,** for example—you may want to wait until you get to your destination and rent a bike for the day at the local train station. The **RER** stations in **Noisiel-le-Luzard, Vincennes, St-Germain-en-Laye, Courcelle Vallée de Chevreuse,** and **Vallée de la Marne** all have bikes for rent. During the summer, cycling trips outside Paris are sponsored by the **Bicy-Club de France** (8 Pl Porte-de-Champerret, at Ave de la Porte-de-Champerret and Blvd Gouvion-St-Cyr, 01.47.66.55.92). For general cycling information, contact the **Fédération Française de Cyclotourisme** (8 Rue Jean-Marie-Jégo, between Rues de la Butte-aux-Cailles and Samson, 01.44.16.88.88).

Boat

The **Batobus,** operated by **Compagnie des Batobus** (01.44.11.33.99), is a boat service that runs up and down the Seine from the beginning of May through the end of September. The circuit covers five stops: **Port de la Bourdonnais** (near the **Eiffel Tower**), **Porte de Solférino** (near the **Musée d'Orsay**), **Quai Malaquais** (opposite the **Louvre**), **Quai de Montebello** (near **Notre-Dame**), **Quai du Louvre** (near the **Louvre**), and **Quai de l'Hôtel-de-Ville** (near the **Hôtel de Ville**). For information on boat tours, see "Tours" on page 12.

In response to the city's worsening air pollution problem, a new system of pollution warnings was implemented in Paris in 1994. Under the system, motorists are asked—but not required—to leave their cars at home when air pollution levels are dangerously high. On 13 July, 1995, the Environmental Ministry told Parisians for the first time ever "not to use their cars except in absolute emergencies."

Bus

Riding the métro may be the quickest and easiest way to get around town, but buses are a far more pleasant means of transportation in Paris. The tourist office on the Champs-Elysées has selected more than a dozen get-acquainted bus routes for tourists, and it provides maps and trilingual (English, German, and Italian) commentary on the sights along the way. The *No. 24* bus, for example, makes a marvelous circuit of Paris. It crosses the Seine four times; passes **Place de la Concorde,** the **Assemblée Nationale,** the **Louvre, Pont-Neuf, Notre-Dame,** Ile St-Louis, and **Place St-Michel;** goes down Boulevard St-Germain; and finally turns back past the **Jardin des Plantes** and the **Musée d'Orsay**—all for just a few francs. The *No. 30, 48, 82,* and *95* routes are equally enjoyable.

Maps of the bus system are usually posted on the walls of bus shelters. **SITU (Système d'Information des Trajets Urbains)**—a computer that prints out the fastest routing onto a wallet-size piece of paper, complete with the estimated length of the trip—is located in such high-traffic spots as the **Châtelet** métro station, the **Gare Montparnasse,** and the Boulevard St-Germain. These handy streetside bus and métro directions are available free of charge.

When planning a sight-seeing excursion, remember that bus service is limited in the evening and on Sunday. The standard fare is one métro ticket; an additional ticket will be needed if you transfer to another bus. Bus tickets may be purchased from all métro stations, or you may buy a single ticket (for 8 francs) on the bus. Be sure to punch your ticket in the machine beside the driver when you board and hold onto your punched ticket throughout the trip; occasionally a *contrôleur* in a blue uniform boards the bus to check them. Those without punched tickets receive heavy fines. For discount ticket and pass information, see "Métro" below; for information on bus tours, see "Tours" below.

Car

Those planning on driving in Paris stand forewarned: The most civilized Parisian becomes a homicidal maniac on the road. Stoplights are routinely ignored and one-way streets simply imply a challenge. Rush hour is from 8 to 10AM and 5 to 7PM on weekdays. Conditions are also rough on Sunday nights between 5 and

9PM, when weekend travelers are heading back into the city. If you have a suicide wish, hire a car and drive around the **Arc de Triomphe** a few times. *Bonne chance.*

If you dare to drive, the main car rental agencies are: **Avis** (5 Rue Bixio, at Ave de Ségur, 01.44.18.10.50, or 60 Rue de Ponthieu, at Rue de Berri, 01.45.62.82.50); **Hertz** (92 Rue St-Lazare, at the Gare St-Lazare, 01.42.80.35.45, or Esplanade des Invalides, 2 Rue Robert-Esnault-Pelterie, between Rue de l'Université and Quai d'Orsay, 01.45.51.20.37); and **Europcar** (48 Rue de Berri, between Rue du Faubourg-St-Honoré and Blvd Haussmann, 01.53.93.73.40). These companies also have offices at **Roissy–Charles-de-Gaulle** and **Orly Airports.** *Europcar* offers a nonresident discount, but you must make your reservations 24 hours before arriving in France, and there is a minimum rental period of three days and a maximum of 99 days. Be sure to take out car insurance if you aren't covered by your own auto insurance or insurance offered by your credit card company. Auto insurance coverage offered by American Express and Visa is valid in Europe.

Métro

It's one of the oldest—and best—subway systems in Europe. The first line, designed by engineer Fulgence Bienvenue, opened on 19 July 1900 between **Porte Maillot** and **Vincennes.** In the early 1900s, the station entrances were Art Nouveau masterpieces designed by Hector Guimard. These days, the symbol of the system is the aqua-and-brown ticket of the **RATP (Réseau Autonome du Transport Parisien).**

Nearly 120 miles of rail snake beneath the streets of Paris, connecting about 300 stations. Aboveground, you're never very far away from a métro stop, and for the cost of a single ticket you can ride all day anywhere within the system, which operates between 5AM to about 12:45AM (each train pulls into its final destination at 1:15AM). Hang onto your ticket: occasionally a *contrôleur* in a blue uniform boards the train to check them.

Getting lost in Paris takes some effort. Métro maps (see inside back cover) are everywhere—inside and outside the stations. And the métro lines are named for the stations at which they end. Simply follow the signs for the terminus in the direction you are headed. If, for example, you want to go from the **Louvre** to **Concorde,** take the line marked **Direction Neuilly.** To transfer from one line to another, look for an orange-and-white *correspondance* sign on the station platform. Each station has a map of the neighborhood surrounding it, so you can get your bearings before you emerge aboveground.

When purchasing tickets, it's cheaper to buy a *carnet* (book) of 10 (46 francs), which cuts the price of a single ticket (8 francs) nearly in half. Also available are tourist passes, which are valid for both the métro and the bus. The *Formule 1* pass (30 to 100 francs, depending on the number of zones covered) is valid for one day; *Le Paris Visite* pass is good for two days

(70 to 170 francs) or five days (165 to 315 francs); and the *carte orange* offers a week (72 to 213 francs) or month (243 to 741 francs) of travel privileges and requires a photograph.

Slip the magnetized ticket into the slot by the turnstile, retrieve it when it pops up, and pass through. Remember that when getting on and off the métro you must open the car door yourself; it closes automatically behind you.

A métro ticket also allows you to use the **RER** rail system (an express métro) within Paris, but study its route before you board because it is primarily a suburban line, and the stops within the city are few and far between. Always hang onto your tickets; you may need them to get in and out of the station. Call 01.36.68.77.14 for métro information.

Parking

If you think driving in Paris is tough, wait until you try to park your car. Vehicles may not be left in one spot on Parisian streets for more than 24 hours. Signs indicate special parking zones, including streets on which parking is allowed on the odd-number side for the first half of the month and the other side for the second half; parking-meter zones (meters are in effect from 9AM to 7PM except Sunday and holidays; August is classed as a holiday in certain quarters of Paris); and "Zone Bleu" areas, in which cars may not be parked for more than one hour between 9AM and 12:30PM and 2:30 and 7PM. Your best bet is to find an underground parking lot, which are located throughout the city; look for "Parking" signs. If your car is towed be prepared to pay a 450-franc fine plus an additional daily charge to recover the vehicle.

Taxis

Most of the time, Paris's 15,000 taxis are clustered at *têtes de station* (taxi stations) throughout the city—except, of course, when you really need one. Hailing a cab is not an acceptable practice in Paris; taxis will not stop in the middle of the street to accept passengers. Your best bet is to locate a *tête de station* (look for the blue-and-white sign) and wait for the next taxi with a bright roof light (a dim light means the cab is occupied). Even then drivers may not pick you up, because if you're not going in their direction, *tant pis* (tough luck). Fake some understanding of the city and tell drivers the main street or métro station closest to your destination; given that guidance they are less likely to take you out of your way. Taxis usually aren't expensive, but the rates increase between 10PM and 6:30AM, on Sunday, and if you're picked up at a train station, hotel, or outside the city. If you need to be somewhere at a specific time (including the airport), call ahead for a taxi; the meter starts running the moment the driver receives the call, but the dispatcher will tell you how long it will take for the cab to arrive (it's usually less than 10 minutes). Tip the driver 10 to 15 percent. To call for a taxi, dial 01.49.36.10.10, 07.55.90.70, 01.47.39.47.39, or 01.46.85.85.85.

Tours

To observe the city through the windows of a climate-controlled, double-decker tour bus, climb aboard one of the coaches of **Cityrama** (4 Pl des Pyramides, at Rue de Rivoli, 01.44.55.61.00) or **Paris Vision** (214 Rue de Rivoli, between Rues du 29-Juillet and d'Alger, 08.00.03.02.14). Both companies offer tours (in several languages) past all the main attractions, as well as separate excursions to Versailles, **Malmaison,** Chantilly, **Chartres,** Fontainebleau, **Mont St-Michel,** the **Loire Valley,** and **Barbizon.** They also run "Paris by Night" tours to the **Moulin Rouge, Lido,** and **Folies Bergère.**

On a late summer afternoon, nothing could be better than spending an hour touring the Seine river in a *bateau mouche* (a small passenger steamer), especially if you take along some creamy goat cheese, a fresh baguette, and a bottle of cool St-Joseph. Take a seat at the rear of the boat out of range of the irritating tape-recorded commentary, then put your feet up and watch the sun set over the City of Light. For a more luxurious trip, book one of the expensive candlelit dinner cruises. Tours lasting between one and three hours (the longer ones feature lunch or dinner) are available from **Bateaux Mouches** (Embarcadère du Pont de l'Alma, at Pont de l'Alma, Right Bank, 01.42.25.96.10), **Bateaux Parisiens** (Port de La Bourdonnais, at the foot of the Eiffel Tower, 01.44.11.33.44), and **Vedettes du Pont-Neuf** (Sq du Vert-Galant, just west of Pl du Pont-Neuf, Ile de la Cité, 01.46.33.98.38). The boats operated by **Vedettes du Pont-Neuf** tend to be smaller and have live guides rather than recorded commentary.

Tours of the **Canal St-Martin** are offered from April through November by **Paris Canal** (01.42.40.96.97). The offbeat three-hour cruises run between the **Musée d'Orsay** and the **Parc de la Villette,** pass through 1.5 miles of subterranean tunnel under the **Place de la Bastille,** and encounter nine locks and two turning bridges en route. Reservations are required.

For serious shoppers who want the inside scoop on where and what to buy, **Chic Promenade** (7 Rue Le Châtelier, between Ave de Villiers and Blvd Berthier, 01.43.80.35.35) offers four shopping tours (each about four hours long) with bilingual guides on weekday afternoons and Saturday mornings. Stroll the Left Bank or the Marais, peruse the flea markets, or go whole hog with the VIP tour—a private shopping spree in a chauffeur-driven limousine for you and a few of your closest friends.

France has the fourth biggest economy in the world according to figures published by *The Economist.* It is the home of four of the world's largest banks and has the 12th-highest GDP per head, following Switzerland, the United States, and Japan.

Walking

Whether by promenading along the broad boulevards or threading your way through intimate medieval neighborhoods, the best way to discover Paris and its environs is on your own two feet. As you will learn on the itineraries outlined in this book, strolling yields the joy of discovering the little things—the grace notes, embellishments, and architectural details that define the feel and texture of Paris. But walking can be a somewhat perilous proposition: On the street you're fair game for distracted drivers, and on the sidewalk you're likely to tread on what dogs have left behind. Every third Parisian owns a dog, and someone in city hall has calculated that the average pedestrian sets foot in canine droppings every 286th step. As a result, ever-vigilant squads of sanitation workers on motorcycles sweep and vacuum the sidewalks of Paris constantly.

FYI

Accommodations

Hotel reservations are essential in Paris not only in the summer months but also during the heavy convention and trade-show months of March and October. Many hotels require a credit card number to hold your reservation, while some of the smaller budget hotels do not accept credit cards at all. Keep in mind that hotel rates rise regularly and renovations often prompt hotels to raise their prices, so it is always sensible to call in advance to check rates. If you do arrive without accommodations, contact the **Office de Tourisme de Paris** (see "Visitors' Information Office," page 17). The tourist office also offers a free brochure charting room availability throughout the year.

For those looking for an alternative to the traditional hotel room, the **Organisation pour le Tourisme Universitaire (OTU)** maintains more than 700 clean, safe, inexpensive beds in youth centers throughout the Paris area. Reservations must be made in person, and those 35 years of age and under have priority. Rooms generally sleep one to eight people, and bathrooms are shared. The centers in the Marais quarter, housed in 17th-century mansions, are the most desirable.

There are three **OTU** offices in Paris (for information call 01.40.29.12.12): **OTU Beaubourg** (119 Rue St-Martin, at Pl Georges-Pompidou); **OTU Port Royal** (39 Ave Georges-Bernanos, between Blvds de Port-Royal and St-Michel); and **OTU Jussieu** (2 Rue Malus, at Rue de la Clef). To secure a room, get to one of the offices by 9AM, when they open.

If you prefer renting an apartment, contact **Paris-Accueil Locaflat** (63 Ave de la Motte-Piquet, 75015 Paris, 01.40.56.99.50). **The French Experience** (370

Lexington Ave, New York, NY 10017, 212/986.1115) also arranges bed-and-breakfast accommodations, as well as apartment and country cottage rentals and hotel reservations.

Addresses

Parisian addresses include a street name and a number, *plus* which of the 20 arrondissements (quarters) it is in. For instance, an address in the Latin Quarter (fifth arrondissement) might be "23 Quai St-Bernard, 5e, or 75005 Paris" (the small "e" is the French equivalent of an English "th"), while an address in the Ile St-Louis (first arrondissement) would read "25 Place Dauphine, 1er, or 75001 Paris" ("er" standing in for the English "st").

Cafes

As noble a French institution as the **Académie Française,** cafes serve light meals and a variety of beverages throughout the day. Try a *crème* (strong coffee with hot, frothy milk) in the morning; in the afternoon you might switch to *vin rouge* (red wine), *un demi* (a 25-centiliter draft beer), or a *citron pressé* (fresh lemonade). Drinks are cheaper at the *zinc* (bar), and coffee is more expensive after 10PM, but by then you'll probably have moved on to cognac, Armagnac, or perhaps eau de vie.

Cinema

Parisians are film fanatics. Each week more than 300 films are shown in the city; all are listed along with their show times in the weekly publications *Pariscope* and *L'Officiel des Spectacles.*

The *v.o. (version originale)* after a film title means the movie is being shown in its original language with French subtitles; *v.f. (version française)* means it's dubbed in French. If you arrive in time for the *séance* (previews), you'll see the ads, which are sometimes risqué, usually silly, and often themselves worth the price of admission. Once in the movie theater, be prepared to surrender a franc to the usher, who may do no more than tear your ticket and gesture toward an empty seat. If you resent this practice, go to the movies on Monday, when ticket prices are uniformly reduced by 30 percent.

Climate

Chances are that fabled Paris in the springtime will be soggy. The city logs more rainy days a year than London, so bring an umbrella or trench coat. Winters are cold and damp, and summers can be as cool and dry as the martinis at the **Ritz** bar. The average temperature ranges from 38 degrees in January to 75 degrees in July. May and September are the best times for finding decent weather and fewer tourists. August, when most Parisians leave the city, can be hot.

Months	Average Temperature (°F)
December-February	46
March-May	58
June-August	76
September-November	61

Drinking

The legal drinking age is 18. Bars typically are open from 10 or 11AM until 2 or 4AM. Drunk driving has become a problem, so police often stop erratic drivers for breath tests and fine them on the spot.

Embassies and Consulates

American Embassy (2 Ave Gabriel, at Rue Boissy-d'Anglas, 01.43.12.22.22)

American Consulate (2 Rue St-Florentin, at Rue de Rivoli, 01.40.20.01.99)

Australian Embassy (4 Rue Jean Rey, between Ave de Suffren and Quai Branly, 01.40.59.33.00)

British Embassy (35 Rue du Faubourg-St-Honoré, between Rues Boissy-d'Anglas and de l'Elysée, 01.44.51.31.00)

British Consulate (9 Ave Hoche, between Rues de Courcelles and du Faubourg-St-Honoré, 01.42.66.38.10)

Canadian Embassy/Consulate (35 Ave Montaigne, at Rue François-1er, 01.44.43.29.00)

Metric Conversions

France uses the metric system. Equivalents are the following:

one kilometer = .6214 miles

one meter = 3 feet, 3.37 inches

one centimeter = .394 inches

one square meter = 10.76 square feet

one hectare = 2.471 acres

one liter = I liquid quart, .1134 pints

one liter = .2642 gallons

one kilogram = 2.20 pounds

one degree celsius = 1.8 degrees Fahrenheit

Entry Requirements
In 1989 France and the United States reached a bilateral accord eliminating the tourist visa requirements between the two countries. Passports are always required when traveling abroad.

Health and Medical Care
For round-the-clock medical house calls, call **SOS Médecins** (01.43.37.77.77). The **American Hospital** is just outside Paris (63 Blvd Victor-Hugo, between Blvds du Château and de la Saussaye, Neuilly-sur-Seine, 01.47.47.70.15); most of the physicians there speak English. An English-language crisis line (operated 3-11PM) can be reached by dialing 01.47.23.80.80.

In Paris, all pharmacies are marked by a neon green cross on the front of the building. When the cross is lit, it means the pharmacy is open for business. Although many pharmacists speak English, you will be certain to get English prescriptions translated and filled with equivalent medicines at the following places: **British and American Pharmacy** (1 Rue Auber, at Pl de l'Opera, 01.47.42.49.40), **Pharmacie Anglaise** (130 Rue La Boétie, at Ave des Champs-Elysées, 01.43.59.22.52), and **Pharmacie Swann** (6 Rue de Castiglione, between Rues de Rivoli and du Mont-Thabor, 01.42.60.72.96).

Holidays
On *jours feriés* (national holidays) most shops and businesses, including banks, are closed, while many museums and restaurants stay open. Buses don't run, but the métro remains operational.

Jour de l'An (New Year's Day), 1 January

Lundi de Pâques (Easter Monday), 12 April 1998

Fête du Travail (Labor Day/May Day), 1 May

Fête de la Victoire (VE—Victory in Europe—Day), 8 May

Fête de l'Ascension (Ascension Day), 21 May 1998

Fête Nationale/Jour de la Bastille (Bastille Day), 14 July

Fête de l'Assomption (Assumption Day), 15 August

Toussaint (All Saints' Day), 1 November

Armistice (Armistice Day), 11 November

Noël (Christmas), 25 December

Hours
Shops are usually open from 10AM to 7PM Monday through Saturday, but many observe the tradition of closing on Monday or for lunch (noon-2PM). Some larger department stores stay open one night a week, usually Thursday; they also may offer additional hours during busy holiday seasons. Most Parisian museums are open from 10AM to 6PM; many stay open until 10PM one night a week. Museums are open on Sunday, but many are *fermé* (closed) on Monday or Tuesday. Restaurants and cafes generally are open from noon to 2PM and 7 to 10:30PM.

While August is still the *fermeture annuelle,* when many Parisians flee the city on vacation and leave countless shops and restaurants closed in their wake, more and more stores and restaurants are staying open during this time. Annual closing times may vary from one year to the next.

In this book, opening and closing times for shops, attractions, cafes, etc., are listed by day(s) if the normal hours described above apply. In all other cases, specific hours will be given (e.g., 6AM-2PM, daily 24 hours, noon-5PM).

Laundry
Self-serve *laveries* are peppered throughout the city. Try the **Dorvag** (25 Rue des Rosiers, between Rues des Ecouffes and Vieille-du-Temple, 01.48.87.37.33); **Laverie Self-Service Monge** (113 Rue Monge, between Ave des Gobelins and Rue Censier, 01.47.07.68.44); or **Louise Delpuech** (24 Pl du Marché-St-Honoré, between Rues du Marché-St-Honoré and Gombaust, 01.42.61.04.49). Most are open Monday through Saturday, 8AM to 8PM.

Money
The basic unit of French currency is the franc (abbreviated F), which is divided into 100 centimes. There are 500F, 200F, 100F, 50F,

and 20F bills, and 20F, 10F, 5F, 2F, 1F, ½F, 20-centime, 10-centime, and 5-centime coins.

Banks are generally open from 9AM to 4:30PM, but they close at midday the day before a holiday. They will display a sign reading *"change"* if they exchange foreign currency. For the best exchange rates, try **American Express** (11 Rue Scribe, at Rue Auber, 01.47.77.77.07), which is open on Saturdays. If you're stuck with dollars and the banks are closed, you can change money at these train stations: **Gare d'Austerlitz** (until 8PM), **Gare de l'Est** (until 7PM), **Gare St-Lazare** (until 7PM), and **Gare de Lyon** (until 11PM). (For train station locations, see page 9.)

Credit cards are in wider use here than elsewhere in Europe. Automatic teller (ATM) machines are common; check with your bank or credit card company about using cash machines in Paris.

Museums
Most Parisian museums stay open late one night a week and are open on Sunday, but many are closed on Monday or Tuesday. If you're planning on some serious museum-hopping, buy a *carte* pass, which allows you to pay reduced admission fees at more than 60 Parisian museums and monuments and costs between 80 and 240 francs. You can buy a pass that's valid for one, three, or five days. They are sold in major métro stations and at most of the participating attractions.

Personal Safety
As recently as 1996 Paris was shocked by several terrorist bombings, all in the city center. The bombs,

planted in or near subway and train stations, outdoor markets, and in other crowded spots, killed nine people and injured nearly 200 others.

French authorities believe the bombings are the work of Islamic militants who are protesting France's ties to the military government in Algeria. Two related bombings took place in Lyons during 1995.

In response to the bombings, at press time there was an increased police presence at borders, airports, and railway stations, and additional police patrolled the streets and the city's public transportation system. Police officers and the military were conducting random checks of métro and bus passengers' identification and bags, and announcements and signs throughout the transit system requested passengers' cooperation and their assistance in reporting suspicious parcels. In addition, the army had been called in to protect the **Arc de Triomphe** and the **Eiffel Tower;** trash cans throughout the métro system and on Paris streets had been sealed; and security agents routinely checked customers' bags in department stores, theaters, and museums.

Authorities were not recommending any special precautions at press time, although travelers were advised to carry passports in the unlikely event of being stopped by police for an identity check.

Aside from this unusual situation, Paris is normally a safe city and visitors generally need only to concern themselves with pickpockets, who flock to tourists like fruit flies to bananas. The busy métro lines, such as **Grande Arche de La Défense** to **Château de Vincennes,** are these thieves' natural habitat. In general, be aware of your surroundings. Watch your money pouch, keep the clasp of your purse against your body, and don't put your wallet in your back pocket, especially if it bulges. Beware of bands of children—sometimes they possess a sleight of hand Fagin would have envied. Don't wear jewelry in crowded places (like on the métro or at Montmartre) and don't leave possessions unattended.

Post Offices

Post offices are marked **PTT** and are open from 8AM to 7PM on weekdays and 8AM to noon on Saturday. The main post office (52 Rue du Louvre, at Rue Etienne-Marcel) is open 24 hours a day. If you want to buy stamps, make sure you're in the correct line and not wasting your time queuing up at the window where Parisians pay their gas and telephone bills. Stamps are also sold at *tabacs* (tobacco shops), hotels, and some newsstands.

Publications

The English-language *International Herald Tribune* (a felicitous child of the *Washington Post* and *The New York Times*) will keep you abreast of world events and Parisian happenings. It appears at newsstands every morning except Sunday. The French dailies in Paris are *Le Monde, Le Figaro,* and *Libération.*

For weekly listings of exhibitions, movies, concerts, plays, discos, and restaurants, pick up a copy of

Pariscope or *L'Officiel des Spectacles,* which both come out on Wednesday. They are sold for a few francs at newsstands, and although they're written in French, they are possible to decipher even if you do not speak the language. *Pariscope* includes a guide in English published by *Time Out,* highlighting restaurants and giving the entertainment schedules for the week.

Radio Stations (English-language)

The only English-language radio station in Paris is the **European News Service (ENS),** a cable station that broadcasts to 30 major hotels. If you have a very strong receiver, however, you may be able to pick up the BBC or even Voice of America.

Rest Rooms

You can usually walk into any cafe and use the toilet, though in some cases you must tip the *gardienne* (keeper) a couple of francs. Such a facility may be a hole or a throne, with or without toilet paper. Your alternative is using the beige automatic toilets in the streets. For a couple of francs, these clever contraptions automatically let you in and out and disinfect themselves between visits. Warning: Don't let young children into the automatic toilets alone; they may not be strong enough to push open the doors to get out.

Restaurants

The French generally lunch between noon and 2PM, and dine between 7:30 and 10PM. To dine at a particularly popular restaurant such as **Taillevent** or **Lucas-Carton,** you might have to book reservations months in advance, but in most cases advance notice of one week, or even a day or two, should suffice. In less expensive restaurants, reservations are not usually necessary. In many dining spots you may either order à la carte or choose a less expensive fixed-priced menu, which often includes the day's special. The fancier restaurants usually offer a *dégustation* (sampler) of the chef's specialties. If the wine list puzzles you, ask the waiter or the sommelier for advice; remember, the quality of the wine does not necessarily increase with the price. A 15-percent service charge is almost always included in the bill.

Shopping

Perhaps no other city in the world enjoys such a reputation as a shoppers' mecca. Haute couture, jewelry, perfume, and gourmet delights are all here. The big department stores are mostly located near **Boulevard Haussmann** and the **Opéra** district. The most chic boutiques are located in the 6th, 7th, 8th, 16th, and 17th arrondissements.

Big department stores include

Galeries Lafayette (40 Blvd Haussmann, at Rue de Mogador, 01.42.82.34.56, and other locations), **Printemps** (64 Blvd Haussmann, at Rue de Caumartin, 01.42.82.50.00), **La Samaritaine** (19 Rue de la Monnaie, between Quai du Louvre and Rue de Rivoli, 01.40.41.20.20), **Le Bazar de l'Hôtel de Ville (BHV,** 52 Rue de Rivoli, at Rue des Archives, 01.42.74.90.00), and **Au Bon Marché** (main store, 22 Rue de Sèvres, at Rue Velpeau, 01.44.39.80.00). Also worth a visit are such major shopping centers as **Porte Maillot** (Pl de la Porte-Maillot, at Aves de la Grande-Armée and de Neuilly, 01.45.74.29.09), **Maine Montparnasse** (Pl du 18-Juin 1940, at Blvd du Montparnasse and Rue de Rennes), **Forum des Halles** (at Rues Pierre-Lescot and Rambuteau, 01.44.76.96.56), the glass-roofed **Galerie Vivienne** (main entrance at 4 Rue des Petits-Champs, between Rues des Petits-Pères and Vivienne, 01.42.60.08.23), **Carrousel du Louvre** (beneath the Arc de Triomphe du Carrousel, 01.46.92.47.47), and the posh **Passy Plaza** (53 Rue de Passy, at Pl de Passy, 01.40.50.09.07).

In addition to elegant designer boutiques for fashion, shoes, and leather goods, the best (and most expensive) antiques dealers are along the **Rue du Faubourg-St-Honoré** on the Rive Droite. On the Rive Gauche, there's **Le Carré Rive Gauche,** an association of more than 100 antiques shops in the area bordered by **Rues des Sts-Pères** and **Rue du Bac,** and **Rue de l'Université** and **Quai Voltaire.** Antiques and curio collectors also should explore such flea markets as **Puces de la Porte de Montreuil** (at Ave de la Porte-de-Montreuil), especially good for secondhand clothing; **Puces de la Porte de Vanves** (at Aves Georges-Lafenestre and Marc-Sangnier), for furniture and fine bric-a-brac; and the largest and best known, **Marché aux Puces de St-Ouen** (more commonly called the **Puces de Clignancourt;** Blvd Périphérique, at Porte de Clignancourt), which offers an admirable array of antiques. The **Marché Biron** is one of the best of the smaller markets that make up the **Puces de Clignancourt;** it is especially good for fine bric-a-brac. Most of the flea markets are held weekends year-round, no matter the weather.

To protest the proliferation of puppy poop on the sidewalks of Paris, 12 professors and artists got down and dirty during the summer of 1995. On Rue Legouvé in the 10th arrondissement, the team transformed 200 sidewalk specimens into still lifes by circling each mess with chalk to form a plate, then adding real spaghetti, salad, flatware, and glasses. Passersby were disgusted, which was just the point: to shame Parisians into curbing their dogs. "Telling the French not to do something doesn't do a bit of good," said an organizer. Every year 650 pedestrians land in the city's hospitals after slipping on dog doo.

Smoking

French law prohibits smoking in the métro and requires that all restaurants provide separate smoking and nonsmoking areas. However, most smokers still consider it only a politeness, certainly not a mandate, to refrain from smoking in no-smoking zones.

Street Plan

At first glance, Paris's broad expanse looks like one great tangle of medieval streets. Don't be dismayed, however, for there's logic in the layout that, once grasped, makes Paris as easy to navigate as your average college campus. The reference points provided by the major monuments (**Eiffel Tower, Panthéon, Arc de Triomphe,** etc.) and the Seine river make locating yourself and your destination surprisingly easy. The series of axes that cut through the city also is a splendid means of orientation. The most obvious axis runs in a straight line from **La Défense** in the west, eastward through the **Arc de Triomphe,** and down the Champs-Elysées to the **Louvre.** Part of the logic is that the city is subdivided into 20 arrondissements, or quarters. Starting from the first arrondissement (the area around the **Louvre**), they spiral outward like the compartments of a snail's shell to the city limits.

While this overall understanding of Paris's layout is helpful, it won't change the fact that the streets are labyrinthine. For navigating the city's streets, Parisians carry a map of the métro in their heads and a *Paris par Arrondissement* guide in their pockets. Sold at most Parisian newsstands and bookshops, and at some travel bookstores in the US, this little book lists every street in Paris, with indexed references to maps of each of the city's 20 arrondissements (indicating the nearest métro station). Don't leave home without it.

Taxes

Included in the purchase price of many items is a 17.1 percent VAT (value-added tax). Tourists are entitled to VAT refunds on items that they take out of France; a minimum purchase of 1,200 francs (about $240) per store is required. To get a refund, ask for the VAT refund forms when you make your purchase and be prepared to produce the items and the forms at the airport *détaxe* (refund) desk.

Telephones

Phone booths adorn half the street corners in Paris, but it's a minor miracle to find one that works. Most operate only with *télécartes,* special phone cards that are sold at post offices and *tabacs.* To use phones in cafes, you may have to purchase a *jeton* (phone token) at the bar. Make international calls from the post office or your hotel.

Since October 1996 all telephone numbers in France have ten digits. All numbers in the Paris area are preceded by 01. Numbers in the northwest are preceded by 02; in the northeast the number is 03; in the southeast and Corsica, it's 04; and in the southwest dial 05.

Placing Calls to Paris

To call Paris from the US, dial 011.33, followed by the nine digit phone number (drop the zero from the "01" Paris regional code). This applies to all numbers in France. To call Paris from elsewhere in France, dial the ten digit number. For example, to call **Tourist Information** from the US dial 011.33.1.49.52.53.54; when calling from anywhere in France dial 01.49.52.53.54.

Placing Calls from Paris

Telephone calls made from hotels are expensive; if making a long-distance call, it is worth having a phone card. Direct-dial to the US can be made by dialing 001, followed by your area code and number.

Tickets

"Everything that exists elsewhere exists in Paris," said Victor Hugo in *Les Misérables.* So it goes for the array of entertainment options available to both the spectator and the participant in this city. For a daily recording (in English) of exhibitions and concerts, call 01.49.52.53.56.

There are two kiosks that sell half-price tickets to about 120 different events in Paris—including plays, concerts, ballets, and operas—on the day of the performance. One is in the **Châtelet–Les Halles** métro station and the other is located at the **Place de la Madeleine.**

Time Zone

France is one hour ahead of Greenwich Mean Time (GMT); throughout most of the year, when it's 9PM in Paris it's 8PM in London, 3PM in New York, and noon in Los Angeles. However, Europe starts and ends *l'heure d'été* (daylight saving time) several weeks before North America, so from about the end of March to the end of April France is seven hours ahead of New York, and from the end of September to the end of October it is five hours ahead.

Tipping

Since a 15-percent service charge is almost always added to your restaurant bill in Paris and throughout France, a supplementary tip is not necessary, although you may leave an additional five percent for *service extraordinaire.* Tip cab drivers 10 to 15 percent of the fare. It is not customary to tip hotel porters and maids.

Visitors' Information Office

The **Office de Tourisme de Paris** (127 Ave des Champs-Elysées, between Rues Galilée and de Presbourg, 01.49.52.53.54) is the home of the city's official tourist bureau, where you can find free maps and sight-seeing information; it's open daily except

May 1. From May through September, another tourist office operates daily at the **Eiffel Tower.**

Four smaller *Bureaux d'Accueil* operate in the following train stations: **Gare du Nord** (01.45.26.94.82), **Gare de Lyon** (01.43.43.33.24), **Gare de l'Est** (01.46.07.17.73), **Gare Montparnasse** (01.43.22.19.19), and **Gare d'Austerlitz** (01.45.84.91.70). The **Gare de l'Est** and the **Gare de Lyon** *Bureaux d'Accueil* branches are open daily; the others are closed Sunday. (For train station locations, see page 9.)

Phone Book

Emergencies

Ambulance...15
Burn Center.....................................01.42.34.17.58
Crisis Line (English-language, 3-11PM)..................
....01.47.23.80.80
Dental Emergency (SOS Dentaire)....01.43.37.51.00
Doctor (SOS Médecins) 01.43.37.77.77
Fire..18
Hospitals
American Hospital 01.47.47.70.15
British Hospital.................................01.46.39.22.22
Pharmacy (British and American).....01.47.42.49.40
Poison Center...................................01.40.37.04.04
Police (emergency) 17
Police (nonemergency) 01.53.73.53.73
Roadside Emergency (Automobile Club de l'Ile-de-France)....................................01.43.80.68.58

Visitors' Information

American Youth Hostels..................01.43.61.08.75
Métro 08.36.68.77.14
Road Conditions..
     Paris 01.48.99.33.33,
     all regions 08.36.68.20.00
Time...36.99
Tourist Information 01.49.52.53.54
....01.59.52.53.56
Weather 08.36.68.00.00

Fêtes et Foires (Festivals and Fairs)

Paris has a full calendar of special events, celebrations, and trade expositions throughout the year that attract Parisians and visitors alike. For additional details on the events listed, consult the **Office de Tourisme** (127 Ave des Champs-Elysées, between Rues Galilée and de Presbourg, 01.49.52.53.54), which publishes a free annual calendar of events, or the weekly listings in *Pariscope* and *L'Officiel des Spectacles* (available at newsstands).

January

Fashion Shows The haute-couture summer season kicks off this month with much fanfare. Most of the shows are held in the **Cour Carrée** at the **Louvre.**

Fête des Rois (Feast of the Kings) Called the **Feast of the Epiphany** in English-speaking countries, this religious holiday (6 January), which commemorates the visit to the infant Jesus by three kings, is also an excuse for a tasty treat: a round, buttery, almond-paste cake called a *galette des rois.* Inside the cake is hidden a tiny charm, and whoever finds it gets to be king or queen for the day, donning the crown that comes with the cake. The cakes are sold all month long.

February

Découvertes An international art show for new galleries and artists is held at the **Grand Palais** the first week in February.

Tournoi des Cinq Nations (Five Nations Trophy) This international rugby tournament is held in mid-February at the **Parc des Princes.**

March

Salon International d'Agriculture This is a vast farming fair featuring the animals and products of French and foreign *fermiers* (farmers) and a sampling of regional food and wine. It's held the first week in March at the **Parc des Expositions de Paris.**

Foire du Trône The largest fair and carnival in France takes place from the last week of March until the end of May in the **Bois de Vincennes.**

Salon de Mars Paris's most important antiques fair is held in the **Parc du Champ-de-Mars** during the last week of March.

April

Paris Marathon The race, held during the first week of April, starts from the **Place de la Concorde** and ends on **Avenue Foch.** The best place to catch a glimpse of

the runners is along the **Avenue des Champs-Elysées.**

Salon de la Jeune Peinture The work of young contemporary artists is exhibited at the **Grand Palais** for two weeks in mid-April.

Shakespeare Garden Festival In a small open-air theater in the **Bois de Boulogne,** set in a garden blooming with flora described by Shakespeare, classic plays (usually by French writers such as Beaumarchais and Molière) are performed from the end of April until the beginning of October. Occasionally there are English-language performances.

May

May Day On the French **Labor Day** (1 May), most shops and museums are closed and trade unions and left-wing parties organize marches. Bouquets of *muguet* (lily of the valley) are sold all over Paris.

French Open This prestigious tennis tournament, held in the **Stade Roland Garros** during the last week of May or the first week of June, is the Wimbledon of France. Advance tickets can be purchased starting in January (write to Stade Roland Garros, 2 Ave Gordon-Bennett, 75016 Paris); they're also available one week before tournament at the stadium. Call 01.47.43.48.00 for information.

June

Fête du Cinéma On one day in June, cinema lovers who pay the normal ticket price for one film can see a second film for only one franc at any movie theater in the city.

International Rose Competition at Bagatelle Prizes for the best roses are given on 21 June, but the public can view the competitors in the **Bois de Boulogne's Jardins de Bagatelle** from 22 June though the end of September.

Fête de la Musique On the longest day of the year (21 June) live bands play throughout the city until the wee hours. It's a great party.

Gay Pride Parade The largest gay and lesbian parade in France takes place on the last Saturday in June. It starts at the **Place de la Bastille,** the country's symbol of liberation.

Garçons de Café This race sends hundreds of cafe waiters and waitresses running around the city, each carrying a tray with a bottle and glass; any spillage or breakage disqualifies the entrant. The race, which takes place at the end of June, starts at the **Place de la République** and ends at the **Place de la Bastille.** You'll never see cafe servers move this fast on the job.

Tour de France After pedaling for three weeks and 2,301 miles (3,835 kilometers), cyclists in the world's most famous bicycle race arrive at the finish line on the Champs-Elysées as throngs of cheering supporters line the avenue.

July

Fashion Shows Winter haute-couture collections are launched in the **Louvre**'s **Cour Carrée** during several days of fashion shows this month.

Bastille Day The French national holiday (14 July) celebrates the 1789 storming of the **Bastille** prison by the revolutionary masses with an impressive military parade down the Champs-Elysées and a fireworks show at the **Palais de Chaillot.**

Festival Estival Classical music concerts are held in churches and concert halls all over Paris from July through September.

August

Fête de L'Assomption (Feast of the Assumption) The 15 August procession in front of **Notre-Dame** and the accompanying Mass are memorable experiences.

September

Portes Ouvertes Monuments Historiques On the third Sunday of September, 300 historic buildings and sites that are usually closed to the public are open free of charge, giving history and architecture buffs the chance to explore private houses, *hôtels particuliers,* and other historic structures.

Festival de Musique de Chambre de Paris The chamber music concerts held during the second half of September are made even more pleasant by the historical settings, such as the **Musée Carnavalet,** that host them.

October

Fêtes des Vendanges à Montmartre (Wine Harvest Festival) The only vineyard left in Paris is no bigger than a baseball diamond and produces 500 bottles of Clos Montmartre every year. On the first Saturday in October, the basement of the 18th arrondissement *mairie* (town hall) becomes a winery, and festivals

and parades liven the tiny crooked streets of **Montmartre.**

Prix de l'Arc de Triomphe This event marks the opening of the horse-racing season and is attended by the fashionable Chanel-suit, Hermès-scarf, and Gucci-bag crowd. The races take place during the first week of October at the **Hippodrome de Longchamp** in the **Bois de Boulogne.**

FIAC (Foire Internationale d'Art Contemporain) During the first week of October, French and foreign gallery owners gather in the large exhibition space of the **Grand Palais** to show artists' work. This is an increasingly important event for the international contemporary art world.

November

Armistice Day In a somber ceremony in remembrance of those who died in the two World Wars, the French president lays wreaths at the **Tomb of the Unknown Soldier** under the **Arc de Triomphe** on 11 November.

Beaujolais Nouveau Day Posters proclaiming that the "*Beaujolais Nouveau est arrivé*" announce the day (the third Thursday in November) that the first wine of the Beaujolais vintage, pressed and drunk without the aging process, arrives in Paris. Cafes, wine bars, bistros, and wine shops, all join together in a country-wide wine-tasting party. Beaujolais Nouveau is never a sophisticated wine but, depending on the year, it can be pleasantly light and fruity or have less pleasing banana or bubblegum undertones.

December

La Crèche de François d'Assise A life-size Nativity scene stands under a large tent in the **Place de l'Hôtel-de-Ville** from early December through early January. Proceeds go to charity.

Christmas Eve Mass Both **Notre-Dame** and **St-Eustache Cathedrals** have memorable Masses, which include impressive organ music on Christmas Eve (24 December). The holday services draw ample crowds.

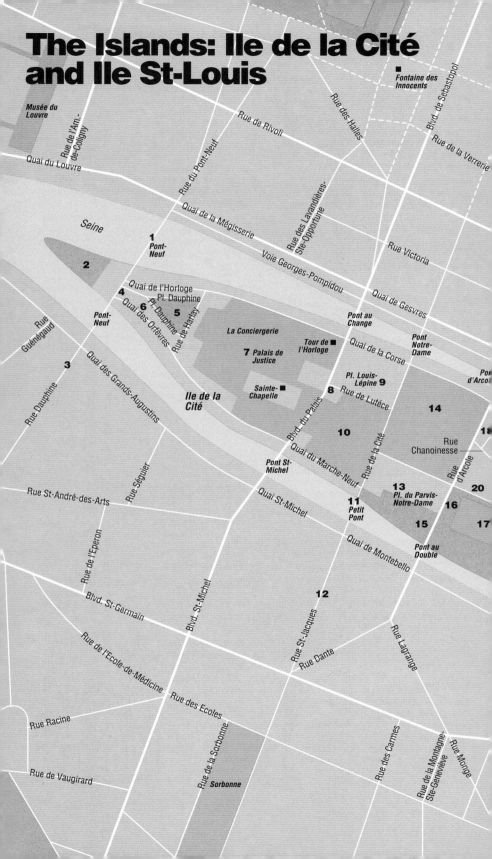

The Islands: Ile de la Cité and Ile St-Louis

Fontaine des Innocents

Musée du Louvre

Rue de l'Am-de-Coligny

Rue de Rivoli

Rue des Halles

Blvd. de Sébastopol

Rue de la Verrerie

Quai du Louvre

Rue du Pont-Neuf

Quai de la Mégisserie

Rue des Lavandières-Ste-Opportune

Seine

1 Pont-Neuf

Voie Georges-Pompidou

Rue Victoria

2

Quai de l'Horloge

Pl. Dauphine

Quai de Gesvres

4

Pont-Neuf

6

5

Pl. Dauphine

Quai des Orfèvres

Rue de Harlay

La Conciergerie

Pont au Change

Pont Notre-Dame

Rue Guénégaud

7 Palais de Justice

Tour de l'Horloge ■

Quai de la Corse

Pon d'Arco

3

Quai des Grands-Augustins

Ile de la Cité

Sainte-Chapelle ■

8

Pl. Louis-Lépine **9**

Rue de Lutéce

14

Rue Dauphine

Blvd. du Palais

10

Rue de la Cité

Rue Chanoinesse

18

Rue Séguier

Quai du Marche-Neuf

Rue d'Arcole

20

Pont St-Michel

13

Pl. du Parvis-Notre-Dame

Rue St-André-des-Arts

Quai St-Michel

11 Petit Pont

16

Rue de l'Eperon

15

17

Pont au Double

Quai de Montebello

Blvd. St-Germain

Blvd. St-Michel

12

Rue St-Jacques

Rue Lagrange

Rue de l'Ecole-de-Médicine

Rue Dante

Rue des Ecoles

Rue Racine

Rue de la Sorbonne

Rue des Carmes

Rue Monge

Rue de la Montagne-Ste-Geneviève

Rue de Vaugirard

Sorbonne

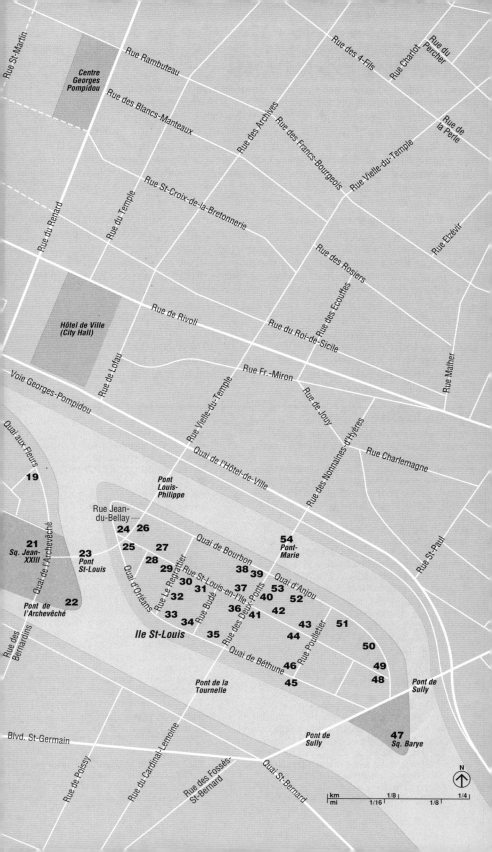

The Islands: Ile de la Cité and Ile St-Louis

At the heart of Paris are two islands: the sloop-shaped Ile de la Cité, which cradles the **Cathédrale de Notre-Dame de Paris** in its stern, and Ile St-Louis, which follows in the wake. Although the islands have no grand hotels, banks, major restaurants, theaters, or designer shops, they do possess two gems of Gothic architecture (**Notre-Dame** and **Sainte-Chapelle**), a world-famous prison, an elegant 17th-century subdivision, some of the city's most beautiful private mansions, the nation's law courts and police headquarters, an Art Nouveau métro station, a flower and bird market, 15 bridges, and one too many souvenir shops selling miniature Napoléon busts and "I Love Paris" bumper stickers.

The following sites serve as an introduction to the islands. If you happen to tour this area on a Sunday, additional attractions include **Notre-Dame's** morning Mass (10:30AM) and late-afternoon organ concerts, and the bird market at **Place Louis-Lépine.** If visiting the Ile St-Louis galleries and boutiques and the **Palais de Justice** is more your style, a weekday would be a better time to drop by. You might begin with a stop at a pastry shop to purchase croissants and brioches in time for a boat trip up the **Seine** (tour boats leave from the **Pont-Neuf**). Then, after stopping at the flower market and **Notre-Dame,** have lunch at a tea salon on Ile St-Louis before strolling down to look at the exterior of the 17th-century **Hôtel de Lauzun.** Top off your day with a candlelit concert in **Sainte-Chapelle,** followed by dinner at the exceedingly fancy **L'Orangerie** or the more plebian, all-you-can-eat **Nos Ancêtres les Gaulois.**

Ile de la Cité

The birthplace of Paris, the Cité (as the island is called) was founded by the Parisii in the third century BC and overtaken by the Romans in 52 BC. It survived attacks by Germans and barbarians, floods, and famine, but succumbed to a Frenchman, Baron Georges-Eugène Haussmann, Napoléon III's prefect (1853-1870). Baron Haussmann ordered the Cité's "hygienizing," in the process destroying 90 streets and most of its medieval and Louis XIII homes. In their place, he constructed four architecturally dull buildings (**Hôtel-Dieu Hospital,** the **Préfecture de Police,** the **Tribunal de Commerce,** and the **Palais de Justice**) and increased by six times the size of the square in front of **Notre-Dame.**

1 Pont-Neuf Despite its name (New Bridge), Paris's most famous bridge is also its oldest. Completed in 1607, it was the city's first pedestrian bridge as well as the first in Paris to be constructed without houses on top of it. Crossing the Seine at the river's widest point, it's also the city's grandest bridge; designed by **Androuet du Cerceau,** it features 12 broad arches and a series of turrets for street vendors, jugglers, and acrobats. It was completed under the popular Henri IV (Henri of Navarre), who inaugurated the bridge by galloping his charger across it. The bronze equestrian statue of *Henricus Magnus* (Henri the Magnificent, as the king was also called) at the bridge's center is an 1818 replacement; the original, erected two centuries earlier by the king's wife, Marie de Médicis, was melted down to make cannons during the Revolution. The cornices overlooking the river have a carved frieze of grimacing caricatures, perhaps of King Henri's ministers and courtiers.

The bridge became such a well-traveled thoroughfare that, legend held, it was impossible to cross without encountering a monk, a prostitute, and a white horse. One of the most notorious Pont-Neuf charlatans was the Great Jean Thomas, who in 1715 set up a stall on the bridge to peddle bottles of an odorous elixir called Solar Balm. As part of an inventive advertising campaign, he hawked his wares dressed in a scarlet suit, a hat of peacock feathers, and a string of human teeth hung around his neck. The bridge has been sketched by J.M.W. Turner among others, rhapsodized by poets such as Victor Hugo and Jean Loiret, and (in 1985) wrapped by Bulgarian artist Christo in acres of beige canvas and more than seven miles of rope. ◆ Between Quais des Grands-Augustine and de la Mégisserie. Métro: Pont-Neuf

2 Square du Vert-Galant Borrowing Henri IV's nickname (which translates roughly as "Gay Old Dog" or "Old Flirt"), this cobblestoned spit of land may be reached by steps behind the king's statue in the middle of Pont-Neuf. Lush with chestnut trees and a haunt of anglers by day and of lovers on warm summer nights, the square affords the best fish-eye view of Paris. Departing from here are one-hour boat tours of the Seine offered by Les Vedettes du Pont-Neuf (01.46.33.98.38, 01.43.29.86.19). The tours leave every 30 minutes from 10AM to noon and from 1:30 to 6:30PM daily. "Lights of Paris" boat tours, departing from 9 to 10:30PM, are offered daily from May to 15 October; on Fridays through Sundays the rest of the year. ♦ Just west of Pl du Pont-Neuf. Métro: Pont-Neuf

3 Rue Dauphine The construction of the Pont-Neuf channeled traffic over to the Left Bank and led to this street's construction. When Henri IV's original request to put a highway through a monastery's vegetable gardens was denied, he snapped: "I will open the new road with cannonballs!" The gardens were sacrificed and the new road, named after the king's son, was built. Today the narrow road is lined with shops. ♦ Between Carrefour de Buci and Pont-Neuf. Métro: Pont-Neuf

4 Taverne Henry IV ★★$ Named after the king in bronze across the street, this reasonably priced bistro serves delicious charcuterie, regional cheeses, and goose rillettes and is well stocked with Bordeaux and Burgundy. ♦ M-F lunch and dinner; Sa dinner; closed 15 August to 15 September. No credit cards accepted. 13 Pl du Pont-Neuf (at Rue Henri-Robert). 01.43.54.27.90. Métro: Pont-Neuf

5 Place Dauphine Once the royal garden, this tranquil triangle of stone and redbrick town houses dates from 1607 and takes its name from Henri IV's son, the princely dauphin who became Louis XIII. The square was one of Henri IV's first city-planning projects in the 17th century and regrettably lost its third side with the expansion of the **Palais de Justice.**

Surrealist poet André Breton (1896-1966) called it "one of the most secluded places I know." ♦ Between Rues de Harlay and Henri-Robert. Métro: Pont-Neuf

On Place Dauphine:

Laine en Couleur Végétale True to its name, this shop specializes in richly colored, hand-dyed wool yarns as well as natural vegetable dyes used for creating and restoring tapestries. The delightful owner, Anne Rieger, derives her reds from red cabbage, her blues from indigo, and her yellows from the leaves of the chestnut trees right outside her door. ♦ M-F 3-7PM (hours vary); closed in August. No. 18 (north side). 01.40.51.72.65

La Rose de France
★★$$ This tiny restaurant with an outdoor terrace specializes in tasty *côtelettes d'agneau* (lamb chops with *herbes de Provence*), mussels in vermouth, and *filet de boeuf en croûte* (tenderloin of beef in a pastry crust). ♦ M-F lunch and dinner; closed the last three weeks of August and Christmas through New Year's Day. No. 24 (north side). 01.43.54.10.12

Hôtel Henri IV $ The wallpaper is peeling, the rooms are tiny, and the showers and bathrooms are in the hall, but that's a minor price to pay for a room with a view of one of the prettiest squares in Paris and a daily rate that's less than the cost of a decent bottle of wine. There are only 22 rooms at this very popular hostelry, so reserve well in advance. There's no restaurant. ♦ No credit cards accepted. No. 25 (south side). 01.43.54.44.53

Pont-Neuf

MICHAEL STORRINGS

Le Caveau du Palais ★★$$ A charming, comfortable restaurant (illustrated above) is wedged between the Quai des Orfèvres and the Place Dauphine. Sample the salad of lamb sweetbreads in a raspberry vinegar, *filet de boeuf à la moutarde de Meaux* (tenderloin of beef with mustard sauce), grilled grouper with basil, and *fondant au chocolat*. Dine inside under the exposed wood beams in winter, on the terrace facing the Place Dauphine in summer. ◆ M-Sa lunch and dinner; closed Saturday mid-October through March. No. 19 (south side). 01.43.26.04.28

Le Bar du Caveau ★$ Managed by **Le Caveau du Palais** next door, this wine bar serves light meals: charcuterie, country cheese, and a variety of Bordeaux and Beaujolais. ◆ Daily breakfast, lunch, and snacks until 8PM. No. 19 (south side). 01.43.54.45.95

Chez Paul ★★$$ Long marble tables set with cloth napkins as big as dish towels dominate this spot. Try the lobster salad with curry sauce, the *mignon de veau en papillote* (veal tenderloin steaks baked in parchment), and, for dessert, the *baba au rhum flambé* with red currant jam. During the summer months don't miss the wild strawberries. ◆M lunch, Tu-Su lunch and dinner. 15 Pl Dauphine/52 Quai des Orfèvres. 01.43.54.21.48

6 **Quai des Orfèvres (Goldsmiths Quay)** This is the Scotland Yard of Paris, home of the city's detective force, the *police judiciare* or "PJ." Perhaps the most famous member of the PJ is Inspector Maigret, the protagonist of the detective stories by the late Georges Simenon. ◆ Between Blvd du Palais and Pont-Neuf. Métros: Pont-Neuf, St-Michel

On Quai des Orfèvres:

"... covered with cardinals mitred like Assyrian kings, and knights leaning on long swords, and saints and angels, and beautiful naked Greek figures that have no religious significance whatever, and gargoyles—creatures with heads of goats and dogs, and claws and wings on men's bodies, all staring down in a jeering sardonic mirth."

William Faulkner, describing
Notre-Dame Cathedral

Au Rendez-Vous des Camionneurs ★$$ A pretty restaurant that boasts yellow-, blue-, and white-checkered tablecloths and fresh flowers is where owner-chef Alain Haye creates simple but tasty fare. Start with his *poelon de moules et de crevettes à la fondue de poireaux* (mussels and shrimp with minced leeks and cream) or *émincé de haddock à la sauce Coulibiac* (smoked minced haddock with cream-and-lemon sauce). Follow with *oeufs pochés à la confiture d'oignons* (poached eggs with onion chutney) or *sauté de porc à l'ancienne* (traditional sauté of pork). Desserts are especially good— the *truffé au chocolat* and *charlotte aux fraises* (trifle with strawberries) should satisfy any sweet tooth. ◆ Daily lunch and dinner. No. 72 (between Rue de Harlay and Pont-Neuf). 01.43.54.88.74

7 **Palais de la Cité** This massive interlocking series of structures has been occupied by the French government since 52 BC, first as the palace of Roman prefects, later as the Gothic palace of the first 12 kings of France. In the 13th century it was the residence of St. Louis (Louis IX), who lived in the upper chambers (now the **First Civil Court**). The king meted out justice beneath a tree in the courtyard. All that remains of the original palace is the breathtaking **Sainte-Chapelle** and the gloomy **Conciergerie,** one of history's most hideous and brutal prisons (see below for details on both places). Most of the original site was covered by the **Palais de Justice,** which was built after the great fire of 1776. ◆ Bordered by Blvd du Palais and Rue de Harlay, and Quais des Orfèvres and de l'Horloge. Métros: Pont-Neuf, St-Michel

Within the Palais de la Cité:

Tours de Bonbec, d'Argent, and de César (Babble, Money, and César Towers) Along the Quai de l'Horloge side of the old palace is a set of round, imposing towers. The first is **Tour de Bonbec,** nicknamed the "babbler" because it was used as a torture chamber during the Reign of Terror, a period of brutal purges following the Revolution. Next are the **Tour d'Argent,** where the royal treasure was once kept, and the **Tour de César,** two steepled gate towers beside the entrance to the **Conciergerie.** The tower interiors are not open to the public. ◆ Quai de l'Horloge (between Blvd du Palais and Rue de Harlay)

La Conciergerie After the bloody mob revolt led by Etienne Marcel in 1358, young King Charles V moved the royal residence to the Marais but left behind the royal dungeon and Supreme Court in the charge of the king's caretaker, known as the *Comte des Cierges* (Count of Candles) or *Concierge.*

Among the dungeon's long list of former residents are notorious criminals such as Ravaillac, the fanatic who murdered popular

Henri IV and was imprisoned and tortured here before his execution. During the Revolution, the Tribunal commandeered the palace and administered its own ruthless form of justice. The **Conciergerie** became the antechamber to the guillotine during the Reign of Terror between January 1793 and July 1794. About 2,600 Parisians were condemned to death, among them Charlotte Corday, who had stabbed Marat in his bath, and, perhaps the best-remembered inmate, Marie Antoinette, the Austrian queen who had reputedly scoffed at the starving French masses with the phrase "Let them eat cake." Shortly after the Tribunal executed her husband, King Louis XVI, she was held here in a tiny cell from August until October 1793, when she was delivered to the guillotine. Royalty were not the only victims during this tumultuous time; no one in a position of authority was safe. Revolutionary Danton, who had ordered the execution of 22 people, was in turn condemned to death by citizen Robespierre, who later was sent to the guillotine by a panel of judges, the Thermidor Convention. At the end of the Terror, the Tribunal's own public prosecutor, Fouquier-Tinville, was dragged off to the gallows shouting "I am the ax! You don't execute the ax!"

Put yourself in the shoes of Marie Antoinette as she walked down the prison's Rue de Paris (which during the Terror led to the quarters of an executioner known as *Monsieur de Paris*). She was jailed in dank cell **No. VI**; in the cell next door, both Danton and Robespierre were held on death row and, in the adjoining chapel, the 22 condemned Girondins heard Mass before their execution. All these rooms, as well as the *salle de la dernière toilette,* from which prisoners were led to the block, have been restored to their original state.

On your way out, duck into the magnificent medieval vaults of the four-aisled **Salle des Gens d'Armes** (Hall of the Men-at-Arms), frequently used these days for classical concerts, theater performances, and wine tastings. The spiral staircase at the far end of the hall is worth a peek. Also be sure to stroll through the 14th-century kitchen that served some 3,000 guests and had large walk-in ovens. The souvenir shop near the exit sells replicas of Revolutionary playing cards that replace kings, queens, and jacks with humbly clothed men and women personifying common virtues such as Industry and Justice. The original deck (1793) by Jaume and Dugorc is kept in the **Bibliothèque Nationale.** ◆ Admission. Daily; guided tours available at 11AM and 3PM. 1 Quai de l'Horloge (at Blvd du Palais). 01.53.73.78.50

Tour de l'Horloge (Clock Tower) This tower was the site of the city's first public clock (1334). Today's more Baroque version is set in a constellation of golden fleurs-de-lis and flanked by angels, rams, and royal shields. Until the French Revolution, the clock signaled royal births and deaths by pealing nonstop for three days. ◆ Quai de l'Horloge (at Blvd du Palais)

Palais de Justice (Law Courts) Behind the lusciously gilded Louis XVI railing and portal gates on the Boulevard du Palais is the main entrance to the **Palais de Justice** and the **Cour du Mai** (May Courtyard). The courtyard was the last stop for the condemned before they left by wooden carts, or tumbrils, for the gallows in the **Place de la Concorde.** Look above the door at the top of the marble steps for the words *Liberté, Egalité, Fraternité.*

On the right in the lobby (**Salle des Pas-Perdus,** literally "Room of the Wasted Steps") is an amusing statue of Berryer, a 19th-century barrister. To his right sits a sculpted muse with her foot on a turtle, a jab at the speed of the legal process. Behind the door to the left is the gorgeous blue-and-gold **Première Chambre,** also known as the **Chambre Dorée** (Gilded Chamber), where the Revolutionary Tribunal sat on 6 April 1793 and sentenced Queen Marie Antoinette to death.

In the "cathedral of chicanery," as Balzac called the Law Courts, a thicket of police, public *écrivains* (letter writers), and prisoners used to gather while hawkers sold newspapers and rented black judicial robes. Today, the lobby is still a chaos of black-robed barristers, plaintiffs, and judges dashing about. If you'd like to see a French Perry Mason putting *liberté, égalité,* and *fraternité* into action, visit on a weekday, when courtroom proceedings (except the juvenile court) are part of the tour. ◆ Tours by appointment only. 2 Blvd du Palais (between Quais des Orfèvres and de l'Horloge). 01.44.32.50.00. Métro: Cité

"You got very hungry when you did not eat enough in Paris because all the bakery shops had such good things in the windows and people ate outside at tables on the sidewalks so that you saw and smelled the food. When you had given up journalism and were writing nothing that anyone in America would buy, explaining at home that you were lunching out with someone, the best place to go was the Luxembourg gardens where you saw and smelled nothing to eat all the way from Place de l'Observatoire to the rue de Vaugirard. There you could always go into the Luxembourg museum and all the paintings were sharpened and clearer and more beautiful if you were belly-empty, hollow-hungry. I learned to understand Cézanne much better and to see truly how he made landscapes when I was hungry."

Ernest Hemingway, *A Moveable Feast*

Parlez-Vous Français?

The French take great pride in their culture and their language. If you attempt to speak their language, no matter how poorly, they will take it as a compliment. Don't be put off if they respond to you in English, however—be glad. It will be that much easier to understand one another. Here are some phrases that will enable you to start communicating *en français*. When there is both a masculine and a feminine spelling, the feminine is in parentheses. *Bon voyage!* (Have a good trip!)

Hello, Good-bye, and Other Basics

Hello/Good morning/ Good afternoon	*Bonjour*
Good evening	*Bonsoir*
How are you?	*Comment allez-vous?*
Good-bye	*Au revoir*
Yes	*Oui*
No	*Non*
Please	*S'il vous plaît*
Thank you	*Merci*
You're welcome	*De rien* or *Je vous en prie*
Excuse me	*Excusez-moi* or *Pardon*
I don't speak French	*Je ne parle pas français*
Do you speak English?	*Parlez-vous anglais?*
I don't understand	*Je ne comprends pas*
Do you understand?	*Comprenez-vous?*
More slowly, please	*Plus lentement, s'il vous plaît*
I don't know	*Je ne sais pas*
My name is. . .	*Je m'appelle. . .*
What is your name?	*Comment vous appelez-vous?*
miss	*mademoiselle*
madame, ma'am	*madame*
mister, sir	*monsieur*
good	*bon(ne)*
bad	*mauvais(e)*
open	*ouvert(e)*
closed	*fermé(e)*
entrance	*entrée*
exit	*sortie*
push	*poussez*
pull	*tirez*
today	*aujourd'hui*
tomorrow	*demain*
yesterday	*hier*
week	*semaine*
month	*mois*
year	*an*

Hotel Talk

I have a reservation	*J'ai une réservation.*
I would like to reserve. . .	*Je voudrais réserver. . .*
a double room	*une chambre pour deux personnes*
with (private) bath	*avec une salle de bain (privée)*
with air-conditioning	*avec la climatisation*
Are taxes included?	*Est-ce que les taxes sont comprises?*

Is breakfast included?	*Est-ce que le petit déjeuner est compris?*
Do you accept traveler's checks?	*Prenez-vous des chèques de voyage?*
Do you accept credit cards?	*Prenez-vous des cartes de crédit?*

Restaurant Repartee

Waiter!	*Monsieur!*
I would like. . .	*Je voudrais. . .*
a menu	*la carte*
a glass of	*un verre de*
a bottle of	*une bouteille de*
The check, please	*L'addition, s'il vous plaît*
Is the service charge (tip) included?	*Est-ce que le service est compris?*
I think there is an error in the bill	*Je crois qu'il y a une erreur avec l'addition.*
lunch	*déjeuner*
dinner	*dîner*
tip	*service, pourboire*
bread	*pain*
butter	*beurre*
pepper	*poivre*
salt	*sel*
sugar	*sucre*
soup	*soupe*
salad	*salade*
vegetables	*légumes*
cheese	*fromage*
eggs	*oeufs*
beef	*boeuf*
chicken	*poulet*
veal	*veau*
fish	*poisson*
seafood	*fruits de mer*
pork	*porc*
ham	*jambon*
chop	*côtelette*
dessert	*dessert*

As You Like It

cold	*froid(e)*
hot	*chaud(e)*
sweet	*sucré(e)*
dry	*sec (sèche)*
broiled, roasted	*rôti(e)*
baked	*au four*
boiled	*bouilli(e)*

fried	frit(e)
raw	cru(e)
rare	saignant(e)
well done	bien cuit(e)
spicy	épicé(e)

Thirsty No More

water	l'eau
coffee	café, express
coffee with steamed milk	café au lait
tea	thé
beer	bière
rosé wine	vin rosé
red wine	vin rouge
white wine	vin blanc
milk	lait
mineral water	l'eau minérale
carbonated	gazeuse
not carbonated	non-gazeuse
orange juice	jus d'orange
ice	glaçons
without ice	sans glaçons

Sizing It Up

How much does this cost?	Combien coûte-il?
inexpensive	bon marché
expensive	cher (chère)
large	grand(e)
small	petit(e)
long	long(ue)
short	court(e)
old	vieux (vieille)
new	nouveau (nouvelle)
used	d'occasion
a little	un peu
a lot	beaucoup

On the Move

north	nord
south	sud
east	est
west	ouest
right	droite
left	gauche
highway	autoroute
street	rue
gas station	station-service
here	ici
there	là
bus stop	l'arrêt de bus
bus station	gare routière
train station	gare
subway	métro
airport	aéroport
road map	carte routière
one-way ticket	aller-simple

round-trip ticket	aller-retour
first class	première classe
second class	seconde classe or deuxième
smoking	fumeur
no smoking	non-fumeur
Does this train go to. . . ?	Est-ce que ce train s'arrête à. . . ?
Where is/are. . . ?	Où est. . . ?/Où sont. . . ?
How far is it from here to. . .	Quelle est la distance entre ici et. . . ?

The Bare Necessities

aspirin	aspirines
Band-Aids™	pansement adhésif
barbershop, beauty shop	coiffeur, salon de beauté
condom	préservatif
dry cleaner	teinturerie
laundromat, laundry	blanchisserie
letter	lettre
post office	bureau de poste
postage stamp	timbre
postcard	carte postale
sanitary napkins	serviettes hygiéniques
shampoo	shampooing
shaving cream	lotion à raser
soap	savon
tampons	tampons périodiques
tissues	mouchoirs en papier
toilet paper	papier hygiénique
toothpaste	dentifrice
Where is the bathroom/ toilet?	Où est la salle de bains?/ Où sont les toilettes?
Men's room	WC pour hommes
Women's room	WC pour dames

Days of the Week

Monday	lundi
Tuesday	mardi
Wednesday	mercredi
Thursday	jeudi
Friday	vendredi
Saturday	samedi
Sunday	dimanche

Numbers

zero	zéro
one	un
two	deux
three	trois
four	quatre
five	cinq
six	six
seven	sept
eight	huit
nine	neuf
ten	dix

SAINTE-CHAPELLE

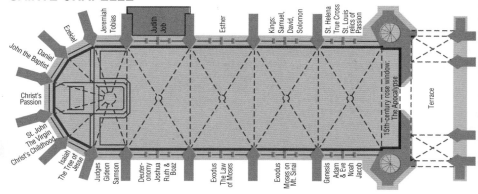

Labels on the diagram:

Top row (left to right): Ezekiel, Jeremiah / Tobias, Judith / Job, Esther, Kings: Samuel, David, Solomon, St. Helena / True Cross / St. Louis / relics of Passion

Left apse (top to bottom): John the Baptist, Daniel, Christ's Passion, St. John / The Virgin / Christ's Childhood, Isaiah / The Tree of Jesse

Right: 15th-century rose window: The Apocalypse, Terrace

Bottom row (left to right): Judges / Gideon / Samson, Deuteronomy / Joshua / Ruth & Boaz, Exodus / The Law of Moses, Exodus / Moses on Mt. Sinai, Genesis / Adam & Eve / Noah / Jacob

Sainte-Chapelle After **Notre-Dame**, this is the city's most significant medieval monument. St. Louis (Louis IX, 1214-1270), France's only canonized king, erected this Gothic jewel of a chapel in 1248 to enshrine the relics he bought from Venetian merchants during his first crusade. His purchases included Christ's Crown of Thorns, two pieces of the True Cross, a nail from the cross, the Roman soldier's lance that pierced Christ's side, and several drops of Christ's blood. For the relics, he paid 35,000 livres in gold, a sum far in excess of what it cost to construct **Sainte-Chapelle.**

Sainte-Chapelle (the name means "holy chapel") was built in less than five years and is thought to have been designed by **Pierre de Montreuil.** It soars 67 feet without the aid of flying buttresses, a daring architectural feat in those days. In medieval times the chapel was connected to the palace of Louis IX, but today it's hidden away in a side courtyard of the 19th-century **Palais de Justice.** The interior has two tiers—the royal family worshiped upstairs in the light and airy **Chapelle Haute,** out of view of the court members who prayed on the somber ground floor.

The chapel suffered considerable damage during the Revolution, when the gold reliquary was melted down and the structure was put to use as a flour warehouse. In the 19th century the chapel was thoroughly made over by **Eugène-Emmanuel Viollet-le-Duc** (1814-1879), one of the Baron Haussmann–hired architects who also restored **Notre-Dame** and cathedrals at Amiens and St-Denis. **Louis Charles Auguste Steinheil,** a compatriot of Balzac and Baudelaire, restored the windows. Of the 12 apostle statues, only one (the bearded apostle fifth down on the left side) is original. Portions of the damaged originals

are on exhibit in the **Musée de Cluny.** The chapel's spectacular windows (see diagram above) are older than **Notre-Dame**'s and comprise the largest expanse of stained glass in the world—1,500 square yards, enough to cover three basketball courts. Created in an age of mass illiteracy, this pictorial Bible consists of 1,134 scenes. Start at the lower-left panel of each window and read from left to right, row by row from bottom to top. The narrative begins with Genesis and continues through the Crucifixion (illustrated in the choir apse), with scenes and figures from both the Old and New Testaments interspersed throughout. The concluding windows (on the left side of the church as you face the rose window) depict Louis IX's acquisition of the holy relics, the construction of

Sainte-Chapelle

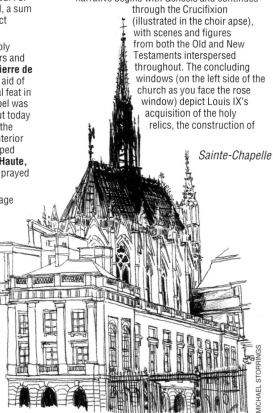

MICHAEL STORRINGS

Sainte-Chapelle, and, finally, the Apocalypse. Notice that a liberated Louis IX devoted entire windows to two women of the Old Testament, Judith and Esther.

Because the windows are backlit by the sun, different ones are more brightly illuminated at different times of day; you have to get up early to catch the Battle of Jericho and must come after lunch for David and Goliath. If the flies on Pharaoh's face interest you, bring your opera glasses, because many of the panels, particularly the highest ones, are nearly impossible to decipher with the naked eye. Anyone who identifies even a few Bible characters in a short visit is doing well. Not long ago a Belgian Benedictine monk arrived here with his Bible and a pair of binoculars; it took him two full weeks, gazing every day from dawn to dusk, to complete the cycle.

For an initial visit, the best approach is to set aside your guidebook and gaze upward. Note how the thick, predominantly red and blue dyed glass of the 15 main windows contrasts sharply with the green and yellow hues of the flamboyant rose window (restored by Charles VIII in 1485) illustrating the Apocalypse. Imagine yourself among the royal family in the 13th century watching as Louis IX mounted the stairs to the gold reliquary to display the sacred Crown of Thorns. (The crown now resides in **Notre-Dame** and is exhibited only on Good Friday.) In addition to its visual splendors, **Sainte-Chapelle** is renowned for its acoustics; Couperin played the organ here in the 17th century. Nowadays, rather expensive evening concerts of classical music are held here several times a week between March and November. ♦ Admission. 2 Blvd du Palais (between Quais des Orfèvres and de l'Horloge). 01.53.73.78.51

8 Les Deux Palais ★$ This corner cafe with 1920s-style mirrored columns serves omelettes, good coffee, and hot lunch specials. ♦ Daily breakfast, lunch, and dinner. 3 Blvd du Palais (at Rue de Lutèce). 01.43.54.20.86. Métro: Cité

9 Place Louis-Lépine Named after a Belle Epoque police chief remembered for having armed Parisian *gendarmes* with whistles and truncheons, this square is a charming urban Eden surrounded by the grim walls of **Hôtel-Dieu Hospital,** the **Préfecture de Police,** and the **Tribunal de Commerce.** One of the largest flower markets in Paris blooms here year-round with everything from chrysanthemums to lemon trees. On Sunday, the square is transformed into a bird market selling cages, seed, and a palette of colorful canaries, finches, and parrots. ♦ Off Rue de la Cité, between Rue de Lutèce and Quai de la Corse. Métro: Cité

On Place Louis-Lépine:

Cité Métro Station This is one of the original 141 Art Nouveau "dragonfly" métro station entrances designed by **Hector Guimard** in 1900.

10 Préfecture de Police This bunker of a building is the headquarters of the fictional Inspector Clouseau of *Pink Panther* fame and the very real Paris police. On 19 August 1944, during the liberation of Paris, about a thousand Paris police officers revolted against the German occupation, barricaded themselves in the **Préfecture,** hoisted the tricolor to a rousing chorus of the *Marseillaise,* and held off Nazi tanks and artillery for four days until the Allies arrived. In the ensuing battle 280 died, and buildings around **Notre-Dame**'s parvis are still pock-marked with bullet holes. ♦ 1 Rue de la Cité (between Quai du Marché-Neuf and Rue de Lutèce). Métro: Cité

11 Petit Pont The "Little Bridge" was first built in 1185 by Bishop Maurice de Sully, who also oversaw the construction of **Notre-Dame.** In the Middle Ages, minstrels were allowed to cross the bridge without paying the toll. A 19th-century version now stands. ♦ Between Quais St-Michel and du Marché-Neuf. Métros: Cité, St-Michel

12 Rue St-Jacques The city's oldest street, which begins at the Petit Pont, originated as a Roman road. A thousand years later, it was named after St-Jacques (St. James), whose body is believed to have miraculously appeared in Spain in the ninth century. Paris was the principal starting point of a thousand-mile pilgrimage to Santiago de Compostela in Spain, where the saint's body was buried. In medieval times, pilgrims wearing scallop shells (the symbol of St. James) would set off down this street. The delicious contents of such shells are now served throughout Paris as *coquilles St-Jacques.* ♦ Between Blvd de Port-Royal and Petit Pont. Métros: Cité, St-Michel

13 Place du Parvis Notre-Dame In the Middle Ages, when miracle plays were performed, the square in front of **Notre-Dame** represented *paradis,* or paradise, a name contracted over the centuries to "parvis." Critics of Baron Haussmann, who enlarged the parvis sixfold in the 19th century, called it the "paved prairie." ♦ Between Rues d'Arcole and de la Cité. Métros: Cité, St-Michel

Beneath the Place du Parvis-Notre-Dame:

Crypte Archéologique (Archaeological Crypt) In 1965, while excavating for an underground parking lot, city workers unearthed Gallo-Roman and medieval ruins, now preserved in this slightly eerie but intelligently designed archaeological site/museum beneath the Place du Parvis Notre-Dame. The crypt, designed by **André Hermant,** is worth a quick visit, if only to see the museum's interesting scale models of Paris, which show its evolution from a Celtic

Notre-Dame

settlement during the Second Iron Age to a Roman city in 50 BC. Notice that the Romans, in anticipation of another barbarian invasion, reinforced the original ramparts with a second wall. This is one of the city's most accessible museums, with information in English and French. If you're lucky, you may even see a few archaeologists still carefully digging away. ♦ Admission. Enter at the west end of Place du Parvis-Notre-Dame. 01.43.29.83.51

On the Place du Parvis-Notre-Dame:

Rue de Venise Paris in the Middle Ages was a snarl of narrow horse paths. Marked in the pavement of the parvis in front of the cathedral is the former position of this one-yard-wide medieval alley, no doubt once the narrowest street in Paris.

14 Hôtel-Dieu Hospital Behind the double row of chestnut trees along the north end of the parvis is "God's Hostel," founded by St. Landry, Bishop of Paris. The original hospital building was erected here in AD 651. In 1400, this became the site of the oldest known cabaret in Paris, **La Pomme de Pin;** it was frequented by Rabelais, Villon, Molière, and Racine. The present hospital building was built here in the mid-19th century by Baron Haussmann as part of his urbanization project; in the latter part of that century it was an important training facility for American doctors. ♦ Pl du Parvis Notre-Dame (between Rues d'Arcole and de la Cité). Métros: Cité, St-Michel

15 Statue de Charlemagne On the south side of the parvis rests a bronze statue, created in 1882, of Charlemagne, the Frank who was crowned the first Holy Roman Emperor in AD 800. The center of Charlemagne's empire was at Aix-la-Chapelle; under Charlemagne and his successors, Paris was merely a provincial town. (If you happen to be looking for public toilets, follow the tail of Charlemagne's prancing horse; it points west to nearby stairs leading underground.) ♦ Pl du Parvis Notre-Dame (at Pont au Double). Métros: Cité, St-Michel

16 Point Zéro All distances in France are measured from this brass compass star *(Point Zéro des Routes de France)* fixed in the pavement in front of **Notre-Dame.** Throughout France, highway signs tell you how far away you are (in kilometers) from Paris **Notre-Dame.** ♦ Rue d'Arcole (between Pont au Double and Rue du Cloître-Notre-Dame). Métros: Cité, St-Michel

17 Cathédrale de Notre-Dame de Paris (Cathedral of Our Lady of Paris) "The cathedral of **Notre-Dame,**" wrote e. e. cummings, "does not budge an inch for all the idiocies of this world." For six centuries, this world-famous masterpiece of the Middle Ages has endured as a sonnet in stone, harmonizing mass and elegance, asymmetry and perfection. Among its architectural triumphs are the Gothic ribbed vaulting and the flying buttresses, which opened up the church by permitting the erection of higher, more slender walls pierced by glorious stained glass.

In 1163 no less a personage than Pope Alexander III laid the cathedral's foundation stone, and the final masterful touches were not completed until 1345—more than two centuries later. (**Sainte-Chapelle,** by comparison, was erected in five years.) The design followed the sketches executed in 1159 by Bishop Maurice de Sully and was implemented by architects **Pierre de Montreuil** who was responsible for **Notre-**

Dame's south transept, and **Jean de Chelles,** as well as generations of anonymous workers.

To tour **Notre-Dame** is to stroll through French history. On this site the Romans built a temple in antiquity to Jupiter and the emperor Tiberius. In the cathedral during the Middle Ages, the homeless slept and were fed; trade unions met; passion plays were performed; and merchants from the Orient sold everything from ostrich eggs to elephant tusks. During the 12th century **Notre-Dame**'s adjoining school became an intellectual center known throughout Europe; it eventually gave birth to the **Sorbonne.** During the Revolution the cathedral was rechristened the "Temple of Reason"; shortly thereafter, it was auctioned off to a demolition contractor for scrap building material. Though never demolished, **Notre-Dame** was in shambles in 1804 when Napoléon Bonaparte called Pope Pius VII from Rome to officiate at his coronation, which was held before the cathedral's high altar. After the anointing, Napoléon defiantly snatched the crown from the pontiff and crowned himself emperor, a dramatic scene captured by Jacques-Louis David in his famous painting, which hangs in the **Louvre.**

West Facade At the base of the west facade, which is topped by two 69-meter (226-foot) towers, are three famous portals. The ones on the left and right honor the Virgin Mary and her mother, St. Anne, respectively; the one in the center depicts the Last Judgment. Royalty also managed to get into the picture; in the tympanum of the portal to St. Anne, a kneeling King Louis VII (far right) dedicates the cathedral with Bishop Sully (on the left with a crook in his hand), as the bishop's faithful secretary takes notes straddling a Gothic stool. The presence of Barbedor, the scribe, represents one of the first times an intellectual was honored in a cathedral facade.

Above the three portals is the **Gallery of Kings, Eugène-Emmanuel Viollet-le-Duc**'s 19th-century replicas of medieval masterpieces, which were once painted in vibrant yellow, cobalt, and scarlet. The 28 kings represent the kings of Judea and Israel, thought by the Catholic Church to be the ancestors of Christ. In 1793 Revolutionaries mistook them for the kings of France and toppled and decapitated them. Fortunately, an educator spirited away the heads and buried them in his yard at 20 Chaussée d'Antin, near the present site of the **Opéra Garnier.** They languished there until 1977, when they were unearthed during excavations for a bank vault and put on exhibit at the **Musée de Cluny.** The facade will be partially obscured by scaffolding for the remainder of the decade as, section by section, it is carefully cleaned. This delicate process, in which only warm water (no soap, solvent, or sandblasting) is used, won't be completed until the year 2000.

North and South Towers
Enter the **North Tower** from a separate entrance at its foot. At the end of a spiraling 255-step climb you will find not Victor Hugo's tormented hunchback, Quasimodo, but an equally unsettling sight: architect **Viollet-le-Duc**'s stone bestiary of gargoyles, gremlins, and

MICHAEL STORRINGS

demons. It was believed that the gargoyles kept evil spirits from the cathedral; a number of them also serve as downspouts, squirting rain from their mouths—an entertaining sight during spring showers. The 90-meter (297-foot) spire was added during the heavy-handed Gothic Revival restoration of 1860. **Viollet-le-Duc** placed a statue of himself alongside the copper apostles and evangelists. The apostles stand on the cathedral roof looking outward, blessing the city, but the architect looks upward, admiring his work. For a bird's-eye view of the **Viollet-le-Duc** statue, the celebrated flying buttresses, and the splendid chain of bridges over the Atlantic-bound Seine, climb the last 125 steps to the top of the **South Tower.** The tower also houses the cathedral's famous 13-ton **Emmanuel Bell,** tolled on solemn occasions.

Interior As you enter the cathedral, the nave appears more somber than the transept and altar. This is due, in part, to your eyes adjusting to the darkness, but the difference in hue is mostly a matter of dirt. The cleaning process was brought to a halt in the early 1990s when it was found that even warm water sponge baths would be harmful to the westernmost portion of the nave. The remaining bays have suffered more pollution damage than the rest of the interior, and unlike the facade had not been protected for centuries by decorative paint. Restorers will continue with the cleanup only after they have developed a suitably safe technique.

The massive organ is France's largest, a masterwork installed in the mid–19th century by Aristide Cavaillé-Coll. Following in the tradition of François Couperin, César Auguste Franck, and Olivier Messiaen, all of whom performed here, some of Europe's greatest organists offer free recitals every Sunday afternoon. These concerts, as well as the candlelit Easter vigil and Christmas Eve Mass, draw ample crowds, as does the deeply moving cathedral service held each 11 November, when the Royal British Legion honors British and Commonwealth soldiers who died on French soil during World War I. The cathedral's seating capacity is nearly 10,000.

Mays Paintings During the Middle Ages, the *Orfèvrerie* (the gold workers' union) presented paintings to the cathedral each May. The paintings, called *Mays,* were originally hung between the church pillars; today, they are displayed in the side chapels. Among them are works by Charles Le Brun (1619-1690) and Eustache Le Sueur (1616-1655).

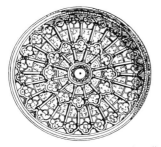

Windows New windows were installed in the cathedral's clerestory after World War II, but not because of damage caused by the Germans. In the 18th century Louis XV declared stained glass déclassé and destroyed the Gothic glass in the upper-level nave windows, replacing it with clear glass (the rest of the stained-glass windows were left intact). The change gave the interior a bright, Protestant appearance. It was not until after the war that contemporary glass replicas of the original upper-nave Gothic windows were installed. Of **Notre-Dame**'s three famous rose windows (north, south, and west), only the north has the original 13th-century glass. The south and west rose windows glow most brilliantly at twilight, while the north window is best viewed in morning light. The stained-glass windows of the 13th and 14th century are thick, with small images and a predominance of deep reds, blues, and purples (the colors are actually dyed into the glass). Over the centuries, it became possible to make thinner glass. Images became larger and were handpainted on the glass surface, and ways of making brighter greens and yellows were discovered. These developments are evident in the differences between the original windows and the modern replicas.

Wood Sculpture One of the cathedral's most charming decorations is the 14th-century Gothic relief on the north side of the chancel that depicts the life of Christ from the Nativity to the Last Supper.

The new altar (in front of the old altar) reflects the liturgical changes in the 1960s that allowed the priest to say Mass facing the congregation instead of turning his back. In addition, Mass is now said in French instead

of Latin (although the cathedral's echoing acoustics sometimes make it hard to figure out what language is being spoken). ♦ 6 Pl Parvis de Notre Dame (at Rue du Cloître-Notre-Dame. 01.42.34.56.10, 01.44.32.16.70 for tour information. Métros: Cité, Maubert–Mutualité

18 Rue de la Colombe This medieval street was cut along the former site of the old Roman wall, which protected Paris against barbarian invasions. ♦ Between Rue Chanoinesse and Quai aux Fleurs. Métros: Cité, Hôtel de Ville

On Rue de la Colombe:

No. 4 Originally a 13th-century tavern and later a famous cabaret in the 1950s, this building was until the mid-1990s the home of **La Colombe** restaurant, which was classified as a French historic landmark and, according to *Le Figaro* magazine, is the most photographed house in Paris. Today the faded sign proclaiming the former restaurant's landmark status and the sculpted doves over the door (*la colombe* is French for "the dove") are the only reminders of the home-style menu of *confit de canard* (duck confit) and *foie gras de maison* that were dished up at this old tourist favorite, which was closed and boarded up at press time.

19 9-11 Quai aux Fleurs The sculpted heads on the facade of this 19th-century building commemorate two of history's most famous lovers, Héloïse and Abélard, who today cast plaintive glances at couples strolling arm-in-arm along the Quai aux Fleurs (where, by the way, no flowers are sold). In 1118 Pierre Abélard (1079-1142), an iconoclastic theologian who helped found the **University of Paris,** fell in love with one of his students. She was Héloïse (1101-1164), the brilliant niece of Fulbert, the foul-tempered canon of **Notre-Dame.** "Under the guise of study, we gave ourselves to love," wrote Abélard. ". . . We exchanged more kisses than sentences." The passionate affair was brought to an abrupt, brutal, and tragic end by Fulbert, whose thugs emasculated Abélard. Héloïse and Abélard lived on, cloistered separately for many years, but were buried side-by-side in **Père-Lachaise Cemetery.** ♦ 9-11 Quai aux Fleurs (at Rue des Chantres). Métros: Cité, Hôtel de Ville

20 Le Vieux Bistro ★★$$ Far removed from the traffic and crush of tourists is this quiet, charming restaurant featuring the cuisine of Lyons. The *civet de canard* (duck stew) and the Burgundy sausage are both delicious choices. ♦ Daily lunch and dinner. Reservations recommended. 14 Rue du Cloître-Notre-Dame (between Rues Massillon and d'Arcole). 01.43.54.18.95. Métro: Cité

Restaurants/Clubs: Red	Hotels: Blue
Shops/ 🍴 Outdoors: Green	Sights/Culture: Black

What Could be More Romantic?

On one of those chilly Paris days, nothing warms the soul and ignites the heart more than dinner in front of a crackling fire. Reserve a table by the *cheminée* at a rustic **Latin Quarter** restaurant and start your meal with some creamy foie gras and a chilled bottle of Sauternes, preferably a Château d'Yquem.

Our favorite hearth-side dining spots include **Atelier Maître-Albert** (1 Rue Maître-Albert, at Quai de la Tournelle, 01.46.33.13.78), which has an imposing 17th-century fireplace; **La Bûcherie** (41 Rue de la Bûcherie, between Rues St-Julien-le-Pauvre and du Petit-Pont, 01.43.54.78.06), with a lovely old hearth in a wainscoted dining room; and **Auberge des Deux-Signes** (46 Rue Galande, between Rues Dante and St-Julien-le-Pauvre, 01.43.25.00.46), a historic old inn complete with a medieval fireplace. Also cozy and intimate are **Le Coupe-Chou** (11 Rue de Lanneau,

at Impasse Chartière, 01.46.33.68.69), with a 14th-century fireplace made of stone and wood, and **La Truffière** (4 Rue Blainville, between Pl de la Contrescarpe and Rue Tournefort, 01.46.33.29.82), which boasts a beautiful Louis XIII *cheminée*.

21 Square Jean XXIII Cherry trees blossom here in the spring, lime trees provide shade in the summer, and the chestnut leaves are heaped ankle-deep in autumn. **Notre-Dame**'s west face is towering but flat compared to the south and east sides, shored by dramatic flying buttresses that loom above this park. Here is a place to pause and feed the birds or to perch on a wooden bench during one of the occasional outdoor concerts given by a local police officers' orchestra. ♦ Quai de l'Archevêché and Rue du Cloître-Notre-Dame. Métros: Cité, Maubert–Mutualité

22 Mémorial de la Déportation (Deportation Memorial) Designed by G.H. Pingusson in 1962, this structure commemorates the 200,000 French citizens, most of whom were Jewish, who died during the Holocaust. Some 30,000 people from Paris alone were deported to Nazi death camps during World War II. Reflecting the Jewish tradition of paying homage to the dead by placing a stone on the grave, the memorial is constructed around a tunnel of 200,000 quartz pebbles. It also contains small tombs with earth from each of the concentration camps.

Visitors descend a narrow stair to an open space where they can look out at water through iron-barred windows. From there they pass through a door to a low, enclosed room where they can look through other barred windows into the tunnel of pebbles. The visitor here feels trapped visually and psychologically by the low ceiling and iron bars. Stark and simple, the memorial is one of city's most moving monuments. ♦ Free. Daily. Sq de l'Ile-de-France (off Quai de l'Archevêché). Métros: Cité, Maubert–Mutualité

23 Pont St-Louis Step lightly; this pedestrian bridge is the ninth on a site that has had a shaky history. The first bridge linking Ile de la Cité and Ile St-Louis was erected in 1634 by developer Jean-Christophe Marie; it crumbled on opening day, drowning 20 people. But, that wasn't the worst of Marie's bridge disasters; his Pont-Marie, built the following year, later collapsed during a flood, killing 121 people. ♦ Between Quais d'Orléans and de l'Archevêché. Métros: Cité, Pont-Marie

Ile St-Louis

A world apart from the rest of Paris, this once-bucolic cow pasture and site of sword duels is jammed today with grand 17th-century town houses (which with few exceptions are closed to the public) and fashionable shops. Somehow it remains a peaceful oasis in the heart of a bustling city. Ile St-Louis is named after Louis IX, the saintly French king who recited his breviary here among the cows. Voltaire considered this island the "second best" location in the world (his first choice was the straits of the Bosporus separating Europe from Asia).

People have only lived here for 300 years, yet the island is the oldest preserved section of the French capital, bisected by a single commercial street. When Henri IV decided to "urbanize" the pastoral Ile St-Louis for his courtiers as an extension of Place des Vosges, he hired developer Jean-Christophe Marie. Between 1614 and 1630, Marie laid out one of the city's first real estate developments with straight streets on a grid, an avant-garde idea in an age when streets followed meandering medieval cow paths.

Only six blocks long and two blocks wide, Ile St-Louis is an isolated village with no subway stop, four small hotels, and a baker whose ovens are fueled with wood. The 6,000 *Louisiens* (as island residents are called) are a proud, independent breed who don't always take kindly to interlopers (Ile St-Louis was the first quarter in Paris to chase out the Nazis during the Liberation). The list of former island residents includes Apollinaire, Balzac, Voltaire, Zola, Baudelaire, Cézanne, Courbet, Daumier, Delacroix, Colette, George Sand, and Georges Pompidou. When Louisiens leave the island, they say they are going "to Paris" or "to the continent" or "to the mainland," a voyage that's less than the length of a football field. Many of the elder residents have not been off the island in years, and less than 25 years ago there was so little traffic here on Sundays that the islanders played *boules* in the streets.

Soon after **Berthillon** opened its doors here, ice cream became the rage of Paris and the island was rediscovered. Along with the notoriety came the inevitable chic tea salons and hordes of tourists. Nonetheless, Ile St-Louis retains its own distinctive identity and charm and remains one of the most exclusive addresses in the city.

24 Brasserie de Isle St-Louis ★★$$ This Alsatian brasserie/tavern comes complete with the regional mascot—a stork perched on the old wooden bar. The bird, of course, is stuffed, and soon so are the neighborhood habitués who sit elbow-to-elbow dining on sausage, sauerkraut, ham knuckles, blueberry tarts, and *chopes* (steins) of Mutzia beer served by gruff waiters. The 1913 silver-plated espresso machine is a museum piece, as is the bartender Yvon Cottet. This feisty Breton, who has worked for Brigitte Bardot, Charles de Gaulle, and François Mitterrand, has served in this noisy brasserie for the last 40 years. He's even immortalized in a statue that's now in New York's Museum of Modern Art. Ask him for that story. ◆ M-Tu, Th-Su lunch and dinner (to 1:30AM); closed in August. No credit cards accepted. 55 Quai de Bourbon (at Rue St-Louis-en-l'Ile). 01.43.54.02.59. Métro: Pont-Marie

25 Le Flore en l'Ile ★★$ This Viennese-style tearoom boasts a three-star view of the **Panthéon** on the Left Bank and the flying buttresses of **Notre-Dame.** Highlights here are music by Mozart, good breakfasts, a hearty onion soup, traditional *plats du jour,* and delicious fruit tarts. ◆ Daily breakfast, lunch, and dinner until 2AM. 42 Quai d'Orléans (at Rue Jean-du-Bellay). 01.43.29.88.27. Métro: Pont-Marie

La Chaumière en l'Ile

25 La Chaumière en l'Ile ★$$ Enjoy traditional French dishes like onion soup, foie gras, roast salmon, and cod with red peppers in a rustic setting of stone walls and oak beams. Desserts—including the chocolate mousse and fresh fruit sorbets—are just as satisfying. ◆ Daily lunch and dinner. 4 Rue Jean-du-Bellay (at Rue St-Louis-en-l'Ile). 01.43.54.27.34. Métro: Pont-Marie

26 La Maison Lafitte *Magret de canard* (duck fillet), *confit d'oie* (confit of goose meat), foie gras, and other gourmet by-products of force-fed fowl are preserved, packaged, and ready to take home in your suitcase. ◆ Tu-Sa. 8 Rue Jean-du-Bellay (between Rue St-Louis-en-l'Ile and Quai de Bourbon). 01.43.26.08.63. Métro: Pont-Marie

27 Alain Carion You'll find minerals, geodes, meteorites, and minuscule fossilized black nautiluses fashioned into earrings at this rock collector's paradise. ◆ Tu-Sa. 92 Rue St-Louis-en-l'Ile (between Rues Le Regrattier and Jean-du-Bellay). 01.43.26.01.16. Métro: Pont-Marie

28 Hôtel St-Louis $$ The cousin of **Hôtel de Lutèce** and **Hôtel des Deux-Iles,** this recently renovated 21-room hostelry has exposed wooden beams, Louis XIII furniture, thick carpeting, and modern bathrooms, but *petits* bedrooms. Fifth-floor rooms have a view. There's no restaurant. ◆ 75 Rue St-Louis-en-l'Ile (at Rue Boutarel). 01.46.34.04.80; fax 01.46.34.02.13. Métro: Pont-Marie

28 Le Monde des Chimères ★★$$ This stone-and-beam bistro is a strong favorite of Ile St-Louis natives. Among the specialties of chef Cécille Ibane are 40-garlic chicken, *la brandade de morue* (codfish puréed with olive oil, garlic, and milk), and duck with apples. ◆ Tu-Sa lunch and dinner; closed two weeks in February. 69 Rue St-Louis-en-l'Ile (between Rues Le Regrattier and Boutarel). 01.43.54.45.27. Métro: Pont-Marie

29 Hôtel de Lutèce $$$ Named after the first Roman settlement in Paris, this restored 17th-century town house is now a hotel offering 27 comfortable rooms. The small breakfast room opens onto a flowered atrium. Ask for one of the brighter rooms on the top floor; they offer exquisite views of the island's rooftops and the dome of the **Panthéon** across the river. ◆ 65 Rue St-Louis-en-l'Ile (between Rues Le Regrattier and Boutarel). 01.43.26.23.52; fax 01.43.29.60.25. Métro: Pont-Marie

30 Aux Anysetiers du Roy ★$$ Originally called *Au Petit Bacchus* (the scorched remains of a 300-year-old effigy of the god of drink and revelry slouch above the entrance), this tavern used to serve the gamblers and jocks who frequented the ancient *jeu de paume*

(tennis) court across the street at **No. 54.** The chef recommends the *moules marinières* (mussels cooked in white wine and shallots) and the *profiteroles au chocolat*. Don't leave without washing your hands in the 17th-century pewter bathroom sink upstairs. ◆ Daily lunch and dinner. Reservations recommended. 61 Rue St-Louis-en-l'Ile (at Rue Le Regrattier). 01.40.46.87.85. Métro: Pont-Marie

30 Hôtel des Deux-Iles $$$ An abundance of fresh flowers adorns this 17th-century mansion-turned-hotel. The hotel bar, which has a fireplace, and the Renaissance-style ceramic tiles in the bathrooms are adequate compensation for the 17 smallish Provence-inspired rooms. There's no restaurant. ◆ 59 Rue St-Louis-en-l'Ile (between Rues Budé and Le Regrattier). 01.43.26.13.35; fax 01.43.29.60.25. Métro: Pont-Marie

30 Pylones The fanciful rubber jewelry and accessories displayed here sell as briskly as hot chestnuts on a winter afternoon. In lieu of that Boucheron diamond bracelet, wouldn't you rather be wearing a fanciful cactus, fish skeleton, monkey, or maybe the Pyramids of Giza on your wrist? Other novelties include children's bibs and rubber suspenders, plus whimsical alligator knives, Flintstone chess sets, and New Wave egg cups. ◆ Daily. 57 Rue St-Louis-en-l'Ile (between Rues Budé and Le Regrattier). 01.46.34.05.02. Métro: Pont-Marie

31 Hôtel Chenizot This former residence of the city's archbishops was also the home of Theresa Cabarrus, a noblewoman of insatiable sexual appetite. She offered herself to drawing-room Revolutionaries and as a result of this gesture was dubbed *Notre Dame de Thermidor*. While the plaster cornucopia and ferns in the first courtyard date from an 18th-century restoration, the mythological sea god over the front door and the sundial in the damp rear courtyard are original 17th-century decorations. This is now an apartment building with a restaurant and shop on the ground floor (see below). ◆ 51 Rue St-Louis-en-l'Ile (between Rues Budé and Le Regrattier). Métro: Pont-Marie

LA CASTAFIORE

SPÉCIALITÉS ITALIENNES

31 La Castafiore ★★★$$ In 1988 an American and an Englishman left the advertising business to open Ile St-Louis's only Italian restaurant. The result was this dining spot with terra-cotta walls, white tablecloths, and a warm ambience in which to enjoy *tagliatelles aux cèpes* (pasta with mushrooms) or chicken Bolognese. Don't pass up the homemade tiramisù or the

naughty *Coupe Amarena* (ice cream with chestnut purée and warm chocolate sauce) for dessert. ◆ Daily lunch and dinner. Reservations recommended. 51 Rue St-Louis-en-l'Ile (between Rues Budé and Le Regrattier). 01.43.54.78.62. Métro: Pont-Marie

31 L'Epicerie French gourmands will feel right at home in this tiny shop packed to the rafters with delicacies to do penance for. Champagne mustard, *terrine de lapin* (rabbit casserole), fois gras, homemade wild strawberry jam, and beautifully wrapped bonbons are but a few of the treats. ◆ Daily until 9PM. 51 Rue St-Louis-en-l'Ile (between Rues Budé and Le Regrattier). 01.43.25.20.14. Métro: Pont-Marie

32 Rue de la Femme Sans Teste (Street of the Headless Woman) Shortly after the Revolution, the Rue Le Regrattier (named in the 17th century for an entrepreneur in the island development consortium) was dubbed the "Street of the Headless Woman" (in old French, *tête* was spelled with an *s*) after a decapitated statue at the corner of Rue Le Regrattier and Quai de Bourbon. "Headless woman" is a misnomer, however; the robed stone figure, severed at the torso, is believed to be St. Nicholas, the patron saint of boatmen. His statue stands at the top of the stairs that once led down to the ferry. ◆ Rue Le Regrattier (between Quais d'Orléans and de Bourbon). Métro: Pont-Marie

32 6 Rue Le Regrattier Jeanne Duval, the voluptuous West Indian mistress of Charles-Pierre Baudelaire who was known as the "Black Venus," lived here. It's still a private residence. ◆ Between Quai d'Orléans and Rue St-Louis-en-l'Ile. Métro: Pont-Marie

33 18-20 Quai d'Orléans Columnist Walter Lippmann lived here in 1938. It remains a private residence. ◆ Between Rues Budé and Le Regrattier. Métro: Pont-Marie

34 10 Quai d'Orléans James Jones, the author of *From Here to Eternity*, resided here with his family from 1958 to 1975 and entertained such famous writers and artists as Henry Miller, Alexander Calder, William Styron, Sylvia Beach, and James Baldwin. This is still a residential building. ◆ At Rue Budé. Métro: Pont-Marie

35 Musée Adam Mickiewicz The life and times of exiled Mickiewicz, the "Byron of Poland," as well as the poet's relationships with great Romantic French authors and musicians, are brought to life on the second floor of this library and museum. The private library, established in 1852, contains some 200,000 volumes as well as copies of nearly every Polish newspaper published in the 19th century. In the **Chopin Room** on the first floor are composer Frédéric Chopin's frayed armchair, his hand-penned mazurka scores, a death mask, and the world's only daguerreotype of the young pianist. ♦ Admission. Tu-F 2-6PM; Sa 10AM-1PM. Guided tours: Th 2-5PM on the hour. 6 Quai d'Orléans (between Rues des Deux-Ponts and Budé). 01.43.54.35.61. Métro: Pont-Marie

35 Isami ★★$$ Small, simple, and casual, the only Japanese restaurant on the island specializes in sushi and sashimi, but also serves dishes such as oyster salad with vinegar and steamed *daurade* (sea bream). ♦ Tu-Sa lunch and dinner; Su dinner. 4 Quai d'Orléans (between Rues des Deux-Ponts and Budé). 01.40.46.06.97. Métro: Pont-Marie

Librairie Ulysse

36 Librairie Ulysse I In 1971 the free-spirited Catherine Domain opened this vest-pocket shop specializing in travel books. She has crammed in, higgledy-piggledy, 20,000 French and English titles on everything from trekking in the Himalayas to canoeing in South America. Her second bookshop, **Ulysse II** (26 Rue St-Louis-en-l'Ile, between Rues Poulletier and des Deux-Ponts, 01.43.29.52.10) specializes in volumes on France, maps, and travel magazines. ♦ Tu-Sa 2-8PM. 35 Rue St-Louis-en-l'Ile (between Rues des Deux-Ponts and Budé). 01.43.25.17.35. Métro: Pont-Marie

36 Nos Ancêtres les Gaulois ★$$ Tackily decorated with sheepskins, battered shields, and mounted heads of wild boars (in sunglasses) to loosely evoke the Middle Ages, this cavernous, all-you-can-eat establishment seats 240 people. Earthy do-it-yourself salads, greasy sausage platters, grilled meat, chocolate mousse, and barely drinkable red wine are perennial hits with starving students and rowdy German tour groups. It's always crowded; arrive early and avoid Saturday nights, when the ambience is raucous, bordering on Neanderthal. ♦ M-Sa dinner until 1:30AM; Su lunch. Reservations required. 39 Rue St-Louis-en-l'Ile (between Rues des Deux-Ponts and Budé). 01.46.33.66.12. Métro: Pont-Marie

Hôtel du Jeu de Paume

37 Hôtel du Jeu de Paume $$$ Deftly fashioned around a royal tennis court dating from 1624 (*jeu de paume* is the medieval precursor of the game now played at Wimbledon and Flushing Meadow), this refined 32-room hotel, opened in the 1980s, is the first new hostelry on the islands in two decades. **Room No. 4** overlooks the garden, and **No. 7** features a terrace. There's no restaurant. ♦ 54 Rue St-Louis-en-l'Ile (between Rues des Deux-Ponts and Le Regrattier). 01.43.26.14.18; fax 01.40.46.02.76. Métro: Pont-Marie

38 Au Pont Marie ★★$$ Run by the Griffoul family from southwest France, this small, rustic restaurant features specialties from the Rouergue region in the south of France. Deserving of hearty appetites are the cabbage stuffed with beef and herbs and the cassoulet. ♦ M-F lunch and dinner; Sa dinner. 7 Quai de Bourbon (between Rues des Deux-Ponts and Le Regrattier). 01.43.54.79.62. Métro: Pont-Marie

39 3 Quai de Bourbon Explaining the plainness of the facade of this real-estate agency is a story in itself. The sumptuous Empire-style windows and storefront that once adorned the building were purchased by J. Pierpont Morgan and in 1926 moved to the Metropolitan Museum of Art in New York. They now serve as the entrance to the museum's Wrightsman Galleries, which house a superb collection of Louis XVI furniture and porcelain. ♦ Between Rues des Deux-Ponts and Le Regrattier. Métro: Pont-Marie

39 Boulangerie Rioux Old-fashioned bread is baked in a *four chauffé au bois* (wood-burning oven) at this traditional bakery. ♦ M-W, Sa-Su. 35 Rue des Deux-Ponts (between Rue St-Louis-en-l'Ile and Quai de Bourbon). 01.43.54.57.59. Métro: Pont-Marie

39 Les Fous de l'Ile ★★★$ Fresh-cut flowers on the bar and brass candlesticks on old wooden bistro tables, combined with wacky monthly art exhibitions, surrealist postcards, and music from Paganini to Pearl Jam make this converted *épicerie* the island's most relaxing and hip restaurant/cafe. At lunch, famished students arrive for the warm goat cheese salad, *tagliatelles au saumon fumé* (pasta and smoked salmon) with caviar, steak with roquefort sauce, and all-American cheesecake. ♦ Tu-Sa lunch and dinner; Su brunch and dinner. 33 Rue des Deux-Ponts (between Rue St-Louis-en-l'Ile and Quai de Bourbon). 01.43.25.76.67. Métro: Pont-Marie

40 La Poste (Post Office) Booths are available for making international phone calls. ♦ M-F 8AM-7PM; Sa 8AM-noon. 16 Rue des Deux-Ponts (between Rue St-Louis-en-l'Ile and Quai d'Anjou). 01.43.25.37.79. Métro: Pont-Marie

The first true restaurant opened in 1765 when a Parisian tavern keeper named Boulanger defied a monopoly held by city caterers and began to sell cooked meat at his tavern on Rue Bailleul. Boulanger served a dish of sheeps' meat in white sauce, which he called a *restaurante* (restorative).

41 Berthillon This Ile St-Louis landmark is so popular that around Christmastime police officers direct the flow of Parisians queuing up for what is undeniably the best ice cream and sorbet in Paris. Its position as the city's preeminent ice cream shop is so secure that it has the chutzpa to close two days a week, on school holidays, and for six weeks in summer, the prime ice-cream–eating season. Surly women in pink aprons scoop up more than 50 flavors, all made without a single artificial ingredient. Sample the exotic fruit flavors in season: rhubarb, black currant, fig, kumquat, and fresh melon. ♦ W-Su; closed school holidays and mid-July through August. 31 Rue St-Louis-en-l'Ile (between Rues Poulletier and des Deux-Ponts). 01.43.54.31.61. Métro: Pont-Marie

42 Au Gourmet de l'Isle ★★$$ This bustling bargain bistro is famous for its *andouillette* (sausage with tripe)—a nice dish if you can stomach it. Other less challenging specialties: artichoke hearts and pork in red wine sauce, strawberry tarts, and Auvergne wines. ♦ W-Su lunch and dinner. Reservations recommended for dinner. 42 Rue St-Louis-en-l'Ile (between Rues Poulletier and des Deux-Ponts). 01.43.26.79.27. Métro: Pont-Marie

43 L'Auberge de la Reine Blanche ★$$ Named for the mother of the island's patron, St. Louis, this pretty pink dining room offers dependable French classics: *canard* (duck) *à l'orange, coq au vin,* and *boeuf* (beef) *bourguignon.* Catch the cute dollhouse furniture displayed on the walls. ♦ M, Tu, F-Su lunch and dinner; W-Th dinner. Reservations recommended. 30 Rue St-Louis-en-l'Ile (between Rues Poulletier and des Deux-Ponts). 01.46.33.07.87. Métro: Pont-Marie

43 L'Orangerie ★★$$$
A mini **Maxim's,** with 18th-century decor and background harpsichord music, this restaurant specializes in elegant late suppers. The ribs of beef, leg of lamb (cooked over a wood fire), and rich Bordeaux reds cause Rolls-Royce traffic jams out front. ♦ Daily dinner. Reservations required. 28 Rue St-Louis-en-l'Ile (between Rues Poulletier and des Deux-Ponts). 01.46.33.93.98. Métro: Pont-Marie

L'Orangerie

43 La Charlotte de l'Isle ★★$ For a diabolically delicious treat, order *gâteau du diable* (devil's cake), half-moon cookies, or witch's brooms (chocolate-dipped orange rinds) at this little-known tea salon. Charlotte, the hospitable, kimono-clad owner, seems strangely obsessed with Halloween but swears she has yet to turn a customer into a toad. Sip freshly brewed Chinese tea at one of three tiny tables nestled in the back room among the clutter of puppets, dried-flower bouquets, and an old stereo playing Poulenc. Poetry readings, puppet shows, and piano concerts are regular events here. ♦ Tu-Su tea (2-8PM); poetry readings Tu 8:30PM; puppet shows W 2:30PM and 4PM (reservations required); piano concerts F 6-8PM; closed July and August. 24 Rue St-Louis-en-l'Ile (between Rues Poulletier and des Deux-Ponts). 01.43.54.25.83. Métro: Pont-Marie

44 St-Louis-en-l'Ile Popular for weddings and candlelit concerts, this Jesuit Baroque–style church was built in 1726; it follows plans created by island resident **Louis Le Vau,** the great French architect who designed portions of the **Louvre** and **Versailles.** Inside is a statue of St. Louis in chain mail and crusader's sword, and next to the tomb of a Polish freedom fighter with a daunting name (Damaiowice-strzembosz) is a 1926 plaque that bears the inscription: "In grateful memory of St. Louis in whose honor the City of St. Louis, Missouri, USA, is named." The church was vandalized during the Revolution. For example, the empty-handed carved cherubs over the massive wooden west portal once held the king's fleur-de-lis. The only reason the statues of St. Geneviève and the Virgin Mary survived the Revolution is that they were disguised as the goddesses of Reason and Freedom. Evening concerts are held here frequently. ♦ 3 Rue Poulletier (at Rue St-Louis-en-l'Ile). 01.46.34.11.60. Métro: Pont-Marie

45 Flood Marker Written on the wall along Quai de Béthune are the words *Crue Janvier 1910* and a line marking the astounding level, or *crue,* the Seine reached during the *inondation* (flood) of January 1910, when many streets became canals and rowboats were the preferred form of transportation. ♦ Quai de Béthune (between Blvd Henri-IV and Rue des Doux-Ponts). Métro: Pont-Marie

46 24 Quai de Béthune In 1935 Helena Rubinstein demolished one of the island's finest town houses (constructed in 1642) and built an Art Deco structure in its place. She reigned from the new building's rooftop apartment. This remains a residential building. ♦ At Rue Poulletier. Métro: Pont-Marie

47 Square Barye At the eastern tip of Ile St-Louis, this pocket park is all that remains of the terraced gardens of Duc de Bretonvillier. You might glimpse sunbathers or witness a schoolboys' fishing competition here on the cobblestone quay. ♦ Off Blvd Henri-IV (at Pont de Sully). Métros: Pont-Marie, Sully–Morland

48 5 Rue St-Louis-en-l'Ile The expatriate literary agent William Aspenwall Bradley, who represented such authors as Thornton Wilder, Edith Wharton, Katherine Anne Porter, and John Dos Passos, lived in this apartment building. Bradley was the one who closed the deal for publication of the *Autobiography of Alice B. Toklas* by Gertrude Stein. ♦ Between Quai d'Anjou and Rue de Bretonvilliers. Métro: Pont-Marie

49 Hôtel Lambert Probably the most opulent of 17th-century private residences in Paris, this frescoed and pilastered *hôtel particulier* was designed by **Louis Le Vau** in 1640 for Lambert the Rich. Its lavish gilded ceilings by Charles Le Brun predate and rival his **Great Hall of Mirrors** at **Versailles.** After the 1830-31 insurrection, Polish prince Adam Czartoryski fled to France, married King Louis-Phillipe's granddaughter, and bought the **Hôtel Lambert** for his personal residence. Over the years, Czartoryski's home served as a salon for expatriate Polish royalty and intelligentsia, as well as a rehearsal hall for Frédéric Chopin. Later it functioned as a girls' finishing school and a safe house for Allied fighter pilots who had been shot down in France. Voltaire briefly nested here with his lover, the Marquise de Châtelet, while writing the *Henriade*. Since 1972 the house has belonged to the Rothschilds. Behind the locked gate is a horseshoe-shaped courtyard and the famous **Galerie d'Hercule,** containing the Eustache Le Sueur frescoes and Jacques Rousseau trompe l'oeil landscape paintings. The building is open to the public only on rare occasions. ♦ 2 Rue St-Louis-en-l'Ile (at Quai d'Anjou). Métros: Pont-Marie, Sully–Morland

50 9 Quai d'Anjou The 19th-century illustrator and satirist Honoré Daumier lived in this apartment building off and on for 17 years in the company of distinguished islanders such as poet Charles Baudelaire and fellow artist Ferdinand Delacroix. It was on the Ile St-Louis that Daumier sketched his mordant portrayals of life and politics and painted masterpieces such as *La Blanchisseuse* (The Washer Woman), which hangs in the **Louvre.** ♦ Between Rues St-Louis-en-l'Ile and Poulletier. Métros: Pont-Marie, Sully–Morland

51 Hôtel de Lauzun Louis Le Vau built this mansion in 1656 for a corrupt French army caterer, Charles Gruyn des Bordes, who was arrested soon afterward. That is why the building is named for its second tenant, the dandy Duke of Lauzun. The roll call of residents and visitors to the **Hôtel de Lauzun** includes Rilke, Wagner, Daumier, Delacroix, and **Louis Charles Auguste Steinheil** (who

restored the **Sainte-Chapelle** windows). In 1834 Baudelaire gathered his bohemian "hashish club" in an upstairs room and conducted the hallucinatory research for his book *Les Paradis Artificiels.* Some of the gaudiest suites in all of Paris are the **Chambres de Parade** (parade rooms), which are cluttered with golden nymphs, cut-velvet walls, trompe l'oeil murals, and allegorical figures. In 1928 the city bought and restored it as a residence for visiting heads of state. The building is currently under renovation; there are no plans to open it to the public. ♦ Tours by appointment only. 17 Quai d'Anjou (between Rues St-Louis-en-l'Ile and Poulletier). 01.42.76.57.99. Métros: Pont-Marie, Sully–Morland

52 29 Quai d'Anjou In 1922, with a hand-printing press, American William Bird established his Three Mountains Press in this building. Under the editorial aegis of Ezra Pound, it published Ernest Hemingway and Ford Madox Ford. ♦ Between Rues Poulletier and des Deux-Ponts. Métros: Pont-Marie, Sully–Morland

53 37 Quai d'Anjou When he arrived in France in 1921 after the acceptance of his first major novel, *Three Soldiers*, John Dos Passos rented a room in this apartment building. ♦ Between Rues Poulletier and des Deux-Ponts. Métros: Pont-Marie, Sully–Morland

54 Pont-Marie King Louis XIII laid the first stone of this bridge, which was completed in 1635. Twenty-three years later, a spring thaw caused a flood that partially destroyed the bridge; 22 of the four-story houses above the structure fell into the Seine, drowning 121 residents and shopkeepers. The bridge is not named after Marie de Médicis, Henri IV's widow, who commissioned the work, but after Jean-Christophe Marie, the contractor hired to develop Ile St-Louis and the *quais*.♦ Between Quais d'Anjou and des Célestins. Métro: Pont-Marie

---

The first tree to show its green buds in springtime is situated at the western tip of the Ile de la Cité at the Square du Vert-Galent.

"No one can understand Paris and its history who does not understand that its fierceness is the balance and justification of its frivolity. It is called a city of pleasure; but it may also very specially be called a city of pain. The crown of roses is also a crown of thorns. Its people are too prone to hurt others, but quite ready also to hurt themselves. They are martyrs for religion; they are martyrs for irreligion; they are even martyrs for immorality."

G.K. Chesterton

Bests

Fern B. Creelan
Psychotherapist and muse for as many creative people as possible

The way I feel when I round the bend in back of the **Panthéon** past the graceful spires of **St-Etienne-du-Mont** and into the small, twisted streets of the fifth arrondissement.

The look of **La Samaritaine** from across the river, looking like the prow of a ship from **Rue Dauphine.**

"La Vie de Bohème" as felt in **Place du Tertre** in **Montmartre** and **Place de la Contrescarpe** in the fifth arrondissement.

Sunlight steaming into **Sainte-Chapelle** the morning after hearing a glorious Bach concert in the very same edifice.

Marc Mimram
Engineer/Architect

The **Seine** is always the best way to discover the interior of the city: Travel by car from the **Pont au Change** to the **Pont de Bercy,** or by *bateau mouche* from the **Eiffel Tower.** Night or day, stop in front of the **Jardin des Tuileries** or **Musée d'Orsay**—the **Passerelle de Solférino** connects the two.

In the evening, buy a book at **La Hune** near **Café de Flore** on the **Boulevard St-Germain.**

Find the best cigars at **A la Civette** on **Rue St-Honoré** and then go to **Place Pigalle** and listen to some good music.

Before you turn in for the night, enjoy a drink at **Les Bains-Douches.**

You can spend the night at the **Quai Voltaire** hotel or the **Hôtel des Grands Hommes** at the **Panthéon.**

The next day see the latest exhibition at the **Centre Georges Pompidou** in Beaubourg.

Jack Lang
France's Former Minister of Culture

Passage des Panoramas—This old covered passage in the neighborhood around **La Bourse** begins at **Boulevard Montmartre** and opens onto **Rue St-Marc.** During the brief regime called the Directoire (1795-99), people paraded here in eccentric but beautiful outfits. The free-spirited feeling of this place still remains, preserved by its very inexpensive restaurants and its *salons de thé.*

Place d'Aligre Market—In this popular colorful market, a combination flea market and food market, you can find marvelous vegetables and specialty items sold by street vendors, as well as classic secondhand goods.

Rue Myrha—In the 18th arrondissement, Rue Myrha leads to **Boulevard Barbès,** a neighborhood that is a blend of the Orient and the West.

At the time of Ramadan, the sidewalks of Rue Myrha at night are filled with lots of small stands selling delicious Oriental pastries. This is also a place where you can buy a live chicken and the freshest eggs.

The lesser known works of Delacroix—I have discovered that many Parisians are not aware of the existence—even though they are easily accessible—of the magnificent works of Eugène Delacroix that are located in a church in the heart of Paris. Three biblical frescoes, from the artist's later work, are in **St-Sulpice.**

Parisian restaurants—For the best cuisine, I believe that Alain Senderens, Alain Dutournier, and Guy Savoy are forever at the peak of creativity.

La Marée Verte restaurant offers oysters from Colchester and New Zealand which, in my opinion, are the best in Europe.

Finally, like every lover of food, I have my favorite bistros. I keep having the pleasure of rediscovering **Ma Bourgogne (Marais),** the charm of its terrace under the archway of the **Place des Vosges,** and its simple, but high quality, fare.

Alain P. Zivie
Egyptologist/Archaeologist/Research Director, National Scientific Research Center

To be in different neighborhoods during the week, when they are full of activity. The weekend will not give you an accurate impression of Paris, except for early Sunday morning, when the town is empty.

The **Seine** and the light from the *bateaux mouche* reflecting on the houses along the banks of the river, thinking about the books of Patrick Modiano, the great poet of Paris. During these times the town resembles a theater set.

The authentic cafes with their authentic 1950s decor.

The **Musée Delacroix**'s studio and garden on the **Rue de Furstemberg.** The African, Chinese, and Arabic neighborhoods, including **Boulevard Barbès.** The **Palais Royal** on an ordinary day. The bar at the **Plaza Athénée** and the **Raphael** bar.

The winter nights when the city is blanketed with snow. The **Passy** station and its gardens that meet the Seine. The American in Paris in the 1950s. The square courtyard of the **Louvre** seen from the Egyptian rooms on the first floor. The artisans and shopkeepers. The retirees who play cards in the **Café de la République.** Paris, city of memories and nostalgia, as well as possibility.

The best bird's eye views of Paris are from the **Eiffel Tower,** the 56th floor of the **Montparnasse Tower,** the cafe on the 10th floor of **La Samaritaine, Notre-Dame**'s south tower, and the dome of **Sacré-Coeur** in **Montmartre.**

The Latin
Quarter

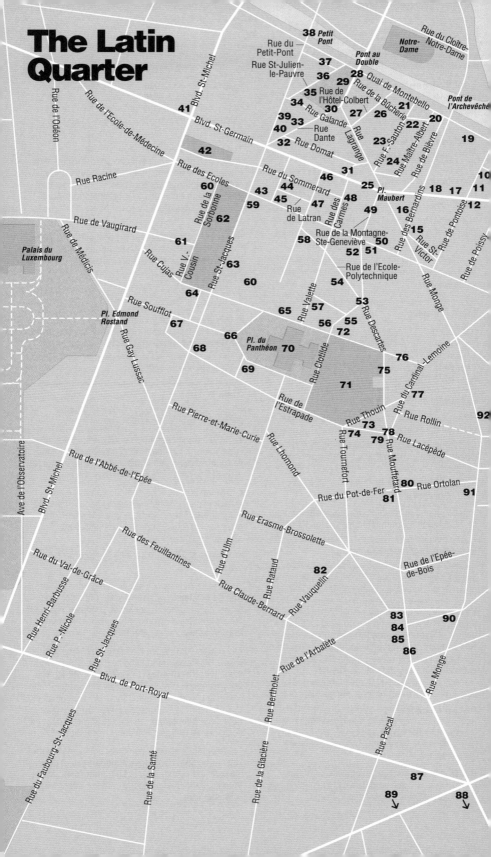

Rue de l'Odéon

Rue de l'Ecole-de-Médecine

Blvd. St-Michel

Rue du
Petit-Pont

Rue St-Julien-
le-Pauvre

38 Petit
Pont

37

36

35 Rue de
l'Hôtel-Colbert

34

33

32 Rue Domat

41

Blvd. St-Germain

39

40

Rue
Dante

28

29

30 Rue Galande

27

Rue Lagrange

Pont au
Double

Quai de Montebello

Rue de la Bûcherie

Notre-
Dame

Rue du Cloître-
Notre-Dame

Pont de
l'Archevêché

21

26

23

24

22

20

19

Rue F.-Sauton

Rue Maître-Albert

Rue de Bièvre

Rue St-Victor

42

Rue Racine

Rue des Ecoles

Rue du Sommerard

46

Rue de Vaugirard

Rue de la Sorbonne

60

43

44

45

47

48

49

31

25

Pl.
Maubert

Rue des
Carmes

Rue
de Latran

Rue de la Montagne-
Ste-Geneviève

18

17

16

15

Rue des Bernardins

11

10

12

Rue St-
Victor

Rue de Poissy

Rue de Pontoise

59

62

Rue de Médicis

Rue Cujas

61

Rue V.-
Cousin

Rue St-Jacques

63

60

58

50

52 51

54

Rue de l'Ecole-
Polytechnique

Rue Monge

Palais du
Luxembourg

64

Rue Soufflot

Pl. Edmond
Rostand

67

68

65

66

Pl. du
Panthéon

70

69

Rue Valette

57

56

55

72

Rue Clotilde

53

Rue Descartes

71

75

76

Rue du Cardinal-Lemoine

77

92

Rue Gay-Lussac

Rue Pierre-et-Marie-Curie

Rue de
l'Estrapade

Rue Thouin

73

74

79

78

Rue Rollin

Rue Lacépède

Rue Tournefort

Rue Mouffetard

Rue L'homond

Ave de l'Observatoire

Blvd. St-Michel

Rue de l'Abbé-de-l'Epée

Rue Erasme-Brossolette

Rue du Pot-de-Fer

80 Rue Ortolan

81

91

Rue des Feuillantines

Rue d'Ulm

Rue Claude-Bernard

Rue Rataud

Rue Vauquelin

82

Rue de l'Epée-
de-Bois

Rue du Val-de-Grâce

Rue Henri-Barbusse

Rue P.-Nicole

Rue St-Jacques

Blvd. de Port-Royal

Rue Berthollet

Rue de l'Arbalète

Rue Monge

83

84

85

86

90

Rue du Faubourg-St-Jacques

Rue de la Santé

Rue de la Glacière

Rue Pascal

87

89

88

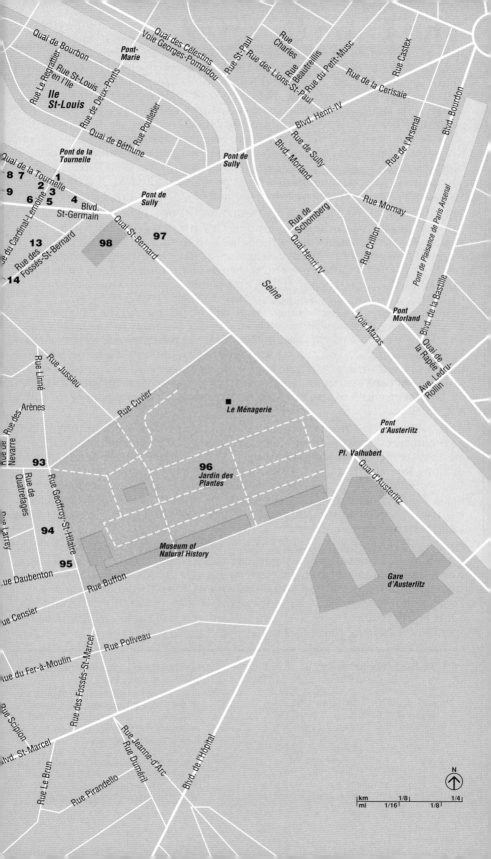

The Latin Quarter

This section of the city is where you'll find Roman Paris, the university, and the bohemian quarter. The Henri Burger novel *Scènes de la Vie de Bohème,* which became the Puccini opera *La Bohème,* was set here. The Latin Quarter was once the home of Verlaine and Descartes, and is still the home of the **Sorbonne,** old bookshops, student cafes, publishing houses, jazz clubs, and, more recently, expensive boutiques. For seven centuries, this was a city within a city, inhabited by Latin-speaking scholars who were exempt from the civil law and recognized no authority other than the pope. Latin, which hasn't been spoken here since the Revolution, has been replaced on the streets of the Left Bank by the Moroccan, Greek, and Vietnamese of immigrant families selling couscous, souvlaki, and imperial rolls to supplement the basic bohemian diet of coffee and cheap cigarettes.

This overview of the Latin Quarter begins at the **Pont de la Tournelle,** in front of the famed penthouse restaurant **La Tour d'Argent.** From here you can browse the bookstalls along the **Seine** and enjoy a splendid view of **Notre-Dame**'s flying buttresses. Next comes François Mitterrand's house; two funny, offbeat museums—the **Musée des Hôpitaux de Paris–Assistance Publique** (Museum of Public Health and Welfare) and the **Musée des Collections Historiques de la Préfecture de Police** (Police Museum); and then the **Rue des Ecoles,** which leads to the **Sorbonne** and the **Collège de France,** for centuries the most celebrated seats of learning in Europe. At the end of the street are the **Roman Baths** adjoining the extraordinary medieval **Musée de Cluny.** As you climb **Montagne Ste-Geneviève,** named after the patron saint of Paris, you'll pass King Philippe Auguste's 13th-century city wall; **Le Raccard** restaurant, a landmark for fondue lovers; and the **Panthéon,** a Classical monument and the final resting place of Voltaire, Rousseau, and Victor Hugo.

At the **Place de la Contrescarpe,** visitors can embark on a detour that passes a Roman arena and a Turkish mosque en route to the zoo and botanical gardens—a nice spot for a picnic lunch purchased in the **Place-Monge** market or along **Rue Mouffetard.** On Rue Mouffetard, a medieval market street frequented this century by the likes of Ernest Hemingway and Josephine Baker, you can meander past stalls selling everything from tropical mangoes to African monkey bread, and then end up at **Gobelins,** the old royal weaving mills, for an afternoon tour.

For a quick bite while sightseeing, stop at one of the many inexpensive Vietnamese or Greek shish kebab restaurants along Mouffetard around **Gobelins.** To find the Latin Quarter's fancier restaurants, including **Dodin-Bouffant, La Bûcherie,** and **La Tour d'Argent,** head toward the Rue des Ecoles and the Seine. The area's nightspots, including **Paradis Latin** and **Les Trois Maillets,** are also located here and are an appropriate way to end a day spent in the bohemian Latin Quarter.

---

1 Statue de Ste-Geneviève On the Pont de la Tournelle, one of the Seine's newest bridges (1928) and the fifth in a long line that dates back to 1369, is a missilelike statue of the city's patron saint. Apparently ready for a heavenly liftoff, the angular obelisk of St. Geneviève by Landowski turns her back on **Notre-Dame** and faces upriver, guarding the city as her spirit has done since 450. In that year, the prayers of the then 27-year-old nun were credited with halting Attila the Hun's advance on Paris, after his army of barbarians had just sacked Cologne and brutalized 10,000 of its maidens.

In 473, while the city was under siege by the Franks, Geneviève courageously smuggled 11 boatloads of food through enemy lines to feed starving Parisians. She lived on **Montagne Ste-Geneviève** until the age of 89. Like France's other virgin saint, Joan of Arc, Geneviève was eventually consigned to flames, but not until 1,281 years after her death. The fanatic anticlerics of the Revolution burned her remains and cast the ashes into the river. ♦ Pont de la Tournelle (between Quais de la Tournelle and de Béthune). Métros: Cardinal-Lemoine, Pont-Marie

2 Les Comptoirs de la Tour d'Argent If you want to take one of the **Tour d'Argent** restaurant's trademark blue-and-white Limoges plates home as a souvenir, walk across the street to the gourmet boutique of Claude Terrail, the enterprising restaurateur who has become the Pierre Cardin of French cuisine. Here, instead of dinner for $180, you can buy a menu for $18, fresh *foie gras de canard* to go, or an entire **Tour d'Argent** place setting, including fluted Champagne glass, coffee spoon, and ashtray. Prices start at $3 for 90 grams of Dijon mustard and escalate to $105 for a bottle of wine. ♦ Tu-Su until midnight. 2 Rue du Cardinal-Lemoine (at Quai de la Tournelle). 01.46.33.45.58. Métros: Cardinal-Lemoine, Maubert–Mutualité

3 La Tour d'Argent ★★★★$$$$ This may no longer be the best restaurant in Paris, but its penthouse panorama of **Notre-Dame**'s flying buttresses and the barges passing on the Seine have helped make it the city's most famous, expensive, and spectacular eating establishment. The renowned dining spot stands on the site of the **Café Anglais,** which opened in 1582. The cafe was mentioned by Mme. de Sévigné in her famous letters and provided the setting for a Dumas novel; it is also said to be where the fork was first used in Paris. On the ground floor of the restaurant is a table set with the silver, crystal, and china used at a dinner here on 7 June 1867 that was attended by Czar Alexander II, the Czarevitch, Wilhelm I, and Bismarck.

Touches of class are found throughout the **Tour d'Argent,** from the Grand Siècle–style elevator to the traditional blue cornflower in the jacket lapel of restaurant owner and dandy Claude Terrail. The kitchen's pièce de résistance is pressed duck flambé, first served in 1890 to Edward VII, then Prince of Wales. More than 600,000 ducklings later, the dish is still a hit. The kitchen keeps a running tally of the number of ducklings pressed, and each order arrives at the table with a numbered card. Other recommended dishes include *filet de sole Cardinal* (fillet of sole with crayfish), flambéed peaches, and bittersweet chocolate cake. The wine list draws from the 300,000 bottles in the vaulted cellars underground.

Diners can tour the cellars after dessert and watch Terrail's little sound-and-light show while sipping a vintage liqueur. Tables in the rooftop dining room must be reserved far in advance; ask for one by the picture window. Bear in mind, however, that lunch is half the price of dinner and midday is when Parisians eat out. The restaurant is popular with American and Japanese tourists, and at dinnertime the waiters may be the only French speakers in the place. ♦ Tu-Su lunch and dinner. Reservations required. 15-17 Quai de la Tournelle (between Blvd St-Germain and Rue du Cardinal-Lemoine). 01.43.54.23.31. Métros: Cardinal-Lemoine, Maubert–Mutualité

3 La Rôtisserie du Beaujolais ★★$$ Owned by Claude Terrail of the pricey **Tour d'Argent** next door (see above) and managed by Alain Robert, this boisterous bistro serves Lyonnais specialties and rotisserie-roasted meat. Try the *pieds de cochon farcis* (stuffed pigs feet) and the *canette rôtie* (roast duck, which comes from the same farm that supplies **La Tour d'Argent** with its birds). Drink in the warm, jolly atmosphere along with a bottle of Moulin-à-Vent, the richest of the Beaujolais, while you consider Terrail's philosophy: "Simple things are what people want, even those in fur coats." ♦ Tu-Su lunch and dinner. 19 Quai de la Tournelle (at Rue du Cardinal-Lemoine). 01.43.54.17.47. Métros: Cardinal-Lemoine, Maubert–Mutualité

4 Le Rallye ★$ Locals lunch on sandwiches and the plat du jour here, but when an earthy crowd takes over at night, the cafe comes to resemble an Amsterdam bar. Just down the street but a world away in spirit from **La Tour d'Argent,** it has a collection of Tintin cartoon memorabilia on display, a friendly boxer named Figaro underfoot, and music ranging from opera to Jimi Hendrix. Avoid the bathroom. ♦ Daily breakfast and lunch; bar open until 2AM. No credit cards accepted. 11 Quai de la Tournelle (between Blvd St-Germain and Rue du Cardinal-Lemoine). 01.43.54.29.65. Métros: Cardinal-Lemoine, Maubert–Mutualité

5 L'Atlas ★★$$ Chef El Jaziri Bijamin likens himself to a culinary ambassador promoting unique dishes from his native Morocco. The tastly *tajines* (stews) include lamb with forest mushrooms and lustily spiced fish with saffron. The elegant *couscous de L'Atlas,* which includes veal, meatballs, and lamb, is another fine main course. Have sweet mint tea with orange blossom nectar to end the meal on a soothing note. ♦ Daily lunch and dinner. 12 Blvd St-Germain (at Rue du Cardinal-Lemoine). 01.46.33.86.98, 01.44.07.23.66. Métros: Cardinal-Lemoine, Maubert–Mutualité

6 Chez René ★$$ An authentic bistro with amusing waiters, this eatery offers tasty daily Lyonnaise specials that range from Monday's pot-au-feu to Friday's *blanquette de veau* (veal in white sauce). Also on the menu are cucumbers and cream, country sausages, mutton with white beans, entrecôte, and, in autumn, *pleurottes Provençales* (fresh wild mushrooms baked with garlic). ♦ M-F lunch and dinner; closed in August. Reservations recommended. 14 Blvd St-Germain (at Rue du Cardinal-Lemoine, Maubert–Mutualité

Campagne et Provence
Restaurant

7 Campagne et Provence ★★★$$ Patrick Jeffroy's classy little restaurant is a treat to behold. Here chef Bonnefoy prepares a palette of dishes with flavors ranging from soothing to robust. Choose from the fresh cod with aioli or saddle of roast lamb with coriander and polenta. Those who habitually abstain from dessert may be tempted by the *soupe de melon à la menthe vanillée* (melon soup with mint and vanilla) or the superb mille-feuille with dried fruits and chocolate. ♦ M dinner; Tu-F lunch and dinner; Sa dinner. 25 Quai de la Tournelle (between Rues du Cardinal-Lemoine and de Poissy). 01.43.54.05.17. Métro: Maubert–Mutualité

8 Vivario ★★$$ This small neighborhood restaurant is serious about the quality of Corsican meals it serves. Its menu changes every day to make the most of what's fresh, but it always includes delicious pasta dishes. ♦ M, Sa dinner; Tu-F lunch and dinner; closed mid-August to mid-September and Christmas. 6 Rue Cochin (between Rues de Poissy and de Pontoise). 01.43.25.08.19. Métro: Maubert–Mutualité

9 Boulangerie Beauvallet Julien Modesty may prevent M. Ousbih and his family from putting their bakery's name in the window, but they won't divulge the recipe that results in the best baguettes in the Latin Quarter. Thin, crusty, with the tang of sourdough, one of these baguettes is the perfect base for building a picnic to take down to the quay. Fresh loaves come out of the oven at 7AM, 11AM, and 1PM. ♦ M-Tu, Th-Su; closed in August. 6 Rue de Poissy (at Rue Cochin). 01.43.26.94.24. Métro: Maubert–Mutualité

10 Chez Toutoune ★★$$ Colette Toutoune and Christophe Paucod offer fine home-style *Provençale* cuisine with a Southern accent and at old-fashioned prices. The five-course menu chalked on the blackboard in the cozy dining room changes daily, but you can count on hot and cold soups, *caviar d'aubergine* (eggplant puree), roast lamb with thyme, iced nougat, and creamy brie. ♦ M dinner; Tu-Su lunch and dinner. Reservations recommended for dinner. 5 Rue de Pontoise (at Rue Cochin). 01.43.26.56.81. Métro: Maubert–Mutualité

11 La Marée Verte ★★★$$ Traditional French cuisine and friendly service are what make this neighborhood restaurant a popular favorite. A steamship decor of marine blue with yellow accents along with nautical posters make for a charming setting in which to enjoy the ever-popular fisherman's platter of salmon, cod, scallops, and scorpion fish; skate wings with olives and capers; or roast duckling with blueberries. There's a good and very affordable wine list. ♦ M dinner; Tu-Sa lunch and dinner. Reservations recommended. 9 Rue de Pontoise (between Blvd St-Germain and Rue Cochin). 01.43.25.89.41. Métro: Maubert–Mutualité

12 Club Quartier Latin The pretty indoor pool at this athletic club is one of the few in Paris where lap swimming is the norm and lane markers are respected. Downstairs are four squash courts, a Jacuzzi, saunas, dance classes, a lounge, and a snack bar where salads, steaks, and fruit juices are served. Day passes are available. ♦ M-Sa 9AM-midday; Su 9:30AM-6:30PM. 19 Rue de Pontoise (between Rue des Ecoles and Blvd St-Germain). Gym and squash club 01.43.54.82.45; pool 01.43.54.06.23. Métros: Cardinal-Lemoine, Maubert–Mutualité

13 Moissonnier ★★★$ Earthenware bowls spilling over with Lyonnaise salads, friendly waiters, generous charcuterie, and a homey setting have earned this Left Bank establishment a loyal clientele. Specialties include kidneys with mustard, tripe baked with onions and white wine, creamy au gratin potatoes, and delicious Bordeaux. ♦ Tu-Sa lunch and dinner; Su lunch; closed in August. 28 Rue des Fossés-St-Bernard (between Rues des Ecoles and des Chantiers). 01.43.29.87.65. Métros: Jussieu, Cardinal-Lemoine

Restaurants/Clubs: Red   **Hotels:** Blue
Shops/ ♥ Outdoors: Green   **Sights/Culture:** Black

PARADIS LATIN
Cabaret

14 Le Paradis Latin Jean Kriegel's glittering nightclub stages one of the city's top 10 floor shows. The food is not the main focus here, but dinner and the show make for a nice evening out. It's also possible to see the show without dining. ◆ Cover. M-Tu, Th-Su. Dinner 8PM; show starts at 9:45PM, but arrive 30 minutes in advance. Reservations required. 28 Rue du Cardinal-Lemoine (between Rue des Ecoles and Blvd St-Germain). 01.43.25.28.28. Métro: Cardinal-Lemoine

15 St-Nicolas-du-Chardonnet Built in 1709, this church was originally a 13th-century chapel standing in a field of *chardons* (thistles). Later redesigned by Charles Le Brun, it now houses the Le Brun family chapel, along with Charles Le Brun's painting *The Martyrdom of Saint John*. The beautiful wood carving over the side door on the Rue des Bernardins is also his work. This also happens to be one of the most conservative churches in Paris: Mass is still said entirely in Latin. ◆ Sq de la Mutualité (at Rues St-Victor and Monge). Métros: Cardinal-Lemoine, Maubert–Mutualité

16 Les Deux Tisserins Marie-Claude Leblois's little toy shop, crammed with some of the most unusual playthings in Paris, is a veritable wonderland of rocking horses, marionette theaters, finger puppets, mobiles, sailboats, wooden trains, spinning tops, stuffed animals, dolls, and music boxes. Lebois's famous line of childrens' clothing includes gaily patterned flannel pajamas, hooded jackets, and cotton dresses; her monogrammed *sacs à dos* (backpacks) have been favorites of Parisian children for years. ◆ Tu-Sa. 36 Rue des Bernardins (between Rue Monge and Blvd St-Germain). 01.46.33.88.68. Métro: Maubert–Mutualité

17 Diptyque Run by English and French artists who met while studying at the **Ecole des Beaux-Arts** after World War II, this tiny corner shop specializes in elegant antique bead necklaces, rose-petal sachets, perfumed soaps, eau de toilette and candles scented like the forest floor on a damp May morning. ◆ Tu-Sa. 34 Blvd St-Germain (at Rue de Pontoise). 01.43.26.45.27. Métro: Maubert–Mutualité

Jazz Joints

In the 1940s and 1950s, when the **Latin Quarter**'s underground dives resonated to the sounds of saxophones, Paris was the undisputed jazz capital of the world. In the next three decades, cities in the United States and Japan laid claim to that fame, but now Paris is staging a comeback. Here are some of the city's hottest spots for jazz:

Au Duc des Lombards 42 Rue des Lombards (off Blvd Sébastopol). 01.42.33.22.88

Jazz Club Lionel Hampton Hôtel Méridien, 81 Blvd Gouvion-St-Cyr (between Pl de la Porte-Maillot and Rue Belidor). 01.40.68.30.42

Latitudes 7-11 Rue St-Benoît (between Rues Guillaume-Apollinaire and Jacob). 01.42.61.53.53

La Villa 29 Rue Jacob (between Rues de l'Echaudé and Bonaparte). 01.43.26.60.00

Le Bilboquet 13 Rue St-Benoît (between Rues Guillaume-Apollinaire and Jacob). 01.45.48.81.84

Le Petit Journal/Montparnasse 13 Rue du Commandant-René-Mouchotte (between Pl de Catalogne and Ave du Maine). 01.43.21.56.70

Le Petit Journal/St-Michel 71 Blvd St-Michel (at Rue Royer-Collard). 01.43.26.28.59

Le Petit Opportun 15 Rue des Lavandières-Ste-Opportune (between Rues Jean-Lantier and des Deux-Boules). 01.42.36.01.36

Le Sunset 60 Rue des Lombards (near Rue St-Denis). 01.40.26.46.60

L'Eustache 37 Rue Berger (between Rues des Prouvaires and Vauvilliers). 01.40.26.23.20

New Morning 7-9 Rue des Petites-Ecuries (between Rues du Faubourg-St-Denis and d'Hauteville). 01.45.23.51.41

Slow Club 130 Rue de Rivoli (between Rues des Bourdonnais and du Pont-Neuf). 01.42.33.84.30

17 H. G. Thomas The boutique of Hervé Gerald Thomas features such *très chic* gifts as Italian luggage, double umbrellas, hunting knives, Braun clocks, and whiskey flasks. The inventory ranges from designer ballpoints to Weber barbecues. And the chicest note of all: Most everything here comes in black. ◆ Tu-Sa 10AM-8PM 36 Blvd St-Germain (between Rues de Pontoise and des Bernardins). 01.46.33.57.50. Métro: Maubert–Mutualité

18 Au Pactole ★★$$$ The delicacies of chef Roland Magne encompass *filet de rouget graine sésame* (red mullet with sesame), lobster sautéed with *girolles* (chanterelle mushrooms), and venison steak with a red wine sauce. The formal dining room, decorated in soft peach tones, provides a refined backdrop for your meal. ◆ M-F lunch and dinner; Sa dinner. Reservations recommended. 44 Blvd St-Germain (between Rues de Pontoise and des Bernardins). 01.43.26.92.28. Métro: Maubert–Mutualité

19 Musée des Hôpitaux de Paris–Assistance Publique (Museum of Public Health and Welfare) Tucked away in this 17th-century mansion, which was converted into the central pharmacy for the city's hospitals after the Revolution, is one of Paris's most offbeat yet entertaining museums. Unknown to most Parisians (and visitors), this repository of French medical history contains an extraordinary collection of old ceramic apothecary jars, Roman medicine vials, hospital rosters, pewter syringes, copper basins, blocks of marble that were pulverized to powder baby bottoms, and a model of a quasi–night deposit box that 19th-century nuns invented for abandoned babies. ◆ Admission. Tu-Sa; closed in August and holidays. 47 Quai de la Tournelle (between Rues de Pontoise and des Bernardins). 01.40.27.50.05. Métro: Maubert–Mutualité

19 45 Quai de la Tournelle Shortly after being discharged from the American Ambulance Corps in the spring of 1919, John Dos Passos subiet a playwright's apartment here and began what would become his first successful novel, *Three Soldiers*. It remains a residential building. ◆ Between Rues de Pontoise and des Bernardins. Métro: Maubert–Mutualité

Parisians continue to view the French law outlawing smoking in the métro and requiring no-smoking sections in restaurants as more a suggestion than a commandment. Despite *Ne Pas Fumer* signs, smokers continue to light up with impunity. Some restaurateurs even gather up all the ashtrays from the tables—only to leave them conspicuously piled on a nearby sideboard for the asking.

20 Jean-Pierre Stella Legions of lead soldiers stand at attention in Stella's little shop on the quay. Military medals, samurai armor, Napoleonic helmets, and vintage weaponry are also sold. ◆ M-Sa 2-4PM, and by appointment in the mornings; closed from mid-July to September. 67 Quai de la Tournelle (between Rues de Bièvre and Maître Albert). 01.46.33.40.50. Métro: Maubert–Mutualité

21 Galerie Urubamba Traditional Indian art and culture from the Americas—weavings, masks, headdresses, and more —is the specialty of this gallery/folk art shop. A bookshop affords visitors a selection of over 2,000 titles and catalogues. The gallery also organizes classes in Indian language and fabric weaving. ◆ Tu-Sa 2-7:30PM. 4 Rue de la Bûcherie (at Rue du Haut Pavé). 01.43.54.08.24. Métro: Maubert–Mutualité

22 Patchworks du Rouvray Like the **Galerie Urubamba** across the square, this quilt emporium is run by an American woman. Diane de Obaldia's shop is named after a 14th-century farmhouse near Chartres, where she started her business. Today she sells traditional American Midwest patchwork quilts of the 1930s. She also offers about 40 quilting classes (in French and sometimes in English) and 700 varieties of cotton fabric for inspired quilters. ◆ M 2-6:30PM; Tu-Sa. 1 Rue Frédéric-Sauton (at Impasse Maubert). 01.43.25.00.45. Métro: Maubert–Mutualité

23 Chieng-Mai ★★$$ An excellent Thai restaurant, this eatery serves beef satay, squid and mint salad, spicy pork brochette, and, for dessert, grilled flan with coconut milk. The pineapple salad is divine. Red is the predominant color in the two warm and inviting dining rooms. ◆ M-Su lunch and dinner. Reservations required. 12 Rue Frédéric-Sauton (at Rue des Trois-Portes). 01.43.25.45.45. Métro: Maubert–Mutualité

24 Dodin-Bouffant ★★$$ One of the best seafood restaurants in Paris, this dining spot (named after a character in a Marcel Rouff novel who's an extravagant gourmet) goes through 500 pounds of fish each day, smokes its own herring and salmon, and has oysters delivered daily from Brittany and Ireland. Order the curried sole with squash fondue or the *tête de veau* (calf's head) and discover why this warm, casual bistro was one of François Mitterrand's favorite neighborhood restaurants. ◆ M-F lunch and dinner; Sa-Su dinner. Reservations recommended for dinner. 25 Rue Frédéric-Sauton (between Rue Maître-Albert and Impasse Maubert). 01.43.25.25.14. Métro: Maubert–Mutualité

25 Place Maubert The name "Maubert" is probably a contraction of Maître (Master) Albert, who was a Dominican teacher at the **University of Paris** in the Middle Ages. For centuries, this wide spot in the road was a crime-ridden skid row, a resort for tramps drinking *gros rouge* (cheap red wine), and the site of public executions. Here, in 1546, during the reign of François I, printer and humanist philosopher Etienne Dolet was burned at the stake as a heretic; his own books were used to kindle the fire. In addition to serving as an execution ground, from the Middle Ages hence this crossroads has been a bustling open-air market. ♦ Market: Tu, Th, Sa 7AM-1PM. At Blvd St-Germain and Rues Monge and Lagrange. Métro: Maubert–Mutualité

On Place Maubert:

Than Binh This little Vietnamese grocery store supplies the many Southeast Asian restaurants and families clustered around Place Maubert. The exotic spices and bewildering assortment of food (rice steamed in banana leaves, tapioca in grape leaves, shrimp muffins) will transport you to the Mekong Delta. ♦ M-Sa. No. 29 (at Blvd St-Germain). 01.40.46.06.15

26 Colbert $$$ From nine of the 34 rooms in this former 17th-century residence, you can contemplate **Notre-Dame** while having breakfast in bed. The decor is a bit grim, but the rooms are quiet and simply furnished, and the beds have luxuriously smooth sheets. The place has an interesting history: Parts of the building date back to 1500, and an animal hospital sponsored by the Duke of Windsor once stood on the site of the present courtyard garden. There's no restaurant. ♦ 7 Rue de l'Hôtel-Colbert (at Rue de la Bûcherie). 01.40.46.79.50; fax 01.43.25.80.19. Métro: Maubert–Mutualité

27 Les Bouchons de François Clerc ★★★ $$ François Clerc has hit upon an idea that's got people talking: the well-selected wines and Champagnes in his cellar are sold in his restaurant at cost. Take advantage of the deal and try a bottle of 1991 Mission Haut-Briand or 1987 Pichon-Longuelle for about 70 percent of what you'd pay anywhere else. The wine prices are only one reason to rush to this dining spot: The wood-beamed dining room is sophisticated and cozy, the homemade bread is warm and crusty, the waiters are young and bubbly, and the four-course prix-fixe menu features original dishes such as *croustillant de rouget* (a light, red mullet cake), *tournedos Rossini* (a sublime version of the classic made with tuna steak instead of the traditional beef), and braised pigeon with cèpes. This place is popular, so reserve well in advance. ♦ M-F lunch and dinner; Sa dinner. Reservations required. 12 Rue de l'Hôtel-Colbert (between Rues Lagrange and de la Bûcherie). 01.43.54.15.34. Métro: Maubert–Mutualité

MICHAEL STORRINGS

28 Quai de Montebello Booksellers The *bouquinistes* who work in the shadow of **Notre-Dame** practice one of the city's oldest trades, selling old Daumier prints, volumes on everything from Balzac to bebop, and the occasional naughty postcard out of their green boxes on the quay (see illustration above). These famous, free-spirited cowboys of the book business open and close their sidewalk stalls when they please and sell only what interests them. ♦ Daily, depending on the weather. Quai de Montebello, between Pont de l'Archevêché and Petit Pont. Métro: St-Michel

28 Pont au Double The name derives from the fact that this was the only bridge in Paris whose toll was two *sous* instead of one. ♦ Between Quai de Montebello and Pl du Parvis-Notre-Dame. Métro: St-Michel

29 Square René-Viviani In this lovely little park stands what is reputed to be the oldest tree in Paris. This false acacia *(Robinia pseudoacacia)* leans on concrete crutches, infirm but erect, and blooms every spring. Not bad for a sprout that crossed the ocean from Guyana to be planted in 1680 by Jean Robin. Sit for a moment on one of the park benches and notice the pieces of worn and broken statuary surrounding you; they were once part of **Notre-Dame.** ♦ Bounded by Rues Lagrange and St-Julien-le-Pauvre and Quai de Montebello. Métros: Maubert–Mutualité, St-Michel

30 Rue du Fouarre Seated on *fouarres* (bundles of straw), undergraduates in the Middle Ages attended open-air lectures presented in this alley by rowdy intellectuals, notorious throughout Europe. In an attempt to ease tensions in 1358, Charles V chained the street at both ends and closed it at night. During his visit to Paris in 1304, even Dante harkened to the scholars here and later made reference in his writing to this *vico degli strami* (the road of straws). ♦ Between Rues Galande and Lagrange. Métro: Maubert–Mutualité

On Rue du Fouarre:

La Fourmi Ailée ★★$ This women's bookstore has a tearoom in the rear, where on a chilly day you can order a hot goat cheese salad, sit back in a caned bentwood chair by the fireplace, and peruse a book by Simone de Beauvoir. ♦ M, W-Su lunch and afternoon tea. 01.43.29.40.99

31 Rue des Anglais In medieval times this street was a favorite haunt of English students attending the **Sorbonne.** ♦ Between Blvd St-Germain and Rue Lagrange. Métro: Maubert–Mutualité

32 A l'Imagerie The largest old print and poster shop in Paris specializes in original Art Deco, Art Nouveau, and late 19th-century Japanese prints and stamps. ♦ M-Sa. 9 Rue Dante (at Rue Domat). 01.43.25.18.66. Métros: Cluny–La Sorbonne, Maubert–Mutualité

33 Librairie Gourmande The celebrated *bouquiniste* Mme Baudon has graduated from her stall on the quay to a shop where she sells books on food and wine from the 17th century to the present. ♦ Daily. 4 Rue Dante (between Blvd St-Germain and Rue Galande). 01.43.54.37.27. Métros: Maubert–Mutualité, St-Michel

33 Album From Action comics to Zot, Donald Duck to Dick Tracy, this *bande dessinée* (comic strip) shop specializes in new and vintage American comic books. For the seriocomic art collector, there are oil paintings of Batman and portraits and statues of Mr. Spock. ♦ Tu-Sa. 6 Rue Dante (between Blvd St-Germain and Rue Galande). 01.43.54.67.09. Métros: Maubert–Mutualité, St-Michel

34 Rue Galande The beginning of the old Roman road to Lyon, this meandering street was named in 1202 after a family who lived nearby. It was one of the fancier neighborhoods in 17th-century Paris. ♦ Between Rues Lagrange and St-Jacques. Métro: Maubert–Mutualité

On Rue Galande:

Studio Galande Catch one of the cinema's nightly showings of *The Rocky Horror Picture Show.* Watching funkily costumed French college students enjoying their umpteenth viewing of this crazy cult film—singing, dancing, and shouting at the on-screen characters—is guaranteed to have you in stitches. Outside the theater, glance up at the 14th-century stone relief of St. Julien crossing the Seine, which originally stood over the portal of nearby **St-Julian-le-Pauvre** church. ♦ No. 42 (between Rues Dante and St-Julien-le-Pauvre). 01.43.26.94.08

Auberge des Deux Signes ★$$ Restaurant owner M. Dhulster shops every day before dawn at the Rungis market for the raw materials that his chef, Nicolas Cano, transforms into a sublime array of dishes such as *soufflé de sole* with prawn ravioli and *foie gras d'oie en brioche* (goose liver in brioche). With its stone spiral staircase and views of **Notre-Dame** (splendid at night) and **St-Julien-le-Pauvre**'s gardens, the setting could not be more medieval. ♦ M-F lunch and dinner; Sa dinner. Reservations recommended. No. 46 (between Rues Dante and St-Julien-le-Pauvre). 01.43.25.46.56

Les Trois Maillets The "Three Mallets" began in the 13th century as a tavern that served the stonemasons constructing **Notre-Dame.** Some 700 years later it was transformed into a postwar jazz club first frequented by American GIs. Entertainment now includes belly dancing and rap, and it has one of the best piano bars in Paris. ♦ Cover. Daily, 6PM-6AM. No. 56 (at Rue St-Julien-le-Pauvre). 01.43.54.00.79

35 St-Julien-le-Pauvre Named in honor of St. Julian the Poor, a martyred third-century bishop who gave all his money to the penniless, this church, an odd, graceless amalgam of Romanesque and Gothic architecture, has no bell tower, transepts, or organ, and squats on a small square lined with acacia trees. With its iron-caged well in front, it looks more like a humble country church than a Parisian monument. Founded in 1165 (and restored in 1250 and 1651), this is one of several structures that claims the title of oldest church in Paris. Although the construction of **Notre-Dame** began two years earlier, **St-Julien-le-Pauvre** was completed first, and while **St-Germain-des-Prés** is older, it originally stood outside the city walls and therefore was not, strictly speaking, a Parisian church.

In the 12th century, when renegade theologian Pierre Abélard quit **Notre-Dame,** he took more than 3,000 students along with him and established a new university here. The church thus became the seat and meeting place of the new **University of Paris.** In 1524, students critical of a new rector ransacked and nearly destroyed the church. After the Revolution, **St-Julien-le-Pauvre** was used variously as a salt storehouse, a wool market, and a flour granary. Since 1889 it has belonged to the Greek Orthodox church. The enormous stone slab beside the well came from the fourth-century Roman highway that became the Rue St-Jacques. ♦ 1 Rue St-Julien-le-Pauvre (between Rue Galande and Quai de Montebello). 01.43.54.52.16. Métros: Maubert–Mutualité, St-Michel, Cité

36 Rue St-Julien-le-Pauvre The magnificent gate at **No. 14** marks the 17th-century home of the governor of the old **Petit-Châtelet** prison. Also don't miss the house of the dwindling windows at **No. 10;** they start with the largest ones on the ground floor and shrink all the way up to the maids' rooms in the attic. ♦ Between Rue Galande and Quai de Montebello. Métros: Maubert–Mutualité, St-Michel, Cité

On Rue St-Julien-le-Pauvre:

The Tea Caddy ★$ Looking like your prim and proper English great-aunt's library, with dark wood paneling and thick-paned windows, this is the place for afternoon tea and crumpets. Light meals of quiche, salads, and omelettes are also served. ♦ M-Tu, Th-Su lunch and afternoon tea. No credit cards accepted. 14 Rue St-Julien-le-Pauvre. 01.43.54.15.56

Esmeralda $$ This run-down 19-room hotel is a favorite of traveling actors and artists. Rooms with views of **Notre-Dame** are subjected to the midnight noise of *The Rocky Horror Picture Show* crowd exiting the **Studio Galande** cinema (see page 48). There is no restaurant. No credit cards accepted. ♦ 4 Rue St-Julien-le-Pauvre. 01.43.54.19.20; fax 01.40.51.00.68

37 Rue de la Bûcherie A *bûcherie* is a wood-shed, and this part of the quay is where firewood-laden barges dropped their cargo. ♦ Between Rues St-Julien-le-Pauvre and du Petit-Pont. Métros: Maubert–Mutualité, St-Michel, Cité

On Rue de la Bûcherie:

Shakespeare and Company Octogenarian George Bates Whitman—who was raised in China, speaks five languages, and claims the poet Walt as a distant forebear—has for the last 45 years run this charitable bookstore/inn for authors, vagabond intellectuals, and literature professors. Spiritual heir to Sylvia Beach, whose famous Paris bookstore of the same name on the Rue de l'Odéon supplied Hemingway with free reading material and was the only house that would publish Joyce's *Ulysses,* Whitman bought part of her collection and borrowed the name **Shakespeare and Company.** In his late sixties he fathered a daughter whom he named Sylvia Beach Whitman. Throughout the years, Whitman's chaotic stacks, which defy the Dewey decimal or any other system of categorization, have been frequented by the likes of Lawrence Durrell, Henry Miller, J.P. Donleavy, and Beat poet Lawrence Ferlinghetti. Whitman is always in the bookstore; while you're browsing he may offer you a cup of tea and, if you happen to be penniless and show promise as a writer, may invite you to spend a night in the **Writer's Room** or to bed down on the floor of his upstairs library. To the left of the bookshop, which has one of the world's most eclectic bulletin boards, Whitman keeps his own private collection and his motor scooter. Each book purchased in the shop is stamped with an inscription that reads: Shakespeare and Co. Kilometer Zero Paris. ♦ Daily noon-midnight. 37 Rue de la Bûcherie. 01.43.26.96.50

La Bûcherie ★★★$$$ Bernard Bosque's menu, featuring cabbage leaves stuffed with langoustines, ocean salmon with chives, and wild duck and oysters in Champagne, hasn't changed in years and neither has the popularity of this restaurant. In summer, reserve a table on the terrace overlooking **Notre-Dame,** and in winter try to get a table near the crackling fireplace. Expect a crowd, and at all costs avoid sitting behind the chimney, where famished customers can go unnoticed for days. Bosque hosted the late Jaqueline Kennedy Onassis in his dining room, and Rosanna Arquette and Isabelle Adjani are regulars. ♦ Daily lunch and dinner. Reservations recommended. 41 Rue de la Bûcherie. 01.43.54.78.06

38 Petit Pont Bishop Maurice de Sully was responsible for the construction of this little bridge, built in 1185 and rebuilt in the 19th century. (Also see page 29.) Formerly located at the end of the bridge was the **Petit Châtelet** fortress and prison, a more diminutive version of the **Grand Châtelet** on the Right Bank. ♦ Between Quais St-Michel and du Marché-Neuf. Métros: St-Michel, Cité

39 Mirama ★★$ With glazed, roasted ducks hanging in the window and a cauldron whose contents bubble mysteriously just inside the door, this informal Chinese restaurant at first seems suspect. Yet it's crowded all day long, and deservedly so: The ingredients are fresh and the price is right. Try the noodle soup with shrimp dumplings, sweet-and-sour chicken, crispy mixed vegetables, pork ribs in black bean sauce, and, of course, the *canard laqué* you saw on the way in. ♦ Daily lunch and dinner. 17 Rue St-Jacques (between Blvd St-Germain and Rue Galande). 01.43.29.66.58. Métros: Maubert–Mutualité, St-Michel

40 27 Rue St-Jacques More than a hundred sundials can be found in Paris, but few were created by artists of worldwide repute. Surrealist Salvador Dalí designed this *cadran solaire* for friends whose furniture store was located here. The timepiece's completion in 1968 was televised, with Dalí mounting a cherry picker to carve his signature into the still-wet cement. Set on the south face of the building, the sundial depicts a female face in the form of a *coquille St-Jacques* (scallop shell). ♦ Between Blvd St-Germain and Rue Galande. Métros: Maubert–Mutualité, St-Michel

40 Le Bar à Huitres
★★$$ This seafood restaurant has the best and least expensive shellfish served in the city. Fresh oysters and scallops arrive daily from the Normandy and Brittany coasts to become components in sumptuous platters of

mollusks and crustaceans. Fish specialties include monkfish curry in winter and roast turbot with wine and butter sauce in summer. Served with velvety beurre blanc for dipping, the grilled lobster is heavenly. The bar outside sells oysters and such for take-out, making this place truly a paradise for shellfish lovers. ♦ Daily lunch and dinner until 2AM. 33 Rue St-Jacques (between Blvd St-Germain and Rue Galande). 01.44.07.27.37. Métros: Maubert–Mutualité, St-Michel. Also at: 112 Blvd du Montparnasse (at Blvd Raspail). 01.43.20.71.01. Métro: Vavin; 33 Blvd Beaumarchais (at Rue du Pas-de-la-Mule). 01.48.87.98.92. Métro: Bastille

Café de Cluny

41 Café de Cluny ★$ Set at one of the Latin Quarter's busiest corners, this sprawling cafe commands a front-row seat on the boulevards St-Michel and St-Germain. Upstairs in the quiet, plush booths, **Sorbonne** professors take their morning coffee or have a dish of ice cream with their graduate students in the afternoon. ♦ Daily breakfast, lunch, and dinner until 2AM. 102 Blvd St-Germain (at Blvd St-Michel). 01.43.26.98.40. Métro: Cluny–La Sorbonne

42 Hôtel de Cluny, Musée de Cluny (Musée National du Moyen-Age), and Palais des Thermes This magnificent mansion, built by the abbots of Cluny in 1330 and rebuilt in 1510, is one of the oldest private residences in Paris. It straddles the ruins of second-century Roman baths and contains one of the world's finest collections of French medieval art, including the beautiful *Lady and the Unicorn* tapestries.

The baths date from Marcus Aurelius (AD 161-180); Julian the Apostate, proclaimed Roman Emperor in 360, lived in the adjoining palace. The baths and palace were sacked during numerous barbarian invasions, and in 1340 Pierre de Châlus, abbot of Cluny, the wealthy Benedictine abbey in Burgundy, bought the ruins and erected the **Hôtel de Cluny** as a pied-à-terre for the abbots when they visited Paris. Shortly after the Revolution, the **Hôtel de Cluny** was occupied by a cooper, a laundress, French Navy astronomers, and a surgeon who used the chapel for his dissections. Among the mansion's tenants in 1833 was Alexandre du Sommerard, an art collector who had specialized in Gothic and Renaissance art. When he died in 1842, the state bought the building as well as du Sommerard's collection and appointed his son Edmond as the first curator of the **Musée de Cluny,** which is also known as the **Musée National du Moyen-Age** (National Museum of the Middle Ages).

As you enter the museum courtyard by the Rue du Sommerard, notice the polygonal stair tower sprinkled with carved shells *(coquilles St-Jacques),* the symbol of the patron saint of Jacques d'Amboise, the abbot of Jumièges, who between 1485 and 1510 rebuilt the *hôtel* in its present Flamboyant Gothic style. The first rooms of the museum are replete with delicate ivory carvings, embroidered Egyptian silks, and Flemish tapestries of gentlemen setting off for the hunt. ♦ Admission. M, W-Su. 6 Pl Paul-Painlevé (at Rue du Sommerard). 01.53.73.78.00. Métros: Cluny–La Sorbonne, Maubert–Mutualité, St-Michel, Odéon

Within the Hôtel de Cluny, Musée de Cluny, and Palais des Thermes:

Notre-Dame Gallery In this stark white room are the sculpted stone heads (1210-30) of 21 noseless but nevertheless majestic monarchs. They represent the kings of Judea and Israel, who, according to St. Matthew's genealogy, were ancestors of Christ. Like most men too closely associated with religion and royalty at the time of the Revolution, they lost their heads. But theirs was a case of mistaken identity. The full-length statues of the kings were originally enshrined in the **Gallery of Kings** on **Notre-Dame**'s west facade, but they were beheaded in 1793 by an angry mob who assumed they depicted the kings of France. The statues have stood decapitated since that time, and for nearly two centuries the heads were considered lost. But in 1977, during excavations for a new bank in the **Hôtel Moreau** near the **Opéra**, they were unearthed; the discovery is considered one of the 20th century's major archaeological finds.

Roman Baths The towering roof of the *frigidarium* (cold bath) is the largest Roman vault in all of France. The ceiling has survived 18 centuries of wear and tear, even with-standing being topped with eight feet of topsoil and an abbot's apple orchard and kitchen garden. The ship prows decorating the base of the groined vaulting are the building signatures of the powerful Boatmen's Guild of Paris. Nearby is the *Boatmen's Pillar*, one of the oldest pieces of sculpture in Paris. It was dedicated to the god Jupiter by the Boatmen's Guild during the reign of Roman emperor Tiberius (AD 14-37) and was later discovered beneath **Notre-Dame.**

Treasury Upstairs, above the baths, is a dazzling display of Gallic, Barbarian, and Merovingian jewelry, including six gold Visigoth crowns, two 13th-century gold double crosses, and the sublimely delicate 14th-century *Golden Rose* that was presented to the Bishop of Basel by Pope Clement V.

Stained Glass Among the medieval stained-glass windows in the upstairs corridor are religious scenes from **Sainte-Chapelle** and the **Basilique de St-Denis**. Take a close look; in the actual churches—even with a strong pair of opera glasses and a craned neck— you won't get this good a view. Three large windows and the surrounding stonework come from the church of **St-Jean-de-Latran,** demolished in 1859 to make way for the Rue des Ecoles built between the **Cluny** and the **Sorbonne.**

Abbots' Chapel One of the few surviving interior details of the original mansion, this chapel was the abbots' oratory and is an architectural masterpiece. The elaborate vaulting sprouts palmlike from a single slender pillar. In a room near the chapel is a 1383 eagle lectern and a 12th-century gilt copper altar table.

Tapestries Saving the best for last, enter the rotunda on the top floor, dimly lit to protect the world-famous *Lady and the Unicorn* tapestry series. In 1844, quite by accident, writer George Sand discovered the tapestries hanging at the **Château de Boussac;** supposedly they were a wedding present in the 15th century from magistrate Jean Le Viste to his bride (the Le Viste coat of arms appears in each panel). The artist, who remains unknown, is thought to have designed the similar set of six tapestries that is now hanging in the Cloisters museum in New York City. The delicate tapestries allegorically depict the five senses. In the one representing sight, for instance, the noble unicorn gazes into the mirror of a bejeweled blond woman. In the mysterious sixth tapestry, the woman's tent is emblazoned with the words "A Mon Seul Désir" (To My Only Desire), thought to represent mastery of all five senses. Notice that the woman on the red *millefleur* (literally, one thousand flowers) background changes from one sumptuous gown to another in a veritable fashion show as you progess around the room.

43 Rue des Ecoles This street name celebrates the presence of all the academic institutions and universities hereabouts. ♦ Between Rue du Cardinal-Lemoine and Blvd St-Michel. Métro: Maubert–Mutualité, Cardinal-Lemoine

43 Au Vieux Campeur France's best mountain-climbing outfitters this side of Chamonix carry pitons, ice axes, alpine sleeping bags, and giant spools of brightly colored climbing rope for your next ascent of Everest or the **Eiffel Tower.** Even if a bivouac at a wine bar atop the Montagne Ste-Geneviève's slopes is more your style, pause on the sidewalk and watch France's next generation of rock climbers testing new equipment, rappelling down an indoor version of what looks like the Eiger's North Face. This is one of a chain of nine stores on the Left Bank. ♦ M afternoon; W until 9PM; Th-Sa. 48 Rue des Ecoles (between Rues Thénard and St-Jacques). 01.43.29.12.32. Métros: Maubert–Mutualité, St-Michel

The croissant, that most French of pastries, actually originated in Budapest. According to the story, when the Turks besieged Budapest in 1686, they dug underground passages to reach the city center. Bakers, working during the night, heard the noise made by the invaders and sounded an alarm. The Turks were defeated and the bakers who had saved the city were granted the privilege of creating a special pastry, which took the form of a *croissant* (crescent), the emblem on the Ottoman flag.

Paris in Print

Some of history's most compelling stories have been set in the French capital. The following is a survey of three centuries of Paris-inspired literature.

The Age of Reason by Jean-Paul Sartre (Vintage Books, 1992). The author's 1945 novel is set in 1938 Paris. This is the story of Mathieu, a professor of philosophy, who is motivated by an idealistic obsession to remain free, particularly when his mistress becomes pregnant.

The Ambassadors by Henry James (Oxford University Press, 1986). In this Henry James 1903 classic, Lambert Strether is sent to Paris by Mrs. Newsome, a wealthy widow whom he plans to marry, in order to persuade her son Chad to come home. Strether gradually realizes that life may hold more meaning for Chad in Paris than in Massachusetts.

The American by Henry James (Buccaneer Books, 1990). This 1877 tome describes how a rich, self-made American goes to Europe to enjoy his wealth and becomes engaged to a French widow from a noble family. Problems develop as cultural differences between the two emerge.

An American in Paris by LeRoy Neiman (Harry N. Abrams, 1994). One of America's most celebrated artists illustrates his impressions of Paris.

Banners of Silk by Rosalind Laker (Doubleday, 1981). A historical romance portraying the rags-to-riches story of two *couturiers,* Charles Worth and Louise Vernet, in the world of 19th-century Paris fashion.

The Blessing by Nancy Mitford (Carroll & Graf, 1989). Grace, a beautiful but dull English woman, marries a dashing French marquis and is swept into the complexities of Parisian society.

Camille by Alexandre Dumas (New American Library, 1984). First published in 1848, this novel depicts Camille, a beautiful courtesan, who becomes part of the fashionable world of 19th-century Paris and rejects a wealthy count for his penniless lover Armand Duval. They escape to the country, but at the request of his family she pretends she no longer loves him and goes back to her life in Paris. The story ends with a tragic reunion between the lovers.

The Cardinal and the Queen by Evelyn Anthony (Putnam Publishing Group, 1968). The story of the beautiful Anne of Austria, her humiliating marriage to Louis XIII, and her passionate love affair with Cardinal Richelieu, the king's minister. The **Louvre,** the **Palais du Luxembourg,** and other royal buildings of 17th-century Paris are the backdrops for this historical novel.

Cousin Pons by Honoré de Balzac (Viking Press, 1978). Part of the 1848 series *Scenes of Parisian Life,* this book focuses on the friendship of two old musicians, Schmucke and Cousin Pons, and is set in the sordid mid-19th-century Parisian society of minor theaters, innkeepers, and impoverished artists and other bohemians.

Gigi by Colette (French & European Publications, 1979). The 1952 story of a young girl brought up to be a prosperous gold digger who maneuvers a marriage proposal from a sophisticated man-about-town.

Giovanni's Room by James Baldwin (Laureleaf, 1985). A classic early gay novel, most of the story takes place in Paris during the 1950s, where a young American man is involved with both a woman and another man.

Good Morning, Midnight by Jean Rhys (W.W. Norton & Company, 1986). A middle-aged woman, lonely and adrift in Paris, seeks consolation in a relationship with a gigolo.

Héloïse and Abélard by George Moore (W.W. Norton & Company, 1974). This fictionalized version of the tragic 12th-century love affair between Héloïse, a beautiful and learned woman, and Pierre Abélard, the brilliant philosopher who served as her tutor, was first published in 1921.

The Hunchback of Notre Dame by Victor Hugo (Longmeadow Press, 1991). First published in 1830, this classic is set in Paris during 1482. With the harshness of medieval life and the grandeur of **Notre-Dame** as backdrops, the strange and fantastic romance between the hunchback Quasimodo and his Esmeralda unfolds.

I'll Always Have Paris: A Memoir by Art Buchwald (Putnam Publishing Group, 1996). The famed columnist recalls when he was a 22-year-old Paris-based writer for the *International Herald Tribune* during the 1940s and 1950s.

Imagining Paris: Exile, Writing, and American Identity by J. Gerald Kennedy (Yale University Press, 1993). An exploration of the imaginative process of five expatriate American writers (Gertrude Stein, Ernest Hemingway, Henry Miller, F. Scott Fitzgerald, and Djuna Barnes) demonstrates how the experience of living in Paris shaped their careers and literary works.

Is Paris Burning? by Larry Collins (Simon & Schuster, 1965). A suspenseful and exciting retelling of the story of the liberation of Paris in 1944 and one German general's decision to save the city from being burned to the ground.

Le Rouge et le Noir (The Red and the Black) by Stendhal (French & European Publications, 1958). Published in 1830, this tale follows the fall of Napoléon, as protagonist Julien's scandalous adventures take him to Paris.

Les Claudine by Colette (French & European Publications, 1969). Four semiautobiographical novels written from 1900 to 1903 follow Claudine through precocious girlhood, young womanhood in Paris, marriage, and an unusual love affair.

Les Enfants Terribles by Jean Cocteau (EMC Corp., 1977). In this historically and psychologically significant novel, two wild, poetic children withdraw to a small room in the midst of Paris after their mother's death.

Les Liaisons Dangereuses (Dangerous Liaisons) by Pierre Choderlos de Laclos (Knopf, 1991). Condemned in 1782 for being scandalous, this ruthless portrayal of sexual intrigue is a powerful moral analysis of the decadent society of mid-18th-century France.

Les Misérables by Victor Hugo (Penguin USA, 1982). A tale of the poor and the outcast in the early 19th century. First published in 1862, it recounts how an unjust system labels the noble Jean Valjean a criminal; other suffering victims of society are Fantine, her daughter Cosette, and Cosette's lover Marius.

Love in the Days of Rage by Lawrence Ferlinghetti (E.P. Dutton, 1988). Set against the turbulence and energy of the 1968 student riots in Paris, the love between a French banker and an expatriate American woman grows as revolutionary ideas are debated in cafes.

The Mandarins by Simone de Beauvoir (W.W. Norton & Company, 1991). This 1954 book paints a portrait of the Existentialist clique and its adversaries, and re-creates the ambience of Paris after the German occupation.

Mrs. 'arris Goes to Paris by Paul Gallico (International Polygonics Ltd., 1989). A middle-aged London cleaning woman, determined to own a designer gown, invades Paris's Christian Dior salon in this 1958 classic tale.

A Moveable Feast by Ernest Hemingway (Scribner, 1996). These sketches of Hemingway's years in Paris (1921-1926) were published posthumously in 1964.

Naked I Came by David Weiss (Wm. Morrow & Company, 1970). A fictionalized account of the life and work of sculptor Auguste Rodin portrays the controversies and love affairs that marked his life.

The Notebooks of Malte Laurids Brigge by Rainer Maria Rilke (W.W. Norton & Company, 1992). A young Danish poet of noble birth moves to Paris and lives in poverty. This 1910 novel is written as if it were a series of diary entries, with observations of the poet's suffering and squalor and speculations on art and life.

Overhead in a Balloon: Twelve Stories of Paris by Mavis Gallant (W.W. Norton & Company, 1988). Twelve stories interconnected by characters who jump from one tale to another. Parisian life is well captured in pieces about a bourgeois debate over real estate law, roommates discussing domestic arrangements, and dissatisfied lovers.

The Scarlet Pimpernel by Baroness Emmuska Orczy (Buccaneer Books, 1984). Sir Percy Blakeney, a foppish young Englishman, is found to be the daring Scarlet Pimpernel who rescues aristocrats from the guillotine during the French Revolution.

The Short Reign of Pippin IV by John Steinbeck (Penguin USA, 1994). In this satire on French politics published in 1957, the French run out of governments and decide to revive the monarchy. They choose Pippin, an amateur astronomer who is a descendant of Charlemagne.

A Tale of Two Cities by Charles Dickens (Buccaneer Books, 1987). This 1859 Dickens classic, set against the bloody French Revolution, has memorable scenes in the **Bastille** prison and the working-class **Faubourg St-Antoine** quarter.

Tropic of Cancer by Henry Miller (Grove Press, 1989). This autobiographical novel recounts Miller's experiences as a penniless American in the Paris of the early 1930s.

44 Hôtel Collège de France $$ Some of the sixth-floor rooms of this quiet, simple-but-comfortable 29-room bed-and-breakfast inn offer a glimpse of the **Notre-Dame** towers. There's no restaurant. ♦ 7 Rue Thénard (between Rues de Latran and du Sommerard). 01.43.26.78.36; fax 01.46.34.58.29. Métros: Maubert–Mutualité, St-Michel

45 Société Centrale de Produits Chimiques This store stocks supplies for high school biology classes and all the **Collège de France** research laboratories. Amid the test tubes and life-size plastic skeletons (shrouded in tinsel at Christmas) are the glass beakers and white porcelain pitchers that French householders love to buy as measuring cups for the kitchen. The 125-centiliter pitchers make dandy creamers. ♦ Tu-Sa. 44 Rue des Ecoles (at Rue Thénard). 01.46.34.56.56. Métro: Maubert–Mutualité

JEAN DE BEAUVAIS

46 Club Jean de Beauvais Work off those gourmet French meals at this classy health club, where visitors to Paris are welcome to sign up for daily or weekly memberships. The good-looking staff offer advice and support while members huff and puff through their cardiovascular circuits and weight-training programs. Classes in aerobics, stretching, toning, and yoga are given daily. Somehow, the modern exercise equipment is right at home amidst the beautifully renovated stone walls and wood-beamed ceilings of the 17th-century salons. This is where Jodie Foster exercises when she is in Paris. ♦ Daily. 5 Rue Jean-de-Beauvais (between Rue du Sommerard and Blvd St-Germain). 01.46.33.16.80. Métro: Maubert–Mutualité

47 Eglise Roumaine (Romanian Church)/Beauvais College Chapel One of the **Sorbonne**'s first college chapels, it was built in 1380. The recently restored sanctuary has been used since 1882 by the Romanian Orthodox church. ♦ 9 *bis* Rue Jean-de-Beauvais (between Rues des Ecoles and du Sommerard). 01.43.54.67.47. Métro: Maubert–Mutualité

48 Musée des Collections Historiques de la Préfecture de Police (Police Museum) This fascinating, often grisly little collection surveys the city's most notorious crimes, from the 16th century to the present. Exhibits include a graphic representation of the 1563 punishment accorded the Duc de Guise's murderer (quartering by four horses); orders for the arrest of Dr. Guillotin in 1795; an account of Charlotte Corday's murder of Marat in his bath; a book stained with blood from the 1932 assassination of French President Paul Doumer; and Verlaine's statement of his attempted murder of fellow poet Rimbaud. Among the more ingenious weapons on display are a strangling cord made of twisted paper and a knife concealed in a lady's fan. There's also a guillotine blade used during the Revolution. This *petit guignol* requires Holmesian perspicacity to find. Enter the lobby of the fifth arrondissement police headquarters, gumshoe your way up the stairs, and knock on the door marked Musée. ♦ Free. M-Sa. 1 *bis* Rue des Carmes (between Rue Basse-des-Carmes and Blvd St-Germain). 01.44.41.52.50. Métro: Maubert–Mutualité

49 Montagne Ste-Geneviève This French Parnassus, the central point of the old **University of Paris,** is named after the city's saintly patroness (St. Denis is her male counterpart). It is admittedly steep, but to call any of the city's seven hills a mountain is certainly an example of Roman grandiloquence. The summit of Ste-Geneviève is gracefully crowned with the **Panthéon** (see below), whose columned dome dominates the Left Bank. This is a vicinity rich in intellectual history: Here was the convent where St. Thomas Aquinas wrote his *Summa Theologica,* upon which the orthodox philosophy of Catholicism is based; here both St. Ignatius Loyola and Calvin studied; here Marat drew up his pamphlets; and here Pascal died a stone's throw from the place where Verlaine was to pass away many generations later. The hill counts among its educational institutions the world-famous **Sorbonne,** the **Collège de France,** prestigious medical and law schools, and three large secondary schools, and was at one time the site of the **Ecole Polytechnique,** the French equivalent of

MIT. In 1804 the Rue de la Montagne-Ste-Geneviève was the scene of a plot to murder Napoléon Bonaparte. ♦ Métro: Maubert–Mutualité

50 Da Capo Charles Recht runs this postage stamp–size shop dealing in 78-rpm records, old sheet music, and opera programs. ♦ Tu-Sa noon-6:30PM; closed in August. 14 Rue des Ecoles (between Rues des Bernardins and de la Montagne-Ste-Geneviève). 01.43.54.75.47. Métros: Maubert–Mutualité, Cardinal-Lemoine

51 Librairie Présence Africaine Need a few Wolof lessons before visiting Gambia? Looking for a Senegalese cookbook? Want to hear a black gospel concert on the Left Bank? This African bookstore includes a Third World periodical section and a bulletin board. ♦ M-Sa. 25 *bis* Rue des Ecoles (between Rues des Bernardins and de la Montagne-Ste-Geneviève). 01.43.54.15.88. Métros: Maubert–Mutualité, Cardinal-Lemoine

52 Shobudo International Europe's oldest judo school is set in a tranquil 17th-century courtyard. If you don't have time for a self-defense class, you can fake it by buying a black belt and the latest kung fu paraphernalia in the **Budo Store** on the second floor. Or walk to the end of the courtyard, turn left, and squeeze into the spectators' gallery to watch a few bouts of *ken jitsu,* a Japanese martial art predating the shoguns. The judo school is in a building that was once part of the **Hostel of the 33** (named for the number of years Christ lived), established by monk Claude Bernard as a dormitory for theology students. ♦ M-Sa 9AM-10PM. 34 Rue de la Montagne-Ste-Geneviève (between Rues de l'Ecole Polytechnique and des Ecoles). 01.44.41.63.20. Métro: Maubert–Mutualité

53 La Nef Parisienne Affixed on this small square, as on city schools and other public structures throughout Paris, is the image of a sailing vessel known as *La Nef Parisienne.* The image has been Paris's coat of arms since 1260, when St. Louis appointed the Boatmen's Guild to administer the affairs of the city. *Fluctuat nec mergitur* (float never sink) is the city motto. In addition to adorning buildings, the coat of arms is embossed on everything from the mayor's stationery to police officers' badges. ♦ At Rues Descartes, de l'Ecole Polytechnique, and de la Montagne-Ste-Geneviève. Métros: Cardinal-Lemoine, Maubert–Mutualité

54 Ecole Polytechnique These massive buildings once housed the French MIT. The **Ecole Polytechnique** was founded as an Army-run engineering school by Gaspard Monge, the mathematician who accompanied Napoléon to Egypt, and its best-known graduates are car designer André Citroën and former French president Valéry Giscard d'Estaing. Its annual grand ball at the **Opéra** is also fairly famous. In 1976 the prestigious university moved to the suburbs; the buildings here are now used for scientific research. ♦ Rue de l'Ecole Polytechnique (between Rues de la Montagne-Ste-Geneviève and Valette). Métros: Cardinal-Lemoine, Maubert–Mutualité

55 51 Rue de la Montagne-Ste-Geneviève The Irish writer James Joyce shared a flat here with French writer Valéry Larbaud. It's still a residential building. ♦ Between Rues St-Etienne-du-Mont and Descartes. Métro: Cardinal-Lemoine

56 Crocojazz This cubbyhole of a record shop resounds with the music of Art Blakey, Miles Davis, Louis Armstrong, and Coleman Hawkins. Jack Daniels whiskey bottles on the wall, the occasional country twang of Hank Thompson and Ricky Skaggs, and the worn Levis and ersatz cowboy boots of the French clientele round out the ambience at this treasure chest of American LPs. ♦ Tu-Sa. 64 Rue de la Montagne-Ste-Geneviève (between Pl du Panthéon and Rue Laplace). 01.46.34.78.38. Métro: Maubert–Mutualité

56 Au Vieux Paris ★$$ In the shadow of the **St-Etienne-du-Mont** church, Jean Vergez's restaurant of wooden beams and stone pillars serves rich food from France's southwest: foie gras, *confit de canard* (duck confit), and blood sausage. Dessert might be a pleasing *charlotte aux poires* (pear charlotte). ♦ M-Sa lunch and dinner. Reservations recommended. 2 Pl du Panthéon (at Rue de la Montagne-Ste-Geneviève). 01.43.54.79.22. Métros: Cardinal-Lemoine, Luxembourg (RER)

57 Le Raccard ★★$$ The Swiss chalet decor may be heavy-handed, but the all-you-can-eat raclette (melted cheese on bread) is as authentic and delicious as it comes. In winter, fondues made with gruyère or *vacherin* are served. ♦ Tu-Su dinner; closed in August.

Reservations recommended. 19 Rue Laplace (between Rues de la Montagne-Ste-Geneviève and Valette). 01.43.25.27.27, 01.43.54.83.75. Métro: Cardinal-Lemoine

58 Le Coupe-Chou ★$$ This seductive inn occupies the site of a famous Parisian barbershop whose proprietor slit the throats of his customers and then gave their bodies to a butcher to be made into pâté. If you can cast that grisly chapter from your mind, you will probably enjoy this attractive dining spot, which serves salmon ravioli, lamb with mint, *magret de canard* (duck fillet) with peaches, and hot homemade puff pastries—although you may opt to stay away from the pâté. ♦ M-Sa lunch and dinner; Su dinner. Reservations recommended. 11 Rue de Lanneau (at Impasse Chartière). 01.46.33.68.69. Métro: Maubert–Mutualité

59 Collège de France First called the **Collège des Trois-Langues** (Three-Language College) because Hebrew and Greek were taught here as well as Latin, this institution, founded by François I in 1529, counts among its famous faculty Frédéric Joliot-Curie (son-in-law of Marie and Pierre Curie), who split the uranium atom; the physicist André-Marie Ampère, after whom a unit of measuring electric current is named; poet Paul Valéry; and the more contemporary scholars Roland Barthes, Michel Foucault, and Claude Lévi-Strauss. ♦ 11 Pl Marcelin-Berthelot (at Rue St-Jacques). 01.44.27.12.11. Métro: Maubert–Mutualité

BRASSERIE BALZAR

60 Brasserie Balzar ★★$$ Camus and Sartre had their last argument at the **Balzar,** and James Thurber, Elliot Paul, William Shirer, and the old *Chicago Tribune* crowd gathered here for the beer and *choucroute* (sauerkraut) *garni.* The literary clientele, old wood paneling and mirrors, and waiters in long white aprons create an ambience that makes this one of the best brasseries in Paris. Getting a table for lunch is not difficult; dinner, however, is a different story. At night, especially after the theater, the vinyl banquettes are jammed with university professors, actors, editors, journalists, and aspiring poets dining on hearty fare such as *cervelas rémoulade* (sausage with mustard and herb dressing), cassoulet, and calf's liver *niçoise* (with tomatoes, anchovies, and olive oil), all washed down with a bottle of Bordeaux.

This restaurant is worth a visit even if you only stop for a Kir or coffee on the terrace. Conveniently, when the **Balzar** is closed, the **Lipp,** another literary shrine (151 Blvd St-

Germain, between Rues de Rennes and du Dragon, 01.45.48.53.91) stays open, an arrangement dating from the days when they were under the same management. ♦ Daily breakfast, lunch, and dinner; closed in August. Reservations recommended. 49 Rue des Ecoles (at Rue de la Sorbonne). 01.43.54.13.67. Métro: Cluny–La Sorbonne

61 Place de la Sorbonne This square, lined with cafes and lime trees, was a focal point of the student-worker protest of 1968. That year, on 10 and 11 May, police and students clashed violently, resulting in the injury of 400 participants and the arrest of hundreds of others. In the square stands a graffiti-marred statue of Auguste Comte (1798-1857), who was fired from his job as examiner in mathematics at the prestigious **Ecole Polytechnique** for his revolutionary ideas. Comte is best remembered as the founder of Positivism, a philosophy that strongly influenced John Stuart Mill. ♦ Between Rue de la Sorbonne and Blvd St-Michel. Métros: Cluny–La Sorbonne, Luxembourg (RER)

On Place de la Sorbonne:

Hôtel Select $$$ Basic, comfortable, and conveniently located on the Place de la Sorbonne, this 68-room hotel is an ideal base for exploring the Latin Quarter. In 1937, 25-year-old Eric Sevareid checked into a 50-cents-a-night room here and headed off to work for the *Paris Herald,* soon accomplishing feats such as an interview with Gertrude Stein. There's no restaurant. ♦ No. 1 (at Rue Victor-Cousin). 01.46.34.14.80; fax 01.46.34.51.79

62 Sorbonne France's most famous university began in 1253 as humble lodgings for 16 theology students. In medieval times, the university was not a mass of edifices, pedants, and bureaucrats; it was a loose assembly of soapbox academics giving street-corner lectures to students who boarded at inns throughout Paris. However, by the end of the 13th century, when the **Sorbonne** became the administrative headquarters of the **University of Paris,** there were 15,000 undergraduates studying in the city. St. Thomas Aquinas and Roger Bacon were among the **Sorbonne**'s great teachers; St. Ignatius Loyola, Dante, Erasmus, and John Calvin were students here. As the **Sorbonne** grew in size and power, it frequently contradicted the authority of the French throne. During the Hundred Years' War (1337-1453), the university had the audacity to side with England against France. It recognized Henry V as king of France and cravenly sent one of its best prosecutors to Rouen to try Joan of Arc.

In 1642 Cardinal Richelieu (pictured below) was elected grand master of the Sorbonne; he commissioned architect **Jacques Lemercier** to restore the dilapidated college buildings and erect a Jesuit-style church. During the Revolution the university closed down and remained empty until 1806, when Napoléon headquartered his **Académie de Paris** here. Following the May 1968 student-worker demonstration, the state unceremoniously rechristened the **Sorbonne "Paris University IV,"** tossing it into the archipelago of institutions of higher learning scattered about the city.

Don't be shy about wandering down the university's long stone corridors or visiting the lecture halls, including the **Amphithéâtre Descartes** and the **Salle Doctorat.** (Unfortunately, the ornate **Grand Amphithéâtre** with its famous Puvis de Chavannes fresco is strictly reserved for ceremonies of state.) If you decide to enroll in a four-month crash course in French (as hundreds of Americans do every year), you will come to know the dusty domed ceiling and stiff wooden benches of the **Amphithéâtre Richelieu** intimately. For an admission application, contact: Cours de Civilisation Française de la Sorbonne, Galerie Richelieu, 45-47 Rue des Ecoles, 75005 Paris. ♦ 45-47 Rue des Ecoles (between Rues St-Jacques and de la Sorbonne). 01.40.46.22.11. Métros: Cluny–La Sorbonne, Luxembourg (RER)

MICHAEL STORRINGS

Cardinal Richelieu

Beside the Sorbonne:

Ste-Ursule-de-la-Sorbonne Nothing of Cardinal Richelieu's **Sorbonne** remains save **Jacques Lemercier**'s chapel (1642), which was the first completely Roman-style building in 17th-century Paris. Richelieu is buried here. Above François Girardon's beautiful white marble tomb (1694), which depicts a half-recumbent Richelieu, his red cardinal's hat still hangs by a few slender threads from the ceiling. According to tradition, the hat will remain there until Richelieu's soul is freed from Purgatory, at which time the threads will rot and the hat will drop. ◆ The chapel is closed to the public except during special exhibitions of stained glass, tapestry, and old manuscripts. Church services are held in the chapel on 21 October (the feast day of St. Ursula) and 4 December (the anniversary of Richelieu's death). Pl de la Sorbonne (between Rues Victor-Cousin and de la Sorbonne). 01.40.46.20.52

63 **Lycée Louis Le Grand** Founded in 1550, this 1,500-student state-run high school numbers among its former pupils Molière, Voltaire, Robespierre, Hugo, Baudelaire, Pompidou, Giscard d'Estaing, Chirac, and Senghor (the former president of Senegal). It's closed to the public. ◆ 123 Rue St-Jacques (between Rues Cujas and des Ecoles). Métros: Luxembourg (RER), Cluny–La Sorbonne

CHEZ PENTO
Le Restaurant des Illustrateurs

64 **Chez Pento** ★★$$ Professors from the **Sorbonne** and nearby *lycées* frequent this 1930s-style bistro at midday, drawn by its reasonably priced lunch menu. At dinnertime, a less homogeneous crowd of Parisians settles into the faux-leather banquettes, choosing among such entrées as *magret de canard au vinaigre de cassis* (breast of duck with black currant vinegar), quail with grapes in rum sauce, and guinea hen marinated in lime. The *mousse de banane sur coulis de fruit rouge* (banana mousse with red fruit sauce) is a divine dessert. ◆ M-F lunch and dinner; Sa dinner. 9 Rue Cujas (at Rue Toullier). 01.43.26.81.54. Métro: Luxembourg (RER)

65 **Bibliothèque Ste-Geneviève** This library, constructed in 1850 on the Place du Panthéon, occupies the site of the old **Collège Montaigu** where Erasmus, Calvin, and St. Ignatius Loyola studied. Architect **Henri Labrouste**'s revolutionary use of steel-frame-and-masonry construction (further elaborated in his other library, the **Bibliothèque Nationale,** which was finished in 1868) makes this building one of the most important 19th-century forerunners of modern architecture. While you may peek inside, the library itself is restricted to visitors with valid readers' cards except during limited touring hours. ◆ Tours: 9-10AM by appointment only. Pl du Panthéon (between Rues Valette and Cujas). 01.43.29.61.00. Métro: Cardinal-Lemoine

66 **Rue Soufflot** Looking down this street (named for the architect of the **Panthéon**), you will see two matching buildings: the **City Hall** of the fifth arrondissement and the **University of Paris Faculty of Law** building, with the **Luxembourg Gardens** and **Eiffel Tower** in the distance. Eighteen feet below Rue Soufflot lie the remains of a Roman forum, discovered by 19th-century archaeologists; the ruins are not open to the public. ◆ Between Pl du Panthéon and Blvd St-Michel. Métro: Cardinal-Lemoine

LES ⁰⁰⁰ FONTAINES

67 **Les Fontaines** ★$$ This bustling bistro may look as if it lost its soul somewhere in all the cigarette smoke, but it serves surprisingly good, hearty fare for quite reasonable prices. Main courses include gigot (leg of lamb), sweetbread with mushrooms, venison with pepper sauce, and John Dory fillet cooked in fifteen spices. For dessert, only if you're starved for sweets, try the less impressive *crêpe soufflé à l'orange* or *feuilleté de poire au chocolat chaude* (pears in flaky pastry with hot chocolate sauce).◆ M-Sa lunch and dinner. 9 Rue Soufflot (at Rue Paillet). 01.43.26.42.80. Métro: Luxembourg (RER)

68 **Perraudin** ★★★$ Popular among **Sorbonne** students and their profs, this bargain canteen with archetypal bistro decor (lace curtains, red-and-white-checkered tablecloths, and Art Deco tile floors) offers a panoply of *cuisine bourgeoise:* lamb and kidney beans, beef stew, au gratin potatoes, and rough red wines. ◆ M, Sa dinner; Tu-F lunch and dinner; closed the last two weeks of August. 157 Rue St-Jacques (between Rues des Fossés-St-Jacques and Soufflot). 01.46.33.15.75. Métro: Luxembourg (RER)

"To know Paris is to know a great deal."

Henry Miller

Restaurants/Clubs: Red   **Hotels:** Blue
Shops/ ❦ Outdoors: Green   **Sights/Culture:** Black

69 Hôtel des Grands Hommes $$$

Comfortable and right in the heart of the Latin Quarter, this 32-room hotel boasts views of the **Panthéon** and the spire of **Notre-Dame** from some of its top-floor rooms. Surrealism may have had its start at this hotel, as André Breton and Philippe Soupault invented automatic writing here in 1919. The apartment of Laurent Fabius, former prime minister under François Mitterrand, is next door at 15 Place du Panthéon. There's no hotel restaurant. ◆ 17 Pl du Panthéon (between Rues d'Ulm and Clotaire). 01.46.34.19.60; fax 01.43.26.67.32. Métro: Luxembourg (RER)

70 Panthéon

When Louis XV recovered from gout at Metz in 1744, he vowed, in gratitude, to build a great temple honoring St. Geneviève. The architect, **Jacques-Germain Soufflot,** chose to construct a Classical edifice based on the form of a Greek cross (339 feet long and 253 feet wide). **Soufflot,** who had been inspired by his trips to Italy, intended his building to resemble the Panthéon of Agrippa in Rome; however, the Paris **Panthéon**'s lofty 52-pillar dome and handsome Corinthian colonnade wound up being much more reminiscent of St. Paul's Cathedral in London. Finished in 1850 by **Guillaume Rondelet,** one of **Soufflot**'s students, the **Panthéon** was secularized into the **Temple of Fame,** a necropolis for the distinguished atheists of France. In its rather depressing crypt lie Voltaire, Rousseau, Victor Hugo (whose coffin passed a ceremonial night under the **Arc de Triomphe** and was carried to the **Panthéon** in the hearse of the poor), Gambetta, Emile Zola, Louis Braille (the 19th-century Frenchman who, blinded at age three, went on to invent the system of embossed dots that enables the sightless to read), Jean Jaurès (the celebrated leftist politician and orator who was assassinated in 1914), and Jean Moulin (the Resistance leader in World War II who was tortured to death during

the Occupation). After the Revolution, the **Panthéon**'s 42 tall windows were walled up, and today the monument looms over the square like a prison, grandiose and austere. ◆ Admission. Daily. Pl du Panthéon. 01.43.54.34.51. Métros: Cardinal-Lemoine, Luxembourg (RER)

71 Lycée Henri IV

Dating from Napoleonic times, this is one of the city's most prestigious high schools; Jean-Paul Sartre, the French novelist and playwright who refused the Nobel Prize for Literature in 1964, taught here. The school's most notable architectural feature is the **Tour de Clovis,** a Gothic belfry. The tower is all that remains of the **Abbaye Ste-Geneviève,** built by King Clovis after he was converted to Christianity by his wife, Clotilde of Burgundy, and St. Geneviève herself. St. Thomas Aquinas (1225-74) taught at the abbey. The school is closed to the public. ◆ 23 Rue Clovis (at Rue Clotilde). Métro: Luxembourg (RER)

72 St-Etienne-du-Mont

The combination of a Gothic rose window, triple Classical pediments, a medieval-style belfry, and a Renaissance dome in this church (see picture below) defies the laws of architectural purity. Its low-hanging chandeliers are a menace to anyone over six feet tall. And it must be the only church in Paris that closes for lunch. But *mon Dieu,* it's beautiful! Completed in 1626, **St-Etienne-du-Mont** is home to two graceful 16th-century spiral staircases, an extraordinary

St-Etienne-du-Mont

wooden pulpit (1650) shouldered by a grimacing Samson, and the only rood screen left in Paris, as well as the tombs of Pascal, Racine, and Marat. The church surrounds a shrine to St. Geneviève, which Paris fathers have visited the first Sunday of each year for centuries. During the annual pilgrimage on 3 January 1857, while bowing to bless a child, Monseigneur Sibour, Archbishop of Paris, was stabbed to death by an unfrocked priest named Verger, who apparently objected to the ban on marriage that compelled priestly celibacy. A marker at the rear of the center aisle indicates the spot where the murder was committed. ♦ Pl Ste-Geneviève (between Rues Clovis and St-Etienne-du-Mont). 01.43.54.11.79. Métro: Cardinal-Lemoine

73 La Truffière ★$$
Rich specialties from Périgord—the very antithesis of nouvelle cuisine—are served at this rustic eatery: black truffles, foie gras, and generous portions of goose and duck prepared in every conceivable fashion. Have an aperitif near the fireplace in the sitting room before proceeding to dinner. ♦ Tu-Su lunch and dinner. Reservations required. 4 Rue Blainville (between Rues Mouffetard and Tournefort). 01.46.33.29.82. Métros: Cardinal-Lemoine, Place Monge

74 9 Rue Blainville
The first public library in Paris was once housed in this building. ♦ At Rue Tournefort. Métros: Cardinal-Lemoine, Place Monge

75 Rue Descartes
This street carries the name of French mathematician and philosopher René "I-think-therefore-I-am" Descartes (1596-1650). He lived on Montagne Ste-Geneviève from 1613 to 1619 and again in 1625, but it is doubtful he ever lived on this street, which was then known as la Rue des Bordels (the street of brothels). Descartes emigrated to Sweden, where he died in the arms of Queen Christina. ♦ Between Rues Thouin and de la Montagne-Ste-Geneviève. Métro: Cardinal-Lemoine

On Rue Descartes:

No. 39 A plaque below the awning marks the house where poet Paul Verlaine (1844-96) died. Later there was a hotel at this same address; in 1922 Ernest Hemingway rented a room in the hostelry, which he later described in *A Moveable Feast*. It's now an apartment building with restaurants on the ground floor. ♦ Between Rues Thouin and Clovis

No. 47 At the end of the passageway through this historic 17th-century, half-timbered Norman-style house is a section of King Philippe Auguste's medieval city wall. Visitors may enter the passageway to see the wall. ♦ Between Rues Thouin and Clovis

76 Rue Clovis
This short street is named after Clovis (AD 466-511), king of the Franks, who defeated the Romans at Soissons, ending the Roman Empire's dominion of Gaul and founding France. The narrow sidewalk on the south side of the street (near **No. 5**) is practically blocked by the ivy-draped ruins of King Philippe Auguste's fortified wall. It was originally 33 feet high, with a pathway on top, and was patrolled by city sentries (during the 19th century, a bronze regiment of these sentries was enshrined on the roof of the **City Hall** in the Place de l'Hôtel-de-Ville). Construction of the wall started in 1190, and it marked the city limits of Paris until the 17th century. The wall was pulled down when Louis XIV left Paris for **Versailles.** At the bottom of the hill at **No. 67** Rue du Cardinal-Lemoine is the house where Pascal died in 1662. ♦ Between Rues du Cardinal-Lemoine and Clotilde. Métro: Cardinal-Lemoine

77 Hôtel des Grandes Ecoles $$
Entering the courtyard here is like stepping into an Impressionist painting. This homey, family-run establishment has recently undergone renovations and comprises two ivy-covered houses set in a lush garden. Each of the 51 delightful rooms is decorated differently; ask for one with a garden view. On cool mornings, enjoy your croissants and *café au lait* in the charming lace-curtained breakfast room; in summer, you can eat amid the trees and flowers. (There's no restaurant.) Guests return year after year, so make reservations well in advance. Note: Reservations are taken from 2PM to 6PM only. ♦ 75 Rue du Cardinal-Lemoine (between Rues Rollin and Monge). 01.43.26.79.23; fax 01.43.25.28.15. Métro: Cardinal-Lemoine

78 Place de la Contrescarpe
In the Middle Ages, this dark, dangerous neighborhood lay outside King Philippe Auguste's city wall, beyond the moat, on the counter-escarpment. Since the days of Hemingway's *A Moveable Feast,* the public urinals and bus stop have disappeared, but a certain seediness remains. In winter, the local *clochards* (street people) still huddle over the heating duct and live off spoils from the markets and spare change from tourists. On summer weekends, harmless bikers in black leather congregate here. ♦ Between Rues Lacépède and Mouffetard. Métros: Cardinal-Lemoine, Place Monge

"There is no food in Paris, only cuisine."

Anonymous

59

French Made Fun

The best way to understand a culture is through its language, but the prospect of studying the intricacies of French grammar is daunting to most English speakers. Enter the **Association Civilisation et Culture Françaises,** which offers customized one-on-one lessons and lectures that will help anyone—first-time students, more experienced French speakers looking to brush up on their pronunciation, and those who just want to learn more about the rich traditions and history of France—unravel the complexities of French language and culture. Whether you want a tour of the **Louvre,** a lesson on restaurant etiquette, or the translation of the words of your favorite Serge Gainsbourg song, Hélène Prevost, director of the association, can come up with an individually tailored course for you. You can meet your instructor anywhere—in **Les Deux Magots** for a conversational course over coffee, the **Musée d'Orsay** for a discussion of Impressionist painting, or the **Latin Quarter** for a tour of Roman Paris. For information contact **Association Civilisation et Culture Françaises** (7 Rue Jacquemont, between Rue Lemercier and Ave de Clichy, 01.42.28.22.40).

On Place de la Contrescarpe:

No. 1 The name **Maison de la Pomme de Pin** (Pine Cone Cabaret) is carved into the wall above the *boucherie* (butcher's shop) at this address. It marks the site of an old cafe frequented by satirist François Rabelais (1494-1553), author of *Pantagruel* and *Gargantua.* ♦ At Rue Lacépède

La Chope ★$ Once a Hemingway haunt, this cafe is crowded with stout butchers drinking Calvados and students from the **Lycée Henri IV** playing pinball. The bill of fare runs from chef's salads to banana splits. ♦ Daily breakfast, lunch, and dinner until 2AM. No. 2 (at Rue Cardinal-Lemoine). 01.43.26.51.26

79 Rue Mouffetard Leading out of the Place de la Contrescarpe is the 13th-century Rue Mouffetard. As you descend the narrow street, let your imagination take you back to the time when it was the main Roman road to the southeast, Lyon, and Italy. During the 12th century the area near the Bièvre River was filled with the country homes of rich Parisians. Within four centuries the Bièvre became a foul-smelling stream polluted by the animal wastes and dyes dumped by tanners, skinners, and the Flemish tapestry weavers from the **Gobelins** factory. In 1910 the river was covered over and incorporated into the sewer system.

Some guess that the name "Mouffetard" comes from *mouffette,* French for skunk; more likely it is a corruption of the Roman name of the hill it traverses, Mont Cétar. Prior to the Revolution the poor of Paris lived here in utter wretchedness. The unadorned mansard-roofed 17th-century houses that still line the Rue Mouffetard were built for ordinary folk. In the 1600s one French writer said more money could be found in one single house of the Faubourg St-Honoré than in all of those combined on the Rue Mouffetard.

Today, this thoroughfare is much beloved by gourmets and gourmands. The upper half of the street is filled with restaurants, many Greek, while a bustling pedestrian street market has convened at the bottom of the hill ever since 1350. The outdoor market section (see below) runs from Rue de l'Epée-de-Bois to Rue Censier, with the liveliest area near Rue Censier. ♦ Between Rues Censier and Thouin. Métros: Censier–Daubenton, Place Monge

79 12 Rue Mouffetard Above this charcuterie is an astounding painting that looks more suited to early Atlanta than Paris. *Le Nègre Joyeux* (The Happy Negro) portrays a stereotyped grinning black servant in striped pants serving tea to his mistress. ♦ At Rue Blainville. Métro: Place Monge

80 51 to 55 Rue Mouffetard In 1938 workers discovered 3,351 coins of 22-karat gold weighing 16.3 grams each and bearing the image of Louis XV hidden inside the wall here. The buried treasure, according to an accompanying note, belonged to Louis Nivelle, the royal counselor who mysteriously disappeared in 1757. ♦ At Rue Ortolan. Métros: Censier–Daubenton, Place Monge

81 Fontaine du Pot-de-Fer What appears to be an Italianate roadside dungeon is actually a restored historic monument. Behind this wall is one of the 14 fountains constructed in 1624 at the behest of Marie de Médicis. The fountain was designed to handle the overflow from the Gallo-Roman aqueduct that she had refurbished to supply water for her new palace in the **Luxembourg Gardens.** ♦ 60 Rue Mouffetard (at Rue du Pot-de-Fer). Métros: Censier–Daubenton, Place Monge

81 Chaussures Georges This dinky hundred-year-old shoe store run by a garrulous Armenian named Georges supplies the neighborhood butchers, fishmongers, and masons with their rubber boots and wool-lined French and Swedish sabots. These are shoes for function, not fantasy, proclaims Georges, who keeps all his footwear in 19th-century boxes with pewter handles. He also sells plain espadrilles—the real ones from the French Pyrenées, not Chinese imitations. ♦ Tu-Sa; Su 9:30AM-12:30PM. 64 Rue Mouffetard (between Rues Jean-Calvin and Pot-de-Fer). 01.47.07.16.66. Métros: Censier–Daubenton, Place Monge

82 10 Rue Vauquelin Working in a ramshackle ground-floor laboratory here at the **Sorbonne School of Physics and Chemistry** (which is now housed in a shiny new redbrick-and-glass building), Marie Curie and her husband, Pierre, discovered radium on 26 December 1898. The discovery of radioactivity not only earned them a Nobel prize in 1903 (the first of two for Marie) but triggered a fundamental rethinking of theoretical physics. A few months after their achievements, the quantum theory was published. ♦ Between Rues Claude-Bernard and Lhomond. Métro: Censier–Daubenton

Le Mouffetard

83 Le Mouffetard ★★$ The croissants, brioches, and fruit tarts are made fresh daily by the friendly Chartrain family, owners of the best cafe on the street. It's noisy, always crowded with vendors and students, and in winter the windows steam up, thanks to the animated conversation. ♦ Tu-Sa breakfast, lunch, and dinner; Su breakfast and lunch; closed in July. No credit cards accepted. 116 Rue Mouffetard (at Rue de l'Arbalète). 01.43.31.42.50. Métro: Censier–Daubenton

84 A la Bonne Source This bas-relief of two boys drawing water, whose title means "At the Good Spring," dates from the time of Henri IV (1589-1610). It's the oldest house sign on the street. ♦ 122 Rue Mouffetard (between Rues Edouard-Quénu and de l'Arbalète). Métro: Censier–Daubenton

85 Facchetti & Co. Charcuterie Fine Although it's a first-rate gourmet Italian delicatessen, the main reason for stopping here is not to buy pasta and parmesan but to admire the bucolic outdoor mural of peasants at work below a pair of stags and wild boars. ♦ Tu-Sa 8:30AM-8PM; Su 8AM-1:30PM. 134 Rue Mouffetard (between Rues Edouard-Quénu and de l'Arbalète). 01.43.31.40.00. Métro: Censier–Daubenton

86 Rue Mouffetard Market Among the gastronomical items purveyed at this outdoor market are mangoes, blood oranges, horse meat, wild boar, sea urchins, Colombian coffee, and hundreds of marvelously smelly cheeses. Take a self-guided tour: Just follow your nose. Be sure to go down the Rue Daubenton and Passage Passé Simple to visit the flower shops and the stalls specializing in Auvergnat sausage. As you wander, remember the two cardinal rules of marketing in Paris: First, don't touch the produce; and second, the vendor, not the customer, is always right. ♦ Tu-Sa; Su 9AM-1PM. Between Rues Censier and de l'Epée-de-Bois. Métro: Censier–Daubenton

86 St-Médard This rustic village church, built in 1773, is an architectural conglomeration of Flamboyant Gothic and Renaissance styles and has a story for every predilection. French literature majors may remember this as the church in which Jean Valjean accidentally encounters Javert in Victor Hugo's *Les Misérables*. Trade unionists point out that the church was turned into the **Temple of Labor** during the Revolution. Art historians will recall the notorious painting of St. Geneviève, which for centuries was erroneously ascribed to Watteau. And the occultists in the crowd will appreciate a most famous corpse buried here, that of a church deacon named François Paris, a saintly young Jansenist who died in 1727. Rumors of miraculous cures drew huge crowds of hysterical convulsionaries to his grave within two years of his death. (The frenzied gatherings were finally outlawed by Louis XV in 1732, but Paris's tomb remains beneath the unmarked stones of what is now the **Chapel of the Virgin.**) The majority of the church's construction was financed by fines imposed on Protestants; the money ran out while the vaulted ceiling was being installed, so it was completed in wood. At least that's how the story goes. ♦ 141 Rue Mouffetard (between Rues Censier and Daubenton). 01.44.08.87.00. Métro: Censier–Daubenton

87 Le Petit Marguery ★★$$ This lively 1900s-style neighborhood bistro presents hearty dishes such as *cassolette de gros escargots de Bourgogne* (Burgundy snails in ramekin) and venison (in season). ♦ Tu-Sa lunch and dinner; closed in August. Reservations recommended. 9 Blvd de Port-Royal (between Blvd Arago and Rue Pascal). 01.43.31.58.59. Métro: Les Gobelins

Tourists often hum "April in Paris" with great hopes of clear weather, but Parisians know that sunshine and spring don't hit town until May, when three long weekend holidays (Labor Day, Ascension Day, and Pentecost) offer a taste of the summer vacations ahead. May is also the month for polo matches at the Club de Paris (otherwise closed to the public) and the glamorous French Tennis Open at Roland-Garros (but tickets are as rare as counterfeits are rife: center court seats are sold out by January to corporate clients).

88 Manufacture des Gobelins (Gobelins Tapestry Factory)

The factory, the avenue, and the neighborhood all take their name from the brothers Jean and Philibert Gobelin, who in the 15th century established their famous dye works along the stinking Bièvre River. Although the name "Gobelins" has become synonymous with tapestry, the two brothers never wove a thread. Their claim to fame in the tapestry world was making a special scarlet dye. In 1662 Jean-Baptiste Colbert, Louis XIV's famous minister, persuaded the king to take over the Gobelins property. There, under the management of court painter Charles Le Brun, Colbert assembled a crafts colony of about 250 Flemish weavers. His goal was twofold: to compete with Flanders's tapestry industry and to cover the vast expanse of walls in the Sun King's sumptuous palace at **Versailles.** (Within Gobelins' first courtyard stands a marble 1907 statue of Le Brun by Cardier, followed in the next courtyard by an 1894 statue of his boss, Colbert, by Aube.) In time, the tapestry factory became so celebrated that Marie Antoinette and Louis XVI (in 1790) and the Pope (in 1895) paid personal visits to the humble workshops.

Today scores of weavers at the factory manufacture tapestries using ancient techniques, working on century-old wooden looms. Using wools from a palette of 14,920 colors, weavers may spend two to four years completing woven panels, the designs of which are based on modern paintings by artists such as Matisse, Picasso, and Miró. Three days a week, the state-owned mills offer 75-minute guided tours of the tapestry factory and the allied **Savonnerie** (carpet) and **Beauvais** (horizontal loom weaving) workshops, a treat for anyone interested in weaving and crafts. You can visit the studios where weavers, trained from the age of 16, work quietly, occasionally glancing up at mirrors before them to view the reverse side of the tapestry. If you can't get to the factory, you can see Gobelins tapestries hanging at **Versailles** as well as other places reserved for the privileged: the **Paris Opéra,** the **National Library,** the **Elysée Palace,** and the **Luxembourg Palace.** ♦ Admission. Tours: Tu-Th 2:45PM. To arrange group tours, call **Caisse Nationale des Monuments Historiques,** 01.44.61.21.69. 42 Ave des Gobelins (between Rues Croulebarbe and des Gobelins). 01.44.08.52.00. Métro: Les Gobelins

89 Mobilier National (National Storehouse)

What institution is as supersecret as the French CIA, answers directly to the president, and is littered with Napoléon-era love seats and andirons? Answer: the **Mobilier National,** France's national attic. This singular government entity was created in 1667 by Colbert as a royal storehouse when he was transforming the **Gobelins Tapestry Factory.** It is the state's interior decorator, responsible for furnishing government ministries and embassies with everything from inkwells to curtains. The institution, which at one time also kept the crown jewels, is quartered within the **Gobelins** complex in an unremarkable redbrick structure designed by **Auguste Perret.** In 1964 André Malraux, then Minister of Culture, offered studio space in the storehouse to contemporary French furniture designers who would be willing to create and sell their prototypes to French manufacturers. Thus, the **Mobilier National** takes credit for the boldly modern furniture used in former president Georges Pompidou's office at the **Elysée Palace.** You can pass by this warehouse on the **Gobelins** tour, but it's off-limits to the public. ♦ Rue Berbier-du-Mets (between Rues Croulebarbe and Emile-Deslandres). Métro: Les Gobelins

90 La Tuile à Loup

Run by the affable Marie-France and Michel Joblin, this crowded shop specializes in French regional arts and crafts. The shelves are stocked with earthenware dishes, hand-carved wooden bowls, toys by well-known French artist Roland Roure, and a vast selection of books on French folklore, rural architecture, and ecology. ♦ Tu-Sa; Su 10AM-1PM (call ahead to confirm Sunday hours). 35 Rue Daubenton (between Rues Monge and de Candolle). 01.47.07.28.90. Métro: Censier–Daubenton

91 Place Monge

This square is named for the mathematician Gaspard Monge (1746-1818), who in 1794 founded the prestigious **Ecole Polytechnique.** Near the bustling small farmers' market is the old barracks of the Garde Républicaine, whose famous horse guards parade up the Champs-Elysées on Bastille Day, 14 July. ♦ Market: W, F, Su 7AM-1PM. Between Rues Monge and Gracieuse. Métro: Place Monge

92 Arènes de Lutèce (Roman Arena)

After the **Roman Baths** at the **Musée de Cluny** (see page 51), this enormous first-century amphitheater is the city's most important Roman ruin. Accidentally discovered (and partially destroyed) in 1869, the 325- by 425-foot oval once seated 15,000 spectators. With its surrounding gardens and benches, the arena provides an island of tranquillity for young parents pushing strollers and old men playing *boules;* in summer, campy medieval jousts take place here. It's a nice spot for a picnic lunch of sourdough rye bread and charcuterie from the Place Monge market. ♦ Enter at Pl Emile-Mâle (at Rues de Navarre and des Arènes). Métros: Cardinal-Lemoine, Jussieu, Place Monge

93 Hôtel Jardin des Plantes $$ Guests of this tranquil 33-room hotel in a quiet neighborhood can enjoy breakfast and lunch surrounded by flowers on the rooftop terrace. Many of the rooms have views of the magnificent botanical garden nearby. ♦ 5 Rue Linné (between Rues Lacépède and des Arènes). 01.47.07.06.20; fax 01.47.07.62.74. Métros: Jussieu, Place Monge

94 La Mosquée de Paris This Moorish ensemble of soaring minarets, pink marble fountains, and crescent moons is the oldest mosque in France. In gratitude for North African support during World War I, France gave the French Arab community the funds to build the mosque. It was constructed in 1926 by Arab artisans and three French architects. Arabs from the poor Belleville and Barbès quarters gather at this enclave of Islam to read the Koran at the **Institut Musulman.** During Ramadan, hundreds of North Africans kneel facing Mecca and pray to Allah on a sea of Persian carpets spread beneath the mosque's delicately carved dome. Nearby, behind a dark curtain, the women intone their prayers. While unfortunately brief, the guided tour of the building, central courtyard, and Moorish garden offers a worthwhile introduction to Islam. You may leave feeling as though you've passed the time in Riyadh or Istanbul. ♦ Admission. M-Th, Sa-Su. Pl du Puits-de-l'Ermite (between Rues Georges-Desplas and Quatrefages). 01.45.35.97.33/34/35. Métro: Place Monge

95 Café de la Mosquée ★$ Flaky Moroccan pastries, sweet mint tea, and Turkish coffee are served during the summer on a white patio shaded by leafy fig trees. In winter, warm up with tea in a quiet lounge adjoining the *hammam* (Turkish steam bath). No alcohol is served. ♦ Daily breakfast, lunch, and dinner until 10PM; closed in August. 2 Rue Daubenton (at Rue Geoffroy-St-Hilaire). 01.43.31.18.14. Métros: Censier–Daubenton, Place Monge

96 Jardin des Plantes It was begun in 1626 by Louis XIII as a royal medicinal herb garden planted on an old rubbish heap. Today the 74-acre botanical garden hosts a floral orgy of peonies, irises, roses, geraniums, and dahlias from April through October. The garden, bounded by streets named after great French naturalists and botanists (Jussieu, Geoffroy St-Hilaire, and Buffon), contains a pedestal inscribed to the French scientist Lamarck, the author of the doctrine of evolution (tough luck, Charles Darwin), and another honoring Chevreul, the director of the **Gobelins** dye factory who lived to 103 and whose color-spectrum research informed the Impressionist painters.

Within the park is France's oldest public zoo, **Le Ménagerie,** which has a rather pathetic history. Established shortly after the Revolution to display survivors from the **Royal Menagerie** at **Versailles** (one hartebeest, one zebra, one rhinoceros, and a sheepdog), it was originally called the **People's Democratic Zoo.** In 1795 the first elephants arrived, in 1805 the bear pit opened, and in 1827 an Egyptian prince contributed a giraffe. The zoo grew in size and popularity until the Siege of Paris in 1870 and 1871, when the poor beasts were eaten. For several weeks, it is said, the privileged of Paris dined on elephant steaks the size of manhole covers. The zoo has never recovered from the

Hôtel Jardin des Plantes

slaughter, and conditions remain on the shabby side (animals are still jailed in Second-Empire pavilions, and rumors of stray cats being fed to snakes and reptiles proliferate). Children still seem to love it, though.

Legend holds that the park's famous **Cedar of Lebanon,** now 40 feet in circumference, traveled in 1735 as a seedling in the hat of naturalist Bernard de Jussieu, who had carefully preserved it during confinement as a prisoner of war. But in truth, it was given to him after his release.

The park's **Museum of Natural History** has five departments (Paleontology, Paleobotany, Mineralogy, Entomology, and Zoology) and it possesses one of the world's richest mineral collections and some of the oldest fossilized insects on earth. The renovated **Grande Galerie,** opened in 1994 after being closed for 30 years, houses a superb display on the evolution of life. Highlights include a giant whale skeleton, stuffed African Savannah animals, and an extinct and endangered species exhibit. ◆ Admission to zoo and museum. Garden and zoo: daily. Museums and greenhouses: M, W-Su. Enter at Rue Buffon, Rue Cuvier, or Pl Valhubert. 01.40.79.30.00. Métros: Gare d'Austerlitz, Jussieu, Place Monge

97 Musée de Sculpture en Plein Air This outdoor sculpture museum, built in 1980, was once the site of Henri IV's bathing beach. Here the king would pour water from a royal hat over the young Dauphin as the preamble to a swimming lesson. Today this spot on the banks of the Seine holds permanent and temporary exhibitions. But don't come here after dark; a less desirable brand of exhibitionist prowls then. ◆ Quai St-Bernard (between Ponts d'Austerlitz and de Sully). No phone. Métros: Gare d'Austerlitz, Jussieu

98 L'Institut du Monde Arabe (Arab Institute) Opened in December 1987, this sociocultural institution was established to promote relations between France and the Arab world. It contains a library, exhibition space, and a top-floor restaurant that serves Moroccan specialties (see below). The architect, **Jean Nouvel,** who received the Agha Kahn prize for his design, has given Islamic architectural elements a stunning space-age interpretation. Notice Nouvel's treatment of the south facade: The wall is made up of thousands of cameralike shutters that open and close automatically according to the sun's brightness, thus regulating the amount of light let inside the building. ◆ Tu-Su. 1 Rue des Fossés-St-Bernard (at Blvd St-Germain). 01.40.51.38.38. Métros: Jussieu, Cardinal-Lemoine

Within L'Institut du Monde Arabe:

Le Ziryab ★★$$ The river view from this rooftop Moroccan restaurant is better than that of La Tour d'Argent—at a fraction of the price. You may want to start your meal with one of the hot and cold hors d'oeuvres, such as marinated salmon, mini-chicken brochettes, *zaalouk d'aubergines* (eggplant pâté) or *kefta* (a mixture of minced beef and lamb with seven spices). Follow with an assortment of Oriental pastries and mint tea. Linger at a table on the terrace on a balmy summer evening. ◆ Tu-Su lunch and dinner. Reservations recommended. Ninth floor. 01.40.46.84.62

Bests

Claude Terrail
Caterer, La Tour d'Argent

I must admit that I am slightly spoiled. From my earliest youth, every day I have contemplated with an ever-renewed amazement (could it be any other way?) the **Ile St-Louis** and the **Ile de la Cité**: all of Paris offered to my eyes. I cannot do without the lacy facade of **Notre-Dame,** which dominates the **Seine.** The river, in turn, amiably divides into two arms to better embrace these so very unique islands.

The river, always the same, always changing, seems to match its colors to the moods, to the whims of the sky: From the **Tour d'Argent** I experience the magical attraction. This irreplaceable scenery sampled by all of my guests does not divert me from other discoveries: I stroll, whenever I have the time, in the **Marais,** chasing down its solid yet refined structures, its prestigious mansions— the **Hôtel de Sens** and so many others—I relearn history that no school had taught me.

A glance at the **Hôtel de Sully** and I stroll through the **Place des Vosges.** There I find my "children" again, **Coconnas** and **La Guirlande de Julie,** which I watch over jealously. But this doesn't stop me at all from going to greet my sister at **L'Escargot Montorgueil,** where I admire the 19th-century decor.

Guy Castelain Perry
Architect/Developer

The business day in the **Place Vendôme/Opéra/Madeleine** area:

Italian wine and pasta at **L'Enoteca** in the **Marais.**

Save a few francs for later: Have lunch at **La Tour d'Argent,** rather than dinner.

A walk along the quays of **Ile St-Louis** on a damp evening.

Sleeping on the rooftops of the Marais.

An evening in the west (by car):

Dinner at **Les Salons de l'Arc de Triomphe.**

To aid digestion, a convertible or limo ride up and down the *"Grand Axe"* from **Place de la Concorde** to **La Défense** before the lights go out.

Return to **Les Salons** (downstairs).

An evening in the east (on foot):

Linger on **Rue St-Antoine** from **St-Paul–St-Louis** to **Place de la Bastille** in the early evening.

Dinner at **Bofinger,** the oldest brasserie in Paris.

Drinks upstairs at the **China Club.**

The **Casbah** after 1AM (the neighborhood looks the part).

How to get away from it all. . .

Within the city:

The **Parc André Citroën** in the 15th arrondissement. This impressive modern landscape is on a par with the traditional ones for which the French are most famous.

In the suburbs:

The view from the château at **St-Germain-en-Laye.** (Take the *A* line on the **RER.**)

In the countryside (go on a weekday to avoid traffic and crowds):

Relaxing on the lawn at the far end of **Vaux-le-Vicomte's** gardens.

Gerrard Rudd and Ed Kohnke
Owners, La Castafiore

A lot of the "best of Paris" is a bit off the beaten track—another world, just a few métro stops away:

The **Parc de Belleville** (20th arrondissement). A better view than at **Montmartre** with none of the hordes of idling tour buses. Afterward, walk down the hill for great, cheap couscous in one of the neighborhood restaurants.

Dinner in the **Quartier St-Blaise** (20th arrondissement) on a warm summer evening. (Our favorite is the sidewalk terrace at the **Village de Paris.**) A trip *en province* without leaving the city.

Taking a drink on the **Butte aux Cailles** in the 13th arrondissement. It's easy to imagine Paris of the 1930s and Piaf singing on the street corner.

The bustling street market at **Barbès Rochechouart.** All the sights, sounds and smells of the Casbah.

And of course no trip to Paris would be complete without a stroll along the quays of **Ile St-Louis** and an intimate dinner afterward in one of its cozy restaurants (a shameless, but honest, plug).

V. Pimentel
Painter/Artist

I like to walk along the **Pont Alexandre III** at night, to watch the fog on the **Pont-Marie** in winter, and to

stroll on the **Ile St-Louis,** just along the edge of the Seine. I like **Montmartre** and all its history, the **Butte aux Cailles** in the 13th arrondissement, the charm of the **Marais,** the shouting heard at the market at **Place d'Aligre,** the **Louvre,** and the **Musée de l'Homme.** I like breathing amidst the nature of the **Bois de Vincennes** and to collect my thoughts in the church of **St-Julien-le-Pauvre.**

Staff
Hôtel Le Bristol

Special places: the *Lady with the Unicorn* tapestry at the **Musée de Cluny, Sainte-Chapelle** in the morning, **St-Julien-le-Pauvre** church, **Place St-Sulpice, Place des Vosges,** and **St-Etienne-du-Mont** church.

Tea at **Mariage Frères** in the fourth arrondissement: Excellent selection of teas and a pleasant atmosphere.

Cocktails or a pretheater dinner at the **Virgin Cafe** at the **Virgin Records' Megastore** on the **Champs-Elysées.** A very fun and lively atmosphere.

Christine Odile
Business Manager, Hôtel Meurice

Les Saveurs Lyriques au Meurice: Every Thursday night at 8:30PM at the restaurant **Le Meurice** in the **Hôtel Meurice** lovers of music and gastronomy meet to enjoy a gourmet menu. The music of Vivaldi, Mozart, Handel, Rossini, Offenbach and many others is performed by a musical ensemble with a soprano, mezzo-soprano, and baritone while you dine by candlelight.

Musée Rodin: A small museum, with a garden, showcasing the works of Rodin and Camille Claudel.

The **Richelieu** and **Denon Wings** at the **Louvre.**

Paris *lumière* (Paris by night): Visit **l'Opéra Bastille,** the **Eiffel Tower,** the **Louvre Pyramid,** and the **Rotonde de la Villette** at night.

Jean Nouvel
Architect

Notre-Dame—The history, the stained-glass windows.

Sainte-Chapelle—A marvel of light.

Driving on the streets along the quays, under the bridges of Paris.

Le Louvre—The underground portion, above all.

Cité de la Musique in **Parc de la Villette**—The music conservatory that is a small town of music by **Christian de Portzamparc.**

L'Institut du Monde Arabe (The Institute of the Arab World)—The geometry and the light of Islam.

Beaubourg—A monument from the 1970s.

Café Beaubourg—One of the city's fine restaurants.

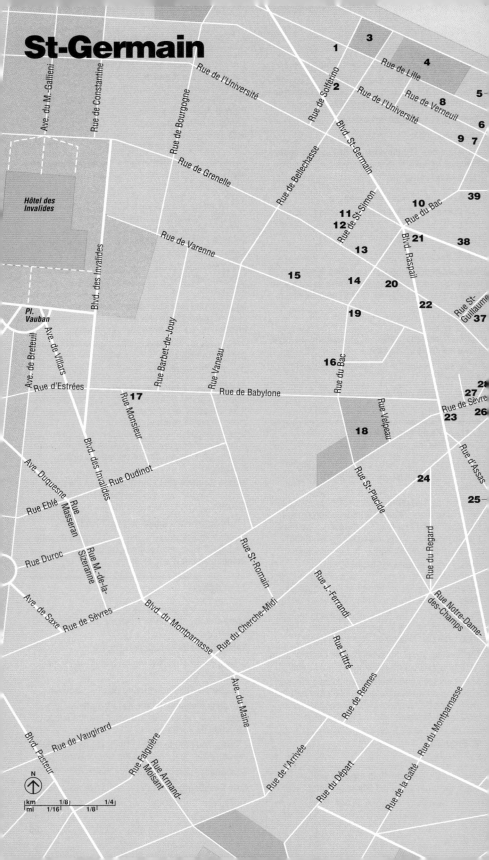

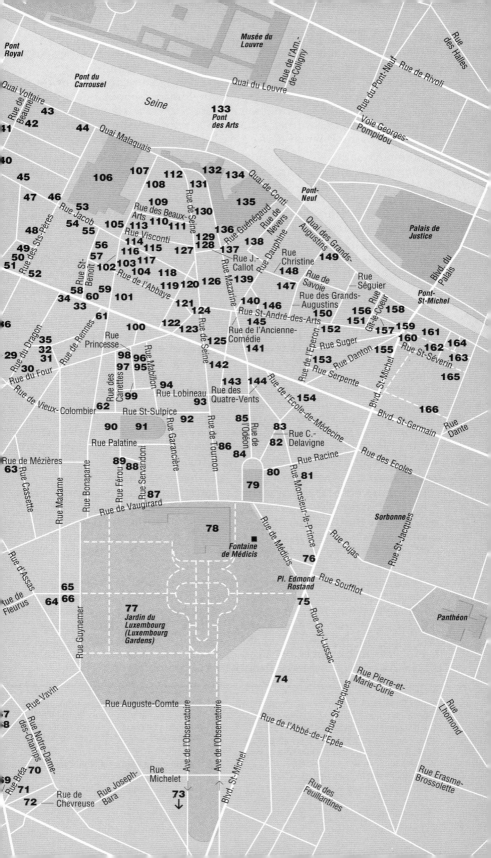

St-Germain

The tree-lined **Boulevard St-Germain** originates near the tip of Ile St-Louis, then traverses the heart of literary Paris, and finally arrives back at the Seine at the **Pont de la Concorde** in the noble faubourg fashionable during the reign of Louis XV. This is the home of the **Académie Française**, the world's oldest cafe (**Le Procope**), prestigious publishing houses, bookbinders, and a conclave of intellectual's watering holes where Fitzgerald, Hemingway, and other American scriveners wrote or drank away rejection-slip depression. And in the 1950s, this is where Sartre gave birth to existentialism.

The St-Germain quarter is also the home of the inviting **Jardin du Luxembourg** (Luxembourg Gardens), the city's **Ecole des Beaux-Arts** (School of Fine Arts), and a plethora of art galleries. In this neighborhood, the painter Corot walked the quays; Manet lived on **Rue Bonaparte**; and Delacroix resided in the **Place de Furstemberg**. Ingres, Baudelaire, and Wagner stayed on **Quai Voltaire**, and Picasso painted *Guernica* on **Rue des Grands-Augustins**.

This St-Germain itinerary covers the boulevard's most interesting portion, in the vicinity of the church of **St-Germain-des-Prés**, site of the remains of the city's oldest abbey. The route leads down alleys where bookshops, poster stores, antiques dealers, and picture restorers do business side by side with chic dress shops and cafes frequented by students.

This is a stroll you can make in blue jeans and a sweater. Start at the **Musée d'Orsay**, a former Belle Epoque train station that is now devoted to art and culture from 1848 to World War I. En route to the Boulevard St-Germain, take **Rue du Bac** and stop at **Deyrolle**, an amusing taxidermy shop. On the boulevard, you'll encounter **Madeleine Gély**'s handmade-umbrella shop, an essential stop during those frequent April downpours. You might consider having an early lunch and watching the world go by at one of the area's literary shrines: **Lipp**, **Flore**, or **Deux Magots**. When you can't eat another bite of **Lipp**'s *choucroute* (sauerkraut), visit the shaded Place de Furstemberg to look for the old studio of Delacroix, browse for antiques along **Rue Jacob**, or tour the African art galleries along **Rue de Seine**.

Also on this tour is the narrow **Cour du Commerce St-André**, where the guillotine was invented and where the firebrand Marat had his printing press. You'll pass **Le Procope**, where Voltaire and Robespierre were among the regulars, and the **Rue de Buci**, the street market where Picasso bought his sausages. At **Rue de Tournon**, nature lovers will want to detour through the **Jardin du Luxembourg**, one of the Queen Marie de Médicis's legacies to the city.

At day's end, consider dining at a classic, Old World bistro such as **Allard**. Or you could catch an early Cary Grant film at the **Action Christine**, then dine in the splendor of **Jacques Cagna** around the corner on Rue des Grands-Augustins. After dinner, wander toward the river, stopping en route at **La Palette**, where you can have a beer at the bar, and afterward take a midnight stroll along the pedestrian bridge **Pont des Arts**, with its superb view of the Ile de la Cité, and ponder the magnificence that is Paris at night.

---

1 Hôtel Solférino $$ Thirty-two small rooms with Oriental rugs, pastel walls, and floral wallpaper are available here. There's also a veranda where you can enjoy breakfast (but no restaurant). ♦ 91 Rue de Lille (at Rue de Solférino). 01.47.05.85.54; fax 01.45.55.51.16. Métros: Solférino, Assemblée Nationale

2 Bonpoint This pricey store offers couture for the little darlings in your life. Sister stores are nearby. ♦ M-Sa. 67 Rue de l'Université (at Rue de Solférino). 01.45.55.63.70. Métro: Solférino

3 Palais de la Légion d'Honneur Built by **Pierre Rousseau** for German prince Frédéric III de Salm-Kyrbourg in 1786, this palace is architecturally the most significant Louis XVI building in Paris. In 1804 Napoléon acquired it for the Légion d'Honneur. The *légion* was a society started by Napoléon to honor men, and later women, for outstanding service to France. Members may wear a woven bud of red wool stitched to their left lapel. The palace houses the **Musée de la Légion d'Honneur et des Ordres de Chevalerie,** which exhibits medals, insignia, and decorations related to the history of the *légion.* Included in the collection is Napoléon's Légion d'Honneur medal and his sword and breastplate. The California Palace of the Legion of Honor in San Francisco, which has an extensive collection of French art, is based on the palace here. ◆ Admission. Museum: Tu-Su 2-5PM. 2 Rue de Bellechasse (at Quai Anatole-France). 01.45.51.87.05. Métros: Solférino, Musée d'Orsay (RER)

4 Musée d'Orsay What was once an imposing turn-of-the-century train station, the **Gare d'Orsay,** is now a magnificent showcase for 19th-century art and culture. Opened in December 1986, this museum houses the art that chronologically links the **Louvre** collections with those of the **Pompidou Center,** bridging the end of Romanticism and the origins of modern art. The museum transports visitors back to a time of grace and wit with the works of such geniuses as writer Henry James, actress Sarah Bernhardt, and artists Edouard Manet and James McNeill Whistler.

The collection (see diagram at right) includes all the Impressionist paintings formerly in the **Jeu de Paume;** the post-Impressionist and Nabi works from the **Palais de Tokyo** (among them are 400 paintings by Odilon Redon); and selected works that were formerly in the **Louvre,** including paintings and sculptures by artists who were born after 1820, such as Courbet and Millet, and various late paintings by Delacroix, Corot, Ingres, and the Barbizon landscape painters.

The Quai d'Orsay site was once occupied by the **Palais d'Orsay,** a government building that was devastated (as were the **Hôtel de Ville** and the **Tuileries Palace**) by the May 1871 fires set by the Commune at the end of France's tragic civil war period. The Orléans Rail Company bought the property and hired **Victor Laloux** (1850-1937), the architect who had rebuilt the **Hôtel de Ville,** to design a railway station and hotel. Construction lasted from September 1898 to July 1900 and was accomplished by a crew of 380 men working in round-the-clock shifts.

At one time, 200 trains a day used the **Gare d'Orsay,** but the growing electrification and lengthening of trains made its short platforms obsolete in the late 1930s. Over the years, the station took on other functions. Prisoners of war were garrisoned here after the Liberation; General de Gaulle announced his return to power at the **Gare d'Orsay** hotel on 19 May 1958; Orson Welles made a film version of the Franz Kafka book *The Trial* here in 1962; and in 1970, Bernardo Bertolucci used it as a setting for part of his film *The Conformist.*

As early as 1961, plans to raze the station and build a modern 870-room hotel complex were nearly realized; **Le Corbusier** even competed for the design job. But in 1971 the station was declared a historic landmark, and eight years later **ACT Architecture** (a group of three associated architects: **Pierre Colboc, Renaud Bardon,** and **Jean-Paul Philippo**) was selected to renovate the building for use as a museum. The famed Italian designer Gae Aulenti planned the interior.

The famous French Impressionist collection is displayed on the ground and upper levels of the museum. The term "Impressionism" was coined by a derisive critic after seeing Monet's painting *Impression: Sunrise.* The name stuck, and the movement effected as dramatic a change in the course of art history as the Renaissance had. Instead of choosing heroes, mythic deities, or saints for their subject matter, the Impressionists painted ordinary people in cafes, as well as trains chugging into Gare St-Lazare, with vivid color and undisguised brush strokes.

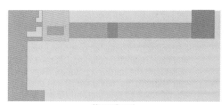

Upper Level

Middle Level

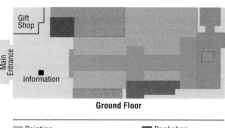

Ground Floor

▨ Painting	■ Bookshop
▨ Sculpture	▨ Café des Hauteurs
■ Decorative Arts	■ Art Nouveau
■ Architecture	▨ Restaurant/tea room
■ Temporary Exhibitions	

The museum collection also features paintings by more than 36 American artists, including John Singer Sargent, William Merritt Chase, Robert Henri, and Winslow Homer, many of whom worked and studied in Paris. And this is where you can visit that emblem of American art, *Arrangement in Grey and Black: The Artist's Mother,* by Whistler. A rooftop cafe, a bookstore, and a 380-seat auditorium round out the museum complex. ♦ Admission. Tu-W, F-Su; Th until 9:30PM; closed Christmas and 1 May. 1 Rue de Bellechasse (at Quai Anatole-France). 01.40.49.48.14, recorded information 01.45.49.11.11. Métro: Solférino, Musée d'Orsay (RER)

Within Musée d'Orsay:

Ground Level This floor features painting, sculpture, photography, and decorative arts dating from 1848 to 1870. The front of the gallery contains sculptures by Rude, Préault, and Pradier, and a great animal bronze by Barye. At the rear of the gallery stands *The Dance* by Carpeaux. Rooms at the end of the courtyard are dedicated to the **Paris Opéra** and its architect, **Charles Garnier.**

To the right of the courtyard are paintings by Romantics such as Delacroix and Ingres, as well as works by the eclectics and symbolists such as Puvis de Chavannes and Gustave Moreau, along with the pre-1870 work of Edgar Degas. To the left of the courtyard are works by Realists, including Daumier, Corot, Millet, and the Barbizon painters. They are neighbors to the masterpieces of Edouard Manet, such as *Olympia* and *Déjeuner sur L'Herbe,* and to the pre-1870 work of Monet, Bazille, and Renoir.

Upper Level To follow the chronological order of the artwork, ascend from the ground floor to the museum's upper level, where the light streaming through the glass roof shows off the post-1870 flowering of Impressionism. Here Manet, Degas, Monet, and Renoir are joined by Sisley, Pissarro, van Gogh, and Cézanne. Nearby, works by post-Impressionists such as Seurat, Signac, Cross, and Gauguin are shown with art from the Pont Aven and Nabi schools, including Denis, Bonnard, Vallotton, and Vuillard. There's also a special room devoted to graphic arts and photography from 1880 to 1914, including the works of early photographers Atget, Emerson, Steichen, and Stieglitz. On a landing between the upper and middle levels are works by Nadar, Legray, Baldus, Carroll, and Cameron.

Middle Level The terraces above the courtyard display the sculpture of Rodin, Maillol, and Bourdelle. The rooms along the Seine have figures created during the Third Republic, including works by symbolists Burne-Jones and Delville. Eight rooms are devoted to the era of Art Nouveau, with works by the Belgians Horta and van de Velde, by

Gallé and Majorelle of the Nancy School, and pieces by Guimard and Thonet, the dean of bentwood furniture. On the Rue de Lille side, you will find the 20th-century paintings of Klimt and Matisse, heralding the advent of modern art. Also on this level is an exhibition showing the evolution of the film industry.

Café des Hauteurs ★$$ Housed in the dining room of the old hotel, the restaurant is an ornately gilded period piece that has a ceiling covered with painted deities by Gabriel Ferrier, winner of the 1872 *Prix de Rome.* The decor is the real attraction here, not the food. Don't bother asking the waiter for absinthe, but try Pernod on ice. ♦ Tu-W, F-Su lunch and afternoon tea; Th dinner. 01.45.49.47.03

5 Rue du Bac The barracks that housed the swashbuckling heroes of *The Three Musketeers* by Alexandre Dumas were located on this street, which was built in 1564 and named after the *bac* (ferry) that used to transport Vaugirard quarry stone across the Seine to the construction site of the **Tuileries Palace.** ♦ Between Rue de Sèvres and Quai Voltaire. Métro: Rue du Bac

JEAN SAFFRAY

6 Jean Saffray Buy an ice-cream bust of your favorite French politician, whether it's Jacques Chirac, François Mitterrand, Georges Marchais, or Valéry Giscard d'Estaing at this *pâtisserie* and ice-cream shop. ♦ Tu-Su; closed in August. 18 Rue du Bac (at Rue de Verneuil). 01.42.61.27.63. Métro: Rue du Bac

7 Lefèbvres Fils Among those who have shopped at this century-old firm selling earthenware china and fanciful trompe l'oeil dishes were Victor Hugo, Marcel Proust, and Georges Feydeau. ♦ M-Sa; closed in August. 24 Rue du Bac (between Rues de l'Université and de Verneuil). 01.42.61.18.40. Métro: Rue du Bac

Christian Constant

7 Christian Constant ★$ This tearoom-cum-chocolate-and-pastry shop serves 36 kinds of tea accompanied by five varieties of sugar, acacia honey, and fresh brioches, as well as great lemon meringue tarts. The pièce de résistance, however, is the pure bittersweet chocolate bar. ♦ Daily breakfast, lunch, and tea. 26 Rue du Bac (between Rues de l'Université and de Verneuil). 01.47.03.30.00. Métro: Rue du Bac

8 Maxoff Restaurant ★$$ Specialties such as *tarama* (salmon roe spread), a Baltic salad, beef stroganoff, Russian caviar, *caviar d'aubergines* (eggplant caviar), Ukrainian borscht, strudel, and blintzes are served in a warm and convivial atmosphere. ♦ M-F lunch and dinner; Sa dinner; closed in August. Reservations recommended. 44 Rue de Verneuil (between Rues du Bac and de Poitiers). 01.42.60.60.43. Métro: Rue du Bac

8 Ravi ★★$$$ Spicy and pricey, this aptly named Indian restaurant (*ravi* means "sun" in Hindi) outshines its competitors with Madras curries, kabobs, and outstanding tandoori prawns. Elephant sculptures stand guard outside, while the small dining room is charming and welcoming. ♦ M-Sa lunch and dinner. Reservations recommended. 50 Rue de Verneuil (between Rues du Bac and de Poitiers). 01.42.61.17.28. Métro: Rue du Bac

TAN - DINH

8 Tan Dinh ★★★$$$ The most elegant—and expensive—Vietnamese restaurant in Paris is conveniently located around the corner from the **Musée d'Orsay.** Delicate smoked-goose ravioli, light noodles with piquant shrimp, lobster beignets, and *coquilles St-Jacques* with ginkgo are prepared by the affable Vifian brothers, who alternate nights in the kitchen. The exotic sorbets and remarkable Bordeaux are also memorable. ♦ M-Sa lunch and dinner; closed in August. Reservations recommended for dinner. 60 Rue de Verneuil (between Rues du Bac and de Poitiers). 01.45.44.04.84. Métro: Rue du Bac

9 50 Rue de l'Université This is the former site of the **Hôtel de l'Intendance,** where Edna St. Vincent Millay wrote her Pulitzer Prize–winning poem, *The Ballad of the Harp-Weaver,* in 1921. The *hôtel* has since been replaced by an unattractive modern structure. ♦ Between Rues du Bac and de Poitiers. Métro: Rue du Bac

10 Galerie Maeght The owner of this bookstore/gallery comes from a famous family of art dealers and sells drawings and prints by modern artists from Matisse to Cucchi, as well as Calder posters, Miró T-shirts, and deluxe art books. ♦ Tu-Sa. 42 and 46 Rue du Bac (between Blvd St-Germain and Rue de l'Université). Book shop 01.45.48.19.55. Gallery 01.49.54.01.50. Métro: Rue du Bac

10 Lenôtre The owner, Gaston Lenôtre, wrote the book on pastry, and this is only one of his five outlets in Paris. You can almost gain weight just by looking in the shop window, so why not slip inside and sample the *palet d'or* (chocolate with gold leaf) or go for broke with

the delectable Concorde chocolate meringue cake? ♦ M-Sa; Su 9AM-1PM; closed in August. 44 Rue du Bac (between Blvd St-Germain and Rue de l'Université). 01.42.22.39.39. Métro: Rue du Bac

10 Deyrolle A 150-year-old taxidermy shop with everything from mounted polar bears, tigers, and bewildered baby elephants to cobras and other citizens of Noah's Ark, all staring out of glass eyes. Deyrolle also acquires rare butterflies, tastefully stuffed cocker spaniels, and just about every crystal, geode, and mineral on earth. Kids could be left here for hours. ♦ M-Sa. 46 Rue du Bac (between Blvd St-Germain and Rue de l'Université). 01.42.22.30.07. Métro: Rue du Bac

11 L'Oeillade ★★$$ An ever-changing, moderately priced three-course menu is offered by chef Jean-Louis Huclin, who makes all the sausages, terrines, and pasta himself. He also serves perfectly stewed pot-au-feu salad, cassoulet in a gleaming copper saucepan, succulent roast chicken, and *mousse au chocolat.* Wine options are limited but affordable and the ambience is warm and welcoming. ♦ M-F lunch and dinner; Sa dinner. 10 Rue de St-Simon (between Rue de Grenelle and Passage de la Visitation). 01.42.22.01.60. Métro: Rue du Bac

HOTEL

Duc de Saint-Simon

PARIS

12 Hôtel Duc de St-Simon $$$$ A Swedish couple runs this cozy antiques-furnished 34-room hotel on a hidden street just off the Boulevard St-Germain. It's popular among transatlantic diplomats, intellectuals, actors (including Lauren Bacall), and writers (Pulitzer Prize–winner Toni Morrison stays here). Reservations for newcomers may be difficult, but keep trying. Garden lovers should ask for room **No. 25,** which has a flower-bedecked terrace. There's no restaurant. ♦ 14 Rue de St-Simon (between Rue de Grenelle and Passage de la Visitation). 01.44.39.20.20; fax 01.45.48.68.25. Métro: Rue du Bac

13 The General Store Homesick Americans can comfort their taste buds with Paul Newman's spaghetti sauce, Hellman's mayonnaise, taco shells, Cheerios, maple syrup, peanut butter, and pecans, thanks to this grocery. Stuffed turkeys and homemade pumpkin pies are sold during Thanksgiving week, and French gourmands researching recipes for meat loaf or succotash will find cookbooks such as *La Cuisine Américaine.*

♦ M-Sa. 82 Rue de Grenelle (between Rues du Bac and de St-Simon). 01.45.48.63.16. Métro: Rue du Bac

14 Superlatif Popular with locals is this stationery shop that sells a wide variety of colored paper, designer pens, and assorted doodads. ♦ M-Sa. 86 Rue du Bac (between Rues de Varenne and de Grenelle). 01.45.48.84.25. Métro: Rue du Bac

14 Olivier de Sercey This tiny printing and engraving shop makes dignified business cards dealt out by ambassadors and government ministers whose offices are nearby. Wedding and party invitations also are made here. ♦ M-F; closed August and holidays. 96 Rue du Bac (between Rues de Varenne and de Grenelle). 01.45.48.21.47. Métro: Rue du Bac

14 La Boîte à Musique This antiques shop specializes in 19th-century music boxes from France, England, and Switzerland. ♦ M 2-7PM; Tu-Sa; open by appointment in August. 96 Rue du Bac (between Rues de Varenne and de Grenelle). 01.42.22.01.30. Métro: Rue du Bac

15 La Cour de Varenne The back door of this snobbish antiques store opens onto a lovely courtyard where the servants' quarters of Madame de Staël still stand. There are two floors of carved wooden columns, clocks, 17th- and 18th-century furniture, Japanese lacquer, mother-of-pearl–framed mirrors, and early 19th-century paintings of hot-air balloons. ♦ Tu-Sa; closed in August. 42 Rue de Varenne (between Rues du Bac and de Bellechasse). 01.45.44.54.73. Métros: Rue du Bac, Sèvres–Babylone

16 110 Rue du Bac After the sale of *Arrangement in Grey and Black: The Artist's Mother* to the French government in 1893, James McNeill Whistler moved into a ground-floor apartment here and consorted with artist-intelligentsia friends such as Henry James, Edgar Degas, Edouard Manet, and Henri de Toulouse-Lautrec. It remains a residential building. ♦ Between Rues de Babylone and de Varenne. Métro: Rue du Bac

17 La Pagode Sigh over your favorite François Truffaut and Jean Renoir classics in this authentic Chinese pagoda, the most unusual cinema in Paris. ♦ 57 *bis* Rue de Babylone (between Rues Vaneau and Monsieur). 08.36.68.75.07. Métro: St-François-Xavier

---

When one of the 170 big clocks found on Paris's public buildings and lampposts breaks down, the city's clock services, by tradition, place the hands at 12 o'clock until repairs can be made.

Restaurants/Clubs: Red   **Hotels:** Blue
Shops/ ♟ Outdoors: Green   **Sights/Culture:** Black

18 Au Bon Marché The oldest department store in Paris is especially famous for its *épicerie* (food market), which is the largest of its kind in the city (9,075 square feet) and sells everything from fresh oysters to foie gras. ♦ M-Sa; épicerie until 9PM. 22 Rue de Sèvres (between Rues Velpeau and du Bac). Store: 01.44.39.80.00; épicerie: 01.44.39.81.00. Métro: Sèvres–Babylone

19 Diners en Ville Tablecloths, candlesticks, china, earthenware, flatware—everything for the well-dressed table is available here. ♦ M 2-7PM; Tu-Sa. 27 Rue de Varenne (at Rue du Bac). 01.42.22.78.33. Métro: Rue du Bac

20 Fontaine des Quatre Saisons (Four Seasons Fountain) In the early 18th century, this, the wealthiest quarter in Paris, was almost totally without water. To remedy that problem, in 1739 sculptor Edme Bouchardon was commissioned to design this fountain to supply water to the residents in the neighborhood. The Ionic-pillared fountain is adorned with a seated figure of Paris looking down on reclining personifications of the Seine and Marne Rivers. The sides are decorated with figures of the seasons and reliefs of cherubs. Voltaire protested the placement of this fountain in a narrow and confined street, arguing that "fountains must be elevated in public places and, like all beautiful monuments, be viewed on all sides." ♦ 57-59 Rue de Grenelle (between Blvd Raspail and Rue du Bac). Métro: Rue du Bac

20 Roland Barthélemy Fromager The **Elysée Palace** buys its cheese at this shop, which offers more than 50 kinds of fresh goat cheese, the finest *vacherin* (from October to February), and its special *boulamour*, a ball of enriched cow's cheese covered with kirsch-soaked raisins. ♦ Tu-Sa. 51 Rue de Grenelle (between Blvd Raspail and Rue du Bac). 01.45.48.56.75. Métro: Rue du Bac

20 Musée Maillol–Fondation Dina Vierny Located near the **Fontaine des Quatre Saisons,** this museum is dedicated to sculptor-painter Aristide Maillol and his model, Dina, whom he met when she was 15. Their collaboration lasted for ten years until his untimely death in 1944. Her beautiful form is used in such works as *La Montagne, L'Air, La Rivière,* and Maillot's ultimate work *Harmonie.* Dina created this foundation dedicated to Maillot and other 20th-century artists such as Dufy, Matisse, Poliakoff, Kandinsky, Kabakov, and Bonnard. A pretty cafe in the vaulted basement serves light meals. ♦ Admission; free for children under 18. M, W-Su 11AM-8PM. 59-61 Rue de Grenelle (between Blvd Raspail and Rue du Bac). 01.42.22.59.58. Métro: Rue du Bac

21 Issey Miyake Artist Shiro Kuramata's white-plaster drapes provide a stunning backdrop for Miyake's sculptural clothes. A fashion purist, this Tokyo-based designer creates all his own fabrics and dresses his followers for maximum comfort and ease of motion. ◆ M-Sa. 201 Blvd St-Germain (at Rue de Luynes). 01.45.48.10.44. Métro: Rue du Bac

22 Kenzo Everyone's favorite Japanese designer splashes gorgeous colors over amusing, informal clothes and accessories. ◆ M-Sa. 17 Blvd Raspail (at Rue de Grenelle). 01.45.49.33.75. Métro: Rue du Bac

HOTEL LUTETIA - PARIS

23 Hôtel Lutetia $$$ Fashion designer Sonia Rykiel spruced up the interior of this 271-room, turn-of-the-century luxury hotel with Art Deco frescoes and elegant gray and violet fabrics. There's a restaurant on the premises. ◆ 45 Blvd Raspail (at Rue de Sèvres). 01.49.54.46.46; fax 01.49.54.46.00. Métro: Sèvres–Babylone

24 Atelier Guillaume Martel Have a special 17th-century portrait or modern print you need framed? Martel, a graduate of the prestigious **Ecole du Louvre,** specializes in *dorure froide* (a cold-gilding technique) frames for both antique and contemporary prints. ◆ Tu-Sa; closed in August. 2 Rue du Regard (at Rue du Cherche-Midi). 01.45.49.02.07. Métro: Sèvres–Babylone

25 Café Parisien ★★$ This modest cafe has garnered a large reputation. Its weekend brunches, hearty *plats du jour,* and *tarte tatin* (apple tart) draw a lively, often literary, throng. ◆ M-F lunch and dinner; Sa-Su brunch and dinner. Reservations recommended. No credit cards accepted. 15 Rue d'Assas (between Rues de Vaugirard and de Rennes). 01.45.44.41.44. Métro: Rennes

26 Poilâne The most famous baker in France, if not the world, Lionel Poilâne continues a family tradition started by his Norman father, Pierre, in 1933. His round sourdough country loaf, baked in wood-fired ovens, is served in some 400 Parisian restaurants and is flown daily to expensive gourmet shops in New York and Tokyo. Catherine Deneuve and Pierre Cardin order specially decorated loaves for their parties, and King Hussein has the bread jetted to his palace.

If he's not too busy and you ask politely, Lionel may even take you down into the bakery's 12th-century cellars, where a bare-chested baker in shorts and a cap, looking like a Daumier cartoon, feeds lumps of dough to a wood-burning brick oven. ◆ M-Sa. 8 Rue du Cherche-Midi (between Rue d'Assas and Carrefour de la Croix-Rouge). 01.45.48.42.59. Métro: Sèvres–Babylone

27 Le Récamier ★★★$$$ Situated in a serene cul-de-sac in the well-trodden St-Germain shopping district, this elegant restaurant caters to the Paris publishing crowd and has one of the city's most peaceful outdoor terraces. Owner and certified wine expert Martin Cantegrit features dishes from his native Burgundy—fricassee of snails and wild mushrooms, *boeuf bourguignon sans pareil,* chateaubriand Récamier—as well as salmon *tartare,* an excellent summer starter. Cantegrit's wine list, which he calls "my little Bible," merits the appellation. ◆ M-Sa lunch and dinner. 4 Rue Récamier (at Rue de Sèvres). 01.45.48.86.58. Métro: Sèvres–Babylone

AU SAUVIGNON

27 Au Sauvignon ★$ This trendy old wine bar is predictably papered with maps of French wine regions. Still, in summer it's not such a bad thing to enjoy a plate of country-cured ham, some cantal cheese, and a Sancerre rosé while sitting at one of the sidewalk tables watching the world stroll by. ◆ M-Sa breakfast, lunch, and dinner until 10PM; closed in August. No credit cards accepted. 80 Rue des Sts-Pères (at Rue de Sèvres). 01.45.48.49.02. Métro: Sèvres–Babylone

28 Rue des Sts-Pères Known in the 13th century as the Chemins aux Vaches (Cow Path), this street became Rue de St-Pierre in the 16th century because of a nearby chapel dedicated to St. Peter. By 1652, people had worn the name down to Rue des Sts-Pères. ◆ Between Rue de Sèvres and Quai Malaquais. Métros: Sèvres–Babylone, St-Germain-des-Prés

29 Maude Frizon More than 1,500 styles of handcrafted haute-couture footwear are carried here. You will also find the lower-priced label Maude Frizon Club; the shoes are almost as pretty as the handcrafted pairs, but they're machine-made and one-third the price. ◆ M-Sa. 83 Rue des Sts-Pères (at Rue de

Grenelle). 01.42.22.06.93. Métro: Sèvres–Babylone

29 Cassegrain There's nothing quite like a proper thank-you note or an engraved-in-gold place card. This stationer has been setting the standard since 1919. ♦ M-Sa. 81 Rue des Sts-Pères (between Rue de Grenelle and Blvd St-Germain). 01.42.22.04.76. Métro: Sèvres–Babylone

30 31 Rue du Dragon The **Académie Julian,** which was once here, admitted hundreds of aspiring American painters who were hoping to study on the GI bill after World War II but were unable to meet the stricter entrance requirements of the **Ecole des Beaux-Arts.** The building now has both residential and commercial space. ♦ Between Rues du Four and Bernard-Palissy. Métro: St-Germain-des-Prés

30 Claude Piau ★$ For more than 25 years, the unfailingly popular restaurant of ex-stuntman Claude Piau has played it safe, serving an unchanging menu of traditional dishes such as steaks, lamb chops, salad, and chocolate mousse in a traditional but casual setting. ♦ M-F lunch and dinner; Sa lunch; closed in August, one week at Easter, and one week at Christmas. Reservations recommended. No credit cards accepted. 27 Rue du Dragon (between Rues du Four and Bernard-Palissy). 01.45.48.29.68. Métro: St-Germain-des-Prés

31 Yakijapo Mitsuko ★★$$ One of the best sushi bars in Paris also serves sashimi and yakitori at reasonable prices in a simple, elegant dining room. ♦ Daily lunch and dinner. 8 Rue du Sabot (between Rues du Four and Bernard-Palissy). 01.42.22.17.74. Métro: St-Germain-des-Prés

32 Via Palissy ★★$$ Climb to the tiny, crooked dining room of this Italian restaurant to sample risotto Milanese, gnocchi with gorgonzola, and homemade tiramisù. ♦ M-Sa lunch and dinner; closed three weeks in August. Reservations recommended. 11 Rue Bernard-Palissy (at Rue du Sabot). 01.45.44.02.52. Métro: St-Germain-des-Prés

33 Brasserie Lipp ★★$$ This famous Alsatian brasserie counts among its clients Yves Saint Laurent and François Mitterrand. A literary landmark, where waiters still dress in black waistcoats and long white aprons, this dining spot is always replete with editors (from Grasset, Gallimard, and Hachette) and politicians. De Gaulle and Pompidou used to lunch at these tables, and Ben Barka, a Moroccan militant, was arrested here.

The ceilings are covered with buxom nudes; the walls are festooned with Art Nouveau ceramics and conveniently hung with mirrors so large you never need to crane your neck to watch the celebrities pass by. The restaurant

used to be run by the formidable Roger Cazes (whose father bought the establishment in 1920 from an Alsatian named Lippman), who didn't seem to care for Americans of less cultural stature than William Styron. At that time, an American's best ploy for getting seated was to arrive on a rainy day in February just before 2AM—or shortly after a morning bomb scare. Anyone who was anyone sat on the main floor; upstairs was Siberia. After Cazes's death, the new management restored the second floor so diners there need no longer feel banished. It is also possible to enjoy a Bavarian dark beer or cup of hot chocolate on the terrace; just don't tell anyone that's where you sat. The food is solid, though often disappointing. Stick with oysters, smoked salmon, and potato salad—they're hard to ruin. ♦ Daily lunch and dinner until 1AM. Reservations required. 151 Blvd St-Germain (between Rues de Rennes and du Dragon). 01.45.48.53.91. Métro: St-Germain-des-Prés

34 Korean Barbecue ★$$ The fare includes marinated beef and vegetables that you grill over a gas stove at your table. The decor is clean, simple, and no-nonsense. ♦ Daily lunch and dinner. No credit cards accepted. 1 Rue du Dragon (at Blvd St-Germain). 01.42.22.26.63. Métro: St-Germain-des-Prés

35 Baxter Old prints, etchings, and lithographs abound in this charming shop that specializes in European architectural and botanical illustrations from the 17th to 19th centuries. The friendly staff has both a knowledge of and affection for the wares. Framing services are available. ♦ M 1-7PM; Tu-Sa. 15 Rue du Dragon (at Rue Bernard-Palissy). 01.45.49.01.34. Métro: St-Germain-des-Prés

36 Sabbia Rosa Sexy teddies and other alluring lingerie can be purchased for or by the femme fatale. ♦ M-Sa; closed last half of August. 71-73 Rue des Sts-Pères (between Rue de Grenelle and Blvd St-Germain). 01.45.48.88.37. Métro: St-Sulpice

36 Y's Yohji Yamamoto Shop here for an outfit that's actually both fashionable and comfortable. This Japanese designer creates baggy high-style clothes for men and women. ♦ M-Sa. 69 Rue des Sts-Pères (between Rue de Grenelle and Blvd St-Germain). 01.45.48.22.56. Métro: St-Sulpice

36 Sts-Pères $$$ This tastefully renovated 39-room hotel was designed in 1658 by **Alphonse Daniel Gittard,** who founded the Academy of Architecture under Louis XIV and whose portrait hangs behind the reception desk. If dozing off while staring up at a 17th-century ceiling painting of the *Crowning of Jupiter* is your idea of luxury, ask for room **No. 100**. There's no restaurant. ♦ 65 Rue des Sts-Pères (between Rue de Grenelle and Blvd St-Germain). 01.45.44.50.00; fax 01.45.44.90.83. Métro: St-Sulpice

37 La Maison de Verre (Glass House)
Seeing the extraordinary glass house of **Pierre Charreau** and **Bernard Bijovet** is a must for any student of 20th-century design. You can get a glimpse of the exterior from the courtyard, but for a look at the inside of the early 1930s building—a tour de force in glass-block-and-steel construction—you must make a reservation. Send inquiries to: A.P. Vellay-Dalsace, 31 Rue St-Guillaume, 75006 Paris. ♦ Donation requested; send with reservations request. 31 Rue St-Guillaume (between Rue de Grenelle and Blvd St-Germain). Métro: Sèvres–Babylone

38 Madeleine Gély Since 1834 the finest umbrella shop in Paris has been selling and repairing handmade *parapluies*. And you needn't have a limp to buy one of Madeleine Gély's 400 unusual canes, which include duck- and bulldog-headed canes, watch canes, whiskey-flask canes, and even a cane to measure the withers of a horse. ♦ Tu-Sa; closed in August. 218 Blvd St-Germain (between Rues St-Guillaume and St-Thomas-d'Aquin). 01.42.22.63.35. Métro: Rue du Bac

39 Hôtel Montalembert

$$$$ The newest and best of the Left Bank's luxury hotels is popular with people from the worlds of publishing, fashion, and fine art. When the building was renovated several years ago, designer Christian Liaigre selected the tasteful furnishings for the lobby and 56 rooms; there's a wondrous attention to detail, from handcrafted leather furniture to cast-bronze door handles. The modern rooms with customized furniture will suit guests who prefer contemporary style, while the Louis Philippe rooms with finely restored period furniture will please traditionalists. Everyone staying here should plan a few long, bubbly soaks in the luxurious bathrooms, done in gray marble and chrome. ♦ 3 Rue de Montalembert (between Rues Sébastien-Bottin and du Bac). 01.45.49.68.68; fax 01.45.49.69.49. Métro: Rue du Bac

Within the Hôtel Montalembert:

Restaurant Montalembert ★★$$
The congenial atmosphere and the creations of chef Fréderic Deswarte have made this intimate cafe a popular meeting place for Parisians. You can't go wrong with the warm quail salad, veal with mushrooms and baked potatoes, grilled lamb chops, scampi ravioli with herbs, or salmon grilled *unilatéral* (on one side). ♦ M-Sa breakfast, lunch, and dinner; Su brunch and dinner. Reservations recommended. 01.45.49.68.68

40 Le Cabinet de Curiosité Lined with panels from a late 18th-century pharmacy, this amusing shop displays scientific instruments, ancient technical books, monkey skeletons from Madagascar, brass hourglasses, ladies' shoes from the Louis XVI epoch, and an exquisite collection of Gothic keys and locks. Owner Jean-Claude Guerin is an expert in fine wrought iron. ♦ M-Sa; closed in August. 23 Rue de Beaune (between Rues de l'Université and de Verneuil). 01.42.61.09.57. Métro: Rue du Bac

41 Bistrot de Paris ★★$$ Michel Oliver, whose father owns the **Grand Véfour**, created this chic bistro, which has an innovative one-two punch: ravishing 1880s decor with Belle Epoque mosaics and a classic menu of crab soup, braised pig's feet, cassoulet, and reliable Bordeaux. ♦ M-F lunch and dinner; Sa dinner. Reservations recommended. 33 Rue de Lille (between Rues de Beaune and du Bac). 01.42.61.15.84. Métro: Rue du Bac

42 7 Rue de Beaune Henry James, whose classic novel *The Ambassadors* featured American expatriates in Paris, came to visit James Lowell here in 1872 and as an added bonus found Ralph Waldo Emerson and his daughter, Ellen, in the sitting room. It's still a residential building. ♦ Between Rue de Lille and Quai Voltaire. Métro: Rue du Bac

42 9 Rue de Beaune While living here at the **Hôtel Elysée** in July 1920, Ezra Pound convinced James Joyce to move from Trieste and bring his family to Paris, where they lived nearby in a small hotel at 9 Rue de l'Université. This is still a residential building. ♦ At Rue de Lille. Métro: Rue du Bac

43 Quai Voltaire This quay honors Voltaire, whose triumphant return in 1778 from 30 years of exile was greeted by a torchlight parade that wound from the **Comédie Française** (where his tragedy *Irène* had just opened) across the river to **No. 27** Quai Voltaire, where he died months later on

30 May 1778. The quay's history involves many artists: Jean-Dominique Ingres died on 14 January 1867 at **No. 11;** Delacroix and Corot, at different times, rented the top-floor studio at **No. 13;** in the hotel at **No. 19,** Baudelaire penned *Les Fleurs du Mal* in 1857; and Wagner composed *Die Meistersinger* here between 1861 and 1862. Today, it is a bazaar of first-rate antiques shops and galleries. Side by side are well-known dealers such as **Huguette Berès Bailly** (No. 25: 01.42.61.27.91) and **Jean Max Tassel** (No. 15: 01.42.61.02.01). ◆ Between Rues des Sts-Pères and du Bac. Métro: Rue du Bac

43 Hôtel du Quai Voltaire $$ Charles-Pierre Baudelaire, Oscar Wilde, Richard Wagner, and Jean Sibelius each came to this hotel looking for a room with a view. Do the same: Ask for a front room (if you don't mind traffic noise) and wake up to a vista of the Seine and the **Tuileries.** There are 33 comfortable guest rooms, but no restaurant. ◆ 19 Quai Voltaire (between Rues des Sts-Pères and de Beaune). 01.42.61.50.91; fax 01.42.61.62.26. Métro: Solférino

44 Sennelier The Left Bank's finest painters patronize this celebrated art-supply store. Even if you couldn't draw an apple to save your life, step inside and rub shoulders with the **Beaux-Arts** students shopping for linseed oil, blocks of brilliantly colored pastel chalks, and wooden palettes. ◆ M-Sa. 3 Quai Voltaire (between Rues des Sts-Pères and de Beaune). 01.42.60.72.15. Métro: Rue du Bac

45 Université $$$ This smugly stylish hotel in a 17th-century town house is embellished with tapestries, antiques, and a small courtyard. It offers 27 comfortable rooms, but no restaurant. ◆ 22 Rue de l'Université (between Rues des Sts-Pères and de Beaune). 01.42.61.09.39; fax 01.42.60.40.84. Métro: Rue du Bac

46 2-4 Rue de l'Université In 1776 Benjamin Franklin lived here at the former **Hôtel d'Entragues** while he was drumming up support for the American Revolution. It's still a residential building. ◆ At Rue des Sts-Pères. Métro: Rue du Bac

47 Lenox $$$ The then–22-year-old T.S. Eliot spent a romantic summer here in 1910 on the old man's money, just before he took a job in a London bank and wrote "The Love Song of J. Alfred Prufrock." Restored with chic simplicity and a slightly New Wave bar, the 34-room hotel is a favorite of visiting fashion models. There is no restaurant. The top floor rooms with balconies and exposed beams are preferable. ◆ Bar: daily 5PM-2AM. 9 Rue de l'Université (at Rue du Pré-aux-Clercs). 01.42.96.10.95; fax 01.42.61.52.83. Métro: Rue du Bac

48 Debauve and Gallais This wood-paneled chocolate shop with a semicircular counter began as a pharmacy nearly 200 years ago, when medicated chocolate was a nostrum for flatulence, anemia, and other ills. Today, in addition to delicious nonmedicinal chocolate, the shop sells such delights as *croquamandes* (almonds roasted with caramelized sugar), hot chocolate mix, and real chocolate gift boxes. The old metal tea canisters date from 1804. ◆ M-Sa. 30 Rue des Sts-Pères (between Rues Perronet and de l'Université). 01.45.48.54.67. Métros: Rue du Bac, St-Germain-des-Prés

49 Coffee Parisien ★★$$ An American brunch is served all day at this eatery, which is decorated with a 1950s Lucky Strike ad, the *New York Times* front page from the day President John F. Kennedy was assassinated in Dallas, and other Americana. Franco-New Yorker Jonathan Goldstein (who also manages **Le Coffee Shop** across the street) serves pancakes with maple syrup, hash browns, bagels and cream cheese, eggs Benedict, bacon cheeseburgers, and more. ◆ Daily lunch, brunch, and dinner until 1AM. Reservations recommended. 5 Rue Perronet (between Rues des Sts-Pères and St-Guillaume). 01.40.49.08.08. Métros: Rue du Bac, St-Germain-des-Prés

50 Than ★★$ Don't let the crowds in the aisle or the swordfish teeth on the wall scare you away. This tiny Asian canteen is a popular bargain in the pricey St-Germain quarter. For more than 25 years the affable Mr. Than has been serving delicious and affordable Cantonese and Vietnamese specialties to neighborhood editors, publishers, and medical students. He brags about the lacquered duck and caramelized spare ribs. ◆ M dinner; Tu-Sa lunch and dinner. 42 Rue des Sts-Pères (between Blvd St-Germain and Rue Perronet). 01.45.48.36.97. Métros: Rue du Bac, St-Germain-des-Prés

51 Jean-Michel Beurdeley and Cie Proprietor of one of the boulevard's most inviting Asian art galleries, Beurdeley displays 18th-century Japanese paintings and eighth-century Chinese porcelain figures, but his most treasured item is an enormous bronze drum from Southwest Asia dating from the second century BC. ◆ M-Sa; closed in August. 200 Blvd St-Germain (between Rues des Sts-Pères and St-Guillaume). 01.45.48.97.86. Métros: Rue du Bac, St-Germain-des-Prés

51 Galerie André-François Petit This fanciful surrealist gallery has whimsical brass door handles, designed by an artist named Jette, that look like a typesetter's nightmare. ◆ Tu-Sa; closed 14 July–15 September. 196 Blvd St-Germain (between Rues des Sts-Pères and St-Guillaume). 01.45.44.64.83. Métros: Rue du Bac, St-Germain-des-Prés

51 Relais St-Germain ★★$$ Dine on respectable cuisine at prices even struggling writers can afford. Profiterole addicts swear by this place, which features Art Deco furniture and reproductions of Picasso and Kandinsky works on the burgundy-colored walls. Diners wait for their tables in a 17th-century salon. ◆ Daily lunch and dinner. Reservations recommended. 190 Blvd St-Germain (between Rues des Sts-Pères and St-Guillaume). 01.42.22.21.35. Métros: Rue du Bac, St-Germain-des-Prés

52 St-Vladimir le Grand Come on a Sunday morning and watch the rosy grandmothers wearing babushkas enter this Ukrainian church. ◆ 49-51 Rue des Sts-Pères (at Blvd St-Germain). Métros: Rue du Bac, St-Germain-des-Prés

53 Rue Jacob Named after the Old Testament patriarch, this street is chock-full of book and antiques shops selling everything from autographs and old manuscripts to theater props and scientific instruments. ◆ Between Rues de Seine and des Sts-Pères. Métro: St-Germain-des-Prés

53 56 Rue Jacob The Treaty of Paris, by which England recognized the independence of the 13 American colonies, was signed in this building, formerly the **Hôtel d'York,** on 3 September 1783. Benjamin Franklin, John Jay, and John Adams signed the document on behalf of the US; England was represented by David Hartley and Richard Oswald. ◆ Between Rues Bonaparte and des Sts-Pères. Métro: St-Germain-des-Prés

November is France's official *Mois de la Photo,* when photography shows are held in dozens of museums and galleries throughout Paris.

ALAIN BRIEUX

SCIENCES · TECHNIQUES · MÉDECINE

53 Alain Brieux This eclectic curio shop specializes in prints, Arabic astrolabes, and rare medical books that date back to the 14th century. Everything in the store is for sale except the alligator hanging from the ceiling. This item was a traditional feature in old apothecaries and alchemists' labs. ◆ M-F; Sa 2-6PM; closed in August. 48 Rue Jacob (between Rues Bonaparte and des Sts-Pères). 01.42.60.21.98. Métro: St-Germain-des-Prés

53 Angleterre $$$ Among the notables who have stayed in this 18th-century hostelry are Washington Irving, Sherwood Anderson, and Ernest Hemingway. It's now a picturesque 27-room hotel with a garden patio. The bar is open 24 hours for hotel guests only; there's no restaurant. ◆ 44 Rue Jacob (between Rues Bonaparte and des Sts-Pères). 01.42.60.34.72; fax 01.42.61.16.83. Métro: St-Germain-des-Prés

Démons et Merveilles

54 Démons et Merveilles You'll find folk costumes from Romania, Hungary, Poland, Afghanistan, Tibet, and India, and all the garb you need to run away with the Gypsies here. Faty, the Tunisian owner, ran away from his law practice to start this shop. ◆ M-Sa. 45 Rue Jacob (between Rues St-Benoît and des Sts-Pères). 01.42.96.26.11. Métro: St-Germain-des-Prés

55 Le Petit St-Benoît ★★$ Offering indigent Left Bank intellectuals the same (including a respectable roast veal with mashed potatoes) for more than 125 years now, this popular coach-house bistro has prices that are difficult to beat. The rest room features a celebrated blue-and-white-checkered washbowl. ◆ M-F lunch and dinner. 4 Rue St-Benoît (between Blvd St-Germain and Rue Jacob). 01.42.60.27.92. Métro: St-Germain-des-Prés

56 Le Muniche ★$$ Delicious fish soup, grilled sardines, fresh briny oysters, four kinds of sauerkraut, and an honest plate of liver and onions are some of the culinary choices at this crowded Alsatian bistro. In summer, reserve a table on the sidewalk. ◆ Daily lunch and dinner until 2AM. 7 Rue St-Benoît (between Rues Guillaume-Apollinaire and Jacob). 01.42.61.12.70. Métro: St-Germain-des-Prés

57 Le Bilboquet ★$$ On the former site of **Club St-Germain,** an old existentialist haunt, this upbeat dinner-jazz club serves grilled rack of lamb and sides of beef. ♦ Daily dinner. Jazz: M-Sa 11PM-2:45AM. 13 Rue St-Benoît (between Rues Guillaume-Apollinaire and Jacob). 01.45.48.81.84. Métro: St-Germain-des-Prés

58 Shu Uemura If you like art supply and stationery stores, you'll love this Japanese cosmetics shop, which has some of the qualities of both. Compacts, lipstick, nail polish, creams, and brushes in every hue and shape imaginable are on display. This is but one of an international 6,000-shop chain created 20 years ago by makeup artist Shu Uemura, who perfected the faces of Japan's most famous movie stars. ♦ M-Sa. 176 Blvd St-Germain (between Rues St-Benoît and des Sts-Pères). 01.45.48.02.55. Métro: St-Germain-des-Prés

58 Café de Flore ★★$$ Jean-Paul Sartre wrote of hanging out in this great cafe during World War II: "Simone de Beauvoir and I more or less set up house in the **Flore.** We worked from 9AM till noon, when we went out to lunch. At 2PM we came back and talked with our friends till 4PM, when we got down to work again till 8PM. And after dinner, people came to see us by appointment. It may seem strange, all this, but the **Flore** was like home to us: even when the air-raid alarm went, we would merely feign leaving and then climb up to the first floor and go on working." You don't have to be Sartre, Camus, or any other brainy regular to divine that the drink to order here in winter is hot grog (rum, tea, and lemon slices); be sure to ask for extra lemon because they never bring enough. If you're an early bird, this is an excellent place to scrutinize *Le Monde* and have a real breakfast of *oeufs sur le plat* (fried eggs), bacon, and croissants. Salads, sandwiches, and other typical cafe fare are served at lunch and dinner. The classic Art Deco interior—all red, mahogany, and mirrors—has changed little since the war. ♦ Daily breakfast, lunch, and dinner until 2AM. No credit cards accepted. 172 Blvd St-Germain (at Rue St-Benoît). 01.45.48.55.26. Métro: St-Germain-des-Prés

58 Le Montana Piano-Bar Champagne at dawn? *Pourquoi pas?* The surly, therefore authentic, bartender serves a seductive *Montana Fantaisie* made of pears, grenadine, orange juice, and Champagne. In the evening the cocktails are accompanied by live jazz. ♦ Daily 6PM-2:30AM. 28 Rue St-Benoît (between Blvd St-Germain and Rue Jacob). 01.45.48.93.08. Métro: St-Germain-des-Prés

59 Arthus-Bertrand This 150-year-old establishment casts reproductions of some of the **Louvre**'s treasures in sterling or in 18-karat gold. It also supplies 80 percent of the military medals and decorations used by African nations. (Business is usually brisk owing to the high turnover in excellencies.) For $6,000 to $20,000, it custom-designs the ceremonial swords worn by the "immortals" accepted into the **Académie Française.** The firm has a seriousness and a price list that will curb any idle browser. ♦ Tu-Sa. 6 Pl St-Germain-des-Prés (at Blvd St-Germain). 01.49.54.72.10. Métro: St-Germain-des-Prés

59 Aux Deux Magots ★★★ $$ If you've read *The Sun Also Rises,* you'll never be alone at this cafe; this is where Jake Barnes meets up with Lady Brett, and it is peopled  with fictitious memories. Hemingway and his cronies met here to drink away the sting of rejection slips, a pastime he later reminisced about in *A Moveable Feast.* The name of the cafe comes from the two statues of paunchy Chinese commercial agents—*magots*—that hang high on one of the pillars. They sit on money boxes, as does the manager of the place, who paid some $1.4 million in 1985 to purchase this literary mecca. Boasting that the cafe is "The Rendezvous of the Intellectual Elite," the menu offers 25 kinds of whiskey and little pots of strong espresso. From May through August, the sidewalk entertainment on the terrace opposite the **St-Germain-des-Prés** bell tower is always amusing and occasionally brilliant. ♦ Daily breakfast, lunch, and dinner until 2AM. 6 Pl St-Germain-des-Prés (at Blvd St-Germain). 01.45.48.55.25. Métro: St-Germain-des-Prés

60 La Hune Wedged between **Café de Flore** and **Aux Deux Magots** is one of the liveliest bookstores in Paris. It provides literary sustenance to the Parisian men and women of letters (and those trying to resemble them) who frequent the nearby shrines to caffeine-driven cogitation. ♦ M-Sa until midnight. 170 Blvd St-Germain (at Rue St-Benoît). 01.45.48.35.85. Métro: St-Germain-des-Prés

61 Embâcle This sculpture (whose name means "blockage") is not a ruptured water main but a practical joke of a fountain by Charles Daudelin. It was created in 1985. ♦ Blvd St-Germain (at Rue de Rennes). Métro: St-Germain-des-Prés

Child's Play

In addition to such obvious child-pleasers as the **Eiffel Tower,** Paris is filled with other attractions that will amuse and amaze young visitors. Here are ten favorites:

1 **Jardin du Luxembourg** is the most marvelous garden in Paris, where children love to play and adults will recapture their childhood. Stroll under the *allées* of chestnut trees and explore the many flower gardens, statues, and fountains. There are special play areas for wee ones, with sandboxes and a lawn where, contrary to the usual Paris law, playing on the grass is allowed.

2 **Théâtre des Marionnettes** puppet shows are joyful, boisterous events. Other delights include: a large playground crammed with numerous slides, swings, and monkey bars; pony, donkey, and go-cart rides; a pond where you can rent toy boats to sail; kiosks selling refreshments and toys; a cafe under the trees; and a pavilion where bands and orchestras perform concerts.

3 **Musée de la Poupée** (Doll Museum) has a collection of more than 200 French porcelain dolls dating from 1860 to 1960. Stuffed animals and limited editions of porcelain dolls can be purchased in the museum's gift shop.

4 **Musée Carnavalet,** housed in a splendid 16th-century mansion, is the **Historical Museum of the City of Paris,** with exhibits on four centuries (1500-1900) of Parisian life. On the ground floor is an entire room full of old shop signs created to be understood by a population that was mostly illiterate—a bakery sign features a stalk of wheat, a butcher sign depicts a pig, and a locksmith sign is in the shape of a giant key. Also of interest to young museum-goers is the exhibit on the French Revolution, which includes a rope ladder used by a prisoner to escape from the **Bastille,** a model of the guillotine, and a pair of Revolutionary drums. Tours for children are offered on Wednesdays, Saturdays, and school holidays.

5 **The Seine** offers tired little feet (and big ones too) boat tours along the river in a *bateau mouche.* These excursions are especially dramatic on summer nights, when the buildings visible from the river are spectacularly, fantastically lit. Highlights include **Notre-Dame,** the **Conciergerie,** the **Louvre,** and the **Eiffel Tower.**

6 **The Sewers** of Paris afford children a place to explore underground Paris. The hourlong visit includes a film and a walk through the tunnels.

7 **Disneyland Paris** is a definite quick fix of American "culture," where kids of all ages can spend a day with Mickey and Minnie. The theme park is similar to those in Florida and California with the requisite **Frontierland, Fantasyland, Adventureland, Discoveryland,** and **Main Street.**

8 **The Zoological Park** in the **Bois de Vincennes,** one of Europe's most beautiful zoos, is home to over 110 species of mammals and 115 types of birds. Visitors can help feed the animals their daily meals: pandas at 9:30AM and 5PM; pelicans at 2:15PM; penguins at 2:30PM; and seals and otters at 4:30PM. On weekends a small train takes passengers on a tour of the zoo.

9 **The Louvre** is a daunting prospect to anyone, so when visiting the world's largest art museum with children, limit your itinerary to one museum department per day. A good place to start is the **Egyptian Antiquities Collection,** always a favorite of fledgling art connoisseurs. Highlights include:Akhout-Hetep's *mastaba* (funeral chapel); Middle Kingdom tomb objects, including model boats to help the deceased on their journey in the afterlife and blue-glazed terra-cotta hippopotami; and furniture, games, jewelry, and other objects illustrating daily life in the New Kingdom period.

10 **The Museum of Natural History** in the **Jardin des Plantes** possesses one of the world's richest mineral collections and some of the oldest fossilized insects on earth. The newly renovated **Grande Galerie,** opened in 1994 after being closed for 30 years, houses a superb display on the evolution of life. Highlights are a giant whale skeleton; an impressive grouping of stuffed African savannah animals, including giraffes, lions, and elephants; and an extinct and endangered species exhibit.

62 Annick Goutal Original perfumes, precious oils, lotions, and soaps are purveyed at this ivory- and gold-toned boutique. Goutal's beautifully packaged products celebrate nature with such women's and men's fragrances as Eau d'Hadrien, Eau du Ciel, Gardénia Passion, and Rose Absolute. The knowledgeable salespeople will cheerfully assist you in choosing the right scent. ♦ M-Sa. 12 Pl St-Sulpice (between Rues des Canettes and Bonaparte). 01.46.33.03.15. Métros: St-Sulpice, Mabillon

Hotel de l'Abbaye

63 Hôtel de l'Abbaye $$$ Stone arches, antique furniture, and fresh-cut flowers enhance this 18th-century convent-turned-hotel. There are 40 peaceful rooms; ground-floor rooms **Nos. 2, 3,** and **4** open onto the trellised garden. There's no restaurant. ♦ 10 Rue Cassette (at Rue de Mézières). 01.45.44.38.11; fax 01.45.48.07.86. Métro: St-Sulpice

64 58 Rue Madame The oldest brother of Gertrude Stein, Michael Stein, and his artist wife, Sarah, moved here in 1903 and began buying the canvases of their close friend Henri Matisse. Within two decades, the Steins had assembled in this apartment one of the finest collections of Matisses, Renoirs, Gauguins, and Picassos in the world. ♦ Between Rues d'Assas and de Fleurus. Métro: St-Placide

Hôtel★★ PERREYVE

65 Perreyve $$ A quiet, 30-room hotel, this place is just a minute's stroll from the **Luxembourg Gardens.** There's no restaurant. ♦ 63 Rue Madame (at Rue de Fleurus). 01.45.48.35.01; fax 01.42.84.03.30. Métro: St-Placide

66 Hôtel de l'Avenir $$ This 35-room hotel near the **Luxembourg Gardens** is tremendously popular with students. There's no restaurant. ♦ 65 Rue Madame (at Rue de Fleurus). 01.45.48.84.54; fax 01.45.49.26.80. Métro: St-Placide

On the Right and Left Banks, addresses on streets perpendicular to the Seine begin at the river with the number 1 and increase as they move away from the river.

67 La Table de Fès ★★$$ Excellent North African couscous, chicken and lemon *tajine* (stew), and peppery *merguez* (lamb sausage) keep this friendly Moroccan restaurant crowded and hopping. The spicy change of pace from all those buttery French cream sauces is welcome. This spot is best late at night, when things are at their liveliest. ♦ M-Sa dinner; closed last two weeks of August. Reservations recommended (call after 5PM). 5 Rue Ste-Beuve (between Blvd Raspail and Rue Notre-Dame-des-Champs). 01.45.48.07.22. Métro: Vavin

67 Hôtel Ste-Beuve $$$ This handsome 52-room hotel, ideally situated equidistant from **La Coupole** and the **Luxembourg Gardens,** was decorated by master designer Christian Badin. Any advice (on restaurants, gallery openings, concerts) received from Alain at the front desk is golden. There's no restaurant. ♦ 9 Rue Ste-Beuve (between Blvd Raspail and Rue Notre-Dame-des-Champs). 01.45.48.20.07; fax 01.45.48.67.52. Métro: Vavin

68 26 Rue Vavin This luxury terraced apartment building was designed in 1925 by French architect **Henri Sauvage.** The splendid blue-and-white-tile complex, complete with ground-floor shops and indoor parking, was an early attempt at a self-contained building—what Le Corbusier would call *unité d'habitation.* ♦ Between Blvd Raspail and Rue Notre-Dame-des-Champs. Métro: Vavin

Within 26 Rue Vavin:

Marie-Papier Attracting customers from Los Angeles to Tokyo, this famous French stationery store sells an elegant line of colored paper in single sheets or large albums. ♦ M-Sa; closed first two weeks of August. 01.43.26.46.44

68 Rouge et Noir Games galore! This handsome shop sells finely crafted miniature billiard tables, roulette wheels, hand-carved dominoes, Chinese checkers, Monopoly, and, yes, even Trivial Pursuit. ♦ Tu-Sa. 01.43.26.05.77

69 La Coupole ★★$$ Along with the **Brasserie Lipp** and **Le Balzar,** this is Paris's most popular cafe with a history. The landmark was conceived in 1926 by René Lafond. While working at the **Dôme Café,** he negotiated a 20-year lease on the wood and coal depot across the street. He transformed the building with red-velvet booths, jazz-age chandeliers, and a dozen columns painted by Montparnasse's artistic community. The story goes that the painter Auffray, whose studio was in Montparnasse, first suggested that real artists paint the columns. Lafond paid for the supplies and gave each artist a few good meals as an honorarium. Léger's contribution is to the left of the bar; the black rat dancing on the head of a flutist is by Vassilief. Other columns were painted by Gris, Ribiera,

Soutine, Chagall, Delaunay, Brancusi, and Foujita. Matching the artist with his pillar has been a favorite diversion over dessert here ever since.

Purchased for more than $10 million and restored by brasserie czar Jean-Paul Boucher, the cavernous dining room has been classified as a historic monument (thus ensuring that its columns will be preserved). Today it's a watering hole for politicos, neighborhood merchants, aspiring actors, wandering poets, Scandinavian models, editors, and, most recently, the suburban hordes that invade the Montparnasse movie theaters on Saturday nights. The restaurant, it is said, has the densest population of beautiful women in all of Paris on weeknights; it is most chic, however, to make an appearance Sunday night. But on any night the atmosphere will be smokily festive. Expect to have a good time, but don't expect haute cuisine; the fare is simple and serviceable. In the basement is an enormous ballroom where dancers literally kick off their shoes. ♦ Daily breakfast, lunch, and dinner until 2AM. Ballroom: F-Sa 9:30PM-4AM; tea dancing Sa-Su 3-7PM. No reservations taken after 9PM. 102 Blvd du Montparnasse (at Rue Delambre). 01.43.20.14.20. Métro: Vavin

70 Dominique ★★$$ This restaurant/deli is as Russian as balalaikas. Grab a stool at the counter and snack on smoked salmon, pressed caviar, hot borscht, and blintzes with sour cream. Takeout is available. ♦ M dinner; Tu-Sa lunch and dinner; closed one week in February and mid-July to mid-August. Reservations recommended. 19 Rue Bréa (between Blvd Raspail and Rue Notre-Dame-des-Champs). 01.43.27.08.80. Métro: Vavin

71 Académie de la Grande-Chaumière Any closet Cézannes, budding Bonnards, or rising Renoirs in your traveling party? At this modest art academy you can draw or paint your own masterpiece from live models and carry it home for less than the cost of those imitation Toulouse-Lautrec posters sold on Rue de Rivoli. ♦ Painting and drawing M-Sa 9AM-noon; sketching M-Sa 3-6PM; closed in August. 14 Rue de la Grande-Chaumière (between Rue Notre-Dame-des-Champs and Blvd du Montparnasse). 01.43.26.13.72. Métro: Vavin

72 La Caméléon ★★$$ A bohemian bastion for famished painters in the 1960s, this eatery has become a thriving neighborhood bistro serving classic veal stew, hot sausage, smoked haddock, and a wide selection of salads. Those with a sweet tooth swoon for the white chocolate mousse and iced tea (with fresh mint) soufflé. Splurge on a delicious old Bourgueil wine with your meal. ♦ M-Sa lunch and dinner; closed in August. Reservations recommended for dinner. 6 Rue de Chevreuse (between Blvd du Montparnasse and Rue Notre-Dame-des-Champs). 01.43.20.63.43. Métro: Vavin

73 La Closerie des Lilas ★★$$ Opened in 1808, this legendary restaurant is where lilacs once bloomed, where Hemingway and Henry James hung out, where the defenders of Dreyfus plotted, and where Gide, Verlaine, Chateaubriand, Ingres, and Trotsky expounded. (Trotsky, Lenin, and the Russian crowd actually preferred **La Rotonde,** which opened down the street around 1911, while serious drinkers convened at **Le Dôme Café,** and the American crowd hung out at **La Coupole**—both also located just down the block.) Today **La Closerie des Lilas** is frequented by young French film stars and other constellations of the pretty and chic. It's expensive and a little pretentious, but not bad for an after-dinner drink or a weekend lunch in the mottled light of its outdoor terrace, especially during August when the rest of Paris shuts down. Try the steak *tartare, pigeon de Bresse rôti* (roasted pigeon from the Bresse region), *rumsteck Hemingway flambé au Bourbon* (beefsteak flambéed with bourbon), or the best-selling *turbotin grillé* (grilled turbot). The piano kindles a certain warmth as well. ♦ Daily lunch and dinner until 1:30AM. Reservations required. 171 Blvd du Montparnasse (at Ave de L'Observatoire). 01.40.51.34.50. Métro: Port Royal (RER)

74 93 Boulevard St-Michel During World War II, the Nazis searched for two years for Sylvia Beach, founder of the famous Paris **Shakespeare and Company** bookstore (see page 84), who hid here in a top-floor kitchen. ♦ Between Rues de l'Abbé-de-l'Epée and Royer-Collard. Métro: Luxembourg (RER)

75 Le Petit Journal Jazz of every type, from Dixieland to fusion and back again to bebop, can be heard in Claude Bolling's favorite club. Other performers here include Sacha Distel, Bill Coleman, Sugar Blue, Doctor Feelgood, and the Metropolitan Jazz Band. ♦ M-Sa until 2AM; closed in August. 71 Blvd St-Michel (at Rue Royer-Collard). 01.43.26.28.59. Métro: Luxembourg (RER). Also at: 13 Rue du Commandant-René-Mouchotte (between Pl de Catalogne and Ave du Maine). 01.43.21.56.70. Métro: Gaîté

76 Dalloyau ★★$$ To sip a civilized cup of Chinese tea and indulge in a scoop of homemade ice cream or a delicate pastry while gazing over the **Luxembourg Gardens** from the terrace of this pastry shop and tea salon is to taste the luxury and leisure of an earlier, more gracious, era. ♦ Daily breakfast, lunch, and afternoon tea. 2 Pl Edmond-Rostand (at Blvd St-Michel). 01.43.29.31.10. Métro: Luxembourg (RER)

Restaurants/Clubs: Red   **Hotels:** Blue
Shops/♥ Outdoors: Green   **Sights/Culture:** Black

76 Rue Monsieur-le-Prince *Monsieur-le-Prince* is what every French king's brother was traditionally called. Since the early 19th century, this street was a veritable American alley, as evidenced by the events that took place at the following addresses. **No. 14:** In March 1959 Martin Luther King Jr. visited black novelist Richard Wright in his third-floor apartment. **No. 22:** In 1892 James McNeill Whistler had a studio on the court-yard, where he completed a portrait of Count Robert de Montesquiou-Fezensac. (Years later, the count sold the painting for an exorbitant sum, thereby greatly offending Whistler. The portrait is now part of the Frick Collection in New York City.) **No. 49:** The poet Henry Wadsworth Longfellow lived here in June 1826. For $36 a week he received a room in the *pension de famille* of Madame Potet, French lessons with her daughters, and free laundry service. **No. 55:** Oliver Wendell Holmes lived here (now the site of the **Lycée St-Louis**) from 1833 to 1835 while he studied to be a doctor. To be on the safe side, the following year he obtained a second medical degree from Harvard. ♦ Between Blvd St-Michel and Carrefour de l'Odéon. Métros: Odéon, Luxembourg (RER)

77 Jardin du Luxembourg (Luxembourg Gardens) As a part of his draconian remodeling of Paris, Baron Haussmann had a plan to change this precious green expanse but was thwarted when 12,000 Parisians signed a petition to save the park. In the heart of the Left Bank, the 60-acre playground is graced with fountains, sculptures, ponds, flower beds, tennis courts, pony rides, a marionette theater, and outdoor band concerts. The open-air cafe is dappled with light filtered through the leaves of the surrounding trees, recalling the most pleasant moods of Impressionism. The park is under heavy surveillance by officious *gardiens* enforcing regulations stating that "The park is out of bounds to the drunk, beggars, and the indecently dressed; the playing of cards is restricted to the northwest corner of the gardens; the kicking of balls and sitting on the grass is prohibited entirely; and the park must be vacated precisely 30 minutes before sunset." These uniformed guards trill their whistles to chase lingerers from the gardens.

As for those ever-amusing Americans in Paris: In 1900 Isadora Duncan was wont to dance here at 5AM, when the gardens opened, and Hemingway's destitute painter protagonist in *Islands in the Stream* captured and strangled pigeons for lunch. Do not miss the gardens' many hidden delights: the small bronze replica of the Statue of Liberty; a series of statues of French queens and famous 19th-century women standing among the crocuses, daffodils, and azaleas; a beekeeping school run by André Lumaire, curator of the apiary, who gives practical classes from April to September through the **Centrale d'Apiculture** (41 Rue Pernety, between Rues Raymond-Losserand and de l'Ouest, 01.45.42.29.08); and the *pétanque* bowlers and chess players sequestered in their respective corners of the gardens. On weekends, smartly dressed Latin Quarter grade-schoolers romp here and compete in the park's tricycle races and toy sailboat regatta held in the octagonal basin at the center of the park. ♦ Bordered by Blvd St-Michel and Rue Guynemer, and Rues Auguste-Comte and de Vaugirard. Métros: Luxembourg (RER), Notre-Dame-des-Champs, St-Sulpice

Within the Jardin du Luxembourg:

Fontaine de Médicis (Medici Fountain) At the end of a long, somewhat slimy pool filled with goldfish is one of the few Italianate stonework remnants of Marie de Médicis's day. White marble nude lovers, *Acis* and *Galatea,* are eyed from above by the bronze Cyclops *Polyphemus,* who waits to do the mythic Greek version of kicking sand in the face of the 98-pound weakling before making off with the girl. Notice that the water appears to flow uphill into the grotto. On the back side of the fountain is a delightful bas-relief of *Leda and the Swan* by Valois. ♦ Near the Rue de Médicis entrance

78 Palais du Luxembourg (Luxembourg Palace) The assassin Ravaillac could hardly have imagined that his murder of Henri IV in

Luxembourg Gardens

MICHAEL STORRINGS

Théâtre de l'Odéon

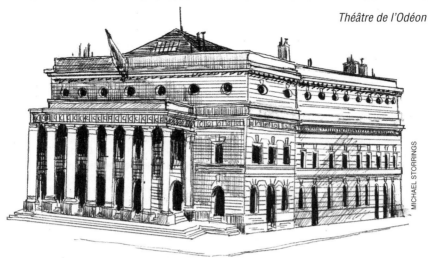

MICHAEL STORRINGS

1610 would result in the creation of this splendid palace and gardens. (Indeed, he didn't live long enough after committing his dastardly deed to imagine much of anything.) The widow of Henri IV, Queen Mother Marie de Médicis, grew tired of the **Louvre** and decided to build a palace that would recall her native Italy. She bought this vast property at the southern edge of the city from Duke François de Luxembourg and dispatched an architect to Florence to study her family residence, the Pitti Palace, before making plans for the new palace. Obediently, **Salomon de Brosse** designed this palace for her. Work began in 1615, but by the time the residence reached completion in 1631, Marie had been banished by her own son, Louis XIII, for turning against Cardinal Richelieu. She died penniless in Cologne 11 years later. During the Revolution, the palace served a short stint as a prison; it was here that "Citizen Paine," the American Thomas Paine, languished as an enemy Englishman for more than 10 months during the 1793 Reign of Terror and narrowly escaped execution.

Subsequently, the palace was remodeled to house the newly created French **Senate**, which met for the first time in 1804 and still resides here. Few of the trappings of Marie de Médicis's time remain; the 19th-century architect **Jean-François Chalgrin** (who also designed the **Arc de Triomphe**) made sure of that in his democratic remodeling. The 24 images of the queen's life story created by Rubens were moved to the **Louvre** and the Uffizi Gallery in Florence. **Chalgrin** festooned the library with the paintings of Delacroix in homage to Virgil, Homer, and Dante. On the one day each month that the palace is open, visitors queue around the block. ♦ Admission. Closed to the public except the first Sunday of each month (call 01.44.61.20.89 or

01.44.61.21.69 before the 15th of the previous month to make a reservation for the guided tour). Rue de Vaugirard (between Rues de Médicis and Guynemer). Métro: Luxembourg (RER)

79 Théâtre de l'Odéon City architects **Marie-Josephe Peyre** and **Charles de Wailly** designed this rather clumsy building (pictured above) in 1782, intending it to look like an ancient temple. With 1,913 seats, it was the largest theater in Paris. Beaumarchais's *Marriage of Figaro* premiered here on 27 April 1784 in an atmosphere of success and scandal; the author was jailed. After World War II, Jean-Louis Barrault and Madeleine Renaud revived interest in the theater with their productions of works by Beckett, Ionesco, Albee, and Claudel that became the talk of the town and, for a short period, made the theater the most popular in Paris. ♦ Box office: Daily 11AM-6:30PM. 1 Pl Paul-Claudel (at Rue Corneille). 01.44.41.36.00. Métro: Luxembourg (RER)

LIBRAIRIE
LE MONITEUR

80 Le Moniteur The best shop in Paris for books on architecture and landscape design also has a large selection of international design magazines and an array of unusual guidebooks and postcards. ♦ M-Sa. 7 Pl de l'Odéon (at Rue Racine). 01.43.25.48.58. Métro: Odéon

81 Polidor ★★$ For more than a century, the home cooking served here has lured writers such as Hemingway, Joyce, Valéry, and Verlaine out of their garrets for the earthy consolations of pumpkin soup, chicken in cream sauce, bacon and lentils, and rabbit in mustard sauce. Since its founding in 1845, little has changed; it's still a classic bistro with the traditional bistro decor, complete with lace curtains and tiny wooden drawers where the regulars store their linen napkins. One customer has dined here every evening for more than 40 years. Even the prices have stayed within a garret-dweller's means. ♦ Daily lunch and dinner. No credit cards accepted. 41 Rue Monsieur-le-Prince (between Rues de Vaugirard and Racine). 01.43.26.95.34. Métros: Luxembourg (RER), Odéon

82 Grand Hôtel des Balcons $$ This comfortable, reasonably priced 55-room hotel is down the street from the **Théâtre de l'Odéon.** There's no restaurant. ♦ 3 Rue Casimir-Delavigne (between Pl de l'Odéon and Rue Monsieur-le-Prince). 01.46.34.78.50; fax 01.46.34.06.27. Métros: Luxembourg (RER), Odéon

83 Chez Maître Paul ★★$$ Like a country cottage hidden deep in the Franche-Comté region of eastern France, this restaurant features white tablecloths and a warm welcome from the Debert family. The kitchen is famous for its variety of wine sauces and a winning way with chicken and veal. ♦ M-F lunch and dinner; Sa dinner. Reservations recommended. 12 Rue Monsieur-le-Prince (at Rue Casimir-Delavigne). 01.43.54.74.59. Métros: Luxembourg (RER), Odéon

84 La Méditerranée ★$$ This old haunt of Marlene Dietrich and Jean Cocteau serves seafood specialties such as marinated mussels, bouillabaisse, and *bar grillé* (grilled sea bass) in a crisp blue-and-white dining room. ♦ Daily lunch and dinner. 2 Pl de l'Odéon (at Rue de l'Odéon). 01.43.26.02.30. Métro: Odéon

85 12 Rue de l'Odéon From 1921 to 1940 this was the famous bookstore **Shakespeare and Company,** run by Sylvia Beach, daughter of a Presbyterian minister from Princeton, New Jersey. Her shop was a Parisian hearth and home for American and British writers such as Ezra Pound, Archibald MacLeish, Thornton Wilder, and F. Scott Fitzgerald, to whom Beach served as guardian angel. She was constantly lending books and money to Ernest Hemingway, who came to Paris in 1921 and, after the publication of *The Sun Also Rises,* became the city's most famous expatriate writer.

Beach was devoted to literature in general and to one writer in particular: James Joyce. If it hadn't been for this amazing woman, the most important literary event of the day—the publication, in full, of *Ulysses*—might never have happened. Beach accomplished that feat by becoming Joyce's secretary, editor, agent, and banker. She nearly went blind typing his illegible manuscript, and the publishing costs practically bankrupted her bookstore. The building now has residential and commercial space. ♦ Between Pl de l'Odéon and Carrefour de l'Odéon. Métro: Odéon

86 19 Rue de Tournon In May 1790 the American Revolutionary naval officer John Paul Jones, having served a year in the Russian navy, moved to Paris, where he was welcomed as a national hero for his epic 1779 capture of the *Serapis,* a British warship. Jones died destitute in a second-floor flat in this building on 18 July 1792; he received a full-scale state funeral paid for by the French government. This is still a residential building. ♦ Between Rues de Vaugirard and St-Sulpice. Métro: Luxembourg (RER)

87 42-44 Rue de Vaugirard In a top-floor flat of this apartment building, William Faulkner set to work on his first novel, *The Mosquitoes,* in the summer of 1925. ♦ At Rue Servandoni. Métro: St-Sulpice

88 Au Bon St-Pourçain ★★$$ This is one of the few remaining authentic Lyonnaise bistros in Paris. Chef Daniel Pesle fuels his regulars from the neighborhood with aioli, cassoulet, and his quick wit. ♦ M-Sa lunch and dinner. 10 *bis* Rue Servandoni (between Rues de Vaugirard and du Canivet). 01.43.54.93.63. Métro: Mabillon

89 Rue Férou This street has housed a number of artists over the years. Painter/photographer Man Ray occupied an atelier with a high ceiling at **No. 2** Rue Férou in 1951. Hemingway lived in the sphinx-protected *hôtel particulier* at **No. 6** in 1926 while writing *A Farewell to Arms,* having left his wife, Hadley, for French *Vogue* staffer Pauline Pfeiffer. Painter Henri Fantin-Latour had an apartment at **No. 13** in 1858, where he was sketched by his friend James McNeill Whistler (whose drawing was later purchased by the **Louvre**). ♦ Between Rues de Vaugirard and du Canivet. Métro: St-Sulpice

90 Place St-Sulpice One of the most serene squares in Paris has a cafe, pink-flowering chestnut trees, and the marvelous stone **Fontaine des Quatre Points Cardinaux** (Fountain of the Four Cardinal Points) by Visconti, featuring four famous French clergymen oriented north, south, east, and west, with four regal lions snarling at their feet. Once flanked by shops peddling ivory crucifixes, rosary beads, and clerical garments, the square today is graced by two

Yves Saint Laurent boutiques. It hosts antiques and book fairs in summer, and what many consider the finest of the Bastille Day balls. ♦ Off Rue Bonaparte. Métro: St-Sulpice

91 St-Sulpice Interrupted by insurrection, insolvency, and even bolts of lightning, the construction of this church required the services of architects, including the notable **Louis Le Vau** over a span of 134 years. Its dramatic Classical style was the inspiration of **Giovanni Servandoni**, a Florentine known for his theater and stage-set designs. The disparity of the two towers, an odd couple indeed, was the result of shifting architectural sands and patronly indecision. Named after St. Sulpicius, the sixth-century archbishop of Bourges, and dubbed the **Temple of Victory** during the Revolution, the church hosted a lavish banquet for 1,200 after Napoléon returned from his victories in Egypt. Inside the front door are two holy water stoups made from enormous shells given to François I by the Venetian Republic. The first chapel on the right was frescoed by an aging Eugène Delacroix. In a chapel at the rear of the church is the extraordinary *Virgin and Child* by Jean-Baptiste Pigalle. The organ, designed in 1776 by **Jean-François Chalgrin**, with 6,588 pipes, numbers among the largest in the world. In the floor, running along the north-south transept, is a bronze meridian line, a testament to France's 19th-century passion for science. Three times a year, on the equinoxes and the winter solstice, sunlight strikes the line so precisely that light runs along the metal strip, glances off an obelisk and globe at its top, and finally illuminates a cross. The inscription on the obelisk translates, more or less, as "Two Scientists with God's Help." ♦ Pl St-Sulpice (between Rues Palatine and St-Sulpice). 01.46.33.21.78. Métro: St-Sulpice

92 Marie Mercié The custom-made hats in Marie's summer and winter collections range from classic chapeaux to the amusing befeathered, beribboned fantasies that are earning her an international reputation. ♦ Tu-Sa. 23 Rue St-Sulpice (between Rues de Tournon and Garancière). 01.43.26.45.83. Métros: Odéon, Mabillon

93 Le Petit Vatel ★★$ One of Paris's smallest and cheapest restaurants is filled with famished students and artists seated around three tables. The tiny room used to be dominated by a large lavender stove until it was judged to be a fire hazard and authorities forced the owner, Mary, to remove it. Now a photograph on the wall is all that's left of the famous stove, but fortunately the food hasn't suffered. Tasty daily specials include Brazilian red beans, ratatouille, moussaka, roast pork, poached fish, and chocolate cake. ♦ M-Sa lunch and dinner; Su dinner. No credit cards accepted. 5 Rue Lobineau (between Rues de Seine and Mabillon). 01.43.54.28.49. Métro: Mabillon

94 Marché St-Germain The old covered market is being renovated to house a new commercial center, but the cobblers, fishmongers, and dairymaids can still be found in the next-door building on Rue Lobineau. Next to the market are an underground basketball court and an 82.5-foot public swimming pool, the **Piscine St-Germain**. ♦ Market: Tu-Sa; Su morning. Pool: Tu-Su hours vary. Rue Mabillon (at Rue Lobineau). 01.46.34.06.45. Métro: Mabillon

95 Castel's ★$$$ The most private of the city's private clubs, this place caters to dandies, back-biting gossips, the most clean-cut "BCBGs" (for *bon chic, bon genre,* the French term for yuppies), and former cabinet ministers with socialite dream girls on their arms. Technically, no one crosses Jean Castel's threshold unaccompanied by a card-carrying member (some 2,500 privileged people), but if you're dressed acceptably (jacket and tie for men) and speak some French . . . *peut-être.* The decor is tacky, the food unremarkable, and the dance floor crowded—so what's all the fuss about? ♦ M-Sa dinner. Disco: M-Sa 11:30PM-dawn. 15 Rue Princesse (between Rues Guisarde and du Four). 01.43.26.90.22. Métro: Mabillon

96 Aux Charpentiers ★★$$ Formerly the lunch hall of an 18th-century carpenters guild, this reasonably priced bistro serves chef Pierre Bardeche's simple but well-prepared bacon and lentils, beef stew, sautéed veal, and other daily specials. ♦ Daily lunch and dinner. Reservations recommended. 10 Rue Mabillon (between Rues Guisarde and du Four). 01.43.26.30.05. Métro: Mabillon

96 Guy ★★$$ Brazilian music, spicy shrimp with pepper, and the delicious black bean stew lure expatriates from Rio. A Brazilian band plays during Saturday lunch and on Wednesday and Saturday evenings. ♦ M-F dinner; Sa lunch and dinner. Reservations required. 6 Rue Mabillon (between Rues Guisarde and du Four). 01.43.54.87.61. Métro: Mabillon

The ornate Luxembourg Gardens employ 80 gardeners, which translates into more than one gardener per acre. Each year, this army plants or transplants 350,000 flowers, and in winter places into safekeeping 150 palm and orange trees, some 200 years old, to shelter them from the cold.

97 Chez Georges On an alley called Duckling Street, surrounded by a wealth of Italian restaurants, the footloose walker stumbles onto this classic old French bar wallpapered with mug shots of the singers who once performed in the old cabaret downstairs. It's a nice place for a glass of Côtes-du-Rhône or Beaujolais before dining on cannelloni and pizza down the street. ♦ Tu-Sa until 2AM. No credit cards accepted. 11 Rue des Canettes (between Rues Guisarde and du Four). 01.43.26.79.15. Métro: Mabillon

98 The Village Voice In the intelligent tradition of those famous Left Bank bookstore/salons run by women such as Sylvia Beach and Adrienne Monnier, the English bookshop of Odile Hellier is a busy crossroads for anglophone writers, artists, and literati in Paris. Hellier has something for everyone: a fine selection of classical, contemporary, and small-press fiction, exceptional author readings, and the latest issues of *The New York Review of Books, The New Yorker,* and (naturally) *The Village Voice.* ♦ M 2-8PM; Tu-Sa. 6 Rue Princesse (between Rues Guisarde and du Four). 01.46.33.36.47. Métro: Mabillon

99 Bistro Henri ★★$ This first-rate neighborhood bistro with a convivial ambience is known for its delicious *magret de canard* (duck fillet), green bean vinaigrette, *foie de veau* (veal liver), baked goat-cheese salad, au gratin potatoes, and homemade tarts. ♦ M-Sa lunch and dinner. Reservations recommended. No credit cards accepted. 16 Rue Princesse (between Rues Guisarde and du Four). 01.46.33.51.12. Métro: Mabillon

99 Birdland The jazzy bar serves chili con carne and plays classic John Coltrane and Charlie Parker. ♦ M-Sa 7PM-dawn; Su 11PM-dawn. 20 Rue Princesse (at Rue Guisarde). 01.43.26.97.59. Métro: Mabillon

100 Rue des Ciseaux Named after a scissors craftsman who once resided here, this short street is home to three Japanese restaurants and a pizzeria. ♦ Between Rue du Four and Blvd St-Germain. Métro: St-Germain-des-Prés

101 St-Germain-des-Prés For more than 15 centuries a church has stood on this corner, which in Roman times was a *pré* (open pasture). The first church, built in AD 452 by Merovingian king Childebert, was repeatedly destroyed by invading Normans and finally rebuilt to last in 1163. The Romanesque western gate tower is faintly reminiscent of the great abbeys on the outskirts of Paris. During the Middle Ages, **St-Germain-des-Prés,** named after St. Germanus (AD 496-576), bishop of Paris, became a focal point for Easter fairs, with hundreds of stalls, performing theater troupes, and dancing bears. (None of this has changed today save the dancing bears, which have been replaced by street musicians of the imitation-Dylan school.)

Inside the church is an altar dedicated to the victims of the September 1793 massacre, a shameful chapter of French history, when Paris was ruled by a bloodthirsty mob called the *sans-culottes* (because they wore linen trousers instead of aristocratic knee breeches). In 1793, after a mock trial on the weekend of 2-3 September, almost 200 prisoners sequestered in the church were led into the courtyard (at the corner of what is now Rue Bonaparte and Boulevard St-Germain), where they were stabbed and hacked to death by hired killers. Ministers of Louis XVI, his father confessor, and the Swiss Guards were slaughtered. The carnage was followed by an auction of the victims' personal effects. The skull of René Descartes, the 17th-century mathematician and philosopher, along with the body of John Casimir, a 17th-century king of Poland who was abbot of St-Germain, are buried inside the church.

Today, however, the edifice is best known for its evening concerts of classical music. It also provides a cool place to meditate on muggy summer days. ♦ Daily; guided tours Tu, Th 1-5PM. Pl St-Germain-des-Prés (off Blvd St-Germain). 01.43.25.41.71. Métro: St-Germain-des-Prés

101 Hommage à Apollinaire In the small park to the left of the main portal of **St-Germain-des-Prés** is a bronze bust of a woman by Pablo Picasso, given to the city in 1958 in memory of his friend, the poet Guillaume Apollinaire (1880-1918), who lived and died at 202-204 Boulevard St-Germain. Of Polish origin (his last name was Kostrowitzki), Apollinaire wrote the famous *Alcools* in 1913 and was an early leader of the Paris avant-garde. Eventually renowned for his poetry, Apollinaire was best known in his time as the man who stole the *Mona Lisa.* The scandal began when Apollinaire's former personal secretary lifted two inconsequential Phoenician statues from the **Louvre** and sold them to Picasso. Coincidentally, the *Mona Lisa* disappeared shortly afterward. Apollinaire, trying to protect his secretary and Picasso from suspicion and incarceration, turned in the statues and was jailed for four days. The *Mona Lisa* eventually resumed her place in the **Louvre,** and Apollinaire was exonerated. He never, however, recovered his self-esteem. A short street nearby also honors Apollinaire. ♦ Pl St-Germain-des-Prés (at Rue de l'Abbaye). Métro: St-Germain-des-Prés

---

Parisians who arrive late to work are hard-pressed to blame the métro. At rush hour, the subway arrives once every 80 seconds. All cars undergo a weekly maintenance to ensure against mechanical breakdowns.

102 St-Germain-des-Prés $$ In the heart of bustling St-Germain, this 30-room hotel is convenient though hardly tranquil. Breakfast is served in the garden room, but there's no restaurant. ♦ 36 Rue Bonaparte (between Rues Guillaume-Apollinaire and Jacob). 01.43.26.00.19; fax 01.40.46.83.63. Métro: St-Germain-des-Prés

103 Librairie Le Divan The bookstore of the Gallimard publishing house has works by all its latest authors, plus other literature and a large collection of *bandes dessinés* (comic books), such as *Tintin Chez le Psychanalyste*. Note the black-and-white author photos tacked to the walls. ♦ M-Sa. 37 Rue Bonaparte (at Rue de l'Abbaye). 01.43.26.84.73. Métro: St-Germain-des-Prés

104 Réunion des Musées Nationaux It's Tuesday. You forgot to buy a poster or catalog at the **Louvre** to take home, and now the museum is closed. Don't fret. This bookstore stocks all the catalogs and posters published by the national museums in France since 1966. ♦ M-F; closed three weeks in August. 10 Rue de l'Abbaye (between Rues de Furstemberg and Bonaparte). 01.43.29.21.45. Métro: St-Germain-des-Prés

105 24 Rue Bonaparte In the spring of 1928, Henry Miller stayed here with his wife, June. The building now has both residential and commercial space. ♦ Between Rue Jacob and Quai Malaquais. Métro: St-Germain-des-Prés

106 Ecole des Beaux-Arts (School of Fine Arts) The city's fine arts school was established by Louis XIV and trained many of the architects and artists who have designed and decorated Paris over the centuries. It's worth a quick detour to view the lovely Renaissance archway, fountain, and sculpture, and the changing exhibitions of student work. Two well-known architects, **Richard Morris Hunt** and **Bernard Ralph Maybeck**, were among the first Americans to be educated here, and each employed his own version of the Beaux Arts style in the US during the late 19th century. ♦ Daily. 14 Rue Bonaparte (between Rue Jacob and Quai Malaquais). 01.44.50.56.00. Métros: Rue du Bac, St-Germain-des-Prés

107 8 Rue Bonaparte The young Corsican conqueror once lived here, but this street wasn't named for him until 1852, when his nephew, Napoléon III, became emperor. ♦ Between Rue Jacob and Quai Malaquais. Métro: St-Germain-des-Prés

108 Restaurant des Beaux-Arts ★★$ Established in 1850, this bargain canteen is usually filled with art students. Go early to miss the lines but not the coq au vin, *boeuf bourguignon, confit de canard* (duck confit), and rabbit in mustard sauce. Wine is included in the prix-fixe menu. ♦ Daily lunch and dinner. No credit cards accepted. 11 Rue Bonaparte (between Rue des Beaux-Arts and Quai Malaquais). 01.43.26.92.64. Métro: St-Germain-des-Prés

109 Robert Duperrier Here you'll find a lively combination of Indonesian, North American, and African art, from Gambian amulets to Ibo statues. ♦ M-Sa; closed in August. 14 Rue des Beaux-Arts (between Rues de Seine and Bonaparte). 01.43.54.38.64. Métro: St-Germain-des-Prés

109 Franco Maria Ricci Editore This is the Paris headquarters of the celebrated Milan publisher, whose eclectic and elegant series of fine arts books and literature ranges in subject from decorative ceramics and iconography to deluxe Italian re-editions of Saki, Kafka, Borges, and Poe. ♦ Tu-Sa. 12 Rue des Beaux-Arts (between Rues de Seine and Bonaparte). 01.46.33.96.31. Métro: St-Germain-des-Prés

L'HOTEL
G.L. Hubricherun

110 L'Hôtel $$$$ Formerly the **Hôtel d'Alsace**, this 27-room place is where Oscar Wilde stayed in 1899 after his release from Reading Gaol (the prison). He expired here the following year, sighing, "I am dying beyond my means." *Dorian Gray* fans can stay in the room where Wilde lived out his last days. Or, if you prefer, book the Art Deco bedroom of dance-hall belle Mistinguett. The hotel's seven-story light well is a triumph of Directoire architecture. ♦ 13 Rue des Beaux-Arts (between Rues de Seine and Bonaparte). 01.43.25.27.22; fax 01.43.25.64.81. Métro: St-Germain-des-Prés

Within L'Hôtel:

Le Belier ★$$ This romantic restaurant maintains a reputation for convivial service. The specialties include veal tournedos with mozzarella, sole and salmon in saffron, and meringue with mangoes and chocolate. ♦ Daily lunch and dinner. Reservations recommended. 01.43.25.27.22

Bar de l'Hôtel Young art and antiques dealers bring their fancy American friends here to experience the Parisian scene. ♦ Daily 6AM-2AM. 01.43.25.27.22

110 Galerie Claude Bernard One of the city's best, this internationally known gallery shows such modern heavyweights as Balthus, Giacometti, David Hockney, Louise Nevelson, and Jim Dine. ♦ Tu-Sa. No credit cards accepted. 7-9 Rue des Beaux-Arts (between Rues de Seine and Bonaparte). 01.43.26.97.07. Métro: St-Germain-des-Prés

111 5 Rue des Beaux-Arts Edouard Manet was born here in 1835. A wall plaque commemorates that truly blessed event. ♦ Between Rues de Seine and Bonaparte. Métro: St-Germain-des-Prés

112 Roger-Viollet With more than eight million black-and-white and color photographs, these archives document the history of mankind from antiquity to the present. Stored here are glossies of the Temple of Ramses at Abou Simbel, the interior of a 14th-century baker's shop, Louis Armstrong, and the demolition of the Berlin Wall. Curious tourists are not admitted, but journalists, students, and other researchers are welcome. ♦ M-F. 6 Rue de Seine (between Rue des Beaux-Arts and Quai Malaquais). 01.43.54.81.10. Métros: Odéon, St-Germain-des-Prés

113 24 Rue Visconti This was once the home of Racine. According to a historian's account, the brilliant 17th-century dramatist died here on 21 April 1699 of a combination of dysentery, erysipelas, rheumatism, a liver ailment, and, possibly, "the chagrin of no longer being in favor with the king." The building is still a private residence. ♦ Between Rues de Seine and Bonaparte. Métro: St-Germain-des-Prés

114 17 Rue Visconti Young Balzac set up his print shop at this address. A few years later, in 1836, Delacroix moved in. It was here that he painted his portraits of George Sand and Frédéric Chopin. It is now a private residential/commercial building. ♦ Between Rues de Seine and Bonaparte. Métro: St-Germain-des-Prés

> Paris "impressed me as the perfect and perfectly beautiful city; and even after I had been there for some time, and seen not only its avenues and palaces, but its most squalid alleys and hovels, this impression was not weakened."
>
> James Weldon Johnson,
> *Autobiography of an Ex-Coloured Man*

114 Claude Boullé For over two decades, Claude Boullé has been selling his landscapes represented in natural stones, cut and polished. Some of them are the mineral counterparts of Turner's seascapes on canvas. ♦ M-Sa. 28 Rue Jacob (between Rues de Seine and Bonaparte). 01.46.33.01.38. Métro: St-Germain-des-Prés

114 La Maison Rustique Green thumbs will enjoy browsing in this agricultural and horticultural bookstore. ♦ M-Sa. 26 Rue Jacob (between Rues de Seine and Bonaparte). 01.43.25.67.00. Métro: St-Germain-des-Prés

115 14 Rue Jacob German opera composer Richard Wagner lived here in 1841-42. The building now has both residential and commercial space. ♦ Between Rues de Seine and Bonaparte. Métro: St-Germain-des-Prés

116 La Villa $$$ If you want to stay on the Left Bank but rustic decor doesn't charm you, this 32-room hotel has a slick contemporary look. After 10:30PM Monday through Saturday you'll find an international assortment of beautiful people downstairs in the **Club la Villa,** listening to live jazz and munching on caviar and foie gras. American filmmaker Spike Lee stays here. ♦ 29 Rue Jacob (between Rues de Furstemberg and Bonaparte). 01.43.26.60.00; fax 01.46.34.63.63. Métro: St-Germain-des-Prés

116 27 Rue Jacob The prestigious French publishing house Editions du Seuil has its offices in the building where Ingres, the master of French classical painting, lived more than 150 years ago. ♦ Between Rues de Furstemberg and Bonaparte. Métro: St-Germain-des-Prés

117 Librairie Maritime et d'Outre-Mer This bookstore specializes in maritime books. ♦ M-Sa. 17 Rue Jacob (between Rues de Furstemberg and Bonaparte). 01.46.33.47.48. Métro: St-Germain-des-Prés

118 Studio V.O./V.F. Want to star in the next Polanski thriller set in Paris? Need to gesticulate more effectively at surly waiters and postal clerks? Adult acting classes in French or English are taught here by highly professional American and French drama instructors. ♦ Tu-F; closed in July and August. 11 Rue Jacob (between Rues de Furstemberg and Bonaparte). 01.40.46.01.92. Métro: St-Germain-des-Prés

118 7 Rue Jacob In 1656, at the age of 17, Racine lived here with his uncle. It's still a residential/commercial building. ♦ Between Rues de Furstemberg and Bonaparte. Métro: St-Germain-des-Prés

119 Yveline Tucked away in the Furstemberg Square (pictured above) is this charming antiques shop. ♦ M-Sa; closed in August. 4 Rue de Furstemberg (between Rues de l'Abbaye and Jacob). 01.43.26.56.91. Métro: St-Germain-des-Prés

119 Musée Delacroix The old atelier of Eugène Delacroix, where he lived, worked, and, in 1863, died, is now a museum displaying his paintings, sketches, and letters. A quick tour will give you some idea of why Baudelaire described Delacroix as a "volcanic crater artistically concealed beneath bouquets of flowers." ♦ Admission. M, W-Su. 6 Rue de Furstemberg (between Rues de l'Abbaye and Jacob). 01.44.41.86.50. Métro: St-Germain-des-Prés

MANUEL CANOVAS

119 Manuel Canovas A showroom exhibiting wallpaper and fabrics by the famed designer whose sumptuous works are often featured in *Vogue* and *Architectural Digest*. Within the shop is a small boutique offering home accessories including bed- and table linens. ♦ M-Sa. 7 Rue de Furstemberg (between Rues de l'Abbaye and Cardinale). 01.43.25.75.98. Métros: Mabillon, St-Germain-des-Prés

119 2 Rue Cardinale The Black Sun Press operated at this address under the aegis of Harry and Caresse Crosby, a couple of wild surrealists of the 1920s. They were the first to publish the D. H. Lawrence book *Sun*. Harry, who was a nephew of J. P. Morgan, died in a double suicide with his mistress at the Hôtel des Artistes in New York. ♦ Off Rue de Furstemberg. Métro: Mabillon

119 Place de Furstemberg Named after Egon de Furstemberg, a 17th-century abbot of **St-Germain-des-Prés,** this hidden treasure attracts French filmmakers, flamenco guitar players, and harpists who like to play in the courtyard because of its extraordinary acoustics. At the center of the square is a white-globed lamppost and four paulownia trees that Henry Miller described as having "the poetry of T.S. Eliot." In spring the trees burst into fragrant lavender bloom; Paris never smells as sweet anywhere else. ♦ Rue de Furstemberg (between Rues de l'Abbaye and Jacob). Métro: St-Germain-des-Prés

120 Hôtel de Seine $$ Once a family-run *pension,* this 30-room hotel no longer has its bohemian charm, but it's nonetheless a well-located and comfortable place that strives to please. Beat poet Lawrence Ferlinghetti, owner of City Lights Bookstore in San Francisco, used to stay here. There's no restaurant. ♦ 52 Rue de Seine (between Rues de Buci and Jacob). 01.46.34.22.80; fax 01.46.34.04.74. Métro: Mabillon

120 Cosi ★★$ This gourmet Italian sandwich and salad counter serves everything from salmon carpaccio to roasted red peppers—all on bread baked in wood-fired pizza ovens. Tuscan wines, opera by Verdi, and daily editions of *La Repubblica* lend to Cosi's Latin charm. Take your order elsewhere or, if you prefer, eat here in the upstairs seating area. ♦ Daily lunch and dinner until midnight. 54 Rue de Seine (between Rues de Buci and Jacob). 01.46.33.35.36. Métro: Mabillon

121 Le Chai de l'Abbaye ★★$ This is one of the few good wine bars in Paris not crawling with yuppies. Typical French fare is served. ♦ Daily breakfast, lunch, and dinner until 2AM. 26 Rue de Buci (at Rue du Bourbon-le-Château). 01.43.26.68.26. Métro: Mabillon

121 2 Rue du Bourbon-le-Château Buzz yourself in and have a look at the circular-well courtyard in this 1824 apartment building. (**L'Hôtel** on Rue des Beaux-Arts is another example of this architectural device.) Try to imagine how items such as grand pianos are hoisted up to the fifth floor. ♦ At Rue de Buci. Métro: Mabillon

122 Rhumerie Martiniquaise ★$ Upper-crust imbibers, along with the rabble out for a good time, keep this place packed. The stiff punches made with 130 kinds of the tropical liquor make it worth fighting for a table. In addition to the usual daiquiris and planter's punch, try the *Père Serge,* which is named after a priest at **St-Germain-des-Prés** and is made with rum, lemon, and sugarcane syrup. The liquid refreshments are the real draw here, but meat and fish dishes are served at lunch and snacks such as *boudin* (sausage), *akra de morue* (fish fritters), and crab *farci* (stuffed and spiced crab) are available throughout the day and night. ♦ Daily 9AM-2AM. No credit cards accepted. 166 Blvd St-Germain (between Rues de Buci and de l'Echaudé). 01.43.54.28.94. Métro: Mabillon

123 Butard Traiteur The windows at this expensive late-night delicatessen/caterer are capable of bringing any passing gourmand to a dead stop. *Duck à l'orange,* curried chicken, ornamented whole poached salmon, and impeccable pastries join a fine selection of wines, liqueurs, breads, and regional French specialties. ♦ Daily. 29 Rue de Buci (between Blvd St-Germain and Rue de Seine). 01.43.25.17.72. Métros: Mabillon, Odéon

124 Rue de Buci One of Paris's prettiest street markets is named after M. Buci, president of the Parliament of Paris during the Renaissance. On Tuesday through Saturday and Sunday mornings, the intersection of Rues de Buci and de Seine is thronged with operatic hawkers hustling endive, homemade fettuccine, freshly ground Colombian coffee, wild strawberries, fresh cherries, hot baguettes, and pink tulips.

From here, Rue de Seine shoots off toward the river, becoming a thoroughfare of art galleries. Bear that in mind when passing by in the early evening: a crowded gallery is most likely hosting a *vernissage* (literally a "varnishing," the French name for an exhibition opening). Put on your best French accent, join the party, and talk art while sipping a glass of Champagne. ♦ Market: Tu-Sa; Su morning. Between Carrefour de Buci and Rue de Seine. Métro: Mabillon

124 Le Fournil de Pierre In the vanguard of the new artisanal bakeries, this place takes particular pride in its whole-grain breads. The *pain de six céréales* (six-grain bread) might even inspire you to buy a toaster for your hotel room. ♦ M-Sa; Su morning. 64 Rue de Seine (between Blvd St-Germain and Rue de Buci). 01.46.34.17.59. Métro: Mabillon

124 La Louisiane $$ If you want to stay right in the heart of Paris, this 80-room property is a good choice. The hotel has hosted some famous French literati, including Jacques Prévert and Jean-Paul Sartre. The noise level is likely to be high, so light sleepers should go elsewhere. Simone de Beauvoir lived in one of the hotel's coveted oval rooms for years. There's no restaurant. ♦ 60 Rue de Seine (between Blvd St-Germain and Rue de Buci). 01.43.29.59.30; fax 01.46.34.23.87. Métro: Mabillon

125 Vagenende ★★$$ With the full effulgence of an 1885 Belle Epoque and Tiffany glass decor, this poor man's **Maxim's** has starred in films such as *Travels with My Aunt* and *Murder on the Orient Express.* Homemade foie gras, fresh shellfish, and pot-au-feu are good dishes to try. ♦ Daily lunch and dinner until 1AM. 142 Blvd St-Germain (between Rues Grégoire-de-Tours and de Seine). 01.43.26.68.18. Métros: Mabillon, Odéon

---

Restaurants/Clubs: Red   Hotels: Blue
Shops/♥ Outdoors: Green   Sights/Culture: Black

126 Galerie Documents

Opened in 1954 by Michel Romand and now run by his daughter Mireille, this is the city's most distinguished antique poster shop, specializing in *affiches* from 1875 to 1930, particularly the works of Toulouse-Lautrec, Grasset, Mucha, and Steinlen. ♦ M-Sa. 53 Rue de Seine (between Rues de Buci and Jacques-Callot). 01.43.54.50.68. Métros: Mabillon, Odéon

127 Galerie Arts des Amériques If pre-Columbian art from Central and South America is your passion, this gallery has treasures in store for you. ♦ M-Sa; closed in August. 42 Rue de Seine (between Rues Jacob and Visconti). 01.46.33.18.31. Métros: Mabillon, St-Germain-des-Prés

128 La Palette ★★$ This bohemian cafe is right out of a Jean Rhys novel. In fact, James Ivory filmed part of that down-and-out tale *Quartet* (with Alan Bates, Maggie Smith, and Isabelle Adjani) here in 1981. The artists' palettes that hang on the wall are more interesting than the paintings themselves, but don't miss the humorous 1920s tiled murals in the back room. House specialties include gruyère omelette, chef's salad, country ham served on Poilâne country bread, and a delicious *tarte tatin* (apple tart). Bearded waiter Jean-François is grouchy but kindhearted and plays the part of a little Bonaparte; you must order quickly and without indecision or he'll ignore you until you've learned your lesson. One Aussie regular calls the crouch-style toilet an "authentic porcelain kangaroo trap." ♦ M-Sa breakfast and lunch until 1:30AM; closed in August. No credit cards accepted. 43 Rue de Seine (at Rue Jacques-Callot). 01.43.26.68.15. Métros: Mabillon, St-Germain-des-Prés

129 Librairie Fischbacher Along with a stunning collection of fine arts editions, this shop has books on history and primitive arts, and autobiographies in French, English, and German. ♦ M-Sa. 33 Rue de Seine (between Rues Jacques-Callot and Mazarine). 01.43.26.84.87. Métros: Mabillon, Odéon

130 Marie & Fils ★★★$$ Marie Steinberg owned her first Left Bank restaurant, **Chez Marie,** for 10 years. As the name of her second venture implies, she now has a

partner, her son Guillaume Barclay. The team has created a refreshing variety of dishes with a range of prices, which in turn has drawn a range of customers. Local artists, editors, and gallery owners lunch here, and at dinnertime the *belle clientèle* arrives, including such neighborhood residents as Catherine Deneuve. Selections change every two months except for two first-class standbys: roast beef with mashed potatoes, and *foie de veau à la sauce aigre-douce* (veal liver in a sweet-and-sour sauce), Guillaume's signature dish. The atmosphere is warm and spirited. ♦ M dinner; Tu-Sa lunch and dinner. Reservations recommended. 34 Rue Mazarine (between Rues Jacques-Callot and de Seine). 01.43.26.69.49. Métros: Odéon, Mabillon

131 12 Rue Mazarine Here the young Molière made his acting debut and later, with an inherited nest egg, opened a theater in an abandoned tennis court; this was the genesis of the **Comédie Française.** In 1673, after he died onstage, the theater company was orphaned and evicted. But the troupe started performing once again in another old tennis court at 14 Rue de l'Ancienne-Comédie after more than a decade of inactivity. ♦ Between Rues Jacques-Callot and de Seine. Métros: Odéon, Mabillon

132 Institut de France Situated across the Pont des Arts from the **Louvre,** this 17th-century masterpiece, designed by **Louis Le Vau** at the same time he was working on the **Louvre,** houses five academies, including the prestigious **Académie Française.** The academy began in 1635 as a salon of intellectuals who gathered informally to discuss French rhetoric and usage. Shortly thereafter, Cardinal Richelieu charged them with the protection and proliferation of the French language, hoping that Parisian French would eventually obliterate the less-refined regional dialects.

Academy membership is limited to 40 "immortals." At their induction ceremonies, the members wear silver-embroidered green robes and cocked admirals' bonnets and carry jeweled swords. The immortals don their robes for secret meetings, which are held every Thursday afternoon. Among their responsibilities are safeguarding the mother tongue and preparing new editions of the academy's dictionary, which first appeared in 1694.

Election to the academy is reserved for great writers, and even the list of runners-up comprises a pantheon of French literature: Descartes, Diderot, de Maupassant, Balzac, Flaubert, Verlaine, Stendhal, and Proust among them. Molière, the playwright/director/actor, was invited to join the academy on the condition that he give up acting. He refused the honor. No actor has ever been admitted to date. Emile Zola campaigned unsuccessfully for election 13 times; Nobel Prize–winners André Gide and Albert Camus never even tried. In 1981, history was made when Marguerite Yourcenar was inducted into the sacred ranks of the academy and became the first female immortal (the cloak she wore at the presentation was personally designed by Yves Saint Laurent).

The left wing of the institute (toward the mint building) is the site of the notorious **Tour Nesle,** from where, according to Dumas, Queen Margot (the first wife of Henri IV) would catapult that night's lover into the Seine. Among the exemplary statuary in the institute rotunda is a nude bust of Voltaire by Houdon. ♦ Open to cultural groups by appointment. 23 Quai de Conti (at Pl de l'Institut). (01.44.41.44.41). Métros: Pont-Neuf, Mabillon

133 Pont des Arts Providing a pedestrian crossing between the **Institut de France** and the **Louvre,** this wooden-planked structure with latticed arches was the first iron bridge in Paris. Designed by an engineer named Dillon in 1804, the footbridge was originally landscaped with potted orange trees, rosebushes, and hothouses full of exotic tropical plants. Hordes of easel-toting artists from the nearby **Ecole des Beaux-Arts** come here to sketch and paint that familiar compact view spanning the Ile de la Cité, the rose-gray facade of Place Dauphine, and the dignified form of the Pont-Neuf, as well as the spires of **Notre-Dame** and **Ste-Chapelle** in the distance. ♦ Between Pl de l'Institut and Quai du Louvre. Métros: Pont-Neuf, Mabillon

134 Galerie Granoff Larock One of the city's most reputable modern art galleries sells works of the masters. ♦ M-Sa. 13 Quai de Conti (at Impasse Conti). 01.43.54.41.92. Métro: Pont-Neuf

134 Impasse de Conti On this street in 1792, a young Corsican named Napoléon Bonaparte rented an attic room in the **Hôtel de Guénégaud** (now part of the **Hôtel des Monnaies**) built by François Mansart in 1659. Twelve years later, he conquered Europe and crowned himself emperor of France. ♦ Off Quai de Conti. Métro: Pont-Neuf

---

Mrs. Allonby: They say, Lady Hunstanton, that when good Americans die they go to Paris.

Lady Hunstanton: Indeed? And when bad Americans die, where do they go?

Lord Illingworth: Oh, they go to America.

Oscar Wilde, *A Woman of No Importance*

135 Hôtel des Monnaies/Musée des Monnaies (Mint/Money Museum) The austere Classical-style French mint is where the nation's centime and franc coins are designed and struck. In 1775, shortly after the original mint by **Jules Hardouin-Mansart** was demolished, the present edifice was built by **Jacques-Denis Antoine.** The museum traces the history of French coins back to Charlemagne's day and houses a collection of medals, currency, and commemorative coins. Hundreds of gold and silver medals are also for sale in the museum shop (2 Rue Guénégaud, 01.40.46.58.58). ♦ Admission. Museum: Tu-Su 1-6PM; Th until 9PM. Tours of mint production area: Tu, F 2PM. Museum shop: M-Sa. 11 Quai de Conti (between Rue Guénégaud and Impasse de Conti). 01.40.46.55.33. Métros: Pont-Neuf, Odéon

136 Galerie J.C. Riedel One of the most successful galleries in Paris, this springboard for European talent boasts the works of such promising and well-received artists as S.W. Hayter and F. Audrum. ♦ Sa afternoon only. 12 Rue Guénégaud (between Rue Mazarine and Quai de Conti). 01.46.33.25.73. Métro: Odéon

136 Michel Cachoux Dig through the fossils, lapis, amethysts, and star-shaped calcites—there's something for everyone's hard-rock fantasy here. ♦ Tu-Sa or by appointment; closed in August. 16 Rue Guénégaud (between Rue Mazarine and Quai de Conti). 01.43.54.52.15, 01.43.25.85.86. Métro: Odéon

137 Le Balto Local architecture students pass their afternoons playing table soccer at this animated bar, which is best for gruyère on Poilâne bread or a nightcap sipped standing up. Every Wednesday at 9:30PM the **Fanfare des Beaux-Arts, a** rowdy horn ensemble, performs. ♦ M-Sa 7AM-1AM. 15 Rue Mazarine (at Rue Guénégaud). 01.44.07.12.37. Métro: Odéon

137 La Cafetière ★★$$ The specialties of this warmly lit restaurant are the beef fillet and hot apple crepes. *Cafetière* means coffeepot, hence the collection that's scattered about. ♦ Daily lunch and dinner. Reservations recommended. 21 Rue Mazarine (between Passage Dauphine and Rue Guénégaud). 01.46.33.76.90. Métro: Odéon

138 Rue de Nevers This 13th-century alley ends near a remnant of the King Philippe Auguste city wall (ca. 1200) and passes beneath an arch chiseled with an excerpt of the 17th-century poem *Le Paris Ridicule* by Claude Le Petit, which forecast the collapse of Henri IV's noble Pont-Neuf. The paper edition of this caustic verse was publicly burned in the Place de Grève, along with its author. ♦ Between Rue de Nesle and Quai de Conti. Métro: Odéon

139 Le Monde en Marche Step into a magical world of wooden toys, puppets, and puzzles that are gaily colored and made by hand. ♦ Tu-Sa 10:30AM-7:30PM; closed in August. 34 Rue Dauphine (between Carrefour de Buci and Passage Dauphine). 01.43.29.09.49. Métro: Odéon

140 Hôtel le Régent $$ This comfortable 25-room hotel is nicely located midway between the Seine and Rue de Buci, which boasts the prettiest outdoor market in Paris. There's no restaurant. ♦ 61 Rue Dauphine (between Rues St-André-des-Arts and Andre-Mazet). 01.46.34.59.80; fax 01.40.51.05.07. Métro: Odéon

141 Hôtel Left Bank St-Germain $$ Best Western comes to France offering 31 rooms with flowered wallpaper, heavy furniture, white marble bathrooms, and such modern amenities as air-conditioning and cable television. The central location near the lively Carrefour de l'Odéon means that street-side rooms are subject to noise from the nearby all-night **Pub St-Germain-des-Prés;** light sleepers might want to ask for a *chambre* opening onto the pretty garden courtyard. The top floor penthouse suite has a splendid rooftop view of **Notre-Dame.** There's no restaurant. ♦ 9 Rue de l'Ancienne-Comédie (between Blvd St-Germain and Rue St-André-des-Arts). 01.43.54.01.70; fax 01.43.26.17.14. Métro: Odéon

141 Le Procope ★★$$ Founded in 1686 by Sicilian Francesco Procopio dei Coltelli, and assured success by the 1689 opening of the **Comédie Française** in a tennis court–turned-theater across the street, this eatery advertises itself as the world's oldest cafe (the second star in its rating is for its history). Customers have included Olympian talents La Fontaine, Rousseau, and Voltaire; 18th-century revolutionaries including Benjamin Franklin, Thomas Jefferson, Robespierre, Danton, Bonaparte, and Marat; ageless literati such as Victor Hugo, Honoré de Balzac, Paul Verlaine, George Sand, and Mallarmé; and in the 1950s, when the tavern/cafe became a restaurant, Simone de Beauvoir and Jean-Paul Sartre. These days, the best part of dining here is adding your name to the distinguished guest list. The restaurant's 18th-century decor, and crystal chandeliers never seem to compensate for the slow service and disappointing cuisine. Safest bets are the classics: pot-au-feu and grilled lamb. ♦ Daily breakfast, lunch, and dinner until 1AM. Piano bar: M-Sa 10PM-1AM. 13 Rue de l'Ancienne-Comédie (between Blvd St-Germain and Rue St-André-des-Arts). 01.40.46.79.00. Métro: Odéon

141 Pub St-Germain-des-Prés ★★$$ Along with 24 brands of draft beer and 450 international varieties of bottled brew, this 600-seat pub offers such basic grub as mussels and beef cooked with—guess what?—beer. By the end of the evening, you may feel that you have been similarly stewed yourself. Open around the clock, it's a favorite of American students abroad. ♦ Daily 24 hours. 17 Rue de l'Ancienne-Comédie (between Blvd St-Germain and Rue St-André-des-Arts). 01.43.29.38.70. Métro: Odéon

142 Hôtel de Fleurie $$ This renovated 18th-century town house in the heart of St-Germain-des-Prés offers 29 quiet, airy rooms, including some in the attic with high ceilings and wood beams. Downstairs is a handsome stone-vaulted breakfast room, where the Marolleau family serves an excellent continental breakfast—slices of *quatre-quarts* (French pound cake), crisp baguettes, cheese, and freshly squeezed orange juice. There's no restaurant. ♦ 32-34 Rue Grégoire-de-Tours (between Rue des Quatre-Vents and Blvd St-Germain). 01.53.73.70.00; fax 01.53.73.70.20. Métro: Odéon

142 Casa Bini ★★$$ Recommended by the concierges at the **Montalembert** and **George V** hotels, this casual, friendly Tuscan restaurant run by Anna Bini and her family has prepared meals for Catherine Deneuve and Marcello Mastroianni. Florentine appetizers include *crostini* with mascarpone and salmon, and swordfish carpaccio with herbs. There are new meat, fish, and pasta specials every day, but the pasta Casa Bini, a filling fettuccine and salmon dish, is always available. The shop next door sells many of the Tuscan products used in the restaurant, including pastas and sauces. Ask about Mme. Bini's tours to Italy. ♦ M-F lunch and dinner; Sa dinner; closed three weeks in August and one week at Christmas. Reservations recommended. 36 Rue Grégoire-de-Tours (between Rue des Quatre-Vents and Blvd St-Germain). 01.46.34.05.60. Métro: Odéon

143 Au Savoyard ★★$$ For 35 years this colorful restaurant has been serving authentic French Alpine cuisine in the midst of Paris. The wooden chairs, wild-game trophies, paintings of mountain scenes, and peacock feathers provide an appropriately rustic setting for raclette (melted cheese, potatoes, and ham), fondue, and smoked Savoie sausages. This is a regional gem. ♦ Daily lunch and dinner; closed last two weeks of July and in August. Reservations recommended. 16 Rue des Quatre-Vents (between Carrefour de l'Odéon and Rue Grégoire-de-Tours). 01.43.26.20.30. Métro: Odéon

144 Carrefour de l'Odéon A crossroads of sorts is ruled over by a great pigeon-christened bronze of Georges-Jacques Danton. This Revolutionary leader's statements such as "We need audacity, more audacity, audacity forever. . . " cost him his head. He was sent to the guillotine by Robespierre in 1794. ♦ At Rues Monsieur-le-Prince and de l'Odéon. Métro: Odéon

On Carrefour de l'Odéon:

Christian Tortu After eight years, Tortu is still one of the hottest florists in town, creating opulent and original designs with flowers and vegetables. Garden furniture is also sold. ♦ M-Sa. 6 Carrefour de l'Odéon. 01.43.26.02.56

145 Rue St-André-des-Arts This eclectic little street seems more like a pedestrian mall. There are always guitar duos here doing imitations of Simon and Garfunkel. ♦ Between Pl St-Michel and Rue Mazarine. Métro: Odéon

145 Le Mazet Street musicians and professional pinball players frequent this down-and-out bar. You know the scene: beer-foamed mustaches, dogs underfoot, and a pall of cigarette smoke in the air. If you choose to slum here, watch your billfold. ♦ Daily 10AM-2AM. No credit cards accepted. 61 Rue St-André-des-Arts (at Cour du Commerce-St-André). 01.43.54.68.81. Métro: Odéon

145 Cour du Commerce-St-André Built in 1776, the city's first covered shopping mall was a hive of activity during the Revolution and inspired 17 other *passages* that sprang up on the Right Bank in the 19th century. Through the windows at **No. 4,** you can glimpse the remains of one of the towers in the city wall. At **No. 8** in 1789, Marat printed revolutionary exhortations in his inflammatory journal *L'Ami du Peuple.* Nearby, a German carpenter named Schmidt patiently perfected the guillotine (named after Dr. Guillotin, who recommended this apparatus for decapitation as a humane means of execution). Schmidt practiced on sheep, and the street ran red with the blood of the unfortunate beasts. It was also here that the artist Balthus had a studio and painted his famous picture *Le Passage du Commerce St-André* in 1954 (don't look for the shop with the golden key in the painting; it has long since been abandoned). ◆ 59-61 Rue St-André-des-Arts (between Rues de l'Eperon and de l'Ancienne-Comédie). Métro: Odéon

Within the Cour du Commerce-St-André:

Monsieur Baudrillart If you decide to have your Paris journal re-covered in leather, the bookbinding shop of M. Baudrillart is the place to go. ◆ M-F. 01.46.33.19.88

A La Cour de Rohan ★★$ This British tearoom is decorated in garden-fresh whites and greens and offers lobster bisque; broiled goat cheese on toast; savory tarts; toothsome cakes, scones, and crumbles; exotic teas; and a 17th-century heirloom recipe for spicy marmalade. No smoking allowed. ◆ M-Th, Su lunch and afternoon tea; F-Sa lunch, afternoon tea, and dinner; closed last two weeks of August. 01.43.25.79.67

146 La Datcha des Arts ★$$ The proprietor of this Central European restaurant keeps a guitar on the wall for those who prefer their own singing to the piped-in mazurkas. Start with borscht, lemon vodka, and a dollop of beluga caviar, then move on to the *assiette Datcha* (a plate of Danish salmon, sprats, salmon roe spread, eggplant caviar, and three kinds of Baltic herring with fresh blintzes). Vodka, blintzes, and salads are also available to go. ◆ Daily lunch and dinner. 56 Rue St-André-des-Arts (between Rues des Grands-Augustins and Andre-Mazet). 01.46.33.29.25. Métro: Odéon

146 St-André-des-Arts $ A friendly staff runs this comfortable, modest 35-room *pension.* There's no restaurant. ◆ 66 Rue St-André-des-Arts (between Rues des Grands-Augustins and Mazet). 01.43.26.96.16; fax 01.43.29.73.34. Métro: Odéon

147 Jacques Cagna ★★★$$$$ In his elegant old inn, Cagna features traditional French cuisine with a nouvelle flourish. The prices are weighty, but the sauces are light and the vegetables are treated with the gentleness

they deserve. Specialties include asparagus, lobster, and wild mushrooms in puff pastry; poached turbot in hollandaise sauce with puréed peas; Scottish beef fillet with Périgord truffles; duck with red Burgundy and orange; veal sweetbreads with almonds and herbs; and a layered meringue and raspberry cake. The wine cellar stocks 60,000 bottles in 550 varieties. ◆ M-F lunch and dinner; Sa dinner two nights per month September through October; closed holidays, in August, and one week at Christmas. Reservations required. 14 Rue des Grands-Augustins (at Rue Christine). 01.43.26.49.39. Métro: Odéon

147 Relais Christine $$$$ A 16th-century monastery was converted into this plush, well-run, fashionable hotel in 1980. It offers 51 rooms with either modern or antique furnishings as well as single or split-level apartments, some of which have luxurious marble bathrooms and access to a secluded courtyard. The basement breakfast room alone is worth the visit to this hotel (there's no restaurant). ◆ 3 Rue Christine (between Rues des Grands-Augustins and Dauphine). 01.43.26.71.80; fax 01.43.26.89.38. Métro: Odéon

147 5 Rue Christine After being ignominiously kicked out of their apartment on Rue de Fleurus, Gertrude Stein and Alice B. Toklas moved here in 1938. During the war, they fled to the countryside; in their absence, 5 Rue Christine was visited by the Gestapo, who attached a note to one of Stein's Picasso paintings reading "Jewish trash, good for burning." Stein died on 19 July 1946, and Toklas lived on here for another 18 years. The two women are buried side by side in the **Père-Lachaise Cemetery.** ◆ Between Rues des Grands-Augustins and Dauphine. Métro: Odéon

RESTAURANT
La Rôtisserie d'en face
JACQUES CAGNA

148 La Rôtisserie d'en Face ★★★$$ Across the street from Jacques Cagna's famous namesake restaurant is his unpretentious bistro, where good, simple meals can be enjoyed in an agreeable setting. The menu features meats cooked on the rotisserie—chicken served with mashed potatoes, rabbit with rosemary, and Scottish lamb with thyme. Cagna's mother has contributed family recipes, including *joues de cochon aux carottes et pommes fondantes,* which translates inelegantly as pig cheeks with carrots and mashed potatoes. For dessert, the specialty is *vacherin glacé au caramel et noix,* a cheese ice cream with caramel and walnuts; in addition, the bistro's chocolate mousse and crème brûlée rival the best. ♦ M-F lunch and dinner; Sa-Su dinner. Reservations recommended. 2 Rue Christine (at Rues des Grands-Augustins). 01.43.26.40.98. Métro: Odéon

148 Action Christine Two adjacent revival movie houses keep aficionados of Hitchcock and Lubitsch, as well as fans of Bogie and Bacall classics, happy. ♦ Daily. 4 Rue Christine and 10 Rue des Grands-Augustins. 01.43.29.11.30. Métro: Odéon

149 7 Rue des Grands-Augustins From 1936 to 1955, Pablo Picasso lived in this imposing house, where he painted *Guernica* in 1937. His friends Gerald and Sara Murphy, the quintessential American expatriates in the 1920s, had an apartment in the pink building around the block on the Quai des Grands-Augustins. It was Picasso who got them work painting sets for Diaghilev and the Ballet Russe. They were also the models Fitzgerald used for Dick and Nicole Diver in *Tender Is the Night.* ♦ Between Rue de Savoie and Quai des Grands-Augustins. Métros: Odéon, St-Michel

149 Quai des Grands-Augustins In 1313, one of the first *quais* (embankments) in Paris was constructed next to the monastery of St. Augustine. Hundreds of years later, Thomas Jefferson idled away many an afternoon here, browsing along this stretch of riverside, which is still known for its book- and print-sellers. ♦ Between Pl St-Michel and Rue Dauphine. Métros: Odéon, St-Michel

149 Lapérouse ★★★$$$ This Old World quayside restaurant is housed in the former town mansion of the Comte de Bruillevert, Master of Waters and Forests under Louis XIV. In 1766 it was transformed by Lefèvre, the king's official wine merchant, into a public meeting place that was renowned for the quality of wines it served. In 1840 the establishment was named in honor of the French navigator Lapérouse, and thrived as a watering hole for such literary figures as Guy de Maupassant, Emile Zola, Alexandre Dumas, Victor Hugo, and Colette. Today chef Guy Krenzer is attracting multitudes of gourmands to this elegant classic with culinary sonnets such as *brochette de langoustines, tournedos Rossini* (a classic dish of beef and foie gras), and heavenly soufflés. ♦ M-F lunch and dinner; Sa dinner. Reservations required. 51 Quai des Grands-Augustins (at Rue des Grands-Augustins). 01.43.26.68.04. Métros: Odéon, St-Michel

150 46 Rue St-André-des-Arts Sixty years ago, in a building housing two bookshops, e. e. cummings rented a single room. The building still has both residential and commercial space. ♦ Between Rues Séguier and des Grands-Augustins. Métros: Odéon, St-Michel

151 28 Rue St-André-des-Arts In *Satori in Paris,* Jack Kerouac described pleasant evenings spent here at what was then a bar called **La Gentilhommière** (ca. 1962) and is now a pizzeria. ♦ At Rue Gît-le-Cœur. Métro: St-Michel

152 Allard ★★$$ One of the old-time, honest bistros, this place has two zinc bars, sawdust-strewn floors, and a rotating selection of *plats du jour* as perennial as the clientele. The Allard family, who played host here to the Aga Khan, Brigitte Bardot, and Georges Pompidou, have sold the restaurant, but it still retains much of the old feeling. ♦ M-Sa lunch and dinner; closed in August. Reservations required. 41 Rue St-André-des-Arts (at Rue de l'Eperon). 01.43.26.48.23. Métros: Odéon, St-Michel

A Matter of Taste

The prospect of dining out in Paris conjures the delicious dilemma of selecting from a menu offering crepes, bouillabaise, *boeuf bourguignon,* and *canard* (duck) *à l'orange*, all standard fare in most restaurants. But beware: That same menu can be a minefield for the finicky diner. Here are some specialties better passed up by more sensitive palates. Those with adventurous appetites, dig in.

Andouillette: sausage made with large chunks of pig intestines

Boudin: sausage or blood pudding

Cervelles: brains

Chasse: venison

Foie: liver

Gésiers: gizzards

Grenouille: frog

Ris de veau: veal sweetbreads

Rognons: kidneys

Tripe: stomach tissue

153 Maroussia ★$ This Russian tea salon has a drawing-room atmosphere in which Chekhov, Tolstoy—or any princeling for that matter—would have been comfortable. Slavic hors d'oeuvres such as borscht, *tarama* (salmon roe spread), caviar, blintzes, and smoked salmon are served, along with cheesecake. It's the perfect spot for afternoon tea or a quick meal. ♦ M-F lunch and dinner; Sa dinner. 9 Rue de l'Eperon (between Rues Serpente and Suger). 01.43.54.87.50. Métros: Odéon, St-Michel

154 Rue de l'Ecole de Médecine During the Revolution, Jean-Paul Marat founded the biting journal *L'Ami du Peuple* and was forced to hide in the Paris sewers. The radical democrat was elected to the National Convention three years later with the support of Danton and Robespierre but soon learned that you can't please all of *le peuple* all of the time. On 13 July 1793 Marat was stabbed while taking a bath in his house on this street. His killer was Girondist Charlotte Corday, who had hidden a knife in her bodice. For a surprisingly ungory depiction of the assassination see David's painting in the **Louvre**'s **Salle des Etats**. ♦ Between Blvds St-Michel and St-Germain. Métro: Odéon

155 La Maison de la Lozère ★★$$ This crowded canteen with bare wooden tables is a trip straight to the Lozère region in France's heartland. Try one of the robust regional specialties such as *confit de porc* (pork confit), mutton tripe vinaigrette, and *aligot d'Aubrac* (a heavenly concoction of mashed potatoes, garlic, and cantal cheese, served only on Thursdays), or snack on slices of country ham, herb sausage, and *bleu d'Auvergne* cheese. ♦ Tu-Sa lunch and dinner; closed mid-July through mid-August and the last week of December. Reservations recommended. 4 Rue Hautefeuille (between Rue des Poitevins and Pl St-André-des-Arts). 01.43.54.26.64. Métro: St-Michel

156 Rue Gît-le-Cœur The name means "Where the heart lies," a French phrase that's a good deal more romantic than the street's preceding moniker: Gilles-le-Cook. **Nos. 1-9** were originally one mansion, built in the 16th century by François I for his love at the time, the Duchesse d'Etampes. ♦ Between Rue St-André-des-Arts and Quai des Grands-Augustins. Métro: St-Michel

On Rue Gît-le-Cœur:

> For the French, *la politesse* is a way of life, so it is best to respect their custom and address them formally: For example, say "*Bonjour Monsieur,*" "*Pardon Madame,*" and "*S'il vous plaît Madame,*" rather than simply "*Bonjour,*" "*Pardon,*" or "*S'il vous plaît.*"

Relais Hôtel de Vieux Paris $$$ In the 1950s this was a pay-as-you-go crash pad for the American Beat generation. John Dos Passos, e. e. cummings, and William S. Burroughs all hung out here at various times and discussed what existentialist effronteries might be perpetrated next. In 1991 it was renovated into a comfortable 20-room hotel and its beatnik atmosphere has now given way to a more traditional charm. There's no restaurant. ♦ No. 9 (at Rue de l'Hirondelle). 01.43.54.41.66; fax 01.43.26.00.15

157 Caveau de la Bolée ★$$ A wooden door leads into a 13th-century dungeonlike cavern filled with late-night chess and checkers players. Dinner is served upstairs starting at 9PM. Downstairs a cabaret act is performed Monday through Saturday nights starting at 10:30PM. ♦ Daily dinner and late-night snacks. 25 Rue de l'Hirondelle (between Pl St-Michel and Rue Gît-le-Cœur). 01.43.54.62.20. Métro: St-Michel

158 L'Ecluse ★★$ This wine bar overlooking the Seine offers a spectrum of 70 reds (18 of which can be ordered by the glass). Bordeaux is the specialty, a wine that goes wonderfully with the plates of smoked goose, carpaccio, and chavignol crottin cheese served here. ♦ Daily lunch and dinner until 2AM. Reservations recommended. 15 Quai des Grands-Augustins (between Pl St-Michel and Rue Gît-le-Cœur). 01.46.33.58.74. Métro: St-Michel. Also at: 64 Rue François-1er (between Rues Lincoln and Quentin-Bauchart). 01.47.20.77.09. Métro: George-V; 15 Pl de la Madeleine (between Blvd Malesherbes and Passage de la Madeleine). 01.42.65.34.69. Métro: Madeleine

159 Boulevard St-Michel This was one of the great boulevards of Baron Haussmann, scythed through the Left Bank from the edge of the Seine in a broad, tree-lined swath. The street was named in 1867 in memory of the ancient chapel of **St-Michel** that stood here once upon a time. ♦ Between Ave de l'Observatoire and Pl St-Michel. Métro: St-Michel

159 Place St-Michel A relatively nonviolent crowd of students, bikers, and drug dealers gathers here on hot Saturday nights. The passable restaurants around the square cater to pizza and souvlaki eaters. ♦ At Quais St-Michel and des Grands-Augustins, and Blvd St-Michel. Métro: St-Michel

On Place St-Michel:

Fontaine St-Michel (St. Michael Fountain) In 1860 Gabriel Davioud designed this 75-foot-high and 15-foot-wide spouting monster. The bronze of St. Michael fighting the dragon is by Duret.

159 Le St-Séverin ★$ The best people-watching perch in Place St-Michel has the famous Berthillon ice cream. The hot choco-late isn't bad either. ♦ Daily 7AM-2AM. No. 3 (at Rue de la Huchette). 01.43.54.19.36

159 St-Michel Métro This is one of the Art Nouveau métro entrances designed by **Hector Guimard** in 1900. ♦ Pl St-André-des-Arts (at Rue Danton)

160 Rue de la Harpe Named after Reginald the Harper, this medieval street, along with Rue de la Huchette, is one of the city's oldest. A youthful air emanates from the cheap restaurants jammed with students along this bustling byway. ♦ Between Blvd St-Germain and Rue de la Huchette. Métro: St-Michel

161 Rue de la Huchette In medieval times this ancient thoroughfare was called Street of Roasters because it had a plethora of barbecue pits. Couscous and shish kebab joints continue the carnivorous tradition by roasting whole lambs and pigs in their front windows. You can always find cheap, sometimes risky, street food here. ♦ Between Pls du Petit-Pont and St-Michel. Métro: St-Michel

161 28 Rue de la Huchette Outside the **Hôtel Mt-Blanc** is a plaque commemorating a World War II Resistance fighter in the Rainbow unit that reads "Here fell Jean-Albert Bouillard, dead in the course of duty, killed by the Gestapo 17 May 1944 at 20 hours." ♦ Between Rue Xavier-Privas and Pl St-Michel. Métro: St-Michel

161 10 Rue de la Huchette For several months here in 1795, a young brigadier general languished in a sparsely decorated back room. Unemployed, unloved, and (he thought) dying of hunger, he saw no hope for the future. Soon thereafter, he dispersed a mob by firing grapeshot into its midst, and from then on Napoléon Bonaparte was never ignored. ♦ Between Rue Xavier-Privas and Pl St-Michel. Métro: St-Michel

162 Théâtre de la Huchette Ever since Eugène Ionesco finished them in the mid-1950s, two of his plays, *The Bald Soprano* and *The Lesson,* have been running nonstop at this 85-seat theater. ♦ Box office: daily. 23 Rue de la Huchette (between Rues Xavier-Privas and de la Harpe). 01.43.26.38.99. Métro: St-Michel

163 Caveau de la Huchette This is another crowded, dingy jazz cellar on a street that once rang with bebop. ♦ Cover; student discount available. M-Th, Su 9:30PM-2:30AM;

F 9:30PM-3AM; Sa 9:30PM-4AM. 5 Rue de la Huchette (between Pl du Petit-Pont and Rue Xavier-Privas). 01.43.26.65.05. Métro: St-Michel

164 Rue du Chat-qui-Pêche The Street of the Fishing Cat, most likely named after a medieval fishmonger, is one of the narrowest and, arguably, grungiest alleys in Paris. ♦ Between Rue de la Huchette and Quai St-Michel. Métro: St-Michel

165 St-Séverin This lesser-known edifice, which was constructed around 1220 on the burial site of a sixth-century hermit named Séverin, is the official church of the **University of Paris**. Recognized as the city's richest example of Flamboyant Gothic architecture, it was expanded between 1414 and 1520 with a bullet-shaped nave, a gaggle of gargoyles, and a five-aisled symphony of ribbed vaulting and stained glass. In 1673, the distinguished **Jules Hardouin-Mansart** tried his hand at enhancing the church, adding a small communion hall.

Don't miss the double ambulatory's slender medieval columns that shoot into vaulted arches, creating an effect that Joris-Karl Huysmans compared to being in a palm grove. The modern windows are by Jean Bazaine, the French abstract painter who created the mosaics for the **UNESCO** building and the **Cluny–La Sorbonne** métro station. Saint-Saëns and Fauré performed on the 18th-century Rococo organ in front of the west window; today the organ is frequently used for recitals. ♦ Rue des Prêtres-St-Séverin (at Rue St-Séverin). Métro: St-Michel

166 Rue de la Parcheminerie This narrow street was crammed with scribes, copyists, and parchment peddlers in the Middle Ages. ♦ Between Rues St-Jacques and de la Harpe. Métro: St-Michel

Bests

Philippe Uzzan
Gallery Owner

Jardin du Luxembourg—in December at 5PM, in April at 10AM.

La Hune's bookshelves.

Being stuck in front of the **Bonpoint** children's store display.

Any kind of terrace of any apartment in any district.

Doing the **Rue du Pré-aux-Clercs** stores—except on Saturday.

Eggs at **Coffee Parisien** and duck at **La Poule au Pot.**

And all that I can discover without a tourist guide.

Eiffel Tower/ Invalides

Eiffel Tower/Invalides

Overshadowed by the lacy mast of the **Tour Eiffel (Eiffel Tower)** and the sparkling gold dome of the **Hôtel des Invalides** (under which rest the remains of Napoléon Bonaparte), this district is one of pomp and grandeur. But nestled among the high-profile monuments are intimate streets lined with fancy food shops that cater to the residents of this upscale *quartier,* and some of the best restaurants in the city.

The following route encompasses two sectors bisected by the **Esplanade des Invalides.** The area to the east of **Les Invalides** is home to the **Assemblée Nationale**, situated in the elegant **Place du Palais-Bourbon,** and is scattered with stately 17th- and 18th-century mansions, including the **Hôtel de Biron,** where the famous sculptor Rodin lived and worked. The mansion is now the **Musée Rodin.**

The affluent neighborhood to the west of the esplanade is dominated by the symbol of Paris, the **Eiffel Tower,** which forms part of the grand axis from the **Ecole Militaire,** along the **Parc du Champ-de-Mars,** and across the river to the **Palais de Chaillot.** To learn some of the secrets of this neighborhood, meander in and out of the side streets off **Rue St-Dominique,** which are lined with exceptional restaurants, small antiques shops, Art Nouveau apartment houses, candy shops, and *pâtisseries;* this is also the site of the city's ritziest street market.

Keep in mind that much of this area shuts down in August, when the French take their annual vacation, and many of the restaurants here are closed for Saturday lunch and all day Sunday year-round.

To begin your explorations, set your watch by the clock over the courtyard facade of the **Assemblée Nationale** in the Place du Palais-Bourbon and grab a breakfast of coffee and croissants alongside publishers, députés (parliament members), and diplomats at the **Brasserie Bourbon** or in the upstairs tea salon at **Rollet Pradier.** If it's Saturday, you can start with a morning tour of the **Assemblée Nationale,** France's parliament building. Otherwise, head down the **Rue de Bourgogne,** taking detours onto **Rue de Varenne, Rue de Grenelle,** and **Rue St-Dominique** to view the neighborhood's 17th- and 18th-century mansions, including the **Hôtel Matignon** and the **Hôtel de Noirmoutiers.** You may only be able to catch a glimpse of these fancy former residences, however; many of them are now ministries and embassies sequestered behind stone portals and off-limits to the public. Upon reaching the **Hôtel de Biron,** spend the remainder of the morning in the **Musée Rodin;** be sure to take some time to stroll in the garden among some of the sculptor's best-known works.

This district's superb restaurants offer lunch possibilities to fit any pocketbook. Indulge in a meal at one of the neighborhood's elegant and pricey establishments such as **Arpège,** or cross the Esplanade des Invalides to **Paul Minchelli** or **Le Divellec.** Less expensive but equally delicious alternatives are lunch at **La Boule d'Or** or the classic family-run bistro **Thoumieux.** Those who want to save their three-star appetites (and budgets) for dinner could pick up a light bite at **Café Lunch,** or a moderately priced meal at **Chez Gilda's** or **Au Petit Tonneau.**

Spend the early afternoon touring the **Hôtel des Invalides,** a monumental 17th-century complex commissioned by Louis XIV to house the nation's veterans. This ensemble of buildings includes the magnificent Baroque **Eglise du Dôme** (Dome Church), which crowns the burial place of Napoléon Bonaparte, and the **Musée de l'Armée,** with its large collection of military paraphernalia.

Wander west along the Rue St-Dominique and notice its distinctly different character as compared to its sister leg to the east. With the distant **Eiffel Tower** beckoning as your final destination, investigate the side streets such as **Rue Surcouf, Rue Malar,** and **Rue Augereau.** Visit the **Musée Seita** (Tobacco Museum), which chronicles the history of the weed in Western Europe. Peruse the city's classiest street market along the **Rue Cler** and take in the beautiful displays of produce, baked goods, cheese, charcuterie, and flowers. If hunger sets in, stop for a coffee and *pain au chocolat* at **Jean Millet** or stroll a little farther for tea and scones at the lovely *salon de thé* **Les Deux Abeilles.**

As you reach the vicinity of the **Parc du Champ-de-Mars** stroll among some of the small side streets, which play peek-a-boo with the **Eiffel Tower,** noticing the elegant apartment houses along the way. Cross the **Pont d'Iéna** to reach the **Palais de Chaillot,** which encompasses four museums, among them the **Musée des Monuments Français** and the **Musée du Cinéma Henri Langlois.** From the building's terrace you will enjoy a striking view of the **Eiffel Tower,** sweeping across the **Champ-de-Mars** to the Ecole Militaire, the military school that numbers Napoléon Bonaparte among its most famous cadets.

Dining spots abound in this neighborhood; you could end your day with dinner at **Vin sur Vin**, or really celebrate Paris with a table at **Le Jules Verne** within the weightless filigree of the **Eiffel Tower.** Linger after dinner over a good Cognac and ponder the glorious nighttime perspective of the City of Light.

1 Palais Bourbon/Assemblée Nationale

The home of the French parliament was constructed in 1728 for the Duchess of Bourbon, one of Louis XIV's daughters. In 1807 **Bernard Poyet** designed the mansion's north facade for Napoléon in the Greek-Revival style, to mirror the **Madeleine** across the river; it now houses the **Assemblée Nationale** (the lower house of the French Parliament). Nearly 600 deputies convene in a chamber decorated in crimson and gold and adorned with a large Napoleonic eagle. Even the president of France is denied entrance into this exclusive club's assemblies. Ordinary people, however, can watch sessions from a public gallery, provided they have a pass signed by a deputy. If you tour the building, don't miss Delacroix's allegorical *History of Civilization* on the library ceiling. ♦ Free. Guided tours: Sa 10AM, 2PM, and 3PM; identification necessary; groups must call in advance. To arrange a group tour or to attend an assembly debate (October through June), call the administrative office of the **Assemblée Nationale** (01.42.97.64.08). Entrance on Quai d'Orsay (between Rues Aristide-Briand and Robert-Esnault-Pelterie). 01.40.63.64.08, 01.40.63.60.00. Métro: Assemblée Nationale

2 Place du Palais-Bourbon

This square boasts an elegant ensemble of Louis XVI buildings constructed in 1776. The *place* is dominated by the main entrance facade of the **Palais Bourbon** and a view of its inner courtyard. The facade and courtyard are the only surviving elements of the original mansion. ♦ Rues de Bourgogne and de l'Université. Métro: Assemblée Nationale

On Place du Palais-Bourbon:

Brasserie Bourbon

Brasserie Bourbon ★★$$ The seasonally changing Alsatian and fish specialties served here are appreciated by the politicians from the **Assemblée Nationale** who lunch in the comfortable dining room and on the terrace. A winter meal could start with *moules marinières* (mussels steamed in white wine) or foie gras soufflé, followed by sirloin steak with *frites* or *saucisson sec de montagne* (dry mountain sausage) and sauerkraut. In spring and summer diners might start with bouillabaisse or salmon and spinach salad, followed by *coquilles St-Jacques à la Provençale* (scallops in a sauce of olive oil, garlic, onions, tomatoes, and herbs) or shrimp kabobs grilled with lime. A good bottle of Gewürztraminer or Riesling will bring out the best in any of these dishes.

♦ M-Sa breakfast, lunch, tea, and dinner; Su breakfast, lunch, and tea. Reservations recommended. No. 1 (at Rue de l'Université). 01.45.51.58.27

Marie-Pierre Boitard Silver napkin rings, a tiny silver escargot-shaped case, a silver baby rattle, and fine Hungarian china are displayed on tables draped with fancy brocades and embroidered fabrics and sold by equally resplendent, but somewhat serious, saleswomen. ♦ M-Sa. Nos. 9-11 (at Rue de Bourgogne). 01.47.05.13.30

3 Rue de Bourgogne Opened in 1719, this street, named for Louis Duc de Bourgogne (1682-1712), the son of Louis XIV, originally extended to the quay, but was modified in 1778 when the Place du Palais-Bourbon was created. ♦ Between Rue de Varenne and Pl du Palais-Bourbon. Métros: Assemblée Nationale, Varenne

3 Hôtel Bourgogne et Montana $$$ This elegant hotel's name has nothing to do with the state of Montana; its previous owner hailed from Montana, Switzerland. The refined decoration of the 33 rooms is in keeping with the upscale neighborhood. The breakfast room (there's no restaurant) features handsome black leather upholstery and crisp white tablecloths. ♦ 3 Rue de Bourgogne (at Pl du Palais-Bourbon). 01.45.51.20.22; fax 01.45.56.11.98. Métro: Assemblée Nationale

3 Chez Marius ★★$$$ At lunch important-looking people speak in hushed tones over *soupe de poissons* (fish soup), *pavé de saumon poêlé à la niçoise* (salmon steak in a light tomato and garlic sauce), bouillabaisse, grilled lobster, or *poulet de Bresse rôtie* (roasted Bresse chicken). In contrast to this seafood restaurant's subdued beige interior, the windows are covered with enough stickers to rival the rear window of a Winnebego; the various labels and logos represent the many guidebooks and organizations that have given the place their stamp of approval. ♦ M-F lunch and dinner; Sa dinner; closed in August. Reservations recommended. 5 Rue de Bourgogne (between Rue St-Dominique and Pl du Palais-Bourbon). 01.45.51.79.42. Métro: Assemblée Nationale

4 Rollet Pradier This is the place that provides the elegant trays of canapés and petits fours at those fancy seventh-arrondissement soirees. Fortunately, you don't have to wait for an invitation to try some of their salmon quiche, langoustine salad with avocado crème, *canard à l'orange,* chicken with *morilles* (morels), chocolate and raspberry Sacher torte, or apricot soufflé; at this *traiteur* (caterer) and *pâtissier* you can order dishes to go or take a table in the upstairs *salon de thé* and sample until you're satiated. ♦ M-Sa. 6 Rue de Bourgogne (between Rue St-Dominique and Pl du Palais-Bourbon). 01.45.51.78.36. Métro: Assemblée Nationale

4 Galerie Naïla de Monbrison If you're looking for a gift or souvenir that's out of the ordinary, you'll find it in this small, narrow jewelry shop and art gallery designed by **Patrick Naggar** and **Dominique Lachevsky.** Unassuming materials such as glass, particle board, oxidized bronze, and lead are fashioned into well-crafted display cases that contrast with and complement the precious materials of the jewelry they contain. Mme de Monbrison offers a superb collection of ethnographic jewelry, and drawers hold bounties of colorful hand-crafted trinkets from Asia, Africa, Siberia, Turkey, and North America. The ethnographic pieces marry well with the contemporary art jewelry that is featured in the gallery's expositions, which change four times a year and are often organized around a theme such as the four elements or the cross. ♦ Tu-Sa; closed in August. 6 Rue de Bourgogne (between Rue St-Dominique and Pl du Palais-Bourbon). 01.47.05.11.15. Métro: Assemblée Nationale

5 Ombeline Maud Frizon has changed her identity: She sold the name of her famous line of haute-couture shoes; switched to her married name, Maud de Marco; and opened this new shop. However, her stunning and creative footwear still has the same high quality and wild heel shapes that made her original line of shoes famous. ♦ M-Sa. 17 Rue de Bourgogne (between Rues de Grenelle and Las-Cases). 01.47.05.56.78. Métros: Assemblée Nationale, Varenne

6 Carole de Villarcy At Carole de Villarcy's tiny boutique you can find top-quality women's haute couture (including clothing by Chanel, Guy Laroche, Yves Saint Laurent, and other designers) from seasons past at a fraction of the original prices. ♦ M afternoon; Tu-Sa; closed in August. 27 Rue de Bourgogne (between Rues de Grenelle and Las-Cases). 01.45.51.28.38. Métros: Assemblée Nationale, Varenne

7 Club des Poètes ★★$ *"La Poésie est vivante. Vive la Poésie!"* (Poetry is alive. Long live Poetry!) proclaims Jean-Pierre Rosnay, well-known French poet and owner of this dimly lit, cozy restaurant, which holds poetry readings in the evenings. Actors read works by Walt Whitman, Lawrence Ferlinghetti, and Jack Kerouac, while diners savor terrine de *lapin* (rabbit pâté), *salade Drômoise* (with tomatoes, St. Marcellin cheese, and walnuts), *grillade St-Tropez* (beef with tomatoes and herbs), and *gâteau de Sarah* (chocolate cake from an old family recipe). Rosnay's wife and son are both poets, and together the family puts out a poetry journal three times a year, runs a radio station devoted to poetry, and started the Festival of Poetry in Paris. Visitors from the States will enjoy a warm welcome here; Rosnay, a resistance fighter during World War II, loves Americans. ♦ M-Sa lunch and dinner; closed in August. Reservations recommended. 30 Rue de Bourgogne (between Rues de Grenelle and St-Dominique). 01.47.05.06.03. Métros: Assemblée Nationale, Varenne

8 Trenta Quattro ★★★$$ Charming Francesca Ciardi serves delectable Italian fare in her cozy dining room. Ricotta and spinach ravioli, risotto with apples and watercress, and veal in white wine or lemon vodka sauce are all worthy entrées. If you have any room left at the end of the meal, share the rich zabaglione and blueberries with your dinner companion. ♦ M-Sa lunch and dinner; Su dinner; closed Saturday in August. Reservations recommended. 34 Rue de Bourgogne (at Rue de Grenelle). 01.45.55.80.75. Métros: Varenne, Assemblée Nationale

9 Hôtel de Varenne $$ The entrance to this tranquil hotel is through a flower-filled courtyard with white iron garden furniture. Guests staying in the 24 fresh, pretty rooms can have breakfast alfresco in the spring and summer. There's no restaurant. ♦ 44 Rue de Bourgogne (between Rues de Varenne and de Grenelle). 01.45.51.45.55; fax 01.45.51.86.63. Métro: Varenne

---

The most famous and celebrated of French monuments, the Eiffel Tower, traditionally gets a new coat of paint every seven years—no small task considering its size. Twenty-five "Alpine painters" and 40 tons of paint are necessary for the operation, which takes about 18 months to complete.

10 Le Garde Manger ★★$$ In the back of this little wine and gourmet-food boutique you can take a table alongside *députés* from the **Assemblée National** and staff members of the **Musée Rodin** to savor a lunch of foie gras or smoked salmon from the shop's shelves. Changing *plats du jour* might include *canard aux lentilles* (duck with lentils), *coquilles St-Jacques* (scallops), and sautéed veal, and desserts such as crème brûlée and *tarte aux pommes* (apple tart). Try one of the fine wines—perhaps the Cahors Château Quatre 1989 or the Côtes-de-Catillon Château Cap de Faugères 1990—with your repast. ♦ Shop: M-F until 8PM. Restaurant: M-F lunch. Closed in August. Reservations required. 51 Rue de Bourgogne (between Rues de Varenne and de Grenelle). 01.45.50.23.93. Métro: Varenne

10 Ariane This narrow shop, piled with dusty cushions, carpets, and tapestries, is the sort of place where you might find an unexpected treasure. The lovely white-haired Ariane has been restoring tapestries and carpets—including many 17th- and 18th-century pieces—for more than 70 years. Her clients include many of Paris's museums and foreign embassies, and some folks from as far away as New York and Washington will trust their tapestry and furniture only to her. She also sells many pieces; at any given time she might have pillows made with original Gobelins tapestry, needlepoint reproductions of Renoir paintings, or tapestries depicting the story of the lady and the unicorn. Her atelier, full of the wools, dyes, and potions that bring life back to worn-out weaving, can be glimpsed at the rear of the shop. ♦ M-Sa. 53 Rue de Bourgogne (between Rues de Varenne and de Grenelle). 01.47.05.18.44. Métro: Varenne

11 Rue de Varenne The name of this street, like that of Rue de Grenelle, evolved over time from the word *garenne* (rabbit warren); Rue de Varenne was laid out in 1605 along a *garenne* belonging to the abbey of **St-Germain-des-Prés.** Today, the street is lined with ministries and foreign embassies housed in attractive old mansions. ♦ Between Rue de la Chaise and Blvd des Invalides. Métro: Varenne

Arpège

11 L'Arpège ★★★★$$$$ Daring but respectful of tradition, young chef Alain Passard executes a first-rate menu that includes *crème de truffe aux oeufs et parmesan* (scrambled eggs with parmesan cheese and truffle cream), sweet-and-sour Brittany lobster with rosemary, and *canard Louise Passard* (duck with orange and date purée and lemon conserve). Desserts include a heavenly lemon soufflé as well as *feuilletage au chocolat* (chocolate cake), and the wine list is one of the best in Paris. The skillful servers may add the final touches to dishes at your table. The mood of the small dining room is modern and subdued, with low lighting, wood paneling, sumptuous carpets, and classical-style nude figurines in crystal. ♦ M-F lunch and dinner; Su dinner. Reservations required. 84 Rue de Varenne (between Rue de Bourgogne and Blvd des Invalides). 01.45.51.47.33. Métro: Varenne

 **Musée Rodin**

12 Musée Rodin The **Hôtel de Biron**, which houses this museum, is a Regency masterpiece of columns and pediments originally built in 1730 by **Jean Aubert** and **Jacques-Ange Gabriel** for a wealthy wigmaker named Abraham Peyrenc. In 1753 it was bought by the Maréchal-Duc de Biron, who indulged quite a passion for gardening in the years before he went to the guillotine during the Reign of Terror; he spent 200,000 *livres* each year on tulips alone. During an unfortunate stint as a convent school, the *hôtel's* gold-and-white wood paneling was ripped out by the Mother Superior, who deemed it too Baroque and materialistic.

The **Hôtel de Biron** was subsequently subdivided into a cluster of artists' studios. In 1908, Auguste Rodin (1840-1917) moved in and stayed until his death. His neighbors in the *hôtel* included Rainer Maria Rilke, Jean Cocteau, Isadora Duncan, and Henri Matisse.

After viewing the ground-floor exhibits of Rodin works, bear left and gradually spiral upstairs. The works are displayed chronologically, beginning with Rodin's academic paintings and his sketches in both classic and modern modes. Notice that Rodin usually depicts only right hands; the one exception to this rule is *The Hand of the Devil,* which shows Satan's left hand crushing humanity.

The room containing Rodin's *Sculptor with his Muse* also displays several works by Camille Claudel, the talented sculptor who became Rodin's muse, model, and lover at the age of 17. Her portrait of Rodin, executed in 1888 at the peak of their affair, when he was nearly 50, reveals a rather cold man with small eyes.

Upstairs is a series of studies of Balzac created in the early 1890s. In one of them, a bronze, the writer stands stark naked and is 90 percent paunch. In the final version, which stands at the corner of Rue Vavin and Boulevard Montparnasse, Rodin draped Balzac in a concealing cloak.

The garden, the third largest of any of the *hôtels* in Paris (after those of the **Elysée Palace** and the **Hôtel de Matignon**), provides the setting for Rodin's best-known works. On 30 January 1937, Helen Keller visited here and was permitted to touch the sculptures with her hands. Of *The Thinker,* she said: "In every limb I felt the throes of emerging mind." Keller said the sculpture of the *Six Burghers of Calais,* who surrendered their lives to the English to save their city, was "sadder to touch than a grave." Unfortunately, this work is no longer part of the museum's collection; in 1988 a Japanese museum bought the figure for $2.5 million. ♦ Admission. Tu-Su. 77 Rue de Varenne (between Rue Barbet-de-Jouy and Blvd des Invalides). 01.44.18.61.10. Métro: Varenne

13 Hôtel de Villeroy This mansion was built in 1724 for actress Charlotte Desmarnes (1682-1753), who debuted at the age of eight at the **Comédie-Française** and performed the roles of queens and maid-servants there for more than 20 years. In the early 18th century the building served as the residence of the ambassador of Holland, then of the ambassador of England. In 1735 it was sold to the Duc de Villeroy. In 1886 a more modern building was erected behind the *hôtel,* dwarfing it. Today it houses the French **Ministry of Agriculture.** ♦ 78-80 Rue de Varenne (between Rues de Bellechase and de Bourgogne). Métro: Varenne

14 Hôtel Matignon Behind the immense porte cochere flanked by two pairs of Ionic columns is one of the most beautiful mansions in the city, built by **Jean Courtonne** in 1721. Inside are beautiful salons sumptuously decorated in period styles, the largest private garden in Paris, and a music pavilion. Former owners include Talleyrand, the statesman and diplomat who lived here from 1808 to 1811 and held infamous parties and receptions, and, later in the century, Mme Adelaïde, the sister of Louis-Philippe. Since 1958 it has been the residence of the French prime minister. It's off-limits to the public. ♦ 57 Rue de Varenne (between Rues du Bac and Vaneau). Métros: Rue du Bac, Varenne

15 Hôtel de Boisgelin This mansion was constructed in 1732 by **Jean Sylvain Cartaud,** and has been the **Italian Embassy** since 1938. ◆ 47 Rue de Varenne (between Rues du Bac and Vaneau). Métros: Rue du Bac, Varenne

16 Hôtel de Gouffier de Thoix This *hôtel particulier,* built in 1719 for the Marquise de Gouffier de Thoix, was confiscated during the Revolution and later won in a lottery by a jeweler. The family of the original owners returned to Paris in the 19th century to reclaim it. Notice the magnificent doorway surmounted by a shell carving. It is now a government administration building. ◆ 56 Rue de Varenne (between Rues du Bac and de Bellechasse). Métros: Rue du Bac, Varenne

16 Hôtel de Gallifet This handsome 1739 mansion, with an Ionic peristyle facing the interior courtyard, is now the **Italian Institute.** The building was enlarged in 1938 with the annexation of **L'Hôtel de Boisgelin,** which stood behind it at 73 Rue de Grenelle. Many of the rooms have their original decoration, and the stairwell is ornamented with false windows framed by Ionic columns and lit by a cupola. The building is closed to the public. ◆ 50 Rue de Varenne (between Rues du Bac and de Bellechasse). Métros: Rue du Bac, Varenne

17 Hôtel d'Estrées Through the courtyard of this mansion, built by **Robert de Cotte** in 1713 for the Duchesse d'Estrées, is a triangular pediment supported by three stories of pilasters. In 1896, when the building served as the **Russian Embassy,** Czar Nicolas II and the czarina lived here. It is now a government administration building. ◆ 79 Rue de Grenelle (between Rues du Bac and de Bellechasse). Métros: Rue du Bac, Varenne

17 Hôtel d'Avaray This *hôtel,* constructed in 1728 by **Jean Baptiste Le Raux,** stayed in the Avaray family for two centuries. In 1920 the government of Holland installed the **Royal Netherlands Embassy.** The garden facade has a triangular pediment with a tympanum framed by carved palm motifs. ◆ 85 Rue de Grenelle (between Rues du Bac and de Bellechasse). Métros: Rue du Bac, Varenne

18 Temple de Pentémont This chapel was built by **Constant d'Ivry** in 1750 for the **Abbaye de Pentémont,** a convent where Joséphine de Beauharnais, future wife of Napoléon, lived for several years. The convent's main buildings (some are still visible at 37-39 Rue de Bellechase) housed an aristocratic school, famous for educating young ladies from the noble families of Paris. Thomas Jefferson's daughter was a student here when he was America's ambassador to France from 1785 to 1789. ◆ 104-106 Rue de Grenelle (between Rues de St-Simon and de Bellechasse). Métros: Rue du Bac, Varenne

19 Rue St-Dominique Between 1355 and 1643 this street had nine different names; its present appellation comes from a monastery for Dominican novices that was once located here. The street originally stretched to Rue des Sts-Pères, but a large portion of it was amputated to make room for the opening of Boulevard St-Germain in 1866. Rue St-Dominique is more like two streets: The segment to the east of Esplanade des Invalides—often called St-Dominique–St-Germain—is characterized by fine *hôtels particuliers* that now hold government offices; the sector to the west of the esplanade—known as St-Dominique–Gros-Caillou—is largely a local shopping street that offers glimpses of the **Eiffel Tower** along its course. ◆ Between Blvd St-Germain and Pl du Général-Gouraud. Métros: Solférino, Invalides, Latour Maubourg

19 1 Rue St-Dominique Known as the **Hôtel de Gournay** or the **Hôtel de Tingry,** this mansion was built in 1695 by **Germain Boffrand** for the Marquis de Gournay. In 1725 it belonged to Christian-Louis de Montmorency, Duc de Luxembourg, Prince de Tingry, and one of the first owners of the **Hôtel de Matignon.** The private residence features a grand concave facade and an oval courtyard. ◆ At Blvd St-Germain. Métro: Solférino

19 3 Rue St-Dominique Dating from 1688, this mansion was at one time part of the **Dames de Bellechasse** convent. It was home to nobility in the 18th century, and a plaque commemorates chemist Jean-Baptiste Dumas, who was a resident in the 19th century. Between the ceiling of the second floor and the floor of the third was a *cachette,* used as a hiding place during *la Terreur.* It is now a government administration building. ◆ Between Blvd St-Germain and Rue de Bellechasse. Métro: Solférino

19 5 Rue St-Dominique Like its next-door neighbor, the **Hôtel de Tavannes** also was once the property of the **Dames de Bellechasse.** Sophie Soymonof, wife of the general Svetchine and known as the Russian Mme de Sévigné, held a literary salon here from 1818 to 1857 that was frequented by many distinguished personalities. Illustrator Gustave Doré, who had his atelier nearby at 27 *bis* Rue de Bellechase, lived here from 1832 until his death in 1883. The private mansion is one of the few in the city that's open to the public (albeit for a limited time). It has an elegant arched doorway surmounted by a scallop and crowned by a triangular pediment. Inside there's a fine stairwell with a wrought-iron balustrade. ◆ Open 20 August to 30 September. Between Blvd St-Germain and Rue de Bellechasse. Métro: Solférino

The exterior edges of the four supports of the Eiffel Tower describe an area of exactly one hectare (2.47 acres).

The City of Light on the Big Screen

With its dramatic buildings, beautiful boulevards, and enduring air of romance, mystery, and sophistication, Paris has an undeniable star quality. It's little wonder, then, that the city has been the setting for scores of films from the early days of the motion-picture industry to the present. The following, arranged alphabetically, are some of the movies in which Paris plays a featured role.

A Bout de Souffle (Breathless; 1959) One of the first and most influential of the French New Wave films, directed by Jean-Luc Godard, tells the story of a young car thief who kills a policeman and goes on the run with his American girlfriend. This classic stars Jean-Paul Belmondo and Jean Seberg.

Allegro Ma Troppo (1963) One night in Paris viewed through accelerated motion.

An American in Paris (1951) Directed by Vincente Minnelli and featuring music by George Gershwin, this enthusiastic MGM musical stars Gene Kelly and Leslie Caron. Many of the sets are inspired by famous French paintings.

Camille (1937) A classic MGM flick starring Greta Garbo shows Paris through the eyes of Hollywood. A dying courtesan falls for an innocent young man (Robert Taylor) who loves her.

Casque d'Or (1952) Simone Signoret, Serge Reggiani, and Claude Dauphin are featured in this tragic romance, set in the Paris slums of 1898.

Charade (1963) The city becomes the perfect setting for Audrey Hepburn and Cary Grant to fall in love in this comedy-thriller directed by Stanley Donen.

Forget Paris (1995) Debra Winger plays an American Air France employee in Paris who helps Billy Crystal find his lost luggage (his father's body) and fulfill his father's dream of being buried in Normandy. This offbeat comedy provides some memorable Paris streetscapes.

Frantic (1988) A Roman Polanski thriller features Harrison Ford as an American doctor in Paris who becomes embroiled with Arab terrorists while hunting for his kidnapped wife.

French Can-Can (1955) This Jean Renoir film explores how the can-can was launched in Paris nightclubs and features great scenes of ramshackle Paris.

French Kiss (1995) A cutesy romantic comedy set in Paris and the South of France co-stars Meg Ryan as an American hunting down her fiancé, who has run off with a young French woman, and Kevin Kline as the faux-French taxi driver who befriends her.

Funny Face (1957) Fred Astaire, Audrey Hepburn, and Kay Thompson star in the story of a fashion editor and photographer who discover a fashion model working in a bookshop. Great music, dancing, and art direction.

Gigi (1958) Based on the novel by Colette, this MGM musical is set in fin-de-siècle Paris. A young girl (Leslie Caron) is trained by her aunt (Hermione Gingold) to be a kept woman, and a dashing, rich gentleman (Louis Jourdan) falls in love with her. Delightful scenes feature 1890s Parisian haunts.

Hôtel du Nord (1938) People with problems congregate at a small hotel in Paris; with Annabella, Louis Jouvet, Jean-Pierre Aumont, and Arletty.

The Hunchback of Notre-Dame (1939) Charles Laughton and Maureen O'Hara star in the Hollywood version of the Victor Hugo novel about the deformed bell ringer of **Notre-Dame** who rescues a young Gypsy woman from her evil guardian.

Irma La Douce (1963) Shirley Maclaine and Jack Lemmon star in this saucy Billy Wilder film about a Paris policeman who falls for a prostitute and becomes her pimp. The street and cafe scenes offer classic images of Paris.

Last Tango in Paris (1972) Marlon Brando stars in this Bernardo Bertolucci film as a middle-aged man who has a doomed love affair with a Frenchwoman. The most memorable scenes take place in a Paris bathtub.

Les 400 Coups (The 400 Blows; 1959) François Truffaut's film, about an unhappy 12-year-old boy who finds himself in a detention center and then escapes and keeps running, provides a vivid portrayal of Paris street life.

Les Amants (The Lovers; 1958) This Louis Malle film starring Jeanne Moreau and Alain Cuny tells the story of the secret life in Paris of a rich wife who has a passionate romance with a young man.

Les Amants du Pont-Neuf (The Lovers of the Pont-Neuf; 1991) An artist who fears she is going blind takes to the streets and ends up on the Pont-Neuf with other down-and-out characters. This movie, directed by Léo Carax, starring Juliette Binoche, Denis Lavant, and Klaus-Michael Gruber, is one of the most expensive French films ever made because it required the construction of an elaborate set re-creating the **Pont-Neuf** and its surroundings.

Les Enfants du Paradis (1945) A street mime falls in love with an elusive young woman whose problems with other men keep them apart. Jean-Louis Barrault, Arletty, and Pierre Brasseur star in this epic melo-drama set in mid-19th century Paris, considered by some to be the greatest French film of all time.

Les Misérables (1935) Based on the Victor Hugo novel, this film tells the story of Jean Valjean (Frederic March), unjustly convicted and sentenced to years in prison, who emerges to rebuild his life but is hounded by the cruel police officer Javert (Charles Laughton).

Paris Holiday (1957) Bob Hope plays an American comedian, and Fernandel a French comedian, who narrowly escape a gang of criminals in Paris.

Paris in the Spring (1935) Four tourists in the romantic city of Paris decide to change partners. Mary Ellis, Tullio Carminati, Lynne Overman, and Ida Lupino star.

Paris Qui Dort (The Crazy Ray; 1923) A mad scientist invents a ray that brings all but six people in Paris to a halt in this silent flick. Henri Rollan, Albert Préjean, Marcel Vallée, and Madeleine Rodrique star.

Paris Underground (1945) Two women (Constance Bennett and Grace Fields) who are caught in Paris when the Nazis invade continue their Resistance activities.

Paris Vu Par . . . (Six in Paris; 1965) Six short stories, set in different parts of Paris, are told by six French New Wave directors.

Paris When it Sizzles (1963) A film writer and his secretary try out several script ideas together. William Holden and Audrey Hepburn star in the Hollywood remake of the 1952 French film *La Fête à Henriette*.

Phantom of the Opera (1925) This silent-film classic is the story of a disfigured man (Lon Chaney) who abducts the prima donna of the **Paris Opéra** (Mary Philbin) and brings her to his lair in the sewers below.

Playtime (1968) Barbara Demek, Jacqueline Lecomte, and Henri Piccoli appear in this Jacques Tati romp in which Hulot and a group of American tourists are bewildered by life in an airport, a business block, and a restaurant.

Prêt-à-Porter (Ready to Wear; 1995) Robert Altman's satirical look at the world of haute couture includes performances by Julia Roberts, Marcello Mastroianni, Sophia Loren, and Lauren Bacall. Paris, the fashion capital of the world, serves as the backdrop for this parody.

Sabrina (1954) Audrey Hepburn plays a chauffeur's daughter who is wooed by Humphrey Bogart and William Holden. A scene in which Hepburn takes a cooking class at the **Cordon Bleu** inspired an actual course at the famous culinary institution.

Seventh Heaven (1927) In this silent film, a Paris sewer worker (Charles Farrell) shelters a street waif (Janet Gaynor), marries her, and then goes off to war.

Sous les Toits de Paris (1930) Albert Préjean, Pola Illery, and Gaston Modet appear in this story of a Parisian street performer who falls in love with a young woman, fights her lover, and proves himself innocent of theft.

Subway (1985) Luc Besson directs Isabelle Adjani and Christophe Lambert in this stylish comedy/melodrama about an eccentric man on the run from thugs who takes refuge overnight in the platforms and tunnels of the Paris métro.

The Trial (1962) Kafka's nightmarish story of a man who is tried and convicted for an unspecified crime is directed by Orson Welles and features Welles, Jeanne Moreau, and Anthony Perkins. The old **Gare d'Orsay** (now the **Musée d'Orsay**) is the set for a huge office space with endless rows of desks.

20 Petit Hôtel de Villars This hôtel was constructed in 1712 by **Germain Boffrand** as an addition to the 1709 mansion he built next door, at **No. 116,** for the Duc de Villars. This one has elegant twin garlanded oval windows. It is now the **Lycée Paul Claudel,** a private high school. ♦ 118 Rue de Grenelle (between Rues de Bellechasse and Casimir-Périer). Métros: Rue du Bac, Varenne

21 Café Lunch ★$ This lunch counter, where young arty-intellectual types serve Italian sandwiches and coffees, might be more at home in San Francisco's North Beach than among the mansions of this stately neighborhood. There's a selection of panini (warm sandwiches) such as the Sicilian (with tomatoes, mozzarella, basil, and olive oil) and the Capri (with gorgonzola, mozzarella, and tomato); *crostini* (open-faced sandwiches) of ham and gruyère or prosciutto, mozzarella, and tomato; various salads; quiche of the day; and desserts such as *tarte au citron* and *mousse au chocolat*. The cappuccino is made with aromatic and rich Segafredo brand coffee beans. Order from the takeout window, perhaps the only one in Paris, or eat inside at the counter. ♦ M-Sa breakfast and lunch until 5:30PM. 130 Rue de Grenelle (at Rue de Martignac). 01.45.55.15.45. Métro: Varenne

22 Basilique Ste-Clothilde Now closed to the public, this Neo-Gothic church, designed in 1846 by **Christian Gau**, was the first of its kind to be built in Paris. It is the product of mid–19th-century enthusiasm for the Middle Ages, inspired by writers such as Victor Hugo. The church is notable for its prominent twin towers, visible from across the river. Composer César Franck was organist here from 1858 until his death in 1890, and a monument commemorating him stands in the pretty neighborhood park opposite the church. ♦ 23 bis Rue Las-Cases (between Rues Casimir-Périer and de Martignac). 01.44.18.62.60. Métros: Solférino, Assemblée Nationale

23 10-12 Rue St-Dominique The **Ministry of Defense** has occupied these buildings since 1804, but they were originally the **Couvent des Filles de St-Joseph,** a convent and home for orphan girls established in 1641. The orphans were taught a skill, such as embroidery, and at 20 were expected to find jobs, become nuns, or marry. In 1645 alone the convent housed 686 girls who worked in an embroidery workshop on the premises. The convent closed in 1790 and became headquarters for the **Ministry of War** in 1793. ♦ Between Rues de Solférino and de Bourgogne. Métros: Solférino, Assemblée Nationale

23 14-16 Rue St-Dominique In the same block as **10-12** Rue St-Dominique, the **Hôtel de Brienne,** built in the early 18th century, was the home of Letizia Bonaparte, Napoléon's mother, from 1806 to 1817. Today it is occupied by the **Ministry of Defense.** ♦ Between Rues de Solférino and de Bourgogne. Métros: Solférino, Assemblée Nationale

24 Chapelle Jesus Enfant The catechism chapel of **Basilique Ste-Clothilde** (see page 107) was built at the same time as its mother church. ♦ 29 Rue Las-Cases (between Rues de Martignac and de Bourgogne). 01.44.18.62.60. Métros: Solférino, Assemblée Nationale

25 Hôtel de Noirmoutiers Also known as the *"Hôtel de Sens,"* this mansion was built in 1722 by **Jean Courtonne** on the lands of the Comte de Noirmoutiers. Mlle de Sens, great-granddaughter of Louis the First of Bourbon, lived here in 1735 and had the interior decorated by Lassurance. The mansion was later the army headquarters, where Marshal Foch resided until his death in 1929. Today, **No. 140** houses the **Ministry of Public Works** and the headquarters of the **Institut Géographique Nationale,** and behind the impressive concave entryway of **No. 138** is the **Ministry of the Sahara.** ♦ 138-140 Rue de Grenelle (between Rues de Bourgogne and de Talleyrand). Métro: Varenne

26 Hôtel du Chanac de Pompadour Designed by architect **Pierre-Alexis Delamair** in 1704, this mansion became the **Swiss Embassy** in 1938. Inside is a subterranean swimming pool, surrounded by 20 Tuscan columns, with five niches for statues. Unfortunately, it is only open to the public once a year. ♦ 142 Rue de Grenelle (between Rues de Bourgogne and de Talleyrand). Métro: Varenne

27 Hôtel du Châtelet This mansion is a fine example of the Louis XV style, built in 1770 for the Duc du Châtelet, who was later beheaded in *la Terreur.* It was confiscated in 1796 to house a civil engineering school. In 1835 it became the **Turkish Embassy,** in 1843 the **Austrian Embassy,** and from 1849 to 1906 it was the **Archbishop's Palace.** Since then it has housed the **Ministry of Employment.** The courtyard facade is ornamented with four composite columns supporting an entablature and balustrade that extend along the whole facade. Several of the salons have their original Louis XV and XVI decoration, and the arched porte cochere is in the Tuscan style. ♦ 127 Rue de Grenelle (at Blvd des Invalides). Métro: Varenne

28 28 Rue St-Dominique This hôtel was constructed in 1703 by **Pierre Lassurance,** one of the builders of mansions in the Faubourg St-Germain area. In 1764 it was owned by Maurice de Riquet, Comte de Caraman, who had a celebrated garden that Marie Antoinette visited in 1771 to get some ideas about how to transform her **Jardin de Trianon** at **Versailles.** In 1929 it became the headquarters for the **Union Internationale de Chimie** (International Union of Chemists). ♦ Between Rues de Bourgogne and de Constantine. Métros: Assemblée Nationale, Invalides

29 53 Rue St-Dominique This 1770 mansion is today home to the **Ministry of Cultural Affairs.** Past renovations united its garden with that of **Nos. 43** and **55** Rue St-Dominique. ♦ Between Rues de Bourgogne and de Constantine. Métros: Assemblée Nationale, Invalides

29 57 Rue St-Dominique This grand mansion, visible through iron gates, is separated from the street by an unpaved courtyard and symmetrical fountains on either side of the entrance. Known as the **Hôtel de Monaco de Sagan,** it was built in 1784 by **Alexandre Théodore Brongniart** for the Princess of Monaco. Until 1825 it was the **British Embassy.** It was acquired in 1838 by Dutch banker William Hope, who distorted it by raising the first floor, moving the stair, and adding three dining rooms. Hope also enlarged the grounds, incorporating a little chapel dating from 1706 belonging to the Filles de Ste-Valère. Today the building houses the **Polish Embassy.** ♦ Between Rues de Bourgogne and de Constantine. Métros: Assemblée Nationale, Invalides

30 British Cultural Center The aim of the center, which is under the aegis of the **British Council,** is to promote cultural and scientific links between Great Britain and France by organizing exchange programs for French and British scientists, offering English-language classes, and operating a lending library of English-language books. The council promotes young artists and musicians, and brings British orchestras and theater companies such as the **Royal Shakespeare Company** to France. ♦ Free. M-F. 11 Rue de Constantine (at Rue St-Dominique). Center: 01.49.55.73.23; library: 01.49.55.73.00. Métro: Invalides

30 Canadian Cultural Services This branch of the **Canadian Embassy** helps Canadian artists find contacts. It often hosts visual-arts shows and theater productions, and changing sculpture exhibits are displayed in the courtyard. ♦ M-F. 5 Rue de Constantine (between Rues St-Dominique and de l'Université). 01.47.05.89.68. Métro: Invalides

31 Rue Robert-Esnault-Pelterie Since 1965 this street has borne the name of the French astronomical engineer and pioneer of aviation (1881-1957), who lived at 23 Rue de Constantine. ♦ Between Rue de l'Université and Quai d'Orsay. Métro: Invalides

On Rue Robert-Esnault-Pelterie:

Gare des Invalides At the Air France *aérogare* (air terminal), you can catch a bus to **Orly Airport,** change your ticket, or rent a car at the **Hertz, Avis,** or **Europcar** desks. Be forewarned: Even the French are confused by the drop-off procedure for rental cars, which involves parking in the lot underneath the Esplanade des Invalides and depositing the key in one of the hard-to-find boxes. ♦ 2 Rue Robert-Esnault-Pelterie. 01.43.23.94.93, 01.43.17.20.20

32 Ministère des Affaires Etrangères (Ministry of Foreign Affairs) The facade, roof, grand stair, and garden statuary of this structure, built by **Jacques Lacornée** in 1845, are classified with the *Monuments Historiques*. ♦ 37 Quai d'Orsay (between Rues Aristide-Briand and Robert-Esnault-Pelterie). Métro: Invalides

33 Hôtel des Invalides Louis XIV ordered **Libéral Bruant** to erect this monumental group of buildings to house the king's old soldiers, many of them invalids who had been reduced to begging or seeking shelter in monasteries. When the *hôtel* (pictured below) was completed in 1676, 6,000 aging pensioners moved in. It is still used as a home for old soldiers, though only a dozen or so still live here. The year after its completion, the "Sun King" (Louis XIV's nickname, derived from his brilliance and his fondness for gold) commissioned a second church for the complex, which was built by **Jules Hardouin-Mansart.** Attached Siamese-twin–style to **Bruant**'s original church, **St-Louis-des-Invalides,** the **Eglise du Dôme** (Dome Church) is one of the most magnificent Baroque churches of the *Grand Siècle*. Its dome is decorated with garlands and crowned with a 351-foot-tall spire.

France's bravest soldiers and greatest warriors are entombed in the **Eglise du Dôme:** Turenne, Vauban, Duroc, Foch, and, of course, Napoléon. "I do not think that there is a more impressive sepulchre on earth than that tomb; it is grandly simple," wrote Theodore Roosevelt of Napoléon's resting place. "I am not easily awestruck, but it certainly gave me a solemn feeling to look at the plain, red stone bier which contained what had once been the mightiest conqueror the world ever saw."

Concealed by the outward simplicity of red porphyry, Napoléon's remains are contained in seven coffins, one inside the other, made of iron, mahogany, lead, ebony, oak, and marble. Napoléon was originally interred on the island of St. Helena, where he died in 1821. The British finally agreed to repatriate his remains in 1840, thus fulfilling the emperor's wish to be buried "on the banks of the Seine among the people of France whom I have loved so much." The tomb of Napoléon's son, the King of Rome, who died in Vienna at age 21, sounds a morbid footnote to history. In 1940 his remains were given to Paris in a grandiose gesture by a heady Hitler.

Bruant's church, **St-Louis-des-Invalides,** where the occupants of the *hôtel* worshiped, is separated by a glass barrier from the domed edifice. One of the church's most impressive features is the collection of captured banners hanging from the upper galleries. Among these tattered mementos of French military victories there is even the flag with the rising sun of Japan, a relic of World War II. In 1837 Berlioz's *Requiem* was performed here for the first time.

Visitors enter **St-Louis-des-Invalides** from the **Cour d'Honneur,** an impressive courtyard also designed by **Bruant.** This is where French army officer Alfred Dreyfus was publicly disgraced and where de Gaulle kissed Churchill. The statue of Napoléon by Seurre, which used to be on the top of a column in Place Vendôme, now stands in this courtyard. Among the other Napoleonic memorabilia exhibited in **Les Invalides** are the emperor's death mask, his dinner jacket, and the dog that was his companion during his years on

Hôtel des Invalides

MICHAEL STORRINGS

the island of Elba, stuffed for posterity. ♦ Admission. Daily. Pl des Invalides (between Blvds des Invalides and de LaTour-Maubourg); enter at Ave de Tourville (at Pl Vauban). 01.44.42.37.38, 01.44.42.30.11. Métros: Latour-Maubourg, Varenne

Within the Hôtel des Invalides:

Musée de l'Armée (Army Museum) At the north end of the **Invalides** complex, this museum houses one of the largest collections of military paraphernalia in the world. Swords, guns, armor, flags, and other articles are on display, along with innumerable models, maps, and images that trace the evolution of warfare from prehistoric times until World War II. Understandably, Napoleonic souvenirs are most conspicuous, but there are also intriguing exhibitions of medieval, Renaissance, and Oriental militaria. ♦ Admission. Daily. Pl des Invalides (between Blvds des Invalides and de La-Tour-Maubourg). 01.44.42.37.70, 01.44.42.54.91. Métros: Latour-Maubourg, Varenne

34 Tai-Yen ★$$ The Thai and Cantonese specialties here include grilled chicken with basil sauce, duck sautéed with fresh mangos, spicy shrimp soup with lemongrass, gingered chicken, roast duck Cantonese style, and an assortment of dim sum, including shrimp rolls and pork ravioli. The informal dining room is decorated in standard Chinese-restaurant style. ♦ Daily lunch and dinner. 36 Rue Fabert (between Rues de Grenelle and St-Dominique). 01.45.51.26.98. Métro: Latour-Maubourg

35 Le Divellec ★★$$$ The tasteful nautical decor of chef Jacques Le Divellec's restaurant emphasizes that the focus here is the sea. Le Divellec's book of seafood recipes, *Les Bons Plats de la Mer,* is none too discreetly displayed at the restaurant's entrance foyer. Some of his exceptional dishes include smoked bass roasted then flambéed with thyme, *homard à la presse avec son corail* (pressed lobster with lobster coral), *gigotin de grenouilles* (frogs' legs), grilled turbot with lobster béarnaise sauce, *tournedos de saumon à la lie de vin* (salmon with foie gras in wine sauce), and *cassolette de St-Jacques aux truffes* (scallop casserole with truffles). Specially prepared desserts such as *crêpes soufflés à l'orange confit* (crepes with candied orange soufflé) and *feuilleté aux pruneaux avec son sorbet d'Armagnac* (prune pastry with Armagnac sorbet) must be ordered at the start of the meal. ♦ Daily lunch and dinner. Reservations required. 107 Rue de l'Université (at Rue Fabert). 01.45.51.91.96. Métro: Latour-Maubourg

36 Petrossian Parisians have flocked here since 1924 for caviar, smoked salmon, and foie gras. Sit down at one of the three tables to sample some of the shop's wares and a glass of 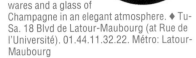 Champagne in an elegant atmosphere. ♦ Tu-Sa. 18 Blvd de Latour-Maubourg (at Rue de l'Université). 01.44.11.32.22. Métro: Latour-Maubourg

37 La Boule d'Or ★★$$ This invitingly calm restaurant, with its blond wood and beige-upholstered banquettes, offers such specialties as *foie gras de canard,* langoustine and leek tart, roast lamb fillet with tarragon cream sauce, and warm lemon soufflé. ♦ M-F, Su lunch and dinner; Sa dinner. Reservations required. 13 Blvd de Latour-Maubourg (at Rue de l'Université). 01.47.05.50.18. Métro: Latour-Maubourg

38 La Mandarin de Latour-Maubourg ★$ Typical of the Chinese restaurants that dot the *quartier,* this informal place serves spring rolls, roasted spareribs, chicken with ginger and scallion sauce, crab and asparagus soup, and roast duck. ♦ Daily lunch and dinner. 23 Blvd de Latour-Maubourg (between Rues St-Dominique and de l'Université). 01.45.51.25.71. Métros: Latour-Maubourg, Invalides

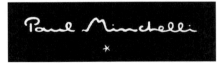

39 Paul Minchelli ★★★$$$ The handsome wood facade and the nautical Art Deco interior of this *restaurant de poissons* provide a fine setting for a meal of simple seafood dishes, extraordinarily fresh, subtle, and impeccably prepared. The chef knows that his high-quality fish and shellfish, often scooped right out of the tank, need little embellishment. Feast on fresh shrimp, *St-Pierre* (John Dory) with olive oil, and lobster with honey and pimiento. ♦ Tu-Sa lunch and dinner; closed in August. Reservations required. 54 Blvd de Latour-Maubourg (between Rues de Grenelle and St-Dominique). 01.47.05.89.86. Métros: Latour-Maubourg, Invalides

39 Le Bistrot du 7ème ★★$ The warmth that emanates from this neighborhood bistro may have less to do with the simple, traditional French food it serves than with Argentinian Mme Beauvallet, who, with her husband, owns this cozy spot. Changing daily specials might include *bavette aux échalottes* (steak with shallots), *soupe de poissons* (fish soup), trout meunière, grilled pork sausage, crème brûlée, iced chocolate charlotte, and a fruit or chocolate tart. The restaurant's only nod to Mme Beauvallet's Argentinian roots is the inclusion of plump little bottles of San Felipe Tinto, an Argentinian red wine, nestled among all the Bordeaux, Bourgognes, and Beaujolais. ◆ M-F lunch and dinner; Su dinner. Reservations recommended. 56 Blvd de Latour-Maubourg (between Rues de Grenelle and St-Dominique). 01.45.51.93.08. Métros: Latour-Maubourg, Invalides

40 Ventose Georges Dupont-Nicolle sells knickknacks galore in his small accessories boutique. Amicable and full of advice, he might recommend a tapestry pillow, a hand-painted ceramic lamp, or one

GEORGES DUPONT-NICOLLE
DECORATEUR

of the lovely frames that he keeps in stock to satisfy the French passion for tables full of framed photos. ◆ M afternoon; Tu-Sa; closed in August. 5 Ave de La Motte-Picquet (between Blvd de Latour-Maubourg and Rue Bougainville). 01.45.51.93.29. Métro: Latour-Maubourg

40 Café Max ★★$$ One of the only beacons in this nighttime desert is this typically French bistro, particularly animated on Saturday nights. The place is agreeably dingy, with banquettes, mismatched chairs and tables, and flea-market memorabilia such as shoe trees, a stuffed swordfish, and street signs hanging from the ceiling. Friendly owner Max presides over the dining room while his wife, Lili, rules in the kitchen. The food is simple and includes the excellent *cassoulet Landais* (a casserole of duck confit, garlic, sausage, beans, and ham), Lyons sausages, ham and potato salad, and *tarte tatin* (apple tart). For an aperitif, order a kir Max, the house cocktail made with sparkling white wine and *crème de cassis*. ◆ M dinner; Tu-Sa lunch and dinner; closed in August. Reservations recommended. 7 Ave de La Motte-Picquet (between Blvd de Latour-Maubourg and Rue Bougainville). 01.47.05.57.66. Métro: Latour-Maubourg

41 Le Chambrelain M. Alexandre's hand-painted Limoges porcelain dishes are exquisitely decorated with fruits, flowers, and fish and come in handsome black gift boxes that accentuate the precious quality of this expensive tableware. Those on tighter budgets might consider buying dishes decorated by the traditional method known as *décalcomanie;* you can take home a set adorned with artichokes, rutabagas, pea pods, roses, and irises for about half the price of the hand-painted porcelains. Alexandre has been in the business for 45 years and had a big workshop that supplied **Bergdorf Goodman** and **Neiman Marcus** before he decided to scale down to this smaller boutique. The smell of turpentine permeating the shop emanates from the back-room atelier where he gives courses in hand-painting porcelain. ◆ M-F; closed in August. 11 Ave de La Motte-Picquet (between Blvd de Latour-Maubourg and Rue Bougainville). 01.45.55.03.45. Métro: Latour-Maubourg

42 Au Liégeur Cork is the name of the game here: cork trivets, cork watches, cork jewelry, sheets of cork, corkscrews, and just plain old corks that come from the company's (what else?) cork factory. The shop carries a nice assortment of decanters, decorative corks, and the coveted bouchon universal, a cork specially designed to fit bottles of all sizes. ◆ Tu-Sa; closed in August. 17 Ave de La Motte-Picquet (between Blvd de Latour-Maubourg and Rue Bougainville). 01.47.05.53.10. Métro: Latour-Maubourg

42 Restaurant Le Champ de Mars ★★$$ At this comfortable restaurant you might start with Normandy oysters, then have a main course of *filet mignon de veau aux morilles fraîches* (veal filet mignon with fresh morels) or stuffed rabbit, followed by a dessert of nougat ice cream with *coulis de framboises* (raspberry sauce) and *profiteroles au chocolat.* ◆ Tu lunch, W-Su lunch and dinner; closed mid-July through mid-August. Reservations recommended. 17 Ave de La Motte-Picquet (at Rue Bougainville). 01.47.05.57.99. Métro: Latour-Maubourg

43 Hôtel Muguet $$ Behind the pink-painted brick exterior of this newly renovated hotel are 45 calm and comfortable rooms with TV sets hung high on the wall, hospital style. Five of the rooms have a view of the **Eiffel Tower** and two look onto the **Hôtel des Invalides.** Breakfast is served, but there's no restaurant. ◆ 11 Rue Chevert (between Rue Louis-Codet and Blvd de Latour-Maubourg). 01.47.05.05.93; fax 01.45.50.25.37. Métros: Ecole Militaire, Latour-Maubourg

44 Le Maupertu ★★$$ This intimate spot will convince you that dining in Paris can indeed be both grand and affordable. The decor is a blend of terra-cotta and marble and the menu is pleasing to the palate. The expertly prepared French specialties include *mille-feuille de torteau aux crevettes* (crab and shrimps in a flaky pastry) and *ravioli de champignons au coulis de cèpes* (ravioli stuffed with wild mushrooms with cèpes). Desserts such as wafer-thin slices of chocolate and white chocolate mousse served with light egg custard are superb. There's also an excellent wine list. ♦ M-F lunch and dinner; Sa dinner. Reservations recommended. 94 Blvd de La-Tour-Maubourg (between Ave de Tourville and Rue Louis-Codet). 01.45.54.37.96. Métros: Ecole Militaire, Latour-Maubourg

45 Auberge d'Chez Eux
★★$$$ In the shadow of the **Hôtel des Invalides,** Jean-Pierre Court and his father have for the last 30 years specialized in a *cuisine familial* from France's southwest. The restaurant's enclosed terrace is draped with red-and-white-striped fabric and is a perfect spot for feasting on the homemade *foie gras d'oie,* which comes with a glass of Château Loubens Bordeaux Blanc; *cuisses de grenouilles Provençale* (frogs' legs sautéed in olive oil, garlic, and tomatoes); *magret de canard* (duck fillets) with honey vinegar; roast lamb chops; or *pavé de saumon d'Ecosse poêlé sauce béarnaise* (sautéed salmon steak with béarnaise sauce). Wines are reasonably priced; the Cahors Chateau Lagineste would be a good choice with any of the dishes. ♦ M-Sa lunch and dinner; closed three weeks in August. Reservations recommended. 2 Ave de Lowendal (at Blvd de Latour-Maubourg). 01.47.05.52.55. Métros: Ecole Militaire, Latour-Maubourg

46 Square de Latour-Maubourg This peaceful private drive dates from 1897 and is decorated with an ornamental pool that matches one in the Place François-1er across the river. ♦ Between Blvd de Latour-Maubourg and Cité du Général-Négrier. Métro: Latour-Maubourg

46 St-Jean This small Lutheran Evangelical church was built in the Neo-Gothic style in 1911; the interior is intimate and full of light, with a timber ceiling of boat hull construction. In 1990 the **American University** took out a 50-year lease on the land directly behind the church and constructed a new building to house its classrooms, computer lab, and faculty offices. The university's main building is located at 31 Avenue Bosquet. ♦ 147 Rue de Grenelle (between Sq de Latour-Maubourg and Cité du Général-Négrier). Métro: Latour-Maubourg

---

The term *hôtel* in Paris often refers not to an overnight lodging place, but rather to an *hôtel particulier,* meaning a town house or mansion.

47 Thoumieux ★★★$$ For those seeking honest regional fare, here is an authentic bistro that has been in Jean Bassalert's family for more than 70 years. The comfortable dining room, with its sophisticated 1930s charm, glows with the warmth of a place well loved, and attentive but discreet waiters deliver impeccable service. The menu includes many specialties from the La Corrèze region in the southwest of France, and changes daily according to what's fresh at the market. Bassalert types each day's bill of fare on an old Remington typewriter and then mimeographs it, adding a wonderful, immediate quality to the experience. Experiment with a Correzien appetizer such as the earthy and sublime *soupe de châtaignes* (chestnut soup) or the *pâté de pomme de terre* (a pastry made with potatoes, pork, and garlic); then have a main course of *steak frites, confit de canard* (duck confit), grilled beef with sauce bordelaise, or *gigot d'agneau rôti* (roast leg of lamb) with ratatouille. Your wine choice might be a lush Bordeaux, such as the Château Cantenac Brown 1989, or a red Burgundy such as the Nuits-St-Georges 1987. For dessert the crème brûlée is warm and velvety, and the *indulgent aux chocolat amer* is as rich and delicious as it sounds. The banquet room is the site of a monthly wine class (normally for groups but there is often an extra space or two) during which six types of wine are served with six accompanying dishes. There's also a small hotel upstairs (see below). ♦ Daily lunch and dinner. Reservations recommended. 79 Rue St-Dominique (between Blvd de Latour-Maubourg and Rue de la Comète). 01.47.05.49.75. Métro: Latour-Maubourg

At Thoumieux:

Hôtel Thoumieux $$ If you can land one of the 10 modern rooms here you will be surrounded by the amiable young staff of the restaurant downstairs. You could even indulge in dinner at **Thoumieux** every night! ♦ 01.47.05.49.75; fax 01.47.05.36.96

48 Hôtel le Pavillon $$ In 1889, when the **Eiffel Tower** was nearing completion and Paris buzzed in anticipation of the World's Fair, many former monastery and convent buildings became hotels to accommodate the flood of visitors to the city. This one, part of a convent built in 1585 by the Ursuline nuns, once sat in a large open field that extended all the way to the Seine. Today it is a humble 18-room hostelry that's inexpensive, well located, and quiet. An arched iron gate and a well-planted courtyard separate the building from the street, and chirping canaries brighten the lobby. Regular guests return year after year. There's no restaurant. ♦ 54 Rue St-Dominique (between Rues Surcouf and Jean-Nicot). 01.45.51.42.87; fax 01.45.51.32.79. Métros: Invalides, Latour-Maubourg

48 Hôtel Saint Dominique $$ Another former-convent-turned-hotel, this one has 34 well-equipped *chambres,* a breakfast room in the vaulted basement (but no restaurant), and exposed beams in the lobby. ♦ 62 Rue St-Dominique (between Rues Surcouf and Jean-Nicot). 01.47.05,51,44; fax 01.47.05.81.28. Métros: Invalides, Latour-Maubourg

48 Boulangerie Gisquet The interior of this bakery is registered as a historic monument; notice the decorative faïence tiles and the trompe l'oeil ceiling painting depicting a view of the sky from underneath an oval balustrade. Much more real are Mme. Gisquet's enticing country breads, fruit tarts, and macaroons. Don't leave without a *mille-feuilleaux* of pears with a caramelized topping, or a *balkon* made with Chantilly cream, fromage blanc, and raspberries. Mme. Gisquet's son is also a *pâtissier,* but she's not worried about the competition—his shop is in San Diego, California. ♦ Tu-Su 7AM-8:30PM. 64 Rue St-Dominique (between Rues Surcouf and Jean-Nicot). 01.45.51.70.46. Métros: Invalides, Latour-Maubourg

49 Rue Surcouf In 1728 this street was called Rue de la Boucherie-des-Invalides because a slaughterhouse was located at its terminus on Rue St-Dominique. By 1867 the *boucherie* had disappeared and the street's name was changed to honor Corsair Robert Surcouf (1773-1827). ♦ Between Rue St-Dominique and Quai d'Orsay. Métros: Latour-Maubourg, Invalides

49 Du Côté 7ème ★★$$ Mme. Renaud and M. Brossard want to be sure there are no unpleasant surprises when the bill arrives at your table, so all meals at this simple but elegant eatery are prix-fixe. A classic French dinner might include an aperitif of kir; an appetizer such as crab and scallop flan or escargots with butter, parsley, garlic, and hazelnuts; a *plat* of *filet d'agneau rôti* (roasted lamb fillet) with garlic purée or *magret de canard* (duck fillet) roasted with spices; a bottle of red, white, or rosé wine (per two people); and either a selection of cheeses or a dessert such as coffee ice cream or *fondant au chocolat* with crème anglaise. It's a great deal. ♦ Tu-Su lunch and dinner. Reservations recommended. 29 Rue Surcouf (between Rues St-Dominique and de l'Université). 01.47.05.81.65. Métros: Latour-Maubourg, Invalides

50 Au Petit Tonneau ★★$$ Ginette Boyer has been preparing *"une cuisine de femme"* for businesspeople, artists, and *habitués du* *quartier* since 1979. In her dining room, with its compelling run-down charm, she serves *le salade Bressane* (with chicken livers in raspberry vinaigrette), *rognons de veau* (veal kidneys) with Madeira sauce, *châteaubriand au poivre,* and chocolate profiteroles. Mme Boyer has connections with the *poissonière,* so she is able to offer a *plat du jour* of fish that changes depending on the day's catch; past specials have included *coquilles St-Jacques* and *turbot au beurre blanc* with fresh sorrel. ♦ Daily lunch and dinner. 20 Rue Surcouf (between Rues St-Dominique and de l'Université). 01.47.05.09.01. Métros: Latour-Maubourg, Invalides

50 Le Bellecour ★★$$$ Chef Gérald Goutany offers classic and refined seasonal Lyonnaise specialties including *truffière de St-Jacques rôties* (roasted scallops with truffles); wild duck and lentils; *beignets de langoustines* with orange and fennel vinaigrette and confit of shiitake mushrooms; and medaillons of *lotte* (angler fish) *à la sauge* (sage) with *jus balsamique* and caramelized endive. The charming dining room recalls the bistros of days gone by. ♦ M-F lunch and dinner; Sa dinner; closed in August. Reservations required. 22 Rue Surcouf (between Rues St-Dominique and de l'Université). 01.45.51.46.93. Métros: Latour-Maubourg, Invalides

50 Marc Farraud This small *depôt-vente* (consignment shop, literally "deposit-sell") specializes in 18th-, 19th-, and 20th-century decorative arts. Treasure hunters might unearth a Lalique vase, a silver serving spoon, a Limoges tea service, or a bronze angel. ♦ M-Sa. 24 Rue Surcouf (between Rues St-Dominique and de l'Université). 01.45.55.51.44. Métros: Latour-Maubourg, Invalides

50 Valérie Barlemont-Antiquités There is an assortment of antiques at this lovely shop. Among those that may strike your fancy: 18th- and 19th-century Russian icons; a silver-plated punch service; the iron grille from a 20th-century elevator; and 19th-century oval frames small enough to tuck into your suitcase. ♦ M-Sa. 28 Rue Surcouf (between Rues St-Dominique and de l'Université). 01.45.51.23.04. Métros: Latour-Maubourg, Invalides

51 La Poule au Pot ★★$ "If God grants me a longer life, I will see to it that no peasant in my kingdom will lack the means to have a chicken in the pot *(une poule dans son pot)* every Sunday," promised King Henri IV. At this dark little bar and restaurant you can enjoy comforting chicken stew every day *but* Sunday (when the place is closed). Other options include warm *saucisson sec de montagne* (dry mountain sausage), steak tartare, or *filet au poivre* flambéed with

Armagnac and served with béarnaise sauce. Dessert might be chocolate mousse or crêpes *soufflés à l'orange*. Come in anytime for a coffee or a *pression* (draft beer) at the zinc bar. ◆ M-Sa breakfast, lunch, and dinner. 121 Rue de l'Université (at Rue Surcouf). 01.47.05.16.36. Métro: Invalides

52 Musée de la Seita (Tobacco Museum) This museum, housed in the administration building of a former tobacco factory, relates the history of tobacco since it was brought to Europe from the New World 500 years ago. The collection, which provides a fascinating insight into the uses and abuses of tobacco, covers smoking, snuff taking, tobacco chewing, and the medical uses of tobacco. Tobacco-related objects on display include Napoleon III's 19th-century cigar chest. ◆ Admission. M-Sa. 12 Rue Surcouf (at Rue de l'Université). 01.45.56.60.17. Métros: Invalides, Latour-Maubourg

53 Chez Gilda's ★★$ Classic French fare is given new life at this cozy, countrified bistro, with such dishes as *croustillant de camembert* (camembert in pastry) with cherry confiture, Norwegian salmon with *purée pomme de terre ancienne* (old-fashioned mashed potatoes), rabbit leg sautéed with basil and eggplant, and apple and blueberry crumble with vanilla ice cream. ◆ M-Sa lunch and dinner; closed in August. Reservations recommended. 3 Rue Surcouf (between Rue de l'Université and Quai d'Orsay). 01.45.55.13.85. Métro: Invalides

53 Bar Au Sel ★★$$ There has been a cafe or restaurant on this site since the beginning of the century. Today Stephan Robinne's intimate, friendly eating establishment features elegant exposed stone walls and entrées of foie gras, roasted duck with sage, and the eponymous *bar en croûte de sel* (salt-crusted sea bass). ◆ M-Su lunch and dinner. Reservations required. 49 Quai d'Orsay (at Rue Surcouf). 01.45.51.58.58. Métro: Invalides

54 53-65, 67-69, and 71-91 Quai d'Orsay From 1829 to 1909 this area was the site of a tobacco manufacturing center. A factory specializing in the fabrication of cigars with tobacco from Havana once stood at **Nos. 53-65**; in 1862 it employed more than 700 workers. ◆ Between Rue Surcouf and Pl de la Résistance. Métros: Invalides, Pont-de-l'Alma (RER)

55 American Church This interdenominational church, built in 1931 by **Carrol Greenough** in the Gothic style, serves the spiritual and social needs of the English-speaking community in Paris. Within the church complex are bilingual **Montessori** and **Lenen Schools,** and a bulletin board renowned by apartment hunters for its listings of housing available in the city. In the basement is the headquarters of the *Paris Free*

Voice, a monthly English newspaper. ◆ 65 Quai d'Orsay (between Rues Henri-Moissan and Jean-Nicot). 01.40.62.05.00. Métros: Pont-de-l'Alma (RER), Invalides

56 Rue Jean-Nicot This street is named after the 17th-century gentleman who introduced tobacco to France. ◆ Between Rue St-Dominique and Quai d'Orsay. Métros: Pont-de-l'Alma (RER), Invalides

56 Conservatoire Municipal With its bold design of intersecting white forms and geometric cutouts, this structure is one of architect **Christian de Portzamparc**'s first well-known projects. After designing it in the 1980s, he went on to the **Café Beaubourg** and, most recently, the **Cité de Musique** at **Parc La Villette.** The building houses the seventh arrondissement's conservatory, where students are trained in music, dance, and dramatic arts. ◆ 135 Rue de l'Université (at Rue Jean-Nicot). Métros: Pont-de-l'Alma (RER), Invalides

57 81 Rue St-Dominique In the mid-18th century this building housed a cabaret called the **Canon-Royal.** It's now the site of several shops. ◆ Between Rue de la Comète and Passage Jean-Nicot. Métro: Latour-Maubourg

57 93 Rue St-Dominique All that is left of the clock maker's workshop that was on this site in the early 19th century is its sign, which is composed of three bells, a lantern, shells, garlands of fruits and flowers, and, of course, a clock. It's classified with the *Monuments Historiques.* The building now has a mix of commercial and residential space. ◆ Between Rue de la Comète and Passage Jean-Nicot. Métro: Latour-Maubourg

58 Jean Millet Pastry chef Denis Ruffel makes dreamy honey madeleines and croissants, and his *pain au chocolat* has two sticks of chocolate instead of the typical one. Indulge in an afternoon snack of a St-Marc pastry (made with chocolate, Chantilly cream, and a caramelized cookie) and an espresso at one of the inviting tables. ◆ Tu-Sa; Su 8AM-1PM. 103 Rue St-Dominique (between Rues Amélie and Cler). 01.45.51.49.80. Métro: Latour-Maubourg

Hôtel de la Tulipe

59 Hôtel de la Tulipe $$ This hotel's lively owner, actor Jean-Louis Fortuit, claims that the rooms in his charming hotel were once the cells of monks, and that the small rounded structure jutting out into the lush plant-filled courtyard was the chapel. Whatever the story, the atmosphere at this cottagelike hostelry is relaxed and friendly, and many of the guests are Fortuit's actor friends. Each of the 20 rooms is slightly different, and many have rustic wood beams and exposed stone walls;

there's no restaurant. The name was inspired by a Belgian tulip seller who rented the entire hotel for four months during a *Salon d'Agriculture* in the 1950s. ◆ 33 Rue Malar (between Rues St-Dominique and de l'Université). 01.45.51.67.21; fax 01.47.53.96.37. Métros: Latour-Maubourg, Pont-de-l'Alma (RER)

60 Chez L'Ami Jean ★$ Here is a Basque restaurant full of sports memorabilia that is frequented by players of rugby and *pelota* (a Basque game similar to jai alai). Owner Jean, himself a former *pelotari* from Basque country, offers paunchy former ballplayers and other patrons such dishes as *confit de canard des Landes* (duck confit), pot-au-feu, paella Valenciana, fresh anchovies, foie gras, and Basque-style chicken, along with a selection of regional red wines. ◆ M-Sa lunch and dinner; closed in August. 27 Rue Malar (between Rues St-Dominique and de l'Université). 01.47.05.86.89. Métros: Latour-Maubourg, Pont-de-l'Alma (RER)

HOI-CHANG

61 Hoi-Chang ★$$ A subdued Chinese restaurant with comfortable banquettes, it features such specialties as lemon chicken, Peking duck, roasted pork, and beef with basil. ◆ M-F, Su lunch and dinner; Sa dinner. 19 Rue Malar (between Rues St-Dominique and de l'Université). 01.45.51.80.69. Métros: Invalides, Pont-de-l'Alma (RER)

61 L'Affriolé ★★★$$ In a pretty dining room with faux marble–painted architectural details, diners can feast on chef Alain Atibard's seasonal offerings such as *côte de veau truffé* (veal ribs with truffles), *coquille St-Jacques* (lightly fried or baked scallops), or *ravioli d'escargots au bouillon d'herbes* (ravioli stuffed with snails and herbs). The wine list is extensive—and expensive. ◆ M-F lunch and dinner, Sa dinner; closed first three weeks of August. 17 Rue Malar (between Rues St-Dominique and de l'Université). 01.44.18.31.33. Métros: Invalides, Pont-de-l'Alma (RER)

62 Michel Chaudun Once chief *chocolatier* at **Maison du Chocolat,** Chaudun now turns out his own confections; particularly dangerous is the diamond-shaped mint truffle. There are also chocolate **Eiffel Towers** for sale, and a white-chocolate Tutankhamen and several African totem sculptures in dark chocolate are on display. ◆ Tu-Sa; closed in August. 149 Rue de l'Université (at Rue Malar). 01.47.53.74.40. Métro: Latour-Maubourg

63 Beato ★★$$ This Italian restaurant is popular with good reason: specialties include the Robespierre (cooked carpaccio perfumed with garlic and rosemary), spaghetti Stromboli (with olives, capers, and anchovies), *scampi alla griglia, scaloppine al limone* (veal scallopini with lemon), osso buco Milanese with saffron rice, and tiramisù with Amaretto. ◆ M-Sa lunch and dinner; closed three weeks in August. 8 Rue Malar (between Rues St-Dominique and de l'Université). 01.47.05.94.27. Métros: Invalides, Pont-de-l'Alma (RER)

64 St-Pierre du Gros Caillou In 1652 the inhabitants of this neighborhood, then called Gros-Caillou, decided that their parish church of **St-Sulpice** was just too far away. It took 86 years to realize, but in 1738 the small chapel of **Notre-Dame-de-Bonne-Délivrance** was erected on this site. The present church, with its austere Doric facade and interior coffered vault, replaced the chapel in 1922. ◆ 92 Rue St-Dominique (at Rue Pierre-Villey). 01.45.55.22.38. Métro: Latour-Maubourg

65 Rue Cler At Paris's most exclusive street market you'll see the best-dressed shoppers in town choosing from the colorful, bountiful displays of butchers, bakers, *traiteurs* (caterers), *fromagers* (cheese sellers), greengrocers, wine merchants, and florists that spill out onto the cobblestone street. This market, like most, is especially lively on Saturday morning. ◆ Tu-Sa morning. Between Ave de La Motte-Picquet and Rue de Grenelle. Métros: Ecole Militaire, Latour-Maubourg

65 Le Repaire de Bacchus This small wine shop has a big selection of *grands vins Français,* as well as many labels from small regional producers. The salespeople are expert wine counselors, able to offer advice on just the right wine to have with a particular dish or to help you select something for your wine cellar back home. You could try an inexpensive bottle of Le Vieille Ferme Côte du Ventoux 1993, with its distinct perfume of wood and raspberries, or splurge with a Château Fonbadet Pauillac 1983 that envelops the mouth with its refined flavors. The shop also carries over 60 types of whiskey, including some rare bottles. ◆ Tu-Sa; Su morning. 29 Rue Cler (between Rues du Champ-de-Mars and de Grenelle). 01.45.56.99.99. Métro: Ecole Militaire. Also at: 147 Rue St-Dominique (between Rue Augereau and Pl du Général-Gouraud). 01.45.51.77.21. Métro: Ecole Militaire, Pont-de-l'Alma (RER)

65 Fromagerie Cler *Bleu de Bresse,* creamy *chèvre,* and *morbier* are just a few of the cheeses sold at this well-stocked shop that you could design a picnic around. ◆ Tu-Sa; Su morning. 31 Rue Cler (between Rues du Champ-de-Mars and de Grenelle). 01.47.05.48.95. Métro: Ecole Militaire

66 Davoli Also known as **La Maison du Jambon** (The House of Ham), this shop has Parma hams hanging from the ceiling and is literally stuffed with sausages and take-out dishes such as lasagna, salads, and an assortment of tarts. ◆ Tu, Th-Sa; W and Su morning; closed 15 July-15 August. 34 Rue Cler (between Rues du Champ-de-Mars and de Grenelle). 01.45.51.23.41. Métro: Ecole Militaire

66 Café du Marché ★★$ Escape the bustling Rue Cler street market by ducking into this cafe for a quick coffee at the attractive copper bar, or stay for a lunch of *confit de canard* (duck confit), hamburgers, or farm chicken. You can also order a crepe at the little stand outside and eat it at a table inside. ◆ M-Sa 7AM-11PM; Su until 4PM. 38 Rue Cler (at Rue du Champ-de-Mars). 01.47.05.51.27. Métro: Ecole Militaire

67 Hôtel Champ-de-Mars $ You'll wake up to the Rue Cler market when you stay at this charming 25-room *hôtel familial.* Also part of the appeal are the accommodating young owners; the friendly resident spaniel, Chipie; and the unbeatable prices. There's a downstairs breakfast room with high-backed tapestry-covered chairs, and rooms **No. 2** and **No. 4** have small terraces where guests can eat breakfast in the summer. There's no restaurant, however. ◆ 7 Rue du Champ-de-Mars (between Rue Cler and Ave Bosquet). 01.45.51.52.30. Métro: Ecole Militaire

67 Ragut Charcuterie The mouthwatering take-out dishes displayed here make it difficult to leave empty-handed. Your choices include trout with almonds, langoustine thermidor, paella, bouillabaisse, avocado stuffed with shrimp or crab, quiche lorraine, Hungarian goulash, beef brochettes, spinach in cream, coq au vin, duck with peaches. . . the list goes on and on. ◆ M-Sa. 40 Rue Cler (at Rue du Champ-de-Mars). 01.45.51.29.35. Métro: Ecole Militaire

67 Le Fournil de Pierre This chain of *artisanal* bakeries offers a selection of breads more fibrous than the traditional baguette. Try the herb bread (with chamomile, parsley, and basil), fruit bread (with raisins and nuts),

sesame bread, or the hearty *pain de campagne* (country bread). ◆ M-Sa; Su morning. 42 Rue Cler (between Rues Bosquet and du Champ-de-Mars). 01.42.43.28.60. Métro: Ecole Militaire

68 3 Rue du Champ-de-Mars Buzz yourself into the entrance foyer of this Art Nouveau apartment house to see how the leaf-and-lily design that appears on the facade's masonry and on the iron gates is repeated in the lovely tile mosaic on the floor. ◆ Between Rues Duvivier and Cler. Métro: Ecole Militaire

69 Le Lutin Gourmand
This candy shop with the whimsical name (it means "gourmet imp") has something for everyone: glass cases full of colorful hard candies and mints; lollipops shaped like animals and hearts; tempting hazelnut treats called *feuilleté noisettes;*

chocolate teddy bears; and pretty bottles of Port and Armagnac. The shop really shines at Easter, when it's chock-full of chocolate rabbits, hens, squirrels, ducks, and fish, as well as delightful marzipan chicks hatching from eggs. All the candy is made right on the premises. ◆ Tu-Sa. 47 Rue Cler (between Ave de La Motte-Picquet and Rue du Champ-de-Mars). 01.45.55.29.74. Métro: Ecole Militaire

70 Hôtel Relais Bosquet $$ The automatic sliding doors are the first tip-off that this 40-room establishment is strong on modern conveniences and limited in the charm department. However, you can count on a comfortable stay enhanced by **CNN**, hair dryers, and an iron and ironing board in your room. Some of the fifth- and sixth-floor rooms have a view of the tip of the **Eiffel Tower.** There's no restaurant. ◆ 19 Rue du Champ-de-Mars (between Rue Cler and Ave Bosquet). 01.47.05.25.45; fax 01.45.55.08.24. Métro: Ecole Militaire

71 Rue de l'Exposition Formerly known as the Passage de l'Alma, this quiet, narrow street received its current name at the time of the **1867 Exposition Universelle.** ◆ Between Rues de Grenelle and St-Dominique. Métro: Ecole Militaire

71 La Serre ★$ Home-style dishes are served up at this casual, lace-curtained bistro. Recommended menu items include onion soup gratinée, steak with roquefort sauce, salmon with leek sauce, crème caramel, and *tarte tatin* (apple tart). ◆ M-Sa lunch and dinner. Reservations recommended. 29 Rue de l'Exposition (between Rues de Grenelle and St-Dominique). 01.45.55.20.96. Métro: Ecole Militaire

72 Hôtel de l'Alma A comfortable 32-room hotel on a calm street offers all the modern conveniences and makes no attempt at false charm. The lobby is decorated with some unfortunate hexagon-shaped red upholstered tables

and chairs. Many Italians stay here. ♦ 32 Rue de l'Exposition (between Rues de Grenelle and St-Dominique). 01.47.05.45.70; fax 01.45.51.84.47. Métro: Ecole Militaire

73 Auberge du Champ de Mars ★$ Michel Duclos wears the chef's hat while his wife, Madeleine, plays hostess in this softly lit, red-velvet-upholstered restaurant. The fixed-price three-course menu includes appetizers such as avocado and smoked salmon salad or *escargots à la Bourguignonne;* a main course of *poulet Normandie* (chicken in a mushroom cream sauce) or turbot in hollandaise sauce; and a dessert of profiteroles with warm chocolate sauce or warm apple tart. ♦ M-F lunch and dinner; Sa dinner; closed in August. 18 Rue de l'Exposition (between Rues de Grenelle and St-Dominique). 01.45.51.78.08. Métro: Ecole Militaire

74 La Fontaine de Mars ★★$$ Ever popular, Mme. Boudon's gem of a bistro is comfortable and cozy, with small dining rooms and a homey atmosphere. Locals keep coming back for the southwest-style cooking. Those looking for lighter fare might try the warm *pâté de cèpes,* poached fillet of turbot, sole meunière, and *pruneaux à l'Armagnac* (prunes in Armagnac), while those with heartier appetites could opt for the *boudin aux pommes* (blood sausage with apples), duck cassoulet, or *côte de veau filet aux morilles* (veal fillet with morels), with a *truffé au chocolat* for dessert. In either case a bottle of Madiran Château Bouscassé or Cahors Château Eugenie will aid in digestion. ♦ M-Sa lunch and dinner. Reservations recommended. 129 Rue St-Dominique (at Rue de l'Exposition). 01.47.05.46.44. Métro: Ecole Militaire

74 Fontaine de Mars This freestanding fountain by **Henri Beauvarlet** was once situated in the center of a semicircle of poplars, replaced in 1859 with the present

arcaded square. The fountain's bas-relief represents Hygeia, the goddess of health, giving a drink to Mars, the god of war. Between the pilasters are vases encircled by serpents, the symbol of Aesculapius, the god of medicine. ♦ 129-131 Rue St-Dominique (at Rue de l'Exposition). Métro: Ecole Militaire

74 La Croque au Sel ★★$ This turn-of-the-century–style bistro offers two different prix-fixe menus with specialties such as winter salad with foie gras, pot-au-feu, grilled meats with herbs, *escalope de saumon, sauté de boeuf,* and grilled pork chops. The high ceilings, whirling fans, and palms give the restaurant a breezy, summery air, and the covered terrace makes a nice dining spot in the warm weather months. ♦ M-F lunch and dinner; Sa dinner. 131 Rue St-Dominique (at Rue de l'Exposition). 01.47.05.23.53. Métro: Ecole Militaire

75 Duchesne Boulanger Pâtissier This pastry shop is most notable for its Louis XV–style interior of ornate wood paneling, mirrors, and mosaics, although the selection of pastries also makes it worth a stop. Enjoy a treat and a cup of coffee or tea at one of the four tables. ♦ M-Sa; closed one month in summer. 112 Rue St-Dominique (between Rues Dupont-des-Loges and Sedillot). 01.45.51.31.01. Métros: Ecole Militaire, Pont-de-l'Alma (RER)

76 Aryllis If you lived in the neighborhood this would be your favorite flower shop. The master florist in the back room makes artful arrangements out of the long-stemmed roses, tulips, lilies, and ferns sumptuously displayed in urns and baskets. Why not take a bouquet of daisies back to your room? ♦ Tu-Sa; Su morning. 141 Rue St-Dominique (at Rue Augereau). 01.47.05.86.26. Métros: Ecole Militaire, Pont-de-l'Alma (RER)

76 Le Chariot du Roy At first glance one wonders whether the vibrant colors of the fruits and vegetables here are due to trickery with lighting: The strawberries, green beans, pencil-thin asparagus, mangoes, kiwis, kumquats, mini bananas, and other deluxe fruits and vegetables look too perfect to be real. There is also a cheese counter, a selection of nuts and dried fruits, and assorted delicacies such as quail eggs. ♦ Tu-Sa; Su morning; closed in August. 145 Rue St-Dominique (between Rue Augereau and Pl du Général-Gouraud). 01.47.05.07.08. Métros: Ecole Militaire, Pont-de-l'Alma (RER)

76 Dubernet Behind the wood-columned facade is a mega-selection of tins and jars of foie gras, *confit d'oie* (goose confit), *boudin blanc truffé* (blood sausage with truffles), pâtés, pot-au-feu, and *gésiers de canard* (duck gizzards). On the last Friday and Saturday of each month the boutique sells its delicacies at a 25- to 30-percent discount.

◆ Tu-Sa; closed in August. 2 Rue Augereau (at Rue St-Dominique). 01.45.55.50.71. Métros: Ecole Militaire, Pont-de-l'Alma (RER)

77 Hôtel de Londres $$ This calm, quiet, 30-room hotel just off Rue St-Dominique has some fifth- and sixth-floor rooms that look out on the top of the **Eiffel Tower;** these are also the smallest rooms on the premises (the double beds are a tight squeeze), but for many that's a small price to pay for a view of Paris's most famous edifice. Traditional-breakfast lovers can order scrambled eggs, ham, or omelettes to accompany the continental breakfast (not included in the room rate) served in the breakfast room; there's no restaurant. ◆ 1 Rue Augereau (at Rue St-Dominique). 01.45.51.63.02; fax 01.47.05.28.96. Métros: Ecole Militaire, Pont-de-l'Alma (RER)

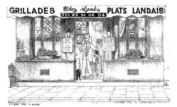

77 Chez Agnès ★★$$ In a small salon with rows of tables in the front room and a discreet dog named Gipsy in the back, Agnès offers daily specials such as *salade au foie gras, pavé de thon au poivre* (tuna steak with black pepper), and *entrecôte sauce roquefort.* Her menu also features unusual crepes: *la contre courante* is filled with smoked salmon, butter, and lemon; the *feux de Bengale* has chicken, curry, mushrooms, and bananas; *l'Emeraude* is filled with mint and chocolate; and *le lemon incest* is stuffed with lots of lemon filling. ◆ Daily lunch and dinner; closed two weeks in August. 1 *bis* Rue Augereau (at Rue St-Dominique). 01.45.51.06.04. Métros: Ecole Militaire, Pont-de-l'Alma (RER)

CAFE
—de—
MARS

78 Café de Mars ★★$$ A strong flavor of California permeates this cool, relaxed restaurant. The US–inspired menu includes chicken brochettes marinated with ginger and lemon, Buffalo wings, brownies, and cheesecake. After 9PM young patrons from the **American University** hang out at the bar. ◆ M-F lunch and dinner; Sa dinner; closed last two weeks of August. Reservations recommended. 11 Rue Augereau (at Rue du

Gros-Caillou). 01.47.05.05.91. Métros: Ecole Militaire, Pont-de-l'Alma (RER)

79 Karlov ★★$$$ Old snapshots in the glass case out front advertise that Robert de Niro, Jon Voight, Alain Delon, and Jacques Chirac have all passed through the carnival-booth facade of this Russian restaurant. Schmoozy *propriétaire* Charles Maman is somewhat of a celebrity himself; his Muses Productions produces the *Traveling Gourmet,* which can be seen on American cable television. Once you pass through the writhing red entrance, you enter a distorted scene that seems to meld the worlds of Peter Max and Dostoyevsky. In this atmosphere everyone looks Russian: The young friendly servers seem to have stepped right off the barge from Odessa, and even the somber groups of French diners spring to life after a fifth glass of Zubrovka.

Regulars come as much for the Gypsy singers and balalaika music as for the cuisine; follow their lead and go straight for a carafe of Russian vodka or a bottle of Bulgarian Cabernet Sauvignon and bask in the faded red-velvet glory while listening to the spirited folk music. The menu is strong on caviar and salmon: good choices would be the *crêpe Tsarivich,* with caviar, smoked salmon, lemon, and olive oil, as a starter; a main course of beef stroganoff, salmon steak, or lamb brochettes; and a dessert of apple strudel or *coupe Pouchkine* (coffee ice cream topped with coffee liqueur). Maman's newest Russian restaurant, **Nikita,** is in the upscale 16th arrondissement (6 Rue Faustin Hélie, between Pl Possoz and Rue de la Pompe, 01.45.04.04.33). ◆ M-Sa dinner; music starts at 10PM. Reservations recommended. 197 Rue de Grenelle (between Aves Bosquet and de La Bourdonnais). 01.45.51.29.21. Métro: Ecole Militaire

80 Le Troubadour ★$ This hole-in-the-wall bar and brasserie seats 18 people and is often filled with **American University** students lunching on ham and gruyère sandwiches or a *plat du jour* of sausage and apples, *blanquette de veau* (veal stew), or *boeuf bourguignon.* ◆ M-Sa breakfast and lunch; bar open until 10PM. 49 Ave Bosquet (between Rues du Champ-de-Mars and de Grenelle). 01.45.51.24.25. Métro: Ecole Militaire, Pont-de-l'Alma (RER)

In 1852, French merchant Aristide Boucicaut took control of a small Parisian shop named Bon Marché and turned it into the world's first true department store. Among the retailing innovations introduced by Boucicaut were fixed and marked prices, free entrance to the store without obligation to buy, and policies allowing customers to exchange merchandise and obtain refunds.

81 The Real McCoy Longing for Pop Tarts, Lays potato chips, a peanut butter and jelly sandwich, or a sesame-seed bagel? You've come to the right place. This small American grocery also has a sandwich counter. ♦ Daily. 194 Rue de Grenelle (between Rue Cler and Ave Bosquet). 01.45.56.98.82. Métro: Ecole Militaire

82 American University Established in 1962 as an independent arts and sciences institution, the university currently has 112 faculty members and almost 1,000 students from 80 countries. Forty percent of the students are American, many on junior-year exchange programs from other schools. The university is strong on art history, comparative literature, European cultural studies, and international economics; its largest department is International Business Administration. This building houses some of the school's administrative offices, a student cafe, and some classrooms. Other school facilities are at 147 Rue de Grenelle. If you want to sit in on a class or enroll in a summer course, contact the director of admissions. ♦ 31 Ave Bosquet (between Rues St-Dominique and de l'Université). 01.40.62.05.73. Métros: Ecole Militaire, Pont-de-l'Alma (RER)

83 Le 6 Bosquet ★★$$ This sophisticated restaurant has smooth service and a smart-looking modern dining room. Burgundy-born owner-chef Emmanuel Joinville creates such sensations as *ravioli de foie gras de canard au bouillon d'épices douces* (ravioli stuffed with foie gras served in a clear broth). Heartier appetites will enjoy *parmentier tortue* (crab with creamed potatoes), roast lamb with carrots in tarragon, and grilled prawns served with apple chutney and basmati rice. Savor

the desserts—especially the chocolate fondant. There's a good selection of Burgundy wines. ♦ M-F lunch and dinner; Sa dinner; closed two weeks in August. Reservations required. 6 Ave Bosquet (at Cité de l'Alma). 01.45.56.97.26. Métro: Pont-de-l'Alma (RER)

84 Place de la Résistance This intersection was named for the French forces who fought to free Paris from Nazi control from 1940 to 1944. ♦ At Quais d'Orsay and Branly and Aves Rapp and Bosquet. Métro: Pont-de-l'Alma (RER)

85 Rue Cognacq-Jay This street was opened in 1928, bisecting the land owned by M. Cognacq and his wife, whose maiden name was Jay; the two were philanthropists and founders of **La Samaritaine** department store. The area between Rue Malar and Avenue Bosquet was occupied in 1910 by a *parc d'attractions* called **Magic City,** which disappeared in 1925. ♦ Between Rue Malar and Pl de la Résistance. Métro: Pont-de-l'Alma (RER)

86 Egouts (Sewers) The *égouts* of Paris are always a popular underground attraction. This 1,305-mile network of tunnels was constructed during the reign of Napoléon III and is considered one of Baron Haussmann's finest achievements. If laid end to end, the tunnels would reach from Paris to Istanbul. The sewers house freshwater pipes, telephone wires, traffic-light cables, and the city's pneumatic postal network, which was shut down in 1984. The hour-long sewer tour includes a film, a photograph exhibition, and a walk through the 18-foot-high by 14-foot-wide tunnels. Ever since a notorious bank heist in which the robbers made their getaway via the sewers, underground boat cruises have not been permitted. ♦ Admission. W-Sa 11AM-5PM May through September; W-Sa 11AM-4PM October through April. Quai d'Orsay (at Pont de l'Alma). 01.47.05.10.29. Métro: Pont-de-l'Alma (RER)

87 13-59 Quai Branly During the First Empire this site served as a wood storage yard for the construction of ships. Half a century later, when the **Mobilier National** (National Storehouse) was located here, it served as a drop-off point for government marble. More recently, the empty expanse was the proposed site of a new **Centre de Conférences International** (International Conference Center), one of François Mitterrand's grand architectural projects. French architect **François Soler** won the 1990 design competition with his controversial proposal calling for three transparent glass boxes, one serving as a reception area, another to be used as diplomatic space, and the third to hold a press center. The design was highly criticized for both budgetary and security reasons, and the project was abandoned in

1992 after construction had begun. The site subsequently was paved over to become a big parking lot; it now contains temporary structures that house art exhibitions and salons. ♦ Between Pl de la Résistance and Ave de La Bourdonnais. Métros: Pont-de-l'Alma (RER), Champ de Mars–Tour Eiffel (RER)

88 Les Deux Abeilles ★★★$ Here is an unpretentious little tea salon that feels like a grandmother's cottage, with pink-flowered wallpaper, terra-cotta tiles, lace curtains, wooden sideboards, and homemade tarts cooling in the window. The food is substantial and good; menu items include *gratiné d'aubergine* (eggplant au gratin), omelettes with cèpes, tomato and thyme tarts, and *salade de feuilleté au roquefort* (salad with roquefort cheese). Desserts include Berthillon ice cream, *tarte aux poires* (pear tart), *tarte tatin* (apple tart), pear crumble, and raspberry tart soufflé. Tea-time treats include scones with butter and confiture, warm cinnamon brioches, and *chocolat à l'ancienne* (old-fashioned hot chocolate) with cream. Pleasant, soft-spoken waitresses serve steamy hot tea in pink-flowered cups. If you want something stronger than tea, a bottle of Lalande de Pommerol, Domaine de Musset will do quite nicely. ♦ M-Sa breakfast, lunch, and tea until 7PM. 189 Rue de l'Université (between Aves Rapp and Franco-Russe). 01.45.55.64.04. Métro: Pont-de-l'Alma (RER)

89 La Flamberge ★★★$$$ This ochre-and-red jewel box of a room is packed with a bustling, cheek-kissing crowd at lunch, and is only slightly less frenetic at dinner. Chef James Baron's traditional French menu is well prepared and includes *filet de daurade poêlée aux artichauts poivrade* (sea bream fillet with peppered artichokes), and *baron d'agneau rôti au thym* (roast lamb with thyme). A good selection of both red and white wines completes the menu. ♦ M-F lunch and dinner; Sa dinner. Reservations recommended. 12 Ave Rapp (at Ave Franco-Russe). 01.47.05.91.37. Métro: Pont-de-l'Alma (RER)

90 Rue de Monttessuy This otherwise unremarkable street is impressive for its angular view of one of the **Eiffel Tower**'s legs. The famous monument, usually depicted in its totality, becomes a revelation when seen at such close proximity and from such a refreshing perspective. ♦ Between Aves Rapp and de La Bourdonnais. Métro: Pont-de-l'Alma (RER)

90 Escrouzailles ★★$$ A refreshingly simple restaurant, it serves *aspic de saumon,* rabbit fricassee with celery purée, and crepes suzette with Cointreau. ♦ Daily lunch and dinner. 6 Rue de Monttessuy (between Aves Rapp and de La Bourdonnais). 01.47.05.93.51. Métro: Pont-de-l'Alma (RER). Also at: 36 Rue du Colisée (between Rue du Faubourg-St-Honoré and Ave Franklin-D.-Roosevelt). 01.45.62.94.00. Métro: St-Philippe-du-Roule

91 American University Library As the semester draws to an end, this small library is full of **American University** students hustling to finish term papers and cramming for final exams. The library is open only to university students and members of the **American Library**, located directly behind it on the Rue du Général-Camou (see below). ♦ Hours vary; call ahead. 9 bis Rue de Monttessuy (between Aves Rapp and de La Bourdonnais). 01.40.62.05.50. Métro: Pont-de-l'Alma (RER)

92 American Library Founded in 1920, this is the largest English-language library in continental Europe, with more than 80,000 volumes. Anyone can become a member (for as little as a day) and partake of a collection that includes the standard fiction, nonfiction, and reference books as well as more than 450 periodicals and 6,000-plus children's books. A free film screening and story reading is held every Wednesday afternoon in the children's room. An added bonus to being a member is access to the **American University Library**, which is linked to the back of this one. ♦ Tu-Sa; limited hours in August. 10 Rue du Général-Camou (between Aves Rapp and de La Bourdonnais). 01.45.51.46.82. Métro: Pont-de-l'Alma (RER)

93 Pâtisserie de la Tour Eiffel ★$$ Before attempting a trip to the summit of the **Eiffel Tower,** enjoy a novel view of the edifice's east leg from the terrace of this *pâtisserie,* which doubles as a tea salon. Fortify yourself for the ascent with a hot chocolate and a tarte de *framboise.* ♦ Tu-Su 6AM-8PM. 21 Ave de La Bourdonnais (at Rue de Monttessuy). 01.47.05.59.81. Métros: Champ de Mars–Tour Eiffel (RER), Pont-de-l'Alma (RER)

93 Vin sur Vin ★★★$$$ There are but eight tables at this honest-to-goodness neighbor-hood restaurant, and the atmosphere is friendly and warm. It's the kind of place where regulars with a craving for a classic dish such as pot-au-feu with foie gras or veal liver *à la diable* (veal liver in a spicy sauce) can order it 24 hours in advance. Otherwise, owner

Patrice Vidal features a seasonally changing menu with original dishes; some past favorites include duck with peaches, *turbot rôti à huile d'olive* (roasted turbot in olive oil), sardine cake with basil, fresh scallop salad, *côtelettes d'agneau "Sirocco"* (lamb chops fried with semolina and grapes in a vegetable sauce), and, for dessert, crème brûlée or a bitter-chocolate tart. The wine list is fabulous and includes some reasonably priced bottles. ♦ Tu-F lunch and dinner; M, Sa dinner. Reservations recommended. 20 Rue de Monttessuy (between Aves Rapp and de La Bourdonnais). 01.47.05.14.20. Métro: Pont-de-l'Alma (RER)

94 Le Sancerre ★★$ Jean-Louis Guillaume's wine bar takes its name from the rich, dry, full-bodied Loire Valley wine that he features on his menu. Wine is the primary focus here; the menu offers very simple fare. Snuggle up in the warm, woody dining room and order a bottle with some *jambon fumé* (smoked ham) and an omelette. ♦ M-F breakfast, lunch, and dinner; Sa lunch; closed two weeks in August. 22 Ave Rapp (between Rues du Général-Camou and de Monttessuy). 01.45.51.75.91. Métro: Pont-de-l'Alma (RER)

95 Pharmacie Rapp Worth a peek even if you don't need *un adhésif* or *l'aspirine,* this corner pharmacy has an 1899 interior that's a pretty assemblage of delicately carved wood cupboards and reliefs of medicinal plants. Notice the original blue glass jars, or *pots à pharmacie,* in the windows. ♦ M-Sa. 23 Ave Rapp (at Rue Edmond-Valentin). 01.47.05.41.25. Métro: Pont-de-l'Alma (RER)

96 7 Rue Edmond-Valentin Irish writer James Joyce lived here from 1935 until 1939. It is still a residential building. ♦ Between Ave Bosquet and Rue Dupont-des-Loges. Métro: Pont-de-l'Alma (RER)

97 Puyricard M. and Mme. Roelandts won the Médaille d'Or at the 1994 International Festival of Chocolate. Their shop was honored as one of the six best *chocolatières* in Europe, thanks to the delectable chocolates from Aix-en-Provence sold here. Heavenly coconut-praline, raspberry-marzipan, apricot-truffle, and mandarin-orange chocolates are some of the irresistible cocoa fantasies available. ♦ M afternoon; Tu-Sa. 27 Ave Rapp (between Sq Rapp and Rue Edmond-Valentin). 01.47.05.59.47. Métro: Pont-de-l'Alma (RER)

97 29 Avenue Rapp Paris's prime example of Art Nouveau architecture won designer **Jules Lavirotte** first prize at the Concours de Façades de la Ville de Paris in 1901. A sense of humor can be seen in this apartment building's glazed terra-cotta decoration of animal and flower motifs intermingled with female figures, which was deliberately erotic and subversive for its day. ♦ Between Sq Rapp and Rue Edmond-Valentin. Métro: Pont-de-l'Alma (RER)

98 Square Rapp This small private way was called Villa de Monttessuy before receiving its current name from the neighboring Avenue Rapp. Notice the trompe l'oeil perspective created by the dark green lattice on the building at the end of the street. ♦ Between Rues St-Dominique and Edmond-Valentin. Métro: Pont-de-l'Alma (RER)

On Square Rapp:

No. 3 Another **Jules Lavirotte** construction, this 1899 apartment building features a wild conglomeration of balconies, railings, glazed brick and terra-cotta decoration, and a watchtower whose finial seems to be a hybrid of Tintin's rocket and the dome of **Sacré-Coeur.**

Société Théosophique de France This curious and ponderous brick building is the headquarters of the **French Theosophical Society.** The interior lobby, a cubic space surmounted by a dome, is somewhat reminiscent of the architecture of India, but unfortunately comes across as heavy and clunky rather than as uplifting and inspirational. The society sponsors some fine lectures (often on Sunday), classes in religion, and music programs featuring international artists such as Ravi Shankar. ♦ Tu-Sa. 4 Sq Rapp. 01.47.05.26.30

At the Société Théosophique de France:

Librairie Adyar The society's bookstore stocks volumes about spirituality, psychology, parapsychology, astrology, and homeopathy, with some titles in English. You will also find candle holders, crystal pyramids, tarot cards, incense, meditation tapes, and anything else you might need to start your journey toward enlightenment. ♦ Tu-Sa. 01.45.51.31.79

99 18 Rue Sedillot The vaguely Baroque overtones of this turn-of-the-century apartment block by **Jules Lavirotte** are typical of the sinuous style employed by the Art Nouveau architect on several Paris apartment buildings. ♦ Between Rues St-Dominique and Edmond-Valentin. Métro: Pont-de-l'Alma (RER)

Restaurants/Clubs: Red **Hotels:** Blue
Shops/ ⌕ Outdoors: Green **Sights/Culture:** Black

100 Avenue de la Bourdonnais Opened in 1770, this avenue once had five entrance gates leading to the **Parc du Champ-de-Mars** along its route. The last survivor, the **Porte Rapp,** existed until 1920. Take time to explore this upscale residential neighborhood by strolling along the short, perpendicular streets (such as Avenue Silvestre de Sacy, Rue du Maréchal-Harispe, and Rue Marinoni) that lead from the Avenue de la Bourdonnais into the park. Here beautiful apartment buildings and gardens are set back from the street behind iron gates, and well-heeled ladies in fur coats walk their well-coiffed dogs. ♦ Between Pl de l'Ecole Militaire and Quai Branly. Métros: Ecole Militaire, Pont-de-l'Alma (RER)

Kniaz Igor

101 Kniaz Igor ★$$ The atmosphere is all red velvet and balalaika music, and Beluga caviar, borscht with sour cream, chicken Kiev, *roulade de filet de boeuf* (rolled beef fillet), and vodka sorbet are featured menu items at this Russian restaurant. Faded photos of past dinner guest Roman Polanski are proudly displayed in the window. ♦ M-Sa dinner; closed last two weeks of July. Reservations recommended. 43 Ave de La Bourdonnais (between Pl du Général-Gouraud and Rue du Général-Camou). 01.45.51.91.71. Métros: Ecole Militaire, Pont-de-l'Alma (RER)

Parlez-Vous Anglais?

If English is your first—or only—language, and you need a book fix in Paris, here are the English-language bookstores of choice:

Albion 13 Rue Charles-V (between Rues Beautreillis and St-Paul). 01.42.72.50.71

Brentano's 37 Ave de l'Opéra (between Rues Danielle-Casanova and d'Antin). 01.42.61.52.50

Galignani 224 Rue de Rivoli (between Rues d'Alger and de Castiglione). 01.42.60.76.07

Shakespeare and Company 37 Rue de la Bûcherie (between Rues St-Julien-le-Pauvre and du Petit-Pont). 01.43.26.96.50

The Village Voice 6 Rue Princesse (between Rues Guisarde and du Four). 01.46.33.36.47

W.H. Smith and Son 248 Rue de Rivoli (at Rue Cambon). 01.44.77.88.99

102 Décembre en Mars British teddy bears, Bauhaus blocks, Native American dolls, hobbyhorses, spinning tops, wooden trains, and rubber ducks are just a few of the colorful delights sold in this little toy store. ♦ Tu-Sa; closed in August. 65 Ave de La Bourdonnais (between Rue de Grenelle and Pl du Général-Gouraud). 01.45.51.15.45. Métros: Ecole Militaire, Pont-de-l'Alma (RER)

103 Ecole Militaire In an attempt to rival the **Hôtel des Invalides** of Louis XIV, Louis XV and his mistress, Mme. de Pompadour, hired **Jacques-Ange Gabriel,** the architect who created **Place de la Concorde** in the 1770s, to design a military school. Raising money for the project was a problem until Beaumarchais, who wrote *The Marriage of Figaro* and gave harp lessons to Louis XV's daughters, came up with the idea of paying for the building through a lottery and a tax on playing cards.

Standing at the foot of the Champ-de-Mars, the school, with its Corinthian columns, statues, dome, double colonnade, and elegant wrought-iron fence, is considered to be one of *Gabriel's* masterpieces. The most famous graduate of the school, which is still in operation, was Napoléon Bonaparte. ♦ By appointment only. For information write to: Direction Générale, Ecole Militaire, 1 Pl Joffre, 75007 Paris. 1 Pl Joffre (at Ave de la Motte-Piquet). No phone. Métro: Ecole Militaire

104 Parc du Champ-de-Mars Named for the god of war, this large rectangular park stretching from the **Ecole Militaire** to the **Eiffel Tower** has long been a site of battles, both actual and preparatory. Here, in 52 BC, Roman legions defeated the Parisii; in 886 the Parisians beat back the invading Vikings; and, in the early 18th century, when this was the parade ground for the **Ecole Militaire,** Napoléon drilled with his fellow cadets.

Now the park, adorned with flowering trees, shrubs, and miniature cascades, is the site of pony rides, marionette theaters, organ-grinders, occasional parades for children, and Christmastime fairs and pageantry. You can do almost anything in the **Champ-de-Mars** except have a picnic on the lawns. French grass is sacred grass, and a bluecoat (guard) will appear and order you off before you've even had time to unwrap your salami and uncork the Bordeaux. ♦ Bordered by Allées Adrienne-Lecouvreur and Thomy-Thierry, and Aves de la Motte-Piquet and Gustave-Eiffel. Métros: Bir-Hakeim, Champ de Mars–Tour Eiffel (RER), Ecole Militaire

The French Revolution, with its emphasis on the spread of ideas, was a boon for Parisian cafes. The city had 2,000 cafes before the Revolution began; that number had doubled by the early 1800s.

105 Tour Eiffel (Eiffel Tower) In 1889, the world was drunk on science. The decade had produced one technological marvel after another: the automobile, the telephone, the electric light, and the **Eiffel Tower.** First dubbed a monstrosity, then considered the definitive symbol of Paris, the tower was built to commemorate the centennial of the storming of the **Bastille** and to stand as the centerpiece of the 1889 International Exhibition of Paris. The now-classic design by **Gustave Eiffel** beat 700 other entries in the design competition. (Among the losers, for obvious reasons, were a giant guillotine and a mammoth lighthouse.) The tower was the tallest structure in the world until 1930, when the title was usurped by the Chrysler Building in New York. **Eiffel,** who also engineered the iron bones of the Statue of Liberty (undergirding the Frédéric Bartholdi copper structure), was himself a diminutive man, only five feet tall.

Spanning 2.5 acres at its base, the tower is made of 18,000 metal parts held together with 2.5 million rivets and covered with 40 tons of brown paint. (The structure is repainted every seven years and at last count received its 17th coat.) A thousand feet high (more than three times the height of the Statue of Liberty), it weighs 7,000 tons and sways no more than 4.5 inches in strong winds. The weight is distributed so elegantly that it exerts no more pressure on the ground per centimeter than does a person seated in a four-legged chair.

When the tower was first completed, much of Paris was unimpressed. Its stark, geometric structure offended the prevailing Beaux Arts sensibility. Prominent critics, including luminaries such as Paul Verlaine, Guy de Maupassant, the younger Dumas, and Emile Zola, denounced it as the "Tower of Babel" and a dishonor to Paris. Maupassant used to say he liked to have lunch at the tower because it was the only place in Paris where he didn't have to look at it.

In later years it was discovered that the tower could function as the world's largest antenna, and during World War I it became one of France's most vital weapons. Since then, it has served as a radio and meteorological post, and in 1985 was fitted with broadcasting equipment for France's fifth television channel.

Despite these eminently utilitarian applications, the **Eiffel Tower**'s primary effect is to excite the imagination. One man tried to fly from it and was killed when his wings failed him. In 1923 a bicycle-riding journalist careened down the steps to the ground from the top floor. A mountaineer scaled it in 1954, and in 1984 two Englishmen parachuted from it.

In 1980, a nine-year renovation program began, which brought great changes to the tower. About 1,500 tons of extraneous concrete (mostly in the form of concession areas) were removed from the first platform; four new electronic glass elevators and new visitors' facilities were installed; and the pavilion, housing the tower's restaurant, **Le Jules Verne** (see page124) was remodeled. The most dramatic change of all, however, was a new 292,000-watt interior lighting system inaugurated on New Year's Eve 1986, replacing the old floodlights. The new lights illuminate the entire structure from within, creating a golden tracery against the sky at night. The renovation program was completed in time for the tower's 100th birthday on the bicentennial of the French Revolution in 1989.

♦ Admission varies for each level. Daily 9:30AM-11PM. Ave Gustave-Eiffel (between Aves Silvestre-de-Sacy and Octave-Gréard). 01.44.11.23.23. Métros: Bir-Hakeim, Champ de Mars–Tour Eiffel (RER)

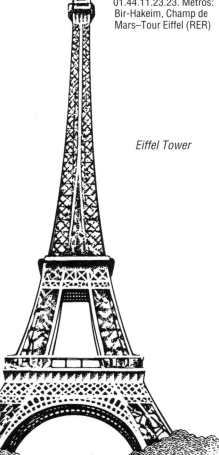

Eiffel Tower

Within the Tour Eiffel:

Le Jules Verne ★★★$$$ One of the most beautiful views of Paris, day or night, is from this perch in the **Eiffel Tower.** Sleek and seductive, the all-black decor is an elegant backdrop for the restaurant's chic clientele and the creative and refined cuisine of chef Alain Reix. *Entrecôte de veau de Corrèze au jus de laitue goût d'herbes* (veal from Corrèze sautéed with herbs), *langoustines rôties et crabe, pommes croustillantes, et asperges* (roasted prawns with crabmeat, fried potatoes, and asparagus), and *tarte au chocolat Caraïbe et glace à la vanille de Tahiti* (a sweet and spicy chocolate tart with exotic vanilla ice cream) are just some of the reasons that reservations here are so difficult to obtain. Be sure, when you reserve, to specify your view preference: a table on the Trocadéro side reveals a perspective all the way to **La Défense,** while the **Ecole Militaire** dining room looks out toward Montparnasse. ♦ Daily lunch and dinner. Reservations required. Second level (elevator at south pier). 01.45.55.61.44

Altitude 95 ★$$ This silvery metallic restaurant wedged in among the 19th-century brown steel girders of the **Eiffel Tower** takes its design inspiration from a 19th-century vision of the future: There are shiny bolts on the tables, silver-riveted bucket seats on wheels, and altimeters reminding you of your elevation of 95 meters (312 feet) above sea level. The menu features dishes from several regions in France that can be mixed and matched to create a meal: You might start with oysters from Brittany, then have a Franche-Comté–inspired fillet of trout, followed by Provençale goat cheeses, and a dessert of crepes flambéed with Grand Marnier from the Ile-de-France. Parents will be pleased with the inexpensive children's menu. Unfortunately the restaurant's inconsistent cuisine doesn't do justice to its spectacular location and four-star view. ♦ Daily lunch, tea, and dinner. Reservations recommended. First level (elevator at north pier). 01.45.55.20.04

106 Palais de Chaillot Perched on its hill across the Seine from the **Eiffel Tower,** this palace serves as the Right Bank termination of the monumental axis that sweeps up across the **Champ-de-Mars** from the **Ecole Militaire.** The white sandstone twin pavilions of the palace were built for the Paris Exhibition of 1937, replacing the earlier **Palais du Trocadéro,** a massive barrel-shaped building erected for the 1878 exhibition. Although its stark forms and groups of heroic statuary uncomfortably recall the type of Fascist architecture that emerged during the period in Germany and Italy, the **Palais de Chaillot** succeeds both as a monument and a cultural complex. Within its two curving wings (which cradle a series of descending gardens and pools) are four museums, two theaters, a library, and a restaurant. Note: the **Musée des Monuments Français,** the **Musée du Cinéma Henri Langlois,** and the screening room of the **Cinémathèque Français** were damaged in a July 1997 fire. All three were closed at press time; call for current details. ♦ Entrance on Ave Albert-de-Mun (between Aves des Nations-Unies and du Président-Wilson). 01.45.53.21.86. Métro: Trocadéro

Within the Palais de Chaillot:

Musée de la Marine Founded in 1827 by order of Charles X and moved here in 1943, the museum displays scale models of ships; artifacts and mementoes of naval heroes; and exhibits on the scientific and technical aspects of the history of navigation. ♦ Admission. M, W-Su. 01.45.53.31.70

Musée de l'Homme (Museum of Mankind) The museum traces human history through a series of anthropological, archaeological, and ethnological displays. ♦ Admission. M, W-Su. 01.44.05.72.72

Musée des Monuments Français Opened in 1880, this museum was the brainchild of **Eugène Emmanuel Viollet-le-Duc,** who restored **Notre Dame** in the 19th century. Through drawings, models, and reproductions, visitors can trace the development of monumental sculpture, statuary, and mural painting from the early Romanesque period to the decoration of the great Gothic cathedrals. ♦ Admission. M, W-Su. 01.44.05.39.10

Musée du Cinéma Henri Langlois This overview of the evolution of filmmaking was put together by Langlois, a film buff extraordinaire. The eclectic collection includes more than 3,000 film-related objects, including costumes, photographic stills, scripts, and the Lumière brothers' kinematograph and photorama. Many film sets are also preserved here, including a street scene from *Les Enfants du Paradis* (considered by many to be the best French film ever made). ♦ Admission. W-Su; guided tours on the hour. 01.45.53.74.39, 01.45.53.21.86

Cinémathèque Français (Film Library) One of the richest film archives in the world, it screens a large selection of movie classics and specializes in retrospectives of stars and filmmakers. Three or four films are shown daily. ♦ Admission. Daily. 01.53.65.74.74

Théâtre National de Chaillot Located beneath the **Palais Terrace,** this theater seats 1,800 people and features productions of mainstream European classics and musical reviews. Within the theater is the smaller **Salle Gémier,** which stages more experimental works. ♦ Box office: daily. 01.45.05.14.50, 01.47.27.81.15

107 Pont de Bir-Hakeim Along the top of this double-decker bridge runs one of the only aboveground métro lines in Paris, which provides a spectacular view of the **Eiffel Tower** as it is approached from the Seine. Board at the **Passy** station, just across the river, and travel toward **Nation.** The lower bridge is for pedestrians. The bridge was constructed in 1903 to replace an inadequate pedestrian bridge, the **Pont de Passy.** ♦ Between Quai de Grenelle and Ave du Président-Kennedy. Métros: Passy, Bir-Hakeim

107 Allée des Cygnes A small narrow islet that divides the Seine provides a pleasant promenade from the Pont de Bir-Hakeim to the Pont de Grenelle with a view of **Radio France** (a modern building that housed the French Broadcasting Service until 1975) on the Right Bank and the **Front de Seine** (a modern urban-renewal project integrating high-rise apartment and office towers, public buildings, and a shopping center) on the Left Bank. On the upriver side of Pont Bir-Hakeim is a 1930s equestrian statue named *La France Renaissante* by Danish sculptor Wederkinch, and downriver on the Pont de Grenelle is a small replica of the **Statue of Liberty** donated by the American community in Paris in 1885. ♦ Between Ponts de Grenelle and de Bir-Hakeim. Métros: Passy, Bir-Hakeim

108 8 Boulevard de Grenelle A plaque records the roundup of thousands of Parisians, most of them Jews, in the *vélodrome* (cycling track) here on 16 July 1942 before their deportation to Nazi concentration camps. Of the approximately 150,000 adults and 20,000 children arrested by the Germans and the cooperating Paris police, only 3,000 adults and six children survived. The *vélodrome* was demolished in 1959. ♦ Between Rue St-Charles and Quai de Grenelle. Métro: Bir-Hakeim

109 Avenue de Suffren Like Avenue de la Bourdonnais, this avenue opened in 1770 as a perimeter road around the **Parc du Champ-de-Mars.** It was named after Vice Admiral *Bailli* Pierre André de Suffren (1726-1788), the justice administrator of St-Tropez and commander of the Ordre de Malte, who fought for the Americans during the Revolutionary War. ♦ Between Blvd Garibaldi and Quai Branly. Métros: Champ de Mars–Tour Eiffel (RER), La Motte-Picquet–Grenelle, Ecole Militaire

109 Paris Hilton $$$ Comprising 11 stories of concrete and glass, this hotel, constructed in 1966, resembles a modern apartment block from the outside, and the slick marble lobby looks more like a bank than a hotel foyer. Overlooking the **Eiffel Tower** and the **Palais de Chaillot,** the property offers 456 rooms and suites, along with several conference rooms and ballrooms. The 10th and 11th floors are the executive floors, with a private lounge and other extras. ♦ 18 Ave de Suffren (at Rue Jean-Rey). 01.44.38.56.00; fax 01.44.38.56.10. Métro: Champ de Mars–Tour Eiffel (RER)

Within the Paris Hilton:

Le Western ★★$$ Saloon doors swing open, revealing this American Southwest–themed restaurant where the waiters and waitresses wear jeans and checkered shirts and the maître d' is dressed as a sheriff. The menu (which is made of leather and weighs almost two pounds) features an abundance of beef, such as T-bone and sirloin steaks, along with spareribs, tacos, barbecued chicken, grilled lobster, cheesecake, and pecan pie. ♦ Daily lunch and dinner. 01.44.38.56.00

Le Bar Suffren Here's a good place to stop for a quick breakfast of coffee and croissants, or a more leisurely pre- or post-dinner cocktail. ♦ Daily 7AM-11PM. 01.44.38.56.00

Le Toit de Paris ★★$$ This rooftop bar, which serves creative cocktails named after Paris monuments, looks out over the **Eiffel Tower,** the most famous monument of them all. The Sunday Champagne brunch buffet features main courses of lobster, prime rib, and salmon, and a selection of *patisserie.* ♦ M-Sa dinner; Su brunch. 01.44.38.56.00

La Terrasse ★$$ The hotel's coffee shop serves French and international specialties in a verdant setting. In the morning there is a continental or American breakfast buffet, at tea time there are cakes and pastries, and lunch and dinner specialties include fresh oysters, onion soup gratinée, escargot Bourgogne, sole meunière, roast chicken, club sandwiches, and vegetarian lasagna. ♦ Daily breakfast, lunch, tea, and dinner. 01.44.38.56.00

You may notice Parisians toting around baguettes with the last two inches munched off; it's traditional to eat *le croûton,* the crusty end, before the baguette makes it home. Serious baguette fans know the baking schedule of their neighborhood *boulangerie* and time their visit for when the bread is fresh from the oven.

The Eiffel Tower is constructed of more than 7,000 tons of iron, 18,038 girders and plates, and 2,500,843 rivets.

Chez Ribe

110 Chez Ribe ★★$$ The exquisite wood paneling dates from 1900, but the specialties on Jean-Antoine Père's prix-fixe menu are as fresh as can be. Start with tartare of smoked salmon or eggplant cake with tomato sauce, then try a *plat* of cod with aioli or duck with lavender honey. For dessert order the apples with warm caramel sauce. ♦ M-F lunch and dinner; Sa dinner; closed in August. Reservations recommended. 15 Ave de Suffren (at Ave Octave-Gréard). 01.45.66.53.79. Métro: Champ de Mars–Tour Eiffel (RER)

111 Le Backgammon For the last 10 years M. Borentain has been selling the shop's namesake games along with chess sets, Chinese solitaire, and casino games, both old and new. ♦ M afternoon; Tu-Sa; closed in August. 62 Ave de Suffren (between Rues de Presles and Alexis-Carrel). 01.45.67.59.18. Métros: Champ de Mars–Tour Eiffel (RER), La Motte-Picquet–Grenelle, Ecole Militaire

112 74 Avenue de Suffren During the Universal Exposition of 1900, this was the site of the **Grande Roue de Paris,** a 350-foot Ferris wheel (one-third the height of the **Eiffel Tower**). The wheel had 40 wooden cars divided into five series of eight cars; it took five stops, boarding eight cars at a time, to load the whole wheel. In what is perhaps a metaphor for the French mentality, each eight-car unit was composed of six second-class cars, one first-class car, and a restaurant. The Ferris wheel's axis was supported by two pylons set in concrete foundations; between them was a garden that was the site of a theater, a restaurant, a hotel, several souvenir stands, and a number of duels. Today the area is built up with a variety of structures, none as fanciful as the late lamented Ferris wheel. ♦ At Rue Dupleix. Métros: La Motte-Picquet–Grenelle, Ecole Militaire

113 Foc Ly ★★★$$
You'll find no dragons or paper lanterns in this chic, contemporary Thai/Chinese restaurant with friendly young servers and a decor of blond wood and peach hues. Faithful clients, many of them patrons of the restaurant's former location of 20 years in the fashionable suburb of Neuilly, come for the *boeuf parfumé au soja noir* (beef in soy sauce), steamed sole *à la*

Cantonnaise, Thai-style *brochettes de gambas* (shrimp kabobs), and sizzling meats cooked at your table on hot stones. ♦ Tu-Su lunch and dinner; closed mid-July through August. Reservations recommended. 71 Ave de Suffren (between Ave de la Motte-Picquet and Rue Jean-Carriès). 01.47.83.27.12. Métros: La Motte-Picquet–Grenelle, Ecole Militaire

114 Le Village Suisse On this site, allotted to the Swiss for the 1900 Universal Exhibition, the Swiss government built a mock-Alpine village, complete with mountains, farms, cows, and a church. Don't expect to find Heidi and snow-capped peaks here today, however; this is now a deteriorating, tacky shopping center (renovated in the 1960s) covered in black and white mosaic tiles and loose paving blocks, unbefitting the upscale antiques dealers and fashionable decorating shops that are located here. All that survives of its former incarnation are the names (Allée de Fribourg, Place de Lausanne, Place de Zurich, Place de Genève) given to the miniature streets and squares of the complex. ♦ M, Th-Su. 78 Ave de Suffren and 54 Ave de la Motte-Picquet. Métros: Dupleix, La Motte-Picquet–Grenelle, Ecole Militaire

115 UNESCO Secretariat This building was designed by architects from three member countries: **Bernard Zehrfuss** of France, **Luigi Nervi** of Italy, and **Marcel Breuer** of the US. When it was built in the late 1950s, the headquarters of the **United Nations Educational, Scientific, and Cultural Organization** was a hopeful symbol of a new era of international cooperation. The complex, however, is better known for the works of art it contains than for its architecture or politics. **UNESCO** headquarters possesses a black metal Calder mobile; Henry Moore's *Reclining Figure;* two ceramic walls executed by Artigas after designs by Miró; sculpture by Giacometti; and a mural by Picasso, appropriately titled *The Victory of the Forces of Light and Peace over the Powers of Evil and Death.*

Casually visiting **UNESCO** is somewhat difficult, as security is tight. Your best bet is to organize or join a group tour and, even then, be sure to bring your passport. ♦ Group tours by appointment. 7 Pl de Fontenoy (between Aves de Saxe and de Lowendal). 01.45.68.10.00, 01.45.68.03.71. Métros: Ecole Militaire, Ségur

---

"I love it here, I want to stay forever . . . I will write here. I will live and write alone. And each day I will see a little more of Paris, study it, learn it as I would a book . . . The streets sing, the stones talk. The houses drip history, glory, romance."

Henry Miller

Bests

Martin Cantegrit
Owner and Managing Director, Le Récamier

Walking:

Palais Royal gardens: Delicious, hidden, far from noise, near the house of Molière/**Comédie Française** and the **Ministry of Culture.** A historical "meeting point" after the Revolution.

Jardin du Luxembourg: Meeting point of students and children. I like particularly the orchard with its exceptional range of pears and apples. A little corner of beauty in the middle of town.

Bercy's district, **Cité des Sciences et de l'Industrie** and **Cité de la Musique:** Paris in 2020!

Restaurants:

Le Récamier: In **St-Germain-des-Prés.** A perfect example of the French tradition with one of the best wine lists in France, a nice terrace, and a beautiful Parisian clientele.

L'Arpège: For a delicate dinner.

Hon-Yin
Fashion Designer/Painter

I love to have a cup of tea at the **Hôtel Montalembert.** I buy tea from **Mariage Frères,** cakes from **Ladurée,** and foie gras from **Dubernet.**

Walking by the **Canal St-Martin,** near where I live. This is the real Paris of the 1930s and 1940s—it's quiet, artistic, but not snobbish.

Ile St-Louis is great at night; there you'll find the best ice cream at **Berthillon.**

Parc de la Villette, with the **Cité des Sciences et de l'Industrie,** is great in the afternoon or on Sunday morning, when it's quieter. Bring something to drink with you.

Henry Pillsbury
Former Executive Director of the American Center

First of all, Paris is the best-run city of the 10 biggest cities in the world. It's as much a museum as Venice and as alive as LA.

After over 30 years here, I'd add the following to all the poetic musings on the city:

Jogging—All of the parks make this the best city for jogging.

Street cleaning and garbage collection—This is the only city where garbage is picked up every day of the year (except for Labor Day and during strikes).

Street Life—Unbeknownst to most Parisians, Paris is one of the most densely populated cities in the world, which explains all the shops, cafes, pedestrians, and effervescence. A model city for the 21st century.

Most telephone booths—The use of telephone cards instead of coins has greatly reduced the number of street phones smashed by thieves. This is

emblematic of the enlightened way Paris and France use electronics, including *Minitels* (computerized phone books and information systems), and more efficient parking, banking, and ticketing.

Street and cafe toilets—Paris has provided pretty well for the most repetitive human need of all. By contrast, compare the availability of toilets in London, New York, or LA.

Veronique Lopez
Owner, Agence Veronique Lopez

Galerie Vivienne—Enter by 4 Rue des Petits-Champs. I fell in love with this place and chose it for my office more than 10 years ago. I relaunched the arcade by introducing new shops and a tearoom.

Palais Royal—The new **Mark Rudkin English Garden,** the shops under the arcades.

Brentano's—All English books and travel guides.

Judith Livingston
Clinical Psychologist

The fixed-price lunch at **L'Arpège** is one of the best bargains in Paris.

Discount shopping at a small store between **Boulevard St-Germain** and the **Buci Market**.

Evelyne de Normandie
Author/Songwriter

To live in **Montmartre** and to breathe the best air in the city.

To meet my friends in its characteristic cafes: **Le Progrès** and **Le Sancerre.**

Paris Opera (Opéra Garnier) or a rock concert at **L'Olympia.**

To rest in the gardens of the **Musée Rodin,** taking in its beautiful sculptures.

Judith Bluysen
Owner, Thanksgiving (American grocery store, catering company, and restaurant)

Rue St-Paul: Browsing in any and all of the *brocante* (semivaluable junk) shops lining this 15th-century street.

Au Pont Marie (bistro): Feasting on real homemade *confit d'oie,* fried potatoes, and a perfect fruit tart.

Pont d'Arcole: Viewing the western tip of **Ile St-Louis** from the **Right Bank** portion of this bridge.

With a glass of wine and a buttered *pain Poilâne,* watching the world go by from the front window of **La Tartine** on **Rue de Rivoli.**

Friday mornings and Sundays on **Rue des Rosiers** (the Jewish quarter), pastry-ogling and eavesdropping.

Les Halles, Marais, and The Bastille

Les Halles, Marais, and The Bastille

This tour traverses three Parisian neighborhoods and 16 centuries of the city's history. It begins in the old **Les Halles** neighborhood, once the site of the great marketplace that Emile Zola called "the belly of Paris." Here you can wake up with the bustle of the marketplace and have a breakfast of coffee and croissants with local workers in one of the many cafes on the **Rue Montorgueil**, one of the surviving remnants of the old Les Halles market. Thus fortified, head over to the fashionable **Place des Victoires** for some power shopping in the fashionable, upscale boutiques (**Victoire** and **Thierry Mugler**, for example). Then proceed to the **Centre Georges Pompidou**, Paris's department store of modern culture, for a fix of modern art. Indulge in a second cup of coffee on the terrace of **Café Beaubourg**, a choice perch from which to watch the myriad street performers in front of the center.

From Les Halles, move on to the city's oldest square, **Place des Vosges**, in a section of the Marais district that was once a snarl of medieval streets inhabited by rich viscounts and poor Jews. Browse the boutiques of Place des Vosges or visit the **Musée Carnavalet** (the **Historical Museum of the City of Paris**) to peruse its collection of Revolution memorabilia and 18th-century shop signs, both of which are a big hit with children. Have lunch at one of the many tea salons (**Le Loir dans la Théière** is a good choice) or pick up a quick falafel or pastrami sandwich somewhere on **Rue des Rosiers**, the main artery of the old Jewish quarter, which is lined with storefront synagogues and kosher bakeries (remember that much of the street closes on Saturday, the Jewish Sabbath). Your dessert will be the **Musée Picasso** in the **Hôtel-Salé** on Rue de Thorigny. (If visiting the Marais during summer, inquire about the **Festival du Marais**, a series of opera, chamber music, and drama performances in the district's exquisite 17th-century mansions.)

The final stop on this tour is the funky **Place de la Bastille**, where the **Opéra Bastille** looms over a neighborhood of artisans and woodworkers existing side by side with trendy designer shops, restaurants, cafes, and clubs. Once the site of the prison whose fall marked the start of the bloody French Revolution, the Place de la Bastille is now best known for the melodramas that take place onstage in the **Opéra Bastille**. But there is plenty to do even if you don't have opera tickets. **Les Grandes Marches, Le Dôme Bistrot, Les Voyageurs sur Mer**, and **Thaï Elephant** are four popular dinner spots. Great dancing is afoot at the trendy **Casbah** and the Latin **Le Balajo**. Complete your Bastille rite of passage by sipping a glass of Champagne at **Sanz-Sans** or a coco loco cocktail at the **Havanita Café**. Art lovers may forgo dancing until dawn at the Bastille clubs and instead backtrack to the **Pompidou Center**, which is open until 10PM. Still later, night owls will want to check out the late-night scene in Les Halles, including the funky **Les Bains Douches**. In the event that hunger strikes, two classic restaurants, **Au Pied de Cochon** and **La Tour de Montlhery**, are open around the clock and are sure to be full of characters with 3AM cravings for steak and Burgundy or oysters and Champagne, providing an appropriately colorful close to this multifaceted tour.

Les Halles

The area known as Les Halles (the marketplace) takes its name from the great wholesale food market that began here in 1100. The market operated on this site until the mid-1970s, when it was moved to Rungis near **Orly Airport**, leaving behind *le trou* (the hole), which later was filled by an underground shopping mall known as the **Forum des Halles,** and a perimeter consisting of **St-Eustache** church and several old all-night restaurants serving onion soup and pig's feet.

As recently as a few decades ago, this area was a run-down garment district and slum that stretched between **St-Merri** church and the old food market. The opening of the **Forum des Halles** and the **Centre Georges Pompidou** in the late 1970s brought new commercial life into the area (as well as architectural controversy). Retired food vendors now share their turf with hordes of tourists, mall-bound French youths, other street performer. as well as upscale professionals who come to take in the local color.

The inclined plaza west of the **Centre Georges Pompidou** is now home to an impromptu circus of folksingers, hypnotists, kerosene garglers, sword swallowers, Hare Krishnas, rowdies, acrobats, jugglers, and (be forewarned) purse snatchers and panhandlers who prey on gawking tourists.

1 Place des Victoires Like the **Place Vendôme,** this circle of noble mansions was designed by **Jules Hardouin-Mansart** to celebrate a triumph of Louis XIV, in this case the Treaty of Nijmegen that marked his victory over Spain, Holland, Piedmont, and Germany. Originally at its center was a gilded bronze statue (1686) portraying the king being crowned by a goddess of victory, with four bound warriors at his feet representing the conquered nations. Destroyed during the Revolution, the statue was replaced in 1822 with the Astyanax Bosio equestrian version of Louis XIV that proudly rears here today. During the 19th century, the Place des Victoires fell into ruin and its buildings were converted into tradesmen's shops, but a recent restoration has turned it into the Right Bank's hub of high fashion. ♦ Rues Etienne-Marcel and Croix-des-Petits-Champs. Métro: Bourse

On Place des Victoires:

Kenzo For the young at heart: This appealing, boutique, decorated with natural wood, has some of the most fanciful fashions and friendliest sales help in town. The menswear collection is downstairs, the ladieswear upstairs. ♦ M-Sa. No. 3 (between Rues Etienne-Marcel and Croix-des-Petits-Champs). 01.40.39.72.00

Cacharel Though company founder Jean Bosquet moved into politics long ago, the design flame remains bright with sensible sportswear and cotton paisley-print fabrics for men and women some of which are produced in collaboration with Liberty of London. Menswear is sold at 20 Rue Tronchet; the children's collection is at 34 Rue Tronchet. ♦ M-Sa. No. 5 (between Rues Etienne-Marcel and Croix-des-Petits-Champs). 01.42.33.29.88. Also at: 33 Rue Tronchet (between Rue des Mathurins and Blvd Haussmann). 01.47.42.12.61. Métro: Havre–Caumartin

Victoire Come here to find out what's new in the current fashion scene. This place takes pride in being the very first specialty store to discover new Paris design talent. ♦ M-Sa. Nos. 10-12 (at Rue Vide-Gousset). 01.42.61.09.02

2 Lina's ★★$ This airy sandwich bar with its ocher walls, blond-wood trim, and acres of windows is the perfect vantage point for spying on the chic fashion show that promenades in the vicinity of the Place des Victoires. Behind the counter, statuesque men in white shirts and smart neckties serve delicious shrimp-avocado, pastrami, and smoked-salmon sandwiches on crusty *pain pavé* (country bread). ♦ M-Sa lunch (until 6:30PM). 50 Rue Etienne-Marcel (at Rue d'Argout). 01.42.21.16.14. Métro: Bourse

Place des Victoires Shopping

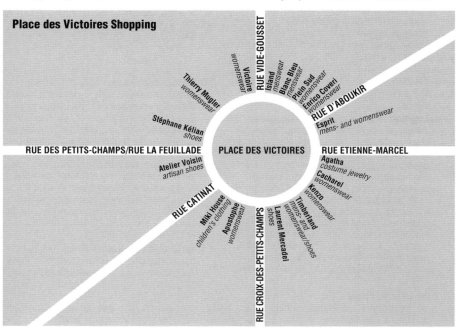

chez Georges

3 Chez Georges ★★$$ Handwritten menus, beveled mirrors, waitresses in black dresses, and an honest platter of beefsteak and fries are the hallmarks of this classic Parisian bistro. ◆ M-Sa lunch and dinner; closed August. Reservations recommended. 1 Rue du Mail (at Pl des Petits-Pères). 01.42.60.07.11. Métro: Sentier

4 Au Panetier Lebon Hundreds of crispy sourdough baguettes are baked daily in the wood-fired oven of Bernard Lebon. ◆ M-F. 10 Pl des Petits-Pères (between Rue des Petits-Pères and Passage des Petits-Pères). 01.42.60.90.23. Métros: Bourse, Pyramides

5 Basilique Notre-Dame-des-Victoires Using the plans of **Pierre Le Muet,** in 1740 architect **Jean Sylvain Cartaud** completed this rather undistinguished church, the name of which commemorates the Louis XIII trouncing of the Protestants in 1628 at La Rochelle. Inside the church are a 1702 bust of the composer Jean-Baptiste Lully, who lived down the street at 45 Rue des Petits-Champs, and an estimated 30,000 tablets blanketing the walls. ◆ Pl des Petits-Pères (at Rue Notre-Dame-des-Victoires). 01.42.60.90.00. Métro: Bourse

6 Legrand It's a joy to behold this renowned wine shop's bright red Belle Epoque facade, glass candy jars on the sidewalk out front, and ceiling covered with corks. For three generations, the Legrand family has run this *épicerie* stocked with an intelligent selection of wine, chocolate, tea, coffee, and jam. Francine Legrand, the daughter of the late Lucien, has a passion for younger, undiscovered (and less expensive) wines from France's smaller vineyards in Burgundy and Bordeaux. Ask her to recommend one—she loves to chat. ◆ Tu-Sa. 1 Rue de la Banque (at Rue des Petits-Pères). 01.42.60.07.12. Métro: Bourse

7 Banque de France The mansion, which became home to the Bank of France in 1812 by order of Napoléon, was originally built for the Comte de Toulouse, the son of Louis XIV and Mlle de Montespan. Among its lavish treasures is a first-class work of art, *Fête à Saint Cloud,* which many art historians say is the best of Fragonard's landscape paintings. That huge (7-by-10-foot) canvas hangs in the private office of the governor of the bank, so unless you have specific business with the governor you'll have to content yourself with the smaller Fragonards down the street at the **Louvre.** The building is not open to the public. ◆ 39 Rue Croix-des-Petits-Champs (between Rues du Colonel-Driant and La Vrillière). Métro: Palais Royal–Musée du Louvre

8 La Coutellerie Suisse You can't miss this consummate cutlery shop with its giant red Swiss Army knife splayed in the window. ◆ M-F; closed August. 44 Rue Coquillière (between Rues Hérold and Croix-des-Petits-Champs). 01.42.33.20.92. Métro: Palais Royal–Musée du Louvre

9 La Fermette du Sud-Ouest ★★$$ Jacky Mayer reigns supreme over this countrified restaurant, which is famous for homemade *boudin* (blood sausage) with onions and sautéed potatoes, cassoulet, magnificent entrecôtes, and hearty Cahors wines. ◆ M-Sa lunch and dinner. Reservations recommended. 31 Rue Coquillière (between Rues du Bouloi and Croix-des-Petits-Champs). 01.42.36.73.55. Métro: Palais Royal–Musée du Louvre

10 Gérard Besson ★★$$$ One of the neighborhood's finest lunch menus (changed every three weeks) begins with owner/chef Besson's *foie gras de canard,* which may be followed by lobster with small vegetables. For dessert, try the *biscuit glacé à la framboise* (a cookie topped with raspberry ice cream). The detailed wine list is strong on Bordeaux. The service is attentive; the ambience, quiet and comfortable. ◆ M-F lunch and dinner, Sa dinner. Reservations recommended. 5 Rue Coq-Héron (between Rues Coquillière and du Louvre). 01.42.33.14.74. Métro: Palais Royal–Musée du Louvre

11 La Cloche des Halles ★★$ This wine bar, named after the *cloche* (bronze bell) that for decades signaled the opening and closing of Les Halles market, offers not only superb Sancerres, Morgons, and Côtes-de-Brouillys, but scrumptious plates of baked country ham, assorted regional cheeses, quiche, and homemade fruit tarts. It's crowded with local merchants, journalists, and the folks in dark suits from the **Bourse** and **Banque de France** up the street. ♦ M-Sa breakfast, lunch and dinner; closed two weeks in August. No credit cards accepted. 28 Rue Coquillière (at Rue Coq-Héron). 01.42.36.93.89. Métros: Les Halles, Palais Royal–Musée du Louvre

12 Dehillerin Half warehouse, half hardware store, this family-run kitchen emporium has been supplying the great chefs of Europe with cooking vessels and utensils since 1820. It even furnishes the French Army with cast-iron frying pans, boxwood knives, spatulas, and the wire skimmers known as "spiders." Mail order is available to civilians anywhere in the world. **Dehillerin** also happens to be the city's leading specialist in re-tinning copper pots. The salespeople speak broken English. ♦ M-Sa. 51 Rue Jean-Jacques-Rousseau and 18-20 Rue Coquillière. 01.42.36.53.13. Métros: Les Halles, Palais Royal–Musée du Louvre

13 Le Pavillon Baltard ★$ This warm and welcoming Alsatian brasserie serves *choucroute* (sauerkraut) with your choice of fish, pork, calf's head, or stuffed pig's tail. Nouvelle cuisine this ain't. Plan a long stroll after dinner. ♦ Daily lunch and dinner (until 1AM). Reservations recommended. 9 Rue Coquillière (at Rue Jean-Jacques-Rousseau). 01.42.36.22.00. Métro: Les Halles

14 La Chambre de Commerce (Commercial Exchange) One of the few buildings to escape the Les Halles demolition, this structure (built in 1887) is a graceful birthday cake of iron and glass. Not to be confused with the **Bourse des Valeurs** (the Roman temple to the north that houses the **Paris Stock Exchange**), here brokers in wheat, sugar, and other commodities do their trading. Beside the **Chambre de Commerce** is a 101-foot Classical column, topped with what appears to be a giant iron birdcage. This curiosity, called the **Horoscope Tower,** was once attached to the **Hôtel de la Reine** of Catherine de Médicis and accommodated her stargazing astrologer, Ruggieri, during the late 16th century. ♦ Reception/information: M-F; open to the public by appointment only. 2 Rue des Viarmes (at Rue Sauval). 01.42.89.78.36. Métro: Les Halles

15 Au Pied de Cochon ★$$ This nostalgic all-night eatery specializes in *fruits de mer* (chilled shellfish) and pig's feet (hence the restaurant's name), and also serves an overrated onion soup gratinée. Local night owls gather here at 4AM, but otherwise it's a tourist spot. For a Parisian version of Sunday brunch, order oysters (a dozen varieties are available) and Champagne at the bar. Though open around the clock, service is as poky as the snails are delicious. ♦ Daily 24 hours. 6 Rue Coquillière (between Rues du Jour and Jean-Jacques-Rousseau). 01.40.13.77.00. Métro: Les Halles

15 agnès b. These cotton T-shirts, chic silk blouses, pajamas, and skirts are comfortable and fashionable—black being the dominant tone. In her three outlets along Rue du Jour, agnès b. outfits the 1990s generation. Her trademark cotton cardigans with mother-of-pearl snaps are de rigueur Parisian attire. ♦ M-Sa. 3 Rue du Jour (between Rues Coquillière and Montmartre). 01.42.33.04.13. Métro: Les Halles. Also at: 6 Rue du Vieux-Colombier (between Rues Bonaparte and Madame). 01.44.39.02.60. Métro: St-Sulpice

16 Le Cochon à l'Oreille ★★$ Beautiful ceramic murals adorn this authentic turn-of-the-century working-class bar/cafe. Butchers, foie gras wholesalers, local merchants, and paunchy men of indefinite occupation wearing blue coveralls hang out here. They come for their coffee and Calvados before dawn or to share a *pastis* at the crowded zinc bar in the afternoon. ♦ M-Sa breakfast and lunch (until 5PM). No credit cards accepted. 15 Rue Montmartre (between Impasse St-Eustache and Rue du Jour). 01.42.36.07.56. Métro: Les Halles

"Of all the Seine bridges the Pont des Arts is the pleasantest to sit or walk on; it is reserved for pedestrians and is really a promenade pitched between sky and water for students, nursemaids, children, old gentlemen, and for painters having another go at the classical view of the Pont-Neuf and the Ile de la Cité, picking out the right light on the Tour St-Jacques, struggling to get that flaking-gray shade of the river buildings. Nothing sacred or secular, joyous or macabre escapes the inflection of French irony. I was chatting with a plump and rosy young man who is in charge of the small lifesaving station that is cozily shaded by the trees close to the bridge. Every couple of days, he said, people jump off the Pont des Arts or the quays close by the river. It is the bridge, he said, most esteemed by those wishing to make a show of the ending of their lives. 'But never at night,' he added. 'No Frenchman ever commits suicide at night. He wants to be seen doing it. *Il veut se faire un drame.*' The stagelike elevation of the bridge, he said, with its fine view of the Louvre on one side and the dome of the Institute on the other, contributing their suggestions of art and poetry, makes the spot appropriate. But between his little boat moored below and the skiffs of the river fire station on the other side of the bridge, he said that the chances of a fatal sucess were small."

V.S. Pritchett, *Down the Seine*

St-Eustache

MICHAEL STORRINGS

17 St-Eustache This massive amalgam of Gothic flying buttresses, rose windows, Flamboyant vaulting, and a Renaissance facade was built in 1640 to rival the likes of **Notre-Dame**. While its dimensions are enormous (346 feet long with a 112-foot-high nave), the church is better known for its musical legacy than its architectural grandeur. The Berlioz *Te Deum* and Liszt *Grand Mass* were first played here, and composer Jean-Philippe Rameau is buried in the church. At midnight Mass on Christmas Eve, the 8,000-pipe organ and talented church choir outshine even **Notre-Dame's**. Notable treasures here are the Rubens painting *Pilgrims at Emmaus,* the Pigalle statue of the Virgin, and a colorful sculpted scene honoring the vegetable vendors forced out of Les Halles in 1969.

The church is dedicated to St. Eustache, a second-century Roman general who converted to Christianity when, like St. Hubert, he saw a vision of the cross poised between the antlers of a stag. (A sculpted stag's head and cross are beneath the gable in the church's Renaissance transept facade.) St. Eustache, as the story goes, was gruesomely martyred; he was roasted alive inside an immense bronze bull with his wife and children. This was once the parish church for the merchants of Les Halles and the nobility from the nearby **Louvre** and **Palais Royal.** It hosted the baptisms of Cardinal Richelieu, Jean-Baptiste Poquelin (Molière), and Mme de Pompadour, as well as the funerals of fabulist Jean de La Fontaine, Colbert (prime minister of Louis XIV), Molière, and Revolutionary orator Mirabeau. During the Revolution the church was vandalized and renamed the "Temple of Agriculture," doubtless in honor of its proximity to Les Halles market. ◆ Fee for tour. Daily; a 45-minute tour is available Sunday at 3PM. 2 Impasse St-Eustache (off Rue Montmartre). 01.42.36.31.05. Métro: Les Halles

18 Rue Montorgueil Paris chefs have continued to shop on this lively market street despite the demolition of the old Les Halles markets. The market begins at Rue Rambuteau. ◆ Market: Tu-Su 6AM-1PM. Between Rues de Turbigo and St-Sauveur. Métro: Les Halles

On Rue Montorgueil:

L'Escargot Montorgueil ★★★$$ One of the most authentic examples of 1830s decor in Paris, this restaurant has a black-and-gilt facade, enormous cut-glass mirrors, tulip chandeliers, and red banquettes. The old cooking allegory gracing the wall came from the dining room of actress Sarah Bernhardt. Champagne is served in carafes; escargots are served in mint, curry, roquefort, or *à la bourguignonne;* and the customers are of the **Maxim's, Lasserre, Grand Véfour,** and **La Tour d'Argent** variety, which is not surprising, as the place is run by Mme. Saladin-Terrail, the sister of Claude Terrail, who owns **La Tour d'Argent**. ◆ Daily lunch and dinner.

Reservations recommended. No. 38 (at Rue Mauconseil). 01.42.36.83.51

19 Jardin des Halles The razing of Les Halles market left 106 acres of open space, which has now been transformed into a tree-lined garden and children's playground in the shadow of **St-Eustache** church. Beneath the park is **Paul Chemetov**'s subterranean sports and culture complex that includes a gymnasium, radio station, billiards hall, art gallery, record-lending library, performing arts conservatory, and a learning center offering instruction on everything from cooking to magic tricks to bridge. There's also an Olympic-size swimming pool.
♦ Gardens free; admission for pool. Daily. Bounded by Forum des Halles and Bourse de Commerce, and Rues Berger and Rambuteau. 01.42.36.98.44. Métro: Les Halles

20 La Tour de Montlhery ★★$$ The owner, Jacques, with his white apron and 1890s mustache, serves his loyal clientele of wine merchants, advertising executives, and visiting English novelists stick-to-the-ribs specialties such as stuffed cabbage, mutton with beans, and steak with shallots. This a nice place to meet friends over a bottle of Brouilly. ♦ M-F breakfast, lunch, and dinner; closed mid-July through mid-August. 5 Rue des Prouvaires (between Rues St-Honoré and Berger). 01.42.36.21.82. Métro: Les Halles

21 Rue de la Ferronnerie Here Henri IV was murdered in his carriage on 14 May 1610 as he passed along Ironmongers Row. His assassin, Ravaillac, was quartered by four horses in the Place de Grève, today called Place de l'Hôtel-de-Ville. ♦ Between Rues St-Denis and de la Lingerie. Métro: Châtelet

On Rue de la Ferronnerie:

Papeterie Moderne If you've got enough patience to sort through this store's marvelous hodgepodge of old Parisian signs (for streets, butcher shops, bakeries, and the like), you can take home a fine souvenir. A copy of anything in the store may be ordered; allow 10 days for pickup. ♦ M-Sa; closed one week in August. 12 Rue de la Ferronnerie. 01.42.36.21.72

Many of the streets in Paris have gutters running down the middle, a holdover from the Middle Ages, when water was channeled through to wash them.

22 Ducs d'Anjou $$ This 34-room hotel sits just off the charming Place Ste-Opportune. Rooms on the courtyard are somber but comfortable. There's no restaurant.
♦ 1 Rue Ste-Opportune (at Rue des Halles). 01.42.36.92.24; fax 01.42.36.16.63. Métro: Châtelet

23 Au Diable des Lombards ★$ Cheeseburgers, rabbit terrine, and homemade ice cream are among the menu items at this trendy bistro. ♦ Daily 9AM-1AM. 64 Rue des Lombards (between Rues St-Denis and Ste-Opportune). 01.42.33.81.84. Métro: Châtelet

24 Fontaine des Innocents During the 16th century, Les Halles fishmongers and butchers drew their water from this fountain (pictured below), which was commissioned by Henri II and designed by **Pierre Lescot** in 1547. An important architectural relic of early Renaissance Paris, it stands on the site of what was once the overcrowded, foul-smelling **Church of the Holy Innocents** cemetery. In 1786 the church was razed and some two million skeletons were transported from the cemetery to a quarry, which was then most appropriately renamed the **Catacombs**. Later, during World War II, the **Catacombs** were the macabre setting for the headquarters of the French Resistance. Today, the area surrounding the fountain is the haunt of tattooed lowlifes and indigent backpackers poring over out-of-print copies of *Europe on $20 a Day*. ♦ Sq des Innocents (between Rues des Innocents and Berger). Métro: Châtelet–Les Halles (RER)

Fontaine des Innocents

MICHAEL STORRINGS

25 Forum des Halles Architect **Victor Baltard's** 12 marvelous 19th-century iron-and-glass food halls were torn down in the 1970s after the 800-year-old wholesale market was moved to near **Orly Airport** in 1969. In its place, architects **Claude Vasconi** and **Georges Pencreach** designed a four-level underground shopping mall along the lines of an inverted hollow pyramid. This crater of consumerism is a labyrinth of walkways, cinemas, snack bars, cafes, 12 restaurants, more than 200 boutiques (the most chic of which are located on the top levels), and a branch of **FNAC**, a popular hangout where teenagers congregate to buy concert tickets and peruse the latest *bandes dessinées* (hardcover comic books). According to a survey conducted by the **McDonald's** here, 80,000 pedestrians walk past its doors every day.

Beneath the **Forum** is the **Châtelet–Les Halles** métro station, the world's largest underground train station, providing direct access to the métro, the **RER** (including lines to the **Roissy–Charles-de-Gaulle** and **Orly Airports**), and various underground parking lots. ♦ Bounded by Rue Pierre-Lescot and Jardin des Halles, and Rues Berger and Rambuteau. Métro: Châtelet–Les Halles (RER)

Beneath Forum des Halles:

Kiosque-Théâtre A kiosk in the **Châtelet–Les Halles** métro station sells half-price tickets to theater, dance, music hall, concert, and cafe theater events, and, occasionally, the opera, on the day of performance. ♦ Daily 1-8PM

BATIFOL

26 Batifol ★$$ While the pre–World War II decor remains, the **Royal Mondétour** (the restaurant formerly located here) and its owners, the beloved Bonnenfant family, alas are no longer. They have been replaced by more professional (and more mercenary) *patrons* who turn out acceptable, affordable bistro fare (hot chèvre salad, pot-au-feu, leg of lamb, and apple tart with Calvados), but rush diners in the interest of squeezing in a second and sometimes even a third seating each night. ♦ Daily lunch, dinner, and late-night meals until midnight. Reservations recommended. 14 Rue Mondétour (between Rues Rambuteau and de la Grande-Truanderie). 01.42.36.85.50. Métro: Les Halles

27 Pharamond ★★$$ This bistro is a remnant of the old Les Halles days, with 19th-century colored tiles and mosaics, handsome woodwork, and lots of mirrors. Try the *tripes à la mode de Caen,* cooked in white wine and Calvados in classic Normandy fashion and served in old-fashioned charcoal-fired brass

braziers. Nobody simmers it better. ♦ M dinner; Tu-Sa lunch and dinner. Reservations recommended. 24 Rue de la Grande-Truanderie (between Rues Pierre-Lescot and Mondétour). 01.42.33.06.72. Métro: Les Halles

Chez Pierrot

28 Chez Pierrot ★★★$$ Walk through the doors of this solid bistro and you'll find yourself back in the old Les Halles market days. Its exuberant decor dates from the turn of the century. A cornucopia of hors d'oeuvres is followed by such entrées as grilled kidneys and marinated mackerel. Many customers end their meals with cheese rather than dessert so that they can order another hearty Bordeaux. ♦ M-Sa lunch and dinner. 18 Rue Etienne-Marcel (between Rues de Turbigo and Française). 01.45.08.05.48. Métro: Etienne-Marcel

29 Duthilleul et Minart For more than a century, this store has sold uniforms and work clothes, from waiters' aprons to chefs' toques, plus an array of uniquely French occupational garb. This is a great spot for gifts, such as the popular French watchmakers' smocks. Same-day service is also available. ♦ M-Sa. 14 Rue de Turbigo (at Rue Etienne-Marcel). 01.42.33.44.36. Métro: Etienne-Marcel

30 Joe Allen ★$$ One of the most popular restaurants in Les Halles, this is a replica of its Los Angeles and Manhattan namesakes right down to the old photographs on the dark brick walls. The menu, which also mirrors its US counterparts, offers spareribs, chili con carne, black bean soup, and apple pie. It's terribly American, or at least the beautiful Parisians think so. ♦ Daily lunch and dinner (until 1AM). 30 Rue Pierre-Lescot (between Rues du Cygne and Etienne-Marcel). 01.42.36.70.13. Métro: Etienne-Marcel

31 Chez Vong aux Halles ★★$$$ Refined Cantonese and Szechuan dishes may be found in the company of excellent French wines at this attractive Chinese bistro. Dim sum, beef in oyster sauce, and lacquered pigeon are good choices. ♦ M-Sa lunch and dinner. Reservations recommended. 10 Rue de la Grande-Truanderie (between Rues St-Denis and Pierre-Lescot). 01.40.39.99.89. Métro: Les Halles

32 Rue St-Denis Once the route by which France's kings entered Paris to be crowned and exited to be buried in the basilica at St-Denis, this street now unfurls a lurid panoply of Parisian sleaze: peep shows, prostitutes, and fast-food joints such as the **Love Burger**. ♦ Between Ave Victoria and Blvd Bonne-Nouvelle. Métros: Châtelet, Châtelet–Les Halles (RER), Etienne-Marcel, Réaumur–Sébastopol, Strasbourg–St-Denis

L'Amandier

32 L'Amandier ★$ This remnant of old Les Halles still offers simple French fare such as onion soup, steak *frites,* and cheap red wine. There's outdoor summer dining, although you may think twice because of its locale: it's in the shadow of neon-splashed sex shops. ◆ Daily lunch and dinner until midnight. 76 Rue Rambuteau (at Rue St-Denis). 01.42.33.07.58. Métro: Les Halles

32 Aux Deux Saules ★★$ The "Two Willows," a holdover from old Les Halles in a wasteland of gaudy, neon-splashed sex shops, offers simple fare such as onion soup, sausages, *pommes frites,* and cheap wine served on outdoor wooden tables. Inside are gorgeous ceramic murals. ◆ Daily lunch and dinner; closed Tuesday in winter. 91 Rue St-Denis (at Rue Rambuteau). 01.42.36.46.57. Métro: Les Halles

33 Au Père Tranquille ★$ French teenagers wearing penny loafers and fake American varsity-letter jackets crowd this late-night corner cafe. On a warm evening, order a kir on the terrace while you sit and watch the Les Halles parade pass by. Act III of e. e. cummings's play *Him* is set here. ◆ Daily breakfast, lunch, and dinner (until 2AM). 16 Rue Pierre-Lescot (at Rue des Prêcheurs). 01.45.08.00.34. Métro: Châtelet–Les Halles (RER)

33 Le Bon Pêcheur ★$ When the adolescents at **Au Père Tranquille** grow up, they graduate to this smoky cafe across the street. Decorated with orange neon lights, mirrored columns, a zinc bar, and maps of Brazil on the wall, it offers salsa music on the stereo, *caipirinha* (the fiery Brazilian drink) for the thirsty, and such fare as quiche Lorraine for the hungry. ◆ Daily breakfast, lunch, and dinner (until 2AM); F-Sa until 6AM. 14 Rue Pierre-Lescot (at Rue des Prêcheurs). 01.42.36.91.88. Métro: Châtelet–Les Halles (RER)

34 Rue de la Cossonnerie On this 13th-century street, Giovanni Boccaccio (1313-1375), considered one of the founders of the Italian Renaissance, was born. He was the author of *Filocolo* and the *Decameron.* ◆ Between Blvd de Sébastopol and Rue Pierre-Lescot. Métro: Châtelet–Les Halles (RER)

35 St-Leu–St-Gilles This 14th-century church is of interest less for its unimposing exterior than for its unusual interior. On a street epitomizing voyeurism, the glass doors of the church appropriately provide their own peep show of medieval architecture. ◆ 92 Rue St-Denis (between Rues de la Grande-Truanderie and du Cygne). 01.40.26.99.75. Métro: Les Halles

36 Les Bains-Douches ★$$$ Architectural whiz kid **Philippe Starck** transformed these old public Turkish baths with their circa-1900 facade into one of the trendiest discos and restaurants in Les Halles. What would former baths patron Marcel Proust have to say? ◆ Daily dinner (starting at 9PM). Disco: daily midnight-dawn. 7 Rue du Bourg-l'Abbé (between Rue St-Martin and Blvd de Sébastopol). 01.48.87.01.80. Métro: Etienne-Marcel

37 Entre des Artistes This whimsical bookstore/gallery specializes in marionettes, Venetian masks, and books on cinema and theater. Ask the owner to crank up the mechanical performing circus, complete with lion tamer, acrobats, and hypnotist. ◆ Daily. 161 Rue St-Martin (between Passage Molière and Rue aux Ours). 01.48.87.78.58. Métro: Rambuteau

38 Passage Molière For now, this ramshackle 19th-century alley with its tiny one-room flats and cheap tailor shops offers a glimpse, in contrast to the glitter and glamour of Les Halles, of what the Beaubourg quarter was like before it got "malled." ◆ Between Rues St-Martin and Quincampoix. Métro: Rambuteau

39 Rue Quincampoix The Scottish financier John Law founded a bank on this street in 1719 after he became France's controller general, prompting a brief rash of speculation in this part of the city. In more recent times, the street has been a magnet for *les femmes de la nuit,* women photographed so remarkably by Brassaï in the early 1930s. ◆ Between Rues des Lombards and aux Ours. Métros: Rambuteau, Châtelet–Les Halles (RER)

39 Pacific Palisades ★★$$ A Les Halles version of Californian nouvelle cuisine is served by French waiters who act like they just stepped off the beach at Malibu. In summer, the terrace is splendid. Any season of the year, the piano bar downstairs is smoky and the crowd trendy. ◆ Daily lunch and dinner. Piano Bar: Th-Sa until 2AM. Reservations recommended. 51 Rue Quincampoix (between Rues Aubry-le-Boucher and Rambuteau). 01.42.74.01.17. Métro: Rambuteau

40 46 Rue Quincampoix This complex contains a cinema, a theater, and the **Cultural Center of Yugoslavia.** Don't miss the startling entryway sculpture of an army of nudes bursting through the seams in the wall. ◆ Between Rues Aubry-le-Boucher and de Venise. Métro: Rambuteau

40 Galerie Jean Fournier The ideal art dealer, Jean Fournier is always amenable to showing and discussing his selections. American artists represented here include Sam Francis, Shirley Jaffe, and Joan Mitchell. The gallery includes a bookstore specializing in painting

as well as ancient and contemporary art.
♦ Tu-Sa; closed August. 44 Rue Quincampoix (between Rues Aubry-le-Boucher and de Venise). 01.42.77.32.31. Métro: Rambuteau

41 Galerie Zabriskie This is the Parisian outpost of New York's first-rate Fifth Avenue photo gallery. ♦ Tu-Sa; closed August. 37 Rue Quincampoix (between Rues Aubry-le-Boucher and Rambuteau). 01.42.72.35.47. Métro: Rambuteau

42 Galerie Alain Blondel Having risen from the ashes of the defunct **Luxembourg Gallery**, this place features early 20th-century works, large canvases from the 1930s, trompe l'oeil, and realism. ♦ Tu-Sa. 4 Rue Aubry-le-Boucher (at Rue Quincampoix). 01.42.78.66.67. Métro: Rambuteau

43 Benoît ★★$$$ You need not take the train to Lyon to savor blood sausage with apples and roast potatoes, duckling with turnips, or mussel soup. This attractive 1912 bistro is frequented by families in the evening. ♦ Daily lunch and dinner; closed August. Reservations required; no credit cards accepted. 20 Rue St-Martin (at Rue Pernelle). 01.42.72.25.76. Metro: Châtelet

44 Hôtel St-Merri $$ A quirky but comfortable 14-room hostelry is attached to the medieval **St-Merri** church. Specializing in irreligious caprice, this hotel uses communion rails as banisters and has a room with a flying buttress and another with a confessional-as-clothespress. There's no restaurant. ♦ 78 Rue de la Verrerie (at Rue St-Martin). 01.42.78.14.15; fax 01.40.29.06.82. Métros: Châtelet–Les Halles (RER), Hôtel de Ville

45 Les Viennoiseries de St-Medard What a treat in this modish neighborhood to find an old-time bakery complete with a rosy-cheeked baker proudly displaying her fresh brioches, croissants, and tarts on the white marble counters. ♦ M, W-Su. 81 Rue St-Martin (between Rues des Lombards and de La Reynie). 01.42.72.84.24. Metros: Hôtel de Ville, Châtelet–Les Halles (RER)

46 Café Beaubourg ★★$$ This intellectual's cafe offers a vantage point on the local wildlife roaming around the **Pompidou Center.** You'll find palatable sandwiches, daily copies of Le Monde and Libération, and a stray cat at architect **Christian de Portzamparc**'s creation. ♦ Daily breakfast, lunch, and dinner (M-F until 1AM; Sa, Su until 2AM). 100 Rue St-Martin (between Rues du Cloître-St-Merri and St-Merri). 01.48.87.63.96. Métros: Châtelet–Les Halles (RER), Hôtel de Ville

47 Centre Georges Pompidou/Centre National d'Art et Culture Critics took to calling the five-story jumble of glass and steel the "gasworks" and asked "Who forgot to take the scaffolding down?" Still, this surrealistic Tinkertoy temple of modern culture is the biggest attraction in Paris, outdrawing both the **Louvre** and the **Eiffel Tower.** A million people visited in 1977 during the first seven weeks it was open; more than half of all visitors are under age 25. Created at the behest of then-president Georges Pompidou (1911-1974) and designed by Italian **Renzo Piano** and Englishman **Richard Rogers** (whose proposal was selected from among a field of 681), the revolutionary (some say revolting) structure houses a modern art museum, the city's largest public library (with more than half a million books), one of the world's most advanced computer music centers, a workshop, a language library, a children's theater and dance workshop, and a fifth-floor restaurant with a four-star view. Pompidou, who was a patron of modern art as well as a politician, is immortalized by Victor Vasarely in a hexagonal portrait that hangs on the ground floor.

The high-tech design concept of the center celebrates the building's functional parts (heating ducts, ventilator shafts, stairways, and elevators) by brightly color-coding them: red for vertical circulation, green for water, blue for air, yellow for electricity, and white for structure. An escalator in a Plexiglas tube snakes up the front of the complex. Even if you aren't interested in seeing the Salvador Dalí portrait of Lenin dancing on piano keys, which is exhibited on the fourth floor, you should still ride up the escalator to scan one of the city's best-loved vistas, the view over the Right Bank rooftops. Unfortunately, innovation and popularity carry a price: the **Pompidou** is showing wear and tear in tarnished steel, peeling paint, and shredded carpets. Architects blame not just the crowds but the design. "To put the bones and intestines outside the skin," said one, "is to invite health problems."

At press time the center was undergoing major renovations and scheduled to reopen in 2001. It is advised to call ahead since not all facilities will be open to the public. Some exhibitions will be housed at the **Grand Palais** (Ave Winston-Churchill, between Cours-la-Reine and Pl Clemenceau, 01.44.13.17.17). ♦ M, W-Su (until 10PM). Entrance at Pl Georges-Pompidou (between Rues St-Merri and Rambuteau). 01.44.78.12.33. Métros: Châtelet–Les Halles (RER), Hôtel de Ville, Rambuteau

Within the Centre Georges Pompidou:

Musée d'Art Moderne One of the world's largest collections of modern and contemporary art is displayed here. Beginning with Rousseau's Snake Charmer and ending with the museum's up-to-the-minute acquisitions, the collection was works by the greatest artists of the 20th century: Picasso, Bonnard, Matisse, Kandinsky, Mondrian, Chagall, Pollock, Magritte, Calder, Moore, and Bacon. Exhibitions are splendidly mounted. ♦ Admission; half-price Sundays 10AM-10PM. M, W-Su (until 10PM). Third and fourth floors

Salle de Cinéma This famous film archive and cinema presents three international classics daily. ♦ Fifth floor

48 IRCAM (Contemporary Institute of Musical and Acoustic Research) One of the world's most advanced computer music centers is located in an innovative building with a brick panel facade by **Renzo Piano.** Toiling away in IRCAM's underground reaches, leading modern composer Pierre Boulez's studio of composers and electronic engineers is creating the music of the future. The building is usually not open to visitors, but you can enter the ground-floor level for information about concerts by **L'Ensemble InterContemporain** and the public lectures that frequently take place here. ♦ By appointment only. 1 Pl Igor-Stravinsky (at Pl Georges-Pompidou). 01.44.78.12.33. Métros: Châtelet–Les Halles (RER), Hôtel de Ville

48 Fontaine de Stravinsky A fantastic and frivolous ballet of animals, serpents, and musical notes floats in this lively fountain created by Niki de Saint-Phalle and Jean Tinguely, making this a great spot for an urban picnic. ♦ Pl Igor-Stravinsky (between Rue du Cloître-St-Merri and Pl Georges-Pompidou). Métros: Châtelet–Les Halles (RER), Hôtel de Ville

ESPACE
VIT'HALLES

49 Espace Vit'Halles This popular health club, started in 1983 by French Olympic wrestler Christophe Andanson and his wife, Claudy, has become one of the hottest underground (in the literal sense) singles spots in the district. Among the more than 1,000 members are **Pompidou Center** staffers flocking to aerobics classes and young Bourse financiers pumping iron as a respite from lusting after gold. The clean and affordable facilities include a sauna, tanning rooms, and bodybuilding equipment. Memberships are available for one day, one week, and longer. ♦ Daily. 48 Rue Rambuteau (at Rue Brantôme). 01.42.77.21.71. Métro: Rambuteau

50 Defender of Time Inspired by the Rathaus clock in Munich, the one-ton Jacques Monestier kinetic sculpture (1975) in oxidized brass sends a sword-brandishing warrior to do battle with a bird, a crab, and a dragon (representing the three elements: air, water, and earth). As every hour strikes, one of the beasts attacks, and at noon, 6PM, and 10PM,

the Defender of Time is forced to take on all the creatures at once, always emerging victorious. A bit kitschy (as is this whole mini-shopping mall, the **Quartier de l'Horloge**), but young children love it. ♦ Rue Brantôme (at Rue Bernard-de-Clairvaux). Métro: Rambuteau

51 Ambassade d'Auvergne ★★$$ Adorned with flickering oil lamps, a roaring fire, and cured hams dangling from heavy wood beams, this rustic restaurant serves hearty Massif Central cuisine. Specialties include *potée au choux* (stew), *alejot* (potatoes, cheese, and cream), roast suckling pig, lentil cassoulet, and blood sausage with chestnuts. ♦ Daily lunch and dinner. Reservations recommended. 22 Rue du Grenier-St-Lazare (between Rues Beaubourg and St-Martin). 01.42.72.31.22. Métro: Rambuteau

52 Porte St-Denis This consciously Roman-style triumphal arch celebrates Louis XIV's victorious battles in Flanders and the Rhineland. **François Blondel** modeled the gigantic arch after the Arch of Titus in Rome; Charles Le Brun's allegorical sculptured adornments were inspired by the reliefs on Trajan's Column. ♦ At Blvd de Bonne-Nouvelle and Rue du Faubourg-St-Denis. Métro: Strasbourg–St-Denis

53 Porte St-Martin In 1674 **Pierre Bullet** constructed this arch after plans made by **François Blondel** for Porte St-Denis. These two triumphal arches, astride the most important routes leading to the north, were erected by the Sun King to announce the grandeur of the French capital to visitors at the very time he had moved to **Versailles** and was tearing down the 13th-century city wall. ♦ At Blvd St-Martin and Rue du Faubourg-St-Martin. Métro: Strasbourg–St-Denis

54 Rue du Vertbois The remains of the walls of **St-Martin-des-Champs** church on this street date from 1270. An inflammatory letter from Victor Hugo is said to have saved the wall from demolition. ♦ Between Rues de Turbigo and St-Martin. Métro: Temple

55 Musée National des Techniques (National Technical Museum) This extraordinary collection of 80,000 machines traces the evolution of technology from the 16th century onward. In an Orwellian juxtaposition of religion and science, part of the museum is in the remains of the **St-Martin-des-Champs** priory, one of the finest naves to survive the Middle Ages. The museum is undergoing a complete renovation and is scheduled to reopen at the end of 1998. The project has been slowed because workers came across important archaeological artifacts in the museum's chapel, many of them dating from before the 10th century. Free temporary exhibitions will be offered during the renovation period. ◆ Admission; free during renovation. Call for hours and information. 292 Rue St-Martin (at Rue Réaumur). 01.40.27.23.71, 01.40.27.22.20, 01.40.27.23.31. Métro: Réaumur–Sébastopol

56 St-Nicolas-des-Champs Construction on this church began in the 12th century, and it has acquired distinguished features throughout the ages: a Flamboyant Gothic facade, a Renaissance doorway, and many 17th-, 18th-, and 19th-century paintings. ◆ 254 Rue St-Martin (at Rue Cunin-Gridaine). 01.42.72.92.54. Métro: Réaumur–Sébastopol

57 404 ★★★$$ The small open kitchen puts bowls of exotic spices, plates of delicate pastries, and simple cooking techniques on display, all of which infuse this North African restaurant with an artistic ambience and heavenly aromas. Tasting one of the *tajines* (succulent stews of meat delicately blended with fruit, vegetables, and spices, and served in ceramic pots) is pure bliss. Choose a bottle of Moroccan wine to go with your meal, lean back on the plump pillows, and observe the hip-looking Parisians at the tables around you. (The restaurant was named after the Peugeot 404, which as car buffs will know, was a very popular car in the 1960s.) ◆ Daily lunch and dinner; closed the last two weeks of August. 69 Rue des Gravilliers (between Rues Beaubourg and St-Martin). 01.42.74.57.81. Métro: Arts et Métiers

58 Le Tango To dance here cheek-to-cheek among Brylcreem dandies and perfumed widows is to enter a time warp that leads back to 1906, when the tango first hit Paris. Patrons dance to calypsos, salsas, beguines—any beat but hip hop—all night long. This club is both authentic and inexpensive. ◆ Cover. W-Sa 11PM-dawn. 11 Rue au Maire (between Rues des Vertus and Beaubourg). 01.42.72.17.78. Métro: Arts et Métiers

59 Musée de la Poupée (Doll Museum) This unusual museum is home to a private collection of over 200 porcelain-headed French dolls dating from 1860 to 1960, amassed by father and son Guido and Samy Odin. Each of the small museum's seven rooms is dedicated to an important phase of French dolldom or to themed temporary expositions often featuring dolls from other countries or dolls in regional costumes. The museum offers lectures on the history of dolls

as well as doll-making classes, and the gift shop carries a nice collection of stuffed animals, limited-edition porcelain dolls, and doll-related accessories. ◆ Admission. Tu-Su. Lectures: Th 5:30PM by reservation. Doll-making courses: M-Tu by reservation. Impasse Berthaud (off Rue Beaubourg). 01.42.72.55.90. Métro: Rambuteau

59 Galerie Daniel Templon Daniel Templon helped launch conceptual art, language art, and a good deal of the "Support Surface" movement in France. His gallery is modeled after those in New York's SoHo. ◆ M-Sa; closed August. 30 Rue Beaubourg (between Rues Rambuteau and Michel-Le-Comte). 01.42.72.14.10. Métro: Rambuteau

60 Café de la Cité ★★$ No wider than a bowling alley, this cafe/luncheonette has become one of the most popular pit stops in the area. Decorated with wooden fans and prints of old Breton sailing vessels (the owner comes from Brittany), it offers tasty *plats du jour*. The management boasts that you can order, eat, and head out the door in less than 30 minutes. ◆ Daily lunch and dinner. Reservations required for dinner. 22 Rue Rambuteau (between Rues du Temple and Beaubourg). 01.42.78.56.36. Métro: Rambuteau

61 The Studio ★★$ In the adjoining dance studio courtyard, this Tex-Mex canteen throws the hottest Fourth of July party in Paris. ◆ Daily dinner; Sa-Su brunch. 41 Rue du Temple (between Rues St-Merri and Simon-Le-Franc). 01.42.74.10.38. Métro: Rambuteau

62 Vieux Marais $$ Decorated with Chinese carpets and floral wallpaper, this 30-room hotel always gives guests a warm welcome. There's a tea room but no restaurant. ◆ 8 Rue du Plâtre (between Rues des Archives and du Temple). 01.42.78.47.22; fax 01.42.78.34.32. Métro: Rambuteau

63 Rue de la Verrerie This narrow street, which takes its name from the 11th-century glassblowers guild, is where Jacquemin Gringoneur once lived. He invented playing cards to amuse King Charles VI ("The Beloved"), who ruled from 1380 to 1422. ◆ Between Rues du Bourg-Tibourg and St-Martin. Métro: Hôtel de Ville

On Rue de la Verrerie:

Lescene-Dura Since 1875 this sprawling wine lover's warehouse has been offering all manner of enological paraphernalia, from corkscrews to Champagne buckets. ◆ Tu-Sa; closed August. No. 63 (between Rues du Temple and du Renard). 01.42.72.08.74

Some of the original stones of the Bastille prison can be found in the small Square Henri-Galli in the fourth arrondissement.

Marais

This district in eastern Paris has been known as the *marais* (marsh) since Roman times. It was a vast, oozy swamp on the northern branch of the Seine until the 12th century, when the marsh was drained, making it habitable for humans. Like New York's fashionable SoHo district, the Marais is now a mélange of ruin and restoration, past and present. The historically rich neighborhood possesses at least one Roman road (along Rues François-Miron and St-Antoine), what may be the city's oldest house (a 14th-century, half-timbered structure at 3 Rue Volta), and numerous twisting, huddled medieval streets.

Among those streets are three (**Rues des Rosiers, des Ecouffes,** and **Ferdinand-Duval**) that are the backbone of the celebrated Jewish quarter, formed in the 13th century when King Philippe Auguste "invited" the Jewish merchants living in front of **Notre-Dame** to move outside his new city wall.

Seven French kings resided in the Marais, starting with Charles V (1337-1380). Henri II (1519-1559) was the last; he died during a freak jousting accident when the shattered lance of Montgomery, the captain of his Scots Guards, pierced the visor of his helmet. Henri's wife, Catherine de Médicis, tried to ease her grief by having their royal **Maison des Tournelles** in the Marais demolished.

A half-century after the accident, Henri IV chose to construct the **Place Royale** on the leveled crown land in the Marais. Its name was changed in 1800 to **Place des Vosges** to honor the Vosges in eastern France, which was the first provincial department to pay its taxes after the Revolution. "It's the blow of Montgomery's lance," Victor Hugo later wrote, "that created the Place des Vosges."

The Marais and Place Royale (des Vosges) figured prominently in Henri IV's building boom in the 17th century, which also included Pont-Neuf, Place Dauphine, and Ile St-Louis. In the Marais, the king employed the leading architects of the day: **Louis Le Vau, François Mansart,** and **Jules Hardouin-Mansart.**

During this era, Mademoiselle de Scudéry, Molière, Racine, Madame de Lafayette, and Madame de Sévigné were exchanging witty party conversation in the great salons of the Marais that Molière parodied in his play *Les Précieuses Ridicules.* Within a century the former swamp had become the heart of intellectual Paris. In 1630 Cardinal Richelieu, a Marais resident, founded the **Académie Française** here, and years later a seven-year-old Mozart played his first Paris concert in the Marais. This area became an island of urban civility and sophistication, far removed from the wild boars and party boors of **Versailles.**

After the Revolution the elegant town houses were abandoned or carved into small factories and rooming houses. Squatters took over, and the Marais fell into a shocking state of ruin. Over the centuries, 29 of the grand *hôtels particuliers* were destroyed;

nearly 100 remained, dilapidated and on the verge of collapse. In 1964 André Malraux, Minister of Culture under Charles de Gaulle, came to the rescue and designated the Marais the first historic preservation district in Paris. Within its boundaries are 1,500 architecturally important structures, making the Marais the largest historic district in France.

Many of the old buildings have been given new life, as you'll see when you visit the **Archives Nationales, Musée Carnavalet** (the city's historical museum), the famous Place des Vosges, and the **Musée Picasso.** The Marais quarter, a juxtaposition of splendor and squalor, is on the rebound.

64 Rue des Archives For generations, the lower section of this street bore the name Rue où Dieu fut Bouilli (street where God was boiled) after the legend of the moneylender who stabbed a communion wafer with his knife, then threw it into a steaming pot, where to his astonishment it began to bleed. ◆ Between Rues de Rivoli and de Bretagne. Métros: Hôtel de Ville, Rambuteau

On Rue des Archives:

Musée de la Chasse et de la Nature (Museum of the Hunt) Housed in a portion of the **Hôtel de Guénégaud** (1654) and designed by **François Mansart,** this museum presents three floors full of hunting paraphernalia and related items, including crossbows, muskets, game trophies, whole stuffed animals, and paintings of hunting dogs and animals by the likes of Rubens and Brueghel. Among the most lavish paeans to the slaughter are the paintings of Desportes, the court artist employed by Louis XIV to portray the royal hunts at **Versailles.** ◆ Admission. M, W-Su. No. 60 (at Rue des Quatre-Fils). 01.42.72.86.43

65 Hôtel de Rohan In 1705 the son of François de Rohan, prince-bishop of Strasbourg, commissioned **Pierre-Alexis Delamair** to build a mansion opposite the **Hôtel Soubise,** where his parents lived. In the courtyard to the right, above the entrance to the former stables, is one of the masterpieces of 18th-century French sculpture: Robert Le Lorrain's superb relief-sculpture *The Watering of the Horses of the Sun.* The building sometimes houses temporary exhibitions. ◆ 87 Rue Vieille-du-Temple (between Rues des Francs-Bourgeois and des Quatre-Fils). Métro: Rambuteau

66 Archives Nationales/Musée de l'Histoire de France The letters of Joan of Arc and Voltaire, the wills of Louis XIV and Napoléon I, a papyrus signed by Merovingian King Dagobert (622-638), the Edict of Nantes, the Declaration of the Rights of Man, and six billion other documents are stored on 175 miles of shelves in this admirable 18th-century mansion, the former **Hôtel Soubise.** Even if you have no interest in French history, the museum's fortified turrets, colonnaded courtyard (72 Corinthian columns in all), and the riot of Rococo in the **Oval Salon** make a visit worthwhile. Designed by **Pierre-Alexis Delamair** for François de Rohan, the prince of Soubise, the mansion has an ornate interior (1739) that was engineered by **Germain Boffrand**, a pupil of **François Mansart.** Boffrand hired the best artists of the day, among them François Boucher and Charles Natoire, to decorate the *hôtel*. The archives, housed in the **Hôtel Soubise** since 1808, expanded into the adjacent **Hôtel de Rohan** in 1927. ♦ Admission. M-Sa. 60 Rue des Francs-Bourgeois (at Rue des Archives). 01.40.27.60.00. Métros: Hôtel de Ville, Rambuteau

67 Picard Surgelés Who said the French are all food snobs? The brave new world of French frozen food is displayed in this chilly, sterile mart (one of a chain of stores in Paris) that sells microwave ovens and anything you might want to defrost in them. Press your nose against the glass, watch Parisians wheel shopping carts around yellow, blue, and red freezers looking for tonight's TV dinner, and ask yourself what Julia Child would say. ♦ Daily. 48 Rue des Francs-Bourgeois (between Rues Vieille-du-Temple and des Archives). 01.42.72.17.83. Métros: Rambuteau, Hôtel de Ville

68 Crédit Municipal de Paris Paris's first municipal pawnshop is still a place for hocking ("putting it on the nail," as the French say). Auctions, especially for jewelry, are frequent and well attended; check the notices posted outside. ♦ Daily. 55 Rue des Francs-Bourgeois (between Rues Vieille-du-Temple and des Archives). 01.44.61.64.00. Métro: Rambuteau

Le Dômarais

68 Le Dômarais ★$$ Covered by a glass rotunda, sumptuously adorned with scarlet walls and bronze statues, this trading house-turned-restaurant features dinner concerts ranging from opera to gospel. Try the *daurade carpaccio* (raw sea bream) with ginger or the *magret de canard* (duck fillet) with cider vinegar. ♦ M, Sa dinner; Tu-F lunch and dinner; closed August. Reservations recommended. 53 *bis* Rue des Francs-Bourgeois (between Rues Vieille-du-Temple and des Archives). 01.42.74.54.17. Métro: Rambuteau

69 Hôtel des Ambassadeurs de Hollande When this Baroque mansion (built in 1660) was named, there were no Dutch ambassadors to France, and none has ever lived here. (The building did, however, belong to the chaplain of the Dutch Embassy from 1720-1727). Subsequently the *hôtel* was

rebuilt by Pierre Cottard; its most famous resident was Beaumarchais, author of *The Marriage of Figaro* and *The Barber of Seville.* The great wooden doors are embellished by what look like howling Medusas or perhaps a pair of baritones warming up. ♦ 47 Rue Vieille-du-Temple (between Rues Ste-Croix-de-la-Bretonnerie and des Blancs-Manteaux). Métro: St-Paul

70 Mariage Frères ★★★$$ The ritual of tea becomes an art at this handsome tea boutique and *salon de thé.* The shop sells 450 varieties of tea stored in smart black canisters lining the walls, along with teapots, sugars, spices, tea cakes, and jams. In the dining room, tea is served with a selection of scones, muffins, and pastries, as well as a superb brunch and lunch. ♦ Daily brunch, lunch, and afternoon tea. 30-32 Rue du Bourg-Tibourg (between Rues du Roi-de-Sicile and Ste-Croix-de-la-Bretonnerie). 01.42.72.28.11. Métros: St-Paul, Hôtel de Ville. Also at: 13 Rue des Grands-Augustin (at Rue de Savoie). 01.40.51.82.50. Métro: St-Michel

71 Hôtel Caron de Beaumarchais $$ Behind the brilliant blue facade of this superbly located hotel is a gem of a hostelry radiating 18th-century elegance and charm. Father and son hosts Etienne and Alain Bigeard are true gentlemen who receive guests with a natural warmth and enthusiasm. The interior is simply and tastefully decorated by Alain: The stone *cheminée* in the lobby boasts a crackling fire in the winter; the 19 guest rooms feature exposed beams, Louis XV–style fabrics, and hand-painted tile in the bathrooms; and the walls are hung with memorabilia from the comedies of playwright Pierre-Augustin Caron de Beaumarchais, the hotel's namesake, who, in 1778, wrote The *Marriage of Figaro* down the street at 47 Rue Vieille-du-Temple. Some rooms on floors 5 and 6 have balconies looking out over the rooftops of the Marais. A continental breakfast with fresh croissants is served until noon, an unusual tradition that's appreciated by those guests who want to sleep in after taking advantage of the late-night spots in neighboring Les Halles and Bastille. There's no restaurant. ♦ 12 Rue Vieille-du-Temple (between Rues de Rivoli and du Roi-de-Sicile). 01.42.72.34.12; fax 01.42.72.34.63. Métros: St-Paul, Hôtel de Ville

72 Au Petit Fer à Cheval ★★★$ Named after its 1903 marble-topped *fer à cheval* (horseshoe) bar, this neighborhood cafe offers lunchtime *plats du jour* in its back room, where one of the booths is an old wooden métro seat. ◆ Daily breakfast, lunch, and dinner (until 2AM). 30 Rue Vieille-du-Temple (between Rues du Trésor and des Rosiers). 01.42.72.47.47. Métros: Hôtel de Ville, St-Paul

73 Le Colimacon ★★$$ A pretty stone facade, built in 1732 by **Louis Le Tellier**, graces this popular restaurant. Inside, guests dine in a romantic setting of fresh floral arrangements, candlelight, and superb service. Specialties such as foie gras and *magret de canard landais au fruits de saison* (duck's breast with seasonal fruit) are popular favorites. There's also a good wine list. ◆ M-Th dinner; F-Su lunch and dinner. Reservations required. 44 Rue Vieille-du-Temple (between Rues des Rosiers and des Francs-Bourgeois). 01.48.87.12.01. Métro: Hôtel de Ville

74 Finkelsztajn A Jewish bakery has operated at this address since 1851, and today Sacha Finkelsztajn carries on the tradition, producing the richest cheesecake this side of Manhattan's Second Avenue. The affable baker offers newcomers a free taste of her Polish herring, chicken liver, and eggplant puree. ◆ W-Su; closed one week in winter and 1 July to mid-August. 27 Rue des Rosiers (between Rues des Ecouffes and Vieille-du-Temple). 01.42.72.78.91. Métro: St-Paul

75 Rue des Francs-Bourgeois Originally called Rue des Poulies (Street of Spools) after a local community of weavers, this thoroughfare became known as the Street of the Free Citizens in the 14th century, when the local parish built an almshouse (on the site of 34-36 Rue des Francs-Bourgeois) for citizens so poor they were *francs* (free) of any obligation to the state tax jackals. ◆ Between Pl des Vosges and Rue des Archives. Métro: St-Paul

75 Boutique Filofax Here you'll find everything to gratify your Filofax fetish. The famous pocket-size, three-ring English notebooks come in myriad styles, from black leather to rubber, and with notepaper of every hue. Also in stock are sheaves of maps, calendars, and metric conversion charts to store in your portable file cabinet as well as a beautiful collection of handmade sterling silver pens. ◆ M-Sa. 32 Rue des Francs-Bourgeois (between Rues Elzévir and Vieille-du-Temple). 01.42.78.67.87. Métro: St-Paul

76 A l'Image du Grenier sur l'Eau Brothers Yves and Sylvain Di Maria have spent the last two decades assembling this remarkable collection of more than a million vintage postcards of locales from Avignon to Zaire, each one for sale. This shop, with its original tiled floors, also features French publicity photos from the 1950s and lithographs from the Art Nouveau period. ◆ M-Sa. 45 Rue des Francs-Bourgeois (between Rues Pavée and Hospitalières-St-Gervais). 01.42.71.02.31. Métro: St-Paul

77 Galerie Yvon Lambert Works by On Kawara, Lewitt, Twombly, Schnabel, Nan Goldin, and Boltanski are showcased here. ◆ Tu-Sa. 108 Rue Vieille-du-Temple (between Rues Debelleyme and des Coutures-St-Gervais). 01.42.71.09.33. Métro: St-Sébastien–Froissart

78 Galerie Philippe Uzzan This is the only gallery in Paris devoted to architecture. Uzzan shows the work of international designers who have become as famous for their concepts as for their constructions. Videos, photos, drawings, sketches, models, and installations are all used to explain the process architects go through in designing a building. The projects of **Thom Mayne, Diller and Scofidio, Daniel Liebeskind, Michele Saee, Peter Eisenman, Steven Holl,** and partners **Odile Decq** and **Benoît Cornette** are exhibited here. ◆ By appointment only. 11 Rue de Thorigny (between Rues Debelleyme and des Coutures-St-Gervais). 01.44.59.83.00. Métro: St-Sébastien–Froissart

79 Musée Picasso When it was finally opened on 23 September 1985 by French president François Mitterrand, this museum had taken two other French presidents, five ministers of culture, and 11 years to establish. In the first month alone, it received 80,000 visitors. "Give me a museum and I'll fill it up," said Pablo

Picasso, perhaps the 20th century's most important and prolific painter. His wish was granted posthumously here in the **Hôtel Salé,** a 17th-century building that undoubtedly would have pleased the artist, who epitomized outlaw Modernism yet preferred old houses. Today the mansion enshrines the artist's collection of his own works, the largest assembly of Picassos in the world: 203 paintings, 158 sculptures, 16 collages, 29 relief paintings, 88 ceramics, 30 sketchbooks, more than 1,500 drawings, and numerous prints, including the *Vollard Suite,* his Neo-Classical etchings created in the 1920s. The museum also houses Picasso's personal art collection, including works by Matisse, Renoir, Cézanne, Braque, Balthus, and Le Douanier Rousseau.

In December 1912, at the age of 31, Picasso began to hoard his own work. He wrote his dealer, Daniel Henry Kahnweiler, that he would keep five paintings a year, as well as his self-portraits, family portraits, and most of his sculpture. For 70 years Picasso also made a habit of holding onto the works he painted during the week of his birthday, 25 October.

When Picasso died on 8 April 1973 with no will, France's tax collectors were quick to pounce on his estate. In lieu of $65 million in inheritance taxes, Picasso's heirs donated one-quarter of his collection to the state. Dominique Bozo (former chief curator of the **Museum of Modern Art** at the **Pompidou Center**) and a team of Picasso experts then carved up the artist's pie for France. Ironically, as late as 1945, there were only three Picassos in public collections in France, a handful far outnumbered by the many in the possession of the Museum of Modern Art in New York.

The **Hôtel Salé** has but a few of Picasso's masterpieces, *Still Life with Caned Chair, Two Women Running on Beach,* and the Neo-Classical *Pipes of Pan* among them. However, the works here are exhibited chronologically, and the collection affords an extraordinary odyssey through the artist's growth and psyche. Furthermore, revealing Picasso memorabilia are sprinkled throughout the museum: photos of Picasso at bullfights, posing on the beach with a fig leaf, hoisting a bull's skull at the beach of Golfe-Juan, playing with his children, and consorting with friends such as Jean Cocteau and Max Jacob. Also throughout the museum are portraits of the women in Picasso's life: Olga Kokhlova, the Russian dancer; Marie-Thérèse Walter, the 17-year-old earth mother; Dora Maar, the intellectual; Françoise Gilot, the painter; and his widow, Jacqueline.

You could spend the entire day wandering through the museum, but if it's 11:30AM and you've got a 1PM lunch date, it is best to concentrate on the second-floor collection, then stroll among the sculptures in the basement on your way out. Here are a few highlights: **Room 1** brings you face-to-face with one of Picasso's Blue Period master-pieces, the wintry 1901 *Self-Portrait at Age 20,* which shows the gaunt-looking artist clothed in an overcoat to ward off the drafts that doubtlessly plagued his bohemian existence. The influences of Toulouse-Lautrec and van Gogh are particularly evident in the Expressionist deathbed portrait of the poet Casagemas. **Rooms 2** and **3** contain sketches and drawings inspired by Cézanne's geometrical style and by the primitive sculpture from Africa and New Caledonia that so fascinated Picasso and ultimately led to the creation of *Les Demoiselles d'Avignon.* **Room 4,** especially *Still Life with Caned Chair,* reflects Picasso's years of Cubist inquiry (1909-1917) with Georges Braque. The next several rooms feature his paper collages and three-dimensional paintings made of cigar-box wood, newspapers, and metal shards. **Room 5** contains the best of the 60 works in Picasso's personal art collection: master-pieces by Matisse, Braque, Rousseau, and Cézanne. Of the latter, Picasso told the photographer Brassai in 1943: "He's my one and only master."The museum crescendos in **Room 6** with *La Lecture de la Lettre* and *The Pipes of Pan* from his classical period. A minuscule side room (**6B**) is devoted entirely to Picasso's theater and costume designs, created in collaboration with Cocteau, Massine, Stravinsky, and Diaghilev. Near the end of his life, Picasso's art became childlike and cartoonish. The last painting in the collection, dated 14 April 1972, is called *Young Painter,* a sketchy image of a smiling dauber. In his final years the artist confessed, "It has taken all my life to learn how to paint like a child again." Picasso's playfulness is perhaps most evident in his sculpture, which is fashioned from an amusing assortment of odds and ends. En route to the exit, descend into the museum's basement to find his sculpture collection, with originals of his celebrated monkey, goat, and skipping girl.

L'Hôtel Salé was built from 1655 to 1659 by architect **Jean Bouillier** for Pierre Aubert de Fontenay, a man who got rich collecting taxes on salt for the king. With the fall of Nicolas Fouquet (1615-1680), Louis XIV's greedy finance minister, Aubert lost his job, his house, and finally, in 1668, his life. Later the **Hôtel Salé** was leased to the embassy of the Venetian Republic and the naval minister of Louis XVI. After the Revolution, in 1793, it became a boys' school (Balzac studied here), a science laboratory, and, from 1887 to 1964, an exhibition hall for a bronze foundry. After Picasso's death, Minister of Culture Michel Guy secured a 99-year lease on the building from the City of Paris, and the government spent some 65 million francs on its restoration.

Roland Simounet, winner of the 1977 Grand Prix for Architecture, was selected to design the museum. Simounet's plan preserved the architectural integrity of the building while doubling its interior space from 9,900 to 19,800 square feet. A design detail lost on most visitors: The museum's extraordinary benches, tables, and light fixtures were fashioned by the late Diego Giacometti, brother of artist Alberto. ◆ Admission. M, W-Su. 5 Rue de Thorigny (at Rue des Coutures-St-Gervais). 01.42.71.25.21. Métros: St-Paul, St-Sébastien–Froissart

Within the Musée Picasso:

Museum Restaurant ★$ Salads, quiche, soups, grilled salmon, and fruit tarts are served in this small, attractive tea salon. ◆ M, W-Su breakfast, lunch, and afternoon tea. 01.42.71.25.21

80 Musée de la Serrure (Lock Museum)/ Bricard Showrooms Roman door knockers, medieval chastity belts, and the key of the now-destroyed **Cimetière des Innocents** may be seen in the changing exhibits of this small, quirky museum, established by the time-honored locksmithing company Bricard and housed in the **Hôtel Libéral Bruant**. (Architect **Bruant** built this mansion as his residence, and it is considered his most important work after the **Hôtel des Invalides** and the **Salpêtrière** chapel.) The museum has been relegated to the building's vaulted cellar while handmade replicas of some of the museum pieces, such as the lock to Marie Antoinette's **Versailles** apartments, are sold in the **Bricard Showrooms**. Here you can also examine the rich detailing and historical styles of other Bricard products. ◆ Admission. Museum: M-F 2-5PM. Showroom: M-F. 1 Rue de la Perle (at Rue Elzévir). 01.42.77.79.62 (museum); 01.42.77.71.68 (showroom). Métros: Chemin Vert, St-Paul

81 Luthier Owner M. Brué buys, sells, makes, and restores violins, violas, bows, and old instruments at these quarters in the **Hôtel de Savourny**. ◆ W-Sa. 4 Rue Elzévir (between Rues des Francs-Bourgeois and du Parc-Royal). 01.42.77.68.42. Métro: St-Paul

81 Musée Cognacq-Jay This marvelously complete collection of 18th-century art was acquired by the husband-and-wife team of Louise Jay and Ernest Cognacq, who created the **Samaritaine** department stores and boasted of never having set foot in the **Louvre**. The collection was moved to the five-story, 16th-century **Hôtel Donon**, and the works of Boucher, Tiepolo, Watteau, Fragonard, Greuze, La Tour, Rembrandt, Gainsborough, and Reynolds are as well displayed here as they were in their old home on Boulevard des Capucines. There's also a remarkable set of perfume cases and snuffboxes as well as Meissen porcelain statuettes. ◆ Admission.

Tu-Su. 8 Rue Elzévir (between Rues des Francs-Bourgeois and du Parc-Royal). 01.40.27.07.21. Métro: St-Paul

82 Gallery Maison Mansart The ground floor of the house **François Mansart** built for himself (and inhabited until his death in 1666) now houses Alain Thiollier's stark, high-ceilinged gallery, which exhibits contemporary works by an international group of artists. On the second floor is a chapel (with an altar inscribed to "Humanism") built by a Brazilian follower of French positivist Auguste Comte. The chapel is not open to the public, but inquire about the occasional string-quartet concerts held here. ◆ Tu-Sa 3-7PM. 5 Rue Payenne (between Rues des Francs-Bourgeois and du Parc-Royal). 01.48.87.41.03. Métro: St-Paul

SMART

SOCIÉTÉ DES MÉTIERS D'ART

83 Société des Métiers d'Art (Smart) Hand-painted tiles and ceramics by a score of French craftspeople from Alsace to Provence are sold here. You can reconstruct the Place des Vosges with terra-cotta tile miniatures of the 17th-century town houses or assemble a fantasy Gallic village with tiles of a French bakery, cafe, butcher shop, school, and church. Other items on **Smart**'s best-seller list are Marseillaise tarot cards in tile, and brass European faucets. A victim of its own success, it is now open only by appointment. ◆ Daily; closed August. 22 Rue des Francs-Bourgeois (between Rues Payenne and Elzévir). 01.42.77.41.24. Métro: St-Paul

83 Marais Plus Formerly a bookstore and tea salon, this jumble is now a *boutique en mouvement,* with an ever-changing stock of postcards, globes, dolls, stuffed animals, Christmas decorations, and handmade ceramic tea services. The tearoom serves delicious tarts, salads, and desserts, plus brunch on Sunday. ◆ Daily. 20 Rue des Francs-Bourgeois (at Rue Payenne). 01.48.87.01.40. Métro: St-Paul

84 Rue Pavée The construction of one of the city's first *pavée* (paved) streets was a pioneer achievement in the 14th century, when the city's muddy roads also served as open sewers and pigsties. ◆ Between Rues de Rivoli and des Francs-Bourgeois. Métro: St-Paul

"Nowhere is one more alone than in Paris . . . and yet surrounded by crowds. Nowhere is one more likely to incur greater ridicule. And no visit is more essential."

Marguerite Duras

84 Le Loft A faint fragrance of fresh polish permeates this three-story warehouse of English and Scandinavian pine. French Anglophiles shop here for old pine desks, mirrors, and three-door wardrobes. ♦ M-Sa. 17 *bis* Rue Pavée (between Rues des Rosiers and des Francs-Bourgeois). 01.48.87.46.50. Métro: St-Paul

85 Association Culturelle Israélite Agoudas Hakehilos The sinuous facade of the only synagogue (1913) designed by **Hector Guimard**, the Art Nouveau architect best known for his sculptural métro entrances, suggests an open book, perhaps the Torah. The building is closed to the public except during Saturday services. ♦ 10 Rue Pavée (between Rues du Roi-de-Sicile and des Rosiers). 01.48.87.21.54, 01.48.87.26.29. Métro: St-Paul

86 Bibliothèque Historique de la Ville de Paris (Historical Library of the City of Paris) Designed in 1611 by **Baptiste du Cerceau,** the **Hôtel Lamoignon** (pictured below) has housed the **Historical Library of the City of Paris** since 1969 and is a mecca for French historians. The mansion was originally the property of Diane de France, the illegitimate daughter of Henri II. As the story goes, young Henri, while traveling in Italy, was in hot pursuit of the Duchess of Angoulême. When she refused to leave her house, he burned it down and had her kidnapped and taken to France. Out of their tumultuous union, Diane was born. At age seven, she was legally adopted by the king and given all the rights of nobility, among them this mansion, where she lived until her death at age 82.

Adorned with a colossal order of Italianate pilasters, this was the city's first private mansion. The low triangular pediment is embellished by a stag with antlers, a tribute to Diana, goddess of the hunt. On a rainy day, the library is one of the best places in Paris to read about Paris. Once in the courtyard, bear right, up the steps to the **Reading Room** door. If you manage to convince the guard you are a visiting scholar, he will give you a reader's card. Take a seat at one of the long wooden tables and gaze up at the gilded beams, one of which is ornamented with a painting of Diana and the hunt. The rest of the library is off-limits to the public. ♦ M-Sa; closed holidays and the first two weeks of August. 24 Rue Pavée (at Rue Malher). 01.44.59.29.40. Métro: St-Paul

87 Rue des Rosiers *Rosiers* means rosebushes and refers to the roses that bloomed nearby within the old medieval city wall, but the fragrances wafting along this narrow, crooked street today are anything but floral. Scents of hot pastrami, steaming borscht, chopped chicken livers, and fresh matzos emanate from the kosher butcher shops, delicatessens, and bakeries that line this street, the *Platzel* of the Jewish quarter since the Middle Ages. The adjoining Rue des Ecouffes takes its name from the Lombardian

Bibliothèque Historique de la Ville de Paris

MICHAEL STORRINGS

pawnbrokers who were derided as *écouffes,* French for kite, a rapacious bird. A terribly haunting reminder of the district's history was a plaque that until recently hung outside an elementary school on the street. It read: "165 Jewish children from this school, deported to Germany during World War II, were exterminated in Nazi camps. Never forget." Down this street the Nazis and Vichy French marched and dragged away 75,000 Jews to concentration camps. ◆ Between Rues Malher and Vieille-du-Temple. Métro: St-Paul

87 Le Roi du Falaffel–Rosiers Alimentation North African grocers offer hummus, Israeli dishes, and falafel sandwiches to go. ◆ M-F, Su. 34 Rue des Rosiers (between Rues Pavée and Hospitalières-St-Gervais). 01.48.87.63.60. Métro: St-Paul

88 Le Loir dans la Théière ★★$ With its flea-market furniture, sprung-out sofas, wooden tables, and raffish air, this comfortable tea salon could be in Seattle or Berkeley. The name, "Dormouse in the Teapot," recalls *Alice's Adventures in Wonderland,* as does the mural of other characters from the Lewis Carroll fantasy. Yet the light, tasty salads and fine homemade cakes and tarts are very real. ◆ Daily brunch, lunch, and afternoon tea. No credit cards accepted. 3 Rue des Rosiers (between Rues Pavée and Ferdinand-Duval). 01.42.72.90.61. Métro: St-Paul

88 Jo Goldenberg ★★$$ The sweet aroma of spiced meat, the clatter of dishes, and, particularly on Sunday afternoon, the babble of strong, animated voices fill this Jewish delicatessen/restaurant. Try the *foie haché* (chopped liver), *poisson farci* (gefilte fish), Cracovian sausages, and strudel, washed down with a cold Pilsen. This famous spot was the site of a tragedy on 9 August 1982, when masked gunmen killed six customers. The PLO took credit, and the gunmen were never caught. ◆ Daily breakfast, lunch, and dinner; closed Yom Kippur. Reservations recommended. 7 Rue des Rosiers (at Rue Ferdinand-Duval). 01.48.87.20.16, 01.48.87.70.39. Métro: St-Paul

89 La Tartine ★★★$ This is the oldest wine bar in Paris, owned for 70 years by the family of M. Bouscarel, who selects the stock of more than 60 wines himself. He buys directly from Burgundy, Bordeaux, Rhône, and Loire Valley producers, keeping the prices down and the quality up. The cafe is always filled with a vibrant mix of ages and personalities, happily sipping wine and munching on *tartines,* simple sandwiches on *pain Poilâne* filled with pâté, cheese, ham, or sausage. ◆ M, Th-Su breakfast and lunch; W lunch. No credit cards accepted. 24 Rue de Rivoli (between Rues Ferdinand-Duval and des Ecouffes). 01.42.72.76.85. Métros: Hôtel de Ville, St-Paul

Teatime

Hoofing around Paris's museums and monuments can be a stimulating but exhausting experience. Take a break at one of the city's many *salons de thé* with a

relaxing pot of hot tea and a rejuvenating piece of pastry. The tea salons mentioned here range in atmosphere from grandma's sitting room to Belle Epoque grandeur, with a few surprises in between.

A La Cour de Rohan Cour du Commerce-St-André, 59-61 Rue St-André-des-Arts (between Rues de l'Eperon and de l'Ancienne-Comédie), 01.43.25.79.67

Angélina 226 Rue de Rivoli (between Rues d'Alger and de Castiglione), 01.42.60.82.00

A Priori Thé 35-37 Galerie Vivienne (off Rue Vivienne), 01.42.97.48.75

Ladurée 16 Rue Royale (at Rue St-Honoré), 01.42.60.21.79

La Mosquée de Paris 39 Rue Geoffroy-St-Hilaire (at Rue Daubenton), 01.43.31.18.14

Le Flore en l'Ile 42 Quai d'Orléans (at Rue Jean-du-Bellay), 01.43.29.88.27

Le Loir dans la Théière 3 Rue des Rosiers (at Rue Pavée), 01.42.72.90.61

Les Deux Abeilles 189 Rue de l'Université (between Aves Rapp and Franco-Russe), 01.45.55.64.04

Les Fous de l'Ile 33 Rue des Deux-Ponts (between Rue St-Louis-en-l'Ile and Quai de Bourbon), 01.43.25.76.67

Mariage Frères 30-32 Rue du Bourg-Tibourg (between Rues du Roi-de-Sicile and Ste-Croix-de-la-Bretonnerie), 01.42.72.28.11; 13 Rue des Grands-Augustins (at Rue de Savoie), 01.40.51.82.50

Muscade 36 Rue de Montpensier (between Rues de Richelieu et de Beaujolais), 01.42.97.51.36

Maison SUBA

90 Maison Suba A stone's throw from the Place des Vosges you will find a shop full of delicious red pepper conserves and oak-smoked Hungarian sausages. Don't pass up the Tokay wine, so loved by King George V, the father of Queen Elizabeth II, that he ordered it in industrial quantities. ♦ Tu-Sa; closed August. 11 Rue de Sévigné (between Rues de Rivoli and des Francs-Bourgeois). 01.48.87.46.06. Métro: St-Paul

91 Hôtel et Musée Carnavalet The laughing carnival mask sculpted in stone above the Rue des Francs-Bourgeois gate of this splendid mansion (illustrated below) is a misleading visual pun: This 16th-century building does not conceal a midway of clowns or a family of dancing bears. A truer clue to the building's contents is found in the ship (the symbol of Paris) on the gate. In 1880, the **Hôtel Carnavalet** was put into service as the **Musée Historique de la Ville de Paris** (Historical Museum of the City of Paris), and today it vividly displays four centuries (1500-1900) of Parisian life. The building's original 1540 design is attributed to **Pierre Lescot,** who was then the architect of the **Louvre.** The *hôtel* (mansion) was spruced up in 1655 by **François Mansart,** the architect for whom the mansard roof is named. The structure's name evolved from that of an early owner, the widow of the Breton Sire de Kernevency, whose surname Parisians constantly mispronounced and permanently corrupted to its present form.

The museum has something for everyone, even the most fidgety youngster. On the ground floor (see diagram at right) is an entire roomful of old metal shop signs and 18th-century billboards dating from an age of mass illiteracy. The baker advertised himself with a golden sheaf of wheat, the butcher with a suckling pig, and the locksmith with an ornate iron key. There is also a lively exhibit on the French Revolution; the royal family's itemized laundry bill; the young dauphin's penmanship book; the rope ladder used by a political prisoner to escape from the Bastille; a model of the guillotine; a pair of drums banged by the Revolutionaries; a *Who's Who* of the Revolution in portraits (from crazed Marat to stern Robespierre); and the penknife Napoléon Bonaparte used during the Egyptian campaign. The ground floor also houses temporary exhibits on topics related to Paris past and present.

On the second floor are exhibitions of fashionable furnishings from the reigns of the last Bourbon kings (Louis XIV, Louis XV, and Louis XVI), salon murals by Jean-Honoré Fragonard and François Boucher, and the apartments of Madame de Sévigné (1626-96). This "Grande Dame of the Marais" (who was born, baptized, and married in the district) lived at the **Hôtel Carnavalet** for the last 19 years of her life. Here she entertained the greatest thinkers of the day and, in her famous *Lettres,* inscribed her witty, incisive

Hôtel et Musée Carnavalet

MICHAEL STORRINGS

observations on the court of Louis XIV. Her association with the royals was not forgotten by well-read Revolutionary hotheads, who a century later exhumed her remains, beheaded the corpse, and triumphantly paraded through Paris with her skull. On your way out, catch Louis XIV, looking rather silly decked out as a Roman general with a wig (the Antoine Coysevox courtyard statue was brought here from the **Hôtel de Ville**). ♦ Admission. Tu-Su. 23 Rue de Sévigné (between Rues des Francs-Bourgeois and du Parc-Royal). 01.42.72.21.13. Métros: Chemin Vert, St-Paul

Ground Floor

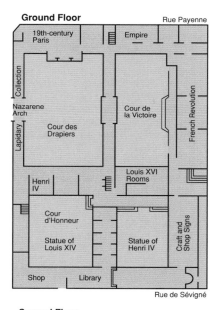

Second Floor

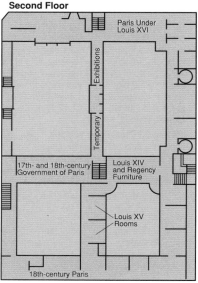

92 Carnavalette Old newspapers, political cartoons, fin-de-siècle theater programs, 19th-century satirical newspapers, and fashion catalogs from the 1930s are for sale here. ♦ Daily. 2 Rue des Francs-Bourgeois (at Rue de Turenne). 01.42.72.91.92. Métro: St-Paul

93 Les Bourgeoises ★★$$ Dining here on the baked St. Marcellin cheese on toast, fresh ravioli stuffed with herbed cheese, lamb stew with coriander and ginger, or Indian specialties such as chicken tandoori is like dining in the living room of owner Martine Robin's grandmother. In fact, the oil paintings, chairs, and tables all come from Robin's grandparents' antiques shop. The homemade raspberry liqueur aging in a jar by the front window is, unfortunately, purely decorative. ♦ Daily dinner; Tu-Sa lunch and dinner. Reservations recommended. 12 Rue des Francs-Bourgeois (between Rues de Turenne and de Sévigné). 01.42.72.48.30. Métro: St-Paul

94 Jean-Pierre De Castro Antique silver and silver-plated articles such as Champagne buckets, candelabras, and sugar tongs are the specialties of this busy boutique. Forks and spoons are displayed by the basketful and sold by the kilogram. ♦ M 2-7PM; Tu-Su. 17 Rue des Francs-Bourgeois (between Rues de Turenne and de Sévigné). 01.42.72.04.00. Métro: St-Paul

95 L'Osteria ★★$$ Friendly service and deliciously prepared Italian fare are the reasons why so many Parisians make repeated stops here. Fresh pasta dishes are the most popular menu choices: Try tagliolini with broccoli and Parma ham, *gnocchi di patate al gorgonzola,* or seafood spaghetti; the osso buco is also highly recommended. ♦ M-F lunch and dinner. Closed in August. 10 Rue de Sévigné (between Rues St-Antoine and de Jarente). 01.42.71.37.08. Métro St-Paul

96 Auberge de Jarente ★$ This simple restaurant serves such Basque specialties as *pipérade* (an omelette with tomatoes and peppers) and paella at modest prices. ♦ Tu-Sa lunch and dinner; closed two weeks in August and at Christmastime. Reservations recommended. 7 Rue de Jarente (between Rues Caron and de Sévigné). 01.42.77.49.35. Métro: St-Paul

96 Bar de Jarente ★★$ Whether you come for coffee and a croissant in the morning or an aperitif before hitting one of the neighboring restaurants, do as the locals do and let the energetic and feisty Mme. Renée take care of you. You will see why her hospitality is known throughout the *quartier.* ♦ M-Sa breakfast, lunch, and snacks; closed August. 5 Rue de Jarente (at Rue Caron). 01.48.87.60.93. Métro: St-Paul

97 Place des Vosges The oldest and perhaps most beautiful square in Paris, this symmetrical ensemble of 36 matching pavilions with red and gold brick and stone facades, steep slate roofs, and dormer windows was designed in 1612 by **Clément Métezeau**. This marked the first time in Paris that an arcade was used to link houses, and balconies were employed for more than decorative purposes.

The original function of the square, commissioned by Henri IV, was to house a silk factory and its workers. The goal was to provide Marie de Médicis, his estranged queen, with lingerie cheaper than what could be imported from Genoa. Despite Henri's good intentions, his silk workers' housing project was gentrified before the last brick was laid. Into the apartments with 16-foot-high ceilings, red marble fireplaces, and parquet floors moved Richelieu, Corneille, Molière, and a covey of courtiers, cavaliers, ministers, and marquises.

It remained a high-class neighborhood until the summer of 1686, when Louis XIV moved to **Versailles** and the French aristocracy followed. In the early 18th century the Marais continued to decline and eventually became the city's industrial East End. Heavy machinery was bolted to the elegant floors of the great spaces, and magnificent salons were subdivided into minuscule apartments. The neighborhood was not pulled out of its nosedive until the early 1960s, when Minister of Culture André Malraux had the Place des Vosges and the Marais declared a historic district. Nowadays, the Place des Vosges is frequented by knitting grandmothers, toddlers digging in the dirt, and perhaps a group of North African immigrants enjoying an impromptu soccer game beside an equestrian statue of a smirking Louis XIII. ◆ Between Rues de Birague and de Béarn. Métros: Bastille, St-Paul

98 Issey Miyake Something of an art gallery for clothes, the newest boutique in the Place des Vosges shows the latest looks from the Japanese master. Many of these pieces are made in limited editions, while the boutique at 201 Boulevard St-Germain (01.45.48.10.44) sells Miyake's regular clothing lines. Like the other newer structures on the square, this building is a masterpiece of trompe l'oeil. The facade is made of plaster on wood framing, and you have to get pretty close to see that the bricks are painted on. ◆ M-Sa; closed two weeks in August. 3 Pl des Vosges (between Rues de Birague and des Francs-Bourgeois). 01.48.87.01.86. Métros: St-Paul, Bastille

98 Hôtel de Coulanges The Marquise de Sévigné, whose correspondence with her daughter in Provence became one of the most famous series of letters in French literature, was born here on 6 February 1626. It's still a private residence. ◆ 1 Pl des Vosges (at Rue de Birague). Métros: St-Paul, Bastille

99 Coconnas ★$$ Boasting a Louis XIII dining room and a sidewalk terrace overlooking the mansions and garden of the Place des Vosges, this casual restaurant (run by Claude Terrail of **La Tour d'Argent**) has built its reputation on serving Good King Henri's *poule-au-pot* (commemorating Henri IV's famous political promise of a chicken in every pot) and *soufflé Grande Marnier*. American tourists and expatriates predominate. ◆ W-Su lunch and dinner; closed mid-December to mid-January. Reservations recommended. 2 *bis* Pl des Vosges (at Rue de Birague). 01.42.78.58.16. Métros: Bastille, St-Paul

99 Musée Victor Hugo This museum was the French writer's home from 1833 until 1848, when Napoléon III came to power and Hugo's voluntary exile in the Channel Islands began. The museum's eclectic assortment of Hugo mementos includes the cap he wore during the 1871 Siege of Paris, his bust sculpted by Rodin, and a model of an elephant sculpture that he proposed for Place de la Bastille. Haunting postage stamp–size pen-and-ink doodles of Rhine castles and ships at sea along with macabre sketches of witches, demons, and the hanging of John Brown show a nightmarish side to the author of *The Hunchback of Notre-Dame* (1831) and *Les Misérables* (1862).

The drawings are counterbalanced by the hodgepodge of oriental furnishings Hugo designed for the Guernsey home of Juliette Drouet, his mistress for more than half a century. Don't leave the museum without viewing the Place des Vosges from one of Hugo's upstairs windows and glancing at the Nadar photo of an old but ageless Hugo on his deathbed, 22 May 1885. ◆ Admission. Tu-Su. 6 Pl des Vosges (between Rues de Birague and du Pas-de-la-Mule). 01.42.72.10.16. Métros: Bastille, St-Paul

100 18 and 23 Place des Vosges These are two of the best portals on the square. Also, don't miss the door knockers at **No. 4** and **No. 17**. ◆ Between Rues de Birague and Pas-de-la-Mule. Métros: Bastille, St-Paul

100 La Chope des Vosges ★$$ Architects working on restorations in the historic district hang out in this simple cafe/restaurant. Not found on any gourmet's restaurant roster, it serves a sumptuous foie gras with a warm welcome. ◆ Daily lunch and dinner; closed for dinner Monday and Sunday from October through April. Reservations recommended.

Restaurants/Clubs: Red   **Hotels:** Blue
Shops/ ♥ Outdoors: Green   **Sights/Culture:** Black

22 Pl des Vosges (at Rue Pas-de-la-Mule). 01.42.72.64.04. Métros: Bastille, St-Paul

101 André Bissonnet Some years ago, a butcher named André Bissonnet laid down his meat cleaver, redecorated his *boucherie,* and began buying antique musical instruments and restoring them in his cold-storage room. On any given day he might be working on a 1747 viola da gamba, a 17th-century harp, a porcelain trumpet, ancient hurdy-gurdies, or a black serpent, a bizarre 18th-century horn used to accompany chanting priests. Bissonnet claims to be an accomplished player of the Breton bombardon and upon request will proudly bleat out a few bars. ♦ M-Sa 2-7PM or by appointment; closed August. 6 Rue du Pas-de-la-Mule (between Blvd Beaumarchais and Rue des Tournelles). 01.48.87.20.15. Métros: Bastille, St-Paul

102 Pavillon de la Reine $$$$ The most elegant hotel in the Marais, this 17th-century mansion, discreetly distanced from the *place* by its own garden courtyard, is quietly opulent, with antique tapestries, Persian carpets, a grand fireplace, marble floors, soft leather couches, and 55 luxurious rooms and suites. There's no restaurant. The property is operated in conjunction with the chic hotel **Relais Christine** across the Seine. ♦ 28 Pl des Vosges (at Rue de Béarn). 01.42.77.96.40. Métros: Bastille, St-Paul

102 Jardin de Flore Founded by renowned French architect **Fernand Pouillon,** this remarkable small publishing house reissues deluxe limited editions of antique manuscripts, illustrations, and maps. Pouillon employs Renaissance bookmaking techniques and prints on handmade paper. The books, sold on the premises, are bound in tooled, gold-leaf leather, and illustrations are colored by hand. Among the wares on display in the lobby are the masterful *Apocalypse* engravings (1498) of Albrecht Dürer, the

illustrated *Venise* (1610) by Giacomo Franco, and the famous three-foot-diameter globes that Venetian cartographer Vincenzo Maria Coronelli created for Louis XIV in 1693. In 1984 another French head of state, President François Mitterrand, ordered a pair of these globes (at $12,000 apiece) for his **Elysée Palace** office—personalized with his portrait floating in the South Atlantic. The Art Nouveau doorway of ersatz marble is by sculptor and jeweler Jean Filhos. ♦ Daily. 24 Pl des Vosges (at Rue Pas-de-la-Mule). 01.42.77.61.90. Métros: Bastille, St-Paul

103 21 Place des Vosges Cardinal Richelieu (1585-1642), the French prime minister under Louis XIII and the founder of the **Académie Française,** lived here.♦ At Rue des Francs-Bourgeois. Métros: Bastille, St-Paul

103 La Guirlande de Julie ★★$$ At his restaurant on the square, Claude Terrail, owner of the celebrated **Tour d'Argent,** presents a small, seasonally inspired menu. Start with something light, such as the *salade de canard* (duck salad) with chestnuts, followed by the excellent pot-au-feu or *dodine de saumon* (salmon with a classic wine sauce) and a bottle of wine from the Cave de la Tour d'Argent. Conclude with the popular chocolate cake with pistachio sauce. The weekday prix-fixe lunch menu is a bargain. In summer reserve a table outside beneath the brick arcade. ♦ W-Su lunch and dinner (until 1AM). Reservations recommended. 25 Pl des Vosges (between Rues de Béarn and des Francs-Bourgeois). 01.48.87.94.07. Métros: Bastille, St-Paul

104 Ma Bourgogne ★★$$ Owned by Aimé Cougoureux, this arcade-sheltered cafe is where the locals go for Sunday breakfast. Specialties include sausages from Auvergne, *foie gras des Landes andouillette* (foie gras from Landes with sausages), veal tripe, and spicy steak *tartare.* ♦ Daily breakfast, lunch, and dinner; closed February and one week in March. No credit cards accepted. 19 Pl des Vosges (at Rue des Francs-Bourgeois). 01.42.78.44.64. Métros: Bastille, St-Paul

105 L'Ambrosie ★★★$$$$ One of the few Michelin three-star restaurants in Paris, this dining spot is owned by chef Bernard Pacaud, who trained under Claude Peyrot at **Le Vivarois.** Pacaud is a perfectionist and his brief bill of fare fulfills the promise of the restaurant's name—a menu fit for the gods. Some favorites have included John Dory braised with fennel, artichokes with foie gras, skate with sliced cabbage, *croustillant d'agneau* (rolled fillet of lamb stuffed with truffles), and the puff-pastry desserts. The dining room is discreetly romantic with subtle lighting, exquisite floral arrangements, and beautiful tapestries adorning the walls. ♦ Tu-Sa lunch and dinner; closed two weeks in

February and three weeks in August. Reservations required (at least one month in advance). 9 Pl des Vosges (between Rues de Birague and des Francs-Bourgeois). 01.42.78.51.45. Métros: St-Paul, Bastille

106 A l'Impasse ★★$$ One of the best-kept secrets in the Marais can be found tucked away in a narrow alley. This old neighborhood bistro serves delightful meals in a pleasantly renovated dining room. Baked goat-cheese salads, terrines of rabbit and *girolle* mushrooms, fillet of duck in blueberry sauce, and rich chocolate profiteroles are offered here at bargain prices. The service is warm and attentive. ♦ M, Sa dinner; Tu-F lunch and dinner; closed two weeks in August. Reservations recommended. 4 Impasse Guéménée (off Rue St-Antoine). 01.42.72.08.45. Métros: Bastille, St-Paul

107 Hôtel de la Place des Vosges $$ Just down the street from the **Pavillon de La Reine** entrance to the famous square sits this cozy, rather than regal, 16-room hotel. There's no restaurant. ♦ 12 Rue de Birague (between Rue St-Antoine and Pl des Vosges). 01.42.72.60.46; fax 01.42.72.02.64. Métro: St-Paul

108 Hôtel de Sully The most richly decorated private mansion in Paris dates from the time of Louis XIII and was designed in 1630 by architect **Androuet du Cerceau** for the notorious gambler Petit Thouars, who is said to have lost his entire fortune in one night. Ten years later, the mansion was bought by the Duc de Sully, a minister to Henri IV. Today this is the site of the information office of the **Caisse Nationale des Monuments Historiques et des Sites** (Bureau of Historic Monuments and Sites), where you may rent any of 40 châteaux or historic mansions throughout France for private receptions, weddings, or conventions. At the far end of the small, well-manicured garden, the orangery opens onto the Place des Vosges. ♦ Garden: Daily. Rental service: M-Sa. 62 Rue St-Antoine (between Rues de Birague and de Turenne). 01.44.61.20.00. Métro: St-Paul

According to a survey by the Tidy Britain Group, an independent association, Paris is Western Europe's third-cleanest city, surpassed in tidiness only by London and Bern.

109 The Hairy Lemon ★★$ This comfortable Irish bar is the perfect drop-in spot for typical pub fare. There are generous burgers, hearty sandwiches, baked potatoes, and daily specials. ♦M-F lunch and dinner; Sa-Su dinner. 4 Rue Caron (between Rues St-Antoine and d'Ormesson). 01.42.72.90.40. Métro: St-Paul

110 St-Paul–St-Louis Built for the Jesuits as part of their monastery in 1627, this Baroque church, with its classically ordered facade, superimposed columns, and dome, is modeled on the Gesù Church in Rome. The spacious interior is well lit and ornate with decoration and sculptures. In the transept is the painting *Christ in the Garden,* by Delacroix. ♦ Rue St-Antoine (between Rues St-Paul and du Prévôt). 01.42.72.30.32. Métro: St-Paul

111 Maison Européene de la Photographie Opened in 1996, this cultural institution is located in a classic 18th-century town house. Parisian architect **Yves Lion** has created a tasteful, contemporary interior that boasts a permanent collection of over 12,000 photographs and a gallery for rotating exhibitions. Exploring the architectural diversity of the center is an adventure: the main promenade features rough stone walls; there's an elegant staircase; and vaults of the original house twist into the adjoining modern, spacious annex. Visitors are invited to participate in workshops, lectures, and conferences and to view films on the institution's various exhibitions. ♦ Admission. W-Su. Tours by appointment only. 5-7 Rue de Fourcy (between Rues de Jouy and François-Miron). 01.44.78.75.00. Métros: St-Paul, Pont-Marie

112 Village St-Paul This jumble of antiques shops crammed into a courtyard often becomes a lively outdoor market. It's one of the few places in Paris to shop on Sunday. ♦ M, Th-Su. Bounded by Rues St-Paul and des Jardins-St-Paul, and Rues de l'Ave-Maria and Charlemagne. Métros: St-Paul, Sully–Morland, Pont-Marie

113 Thanksgiving ★★$ Americans who long for familiar tastes can sate themselves with barbecued ribs or chocolate chip cookies at this American-food restaurant and shop. Also look for California-style chicken, Maryland crab cakes, smoked sausage, and prawns with spicy rice. The shop carries packages of Cracker Jack, Oreos, and Pop-Tarts, as well as Alpo for your dog (at foie-gras prices). When

Thanksgiving approaches, fresh turkey (cooked, if you call ahead), pumpkins, cranberries, and all the fixings are on hand. ♦ Restaurant: Tu-F lunch and dinner; Sa-Su brunch. Shop: Daily. Closed two weeks in August and one week in January. 20 Rue St-Paul (at Rue Charles-V). 01.42.77.68.29. Métros: St-Paul, Sully–Morland, Pont-Marie

l'E N O T E C A

113 L'Enoteca ★★$$ The Italian food served here, beneath colorful glass lamps and wood beams, often varies in specifics but never in quality. Neighborhood residents come for *gigot d'agneau* (leg of lamb), or *soupe de coquillages* (shellfish soup). The wine bar is a pleasant place to pass the afternoon or late evening, with more than 300 Italian wines as well as Italian cheeses for nibbling. ♦ Daily lunch and dinner. Wine bar noon-1AM. Reservations recommended. 25 Rue Charles-V (at Rue St-Paul). 01.42.78.91.44. Métros: St-Paul, Sully–Morland, Pont-Marie

114 Albion Pick up a few paperback classics in English to read at cafes and on train rides. French people who are trying to learn English buy their books here. ♦ M-Sa; closed last three weeks in August. 13 Rue Charles-V (between Rues Beautreillis and St-Paul). 01.42.72.50.71. Métros: St-Paul, Sully–Morland

115 Hôtel St-Louis Marais $$ A rustic 15-room hotel is all that remains of the 18th-century **Hôtel des Célestins** that belonged to the **Celestine Monastery.** Around the corner on Rue Beautreillis is the original entrance to the convent, a stone portal with a weathered wooden door. Beware: The five-story hotel's landmark status prevents the owners from installing an elevator. The rooms are both charming and comfortable. There's no restaurant. ♦ 1 Rue Charles-V (at Rue du Petit-Musc). 01.48.87.87.04; fax 01.48.87.33.26. Métros: St-Paul, Sully–Morland

116 Le Maraîcher ★★$$ It's charming and authentic in every detail, from the wooden beams to the old photos of the Marché St-Antoine. The restaurant's original owner, Valentin Corral, who studied cooking with Alain Senderens, decoration and presentation at Ledoyen, and fine wines in Bordeaux, still stops in from time to time but has been replaced by his understudy Olivier Assan. Nonetheless, the atmosphere remains the same, with exotic flowers, a well-chosen wine list, and, above all, a seasonally inspired menu with gems such as *filet de rouget à l'orange et confiture de tomates* (red mullet fillet with orange and tomato chutney), *magret de canard* (duck fillet) with honey and spices, and *morue dorée aux poivrons* (cod with peppers). Just as impressive are the prices, especially the

incredibly inexpensive lunchtime menu. ♦ M dinner; Tu-Sa lunch and dinner. Reservations recommended. 5 Rue Beautreillis (between Rues des Lions-St-Paul and Charles-V). 01.42.71.42.49. Métro: Sully–Morland

117 Temple de Ste-Marie This circular temple was originally the chapel of the **Convent of the Visitation,** built by **François Mansart** in 1632, and is today a Protestant church. Nicolas Fouquet, the finance minister accused of embezzlement under Louis XIV, and Henri de Sévigné, the husband of Madame de Sévigné who was killed in a duel in 1651, are buried here. ♦ Rue St-Antoine (at Rue Castex). No phone. Métro: St-Paul

118 Statue de Beaumarchais The 18th-century comedies of Pierre-Augustin Caron de Beaumarchais (1732-1799), *The Barber of Seville* (1775) and *The Marriage of Figaro* (1784), were transformed by Rossini and Mozart respectively into operas whose factotum heros were regarded as dangerously, even revolutionarily, independent. The radical sympathies of Beaumarchais were played out in real life, too: His office was secretly running guns to American revolutionaries. In keeping with the dramatist's satiric tradition, residents of the Bastille neighborhood are constantly dressing up his statue in outrageous costumes. ♦ At Rues St-Antoine and des Tournelles. Métro: Bastille

The Bastille

The area around the Bastille, rejuvenated by the relatively new opera house and scores of art galleries, today is often called the SoHo of Paris. But this neighborhood was not always on the cutting edge of fashion. Originally a convergence of roads leading to Paris, it became a center for jobs and industry in the 17th century when Louis XIV attracted artisans and craftsmen guilds to the area by exempting them from taxes. A century later the working-class haven was to become the symbol of freedom, when, in July 1789, a crowd of citizens seized the **Bastille** and freed its prisoners, marking the start of the French Revolution.

In the 1930s, the district was filled with *bougnats,* Auvergnat dispensaries of wine and coal. Today the *quartier* has been discovered by painters and other bohemians, and the neighborhood has undergone a mind-boggling transformation. The once seedy **Rue de Lappe,** just off the **Place de la Bastille,** is now dubbed "the trendiest street in Paris." Quite a change from 1944, when Somerset Maugham wrote in *The Razor's Edge* that Rue de Lappe, "gave the impression of sordid lust." There are artisans' studios and ateliers and a handful of Auvergnat restaurants, side by side with oh-so-trendy bars and cafes, avant-garde art galleries, and more than one too many Tex-Mex restaurants. Upscale establishments like **Bistrot les Sans-Culottes** and Jean Paul Gaultier's headquarters are causing rents to go up and forcing struggling artists and artisans to move to other neighborhoods.

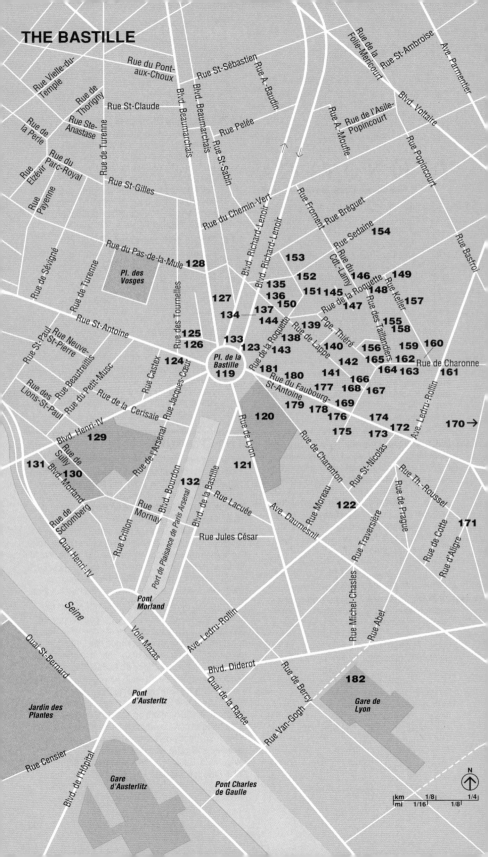

THE BASTILLE

Rue Vieille-du-Temple
Rue de Thorigny
Rue du Pont-aux-Choux
Rue St-Sébastien
Rue A.-Baudin
Rue de la Folie-Méricourt
Rue St-Ambroise
Ave. Parmentier

Rue Ste-Anastase
Rue St-Claude
Blvd. Beaumarchais
Rue Pelée
Rue A.-Mouffe
Rue de l'Asile-Popincourt
Blvd. Voltaire

Rue de la Perle
Rue du Parc-Royal
Blvd. Beaumarchais
Rue St-Sabin
Rue Popincourt

Rue Elzévir
Rue St-Gilles
Rue de Turenne
Rue du Chemin-Vert
Rue Froment
Rue Bréguet
Rue Sedaine

Rue Payenne
Rue du Pas-de-la-Mule
Rue Richard-Lenoir
Rue Richard-Lenoir
Cdt.-Lamy
154

Rue de Sévigné
Pl. des Vosges
128
153
152
151 145
146
149
157

Rue de Turenne
Rue des Tournelles
127
135
136
150
Rue de la Roquette
147
148
Rue Keller

Rue St-Antoine
134
137
144
Pge. Thiéré
155
158

Rue St-Paul
Rue Neuve-St-Pierre
125
126
133
123
143
139
138
Rue de Lappe
140
156
165
159
160

Rue Beautreillis
124
Rue Castex
Rue Jacques-Cœur
Pl. de la Bastille
119
181
180
142
164
162
163
Rue de Charonne
161

Rue des Lions-St-Paul
Rue du Petit-Musc
Rue de la Cerisaie
177
168
167
Ave. Ledru-Rollin

Blvd. Henri-IV
129
Rue de l'Arsenal
Rue du Faubourg-St-Antoine
179
178
176
169
174
172
170 →

Rue de Sully
Blvd. Bourdon
120
175
173
173

131
Blvd. Morland
130
Rue de Lyon
121
132
122

Rue de Schomberg
Rue Mornay
Blvd. Bourdon
Rue de la Bastille
Rue Lacuée
Ave. Daumesnil
171

Quai Henri-IV
Pont de Plaisance de Paris Arsenal
Rue Jules César
Rue de Charenton
Rue Moreau
Rue St-Nicolas
Rue Th.-Roussel
Rue de Prague
Rue de Cotte
Rue d'Aligre

Seine
Pont Morland
Voie Mazas
Rue Michel-Chasles
Rue Traversière
Rue Abel

Quai St-Bernard
Ave. Ledru-Rollin
Blvd. Diderot
Rue de Bercy
182
Gare de Lyon

Jardin des Plantes
Pont d'Austerlitz
Quai de la Rapée
Rue Van-Gogh

Rue Censier
Blvd. de l'Hôpital
Gare d'Austerlitz
Pont Charles de Gaulle
N

km   1/8   1/4
mi 1/16   1/8

MICHAEL STORRINGS

the largest opera house in the world on the Place de la Bastille. The resulting gigantesque and somewhat alienating structure has come under heavy criticism (it has been called the world's largest toilet by some), but despite poor reviews the opera house's presence has been instrumental in the renewal of the Bastille area, helping it to become the trendiest neighborhood in Paris. The facility, billed as the "people's opera house," entertains an estimated 700,000 ticket holders a year and includes an amphitheater and a stage for smaller performances. Its opening was planned in conjunction with the July 1989 bicentennial of the storming of the Bastille and the French Revolution, but dissension among administrators, including the axing (figuratively at least) of the director, delayed the opening of the amphitheater until 1991. The opera house finally opened in 1992, and all opera takes place here. (The **Opéra Garnier** is now reserved for dance performances.) Tours of the building are available for a small charge, but you must reserve in advance. ♦ Box office: M-Sa 11AM-6PM. 120 Rue de Lyon (at Rue de Charenton). 01.44.73.13.00. Métro: Bastille

119 Place de la Bastille On 14 July 1789, 633 people stormed the **Bastille** (the French counterpart to the Tower of London), captured its ammunition depot, released its prisoners (only seven, and none political), lynched its governor, and demolished the fortress, thus sparking the French Revolution. Every year on the 14th of July, these events are celebrated in Paris with parades and dancing in the streets.

The eight-towered **Bastille** was built in 1370 by Provost Hugues Aubriot as a fortified palace for Charles V, and was later transformed by Cardinal Richelieu into a holding tank where political prisoners were detained without trial. During its baleful history, the prison held Voltaire, who was imprisoned for his biting verse, as well as the Marquis de Sade and the notorious, enigmatic "Man in the Iron Mask." Paving stones, laid where Rue du Faubourg-St-Antoine intersects the square, mark the site of the original towers. The figure perched on top of the 170-foot **Colonne de Juillet** (July Column; pictured above) is not an allegory of Liberty as many suppose, but a winged Mercury. ♦ At Rue du Faubourg-St-Antoine and Blvd Beaumarchais. Métro: Bastille

120 Opéra Bastille Not long ago, the French government appointed **Carlos Ott,** a Canadian-Uruguayan architect, to design what was to be

120 Les Grandes Marches ★★$$ This brasserie began as a 17th-century inn patronized by the artisans of the working-class Faubourg St-Antoine quarter, and during the days preceding the Revolution it became a meeting place for patriots. Today the restaurant is frequented by tourists and famished post-opera diners who gather for the less urgent task of consuming *fruits de mer* (seafood), fish, and grilled meat. Begin your meal with oysters and langoustines from the *coquillage* bar, then proceed with the steamed duo of fish (featuring salmon and sole) or the chateaubriand with béarnaise sauce. For a grand finale, order the bitter-dark-chocolate cake with coffee sauce or prunes soaked in red wine. The handsome turn-of-the-century–style dining rooms are decorated in soft blue tones with elegant painted ceilings and enough mirrors to satisfy any narcissist. The best seats in the house are in the upstairs *salon* with its sweeping view over the site of the former **Bastille** prison. ♦ Daily lunch and dinner (until 1:30AM). Reservations recommended for post-opera dinners. 6 Pl de la Bastille (between Rues de Charenton and de Lyon). 01.43.42.90.32. Métro: Bastille

120 FNAC Musique Bastille Your one-stop connection to the music scene carries a complete range of CDs and cassettes and a huge selection of videos and laser discs. Like all stores in the chain, this place is sleek and efficient. It features listening stations with headphones, a ticket outlet, a photo gallery, and frequent music-related events (when Slash's Snakepit released his first solo album, the store raffled off a customized Harley Davidson). ♦ M-Sa; W and F until 10PM. 4 Pl de la Bastille (between Rues de Charenton and de Lyon). 01.43.42.04.04. Métro: Bastille. Also at: Forum des Halles, 1 Rue Pierre-Lescot (at Rue Berger). 01.40.41.40.00. Métro: Châtelet–Les Halles (RER)

121 Dame Tartine ★★$ Chicken with cinnamon and almonds, duck stew with orange and fresh mint, and *saumon* (salmon) *Maltaise* with orange hollandaise sauce are just a few of the interesting combinations featured here. Every delicious dish comes with a piece of *tartine* (toasted bread), the restaurant's namesake. Portions are small, but appropriately inexpensive, so famished diners might want to order two courses. There is an unfortunate view of the ponderous **Opéra Bastille** building. The original **Dame Tartine** restaurant is on the Place Igor-Stravinsky, next to **Centre Georges Pompidou.** ♦ Daily lunch and dinner. 59 Rue de Lyon (between Rue Lacuée and Pl de la Bastille). 01.44.68.96.95. Métro: Bastille. Also at: 2 Rue Brisemiche (at Pl Igor-Stravinsky). 01.42.77.32.22. Métro: Chatelet–Les Halles (RER), Hôtel de Ville

122 China Club ★★$$ This Shanghai-chic place mixes cocktails for the new gentry of the east side. The Chinese-Deco atmosphere features a cozy drawing room with soft leather chairs, a 46-footlong bar, and a Chinese restaurant. Very good renditions of traditional Chinese dishes are served. The bourgeoisie from Paris's conservative west side like to come here, thinking they're living dangerously. ♦ Daily lunch and dinner. Bar daily 7PM-2AM. 50 Rue de Charenton (between Ave Ledru-Rollin and Rue Moreau). 01.43.43.49.14. Métros: Ledru-Rollin, Bastille

---

Although classy restaurants do not take kindly to babies or young children (and Parisians know better than to bring them), a warm welcome is always extended to man's best friend, *le chien.*

123 Indiana Cafe ★$$ There are margaritas and tequila sunrises to go with the nachos, guacamole, bacon cheeseburgers, and barbecued ribs at this formula Tex-Mex restaurant and bar. The sweeter side of the menu features brownies, hot fudge sundaes, and apple pie. ♦ Daily lunch and dinner. 14 Pl de la Bastille (at Blvd Richard-Lenoir). 01.44.75.79.80. Métro: Bastille. Also at: 130 Blvd St-Germain (between Rues de l'Eperon and de l'Ancienne-Comédie). 01.46.34.66.31. Métro: Odéon; 7 Blvd des Capucines (at Pl de l'Opéra). 01.42.68.02.22. Métro: Opéra

124 5 Rue St-Antoine This building marks the position of the **Bastille** courtyard where the angry mob gained access. A plaque at the site reads: *Ici était l'entrée de l'avant-cour de la Bastille par laquelle les assaillants pénétrèrent dans la forteresse le 14 juillet 1789* (Here was the entrance of the forecourt of the Bastille through which the assailants penetrated the fortress the 14th of July 1789). ♦ At Rue Jacques-Cœur. Métro: Bastille

125 Bofinger ★$$ Dating from 1864, this is among Paris's oldest and most overrated brasseries. House legend holds that it was the first in the city to pour draft beer. Specialties are nostalgia, *fruits de mer,* Alsatian *choucroute,* wine from the Côtes-du-Rhône, and more nostalgia. It's popular with Americans, whom the restaurant segregates from its French regulars as a matter of course. ♦ Daily lunch and dinner (until 2AM). Reservations recommended. 5-7 Rue de la Bastille (between Rues Jean-Beausire and des Tournelles). 01.42.72.87.82. Métro: Bastille

126 Le Dôme Bistrot ★★$$ This friendly seafood place features *friture d'éperlans* (fried smelts), salmon tartare and *bar grillé à la Provençale* (grilled bass). With fish, the Mâcon Villages Domaine des deux Roches is an especially nice choice from the wine list. The famous **Le Dôme** in Montparnasse (108 Blvd du Montparnasse, at Rue Delambre, 01.43.35.25.81) is this bistro's *maison mère.* ♦ Daily lunch and dinner. 2 Rue de la Bastille (at Rue des Tournelles). 01.48.04.88.44. Métro: Bastille. Also at: 1 Rue Delambre (at Blvd Raspail). 01.43.35.32.00. Métro: Vavin

126 Le Bistrot de Bofinger ★$$ Spawned by **Bofinger** across the street in 1993, this *decontracté* (easygoing) 1940s-style bistro serves *pâté de tête* (headcheese), *salade*

d'endives with cantal cheese and walnuts, steak tartare, and, in winter, a steamy pot-au-feu. There is also a special menu for children, a rarity in Paris. The mosaic floors and 1945 wall mural depicting the Place de la Bastille were uncovered by workmen during renovation. ♦ Daily lunch and dinner. 6 Rue de la Bastille (between Pl de la Bastille and Rue des Tournelles). 01.42.72.05.23. Métro: Bastille

127 2-20 Blvd Beaumarchais Here once stood the luxurious mansion and gardens of Caron de Beaumarchais (1732-99), the 18th-century dramatist who wrote *The Marriage of Figaro* and who now resides in **Père-Lachaise Cemetery.** The garden was garnished with statues (including one of Voltaire), grottoes, a labyrinth, and an orchard. In 1818 his heirs sold the property to the city for less than a quarter of what Beaumarchais had invested, and it was demolished to facilitate the opening of the Canal St-Martin. The buildings now have residential and commercial space. ♦ Between Pl de la Bastille and Rue Pasteur-Wagner. Métro: Bastille

128 Le Bar à Huitres ★★$$ Known for its fresh and reasonably priced seafood, this restaurant composes delicious platters of *coquillage* (shellfish) and serves fine entrées of grilled salmon and grilled lobster. The crisply decorated dining room is well run and casual. ♦ Daily lunch and dinner (until 1AM). 33 Blvd Beaumarchais (at Rue du Pas-de-la-Mule). 01.48.87.98.92. Métros: Chemin Vert, Bastille. Also at: 33 Rue St-Jacques (at Blvd St-Germain). 01.44.07.27.37. Métro: Maubert–Mutualité; 112 Blvd du Montparnasse (at Blvd Raspail). 01.43.20.71.01. Métro: Vavin

129 Garde Républicaine This massive, rusticated stone complex houses the military barracks and horses' stables of the French National Guard. It was constructed in 1891 on the site of the garden of the former **Celestine Monastery** (founded in 1352), although all that remains today of the vast religious grounds is a stone portal on Rue Beautreillis (off Rue St-Antoine). The compound is open to the public only two days a year (usually in June) but you may be lucky enough to catch the uniformed gendarmes parading on horseback through the streets of Paris on public holidays. Such processions are magnificent, although some of their pomp is diminished by the humorous and necessary presence of one of the city's bright green pooper-scoopers at the end of the parade. ♦ Open to visitors two days a year in June. 12-28 Blvd Henri-IV (between Rues de la Cerisaie and de Sully). 01.42.76.16.32. Métros: Sully–Morland, Bastille

130 Bibliothèque de l'Arsenal Housed in the four stories of this long and slender sandstone building, constructed in 1594 as the mansion of the Grand Master of Artillery under Henri IV, is a library with an unparalleled collection of literature, illuminated manuscripts, French dramatic works, and books on literary history and the history of the theater. The archives encompass over a million printed volumes, 15,000 manuscripts, 100,000 engravings, and 300 musical works. The collection includes Louis IX's Book of Hours, Charles V's Bible, and many documents relating to the **Bastille.** To visit the fine 17th- and 18th-century salons, among them the **Salon de Musique** with its intricate Louis XV woodwork, you must make a reservation for a group tour through the **Caisse Nationale des Monuments Historiques** (62 Rue St-Antoine, 01.48.87.24.15). On the cornice of the south facade (along Boulevard Morland) is a row of eight life-size stone cannons, serving as a reminder of the original function of the building. ♦ Fee for tour. M-Sa; closed 1-15 September. 1 Rue de Sully (at Rue Mornay). 01.53.01.25.04. Métro: Sully–Morland

131 Pavillon de l'Arsenal This building's heavy stone facade hides a glass-and-steel structure constructed in 1879 for Laurent-Louis Borniche, an art lover and patron, as a place to display his almost 2,000 canvases. But Borniche didn't live to see his museum realized, and after his daughter sold the building it was used for various purposes, including workshops for the **Samaritaine** department store and archival storage for the City of Paris. Renovated in 1988 by **Bernard Reichen** and **Philippe Robert,** the building is now a fascinating museum that looks at the urban development of Paris. It also houses a center for documentation on current architectural projects, and a photographic library.

By presenting drawings and models of local urban design and architectural projects, the museum aims to enhance the public's understanding of the city's continual evolution. On permanent display is a model of Paris connected to a computer; at a visitor's request, a videodisc displays one of 30,000 images (of canals, monuments, green spaces, sectors under development, etc.) while a laser ray spots the corresponding locus on the model. There is also an exhibit on the successive phases of the city's construction, from the wall of Philippe Auguste to Haussmann's Paris to present-day developments. The changing exhibitions concentrate on contemporary urbanization. ♦ Free. Exhibitions: Tu-Su. Library: Tu-F 2-6PM. 21 Blvd Morland (between Rue Agrippa-d'Aubigné and Blvd Henri-IV). 01.42.76.33.97. Métro: Sully–Morland

Restaurants/Clubs: Red	Hotels: Blue
Shops/ 🍷 Outdoors: Green	Sights/Culture: Black

132 Canal St-Martin This industrial canal, dating from 1821, was dug to facilitate delivery of materials to the manufacturers in the Faubourg St-Antoine quarter. It flows under Boulevard Richard-Lenoir and the Place de la Bastille and comes out at the Bassin de la Villette (northeast of Place de Stalingrad in the 19th arrondissement). Boat tours are offered from April through November by **Paris Canal** (01.42.40.96.97) and **Canauxrama** (01.42.39.15.00). The unusual cruises pass along the tree-lined canal, through a mile and a half of tunnel and nine locks, and under two swinging bridges and eight footbridges. ◆ Métro: Bastille

133 Boulevard Richard-Lenoir One of the city's most pleasant outdoor markets is situated in the center island of this wide boulevard, between Place de la Bastille and Rue St-Sabin. Fine produce and poultry are sold—one stall features organically grown fruits and vegetables, and one offers roast chickens and ducks. In the fall there's a vendor who deals in wild mushrooms. Sunday is the market's big day, when you'll find merchants earnestly hawking everything from antique furniture, cookware, and Savon (soap) de Marseille to chrysanthemums, pig's feet, and Babar the elephant beach towels.
◆ Market: Th and Su mornings. Between Pl de la Bastille and Ave de la République. Métros: Bastille, Bréguet–Sabin

134 Berc Antoine Everything you need to start your own French cafe is here, from zinc bars, round marble tables, cane chairs, and coat racks to wire egg holders, oil and vinegar cruets, salt and pepper shakers, and those tacky hanging signs depicting *croque-monsieurs* (grilled ham and cheese sandwiches) and omelettes. The only emporium of its kind left in a neighborhood that once boasted over 25 similar suppliers, this shop has been here since 1892 and has been run by four generations; Mme. Berc Sacrispeyre, descended from founder Antoine Berc, is now in charge. Although the shop is meant for professionals, no order is too small.
◆ M-F; Sa morning; closed Saturdays during long weekends and August. 10-12 Blvd Richard-Lenoir (between Pl de la Bastille and Rue Daval). 01.43.55.13.56. Métro: Bastille

The Bic ball point pen, invented by Frenchman Marcel Bich in 1945, is a fine example of the old adage that the best is not necessarily the most expensive. Unless, of course, you go for *le Bic argent,* the same pen made of sterling silver. With a price tag comparable to that of a Mont Blanc or a Waterman, *le Bic argent* is available at Elysées Stylos Marboeuf (40 Rue Marbeuf, between Rue François-1er and Ave des Champs-Elysées, 01.42.25.40.49).

135 Le Sedaine Bastille Mme. and M. Rousseau's small corner bar peaks on Sundays between 10AM and 1PM when market workers escape their stalls for a quick *pastis* or rough Côte du Rhone. The floor is strewn with cigarette butts, sugar wrappers, and napkins.
◆ M-F, Su 6AM-8PM. 18 Blvd Richard-Lenoir (at Rue Sedaine). 01.47.00.90.40. Métros: Bastille, Bréguet–Sabin

136 Café Wah Wah This grungy little rock bar takes its name from the foot pedal used with an electric guitar. Mangy animal skins and a dusty sofa draped with faded French and American flags are mounted from the blood-red walls. A bartender with butchered, shoe-blackened hair serves dishes like *salade Wah Wah, mega croque Wah Wah,* and club sandwiches to heavy-metal wah-wah player wannabes. ◆ Daily 11AM-2AM. 11 Rue Daval (between Rue St-Sabin and Blvd Richard-Lenoir). 01.47.00.08.48. Métro: Bastille

137 Cour Damoye Behind a rusted iron gate lies this deserted street, whose owner rents it out as a movie-filming location. Notice that almost all the shops along this little *allée,* such as the one with the sign reading "Boulanger," are only the false storefronts used in the last filming. ◆ Off Rue Daval (between Rue de la Roquette and Blvd Richard-Lenoir). Métro: Bastille

137 Brûlerie Daval One whiff of the aroma of freshly roasted Moka and Arabica coffee wafting down Cour Damoye is enough to tell you that you've found something real amidst the stage sets. Mme Andrée d'Amico has been in the coffee and tea business for 50 years and just recently moved into this rough, raw space from the Rue de la Roquette. Her coffee blends are secret, but she will tell you all about the film crews that frequent the *cour,* and if you're lucky she may even give you her recommendation on local theater productions that merit seeing. Call ahead to find out when she'll be roasting her coffee so that you can experience the magnificent smell. ◆ Tu-Sa; Su morning. 12 Rue Daval (entrance in Cour Damoye). 01.48.05.29.46. Métro: Bastille

137 Relais du Massif Central ★★$ Softly smiling and amply built Mme. Caroline Coutinho makes sure that no one leaves her restaurant hungry. Auvergne-inspired specialties include frog's legs *Provençale,* grilled shrimp with Cognac-laced lobster sauce, *faux-filet* (beef sirloin) with roquefort cheese, *gratin de coquilles St-Jacques* (scallops au gratin), and sole meunière. Amidst the here-today-gone-tomorrow trendiness of the Bastille, this is the real thing—which is why neighborhood workers, residents, and tourists keep coming back. ◆ M-Sa lunch and dinner. 16 Rue Daval (between Rue de la Roquette and Blvd Richard-Lenoir). 01.47.00.46.55. Métro: Bastille

138 Rue de Lappe Once populated with natives of the Auvergne region of France and now the main artery of the trendy Bastille, this street was named in 1652 for Girard de Lappe, who owned the gardens and marshland through which the street was pierced. On 23 December 1830, Louis Philippe passed down the Rue de Lappe during a royal visit to the Faubourg, filling the residents with such enthusiasm that the following year they named the street after him. In 1848, after the February Revolution in which Louis Philippe was overthrown, the street reverted to its original name. ♦ Between Rues de Charonne and de la Roquette. Métros: Bastille, Ledru-Rollin

138 Chez Teil One of the few remaining Auvergnat establishments in the neighborhood, this shop sells products from the Auvergne region in central France. Take home a jar of *confit d'oie* (goose meat confit), some *saucisson sec* (dry sausages), a tasty nut cake, or a pair of *galoches* (the Auvergnat version of clogs). ♦ Tu-Sa. 6 Rue de Lappe (between Rues de Charonne and de la Roquette). 01.47.00.41.28. Métro: Bastille

138 66 Café ★$ The theme here is—you guessed it—Route 66 in the USA. The red vinyl seats, rough-hewn wood floor, and wagon wheel over the bar (which specializes in drinks such as whiskey sours, Long Island iced tea, and screwdrivers) all contribute to the all-American ambience. US-style grub includes fried chicken, T-bone steak, cheeseburgers, apple pie, and banana splits. The place is full of young Americans and Yankee-loving French. Happy Hour is from 6 to 8:30PM daily. ♦ M-F lunch and dinner (until 2AM); Sa-Su brunch and dinner. 8 Rue de Lappe (between Rues de Charonne and de la Roquette). 01.43.38.30.20. Métro: Bastille

"In Paris a building is never just a building. New public architecture gets served up as a gourmand's feast of allegory and national politics. I.M. Pei's pyramid at the Louvre is not just a new entrance to an old museum but a central eye for all of Paris, regenerating all that is old, redefining the entire city around its single glass point like a magic crystal in Superman's Fortress of Solitude."

Alastair Gordon, *Architecture View,* 1991

139 La Pirada ★$ A gigantic bull's head keeps watch while Spanish-food enthusiasts drink sangria and consume tapas and paella. ♦ Daily lunch and dinner (until 2AM). 7 Rue de Lappe (between Passage Louis-Philippe and Rue de la Roquette). 01.47.00.73.61. Métro: Bastille

139 Le Balajo Once upon a time this was a Belle Epoque dance hall and bar frequented by Maurice Chavalier and Edith Piaf. Today the dance club, announced by a giant neon sign, is full of wild people straight out of a Fellini flick dancing to Latin and swing music on the small, cramped dance floor, or relaxing on sticky red vinyl seats. A deejay spins disks on the balcony where an orchestra once played, and on the opposite wall is a zany model of a fictitious city. ♦ M-Sa 11PM-5AM; Sa-Su lunch. 9 Rue de Lappe (between Passage Louis-Philippe and Rue de la Roquette). 01.47.00.07.87. Métro: Bastille

139 Havanita Cafe ★★$ Buzzing with the warmth of the Caribbean, this Cuban restaurant has well-worn chairs, colorful wall and ceiling murals, and palms galore. Join the **Balajo** crowd which arrives late for dinner and feast on sautéed langoustines with fried bananas, Cuban chicken salad, and exotic fruits, accompanied by mojitos, piña coladas, coco locos, and other Cuban cocktails. ♦ Daily dinner (until 2AM). 11 Rue de Lappe (between Passage Louis-Philippe and Rue de la Roquette). 01.43.55.96.42. Métro: Bastille

140 Hôtel les Sans-Culottes $ If you're lucky enough to land one of the nine rooms in this charming old-fashioned inn, you're getting the best deal in the Bastille. Although small, the rooms are equipped with 20th-century comforts like showers and TV sets, and hotel guests get to have breakfast in the handsome 1900s-style **Bistrot les Sans-Culottes** downstairs (see below). ♦ 27 Rue de Lappe (between Rue de Charonne and Passage Louis-Philippe). 01.49.23.85.80; fax 01.48.05.08.56. Métro: Bastille

Within Hôtel les Sans-Culottes:

Bistrot les Sans-Culottes ★★★$$ Entrepreneurial young owner Lahlou created this fin de siècle–style restaurant two years ago, but a zinc bar, an elegantly curved stair, ornate ceiling details, and wall mirrors make it look as if it's been here for decades. The name *sans-culottes* (without knickers) was given to the French Revolutionaries, who wore the trousers of the working class rather than the knickers favored by the aristocracy, but the menu features both the traditional and the revolutionary: foie gras, grilled salmon with *pistou* (a creamy basil and garlic sauce) and saffron rice, veal kidneys with *pleurottes* (wild mushrooms), *crème brûlée pistaché,* and warm apple tart. The large outdoor terrace, the only one on the street, is the perfect vantage point from which to watch the wild parade along the Rue de Lappe. ◆ M breakfast for hotel guests only; Tu-Su breakfast, lunch, and dinner. 01.48.05.42.92

LILIANE & MICHEL DURAND-DESSERT

141 Galerie Liliane et Michel Durand-Dessert Located behind an art bookstore, this is one of the best-known galleries in Paris. Within its white lofty space is fine art in all mediums from noted artists including Joseph Beuys, Stanley Brouwn, Yan Pei-Ming, Yves Openheim, and Gerard Garouste. ◆ Tu-Sa. 28 Rue de Lappe (between Rues de Charonne and de la Roquette). 01.48.06.92.23. Métro: Bastille

141 Galerie Zone & Phase A popular gallery for its use in *matière* (raw material, textures, and colors), as well as work by contemporary artists who make objects in the *esprit africain*. ◆ Tu-Sa; Mondays by appointment. 30 Rue de Lappe (between Rues de Charonne and de la Roquette). 01.48.04.74.32. Métro: Bastille

141 Storage There's enough American memorabilia from the 1950s, 1960s, and 1970s to move even the most die-hard expatriate to nostalgia. An Arizona license plate, a Marilyn Monroe bust, a bright orange General Electric refrigerator, jukeboxes, gum ball machines, Coca Cola ice chests, and American flags are all for sale here. ◆ M-Sa. 34 Rue de Lappe (between Rues de la Roquette and de Charonne). 01.43.14.90.70. Métro: Bastille

142 La Galoche d'Aurillac ★★$$ Mme and M. Bonnet's *restaurant Auvergnat* is one of the last holdouts from the days when this neighborhood was heavily populated with craftsmen and others from the Auvergne region in central France. The eatery is named for the wooden or leather clogs traditionally worn by French workmen, and numerous examples of *galoches* are hung from the ceiling in neat rows. The menu features *salade du Cantal* (salad with cantal cheese), lentils *à l'Auvergnate* (cooked with bacon and goose

fat), *confit de canard* (duck confit) with apples, and sausage from Auvergne. The regional cheeses such as cabécous, cantal, and bleu d'Auvergne are a good excuse for another bottle of Côtes d'Auvergne or Marcillac. ◆ Tu-Sa lunch and dinner. 41 Rue de Lappe (between Rue de Charonne and Passage Louis-Philippe). 01.47.00.77.15. Métro: Bastille

142 Galerie Alain Gutharc This gallery specializes in exhibiting photographs, video, and sculpture with an emphasis on such young artists as Joël Bartoloméo, Valery Belin, and Claire Chevrier. ◆ Tu-F afternoon; Sa. 47 Rue de Lappe (between Rue de Charonne and Passage Louis-Philippe). 01.47.00.32.10. Métro: Bastille

143 Sukiyaki ★$ It's all here: standard Japanese decor, a sushi bar, and a menu featuring sashimi, sushi, sukiyaki, and Japanese barbecue that you grill at your own table. ◆ M-Sa lunch and dinner; Su dinner. 12 Rue de la Roquette (between Pl de la Bastille and Rue de Lappe). 01.49.23.04.98. Métro: Bastille

144 Slice ★★$ If you crave mozzarella and an aroma of Manhattan, you've come to the right place. Here you'll find the best New York–style pizza in Paris. There are also highly respectable chocolate chip cookies and brownies and a moist banana-chocolate cake. ◆ Daily lunch and dinner. Delivery: noon-2:30PM, 6:30-11PM anywhere in Paris. No credit cards accepted. 11 Rue de la Roquette (between Pl de la Bastille and Rue Daval). 01.43.57.66.67. Métro: Bastille

144 Café Iguana ★★$ This two-story Tex-Mex bar has a woody interior and ceiling fans and serves omelettes, chili, grilled meat, carpaccio, sandwiches, and salads. However, drinking is the main purpose of most who come here, and the cocktail list offers blue lagoons, silver bananas, white Russians, 11 types of vodka, 16 kinds of whiskey, and the darkest draft Guinness this side of Dublin. There's a tiny *non-fumeur* (nonsmoking) room upstairs. ◆ Daily 9AM-5AM. 15 Rue de la Roquette (at Rue Daval). 01.40.21.39.99. Métro: Bastille

145 Vue sur Toi Stylish men's and women's clothes to outfit the elegant Lycra crowd are featured at this small boutique. ◆ M-Sa. 41 Rue de la Roquette (between Rues du Commandant-Lamy and St-Sabin). 01.47.00.17.33. Métro: Bastille

COYOTE CAFÉ

145 Coyote Café ★$ This tiny restaurant offers the standard Mexican repertoire with a few Parisian twists, such as a quesadilla with smoked salmon. There's also a good selection of Mexican beers. ♦ Tu-Su lunch and dinner. 43 Rue de la Roquette (between Rues du Commandant-Lamy and St-Sabin). 01.47.00.70.85. Métro: Bastille. Also at: 27 Rue St-Jacques (between Blvd St-Germain and Rue Galande). 01.44.07.02.22. Métro: Maubert–Mutualité

145 Thaï Elephant ★★★$$ The Tikki Room meets Thailand in this veritable jungle of exotic flora, with a little wooden bridge, a waterfall, and young waiters in silk robes gliding among the tables serving chef Oth Sombath's sweet and spicy specialties. Try the *tom yam khung* (spicy shrimp soup with lemon), *colvert Siamois* (duck with raisins, pineapple, basil, and coconut milk), *massaman d'agneau* (a southern Muslim lamb dish in a sweet sauce), or the chicken soufflé served in banana leaves. Other restaurants under the same ownership in London, Bangkok, Brussels, and Copenhagen go by the name Blue Elephant. ♦ M-F, Su lunch and dinner; Sa dinner. Reservations recommended. 43-45 Rue de la Roquette (between Rues du Commandant-Lamy and St-Sabin). 01.47.00.42.00. Métro: Bastille

146 Notre-Dame d'Espérance A victim of the sometimes overzealous Bastille redevelopment, this 1928 church, which served the neighborhood's former working-class community, was razed in April 1995, despite the petitions and protests of local merchants and residents. The bell tower remains, but the facade, with its relief carvings of furniture makers by Gabriel Dufrasne, is lost. ♦ 51 *bis* Rue de la Roquette (at Rue du Commandant-Lamy). Métros: Bastille, Bréguet–Sabin

147 Cité de la Roquette Pop into this small dead-end passage for a look at the charming brick ateliers of woodworkers and violin makers. This is a favorite location spot for filmmakers. ♦ Off Rue de la Roquette (between Rue des Taillanders and Passage Thiéré). Métro: Bastille

148 Louis Philippe Fountain This stone fountain, decorated with delicately carved fruit, acanthus leaves, shells, and lions' heads was built in 1846 during the reign of Louis Philippe. The now-dry fountain is off-limits to the public, closed off by iron gates (which have been adopted by locals as a bike rack). Notice the ship, the symbol of Paris, carved in the center keystone. A similar fountain was erected on the Rue de Charenton but was demolished in 1906 for the opening of the Rue

de Prague. ♦ 70 Rue de la Roquette (between Rues Keller and des Taillandiers). Métros: Bastille, Bréguet–Sabin

149 Théâtre de la Bastille A red neon sign announces this theater, which, under the direction of the innovative Jean-Marie Hordé, features daring and inventive ventures in contemporary dance and theater. ♦ Box office: M-F 10AM-6PM by phone only; 30 minutes before performances. 76 Rue de la Roquette (between Rues Basfroi and Keller). 01.43.57.42.14. Métros: Bastille, Bréguet–Sabin

HOTEL DAVAL

150 Hôtel Daval $ Didier Gonad's friendly hotel is nothing fancy—the 23 rooms are small and simply decorated—but who could ask for more than a clean, quiet, cheap room in the heart of the lively Bastille quarter? A friendly German shepherd named Malka is in residence. There's no restaurant. ♦ 21 Rue Daval (between Rue St-Sabin and Blvd Richard-Lenoir). 01.47.00.51.23; fax 01.40.21.80.26. Métro: Bastille

151 Galerie Praz/Delavallade Small and intimate, this is one of the Bastille's most popular galleries, focusing on contemporary art in *toutes les formes*. Some of the internationally known artists whose work is shown here are Andrea Busto, Alain Balzac, and Maria Hahnenkemp. ♦ Tu-Sa afternoons. 10 Rue St-Sabin (between Rues de la Roquette and Sedaine). 01.43.38.52.60. Métros: Bastille, Bréguet–Sabin

152 Confiserie Rambaud Artisans Mme. Rambaud and her husband have been making delicious treats in their chocolate laboratory for more than 30 years. At Easter the shop is packed to the gills with the traditional chocolate fish, rabbits, and chickens stuffed with small candies, and with real eggshells filled with chocolate and praline. Available year-round are more than 40 kinds of chocolate bars, including praline, hazelnut, and orange fondant. Buy a bag of orangettes (strips of candied orange peel in chocolate) with no guilt about the calories—as Mme. Rambaud says, "You must have your magnesium." Taped to the counter is a magazine article hailing the benefits of chocolate as a physical stimulant, an antidepressant, a source of minerals, and a cure for broken hearts. ♦ Tu-Sa. 12 Rue St-Sabin (between Rues de la Roquette and Sedaine). 01.48.05.82.02. Métros: Bastille, Bréguet–Sabin

161

152 Café de l'Industrie ★★★$ Chili con carne, carpaccio, roast beef with potatoes, and other basic foods provide sustenance at this airy, informal cafe. This is the epitome of the Bastille, where the food is cheap and good, the patrons are your basic *intello-mode* types, and you may even find yourself being served by a waitress from New York who doesn't speak a word of French. The owner is self-confident enough to close down on Saturdays, the most popular day to dine out. ◆ M-F, Su lunch, dinner, and late-night meals (until 2AM). 16 Rue St-Sabin (at Rue Sedaine). 01.47.00.13.53. Métros: Bréguet–Sabin, Bastille

153 Papeterie Saint Sabin This family-run paper shop sells some classic French paper products such as Rhodia blocks, Canson Paper, and Oberthur agendas (which have been around more than 130 years longer than Filofax). There are also handmade sketchbooks and those wonderful Annonay notebooks and folders adorned with black blotches. ◆ Tu-Sa. 16-18 Rue St-Sabin (between Rues Sedaine and Bréguet). 01.47.00.78.63. Métros: Bastille, Bréguet–Sabin

154 Lire Entre les Vignes ★★★$ "Read Between the Vines" is the English translation of this wine bar's name, and it is overseen by Pablo Balduzzi, an Italian from Rochester, New York. Local clientele nosh on specialties such as the *assiette italienne* (a plate of Parma ham, mortadella, and mozzarella cheese) and apple crumble while sipping Saumur Rouge Château de Beauregard or Chablis Domaine des Marronniers. Relaxed and spacious, the bar has rough wood floors and is decorated with old bottles, scales, and crockery, calling to mind an old Vermont general store. ◆ M lunch, Tu-F lunch and dinner or evening snacks. 38 Rue Sedaine (between Rues Popincourt and du Commandant-Lamy). 01.43.55.69.49. Métros: Bréguet–Sabin, Bastille, Voltaire

155 Les Taillandiers ★★$ The locals don't mind waiting for a table at this popular French bistro serving hearty fare at a reasonable price. Choose from such popular favorites as *petit salé* (salted pork with lentils) and *blanquette de veau* (veal in béchamel sauce with mushrooms and rice). ◆ M-Sa lunch only. 22 Rue des Taillandiers (between Rues de Charonne and de la Roquette). 01.48.05.98.24. Métros: Bastille, Ledru-Rollin

155 Galerie Jorge Alyskewycz For the last several years this gallery's Argentinian-Ukrainian curator has dedicated his space to installations and sculptures, with the occasional painting or photography exhibit. The sculptures of Roland Cognet, Alejandro Martinez, and Léo Delarue, and the conceptual installations of Arnold Schalks have been featured here. ◆ Tu-Sa 2:30-7PM. 14 Rue des Taillandiers (between Rues de Charonne and de la Roquette). 01.48.06.59.23. Métros: Bastille, Ledru-Rollin

156 Galerie Jousse Seguin: Espace Gran Dia Behind this red-and-yellow–painted brick facade is a collection of original-edition architects' and designers' furniture, with a particular emphasis on pieces from the 1950s. There are many works by Jean Prouvé, Alexandre Noll, and Charlotte Perriand. ◆ M-Sa; if closed ask at main gallery (34 Rue de Charonne, 01.47.00.32.35). 5 Rue des Taillandiers (between Rue de Charonne and Passage des Taillandiers). 01.47.00.32.35. Métros: Bastille, Ledru-Rollin

157 Galerie Akié Aricchi Not limited by any particular style, Akié Aricchi shows the work of international painters and sculptors, both abstract and figurative. She is spontaneous and eclectic in her selection—if she likes the spirit of the artist's work, she shows it. Some of the artists she has taken to are Hyung-Dae, Akiko Toriumi, Michel Dalhaye, de Chevallier, and Alan Simon. ◆ Tu-Sa 3-7PM. 26 Rue Keller (between Rues de Charonne and de la Roquette). 01.40.21.64.57. Métros: Bastille, Ledru-Rollin

158 Get Crazy Designer Eric Beaune employs everything from fringe, studs, and patches to sheepskin, quilting, and lace in his leather and suede clothing line. Beaune's designs are manufactured in his Paris workshops, and many of the pieces are one-of-a-kind creations. He also sells belts, buckles, and collars made of turquoise and bone. ◆ M-Sa until 8PM ; occasionally open Sundays, depending on the owner's mood. 23 Rue Keller (between Rues de Charonne and de la Roquette). 01.48.06.35.99. Métros: Bastille, Ledru-Rollin

158 Café Moderne ★★$$ In his 1930s-style brasserie, Omar Guerda offers such dishes as couscous with lamb brochette and *tajines* (North African stews), and *entrecôte grillé* served with fries. There is a changing *plat du jour*, as well as an inexpensive lunch menu. ◆ M-Sa lunch and dinner. 19 Rue Keller (between Rues de Charonne and de la Roquette). 01.47.00.53.62. Métros: Bastille, Ledru-Rollin

158 Galerie Oz Jean Luc Richard coined the phrase *baroque contemporain* to describe the sensual, undulating, joyous art that he likes to show in his gallery. Precious objects and brilliant, glittery things of all mediums, including computer-generated art, are typically exhibited here. ◆ Tu-Sa afternoon. 15 Rue Keller (between Rues de Charonne and de la Roquette). 01.47.00.66.23. Métros: Bastille, Ledru-Rollin

159 La Laverie Four young French and Chinese photographers created this association to promote the exchange of creative ideas between French and Chinese artists. Their photography gallery, with adjoining professional lab, often features the work of Asian artists from other countries. The association also sponsors exhibitions of works of French photographers in Hong Kong, Taiwan, and China. ◆ M-Sa. 9 Rue Keller (between Rues de Charonne and de la Roquette). 01.47.00.11.38, 01.42.74.26.60. Métro: Ledru-Rollin

160 Centre Gai et Lesbien At the city's only gay and lesbian information center, interested folk can find information on the gay scene in Paris, including the inside scoop on restaurants, bars, and clubs. There is plenty of informational literature, a small gallery, a library of books and magazines (including *3 Keller,* the center's monthly magazine), and a small cafe in the corner. Numerous lesbian and gay groups hold meetings here. The friendly staff is happy to answer your questions either in person or by phone. Free *préservatifs* (condoms) are there for the taking. ◆ M-Sa 2-8PM; Su 2-7PM. 3 Rue Keller (between Rues de Charonne and de la Roquette). 01.43.57.21.47. Métro: Ledru-Rollin

160 BPM Progressive music is sold at this techno house, one of the many in the Bastille neighborhood. ◆ M-Sa. 1 Rue Keller (at Rue de Charonne). 01.40.21.02.88. Métro: Ledru-Rollin

160 Pause Café ★★$ On a warm, sunny Paris day pause for a break on the terrace of this corner cafe with a bottle of crisp white Montlouis Domaine Levasseur and a plate of assorted cheeses. Or try the duck with orange, a roast beef sandwich, or warm goat cheese on *pain Poilâne.* If the weather isn't obliging, take a seat at the horseshoe-shaped bar inside. ◆ Tu-Sa lunch and dinner (until midnight); Su lunch. 41 Rue de Charonne (at Rue Keller). 01.48.06.80.33. Métro: Ledru-Rollin

LE BISTROT DU PEINTRE

161 Le Bistrot du Peintre ★★$ This corner cafe is an architectural jewel. It opened in 1907 as a bistro/billiard hall and retains the original Eiffel-era girders, carved wood panels, and peeling gold-leaf lettering. Have a *pastis* or some Berthillon ice cream on the terrace and luxuriate in the faded fin de siècle elegance. Simple fare—omelettes, sandwiches, and the like—is also served. ◆ Daily breakfast, lunch, and dinner (7AM-2AM; Sunday until 10PM). 116 Avenue Ledru-Rollin (at Rue de Charonne). 01.47.00.34.39. Métro: Ledru-Rollin

162 Dream On Furnishings and accessories from the 1950s through the 1970s are featured here, which means lots of plastic furniture, chunky watches, and the official Army-issue lighters given out to US soldiers who served in the Vietnam War. Also featured is the work of contemporary French designer Christian Boitel, who makes furniture and lamps out of aluminum heating pipes. ◆ Tu-Sa afternoons. 31 Rue de Charonne (at Rue des Taillandiers). 01.47.00.41.44. Métro: Ledru-Rollin

163 Galerie Jousse Seguin Since 1989, owners Patrick Jousse and Philippe Seguin have been showing a broad range of works by contemporary international artists. At opposite ends of the spectrum are Karin Kneffe's precise, realist watercolors of fruits and Thomas Grünfeld's disturbing installations of taxidermy misfits, featuring such fantastical creatures as a combination sheep/Saint Bernard, and a fox/pheasant/swan. Also Serge Comte, Stephen Hepworth, and Peter Hopkins. ◆ M-Sa. 34 Rue de Charonne (between Ave Ledru-Rollin and Rue du Faubourg-St-Antoine). 01.47.00.32.35. Métro: Ledru-Rollin

164 Rough Trade Rough types listen to blasting jungle and techno music and consult with owners Stephan and Jerome on which CDs to buy. This chain also has shops in London and Tokyo. ◆ M-Sa afternoons. 30 Rue de Charonne (between Ave Ledru-Rollin and Rue du Faubourg-St-Antoine). 01.40.21.61.62. Métro: Ledru-Rollin

164 La Chaiserie du Faubourg Hundreds of chairs waiting to be repaired or retrieved by their owners are stacked *pêle-mêle* (that's French for higgledy-piggledy) from floor to ceiling, leaving only a small

passage for Gérard Decourbe to squeeze through to his desk. It's a wonder Decourbe is able to find the particular chair he is looking for, but he has a special cataloguing system that makes even the Louvre's look simple. If he's not too busy you may be able to talk him into a tour of the atelier in the **Passage de l'Homme** where chairs are repaired and manufactured. There you'll meet paint-spattered craftsman Gérard Brousset, who jokes with pride that he can make old chairs look new and new chairs that look old. ♦ M-Sa. 26 Rue de Charonne (between Ave Ledru-Rollin and Rue du Faubourg-St-Antoine). 01.43.57.67.51. Métro: Ledru-Rollin

164 Passage l'Homme Take a detour into this pleasant ivy-covered passage and peek through the windows of **Ateliers d'Art** (01.47.00.81.22), where artisans keep alive the traditional craft of binding books with leather and gold leaf. ♦ 26 Rue de Charonne (between Ave Ledru-Rollin and Rue du Faubourg-St-Antoine). Métro: Ledru-Rollin

165 Galerie Lavignes-Bastille In his big, light-filled space, Jean-Pierre Lavignes displays the work of both new and more established artists, whose styles range from the figurative to the abstract. Some notables are artists Jean-Claude Meynard, Martin Dubilé, and Yoo Sun Tai. ♦ M-F afternoons; Sa. 27 Rue de Charonne (between Rue des Taillandiers and Passage Thiéré). 01.47.00.88.18. Métro: Ledru-Rollin

165 Charonne Café ★★$ East meets West at this cozy cafe owned by an Egyptian husband-and-wife team. Popular light-meal choices—such as Oriental cakes with mint tea, charcuterie, or a spicy homemade rice dish—will no doubt satisfy. ♦ M-Sa; Su brunch. 25 Rue de Charonne (at Passage Thiéré). 01.43.57.69.33. Métro: Ledru-Rollin

Les Portes

166 Les Portes ★$ Behind the rustic facade with its namesake doors, this restaurant's harried owner serves lunches of ricotta and tomato tarts; chicken, potato, and tarragon salad; salmon ravioli with peas and creamy fennel sauce; and *plats du jour* such as gingered salmon. At night the dining room becomes a well-populated bar. ♦ M-Sa lunch; bar daily 5PM-2AM. 15 Rue de Charonne (at Rue de Lappe). 01.40.21.70.61. Métros: Bastille, Ledru-Rollin

167 L'Entre-Pots This dark, cavernous bar suggests Paris in the 1940s. Hip French students sip fruit juice and expensive American cocktails and lip-sync to booming Otis Redding and Madonna tunes. ♦ Daily lunch and evenings until 2AM. 14 Rue de Charonne (between Ave Ledru-Rollin and Rue du Faubourg-St-Antoine). 01.48.06.57.04. Métro: Ledru-Rollin

168 Chez Paul ★★★$$ Although the customers look rather trendy, this eatery is unpretentious and old-fashioned, serving authentic bistro fare such as lamb with rosemary, and rabbit stuffed with goat cheese and mint. ♦ M-Sa lunch and dinner. Reservations recommended. 13 Rue de Charonne (at Rue de Lappe). 01.47.00.34.57. Métro: Ledru-Rollin

168 Axis This boutique's humorous collection of kooky objects includes an escargot plate with snail-shaped ceramic cups, Philippe Starck's daddy longlegs juice squeezer, leg-shaped nutcrackers, an assortment of offbeat watches, and a collection of cartoon character Géteon paraphernalia. ♦ M-Sa. Closed two weeks in August. 13 Rue de Charonne (at Rue de Lappe). 01.48.06.79.10. Métro: Ledru-Rollin

169 L'Herbe Verte Behind the beautiful carved wood facade, once the entrance to a *pâtisserie,* young florist Marc Henri casually displays his colorful sunflowers, tulips, daisies, and roses in zinc buckets. Henri, who spent four years working with renowned florist Christian Tortu, designs arrangements for John Galliano. He works with the rhythms of the seasons, creating his splendid arrangements out of the fruits and flowers of the moment; in spring that might mean daisies and tulips, in winter, anemones and berries. He makes an exception for sunflowers, however, which he gets year-round from his native Auvers-sur-Oise, the village where Vincent van Gogh breathed his last and is buried with his brother, Theo. ♦ M-Sa. 5 Rue de Charonne (between Rues du Faubourg-St-Antoine and de Lappe). 01.48.06.50.69. Métro: Ledru-Rollin

169 Bar La Fontaine This busy spot at the junction of Rues de Charonne and du Faubourg-St-Antoine has been a watering hole for more than 100 years. Its location makes for great people watching, so take a sidewalk table, order a carafe of red wine, and observe the world as it strolls by. The bar is named after the 16th-century **Fontaine Trogneux** around the corner on the Rue du Faubourg-St-

Antoine, where two bronze lion heads spout water rather unceremoniously from their mouths into the drains below. ♦ Daily. 1 Rue de Charonne (at Rue du Faubourg-St-Antoine). 01.47.00.58.36. Métro: Ledru-Rollin

170 Casbah Three bouncers at the door decide who will get into this nightclub, where everything from jeans to tuxedos is acceptable as long as you have "the look." Those who pass muster can soak in an atmosphere created by rich colors, dim lighting, and incense, but don't even think of arriving before midnight. ♦ Bar: daily 9PM-dawn. Disco: W-Sa 11PM-dawn. 18-20 Rue de la Forge-Royale (between Rues du Faubourg-St-Antoine and Charles-Delescluze). 01.43.71.71.89. Métros: Ledru-Rollin, Faidherbe–Chaligny

171 Place d'Aligre Market This outdoor market, one of the most famous and cheapest in Paris, has an exotic North African flavor. It is always lively and crowded, with shops, stalls, and a covered market offering fabric, white rum, oriental spices, green bananas, and secondhand goods. ♦ Tu-Su mornings. Rue d'Aligre (at Pl d'Aligre). Métros: Ledru-Rollin, Faidherbe–Chaligny

172 Rue du Faubourg-St-Antoine The main artery of the old working class Faubourg St-Antoine quarter, this street is latticed with courtyards and passages that have enticing names like Etoile d'Or, Le Bel-Air, and St-Esprit. Here you can still find carpenters' and cabinetmakers' workshops adjacent to furniture stores, fashion houses, and funky bars and restaurants. The intersection of Rue du Faubourg-St-Antoine and Avenue Ledru-Rollin was, until 1914, a crossroads where an outdoor furniture market was located; now it is home to discount chain stores like **Monoprix** (the French version of K mart), and **ED l'Epicier**, a no-frills grocery store. ♦ Between Pls de la Nation and Bastille. Métros: Bastille, Ledru-Rollin, Faidherbe–Chaligny, Nation

172 Rémy Here reproductions of antique furniture, chandeliers, curtains, rugs, and anything else you might need to furnish a somewhat stuffy apartment are sold by a somewhat stuffy staff of designer counselors. This is one of three **Rémy** stores in the neighborhood. ♦ M-Sa. 75 Rue du Faubourg-St-Antoine (between Ave Ledru-Rollin and Rue de Charonne). 01.43.43.65.58. Métro:

Ledru-Rollin. Also at: 82 Rue du Faubourg-St-Antoine (at Rue St-Nicolas). 01.43.43.80.72. Métro: Ledru-Rollin

173 80 Rue du Faubourg-St-Antoine In a niche above the door of a bourgeois furniture store (see above) is a statue of St. Nicholas dating from 1895. Its presence recalls the 17th-century orphanage, founded by *prêtre* Antoine Barberé, that once stood on the Rue St-Nicolas. With his outstretched hands, the saint seems to be pontificating, largely unnoticed, to the steady stream of traffic below. ♦ At Rue St-Nicolas. Métro: Ledru-Rollin

174 Cour de l'Etoile d'Or This courtyard, part of which is inhabited by the workshops of the **Rémy** furniture shop down the street, is worth a detour. Just inside the entrance is a trompe l'oeil window display with abundant draperies, mirrors, chairs, vases, and decorative objects. Straight ahead you encounter another trompe l'oeil painting, this one of a woman standing at her ivy-covered balcony; through open doors you can glimpse the interior of her apartment. The delightful chirping birds that frequent the courtyard are real, as is the barely legible 1751 sundial on a plaster wall. ♦ 75 Rue du Faubourg-St-Antoine (between Ave Ledru-Rollin and Rue de Charonne). Métros: Bastille, Ledru-Rollin

175 Passage du Chantier A sign at the entrance invites you to visit the artisans and fabricants whose ateliers and showrooms line this passage. Don't miss **A. Fey et Fils,** where craftsmen inlay leather and gold leaf into desktops (notice the fantastic array of tools hanging from the wall). Look into the workshops of **Atelier Paul,** where reproductions of Louis XVI furniture are created. ♦ 66 Rue du Faubourg-St-Antoine (between Rue St-Nicolas and Pl de la Bastille). 01.46.28.44.83. Métros: Bastille, Ledru-Rollin

One of Paris's newest and most unusual monuments honors 19th-century scientist and politician François Arago. Designed by Dutch artist Jan Dibbets, the monument consists of 135 bronze circles—each bearing only the word "Arago" and an "N" and "S" for the compass points—implanted in city streets and courtyards. The plaques follow the imaginary line between the Earth's poles, known as the meridian of Paris, which Arago had helped trace out before his election to the Academy of Sciences at the age of 23. An ambitious pedestrian can follow the new "monument" from its northernmost point at 18 Avenue de la Porte-de-Montmartre, through the Palais Royal, the Louvre, the Luxembourg Gardens, the Observatory, across Boulevard Arago, and finally to the southernmost point at the Cambodian Pavilion.

176 Librairie L'Arbre à Lettres This bookstore's great collection, strong on art and philosophy, makes you want to improve your French in order to read all the volumes. The shop is beautifully designed by Thierry Claude with

well-organized stacks and great lighting. ◆ M 1-8PM; Tu-Sa 10AM-8PM; Su 2:30-7PM. 62 Rue du Faubourg-St-Antoine (between Passage du Chantier and Pl de la Bastille). 01.43.45.49.04. Métros: Bastille, Ledru-Rollin

177 Sanz-Sans ★★$ This Bastille bar is named after its young owners, Messrs. Sanz and Sans. The exterior is rough and raw, with exposed brick and steel beams, and the interior features a framed video screen running a continuous closed-circuit film of the bar. The eclectic menu offers such dishes as salmon steaks and steak tandoori, and pear tart for dessert. ◆ Daily breakfast, lunch, and dinner (until 2AM). 49 Rue du Faubourg-St-Antoine (between Rue de Charonne and Pl de la Bastille). 01.44.75.78.78. Métros: Bastille, Ledru-Rollin

177 Didier Lavilla Take home a new turquoise-green suede handbag with matching gloves and hat, a pink suede wallet, or maybe a pair of sunglasses with round yellow lenses. ◆ Tu-Su. 47 Rue du Faubourg-St-Antoine (between Rue de Charonne and Pl de la Bastille). 01.53.33.85.55. Métros: Bastille, Ledru-Rollin. Also at: 15 Rue du Cherche-Midi (between Rue d'Assas and Carrefour de la Croix-Rouge). 01.45.48.35.90. Métro: St-Sulpice; 38 Rue de Sévigné (between Rues des Francs-Bourgeois and du Parc-Royal). 01.42.74.76.60. Métros: Chemin Vert, St-Paul

178 La Distillerie ★★$$ The poem posted outside this creole restaurant promises to transport diners to the exotic world of the Antilles. Inside, the pink tablecloths, white ironwork chairs, and rum cocktails with names like *touloulou,* punch Soufrière, and *la vie en rose* will make you feel as if you've stepped into a Jean Rhys novel. Owner Elisabeth de Rozières offers Caribbean-inspired dishes such as red snapper and shellfish terrine with langoustine sauce, spicy fish soup, mutton with Antillean curry sauce, shark with lime sauce, and exotic ice creams such as mango, banana, white rum, pineapple, and coconut. ◆ M-Th dinner (until 2AM), F until 5AM. 50 Rue du Faubourg-St-Antoine (between Passage du Chantier and Pl de la Bastille). 01.40.01.99.00. Métros: Bastille, Ledru-Rollin

Jean Paul GAULTIER

179 Jean Paul Gaultier The man who outfitted Madonna in ice-cream-cone bras has set up shop in the Faubourg, lending an aura of avant-garde establishment to the neighborhood's often trendy fashion design industry. The handsome black-and-white-striped building was derelict and full of squatters when Gaultier moved in. Now the interior has been revamped and features exposed steel beams, a galactic blue ceiling, mosaic floors embedded with video monitors showing the latest fashion shows, and model-thin salesgirls peddling ready-to-wear for men and women, including the designer's trademark striped T-shirts. ◆ M-Sa. 30 Rue du Faubourg-St-Antoine (between Passage du Chantier and Pl de la Bastille). 01.44.68.85.00. Métro: Bastille. Also at: 6 Rue Vivienne (between Rue des Petits-Champs and Pl de la Bourse). 01.42.86.05.05. Métro: Bourse

180 Atelier 33 This discreet 17th-century building was an inn before the French Revolution, and today is one of the few remaining buildings on the street that witnessed the bloody events of 1789. It is notable for its architectural details, including its mansard roofs, balcony, windows, ironwork, and the wood staircase visible through the double doors in the courtyard. Young fashion designer Henry Leparque has renovated this historic building—now the home of his boutique and ateliers—with respect and elegance, leaving the old stone walls as a backdrop for his simple, classic men's and women's clothing.

The young *créateur* helped change the Faubourg from a street of furniture-making workshops to one of fashion houses, yet his fashions are anything but trendy. Leparque uses fine wools and cashmeres for his jackets and coats, which he sells to such established New York department stores as Saks Fifth Avenue and Bloomingdale's. Part of Leparque's success hinges on his interchangeable collections; because his ateliers are upstairs he is able to bring the mix-and-match concept to a new height. Clients can choose their own buttons, ask for another lining in a jacket, or order a pair of gloves and a hat to go with a coat, ending up with a customized ensemble that will be ready in a week. Friendly and excitable, Laparque can easily be persuaded to give you a tour of his upstairs ateliers, where his fashions are made alongside gloves, jewelry, and lovely hats by Akemi. Note the chairs in the dressing rooms, which once graced the winter garden of the Côte d'Azur estate of the Gould family, the dynasty responsible for the first railway line in the US. ♦ Daily. 33 Rue du Faubourg-St-Antoine (between Rue de Charonne and Pl de la Bastille). 01.43.40.61.63. Métro: Bastille

Perrette

180 Perrette Handmade clothes for *les petits,* some with lovely hand-embroidered details, are displayed on racks while women quietly continue stitching more garments. If you don't see exactly what you want for that special little girl or boy, keep in mind that they will do made-to-measure outfits. ♦ Tu-Sa. 29 Rue du Faubourg-St-Antoine (between Rue de Charonne and Pl de la Bastille). 53.17.13.56. Métro: Bastille

181 Les Colonies du Paradis ★$ This schizophrenic restaurant can't decide what it wants to be so it offers a bit of everything. Shrimp and spinach tandoori, coconut daiquiris, mango margaritas, carrot cake, mint tea, chocolate orange mousse, and dishes with such curious names as the Viking Specialty and the Inca Sandwich are served on glass-topped tables displaying compartments of dried pumpkin seeds, rose buds, black-eyed peas, and banana chips. ♦ M-Sa lunch and dinner; Su brunch and dinner. 3 Rue du Faubourg St-Antoine (between Rue de Charonne and Pl de la Bastille). 01.43.44.01.00. Métro: Bastille

181 Galerie Franck & Herve Bordas This gallery has put out its own editions of works on paper since 1978, when the curators established an adjacent atelier where artists can create prints on the premises. Internationally known artists such as Gilles Aillaud, Jean-Paul Chambas, Jan Voss, and Robert Wilson have all exhibited in the light and airy spaces, which are perfect for viewing the original prints, artists' books, and lithographed travel cards. ♦ M-Sa afternoons; closed August. 2 Rue de la Roquette (in the Cour Février off the Passage du Cheval-Blanc). 01.47.00.31.61. Métro: Bastille

RESTAURANT

Le Train Bleu
★★★★

182 Le Train Bleu ★★★$$$ Suspended in time between here and there, this glorious Old World dining room in the monumental **Gare de Lyon** is a train station restaurant in the grand tradition. Named for the luxurious Belle Epoque express train that once took the elite down to the Riviera, it is a traveler's dream, striking wanderlust into the hearts of even the most sedentary. The restaurant, classified as a historic monument, is characterized by vaulted ceilings; extraordinarily intricate gold leaf moldings, friezes, and carvings; and ceiling frescoes by different artists depicting destinations from the **Gare de Lyon**. Images of Mont Blanc, Marseille, Monaco, Evian, Nice, Montpellier, and Algeria are enough to give even those who come here for a meal (and aren't waiting for a train) the travel bug. The restaurant's guest book is signed by the likes of François Mitterrand, Jacques Chirac, and Serge Gainsbourg, and such notables as Sarah Bernhardt, Edmond Rostand, and Salvador Dalí have nourished themselves here.

Upscale brasserie cuisine is prepared by chef Michel Combyres. Appetizers include hot Lyonnaise sausage, duck terrine with pistachios, and caviar from Petrossian; some of the classic main courses are chateaubriand with béarnaise sauce, lamb chops with *herbes de Provence,* and beef fillet flambéed with brandy. The 1990 St-Emilion, Chapelle de la Trinité, or the 1990 Louis Jadot Clos Vougeot would be fine choices from the restaurant's wine list, but Champagne might be more appropriate in this sumptuous space. ♦ Daily lunch and dinner. Reservations recommended. Gare de Lyon, 20 Blvd Diderot (at Cour Diderot). 01.43.43.09.06. Métro: Gare de Lyon

Bests

Sandra and Jay Lampros
Sculptor and Architect

Place des Vosges—especially in the spring when the trees sprout their tiny green leaves and children gather to play.

Au Petit Fer à Cheval—our local cafe and rendezvous point.

The walls lined with every variety of tea imaginable at **Mariage Frères.**

An *andouillette frites* at **Ma Bourgogne** on the **Place des Vosges.**

The garden of the **Hôtel de Sully.**

Michelangelo's *Slaves* in the southwest wing of the **Louvre.**

Louvre and The Champs-Elysées

Rue St-Ferdinand
Rue Brunel
Rue d'Arnaille
Rue des Acacias
Ave. Carnot
Rue Mac-Mahon
Ave. de Montenotte
Rue de Brey
Rue Troyon
Ave. des Ternes
Ave. de Wagram
Rue de Courcelles
Parc de Monceau
Rue du Faubourg St-Honoré
Rue de Moncea
Blvd. Haussma

←105

111
110
109
108

Ave. de la Grande-Armée

Ave. Hoche   Rue Beaujon
Rue Balzac
Rue de Moncea
Blvd. Haussma

104

Pl. Charles-de-Gaulle
106

Ave. de Friedland
Ave. Arsène-Houssaye
Rue de Châteaubriand
Rue Lord-Byron
Rue Lamennais
Rue d'Artois

96
97
98

107

102
101
100

Ave. Foch

Rue de Presbourg

Rue Washington

99

Ave. Victor-Hugo
Rue Lauriston
Rue Paul-Valéry
Rue Copernic
Rue de Belloy
Rue Galilée
Rue La Pérouse

103

Ave. d'Iéna
Ave. Marceau

Ave. des Champs-Elysées

92
93
91
90

95 94

Rue de Berri
Rue de Ponthieu
Rue La Boétie

87 88
63
64

Rue Euler
Rue Magellan
Rue Euler

84
85

Rue C.-Colomb

86

Rue Lincoln

Rue Quentin-Bauchart

83

Rue Pierre-Charron
Rue François-1er
Rue Marbeuf
Rue de Marignan

Rue Boissière
Ave. Kléber
Rue Hamelin

Rue de Bassano

Rue de Chaillot
Rue G.-Bizet

81
82

78
79
80

Rue Ch.-Marot

Rue du Boccador
77

65 66
69 67
68

Rue de Lübeck

Ave. Pierre-1er-de-Serbie

Rue de la Trémoille

71
76
72 70

Ave. Montaigne

55

73 Rue Jean-Goujon

Rue de Longchamp
Ave. du Prés.-Wilson
Ave. d'Iéna

Ave. du Prés.-Wilson

75

Cours Albert-1er

Rue Bayard

Ave. du Albert-de-Mun

Rue de la Manutention

74
Pont de l'Alma

Seine

Palais de Chaillot

Passerelle Debilly

Quai d'Orsay

Ave. des Nations-Unies
Ave. de New-York

Rue de l'Université

Jardins du Trocadero

Pont d'Iéna

Ave. Bosquet

Rue Jean-Nicot

Ave. des Nations-Unies
Ave. du Prés.-Kennedy

Ave. de La Bourdonnais

Rue St-Dominique

Ave. Rapp

Quai Branly

■ Tour Eiffel

Ave. Gustave-Eiffel
Ave. Elisées-Reclus

Ave. Bouvard

Rue de Grenelle

Rue E.-Psichari

N
↑

km   1/8   1/4
mi 1/16   1/8

Ave. de Suffren
Ave. Charles-Floquet

Park du Champ-de-Mars

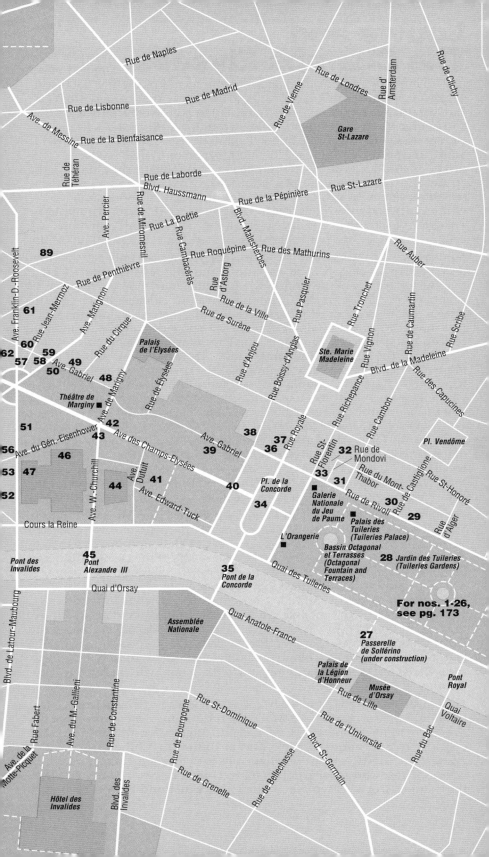

Louvre and The Champs-Elysées

This superlative stroll includes the largest museum in the Western world (the Louvre), the world's most famous boulevard (the Champs-Elysées), the most ancient monument in Paris (the 3,300-year-old Egyptian **Obelisk of Luxor**), the best 360-degree view of Paris (from **La Samaritaine**'s rooftop cafe), the city's grandest hotels (the **Meurice, Crillon,** and **George V**), its oldest métro station **(Franklin-D.-Roosevelt)**, its most elegant tea salon **(Angélina)**, its best English paperback bookshop **(W.H. Smith and Son)**, one of the world's most magnificent squares **(Place de la Concorde)**, the largest concert hall in Paris **(Théâtre du Châtelet)**, the "hautest" of haute couture (the boutiques along **Avenue Montaigne**), the sexiest cabaret in Paris **(Crazy Horse Saloon)**, the city's best restaurant **(Taillevent)**, and the world's biggest triumphal arch **(L'Arc de Triomphe)**. That's a lot to absorb in one day, so get an early start, put on your most comfortable shoes, and *bon courage*—that's French for "keep a stiff upper lip."

Monday may be the best day to visit this area, for it's the only day the **Hôtel de Ville** (City Hall) is open and the lines at the **Louvre Museum** slack off (on the first Sunday of the month, when admission to the **Louvre** is free, it's a mob scene). Monday is also discount night at the cinemas on the Champs-Elysées. Begin your tour with the **Hôtel de Ville**, then walk along the Seine past the pet and plant shops on **Quai de la Mégisserie** and stop for morning coffee and a spectacular panorama atop **La Samaritaine** department store. Next comes the **Louvre Museum**. Ask someone to hold your place in the museum's ticket line so you can run across the street to peek at the Louis XIV royal pew in the artists' church of **St-Germain-l'Auxerrois**. Then prepare yourself for a two- to three-hour whirlwind tour of the history of Western art that includes those three remarkable Mediterranean ladies: *Venus de Milo,* the *Winged Victory of Samothrace,* and the *Mona Lisa.* After the **Louvre** take a break at the nearby **Jardin des Tuileries** (Tuileries Gardens), then either splurge for lunch at Gaston Lenôtre's **Elysée Lenôtre** or join the fashion models with fierce sweet cravings who order the *Mont Blanc* dessert at **Angélina**. En route to the Place de la Concorde, you might stop at **W.H. Smith and Son** for the latest *New Yorker* or an English-language novel to read on the plane home.

From the base of the **Obelisk of Luxor**, it is a mile to the **Arc de Triomphe**. If you need motivation to keep walking, consider the delights that lie ahead: the Vermeer and Rembrandt paintings at the **Petit Palais**, and chef Deligne's hot oysters with truffles at **Taillevent**. The eastern half of the Champs-Elysées is bordered by gardens (designed by André Le Nôtre, a gardener for Louis XIV, who also landscaped **Versailles)** that have not changed since novelist Marcel Proust played there as a child. On the right, you pass behind three fine structures: the **British Embassy**, the **Japanese Embassy**, and the **Palais de l'Elysée**. At **Rond-Point des Champs-Elysées**, a roundabout at the east end of the Champs-Elysées, shoppers should veer left to Avenue Montaigne, the high-fashion row, while art buffs and philatelists will want to go directly to the galleries on **Avenue Matignon** and to the stamp stalls on **Avenue Gabriel**.

The last stretch of the Champs-Elysées, which leads up to Napoléon's triumphal arch, is meant to be strolled in the evening, when Paris more than lives up to its nickname, the "City of Light." High rollers will want a cocktail on the terrace at **Fouquet's**, and dinner at **Taillevent, Chiberta,** or, perhaps, upstairs at **Lasserre**, where the ceiling rolls back for stargazing between courses. Those who are on a tighter budget might catch a first-run movie at the **Gaumont,** or a Beckett play at the **Théâtre du Rond-Point**, and then enjoy a late-night raclette (melted cheese on bread) at **La Boutique à Sandwiches.** When the day's strolling is over, you may feel as if you've completed the Tour de France, the world's greatest bicycle race, which ends each July on the Champs-Elysées—also the finishing line for your one-day "Tour de Paris."

1 Place de l'Hôtel-de-Ville The present seat of the Paris city government, this square is where Etienne Marcel, one of the first mayors of Paris, established his city council in 1357. Marcel incited a mob to rise against the monarchy and storm the royal palace on Ile de la Cité. The next year he was killed—not by the king but by his fellow Parisians. Centered in the granite on the square is the image of a boat, the city symbol, adopted from the 13th-century coat of arms of the Boatmen's Guild.
♦ Between Quai de Gesvres and Rue de Rivoli. Métro: Hôtel de Ville

2 Hôtel de Ville (City Hall) Another example of late 19th-century architectural eclecticism, this building (pictured below) is part Renaissance palace, part Belle Epoque fantasy. Its exterior is embellished with 146 statues, among them bronze effigies of the sentries who patrolled the perimeter of the city wall during the Middle Ages. Visitors on guided tours of the state rooms are shown the splendid staircase by Philibert Delorme, murals by Puvis de Chavannes, and a lesser-known Rodin sculpture, *La République.*
♦ Tours: M 10:30AM, departing from the information desk at 29 Rue de Rivoli; call the previous Friday to confirm time. Pl de l'Hôtel-de-Ville (between Quai de Gesvres and Rue de Rivoli). 01.42.76.50.49. Métro: Hôtel de Ville

Le Trumilou
RESTAURANT

3 Le Trumilou ★$ The perfect way to enjoy this authentic Parisian bistro is at a window table overlooking the Seine and **Notre-Dame.** Jean-Claude Dumond and his family prepare home-cooked food at sensible prices. Favorites include *canard aux pruneaux* (duck with prunes), lamb with white beans, *sole meunière* (fried in butter), and the ever-popular *poulet Provençale* (chicken in tomato sauce with *herbes de Provence*). For dessert, try the *oeufs à la neige* (meringue floating in crème anglaise). ♦ Daily lunch and dinner. Reservations recommended. 84 Quai de l'Hôtel-de-Ville (between Rues du Pont-Louis-Philippe and de Brosse). 01.42.77.63.98. Métro: Hôtel de Ville

4 Miravile ★★★$$$ The word is out: Gilles Epié, the highly regarded young chef, is expected to achieve *grand chef* status by the end of the decade. His elegant restaurant is appropriately named after the word for "marvelous" in Old French. The chic dining room, with marble floors and frescoes on the

Hôtel de Ville

MICHAEL STORRINGS

171

walls, calls to mind a Florentine villa. Windows overlook the Seine, and when the *bateaux mouches* pass by they light up the entire restaurant. Epié's imaginative approach to French cuisine incorporates Italian and *Provençale* elements. Among his celebrated creations are *beignets de foie gras caramélisés au Porto* (foie gras fritters caramelized in Port), prawns marinated in balsamic vinegar with a *tapenade tomatée,* lobster grilled with *jus gras de jambon* served with white beans, and garlic-roasted lamb served with foie gras. For dessert the *chaud chocolat mousse,* a warm, chewy chocolate mousse cake served with coconut sorbet is as divine as it sounds. ♦ M-F lunch and dinner; Sa dinner. Reservations recommended. 72 Quai de l'Hôtel-de-Ville (between Rues du Pont-Louis-Philippe and de Brosse). 01.42.74.72.22. Métro: Hôtel de Ville

A L'OLIVIER

5 A l'Olivier Founded in 1860, this shop still sells every oil imaginable, including hazelnut oil for vinaigrettes, almond-honey oil shampoo, and apricot-nut oil for massages. Tarragon mustard and dried figs are also available. The classic bottles would be worth buying empty, and the giant pottery casks for olive oil are not to be missed. ♦ Tu-Sa. 23 Rue de Rivoli (at Rue du Pont-Louis-Philippe). 01.48.04.86.59. Métro: Hôtel de Ville

6 Bazar de l'Hôtel-de-Ville BHV is every Parisian's hardware store, its five floors replete with the wherewithal to do it yourself. This is a paradise for Monsieur Fix-It. ♦ M-Sa; W until 10PM. 52-64 Rue de Rivoli (between Rues des Archives and du Temple). 01.42.74.90.00. Métro: Hôtel de Ville

7 Avenue Victoria One of the shortest avenues in Paris doesn't commemorate any military victory, but rather the royal visit of the dowager Queen of England to Paris. ♦ Between Quai de Gesvres and Rue des Lavandières-Ste-Opportune. Métro: Hôtel de Ville

8 Tour St-Jacques (St. Jacques Tower) This 1522 architectural anomaly is the Gothic belfry of **St-Jacques La Boucherie,** a church that was destroyed in 1802; the tower was spared to become a factory for manufacturing lead musket balls. The tower now doubles as a weather station, appropriately enough, for at the tower's base is a statue of Blaise Pascal (1623-62), one of

France's first weather forecasters. In 1648, at the top of this very tower, he used a barometer to calculate the weight of air. Cast your eyes up and you will see meteorological equipment lurking among the gargoyles. The tower is closed to the public. ♦ Sq St-Jacques (at Rue de Rivoli). Métro: Châtelet

9 Place du Châtelet Named after a fortress and prison that once stood on this site, Châtelet is the principal crossroads of Paris, a hub of east-west and north-south traffic. The **Châtelet Fountain** in the center of the square, flanked by sphinxes, was designed in 1808 to celebrate the triumphant Egyptian campaign of Napoléon. Below the square, five métro lines intersect, making **Châtelet–Les Halles** the world's largest underground station. ♦ Between Quai de Gesvres and Ave Victoria. Métros: Châtelet, Châtelet–Les Halles (RER)

10 Théâtre de la Ville de Paris Formerly the **Sarah Bernhardt Theatre,** this mid-19th-century stage is now devoted to contemporary dance, jazz, and classical theater, but still preserves the dressing room of the "Divine Sarah." ♦ Box office: daily. 2 Pl du Châtelet (at Quai de Gesvres). 01.42.74.22.77. Métros: Châtelet, Châtelet–Les Halles (RER)

11 Pont au Change "Money-Changers' Bridge" was the ninth-century forerunner of an American Express office: a spot where travelers came to change foreign currency for French funds. Today this Second-Empire bridge is flanked by identical state-owned theaters, both built by architect **Gabriel-Jean-Antoine Davioud** in 1862. ♦ Between Quai de la Corse and Quai de Gesvres. Métro: Châtelet

12 Quai de la Mégisserie Once a malodorous *mégisserie* (sheepskin tannery), today this spot is rife with booksellers, pet shops, fish-tackle dealers, and plant stores where mice and goldfish are sold alongside dahlias and fertilizer. The cacophony of the parakeets, turkeys, and guinea fowls whose cages clutter the pavement vies pleasantly with that of the automobile traffic nearby. If you don't fancy house pets or have a green thumb, stroll here for the splendid views of **La Conciergerie,** the towers of **Notre-Dame,** and the spire of **Sainte-Chapelle.** ♦ Between Pl du Châtelet and Rue du Pont-Neuf. Métro: Châtelet

13 Théâtre du Châtelet Built in 1862, this is the fourth-largest auditorium in Paris (after the **Opéra Bastille, Opéra Garnier,** and the **Palais des Congrès**) and the city's largest concert hall. Seating half as many people as the **Opéra Garnier,** the theater is primarily a venue for symphonies, operas, and ballets. On 21 May 1910, the New York Metropolitan Opera Company made its Paris debut here with *Aida.* Toscanini conducted, Caruso sang, and the audience, which included most of the French diplomatic corps, the Vanderbilts, and Louis Cartier (who estimated that more than

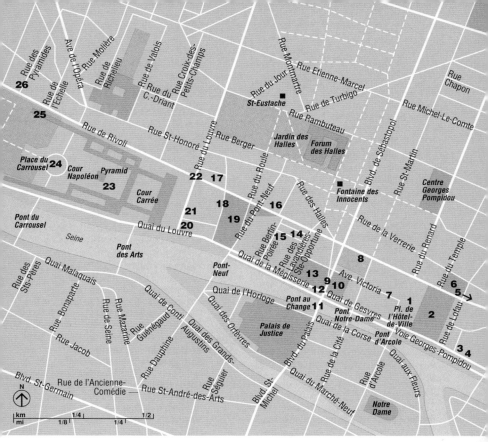

$3 million worth of jewelry was worn that evening), went wild. ◆ Box office: daily. Theater: closed in August. 1 Pl du Châtelet (at Quai de la Mégisserie). 01.40.28.28.28. Métro: Châtelet

14 Le Petit Opportun This popular jazz club headlines such names as Clark Terry, Slide Hampton, and Pepper Adams. Don't expect the cigarette haze that usually hangs around jazz nightclubs: Smoking is not permitted during performances. ◆ Cover. Shows: Tu-Sa 8:30PM and 11PM; buy tickets at least a half-hour in advance. No credit cards accepted. 15 Rue des Lavandières-Ste-Opportune (between Rues Jean-Lantier and des Deux-Boules). 01.42.36.01.36. Métro: Châtelet

𝔊𝔯𝔞𝔫𝔡 𝔥𝔬𝔱𝔢𝔩 𝔡𝔢 𝔄𝔥𝔞𝔪𝔭𝔞𝔤𝔫𝔢

15 Grand Hôtel de Champagne $$$ Small, comfortable rooms (of which there are 42) characterize this hotel, which is a short walk from the Place du Châtelet, the **Louvre, Sainte Chapelle, Notre-Dame,** and the Ile de la Cité. There's no restaurant. ◆ 17 Rue Jean-Lantier (at Rue des Orfèvres). 01.42.36.60.00; fax 01.45.08.43.33. Métro: Châtelet

16 Slow Club Dixieland jazz is alive and well at this former ballroom, now the oldest jazz club in the city. Enjoy Dixieland and swing (and, occasionally, big band and rhythm 'n' blues) in a refreshingly unpretentious, old-fashioned atmosphere. ◆ Cover. Tu-Sa 10PM-3AM. No credit cards accepted. 130 Rue de Rivoli (between Rues des Bourdonnais and du Pont-Neuf). 01.42.33.84.30. Métros: Châtelet, Pont-Neuf

17 Chez la Vieille ★★★$$$ When *mère* Adrienne Baisin retired in 1994 at 73 years of age, young chef Miriam Jenard took over, but the meals still seem to come from the kitchen of a French country grandmother: pork liver pâté or sautéed chicken livers to start, followed by sautéed lamb, chicken fricassee, or peasant pot-au-feu, and, for dessert, a traditional chocolate mousse or chocolate cake. The welcoming owner Marie-José Cervoni presides over the tiny dining room. ◆ M-W, F-Su lunch; Th lunch and dinner; closed in August. Reservations recommended for lunch, required for dinner. 1 Rue Bailleul (at Rue de l'Arbre-Sec). 01.42.60.15.78. Métros: Louvre-Rivoli, Pont-Neuf

18 Rue de l'Arbre-Sec This short street is long and rich in history. D'Artagnan of the Three Musketeers lived at **No. 4** (formerly the **Hôtel des Mousquetaires,** now **La**

Samaritaine department store); at **No. 52** is the **Hôtel de Trudon,** the former home of Louis XV's wine steward; nearby is the **Hôtel de François Barnon,** named after Louis XIV's barber. The name *arbre-sec* (which literally means dry tree) suggests that a gibbet once stood in the street. ♦ Between Pl de l'Ecole and Rue St-Honoré. Métro: Pont-Neuf

19 La Samaritaine One of the city's oldest department stores and possibly its most confusing, this emporium is named for an old Pont-Neuf water pump decorated with an image of the woman of Samaria offering Jesus a drink of water. Today the store sprawls through four grand old buildings offering everything from pop psychiatry books to kitchen sinks, all at bargain prices. Its best deal, however, is the rooftop panorama. On a pleasant summer day, walk into **Magasin II** (Store No. 2), designed by **F. Jourdan,** and ride the elevator to the ninth floor. Sip a *café crème* or *citron pressé* (lemonade) at the cafe, then mount the stairs and enjoy a 360-degree view of Paris. A ceramic legend locates points of interest. ♦ M-W, F-Sa; Th until 10PM. 19 Rue de la Monnaie (between Pl de l'Ecole and Rue de Rivoli). 01.40.41.20.20. Métro: Pont-Neuf

Within La Samaritaine:

Toupary ★$$ Suspended between the sky and the Seine, this apricot, turquoise, and electric blue restaurant designed by **Hilton McConnico** serves such specialties as cream of tomato soup with cardamom, *daurade* (sea bream) in fennel, and lime crepes. Try to get a window table for a panoramic view of Paris. ♦ M-Sa lunch, tea, cocktails, and dinner until 1AM. Magasin II, Fifth floor. 01.40.41.29.29

Pâtisserie St-Germain-l'Auxerrois

20 Pâtisserie St-Germain-l'Auxerrois ★★$$ Embellished with crystal chandeliers, gilded pillars, and marble tables, this elegant 100-year-old pastry shop and tea salon makes all its sweets and ice cream in a basement factory. Be sure to buy a few treats to munch on while you wait in the **Louvre** ticket line. Try the chocolate pastries (*la mousseline* and *le cador*). ♦ Tu-Su; closed two weeks in August and two weeks in September. No credit cards accepted. 2 Rue de l'Amiral-de-Coligny (at Quai du Louvre). 01.45.08.19.18. Métros: Louvre–Rivoli, Pont-Neuf

21 Place du Louvre In 52 BC, Labienus, a lieutenant of Caesar, bivouacked with his troops between the present sites of the **Louvre** and **St-Germain-l'Auxerrois** before capturing the settlement of Lutetia. ♦ Between Rues des Prêtres-St-Germain-l'Auxerrois and Perrault. Métros: Louvre–Rivoli, Pont-Neuf

21 St-Germain-l'Auxerrois On St. Bartholomew's Day (24 August) in 1572, at the orders of Catherine de Médicis and Charles IX, the pealing bells of this church (illustrated below) signaled the beginning of a brutal religious massacre. Some 3,000 Huguenots, Protestant wedding guests of Henri de Navarre and Marguerite de Valois, were slain in their beds. The 38-bell carillon in the Neo-Gothic tower still rings every Wednesday afternoon, a grave reminder of the mass murder. The carillon is the only truly ancient one in Paris; all the others were melted down during the Revolution.

St-Germain-l'Auxerrois

MICHAEL STORRINGS

Musée du Louvre

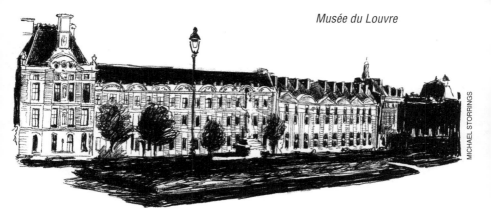

MICHAEL STORRINGS

This gargoyle-laden edifice, designed in 1220 by **Jean Gaussel**, is named for St. Germain, the bishop of Auxerre (378-448), whose students included St. Patrick of Ireland, and St. Geneviève of Paris. When Louis XIV and his court moved to **Versailles**, the artists' colony he had established there took over the **Louvre**, and **St-Germain-l'Auxerrois** became its parish church.

Among the luminaries buried here are architects **Louis Le Vau, Jacques-Ange Gabriel**, and **Jacques-Germain Soufflot;** the sculptor Antoine Coysevox; and painters Nöel Coypel, François Boucher, and Jean-Baptiste Chardin. Every Ash Wednesday a service is held to pray for artists throughout the world who will die in the coming year. Royalists flock here annually to a Mass said for Louis XVI on the anniversary of his 21 January 1793 execution. Notice the ornately canopied and sculpted oak bench on the right side of the aisle; this red-velvet pew was designed in 1682 by painter Charles Le Brun for Louis XIV and his family. ◆ Daily; call for a schedule of Masses in English and organ and bell recitals. 2 Pl du Louvre (at Rue des Prêtres-St-Germain-l'Auxerrois). 01.42.60.13.96. Métros: Louvre–Rivoli, Pont-Neuf

22 **Louvre–Rivoli Métro Station** The platform is a museum in itself, with softly illuminated copies of the sculptures found above it in the **Louvre**. This and the *Varenne* métro station (with replicas of Rodin sculptures) are two of the prettiest in Paris.
◆ Rues de l'Amiral-de-Coligny and de Rivoli

22 **Rue de Rivoli** On this arcaded street, an incongruous mix of luxury hotels and tacky souvenir shops lies demurely behind a graceful but rather monotonous First Empire colonnade designed by **Charles Percier** and **Pierre Fontaine** in 1811 at the behest of Napoléon. The street was named after the Italian town where the emperor thrashed the Austrians in 1797. Strict rules pertaining to the arcades forbade leasing shops to any

entrepreneur using ovens or metal tools, thus excluding such riffraff as bakers and butchers. ◆ Between Rues St-Florentin and de Sévigné. Métro: Louvre–Rivoli

23 **Musée du Louvre** The **Louvre** is the single largest building in Paris, the largest palace in Europe, the largest museum in the Western world, and probably the most dominating symbol of art and culture the world has ever known. "I never knew what a palace was until I had a glimpse of the **Louvre**," said 19th-century American author Nathaniel Hawthorne. It has 224 halls, and its enormous **Grande Galerie** is longer than three football fields. It took seven centuries to build, spanning the lives of 17 monarchs and countless architects.

The origin of the word *louvre,* though obscure, is believed to be either a derivation of the Old French word *louverie,* which meant wolf lodge; a corruption of the word *l'oeuvre,* meaning a work of art; or a variation of an Old Flemish word meaning fortress. In 1190 King Philippe Auguste began surrounding Paris with a 30-foot-high city wall that included the fortified structure known as the **Louvre**. More than three centuries later, François I agreed to live in this fortress at the request of Parisian citizens who had ransomed him from captivity in Italy. In 1527 he tore down most of the old building, and by 1546 he had constructed the **Cour Carrée** (Square Courtyard).

In 1578 Catherine de Médicis built a new palace, the **Tuileries,** at the far end of the present **Louvre**. The two palaces were joined by Henri IV, who created a number of apartments in the long gallery for the use of court painters and their families in 1608. This same Henri was stabbed by an assassin here in 1610 (he was the only king to die within the **Louvre**'s walls). In the late 1660s, Colbert, a minister of finance to Louis XIV, hired the acclaimed Roman architect **Giovanni Bernini** to redesign the **Louvre**. But when Bernini suggested knocking the whole place down and starting from scratch, Colbert sent him

175

packing. Louis XIV proceeded to reconstruct the **Cour Carrée** to his own tastes, consulting the architect **Louis Le Vau,** the painter Charles Le Brun, and Claude Perrault, a Parisian physician whose brother Charles was the author of *Puss in Boots.* After renovating the

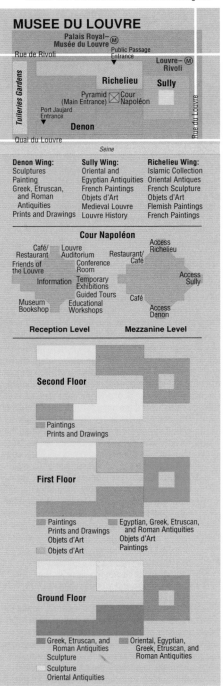

MUSEE DU LOUVRE

Palais Royal–
Musée du Louvre Ⓜ
Public Passage Entrance
Rue de Rivoli
Louvre– Ⓜ
Rivoli

Tuileries Gardens

Richelieu
Sully

Pyramid ☒ Cour
(Main Entrance) ☒ Napoléon
Port Jaujard Entrance

Rue du Louvre

Denon
Quai du Louvre

Seine

Denon Wing:	Sully Wing:	Richelieu Wing:
Sculptures	Oriental and	Islamic Collection
Painting	Egyptian Antiquities	Oriental Antiques
Greek, Etruscan,	French Paintings	French Paintings
and Roman	Objets d'Art	Objets d'Art
Antiquities	Medieval Louvre	Flemish Paintings
Prints and Drawings	Louvre History	French Paintings

Cour Napoléon

Café/ Louvre Access
Restaurant Auditorium Restaurant/ Richelieu
Friends of Conference Café
the Louvre Room
Access
Information Temporary Sully
Exhibitions
Guided Tours Café
Museum Educational
Bookshop Workshops Access
Denon

Reception Level **Mezzanine Level**

Second Floor

■ Paintings
Prints and Drawings

First Floor

■ Paintings ■ Egyptian, Greek, Etruscan,
Prints and Drawings and Roman Antiquities
Objets d'Art ■ Objets d'Art
■ Objets d'Art Paintings

Ground Floor

■ Greek, Etruscan, and ■ Oriental, Egyptian,
Roman Antiquities Greek, Etruscan, and
Sculpture Roman Antiquities
■ Sculpture
Oriental Antiquities

palace, Louis XIV established an artists' colony here; residents included painters such as Coustou, Boucher, and Coypel. Louis XIV left Paris for **Versailles** in 1678, and without royal occupants, the **Louvre** fell into disrepair. Overrun by freeloaders and squatters, it soon became a slum, and a shantytown of bars and brothels sprang up outside its walls.

After being dissuaded from tearing the structure down, Louis XVI magnanimously put some of the royal art collection on display in the **Louvre** shortly before he and Marie Antoinette were beheaded in 1793. Following his rise to power, Napoléon moved into the **Tuileries Palace** and built Rue de Rivoli for quick access to the **Louvre.** Napoléon also built the **Arc du Carrousel,** an arch celebrating some of his military victories (see page 178). During the Second Empire, Napoléon's nephew Napoléon III and Baron Georges-Eugene Haussmann, the radical urban planner, completed the **Louvre** (or so they thought) by building the **North Wing** and the **Flore** and **Marsan Pavilions.** The **Louvre**'s art collection began with 12 paintings—including works by Titian, Raphael, and Leonardo da Vinci—that François I looted in Italy. (He not only took the *Mona Lisa* but also the man who had painted it, inviting Leonardo to his chateau at Amboise, where the artist remained until his death.) By the time of Louis XIV (who reigned from 1643 to 1715), the royal collection numbered more than 2,500 items. Until the Revolution, works in the **Louvre** were strictly for the pleasure of the kings and their courtiers. In 1793, after nearly burning the palace to the ground, the Revolutionaries opened the collection to the masses. Today the museum possesses more than 400,000 works of art, only a fraction of which are on display at any given time. In a morning's hoofing, however, you can see many of the **Louvre**'s greatest hits: the *Venus de Milo,* the *Winged Victory of Samothrace,* the *Mona Lisa,* the **Crown Jewels,** the **David Galleries,** the *Eagle of Sugerius,* the *Law Code of Hammurabi,* the **Rubens Gallery,** Michelangelo's *Slaves,* the *Seated Scribe,* and other highlights of art history.

The collection is divided into seven categories (see floor plan at left): Greek and Roman antiquities, Oriental antiquities, Egyptian antiquities, sculptures, objets d'art, paintings, and drawings. Although the Greek and Roman, Egyptian, and Oriental antiquities warrant at the very least a quick look, the museum's richest collection consists of paintings.

A few words of advice for touring the **Louvre:**
1. Don't even think about trying to see the museum's entire collection—or even half of it—in one day. Visit your favorite artworks the first time around, and come back for more another day. 2. In the summer or other high-

season months count on a half-hour wait to buy tickets. 3. Wear comfortable shoes. Check your coat as you enter, but in winter keep a sweater handy (the museum is drafty). 4. Guided tours in English leave every 20 minutes from the ground-floor information stand. 5. When fatigue sets in, take a break in the museum cafeteria. (If you lunch outside and then decide to re-enter, you'll have to buy a new ticket.) 6. Certain exhibitions (for example, the **Crown Jewels**) close during the lunch hour (noon-2PM) and when there is a shortage of museum guards. ◆ Admission; free first Sunday of the month. Museum: M-W 9AM-9:45PM; Th-Su 9AM-6:30PM. Bookstores and postcard shops: M, W-Su. Entrance by the Pyramid in the Cour Napoléon (off Place du Carrousel); bounded by Rue de l'Amiral-de-Coligny and Ave du General-Lemonnier, and Quai du Louvre and Rue de Rivoli. 01.40.20.51.51. Métros: Louvre–Rivoli, Palais Royal–Musée du Louvre

Within the Musée du Louvre:

Cour Napoléon (Napoléon Courtyard)
Under King Philippe Auguste, this was a patch of sparsely populated farmland. Over time, it sprouted a church, a charity school, a meat market, a menagerie for wild animals, the castle kitchens, and a street for prostitutes frequented by soldiers from the castle garrison. Napoléon III leveled the houses and paved over the courtyard in the late 19th century.

Louvre Pyramid Adding to the **Louvre** museum building seems to be an irresistible French pastime. The latest additions, officially opened in April 1989, were based on the designs of Chinese-American architect **I.M. Pei.** Now topping the **Cour Napoléon**

(Napoléon Courtyard) is a 70.5-foot-tall glass pyramid, flanked by three smaller pyramids, a series of fountains, reflecting pools, and a bronze replica of the Bernini statue of Louis XI. The largest pyramid (see illustration below) serves as the central entrance to the museum and as an enormous skylight above a 70,000-square-foot underground cavern.

The pyramid and its underground space contain an auditorium, an area for temporary art shows, and the remains of the 12th-century fortress that was unearthed prior to the pyramid's controversial construction, as well as ticket offices, conference rooms, laboratories, and museum shops. Tunnels lead from under the pyramid to each side of the U-shaped **Louvre.** Traditionalists fear this latest addition has marred the Louvre's grandeur with a sort of Hyatt Regency glitz. Michel Guy, cultural minister under former French President Giscard d'Estaing, has said that **Pei**'s pyramids turn the **Louvre** into a "cultural drugstore that looks like an airport." However, the design has garnered fans, and, lest we forget, the **Eiffel Tower** was also first greeted with guffaws.

Excavations At the same time President François Mitterrand approved the **Pei** pyramid project, he also set aside close to $2 million for an immense archaeological excavation of the **Louvre**'s courtyard. This ambitious project brought 70 archaeologists to supervise the dig in the **Cour Napoléon,** where the ancient dungeons of the King Philippe Auguste fortress were exposed. More than 11 million objects were retrieved, ranging from Chinese porcelain imported during the Ming Dynasty to coins from the first century AD and an eighth-century human skeleton. Visitors may

Louvre Pyramid

MICHAEL STORRINGS

descend from the pyramid to the 12th-century dungeons and view about 10,000 of the objects uncovered in the dig.

Cour Carrée (Square Courtyard)

This elegant courtyard was built, in part, during the reign of François I, with additions commissioned by Louis XIII and Louis XIV. It becomes a chic circus during the fall and spring, when more than 50 fashion designers parade their ready-to-wear collections through striped tents set up here. Check at the information stand in the courtyard for a schedule of events.

Richelieu Wing Named after the famed 17th-century French cardinal and statesman, this structure was once occupied by France's **Ministry of Finance.** In November 1993 it opened as a new wing of the **Louvre;** it connects to the rest of the complex and allows the museum to display 25 percent more of its art collection.

Le Café Marly

Le Café Marly ★$$ Restaurateurs Jean-Louis and Gilbert Costes's popular cafe in the **Richelieu Wing** of the **Louvre** serves such dishes as salmon tartare, Caesar salad, cheeseburgers, veal liver, lemon tart, and brownies. The interior, with its Venetian red walls, gold leaf, and velvet upholstered armchairs, calls to mind an Italian disco, and the food can be disappointing, but the location can't be beat, especially if you can land a table on the covered gallery overlooking the **Cour Napoléon** and **I.M. Pei**'s glass pyramid. Expect a long wait for a table at lunchtime. ♦ Daily breakfast, lunch, tea, and dinner. 93 Rue de Rivoli (enter from the Cour Napoléon). 01.49.26.06.60

Le Grand Louvre ★★★$$ Run by André Daguin, the chef and proprietor of the Hôtel de France in Auch, this is an exceptional restaurant by any standard. Located under the **Louvre Pyramid,** it features a subdued wood-and-metal decor and such Gascon specialties as foie gras, goose, confit de canard (duck confit) with mushrooms, and prune ice cream. ♦ M, W-Su lunch and dinner. 01.40.20.53.41

Carrousel du Louvre This underground shopping mall is skylit by a 150-ton inverted glass pyramid and features over 35 boutiques and businesses proffering everything from Lalique crystal to miniature Eiffel Tower souvenirs and

château rentals to one-hour film developing. **Restagora,** a 700-seat international food hall, offers fast food of nearly every description—Mexican, Lebanese, Asian, vegetarian, and, of course, French. During the shopping center's construction, architects **I.M. Pei** and **Michel Macary** uncovered a 14th-century moat built by Charles V, which has been incorporated into the design and named the **Fossé Charles V.** ♦ Daily. Main entrance at 99 Rue de Rivoli; also accessible from the Louvre Museum foyer. 01.43.16.47.47.

24 Place du Carrousel Part of the **Louvre** complex, this square was named to commemorate a *carrousel* (equestrian gala) held by King Louis XIV and his court in June 1662 to honor the birth of the king's first child. More than 15,000 spectators watched the king lead a thundering brigade of horsemen dressed as Romans, sporting golden helmets with red plumes, gold breastplates, and red stockings. ♦ Between the Quai du Louvre and Rue de Rivoli. Métro: Palais Royal–Musée du Louvre

On Place du Carrousel:

L'Arc du Carrousel This marble arch with pink pillars (see illustration below) was built in 1808 by Napoléon to celebrate Austerlitz and other military victories. It was then crowned with the famous bronze horses of San Marco, plundered from Venice during one of Napoléon's military campaigns (originally, the horses stood in the Temple of the Sun at Corinth). With the fall of Napoléon in 1815, Italy recovered the horses and copies were placed here. The arch can be used like a gun sight to line up the **Tuileries Fountains,** the Egyptian **Obelisk of Luxor** in the Place de la Concorde (a half-mile to the west), the Champs-Elysées, and the **Arc de Triomphe,** more than two miles away.

L'Arc du Carrousel

MICHAEL STORRINGS

25 Musée des Arts Décoratifs (Museum of Decorative Arts) and Musée de la Publicité (Poster and Advertising Museum) With furnishings that date from the period of Louis XVI through the 19th century, the museum, located in the **Louvre** complex, is something of a composite mansion, with rooms taken wholesale from different periods. Amid too much wallpaper and too many bowlegged chairs from **Versailles,** the patient and searching eye will discover singular treasures such as a Tiepolo painting, exquisitely carved floral *boiserie* (woodwork) by Oudry, and hunting scenes by Desportes.

In the same building is the newly renovated **Musée de la Publicité,** which has in its collection more than 40,000 posters from the 18th century to the present. Beautiful temporary exhibitions are mounted here. ◆ Admission. W-Sa 12:30-6PM. 107 Rue de Rivoli (at Ave du Général-Lemonnier). 01.44.55.57.50. Métro: Palais Royal–Musée du Louvre

25 Musée National des Arts de la Mode (Costume and Fashion Museum) Located in the **Louvre**'s **Pavillon de Marsan,** this newly renovated museum pays homage to the capital of fashion. The 20,000 exhibits and 35,000 accessories are presented by theme and change every six months. There is also a library containing engravings, drawings, journals, photographs, and catalogues. The museum's sleek and chic collection consists of costumes dating back to the 16th century. Among the highlights of the collection are the 17th-century gloves worn by Anne of Austria, Brigitte Bardot's wedding dress (made by Jacques Esterel in 1958), a robe designed for Sarah Bernhardt, and the gown worn by the Empress Eugénie to please Napoléon III when he returned from a hard day of empire-building. The view of the **Tuileries Gardens** from the top floor is spectacular. ◆ Admission. Tu, Th-F 11AM-6PM; W 11AM-10PM; Sa-Su 10AM-6PM. 107 Rue de Rivoli (at Ave du Général-Lemonnier). 01.44.55.59.24. Métro: Palais Royal–Musée du Louvre

26 Statue de Jeanne d'Arc This gilded equestrian statue by 19th-century sculptor Frémiet honors Joan of Arc (1412-31), the French national hero and Roman Catholic saint. Born during the Hundred Years' War (1337-1453), this charismatic peasant girl claimed she heard the voices of saints urging her to save France from the English. She was able to convince the Dauphin Charles VII to provide her with troops that, under her generalship, took back Orléans and routed the English forces in the Loire. In 1429, during an unsuccessful attempt to liberate Paris from the occupying English army, Joan stationed a cannon on Butte St-Roch (leveled some three centuries ago as landfill for the Champ-de-Mars) to attack the St-Honoré Gate (which is now 163 Rue St-Honoré). A year later Joan of Arc was captured by Burgundians and turned over to the English, and the following year she was convicted of witchcraft and heresy by a tribunal of French clerics who supported the English, then burned at the stake in Rouen. She was canonized in 1920, and today France honors her with a national holiday. ◆ Pl des Pyramides (between Rues de Rivoli and des Pyramides). Métro: Tuileries

27 Passerelle de Solférino Still under construction at press time, the city's newest bridge will provide pedestrian passage between the **Jardins des Tuileries** and the **Musée d'Orsay.** Constructed of a special type of steel used in naval architecture, the wood-planked *passerelle* (footbridge), designed by engineer **Marc Mimram,** will be the first to span the Seine with only one arch. The bridge will offer pedestrians direct access from either the upper or lower quays. ◆ Between Quais Anatole-France and des Tuileries. Métro: Tuileries, Musée d'Orsay

28 Jardin des Tuileries (Tuileries Gardens) The gardens were designed in 1649 for Louis XIV by André Le Nôtre, the king's gardener, who was born in a cottage on the royal grounds. Le Nôtre also designed the gardens at **Versailles, Chantilly,** and the **Château Vaux-le-Vicomte.** It's hard to believe that this lovely and serene spot was the site of such violence during the Revolution (the **Tuileries,** then the home of the royal family, was attacked by an angry mob in 1792). Stroll through the manicured hedges and lawns near the 18 bronze nudes by Aristide Maillol. You'll see old women feeding the pigeons, African immigrants lofting mechanical birds into the air in hope of attracting a sale, and kids racing sailboats on the fountain under the watchful eyes of their governesses. You will also find four refreshment stands, a small merry-go-round, a swing set, and subdued pony rides for children.

By purchasing one of the quarterly journals sold on Paris street corners and métros by the homeless (known here as "SDF," for *sans domicile fixe*), you help them earn a living. The three most prominent such publications are *Le Réverbère, Macadam,* and *Le Lampadaire,* containing articles on political and social issues, all written by the homeless.

From the upper terrace of the gardens is a splendid view of the Seine, the **Musée d'Orsay,** and the **Palais de la Légion d'Honneur,** which was begun by Napoléon to laud French accomplishment. Farther in the distance, you can glimpse the stern **Chambre des Députés,** France's congress. The terrace has become known as a gathering spot for gay men. ♦ Bounded by Ave du Général-Lemonnier and Place de la Concorde, and Quai des Tuileries and Rue de Rivoli. Métro: Tuileries, Concorde

Within the Jardin des Tuileries:

Galerie Nationale du Jeu de Paume

Built in 1853 by Napoléon III, this museum has nothing to do with *jus de pomme* (apple juice). Its name refers to the building's original function as an indoor court where royalty played the racket sport that was the precursor of tennis (see "From Kings to Commoners—Tennis Has Come a Long Way" on page 251). In 1907, a group of painters called Impressionists commandeered the building and used it as a gallery. From 1947 until 1986, the **Louvre**'s collection of French Impressionist masterpieces was housed here, making this the most visited museum in the world relative to its size. The Impressionist collection was moved across the river to St-Germain's **Musée d'Orsay,** and since 1991 the renovated galleries here have hosted changing exhibitions by contemporary artists. On the terrace to the south of the museum is a monument to Charles Perrault, the 17th-century fabulist who convinced Colbert to make the **Tuileries** public. ♦ Call ahead for opening times. Hours vary. Northwest corner (at Pl de la Concorde). 01.42.60.69.69

Palais des Tuileries (Tuileries Palace)

Designed in 1564 by **Philibert Delorme,** this palace stood until 1884. It connected the two corner pavilions of the **Louvre** (paralleling what is today Avenue du Général-Lemonnier) and took its name from the *tuile* (tile) factories that had previously stood on the site. Catherine de Médicis, for whom the palace was built, moved out after her astrologer, Ruggieri, told her she would die close to St-Germain. Since **Tuileries** was in the parish of **St-Germain-l'Auxerrois,** Catherine built another palace near what is today the **Bourse du Commerce** (Commercial Stock Exchange), and there she died. As for Ruggieri's prediction: The priest who administered the last rites to Catherine de Médicis was named Julien de St-Germain.

Napoléon's second wife gave birth in the palace to a short-lived imperial heir, l'Aiglon, who was named the king of Rome. Subsequent royal residents included Charles X and Louis Philippe, who ruled from 1831 to 1848 and was popularly known as the "Grocers' King" for his custom of carving the

Sunday roast himself. In 1871, during the Siege of Paris, the Communards set the palace afire. It burned for three days while the **Louvre Museum** staff worked frantically to save the collections. The palace was razed between 1882 and 1884; a single bay was preserved and stands unmarked in a remote corner of the **Tuileries Gardens** behind the **Jeu de Paume.**

Bassin Octagonal et Terrasses (Octagonal Fountain and Terraces)

Between the **Jeu de Paume** and **L'Orangerie** are a series of 18th-century statues representing the Nile, the Tiber, the Loire and Loiret, the Marne, and the Seine Rivers, part of an overall garden design that also includes the adjoining **Octagonal Fountain,** terraces, slopes, and stairways. North of the fountain is a modest bust of André Le Nôtre, the landscape architect. The **Tuileries** is framed from the west by Coysevox's two winged horses, erected in 1719 at the western edge of the garden, along Place de la Concorde.

The first human ascent in a hydrogen balloon, on 1 December 1783, was launched beside the **Octagonal Fountain.** The flight was made by physician J.A.C. Charles and his mechanic, Noel Robert. Thousands packed the park to watch the historic flight; among the spectators were Benjamin Franklin and French philosopher Denis Diderot, who conjectured that one day human beings might go to the moon. The hot-air balloon rose more than 2,000 feet and carried its passengers safely 25 miles to the north of Paris. Now, every New Year's Day, the celebrity-studded Paris-Dakar overland motor race across Europe and North Africa begins here. ♦ Between L'Orangerie and the Jeu de Paume

L'Orangerie This former citrus nursery is the permanent home of the **Walter-Guillaume Collection** of paintings, including 144 masterworks by such artists as Renoir, Monet, Cézanne, Soutine, Picasso, Derain, and Matisse. The artists best represented are Pierre-Auguste Renoir (24 works) and André Derain (28 paintings). The Cézannes are exceptional, particularly *Apples and Biscuits,* whose audacious composition is held together by a drawer latch placed dead center in the picture.

On the lower floor, mounted on curved panels, are Claude Monet's eight giant water lily murals, *Les Nymphéas.* Monet's visual kingdom was centered at his house and gardens in Giverny near Paris (see "Day Trips," page 256). ♦ Admission. M, W-Su. Southwest corner (at Pl de la Concorde). 01.42.97.48.16

29 Galignani The classic French bookstore is liberally sprinkled with selections in English. ♦ M-Sa. 224 Rue de Rivoli (between Rues d'Alger and de Castiglione). 01.42.60.76.07. Métros: Concorde, Tuileries

ANGELINA

29 Angélina ★★★$$ The Rolls-Royce of Parisian tea salons, this place originally went by the name **Rumpelmayer's.** It was founded in 1903 on the former site of the king's stables. Amid marble pedestal tables, landscapes by Lorrant-Heilbronn, red carpet, and gilt decor, the overworked waitresses deliver justly celebrated pastries, sumptuous hot chocolate, and *Mont Blanc,* a weighty concoction of chestnut cream purée (a favorite of the Aga Khan). The whipped cream is fresh and the ice water is served on silver trays. In spring and autumn, get a table near Rue de Rivoli, where you can watch top models and fashion designers returning from the ready-to-wear collection fashion shows. ♦ Daily breakfast, lunch, and afternoon tea; closed three weeks in August. Reservations recommended for lunch. 226 Rue de Rivoli (between Rues d'Alger and de Castiglione). 01.42.60.82.00. Métros: Concorde, Tuileries

HOTEL MEURICE
Paris

29 Hôtel Meurice $$$$ Heads of state (vacationing and exiled), artists, writers, and other celebrities have long favored this refined 180-room property. Alphonse XIII of Spain stayed for years in Suite 112, and Salvador Dalí made the Royal Suite his Paris home for three decades. During World War II, the hotel served as Nazi headquarters. In the immense Suite 108, Commandant General von Cholitz, after disobeying Hitler's orders to burn Paris, surrendered to the Allies in August 1944. Since the hotel opened in 1816, it has attracted many famous American visitors, including Herman Melville, Henry James, Henry Wadsworth Longfellow, and Wilbur and Orville Wright, who stayed here in 1907 while trying to sell their airplane to the French. (The Wrights used the familiar argument that their invention was the weapon to end all wars. The French military didn't buy that, but the public was captivated by the biplane, which the Wrights had shipped all the way to Paris from Dayton, Ohio.) The styles of Louis XV and XVI prevail throughout the property. Tea in the **Salon Pompadour** next to the charming bar is a discreet pleasure, especially in the late afternoon after the pianist settles at the keys. There's also **Le Meurice** restaurant, which boasts one Michelin star. Note: There's no charge for children 14 and under when sharing a room with a parent or guardian; however, owners of dogs must pay for bunking their pets. ♦ 228 Rue de Rivoli (between Rues d'Alger and de Castiglione). 01.44.58.10.10; fax 01.44.58.10.78. Métros: Concorde, Tuileries

30 Hôtel Inter-Continental Paris $$$$ Designed in 1878 by **Charles Garnier** (who built the **Opéra Garnier** and the **Grand Hôtel**), this 150-room establishment has three salons that are classified as historical landmarks. The fanciest receptions in town—including those celebrating the new haute couture collections of Yves Saint Laurent, Guy Laroche, and Jean Patou—take place in these ornate rooms. This hotel has always drawn a varied clientele: Victor Hugo and the Empress Eugénie were fans, as is Jerry Lewis. The rooms offer both turn-of-the-century elegance and modern conveniences. ♦ 3 Rue de Castiglione (between Rues de Rivoli and du Mont-Thabor). 01.44.77.11.11; fax 01.44.77.14.60. Métros: Concorde, Tuileries

Within Hôtel Inter-Continental Paris:

Brasserie 234 Rivoli ★$$ Simple dishes such as omelettes, *croque-monsieurs* (grilled ham and cheese sandwiches), and salads are served at reasonable prices in an informal cafe environment. ♦ Daily breakfast, lunch, and dinner. 01.44.77.11.11

Bar du Lobby The celebrity-studded bar is paneled in dark wood and softly lighted with Tiffany lamps. ♦ Daily 9AM-midnight. 01.44.77.11.11

31 W. H. Smith and Son A bonanza of English paperbacks and magazines is carried here. ♦ M-Sa. 248 Rue de Rivoli (at Rue Cambon). 01.44.77.88.99. Métro: Concorde

32 Lescure ★★$$ This unspoiled bistro serves *confit de canard* (duck confit), rabbit and sorrel, dandelion green salad, and wild game during hunting season (autumn). ♦ M-F lunch and dinner; Sa lunch. Reservations recommended. 7 Rue de Mondovi (between Rues de Rivoli and du Mont-Thabor). 01.42.60.18.91. Métro: Concorde

33 Hôtel Talleyrand/American Consulate Designed by **Jacques-Ange Gabriel,** the architect for Louis XV, and **Jean-François Chalgrin** who designed the **Arc de Triomphe,** this *hôtel* was originally the residence of diplomat par excellence Charles-Maurice de Talleyrand-Périgord and subsequently housed Czar Alexander I, several French Rothschilds, and, during World War II, the German Navy, which kept prisoners of war in the cellars. Today this historic building houses the **American Consulate,** best known among traveling Americans as the office where you replace lost or stolen passports. ♦ 2 Rue St-Florentin (at Rue de Rivoli). 01.40.20.01.99. Métro: Concorde

34 Place de la Concorde The largest square in Paris, covering 21 acres, was a swamp until royal architect **Jacques-Ange Gabriel** was asked by Louis XV to find a setting appropriate for an equestrian statue of the king himself. The statue stood on the square, originally named for Louis XV, less than 20 years; it was removed during the Revolution. On Sunday, 21 January 1793, the guillotine was set up on the square's west side (near the spot where the statue of Brest sculpted by Cortot stands today). Louis XVI was beheaded, and the 13-month Reign of Terror began. Among its thousands of victims were Marie Antoinette, Madame du Barry, Charlotte Corday, and Danton. On the evening of 28 July 1794, more than 1,300 townspeople gathered here to watch the execution of Robespierre. During the Revolution, no fewer than 1,343 victims were executed on the Place de la Révolution (as it was known then), and the square so reeked of gore that herds of oxen balked at crossing it. The *place* subsequently was given the name *concorde* (peace) as a way of laying to rest its violent past. ♦ Between Jardin des Tuileries and Ave des Champs-Elysées. Métro: Concorde

On Place de la Concorde:

Obelisk of Luxor This 3,300-year-old, 220-ton Egyptian obelisk is unquestionably the oldest monument in Paris. Originally erected around the 13th century BC in the Temple of Luxor, the 76-foot-tall monument was a gift to Louis Philippe from Mohammed Ali Pasha, who was viceroy of Egypt in 1831. (He also gave Queen Victoria Cleopatra's Needle, a slightly shorter obelisk taken from Heliopolis.) The pink-granite Paris obelisk, which replaced the equestrian statue of Louis XV that was removed during the Revolution, traveled 600 miles by barge down the Nile to Alexandria, was towed across the Mediterranean and up the Atlantic, was carted through Normandy, and finally was erected at Place de la Concorde in 1836, ending a political squabble over whose monument should adorn a square dedicated to neither a French king nor Napoléon's army. The designs on the pedestal are meant to illustrate the technological wizardry involved in the obelisk's journey from Egypt to Paris.

Visitors be forewarned: Pedestrians crossing the Place de la Concorde on foot are taking their lives in their hands. But go ahead; you only live once, and the obelisk is worth a close look. What's more, the island surrounding it provides an unobstructed view of the Champs-Elysées. Cross at the light!

Sculpture and Fountains Adorning Gabriel's original octagonal square are several groups of statuary, allegorical figures representing Bordeaux, Brest, Lille, Marseilles, Nantes, Rouen, and Strasbourg. Believe it or not, the tiny two-room pavilions underneath the statues were once rented out

as dwellings. North and south of the obelisk stand two fountains, one representing maritime navigation and the other river navigation. The latter, ironically, is the farthest from the Seine. The fountains' sea nymphs and water gods are replicas of those found in fountains on St. Peter's Square in Rome.

35 Pont de la Concorde This five-arched bridge designed in 1791 by civil engineer Jean Rodolphe Perronet is constructed in part with stone souvenirs from the 1789 storming and demolition of the **Bastille,** allegedly so that people could forever trample the ruins of the old fortress. ♦ Between Quai d'Orsay and Cours la Reine. Métro: Concorde

36 North Facade of Place de la Concorde When royal architect **Jacques-Ange Gabriel** designed the Place de la Concorde, he made sure that buildings would face only its north side, and in 1757, work began on the two matching Neo-Classical north facades separated down the middle by Rue Royale. The facade's design was borrowed from the **Louvre** colonnades, which **Gabriel** himself had restored. The **Hôtel de la Marine,** part of the facade east of Rue Royale, was intended to be lodging for foreign ambassadors, but became first a royal-furniture storehouse and then, in 1792, the **Admiralty** (now known as the **Ministry of the Navy**). The building on the opposite corner is now occupied by the prestigious **L'Automobile Club de France** and the very elegant **Hôtel Crillon** (see below). On 6 February 1778, Louis XVI and American diplomats (including Benjamin Franklin) met at the **Crillon** to sign the Treaty of Friendship and Trade, which recognized the independence of the 13 American states. ♦ Between Rues St-Florentin and Boissy-d'Anglas. Métro: Concorde

36 Hôtel Crillon $$$$ The facade of this hotel, one of the swankiest properties in Paris, was designed in 1758 by **Jacques-Ange Gabriel** for the Count of Crillon. The family managed to hold onto the mansion right through the Revolution, in spite of the fact that the guillotine was set up practically on their doorstep. Today the 163-room institution is the last of the grand Parisian hotels to remain 100 percent French-owned. Should you decide that the kids don't need to go to college after all, rent one of the three royal suites (the **Red Suite,** the **White Suite,** or the **Blue Suite**) and enjoy some of the best possible views of the Place de la Concorde, the Seine, and the

Eiffel Tower. Another option is the **Marie Antoinette Apartment,** where the queen is said to have taken her music lessons. Among the famous American couples who have romanced here are Mary Pickford and Douglas Fairbanks, who stopped in during their 1920 honeymoon, and newspaper magnate William Randolph Hearst and his girlfriend, Marion Davies. The hotel's proximity to the American and British Embassies assures a clientele of diplomats, royalty, and wealthy foreigners. ♦ 10 Pl de la Concorde (between Rues Royale and Boissy-d'Anglas). 01.44.71.15.00; fax 01.44.71.15.02. Métro: Concorde

Within the Hôtel Crillon:

Ambassadeurs Restaurant ★★$$$$ Innovative chef Christian Constant concocts such specialties as a savory *St-Pierre* (a fish known as John Dory in the US), *gratin dauphinois* (sliced potatoes baked in cream), Brittany lobster, sea bass with sesame-and-cinnamon fritters, and a tasty chocolate tart. The exemplary fare is complemented by the magnificent setting, with 20-foot-high ceilings, elaborate mirrors, and massive crystal chandeliers. The views of the Place de la Concorde are outstanding. ♦ Daily lunch and dinner. Reservations required. 01.44.71.16.16

Obelisk ★$$$ Serving delicious pasta and regional cheeses, this eatery offers meals suitable for lighter appetites and slimmer purses while remaining in step with the hotel's elegant atmosphere. ♦ M-F lunch and dinner; Sa lunch; closed in August. Reservations recommended. 01.44.71.15.15

Bar du Crillon International journalists and visiting diplomats often stop here for a glass of Champagne before dinner. Its hot *feuilletés* (croissant-like pastries) are great snacks. ♦ Daily 11AM-2AM. 01.44.71.15.39

37 Maxim's ★★$$$$ Paris without Maxim's? *Pas possible.* Where would all those rich business executives lunch? And where would the bona fide blue bloods, glitzy jet-setters, and fashionably late diners find such a Belle Epoque setting? This venerable dining spot has given the royal treatment to Edward VIII of England and Leopold II of Belgium, as well as to prominent Americans such as John Paul Getty, Jackie Onassis, and Elizabeth Taylor. Not everyone is admitted to the Pierre Cardin–owned landmark that has been cloned in New York, Mexico, Tokyo, Singapore, and Beijing. If you are lucky enough to be allowed to pass through the doors, however, expect unsurpassed Champagne and service, disappointing food, and a splendid and expensive Parisian evening. ♦ M-Sa lunch and dinner. Reservations required. 3 Rue Royale (between Pl de la Concorde and Rue du Faubourg-St-Honoré). 01.42.65.27.94. Métro: Concorde

38 American Embassy Designed in 1933 by the New York firm **Delano and Aldrich,** and flanked by two bald eagles in stone, the embassy and nearby consulate are staffed with about 500 Americans working for an alphabet soup of agencies including the IRS, CIA, and FBI, and the Departments of Defense, State, Agriculture, and Commerce. ♦ Rue de Boissy-d'Anglas (between Ave Gabriel and Rue du Faubourg-St-Honoré). 01.43.12.22.22. Métro: Concorde

39 L'Espace Restaurant ★★$$ This Pierre Cardin–designed restaurant with a 1950s Miami Beach decor (floral beach parasols, plastic chairs) serves a dandy buffet of 110 entrées and 40 desserts. It is a favorite with international TV and film glitterati, whose autographed photos festoon the walls. Liza Minnelli, Richard Gere, Brigitte Bardot, and French actress Arletty have all passed through at one time or another. There's dining on the garden terrace in summer. ♦ M-F lunch and dinner; Sa dinner; Su brunch and dinner. Reservations recommended. 1 Ave Gabriel (between Pl de la Concorde and Ave de Marigny). 01.42.66.17.30. Métro: Concorde

40 Chevaux de Marly (Marly Horses) The two sculptures of rearing horses at the entrance to the Champs-Elysées are actually replicas. The originals by Nicolas and Guillaume Coustou, called *Africans Mastering the Numidian Horses,* were taken from the **Château de Marly** (the Louis XIV château that was destroyed in the Revolution) and placed here in 1795. Sixteen horses dragged the statues to Paris in five hours, a transportation feat considered so marvelous that the vehicle in which they were carried is exhibited in the **Conservatoire des Arts et Métiers.** In 1994, the original Coustou sculptures were moved to **La Cour Marly,** a glass-covered courtyard in the **Louvre.** ♦ Ave des Champs-Elysées (at Pl de la Concorde). Métro: Concorde

"There is never any ending to Paris and the memory of each person who has lived in it differs from that of any other. We always returned to it no matter who we were or how it was changed or with what difficulties, or ease, it could be reached. Paris was always worth it and you received return for whatever you brought to it."

Ernest Hemingway, *A Moveable Feast*

40 Avenue des Champs-Elysées The neighborhood that is now the site of the world's most famous boulevard was forsaken marshland, unsafe after dark, until 1616, when Marie de Médicis, the wife of Henri IV, had a fashionable carriage-drive, the Cours-la-Reine (Queen's Way) built west of the Tuileries along the Seine. A half-century later, master landscaper André Le Nôtre planted double rows of chestnut trees to create another avenue to the northwest. Originally called the Grand Cours, this second avenue was later renamed the Avenue des Champs-Elysées (Elysian Fields). In 1724 the boulevard was extended to the top of the Butte de Chaillot. Half a century later, architect **Jacques-Germain Soufflot** leveled it by 16 feet to ease the climb for carriage-towing horses.

Since its creation, the Champs-Elysées has always been the place to promenade. Processions marking the liberation of Paris (26 August 1944), the student-worker demonstrations (30 May 1968), and the death of Charles de Gaulle (12 November 1970) all made their way down this street. If you fancy pomp and pageantry, show up here on Bastille Day (14 July), when the jets of the French Air Force streak overhead; Armistice Day (11 November), when the president lays a wreath on the **Tomb of the Unknown Soldier;** in late July when the grueling three-week Tour de France bicycle race ends here; and at Christmastime, when the avenue's trees twinkle with tiny white lights. The eastern half of the boulevard, from Place de la Concorde to Rond-Point des Champs-Elysées, is bordered by lush gardens of azaleas and mature chestnut trees. Within the gardens are theaters (the **Théâtre de Marigny** and **Théâtre du Rond-Point**) and exclusive restaurants with pretty garden terraces, such as **Laurent, L'Espace,** and **Elysée Lenôtre.** The western half of the avenue, between Rond-Point des Champs-Elysées and Place Charles-de-Gaulle, has lost its aristocratic sheen; today it is a crowded commercial strip of banks, airline offices, cinemas, cafes, fast-food parlors, and shops. A face-lift in the early 1990s gave the avenue new granite paving and the city's fanciest underground parking garage. ♦ Between Pls de la Concorde and Charles-de-Gaulle. Métros: Concorde, Champs-Elysées–Clemenceau, Franklin-D.-Roosevelt, George-V, Charles-de-Gaulle–Etoile

41 Ledoyen ★★★$$$ During the reign of Louis XVI (1774-92), this dining spot on the south side of the Champs-Elysées was a country inn and dairy bar serving fresh milk to travelers. Dinner here can still seem pleasantly bucolic; the view of the Champs-Elysées from the upstairs dining room is superb. The menu of female chef Guislaine Arabian has a Northern Italian twist: Selections include zucchini flowers with truffles, shellfish ratatouille, and mille-feuille of polenta and lobster. Within months of its 1988 opening, the restaurant had earned its first Michelin star; it now boasts two stars. A superb wine list is available. ♦ M-F lunch and

Avenue des Champs-Elysées

MICHAEL STORRINGS

dinner. Reservations required; jacket and tie required. Carré des Champs-Elysées (off Ave Edward-Tuck). 01.47.42.23.23, 01.53.05.10.01. Métro: Champs Elysées–Clemenceau

42 La Table du Gouverneur ★★$$ In a Louis XVI pavilion that has served dinners to a long line of notables from Edward VII to Toulouse-Lautrec, chef Jean-Paul Deyries offers a tripartite menu of Breton, Oriental, and English cuisine. Choose from original combinations like *terrine de canard* (duck terrine) with three chutneys, curried shrimp in banana leaves, *raie* (skate) in cider butter, Aberdeen Angus beef, and mango and papaya dessert soup. ♦ M-F lunch and dinner; Sa dinner. Carré Marigny, 10 Ave des Champs-Elysées (between Pl de la Concorde and Ave de Marigny). 01.42.65.85.10. Métro: Champs-Elysées–Clemenceau

43 Statue de Clemenceau Georges Clemenceau (1841-1929) was the out-spoken French politician who at the end of World War I helped form a coalition govern-ment to rally French morale and fight the Germans. Sculptor François Cogne has captured Clemenceau's trademarks in bronze: the walrus mustache, high leather boots, walking stick, and wool scarf flapping in the wind. ♦ Pl Clemenceau (at Ave des Champs-Elysées). Métro: Champs-Elysées–Clemenceau

44 Petit Palais This little turn-of-the-century palace houses the city's fine arts museum, with a collection specializing in 19th-century French painters such as Delacroix, Courbet, Monet, Cézanne, and Bonnard. The architect, **Charles Girault**, crowned the building with a graceful cupola and decorated its two wings with Ionic columns and Rococo embellishments. ♦ Admission. Tu-Su. Ave Winston-Churchill (between Cours la Reine and Ave Charles-Girault). 01.42.65.12.73. Métro: Champs-Elysées–Clemenceau

45 Pont Alexandre III Between the **Invalides** and the **Grand Palais** is an elegant Belle Epoque bridge embodying the architectural giddiness that celebrated the French spirit of ingenuity and optimism at the turn of the century. The bridge is encrusted with every Greco-Roman frippery in the book: human-size cupids, lavish garlands, huge golden statues of Pegasus and Renown, prides of lions, and a plethora of trumpets, tridents, shells, and shields. Built to commemorate the 1892 French-Russian alliance, the bridge bears the Russian and French coats of arms side by side and teams a sculptural allegory of the Seine with one of the Neva. ♦ Between Quai d'Orsay and Cours la Reine. Métro: Champs-Elysées–Clemenceau

46 Grand Palais Along with the Pont Alexandre III and the **Petit Palais,** this exuberant stone, steel, and glass structure is an example of Art Nouveau architecture at its most excessive. The **Grand Palais** and **Petit Palais** were built for the Universal Exhibition of 1900, the first world's fair in Paris. Famous for its domed and vaulted glass roof and superb staircase, the **Grand Palais** was the work of three architects: **Henri Deglane** designed the principal facade; **Albert Thomas**, the rear facade; and **Louis-Albert Louvet**, the rest. With 54,000 square feet of floor space (equivalent to nearly 14 basketball courts), this structure is used for book fairs, car shows, and blockbuster art exhibitions. ♦ Admission. Open only for special exhibitions and events; call for schedule or check *Pariscope*. Ave Winston-Churchill (between Cours la Reine and Pl Clemenceau). 01.44.13.17.17. Métro: Champs-Elysées–Clemenceau

47 Palais de la Découverte The western part of the **Grand Palais** houses a sprawling science museum offering holography exhibitions, Jacques Cousteau festivals, daily demonstrations on everything from ants to astronomy, and 9,000 stars twinkling on the ceiling of its celebrated planetarium. Kids love the Madagascar agates and, of course, the metal replicas of dinosaurs. ♦ Admission. Tu-Su. Ave Franklin-D.-Roosevelt (between Cours la Reine and Ave du Général-Eisenhower). 01.40.74.80.15, 01.4074.81.82. Métro: Franklin-D.-Roosevelt

48 1 Avenue de Marigny In 1954, when American novelist John Steinbeck and his family moved into this house, he described it in a letter to Richard Rodgers and Oscar Hammerstein: "It is next to the Rothschilds and across the street from the president of France. How's that for an address for a Salinas kid?" It's still a private residence. ♦ At Ave Gabriel. Métro: Champs-Elysées–Clemenceau

49 Résidence Maxim's $$$$ Near the intersection of the Champs-Elysées and the Place de la Concorde, Pierre Cardin has created a 43-room Art Nouveau confection that accommodates visiting executives, sheiks, and the rich and famous for anywhere from $500 to $7,000 per night, depending on whether you prefer, say, the Sarah Bernhardt bed or the Toulouse-Lautrec painting in your room. There's also a classic Belle Epoque lobby, a secluded bar, and a fine restaurant. ♦ 42 Ave Gabriel (between Rue du Cirque and Ave Matignon). 01.45.61.96.33; fax 01.42.89.06.07. Métro: Franklin-D.-Roosevelt

The guillotine was proposed by Dr. Joseph Guillotin in 1791 as an instantaneous and thus more humane means of execution. The beheading device was adopted for all capital crimes in France in 1792. Contrary to common lore, Dr. Guillotin was not killed by the machine that bears his name; he died in his bed in 1814 at age 76.

RESTAURANT LAURENT

50 Restaurant Laurent ★★★$$$$ Just down the street from the official residence of the French president, the parking lot of this restaurant is always crowded with chauffeured limousines bearing diplomatic license plates. The drawing cards here are the lovely garden terrace, impeccable service, and nouvelle cuisine bourgeoise, which includes salmon carpaccio with caviar, rack of lamb, langoustines in pastry crust, roast lobster, and warm raspberry soufflé. The chef is Philippe Braun, a disciple of Joël Robuchon, and the wine list is overseen by the aptly named Philippe Bourguignon. In addition to the terrace, there are tables in a covered garden pavillion and in dining rooms on two floors in a 19th-century building. The interior decor is plush, with high ceilings, Impressionist paintings, and a nostalgic Belle Epoque theme. ◆ M-F lunch and dinner; Sa dinner. Reservations required. 41 Ave Gabriel (between Aves de Marigny and Matignon). 01.42.25.00.39. Métro: Champs-Elysées–Clemenceau

THÉÂTRE
DU ROND-POINT

51 Théâtre du Rond-Point The company of Marcel Marechal took up residence in this newly renovated theater just off the Champs-Elysées in the fall of 1995. Contemporary French theater, including the works of Camus and Claudel, is featured. ◆ Call for box office hours. 2 *bis* Ave Franklin-D.-Roosevelt (between Ave du Général-Eisenhower and Rond-Point des Champs-Elysées). 01.44.95.98.00. Métros: Champs-Elysées–Clemenceau, Franklin-D.-Roosevelt

Within the Théâtre du Rond-Point:

Théâtre du Rond-Point Restaurant ★ $$ On the lower level of the theater, this restaurant serves reasonably priced meals, including traditional French dishes and such unusual items as ostrich meat with mangoes. The *assiette du spectacle* consists of a salad, melon, ham, vegetables, cheese, and wine. Dine on the delightful terrace overlooking the gardens along the Champs-Elysées. ◆ Daily lunch, afternoon tea, and dinner. Reservations recommended. 01.45.61.23.84

52 France Amérique If you want to give a party during your Paris stay and insist on nothing less than a Second-Empire town house for your setting, consider this place, which rents its three Louis XVI rooms (200 square meters/660 square feet) for festivities lasting just until midnight. Have **Angélina** (see page 181) take care of the catering for the perfect lavish bash. ◆ 9 Ave Franklin-D.-Roosevelt (between Rues François-1er and Jean-Goujon). 01.43.59.51.00. Métro: Franklin-D.-Roosevelt

53 Lasserre ★★★$$$$ In the same luxurious league (and price range) as the **Tour d'Argent** and the **Grand Véfour,** this restaurant is famous for its caviar, 1930s ocean-liner decor, and service bordering on perfection (owner René Lasserre got his start in the restaurant business washing dishes at the age of 13, and all that experience shows). Located in a small town house, the main dining room is reached by a velvet-lined elevator. In warm weather, the ceiling, painted by Touchagues, rolls away, providing patrons with a view of the stars and a little cool air. Masterpieces from a rather traditional repertoire include: Belon oysters, *canard* (duck) *à l'orange,* sea bass with sorrel, and *soufflé Grand Marnier.* The restaurant's wine cellar has 140,000 bottles. ◆ M dinner; Tu-Sa lunch and dinner; closed in August. Reservations required. 17 Ave Franklin-D.-Roosevelt (between Rues François-1er and Jean-Goujon). 01.43.59.53.43. Métro: Franklin-D.-Roosevelt

54 7 Rue François-1er During World War II, this building, formerly the **Hôtel du Palais,** was the headquarters of the American Red Cross. It was here that American poet e.e. cummings, a volunteer ambulance driver, spent a glorious May in 1917 detached from his unit. This act of independence resulted, through a tragicomic series of events, in his spending six months in a French prison, an experience that provided cummings with ample material for his autobiographical prose work, *The Enormous Room,* published in 1922. The building is now privately owned. ◆ Between Cours Albert-1er and Pl François-1er. Métro: Franklin-D.-Roosevelt

55 San Régis $$$$ This sophisticated and discreet little 40-room Paris hotel has hosted Raquel Welch and Lauren Bacall. It's decorated with fine antiques and paintings and sits close (but not too close) to the Champs-Elysées. There's a restaurant and a bar. ◆ 12 Rue Jean-Goujon (between Ave Franklin-D.-Roosevelt and Pl François-1er). 01.43.59.41.90; fax 01.45.61.05.48. Métro: Franklin-D.-Roosevelt

56 25 Avenue Franklin-D.-Roosevelt From 1862 until the end of the Civil War, John Slidell, the Confederate commissioner to France, spent his time in a vain attempt to gain diplomatic recognition and financial support for the Southern cause. After the Confederacy's defeat, Slidell chose to remain in this house in Paris. It's still a private home. ♦ Between Rue Jean-Goujon and Impasse d'Antin. Métro: Franklin-D.-Roosevelt

57 Yvan ★★$$$ In his handsome restaurant, *gastronomique* chef Yvan Zaplatilek presents dishes largely influenced by his Belgian roots: potatoes with caviar, pigeon with honey and spices, *filet de dorade* with celery, rabbit with lemon confit, and *gateau au chocolat*. The pastel-and-ivory dining room is filled with fresh flowers and softly lit with chandeliers and candlelight. ♦ M-F lunch and dinner; Sa dinner. Reservations required. 1 *bis* Rue Jean-Mermoz (at Rond-Point des Champs-Elysées). 01.43.59.18.40. Métro: Franklin-D.-Roosevelt

57 Le Petit Yvan ★$ Chef Yvan Zaplatilek's little bistro is cheery, with brightly colored mismatched plates, red paper napkins, a hodge-podge collection of art on the walls, and a polite young staff. It's a tight squeeze, but the beautiful people here don't seem to mind rubbing elbows with each other. The inexpensive prix-fixe menu offers such dishes as langoustine bisque, roast chicken with mushrooms, steak tartare, baba rhum, and poached pears. ♦ M-F lunch and dinner; Sa dinner. Reservations recommended. 1 *bis* Rue Jean-Mermoz (at Rond-Point des Champs-Elysées). 01.42.89.49.65. Métro: Franklin-D.-Roosevelt

58 Avenue Matignon This is "gallery alley" for Right Bank art and antiques. Take note of the stamp-collectors' market along this street and the connecting Avenue Gabriel, which is held Thursdays, Saturdays, Sundays, and holidays. ♦ Between Rond-Point des Champs-Elysées and Rue de Penthièvre. Métro: Franklin-D.-Roosevelt

58 Le Berkeley ★$$ A classic oysters-and-Champagne, steak-and-fries restaurant, it features the red decor of a first-class dining car. ♦ Daily breakfast, lunch, and dinner until 2AM. Reservations recommended. 7 Ave Matignon (at Rue de Ponthieu). 01.42.25.47.79, 01.42.25.72.25. Métro: Franklin-D.-Roosevelt

59 Artcurial In the middle of this sprawling three-story complex of galleries is an extraordinary bookstore for art lovers. ♦ Tu-Sa; closed three weeks in August. 9 Ave Matignon (at Rue de Ponthieu). 01.42.99.16.16. Métro: Franklin-D.-Roosevelt

60 La Place Boisterous Parisian university students dance to very loud music until the very wee hours at this popular nightclub (formerly **Le Privé**). ♦ Cover. Daily midnight until exhaustion. 12 Rue de Ponthieu (between Rue Jean-Mermoz and Ave Franklin-

D.-Roosevelt). 01.42.25.51.70. Métro: Franklin-D.-Roosevelt

61 Le Boeuf sur le Toit ★★★$$ This is the sixth and fanciest of Jean-Paul Boucher's marvelous group of old brasseries (the others are **Chez Flo, Julien, Terminus Nord, Vaudeville,** and **La Coupole**). Note the superb Art Deco interior. Traditional, well-prepared brasserie fare is served. ♦ Daily lunch and dinner until 2AM. Reservations recommended. 34 Rue du Colisée (between Rue du Faubourg-St-Honoré and Ave Franklin-D.-Roosevelt). 01.43.59.83.80. Métro: Franklin-D.-Roosevelt

62 Jadis et Gourmande This candy store is a chocolate-lover's sweetest dream. ♦ M-Sa. 49 *bis* Ave Franklin-D.-Roosevelt (between Rond-Point des Champs-Elysées and Rue de Ponthieu). 01.42.25.06.04. Métro: Franklin-D.-Roosevelt

63 Hôtel Colisée $$ Quilted bedspreads and bamboo furniture embellish the 44 rooms of this comfortable, well-located hotel. There's no restaurant. ♦ 6 Rue du Colisée (between Rue de Ponthieu and Ave des Champs-Elysées). 01.43.59.95.25; fax 01.45.63.26.54. Métro: Franklin-D.-Roosevelt

63 La Boutique à Sandwiches ★★$$ Stop here for the perfect late-night snack: all-you-can-eat Swiss raclette (melted cheese on bread). This crowded two-story restaurant/snack bar also serves 40 kinds of sandwiches, as well as Welsh rarebit, ravioli, corned beef, and strudel. It's a great value. ♦ Daily lunch and dinner until 1AM. 12 Rue du Colisée (between Rue de Ponthieu and Ave des Champs-Elysées). 01.43.59.34.32, 01.43.59.56.69. Métro: Franklin-D.-Roosevelt

64 Franklin-D.-Roosevelt Métro Station This is the oldest métro station in Paris. The Parisian underground railway, or *métro* (short for *métropolitain*), was born on 4 October 1898, when men with picks and shovels began digging a labyrinth beneath the city as directed by engineer Fulgence Bienvenue. ♦ Rue de Marignan and Ave des Champs-Elysées

"As an artist, a man has no home in Europe save Paris."

Friedrich Nietzsche

Paris has grown greener in recent years. Since 1977 more than 120 hectares (300 acres) of park space have been added to the city, twice as much as in the previous century.

Restaurants/Clubs: Red   **Hotels:** Blue
Shops/♥ Outdoors: Green   **Sights/Culture:** Black

65 L'Avenue ★★★$$ In this chic brasserie/restaurant, located on one of the most sumptuous avenues in the world, chef Jean Philippe Liotté prepares appropriate temptations: classic Caesar salad, *gazpacho de tomates du soleil* (gazpacho with sun-dried tomatoes), bouillabaisse, risotto with snails, prawns with ginger, and grilled duck with peaches and *carottes caramélisées*. ◆ Daily breakfast, lunch, afternoon tea, and dinner. Reservations recommended. 41 Ave Montaigne (at Rue François-1er). 01.40.70.14.91. Métros: Alma–Marceau, Franklin-D.-Roosevelt

66 Avenue Montaigne This street is to haute couture what the **Louvre** is to art. The swank avenue is lined with high-fashion temples (**Christian Dior, Nina Ricci, Jean-Louis Scherrer, Valentino, Ungaro,** and **Laroche**). You will also find the **Canadian Embassy,** the luxurious **Plaza Athénée** hotel, and two smart theaters (the **Comédie des Champs-Elysées** and the **Théâtre des Champs-Elysées**). ◆ Between Rond-Point des Champs-Elysées and Pl de l'Alma. Metros: Alma–Marceau, Franklin-D.-Roosevelt

67 Chanel The dashing Chanel collections are displayed here to their best advantage: in a setting of crisp white walls, gleaming mirrors, and spacious dressing rooms. ◆ M-Sa. 42 Ave Montaigne (between Rues Bayard and François-1er). 01.47.23.74.12. Métros: Alma–Marceau, Franklin-D.-Roosevelt

68 Christian Dior In 1949 Dior signed the first designer licensing contract (for stockings). Today, women can dress in his wares from head to toe. Stop in this three-floor, gray-and-white complex, which sells dresses, furs, jewelry, and gifts, to select your ensemble. ◆ M-Sa. 30 Ave Montaigne (between Rue François-1er and Pl de la Reine-Astrid). 01.40.73.54.40. Métros: Franklin-D.-Roosevelt, Alma–Marceau

68 26 Avenue Montaigne In 1857, when he was 14, Henry James moved into this apartment building with his family. ◆ Between Rue François-1er and Pl de la Reine-Astrid. Métro: Alma–Marceau

---

Declared the French national anthem in 1795 (and again in 1879), "La Marseillaise" was first sung by the Army of the Rhine, but it was brought to Paris by volunteer troops from Marseilles.

The French Revolution has been the subject of more than 200 feature films by directors such as Jean Renoir, Abel Gance, D. W. Griffith, Ettore Scola, and Andrzej Wajda.

---

69 Nina Ricci Perhaps the most beautiful lingerie in the world is sold here, along with a stylish array of dresses, scarves, scents, and jewelry. **The Ricci Club,** an elegant menswear shop, is next door at 19 Rue François-1er, and around the corner at 17 Rue François-1er this haute couture designer's fashions from the year before are sold at a discount. ◆ M-Sa. 39 Ave Montaigne (at Rue François-1er). All three stores 01.49.52.56.00. Métros: Alma–Marceau, Franklin-D.-Roosevelt

70 Bar des Théâtres ★★$$ This noisy bar/restaurant is patronized by theater critics before, bored ticket holders during, and worn-out actors after performances. The fare is simple: steak, Welsh rarebit, osso buco, and the like. It's a favorite lunch spot of film director Roman Polanski. ◆ Daily lunch and dinner until 2AM. 6 Ave Montaigne (between Rue François-1er and Pl de la Reine-Astrid). 01.47.23.34.63. Métro: Alma–Marceau

71 Plaza Athénée $$$$ Elegant and charming, this 210-room property has long enjoyed a reputation as the most fashionable palace hotel in Paris, largely because its **Relais Plaza** restaurant (see below) remains the favored lunchtime hangout of Paris couturiers. In fact, when the great designer Pierre Balmain died, the management retired his table. Also on the premises are the one-Michelin-star **Régence** restaurant and a classic Parisian cocktail bar (see below). The Louis XV– and XVI–style decor features a profusion of flowers—the hotel staff boasts that the monthly florist's bill is higher than the electric bill. In 1918 West Point graduate Captain George Patton stayed here while learning to fence at the French Military Academy in Saumur. While in residence, Patton discussed combat with then 28-year-old Charles de Gaulle. Today the hotel's select out-of-town clientele includes Rockefellers, rich Brazilians, and the like. ◆ 25 Ave Montaigne (between Rues Clément-Marot and du Boccador). 01.53.67.66.65.; fax 01.53.67.66.66. Métro: Alma–Marceau

Within the Plaza Athénée:

Relais Plaza ★$$ For a late-night, after-theater meal, try the fillets of sole or braised beef in aspic, accompanied by a good house wine. *Tout Paris* lunches here, particularly during the fashion shows. ◆ Daily lunch and dinner. Reservations recommended. 01.47.23.78.33

Bar Anglais After a performance at the **Théâtre des Champs-Elysées,** the concert crowd may come here and mix with the South American night owls staying at the hotel. There's piano music after 11PM. ◆ Daily 11AM-1AM. 01.47.23.78.33

Régence-Plaza ★★$$$ The most expensive of the hotel's restaurants is peopled, as a rule, by the rich and famous.

Young chef Eric Briffard creates such elegant dishes as *St-Pierre au curry et aux aubergines fondants* (John Dory with curry and melted eggplant) and roast peach with fresh almond and lavender. Patrick Jeanne, the restaurant's manager, has mastered the art of mingling the stars and the not-yet-famous so that everyone can get a look at everyone else. In summer dine on the ivy-decked terrace. ♦ Daily lunch and dinner. Reservations recommended. 01.47.23.78.33

72 Valentino The Milan designer's Paris boutique, all beige marble and glass, shows his sophisticated men's and women's fashions as well as the casual, less expensive clothes sold under his younger label, Oliver. ♦ M-Sa. 17-19 Ave Montaigne (at Rue du Boccador). 01.47.23.64.61. Métro: Alma–Marceau

72 Maison Blanche ★★★$$$$ Fresh from the success of the trendy original **Maison Blanche** (now closed), René Duran took over an even trendier spot atop the **Théâtre des Champs-Elysées.** A restaurant with Paris literally at its feet, it attracts a business and haute couture clientele. The space is decorated in simple monochromes, and the culinary magic of José Martinez is as pleasing to the eye as to the palate: special taste treats include *beignets d'huitres aux neuf saveurs* (oyster fritters with nine flavors), *le pigeon rôti aux coings confits* (roast pigeon with quince chutney), and heavenly desserts. ♦ Daily lunch and dinner. 15 Ave Montaigne (between Rue du Boccador and Pl de l'Alma). 01.47.23.55.99. Métro: Alma–Marceau

72 Théâtre des Champs-Elysées Here, on 29 May 1913, the **Ballet Russe** of Sergei Diaghilev first performed to the music of the Stravinsky piece *Le Sacré du Printemps.* Riots followed the performance, which was shocking in its originality and modernity. Diaghilev, Stravinsky, Nijinsky, and Cocteau fled the mobs for the **Bois de Boulogne** and drove around while Diaghilev wept.

Inaugurated in 1913, the theater was one of the first buildings of reinforced concrete in Paris; it was designed by **Auguste Perret,** who was later hired to reconstruct the entire port city of Le Havre after World War II. Today it is the city's most celebrated classical music venue; it also hosts opera and dance performances.

American footnotes: On 2 October 1925 *La Revue Nègre* opened here; John Dos Passos painted the show's stage set, Sidney Bechet played clarinet, and Josephine Baker danced to "Yes, Sir, That's My Baby." In May 1927 a Charles Lindbergh autograph sold for $1,500 at an auction held at the theater (the name of his plane, *The Spirit of St. Louis,* pleased the French, who associated it not with Missouri, but with the saintliest of their line of kings). And on 16 April 1928, the Gershwins attended the opening of a performance of *La Rhapsodie en Bleu* by the **Ballet Russe.** ♦ Box office: M-Sa 11AM-7PM. No performances holidays and 1 July through the first week of September. 15 Ave Montaigne (between Rue du Boccador and Pl de l'Alma). 01.49.52.50.00. Métro: Alma–Marceau

73 2 Avenue Montaigne Back when this was the **Hôtel Elysée-Bellevue,** Sinclair Lewis passed the winter of 1924 here writing *Arrowsmith.* It is now a private residential building. ♦ At Pl de la Reine-Astrid. Métro: Alma–Marceau

74 Pont de l'Alma Built in 1855 to honor the first French victory in the Crimean War (1854), this bridge is decorated with a statue of a Zouave soldier that acts as a watermark; during the flood of 1910, the Seine reached his chin. The *bateaux mouches* and dinner cruises embark on their tours of the Seine from the quay below Place de l'Alma. ♦ Between Quai Branly and Ave de New-York. Métro: Alma–Marceau

75 Chez Francis ★★$$ Formerly a *relais de poste* (stable for the post office's horses), this bistro boasts a three-star view of the **Eiffel Tower** and the largest outdoor terrace in Paris. A show-biz crowd assembles here for the fresh seafood platters, beef carpaccio with basil, *moules marinières* (mussels steamed in white wine and shallots), grilled sole, and *confit de canard* (duck confit) with sautéed apples. ♦ Daily lunch and dinner. Reservations recommended. 7 Pl de l'Alma (at Ave George-V). 01.47.20.86.83. Métro: Alma–Marceau

75 Avenue George-V Along this grand avenue named after the English king, you will find the **American Cathedral;** the salons of **Givenchy** and **Balenciaga;** the Chinese and Mexican embassies; a swank hotel **(George V);** and the **Crazy Horse Saloon,** with its sophisticated girlie shows. ♦ Between Pl de l'Alma and Ave des Champs-Elysées. Métros: Alma–Marceau, George-V

75 Marius et Janette ★★$$$ For a taste of some of the finest *Provençale* cuisine available in Paris, reserve a table at this gracious seafood restaurant, which is set on a large yacht. Chef Laurent Odiot serves classic bouillabaisse, lobster salad, sea bass flambé, and a selection of dishes representative of the western maritime provinces. A favorite of celebrities (Sylvester Stallone, Michelle Pfeiffer, and Robert de Niro have all dined here), this place has an appropriately nautical feel, with lots of wood and photos of fishermen on the walls. ◆ Daily lunch and dinner. Reservations recommended. 4 Ave George-V (between Pl de l'Alma and Rue de la Trémoille). 01.47.23.84.36. Métro: Alma–Marceau

75 Le Bistrot de Marius ★★$$ Pagnol's Marius may have run away to sea, but the chef here seems to have just returned. The bill of fare at this warm, *Provençale*-style spot revolves around the freshest of seafood, from baby clams on a bed of spinach to *daurade grillé* (a sumptuous grilled sea bream). ◆ Daily lunch and dinner. 6 Ave George-V (between Pl de l'Alma and Rue de la Trémoille). 01.40.70.11.76. Métro: Alma–Marceau

75 Crazy Horse Saloon The saloon's upscale strip show is a knowing display of naughtiness featuring 16 lasses, most British and all of uniform height (between 5 feet, 4 inches, and 5 feet, 5 inches, tall), with silly stage names such as Bianca Sundae, Ivy Speculation, Rita Cadillac, and Pompea Mackintosh. The family of Alain Bernardin, the late impresario of the saloon, now runs the establishment, but the unseen star of the show is the lighting designer, who strobes, tints, patterns, and spotlights dancers with flair. ◆ Cover. Shows: M-F, Su 9PM and 11:30PM; Sa 8PM, 10:30PM, and 12:50AM. Reservations recommended. 12 Ave George-V (between Pl de l'Alma and Rue de la Trémoille). 01.47.23.32.32. Métro: Alma–Marceau

76 Hôtel de la Trémoille $$$$ This impressive-yet-relaxed 107-room hotel is a bit of *Vieux France* in the heart of the high-fashion district. The rooms are furnished with antiques and feature sumptuous bathrooms. After an afternoon of shopping at **Christian Dior** and **Nina Ricci,** dine here or at one of the restaurants in the nearby **Plaza Athénée** or **George V** hotels and charge your meal to your room. ◆ 14 Rue de la Trémoille (at Rue du Boccador). 01.47.23.34.20; fax 01.40.70.01.08. Métro: Alma–Marceau

Within the Hôtel de la Trémoille:

Le Louis d'Or ★★$$$ A fire burns in the *cheminée* of this elegant but cozy dining room. With an emphasis on traditional cuisine, a fine meal here might consist of a starter of potato cakes with truffles and Port or scallop salad with lime, a main course of sole stuffed with herbs or roast lamb with fresh thyme, and a dessert of crème brûlée or assorted sorbets with fruit sauce. ◆ Daily lunch and dinner. Reservations required. 01.47.23.75.12

77 Chez Edgar ★$$ This noisy restaurant thronged with politicians, journalists, and actors serves meals to fit any pocketbook. Try the red mullet *au pistou* (in a creamy garlic basil sauce), salmon tartare, fresh pasta, pot-au-feu, or fresh shellfish. ◆ M-Sa lunch and dinner. Reservations recommended. 4 Rue Marbeuf (at Rue du Boccador). 01.47.20.51.15. Métro: Alma–Marceau

RISTORANTE

Romano

78 Ristorante Romano ★★$$ Highlights of this simple, casual, and warm Italian eatery include its smiling owner Romano and a seasonally changing menu that might include *insalata caprese, spaghetti alle vongole* (with clams), ravioli in a morel sauce, scampi, and saltimbocca with mozzarella. ◆ Daily lunch and dinner. Reservations recommended. 11 Rue Marbeuf (between Rues du Boccador and Clément-Marot). 01.47.20.85.98. Métro: Alma–Marceau

79 La Fermette Marbeuf 1900 ★★★$$ In 1978, when Jean Laurent purchased what had been a self-service restaurant since 1950, he had no idea of the treasure that lay behind the plastic and Formica. Renovations began, and as workers were tearing down the partition walls they discovered the tile, stained glass, and cast-iron pillars of a spectacular Art Nouveau room that had been hidden for 30 years. The room, it turns out, had been created in 1898 by two young, unknown designers named Hutre and Wielharski. Although the real star here is the decor, the cuisine runs a close second; among the delectations are grilled lamb in a light béarnaise sauce, sliced duck breast with fresh rosemary and peaches, grilled sole with *beurre blanc,* nougat ice cream with apricot sauce, and bittersweet chocolate mousse. A fine selection of eaux-de-vie, Cognacs, and liqueurs await the end of your meal. ◆ Daily lunch and dinner. Reservations required. 5 Rue Marbeuf (at Rue du Boccador). 01.53.23.08.00. Métro: Alma–Marceau

79 24 Rue du Boccador In the late 1940s this apartment building was rife with movie stars such as Brigitte Bardot, Ivy League CIA agents posing as novelists, and legitimate American writers, including Theodore H. White, Art Buchwald, and Irwin Shaw. This is where White, after working for six years as *Time* magazine's Beijing bureau chief, wrote his Pulitzer Prize–winning World War II novel, *The Mountain Road.* In a fifth-floor studio, Buchwald wrote his "Paris After Dark" column for the *Herald Tribune,* and Shaw, in much grander digs, completed his best-selling novel *The Young Lions,* which was published in 1948. ♦ Between Rue Marbeuf and Ave George-V. Métro: Alma–Marceau

80 American Cathedral On 6 July 1905, 100 years after his death, a service was held in this spired late 19th-century Gothic cathedral for John Paul Jones, naval hero of the American Revolution. More than 500 Americans attended. Afterwards Jones's casket was taken to Annapolis, Maryland. ♦ 23 Ave George-V (between Pl de l'Alma and Ave Pierre-1er-de-Serbie). 01.53.23.84.00. Métro: Alma–Marceau

81 Claridge-Bellman $$$ Decorated with antiques, paintings, 17th-century tapestries, Chinese vases, and other costly objets d'art, this posh 40-room hotel is home to the Italian couturiers during the seasonal fashion shows. The dining room is open to hotel guests only. Reserve well in advance. ♦ 37 Rue François-1er (at Rue Marbeuf). 01.47.23.54.42; fax 01.47.28.08.84. Métro: Franklin-D.-Roosevelt

82 Chez André ★★$$ Unchanged since 1938, this bistro bustles at lunchtime with the dressed-for-success crowd from the Champs-Elysées and matronly waitresses loping through with hot plates. Recommended: the poached haddock, short ribs, roast leg of lamb with mashed potatoes, sponge cake with rum sauce, and the affordable house Muscadet and red Graves. ♦ Daily lunch and dinner until 1AM. Reservations recommended. 12 Rue Marbeuf (at Rue Clément-Marot). 01.47.20.59.57. Métro: Franklin-D.-Roosevelt

83 George V $$$$ Art Buchwald put it this way: "Paris without the **George V** would be Cleveland." While not everyone would concur with that particular assessment, most guests agree that this 300-room hotel has something special to offer, and it's not just the red-leather elevator. François Dupré, who owned the property from its opening in 1928 until 1968, amassed a vast collection of antique furniture, Baroque statues, Louis XIV tapestries (the value of these alone is estimated at $6 million), and paintings (among them, *Vase de Roses* by Renoir) that still decorates the public and private rooms. The hotel has long attracted the greats of every field. Duke Ellington stayed here in 1933 while he was performing at the **Salle Pleyel.** He wrote in his memoirs that he spent a long time trying to get out of his suite; apparently it was so enormous, with doors opening onto other rooms or closets, that it was difficult to find the exit. ♦ 31 Ave George-V (between Ave Pierre-1er-de-Serbie and Rue Quentin-Bauchart). 01.47.23.54.00; fax 01.47.20.06.49. Métro: George-V

Within the George V hotel:

Les Princes ★★$$$ The menu at this elegant 1930s-style restaurant runs from the delicate (fillet of sole with spring truffles) to the hearty (veal kidneys in mustard cream sauce, flambéed in Cognac). There's dining on the verdant terrace in summer. ♦ Daily breakfast, lunch, and dinner. Reservations required. 01.47.23.54.00

Bar du George V This bar has the glorious feeling of an old-fashioned salon. ♦ Daily 11AM-2AM. 01.47.23.54.00

Le Grill ★★$$ This chic and relaxed 1930s-style bistro is frequented by business people and those from the entertainment and fashion worlds. The decor here is more contemporary than that of the rest of the hotel, with straw-colored stucco walls and deep-brown leather banquettes. The bill of fare offers traditional French dishes. Order the *fruits de mer* (shellfish platter), or opt for *plat du jour,* which is generally another good choice. ♦ M-F breakfast, lunch, dinner, and late-night snacks; closed in August. 01.47.23.54.00

83 37 Avenue George-V On their honeymoon in 1905, Franklin and Eleanor Roosevelt visited Franklin's aunt, Deborah Delano, who had an apartment at this address. She used to take the newlyweds driving; indeed it was in the **Bois de Boulogne** that FDR learned to drive. ♦ Between Ave Pierre-1er-de-Serbie and Rue Quentin-Bauchart. Métro: George-V

84 Hôtel François I $$$$ This luxurious 40-room hostelry off the Champs-Elysées is a favorite of business travelers. The spacious lobby, bar, and restaurant feature tasteful Art Deco decor. All rooms afford luxurious bath amenities, minibar, and room service. ♦ 7 Rue Magellan (between Rues Christophe-Colomb and de Bassano). 01.47.23.44.04; fax 01.47.23.93.43. Métro: George-V

85 16 Rue Christophe-Colomb In 1898 Henry Adams, grandson of John Quincy Adams and professor of history at Harvard University, stayed in several rooms in this apartment building while reading medieval manuscripts for his book on art and culture,

Mont-Saint-Michel and Chartres. ◆ Between Rue Magellan and Ave Marceau. Métro: George-V

86 L'Ecluse ★★$$ The second in a chain of classy wine bars, it offers vintage Bordeaux and light meals of smoked salmon, carpaccio, and goat cheese. ◆ Daily lunch and dinner until 1AM. 64 Rue François-1er (between Rues Lincoln and Quentin-Bauchart). 01.47.20.77.09. Métro: George-V. Also at: 15 Quai des Grands-Augustins (between Pl St-Michel and Rue Gît-le-Cœur). 01.46.33.58.74. Métro: St-Michel; 15 Pl de la Madeleine (between Blvd Malesherbes and Passage de la Madeleine). 01.42.65.34.69. Métro: Madeleine

87 Virgin Records' Megastore This majestic music shop looks like a Cecil B. De Mille movie set, complete with a monumental marble staircase. Its various levels are replete with a mind-bending selection of records, CDs, tapes, and videos (in English and French), as well as books on music and stereo equipment. There's also a lively cafe on the premises. ◆ M-Th, Su until midnight; F-Sa until 1AM. 52-60 Ave des Champs-Elysées (at Rue La Boétie). 01.49.53.50.00. Métro: Franklin-D.-Roosevelt

87 Guerlain Institut de Beauté You must reserve at least eight days in advance if you wish to visit this Regency-paneled beauty salon and undergo the royal treatment from the perfumed ladies in pink. ◆ M-Sa. 68 Ave des Champs-Elysées (between Rues La Boétie and de Berri). 01.45.62.52.57. Métro: George-V

88 Institut Géographique National The French counterpart of the National Geographic Society in Washington, DC, is a cartographer's heaven, selling maps of the entire universe (at least that which is recognized by the French) and more. You may purchase wall-size maps of the Paris métro, navigation charts of the Seine, infrared satellite photos of France, 1618 city maps of Paris, and four-by-four-foot color aerial photographs of different sectors of downtown Paris so detailed you can make out pedestrians on the Champs-Elysées. ◆ M-Sa. 107 Rue La Boétie (between Rue de Ponthieu and Ave des Champs-Elysées). 01.42.56.06.68. Métro: Franklin-D.-Roosevelt

89 Galerie Lambert Rouland This contemporary art gallery features engravings, photographs, lithographs, and illustrated books. ◆ Tu-Sa afternoons. 62 Rue La Boétie (between Ave Percier and Rue de Courcelles). 01.45.63.51.52. Métro: St-Philippe-du-Roule

90 Régine's Régine, the notorious queen of Paris nightlife, puts in only rare appearances at her enticing, dimly lit private club off the Champs-Elysées, but the **Ritz/Tour d'Argent/ Maxim's** crowd keeps coming back anyway. ◆ Cover. Daily 11PM-dawn. 49 Rue de Ponthieu (between Rues La Boétie and de Berri). 01.43.59.21.13. Métro: Franklin-D.-Roosevelt

91 Gymnase Club The largest health club in Paris offers five floors of aerobics studios, body-building equipment, saunas, Jacuzzis, a solarium, and a juice bar. ◆ M-Sa. 6 Rue de Berri (between Rue de Ponthieu and Ave des Champs-Elysées). 01.43.59.04.58. Métro: George-V

92 Lancaster $$$$ Set in a handsome 19th-century town house, this 58-room first class hotel has an atmosphere more like a private home than a grand hostelry. The rooms are furnished with antiques, and each has individual charm. There's also a relaxed and refined restaurant and an old-fashioned bar. Helen Keller stayed here in 1937, John Steinbeck in 1954, and a continuing parade of American luminaries has sojourned here since then. ◆ 7 Rue de Berri (between Rue d'Artois and Ave des Champs-Elysées). 01.40.76.40.76; fax 01.40.76.40.00. Métro: George-V

92 The Chicago Pizza Pie Factory ★★$ Midwesterners pining for a taste of home should descend to the cavernous brick basement, bright with red-and-white checkered tablecloths and reverberating with Chuck Berry, where they can order a deep-dish pizza with such traditional toppings as pepperoni and mushrooms. There's a Happy Hour with half-price cocktails Monday through Friday from 4 to 8PM. ◆ Daily lunch and dinner until 1AM. 5 Rue de Berri (between Rue d'Artois and Ave des Champs-Elysées). 01.45.62.50.23. Métro: George-V

93 1 Rue de Berri On 17 October 1785, 42-year-old Thomas Jefferson succeeded Benjamin Franklin as minister to France and moved into this mansion, the **Hôtel de Langeac,** designed by architect **Jean-François Chalgrin.** Jefferson resided here for the next four years. It's now divided into shops and offices. ◆ At Ave des Champs-Elysées. Métro: George-V

Fouquet's

94 Fouquet's ★★★$$$ Irish writer James Joyce dined almost every night at this old (1899) high-priced cafe/restaurant that has become a watering hole for show-biz celebrities, glamour girls, and rubberneckers. American novelist Ernest Hemingway may have liberated the **Ritz** bar after World War II, but sexism still reigns here. For the last 80 years, a sign at the seven-stool bar has read: *Les dames seules ne sont pas admises au bar* (No unescorted women allowed at the bar). The maître d', one Monsieur Casanova, offers the spurious explanation that the house rule is for the ladies' own protection. The bill of fare features very traditional French cuisine. Among the dishes that have been on the menu for the past 50 years are *maquereaux* (mackerel) in white wine, *merlan au colbert* (fried whiting), and *hachis parmentier* (mashed potatoes mixed with beef and spices). ♦ Daily breakfast, lunch, and dinner until 2AM. Reservations recommended. 99 Ave des Champs-Elysées (at Ave George-V). 01.47.23.70.60. Métro: George-V

95 Bar Fly ★★$$ Food is secondary here—getting a chance to gawk at the international assemblage of the rich and famous is more to the point. However, there is a perfectly acceptable eclectic menu of Japanese sushi or traditional French fare including puff pastry desserts. As reservations can be hard to come by, dropping in for a drink at the bar is the quicker way to check out the scene. ♦ M-F lunch and dinner; Sa dinner. Reservations recommended. 49-51 Ave George-V (at Rue Vernet). 01.53.67.84.60. Métro: George-V

96 Taillevent ★★★★$$$$ This is as close as a restaurant comes to perfection. Jean-Claude Vrinat, the owner and idea man, and chef Philippe Legendre have made this establishment one of the best dining spots in Paris. Set in a town house with high ceilings, oak-paneled walls, and Louis XV furniture, the place has the feel of a grand bourgeois private club. Its namesake is Guillaume Tirel (a.k.a. Taillevent), the 14th-century royal cook who wrote the first treatise on French cooking, and it offers such innovative signature dishes as *fruits de mer* (seafood) with truffles and pistachios, langoustines with fresh pasta, Barbary duck, veal kidneys, and almond ice cream. The wine list draws on a cellar of 130,000 bottles ranging from collector's items such as the Lafite-Rothschild 1806 to a less risky and far less expensive Château Haut Brion. This is the perfect choice for a top-of-the-line business lunch or that once-in-a-lifetime dining experience. ♦ M-F lunch and dinner; closed one week in February and the month of August. Reservations required well

in advance. 15 Rue Lamennais (between Rue Washington and Ave de Friedland). 01.44.95.15.01; fax 01.42.25.95.18. Métro: Charles-de-Gaulle–Etoile

97 Hôtel de Vigny $$$$ This little hotel features sumptuous wood paneling, a lobby resembling a private London club, and 37 bright and airy rooms that are royally furnished with antiques, puffy down comforters, and private Jacuzzis. There's a bar, but no restaurant. ♦ 9-11 Rue Balzac (at Rue Lord-Byron). 01.40.75.04.39; fax 01.40.75.05.81. Métros: George-V, Charles-de-Gaulle–Etoile

98 Pierre Gagnaire ★★★★$$$ One of the year's most-anticipated openings, this elegant dining place has already been awarded two Michelin stars. Chef Gagnaire is one of the most skilled practioners of blending exotic ingredients: His uses of sweet and sour are legendary. In the modern room diners savor poached salmon with chutney, duck foie gras wrapped in bacon, roasted duck topped with lime and served with bitter melons, veal with tomato marmalade and tiny squid, and herbed sea bass with fresh vegetables. Desserts are just as captivating—the dried grapefruit *daquoise* is a hit. ♦ M-F dinner. Reservations recommended. 6 Rue Balzac (between Ave des Champs-Elysées and Rue Lord-Byron). 01.44.35.18.25; fax 01.44.35.18.27. Métro: Charles-de-Gaulle–Etoile

99 Lido The largest cabaret in Paris, this lavish extravaganza outglitters Las Vegas with its newest $15-million revue starring the famous **Bluebell Girls,** whose dance numbers are choreographed by computer and who wear $4 million worth of hi-tech costumes incorporating fiber optics, fake fur, leather, and the obligatory feathers and sequins. Dazzling special effects include aerial and aquatic ballets, a motorized flying dragon, water sprays, and a skating rink that rises out of the floor. Throw in a few jugglers, acrobats, and bare-breasted dancers decorously lowered from the ceiling and you have your basic night at the **Lido.** It's always packed with Japanese tourists, car salesmen, and sailors on leave. ♦ Cover. Shows: Daily 10PM, midnight; doors open at 8PM for the dinner spectacle. Reservations recommended. 116 *bis* Ave des Champs-Elysées (between Rues

Washington and Balzac). 01.40.76.56.00, 01.40.76.56.10. Métro: George-V

99 Burger King $ This bustling establishment (one of 12 in Paris) serves traditional American cuisine, called *le fast food*, to homesick Yankees and a young and foolish international clientele. *Spécialités de la maison* include *Le Whopper avec fromage, les frites*, et *le milk shake*. A bronze plaque notes that on Bastille Day 1985 more Whoppers were sold here than in any other Burger King in the world. ♦ Daily lunch and dinner; F-Sa until 2AM. No credit cards accepted. 122 Ave des Champs-Elysées (between Rues Washington and Balzac). 01.45.62.03.31. Métro: George-V

100 La Boutique Flora Danica ★★$$$ The pleasures of Danish dining—pickled herring, eel, marinated salmon, shrimp salad, roast beef with onions, Tuborg on tap, and the flakiest pastries around—abound in this informal luncheonette with blond-wood tables and cheerful abstract art. In summer, meals are served in an umbrella-shaded courtyard. ♦ Daily lunch and dinner; takeout available in the evening. 142 Ave des Champs-Elysées (between Rues Balzac and Arsène-Houssaye). 01.43.59.20.41. Métro: Charles-de-Gaulle–Etoile

100 Copenhague ★★$$$ Upstairs from **La Boutique Flora Danica,** this restaurant serves slightly higher-priced Danish cuisine in a more intimate and modern setting. ♦ M-F lunch and dinner; Sa dinner; closed in August and the first week of January. 142 Ave des Champs-Elysées (between Rues Balzac and Arsène-Houssaye). 01.43.59.20.41. Métro: Charles-de-Gaulle–Etoile

OFFICE DE TOURISME DE PARIS

101 Office de Tourisme de Paris Home of the city's official tourist bureau, this office provides visitors with free maps, sightseeing information, and same-day hotel reservations for those stuck without a room for the night. ♦ Daily 9AM-8PM. 127 Ave des Champs-Elysées (between Rues Galilée and de Presbourg). 01.49.52.53.54. Métros: Charles-de-Gaulle–Etoile, George-V

102 133 Avenue des Champs-Elysées After World War II, General Dwight D. Eisenhower, supreme commander of the Allied Forces in Europe, had his headquarters here in what was the old **Hôtel Astoria.** He asked for a room with a view of the **Arc de Triomphe,** his favorite structure in Paris. The hotel was destroyed in a fire in 1972; the present

building houses offices and a drugstore. ♦ At Rue de Presbourg. Métro: Charles-de-Gaulle–Etoile

Within 133 Avenue des Champs-Elysées:

Drugstore des Champs-Elysées In addition to aspirin and Band-Aids, this drugstore sells gourmet groceries, quick brasserie meals, wristwatches, banana splits, and Cuban cigars. ♦ Daily 9AM-2AM. 01.44.43.79.00, 01.47.20.39.24

Raphael

103 Raphael $$$$ This luxurious 87-room lodging place with Louis XVI and Louis XV decor attracts Italian and American movie stars. There's a sumptuously decorated restaurant. ♦ 17 Ave Kléber (at Ave des Portugais). 01.44.28.00.28; fax 01.45.01.21.50. Métro: Kléber

104 Le Duplex ★★$$ The beautiful people who frequent this restaurant and nightclub come to see and be seen. If you don't want to stand outside under bright lights hoping you're cool enough to be allowed into the nightclub, make dinner reservations. You'll enjoy typical bistro food along with a stupendous view of the **Arc de Triomphe,** and afterwards you can go directly downstairs to the club, which boasts the best sound system in Paris. ♦ Tu-Sa dinner; nightclub: daily 11PM-4AM. Reservations recommended on weekends. 8 Ave Foch (between Rues de Presbourg and Rude). 01.45.00.45.00. Métro: Charles-de-Gaulle–Etoile

105 Le Méridien Etoile $$$ Conveniently located across from the **Palais des Congrès,** this 1,025-room hotel is perfect for the business traveler. It offers the two-floor **Le Club Président,** which is like a private British club. In addition to traditional business services, **Le Club** features voice mail, individual fax and phone lines on request, personalized check-in/-out service, and small meeting rooms. All rooms in the hostelry have direct-dial telephones, minibar, safe, and satellite television. And with the **Bois de Boulogne** and the **Arc de Triomphe** nearby, the vacationing visitor will be just steps away from two of Paris's pleasures. There are three restaurants (all face a garden, each landscaped to complement the particular dining spot's decor), a Sunday jazz brunch in the lobby, two bars, a **Häagen-Dazs** ice-cream shop, and a jazz club. ♦ 81 Blvd Gouvion-St-

Cyr (between Pl de la Porte-Maillot and Rue Belidor). 01.40.68.34.34; fax 01.40.68.31.31. Métro: Porte-Maillot

Within Le Méridien Etoile:

Le Clos Longchamp ★★★$$$ Furnished in a sophisticated floral motif, this one-Michelin-star dining room is a delight. Jean-Marie Meulien presides over the kitchen, incorporating Asian flavors into French Mediterranean cooking. Try such delicacies as *crevettes aux herbs thaïes* (Thai-style prawns), *agneau en navarin au tandoori* (tandoori lamb stew), and *rognon de veau au jus de noix* (veal kidneys in a nut sauce). Leave room for the wonderful cheese tray and delicious desserts. Ask the very knowledgeable sommelier for a wine selection. ♦ M-F breakfast, lunch, and dinner. Reservations recommended; jacket recommended. 01.40.68.30.40

Lionel Hampton Jazz Club Known throughout Paris for its high-quality music, this hospitable club attracts well-known international jazz and blues players and bands. Performers include B.B. King, Oscar Peterson, the Count Basie Orchestra, Rodney Scott, and Karen Alison. ♦ Cover. M-Sa jazz 10PM-2AM. Reservations recommended. 01.40.68.30.42

106 Place Charles-de-Gaulle Once called Place d'Etoile (Square of the Star), this square was created by Baron Haussmann in 1854 when he added seven avenues to the existing five to form a 12-pointed star. Although the area is a snarl of traffic, it was always the street where the rich and famous, such as Aristotle Onassis, Maria Callas, Claude Debussy, the Shah of Iran, and Prince Rainier of Monaco, lived. One of the avenues that begins here, Avenue Foch, is the widest (390 feet) in Paris; it leads to the **Bois de Boulogne.** ♦ At Aves des Champs-Elysées and de la Grande-Armée, and Aves Kléber and de Wagram. Métro: Charles-de-Gaulle–Etoile

On Place Charles-de-Gaulle:

L'Arc de Triomphe If Emperor Napoléon hadn't changed his mind in the nick of time, Parisians would be staring not at this magnificent arch (pictured at right), but at a 160-foot-high elephant squirting water from its trunk. The decision was so close that a model of the elephant was made and stood for a while at the Place de la Bastille. In the end, Napoléon chose the more tasteful triumphal arch to honor his army's victory at the Battle of Austerlitz. (The sun sets exactly along this axis on 2 December, the anniversary of that victory.) This triumphal arch is 164 feet high and 148 feet wide.

Construction of the arch began in 1806, and the walls had scarcely risen above the ground by the time Napoléon divorced the childless Empress Josephine and wed Princess Marie Louise of Austria in 1810. The bridal procession passed through a fake arch of canvas, hastily constructed for the occasion by the architect **Jean-François Chalgrin.** The arch was not completed until 1836, well after Napoléon's downfall; only four years later, a chariot bearing his body would pass beneath the arch on its way to the **Invalides.** On 14 July 1919, victorious French soldiers marched through the structure. The following month, pilot Sergeant Godefroy flew a plane with a wingspan of 29 feet through the 48-foot-wide arch. On 11 November 1920 the body of the Unknown Soldier was laid in state here to commemorate the dead soldiers of World War I. The eternal flame at the tomb (first kindled in 1923) is lit each evening at 6:30PM. On 26 August 1944, after the Germans had been routed from the capital, General Charles de Gaulle led a jubilant crowd to the arch, then walked down the Champs-Elysées to **Notre-Dame,** where the *Te Deum*

L'Arc de Triomphe

Mass was celebrated in thanksgiving. On state occasions, an enormous French flag hangs inside the arch.

It would be suicide to cross the Place Charles-de-Gaulle on foot (cars have a hard enough time); pedestrians can take an underground passage. An elevator or 284 steps will take you (during daylight hours only) to the platform at the top, which affords a magnificent panorama of Paris.

On the Arc de Triomphe:

Departure of the Volunteers Known as *La Marseillaise,* this sculpture (pictured below) by François Rude is the arch's most inspired and noteworthy stonework. (It is on the right with your back to the Champs-Elysées.) In 1916, on the day the Battle of Verdun started, the sword brandished by the figure representing the Republic broke and fell off. The disarmed sculpture was immediately hidden to conceal the accident from the superstitious, who might have seen it as a bad omen.

107 Chiberta ★★★$$$ The most chic nouvelle-cuisine restaurant in Paris is made even more hip by its Art Deco decor. Chef Eric Coisel offers seasonal specialties such as wild mushroom fricassee in winter, truffle-and-parsley ravioli in autumn, and salmon with fresh artichokes and asparagus come spring. ♦ M-F lunch and dinner; closed in August. Reservations recommended. 3 Rue Arsène-Houssaye (between Aves des Champs-Elysées and de Friedland). 01.45.63.77.90. Métro: Charles-de-Gaulle–Etoile

108 Royal Monceau $$$$ This luxurious 220-room establishment has attracted such celebrities as Arnold Schwarzenegger, Tina Turner, and rock star Sting. A Madonna video and episodes of "Dallas" have also been shot here. The saunas, steam rooms, herbal massages, and "spa cuisine" restaurant at the adjoining **Thermes Health Spa** are open to hotel guests. ♦ 35-39 Ave Hoche (between Ave Berthie-Albrecht and Rue Beaujon). 01.42.99.88.00; fax 01.42.99.89.90. Métro: Ternes

The pyramid designed by I. M. Pei isn't the first to grace the Cour Napoléon. After the murder of revolutionary Jean-Paul Marat, his corpse, along with his writing desk and the bathtub in which he met his demise, was placed in a wooden pyramid that stood near the Carrousel Arch.

"If you are lucky enough to have lived in Paris as a young man, then wherever you go for the rest of your life, it stays with you, for Paris is a moveable feast."

Ernest Hemingway, *A Moveable Feast*

Within the Royal Monceau:

Le Carpaccio ★★★$$ The most celebrated Italian restaurant in Paris has an elegant, airy Venetian decor and a kitchen that's simply topnotch. House specialties by chef Angelo Paracucchi include risotto Milanese, lamb cutlets, and grilled fish. ♦ Daily lunch and dinner; closed in August. Reservations recommended. 01.42.99.98.90

Le Jardin ★★$$$ The lush, flower-filled setting is perhaps the most alluring aspect of this garden pavilion eatery, but the fish dishes are also memorable. Try the simple sardines *grillées en saupiquet* (grilled sardines in a spicy sauce) or *avec leur croûton de foie de volaille* (grilled sardines in a spicy sauce with chicken liver). ♦ M-F lunch and dinner. 01.42.99.98.70.

109 14 Rue de Tilsitt It was April of 1925: *The Great Gatsby* was selling briskly and American novelist F. Scott Fitzgerald was at the height of his fame. He and his wife, Zelda, took an apartment at this address and Fitzgerald's drunken binges began. There were times when he would stumble into the Paris bureau of the *Chicago Tribune* and William L. Shirer and James Thurber would have to pack him home in a taxi to greater ignominies ahead. This is still an apartment building. ♦ At Ave de Wagram. Métro: Charles-de-Gaulle–Etoile

Departure of the Volunteers

MICHAEL STORRINGS

110 Guy Savoy ★★★$$$$ This large, handsome dining room simply decorated with Japanese-style flower arrangements perfectly complements the remarkable cuisine of Chef Savoy, a shining star in the Parisian culinary firmament. Try the artichoke soup with parmesan and truffles or *the bar en écaille grillé aux epices douces* (sea bass grilled in sweet spices). Everything looks as good as it tastes—and vice-versa. ◆ M-F lunch and dinner; Sa dinner. Reservations recommended. 18 Rue Troyon (between Aves de Wagram and Mac-Mahon).

01.43.80.40.61. Métro: Charles-de-Gaulle–Etoile

111 L'Etoile Verte ★★$ This small, inexpensive neighborhood restaurant serves traditional French cuisine. The waitresses can be gruff, but, at these prices, politeness is perhaps too much to expect. Enjoy such fundamental fare as coq au vin, sautéed veal, and chateaubriand béarnaise. ◆ Daily lunch and dinner. 13 Rue Brey (between Ave de Wagram and Rue de Montenotte). 01.43.80.69.34. Métro: Charles-de-Gaulle–Etoile

Bests

Gérard Thiault
Head Concierge, Hôtel Plaza Athénée

My favorite restaurants:

The greatest—**L'Ambrosie** and **Taillevent.**

With character—**Le Grand Véfour, Pré Catelan,** and **Le Jules Verne.**

Romantic—**Beauvilliers** and **L'Orangerie.**

Bistro—**De Chez Eux.**

My favorite places:

Place des Vosges, the **Marais,** the **Jardins de Bagatelle** in the **Bois de Boulogne,** trips on *bateaux mouches,* **l'Ile de la Cité, Montmartre,** the excellent view from the top of the **Grande Arche de la Défense,** the expanded **Louvre,** the **Musée d'Orsay.**

Catherine Davenas
Contemporary Art Lover

Advanced contemporary art galleries are not easy to find—you may pass their opaque glass windows by on the street or have to push a heavy porte cochere and go upstairs. So get the *Galeries Mode d'Emploi* map and listing at the famous and beautiful **Galerie Yvon Lambert.**

Neotu shows producers and sells international young designers.

agnès b. sells unnoticeably noticeable clothes, and art from emerging artists in the next court.

Sanz-Sans club bar for the video mirror, which shows people passing by and coming in. Inexpensive food (great plain steamed vegetables as well as pasta, meat, etc.).

Christian Constant made himself famous for his creative chocolates with exotic tastes.

Exercise in a contemporary way, trying to find the 135 medallions inserted in the pavement with the name of French astronomer Arago on them. The largest and most discreet public monument in the world runs along the Paris Meridian from **Montmartre** to **Montparnasse** and beyond. Two easy ones to find: on **Rue de Seine,** at the corner of

Rue des Beaux-Arts, and the passageway under the **Institut de France.**

Philippe Bourguignon
Assistant Manager/Head Sommelier, Restaurant Laurent

Wine Bars: **L'Angevin,** a "new generation" wine bar; **Au Vin des Rues,** user-friendly wine; **Le Moulin à Vin,** wine at night.

Le Val d'Or, the man from Auvergne with a heart of gold. For the quality of the purchases and the wine bottled by the owner.

Christopher Evans and Victor Wong
Designers, evansandwong

Your basic needs are perfectly fulfilled in Paris:

Air: the blossoming trees during the month of June.

Water: the waterfall in the artificial grotto at the **Parc des Buttes-Chaumont.**

Food: shopping for fresh produce on **Rue du Faubourg-St-Denis.**

Shelter: protection from the elements provided by the canopy of any neighborhood cafe.

Clothing: all you need to make your own at the **Marché St-Pierre.**

Love: anywhere, anytime, anyway—after all, it's Paris.

Christian Ferron
Head Concierge, Hôtel Crillon

Yvan: Yvan is a young chef and host. If one spends both morning and evening in his restaurant it is because one eats well and is well received and the prices are reasonable.

Les Puces de Paris–St-Ouen at the **Porte de Clignancourt**: Very few people know that one can go to this flea market on Friday mornings. It's open from 5AM until noon and it's the best day to make wonderful finds.

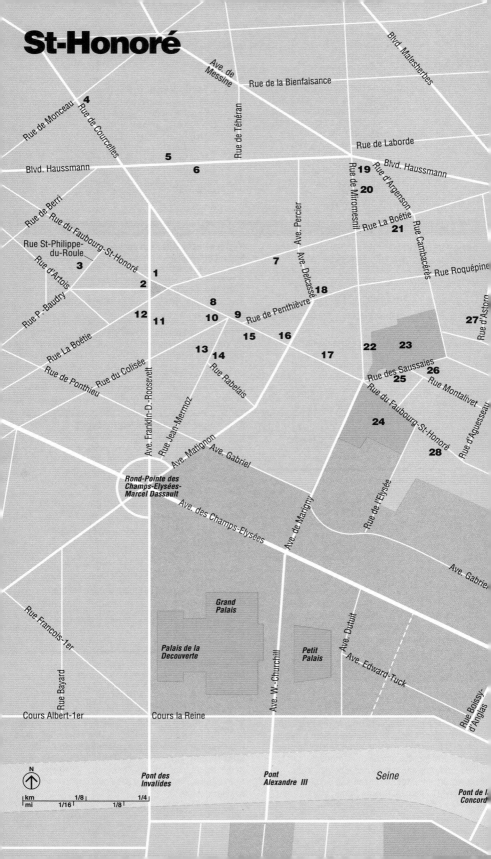

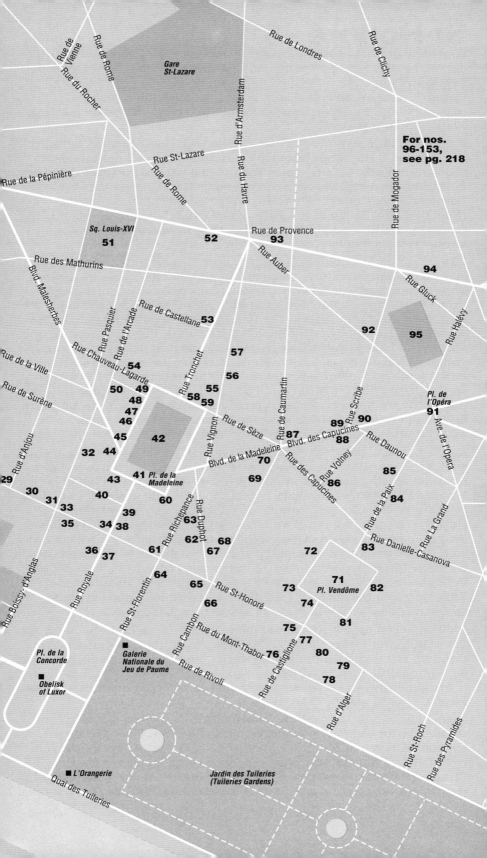

Rue de Vienne

Rue de Rome

Rue du Rocher

Rue de Londres

Rue de Clichy

Gare St-Lazare

Rue d'Amsterdam

For nos. 96-153, see pg. 218

Rue St-Lazare

Rue du Havre

Rue de Rome

Rue de Mogador

Rue de la Pépinière

Sq. Louis-XVI
51

52

Rue de Provence
93

Rue Auber

Rue Gluck
94

Rue des Mathurins

Blvd. Malesherbes

Rue de Castellane
53

92

95

Rue Halévy

Rue Pasquier

Rue de l'Arcade

57

Rue Tronchet

Rue Chauveau-Lagarde

56

Rue de la Ville

54

55

Rue Scribe

Pl. de l'Opéra
91

Rue de Surène

50 49

58 59

89 90

Ave. de l'Opéra

48
47
46

Rue de Séze

Rue de Caumartin

88

Rue Daunou

32 44

45

42

Rue Vignon

87

Blvd. des Capucines

85

Rue d'Anjou

43

41 Pl. de la Madeleine

Blvd. de la Madeleine
70

Rue des Capucines

Rue Volney

86

Rue de la Paix

29

30

40

60

69

84

Rue Boissy-d'Anglais

31 33

39

Rue Richepance

83

Rue Danielle-Casanova

Rue La Grand

35

34 38

Rue Duphot

63

72

36 37

61

62

68

67

71
Pl. Vendôme

82

64

65

Rue St-Honoré

73

74

81

Rue Royale

66

75

80

79

Rue St-Florentin

Rue Cambon

Rue du Mont-Thabor

76

77

78

Pl. de la Concorde

Galerie Nationale du Jeu de Paume

Rue de Rivoli

Rue de Castiglione

Rue d'Alger

Rue St-Roch

Rue des Pyramides

Obelisk of Luxor

L'Orangerie

Quai des Tuileries

Jardin des Tuileries (Tuileries Gardens)

St-Honoré

Forget Fifth Avenue and Rodeo Drive. The **Faubourg St-Honoré,** named after the patron saint of pastry chefs, takes the cake as the world's most glamorous shopping district. *La plus haute* of international haute couture is here: Christian Dior, Yves Saint Laurent, Lanvin, Gucci, Hermès, Pierre Cardin, Guy Laroche, Ungaro, Courrèges, and Jean Paul Gaultier, not to mention countless purveyors of such extravagances as diamonds, crystal, silver, mink, caviar, truffles, and Champagne.

This district includes other dazzling sights as well. There is a small, remarkable art collection at the **Musée Jacquemart-André;** several architectural jewels, including **St-Roch** (the city's finest Baroque church) and the splendid **Palais Royal** and its gardens; the city's two most important theaters, the **Opéra Garnier** and the **Comédie Française;** and several grand hotels, such as **Hôtel Le Bristol, St-James et Albany,** and the **Hôtel Ritz,** whose name is synonymous with luxury. **Rue du Faubourg-St-Honoré** is made for that favorite Parisian pastime, tasteful loitering.

Plan on visiting St-Honoré on a weekday from Tuesday through Friday, since many shops and exhibits are closed on Monday, and the streets are crowded on weekends. Start with an early-bird pastry and coffee at one of the Right Bank's finest bakeries, **Boulangerie St-Philippe** (open at 7:30AM), and continue down Rue du Faubourg-St-Honoré to the street's most fashionable stretch, which lies between the presidential **Palais de l'Elysée** at **Avenue de Marigny** and **Rue Royale.** Those getting a late jump on the day might consider visiting **Le Val d'Or,** a popular neighborhood wine bar, where an elite crowd stands with a mid-morning Bordeaux. While lovers of the Italian Renaissance keep their date with Donatello, Botticelli, and Titian at the **Musée Jacquemart-André,** serious shoppers will head down **Embassy Row** (where the American, British, and Japanese ambassadors hang their hats) and make a mandatory stop at **Hermès,** the world-famous leather and accessories shop.

As you pass onto Rue Royale, which starts at the **Place de la Concorde** and ends at the **Place de la Madeleine,** you will gaze upon the finest in antiques, tapestries, jewelry, and silver. By midday you will have reached Place de la Madeleine. Survey the plaza and whet your appetite with truffles at **La Maison de la Truffe,** chocolates at **Marquise de Sévigné,** and cheese at **La Ferme St-Hubert.** When you're finished with those delicacies, why not spend your life's savings on the four-star nouvelle cuisine at **Lucas-Carton** or on a feast of caviar and Champagne at **Caviar Kaspia?** If you're down to your last few francs, you'll have to settle for a modest, though tasty, repast at **Ladurée** or **L'Ecluse.** Those feeling brash and regal by turns could knock back a shot of one of the 156 whiskeys sold at **Harry's New York Bar** and weave into **Charvet** to buy a cravat, as Edward VII was in the habit of doing not so long ago.

While your companion is changing money at **American Express,** line up for tickets inside the **Opéra Garnier** (also known as the **Paris Opéra**), **Charles Garnier**'s architectural birthday cake. If you're an antiques hound, **Le Louvre des Antiquaires,** with 240 dealers under one roof, will keep you occupied for hours. Otherwise, watch (as everyone from Louis XIV to Colette has) the sun set on the gardens of the **Palais Royal.**

Dinnertime already? Consider the best (and most expensive) sushi in Paris at **Issé** or go for broke at **Le Grand Véfour** or the century-old **Restaurant Drouant.** An evening in the neighborhood might consist of polishing your French at the **Comédie Française,** catching a classical ballet or modern dance performance at the **Opéra Garnier,** taking in a movie on **Boulevard Haussmann,** or people watching from the terrace of **Café de la Paix.** If you still have energy to spare, you can return to where you began the day's outing and spend the night dancing till dawn at **Keur Samba**. Glittering St-Honoré offers glamour and grandeur around the clock.

---

1 St-Philippe-du-Roule Before this church was completed in 1784, its parishioners prayed in the chapel of a local leprosy asylum. Designed by **Jean-François Chalgrin** (better known for his **Arc de Triomphe**), it has three aisles divided by two rows of fluted Ionic columns, a floor plan resembling that of the early Christian basilicas. ♦ 154 Rue du Faubourg-St-Honoré (at Ave Myron-Herrick). 01.43.59.24.56. Métro: St-Philippe-du-Roule

2 Boulangerie St-Philippe ★★$ This bakery's luncheonette (beside the crowded bread counter) features *foie de veau à la vapeur* (steamed veal liver), delicious house terrines, grilled meats, and wine by the glass. Order one of the éclairs, a slice of lime tart, or *tarte tatin* (apple tart) for dessert and find out why the bakery is always crowded. ♦ M-F, Su 7AM-8PM. 73 Ave Franklin-D.-Roosevelt (at Rue du Commandant-Rivière). 01.43.59.78.76. Métro: St-Philippe-du-Roule

Hôtel Bradford

3 Hôtel Bradford $$$ A surprising oasis of calm and friendliness is wedged between the harried Champs-Elysées and Rue du Faubourg-St-Honoré. The 48 rooms are spick-and-span and big enough to dance in. There's no restaurant. ♦ 10 Rue St-Philippe-du-Roule (between Rues d'Artois and du Faubourg-St-Honoré). 01.45.63.20.20; fax 01.45.63.20.07. Métro: St-Philippe-du-Roule

4 C.T. Loo and Co. Located in a fantastic three-story pagoda equipped with a Chinese elevator, Michael Bosc's Asian art gallery traffics in Orientalia. Get a close look at the lacquered hardwood furniture from the Ming Dynasty and the 13th-century Nepalese sculptures. ♦ M-Sa; closed in August. 48 Rue de Courcelles (at Pl du Pérou). 01.45.62.53.15, 01.42.25.17.23. Métro: St-Philippe-du-Roule

5 Musée Jacquemart-André Originally this Neo-Classical building was the private residence of banker Edouard André and artist Nélie Jacquemart. The couple poured considerable amounts of money into their exquisite art collection, which now belongs to the **Institut de France**. The collection features Italian Renaissance and French 18th-century art, including works by Donatello, Botticelli, Tintoretto, Titian, Bernini, Watteau, Fragonard, Tiepolo, Rembrandt, Reynolds, and Murillo. Also noteworthy are the four

Gobelins tapestries. For a quick respite, try the cafe serving light snacks. ♦ Admission. M-Su 10AM-6PM; group tours are available. 158 Blvd Haussmann (between Rues de Téhéran and de Courcelles). 01.45.62.39.94, 01.42.89.04.91. Métro: Miromesnil

6 Ma Bourgogne ★★$$ This reputable wine bar won the coveted *Meilleur Pot* award for the best *bistrot du vin* in 1962 and is known for hot daily lunch specials such as *oeufs en Meurette* (eggs cooked in red wine with bacon) and steak with béarnaise sauce. Bourgogne and Beaujolais wines are featured. ♦ M-F breakfast, lunch, and dinner; closed in July. Reservations recommended for lunch. 133 Blvd Haussmann (between Ave Percier and Rue de Courcelles). 01.45.63.50.61. Métro: Miromesnil

7 Salle Gaveau This concert hall hosts classical and chamber music performances. In June 1921 Harvard's glee club sang here, becoming the first such American student singing group to perform in France. ♦ Admission. Box office daily 11AM-6PM; closed in August. 45 Rue La Boétie (between Ave Delcassé and Rue du Faubourg-St-Honoré). 01.49.53.05.07. Métro: St-Philippe-du-Roule

8 Cailleux This shop is full of works of art, primarily by 18th-century artists, including drawings and paintings by Watteau, Boucher, and Fragonard. ♦ M-F; closed in August. 136 Rue du Faubourg-St-Honoré (between Rues de Penthièvre and La Boétie). 01.43.59.25.24. Métro: St-Philippe-du-Roule

9 Henri Picard et Fils Founded in 1860, this exquisite bookstore deals in bound treasures such as Diderot's 35-volume, 18th-century encyclopedia and *Democracy in America* by Alexis de Tocqueville. ♦ M-Sa; closed in August. 126 Rue du Faubourg-St-Honoré (at Rue de Penthièvre). 01.43.59.28.11. Métro: St-Philippe-du-Roule

10 Dalloyau This dessert shop has been perfecting its chocolate since 1802. Sample the *buisson* (chocolate cake with raspberry), *gâteau mogador* (a confection of chocolate cake and chocolate mousse with a racing stripe of raspberry jam), or the best-selling *Opéra*, with layer upon layer of multi-textured chocolate. The Sunday morning lines attest to the best croissants in town. ♦ Daily. 101 Rue du Faubourg-St-Honoré (between Rues du Colisée and La Boétie). 01.43.59.18.10. Métro: St-Philippe-du-Roule

11 Le Val d'Or ★★★$ On the ground floor of St-Honoré's most popular wine bar you'll find all the ingredients for a delicious quick lunch: quiche, charcuterie, perhaps the best sandwiches in Paris, and wines admirably selected by M. Rongier. Try the Côtes-du-Brouilly and Côtes-du-Rhône and, in November, the new Beaujolais (Rongier always manages to snag some of the best). Under the exceedingly civil house rules, wine must be ordered by the bottle, but you pay only for what you drink. Lunchtime is the liveliest time. Those looking for a more leisurely meal can dine downstairs on hearty *boeuf bourguignon.* ♦ M-Sa breakfast, lunch, and early dinner. 28 Ave Franklin-D.-Roosevelt (between Rues du Colisée and La Boétie). 01.43.59.95.81. Métro: St-Philippe-du-Roule

12 Keur Samba This nightclub uncorks around 2AM when actors, models, musicians, and diplomats of every stripe and color push their way past Kane at the door. This black-upholstered, after-hours playpen is located near **Régine's.** ♦ Cover. Daily midnight-7AM. 79 Rue La Boétie (between Ave Franklin-D.-Roosevelt and Rue de Ponthieu). 01.43.59.03.10. Métro: St-Philippe-du-Roule

13 Chez Germain ★$ This inexpensive bistro serves quick lunches to the models, fashion designers, and art dealers who work in the neighborhood. Sample the coq au vin, *jarret aux lentilles* (ham hock with lentils), or steak in roquefort sauce. The delicious desserts come from **Le Merisier,** the restaurant's elegant cousin across the street. ♦ M-F lunch only. Reservations recommended. 19 Rue Jean-Mermoz (between Rues de Ponthieu and du Faubourg-St-Honoré). 01.43.59.29.24. Métro: Franklin-D.-Roosevelt

Le Merisier

14 Le Merisier ★★★$$ In keeping with this restaurant's name, which means "the wild cherry tree," owners Jean-Paul and Françoise Boyrie have paneled the dining room in cherry wood. The warm and handsome room is often filled with executives from the nearby embassies, who come here for the continental breakfast and the exceptional lunch. Good choices are the *terrine à l'ancienne et sa confiture d'oignons* (duck pâté with Armagnac and onion preserves), the steak *tartare,* and the *pavé de rumsteck aux morilles* (steak with morels). For dessert, the *larme au chocolat griottines* (a tear-shaped chocolate shell filled with chocolate mousse and kirsch-soaked

cherries) is widely acclaimed. ♦ M-F breakfast and lunch; dinner by appointment only for 12 or more. Reservations recommended. 28 Rue Jean-Mermoz (at Rue Rabelais). 01.42.25.36.06. Métros: St-Philippe-du-Roule, Franklin-D.-Roosevelt

15 Galerie Berheim-Jeune Exhibits of works by such masters as Renoir and Picasso are held in this art gallery. Around 1840 William Thackeray took a small pied-à-terre in the same building. ♦ Tu-Sa. 83 Rue du Faubourg-St-Honoré (between Ave Matignon and Rue Jean-Mermoz). Métro: St-Philippe-du-Roule

16 Jullien Cornic This prestigious shop is a Circe's Isle to connoisseurs and collectors of art books. Among its allures are beautifully bound catalogs of the oeuvres of artists as diverse as Edouard Manet and Norman Rockwell, and an eclectic assortment of books on interior design, architecture, and fashion (everything on the rag trade from Balmain to buttons). An annex around the corner specializes in rare art books. ♦ Tu-F. 118 Rue du Faubourg-St-Honoré (at Ave Matignon). Annex: 29 Ave Matignon (at Rue du Faubourg-St-Honoré). 01.42.68.10.10. Métro: St-Philippe-du-Roule

17 Hôtel Le Bristol $$$$ One of the last and perhaps the most prestigious of Paris's grand hotels, this newly refurbished establishment caters to the diplomats and dignitaries who conduct business down the street at the **Palais de l'Elysée.** All 195 rooms and 41 suites feature luxurious silk fabrics, antiques, Persian carpets, crystal chandeliers, and marble bathrooms, placing the hotel in a class by itself. Ulysses S. Grant was a guest here in the fall of 1887, and Sinclair Lewis lived here in 1925, the year he won the Pulitzer Prize (which he declined to accept) for his novel *Arrowsmith.* Most rooms overlook the pretty garden. ♦ 112 Rue du Faubourg-St-Honoré (between Rue de Miromesnil and Ave Matignon). 01.53.43.43.00; fax 01.53.43.43.01. Métros: Champs-Elysées–Clemenceau, Miromesnil, St-Philippe-du-Roule

Within Hôtel Le Bristol:

Le Bristol ★★★$$$$ This formal dining room of the hotel, which has been awarded a Michelin star, brings forth images of elegance with its Regency-style and wood-paneled decor. Chef Michel del Burgo presides over the kitchen, adding the flavors of his Southern

French background to create some of the best cuisine in Paris. Try *gros gnocchi de peau de courgettes au caillé de brebis* (gnocchi made with zucchini and curdled goat milk), *dos de loup clouté de romarin grillé au feu de bois* (grilled sea perch flavored with rosemary), the fragrant truffle-parmesan risotto, or *coquilles St-Jacques* garnished with dried Sicilian tomatoes. A good selection of desserts including coconut ice cream and pineapple poached in rum round out a fine meal. ◆ Daily lunch and dinner. Reservations recommended. 01.42.66.91.45

Bar du Bristol Don't order lemonade from barkeeper Pascal Havel: Try the Nathaly (a drink with Grand Marnier, white Martini vermouth, Cognac, and raspberry brandy). ◆ Daily 10:30AM-1:30AM

17 Le Sphinx Together with its sister shop, L'Aigle Impériale (around the corner at 3 Rue de Miromesnil, 01.42.65.27.33), this place has one of the city's largest collections of antique weapons and Napoléonic memorabilia. Here you will find portraits of the emperor, a bottle of 1811 Cognac he never got around to drinking, and one of Napoléon's trademark hats enshrined in a glass case. The proprietor, Pierre de Souzy, will part with the latter item for a mere $100,000. ◆ M-Sa. 104 Rue du Faubourg-St-Honoré (between Rue de Miromesnil and Ave Matignon). 01.42.65.90.96. Métros: St-Philippe-du-Roule, Miromesnil

18 Trompe-l'Oeil On the corner of Rue de Penthièvre and Avenue Delcassé, a man gazes from his balcony at a bronze nude as two doves flutter away, casting shadows on the walls. Painted by artist Rieti in 1985, this trompe l'oeil enlivens an otherwise unremarkable intersection. ◆ Rue de Penthièvre and Ave Delcassé. Métros: Miromesnil, St-Philippe-du-Roule

19 René-Gérard Saint-Ouen Instead of clay, this sculptor uses bread dough to create shapes—elephants, chickens, half-moons, bicycles, even the **Eiffel Tower**—for any whim or occasion. If you can't bring yourself to eat these yeasty works of art, brush on some varnish and hang them in the kitchen. ◆ M-Sa. 111 Blvd Haussmann (at Rue d'Argenson). 01.42.65.06.25. Métro: Miromesnil

20 Le Marcande ★★$$$ Chef Joël Verron prepares such dishes as pigeon with wild mushrooms, langoustines with Chinese cabbage and balsamic vinegar, lentil and foie gras terrine, and a delicious *chausson aux pruneaux et à l'armagnac* (plum turnover with Armagnac). Ask for a table with a view of the charming courtyard. ◆ M-F lunch and dinner; closed in August. Reservations recommended. 52 Rue de Miromesnil (between Rue La Boétie and Blvd Haussmann). 01.42.65.19.14. Métro: Miromesnil

21 19 Rue La Boétie Thirteen-year-old Henry James developed an addiction to the croissants sold across the street when he lived here from 1856 to 1857. It is still a residential building. ◆ Between Rues Cambacérès and de Miromesnil. Métro: St-Philippe-du-Roule

22 8 Rue de Miromesnil In May 1961, pop artist Robert Rauschenberg's first solo show was held here and received rave reviews. The building now houses several shops. ◆ Between Pl Beauvau and Rue de Penthièvre. Métro: Miromesnil

At 8 Rue de Miromesnil:

Arts et Marine A veritable armada of hand-crafted model wooden sailing vessels floats before your eyes. Among the replicas are the *Navire Négrier* (a 1780s slave ship) and the *Navire Barlaresqué* (a French copy of a Turkish pirate ship). Also for sale are old brass compasses, ivory-clad binoculars, and frigates in bottles. There's sufficient nauticalia to salt up any landlubber. ◆ M-F; Sa 2-6PM; closed in August. 01.42.65.27.85

23 Hôtel de Beauvau Le Camus de Mezières designed this mansion for Prince Charles de Beauvau, but the Revolution transferred its ownership to the state. The **Ministry of the Interior** has resided behind its ornate iron gates since 1861. ◆ 96 Rue du Faubourg-St-Honoré (at Pl Beauvau). Métro: St-Philippe-du-Roule

24 Palais de l'Elysée The most famous address on Rue du Faubourg-St-Honoré, if not in all of France, is the French version of the White House. Built in 1718 according to a design by **Armand-Claude Mollet,** the palace was purchased in 1753 by Mme. de Pompadour, Louis XV's rich and spoiled mistress, who hired the architect **Jean Lassurance** to expand the building and extend the gardens to the Champs-Elysées. Expropriated during the Revolution to serve as a government printing office (for the *Bulletin des Lois*) and dance hall, it later was known as the **Hameau Chantilly** and became a hideaway for the Empress Joséphine after she was divorced by Napoléon. On 22 June 1815 Napoléon signed his second abdication here. The mansion was subsequently the site of a restaurant and fairgrounds run by an ice-cream maker named Velloni. Still later, the Duke of Wellington and Czar Alexander I stayed here. The palace has been the official residence of the French president since 1873. The public is not admitted, but you can glimpse the dignified facade through the gateway. ◆ 55 Rue du Faubourg-St-Honoré (between Rue de l'Elysée and Ave de Marigny). Métro: St-Philippe-du Roule

25 Muriel A remnant of Old Paris, this is one of the few remaining Parisian boutiques that

Rue du Faubourg-St-Honoré Shopping

Christian Lacroix
clothing
RUE DU CIRQUE
Pierre Cardin
menswear
AVENUE DE MARIGNY

RUE DE L'ELYSEE
Ungaro
womenswear
Alimia
womenswear
Jean Lupu
antiques
Apostrophe
womenswear

British Embassy
Hervé Leger
womenswear
Lancôme
cosmetics
Valentino
womenswear
Pierre Balmain
womenswear
Gianfranco Ferré
menswear

RUE DU FAUBOURG-ST-HONORE

RUE DE MIROMESNIL
Perrin
antiques
Armorial
engravers/leather goods
RUE DES SAUSSAIES
Jean Damien
womenswear
Galerie de la Présidence
19th and 20th century art
Maud Frizon
women's shoes
Lilane Romi
womenswear
Louis Féraud
womenswear
Popoff *gallery*
Floriane
children's clothing
Marina
children's clothing
Lecoanét Hemant
women's shoes and clothing
Maxim's *clothing*
RUE DE DURAS
Remy S.
womenswear
Burma *jewelry*
Chopard *jewelry*
Sonia Rykiel
womenswear
Arfan *jewelry*
Etro *accessories*
Pomellato
jewelry
Gianni Versace
womenswear
RUE D'AGUESSEAU
Mont Blanc
writing supplies
Christian Dior
womenswear
Au Vieux Venise
antiques
Fratelli Rossetti
men's and women's shoes
Chloé
womenswear

Map continues on right

Cartier
jewelry
Trussardi
mens- and womenswear
Rena Lange
womenswear
Karl Lagerfeld
womenswear

RUE DU FAUBOURG-ST-HONORE

Cour aux Antiquaires
antiques
Franck Namani
womenswear
JP TOD'S *shoes*
Salvatore Ferragamo
leather goods
Leonard
womenswear
Courrèges
womenswear
RUE D'ANJOU
Maxandre
womenswear
Hôtel de Castiglione
Yves Saint Laurent
womenswear
Jacques Fath
womenswear
Aramis *menswear*
Jun Ashida
womenswear
Yves Saint Laurent
beauty products
Guy Laroche
womenswear
Givenchy
womenswear
Hermès
leather goods/scarves

RUE BOISSY-D'ANGLAS
Lanvin
Cafe Bleu/menswear
Istante
womenswear
Carita
salon
La Bagagerie
leather goods
Façonnable
menswear
Jean de Bonnot
rare books
Poiray
jewelry
Jaeger
womenswear
Igin
womenswear

Lanvin
women's boutique
La Perla
lingerie
André Chékière
menswear
Lolita Lempicka
*womenswear/
wedding gowns*
Iceberg *womenswear*
Loft *menswear*
Joan & David
men's and women's shoes
Christina Richard
jewelry
Les Copains
womenswear
Gucci
mens- and womenswear

sells only gloves. ◆ M-Sa; closed Saturday in August. 4 Rue des Saussaies (between Rue Montalivet and Pl Beauvau). 01.42.65.95.34. Métro: St-Philippe-du-Roule

26 Au Vieux Saussaies This shop trades in 18th- and 19th-century silver—from sugar bowls to samovars, evening bags to Champagne ice buckets, specializing in gifts for weddings and christenings. Here you'll find top-name *orfèvrerie* (silverware) at lower prices than you'll see at some of the other dealers. ◆ Tu-Sa. 14 Rue des Saussaies (between Rues Montalivet and de Surène). 01.42.65.32.71. Métro: St-Philippe-du Roule

ASTOR

WESTIN DEMEURE HOTELS · PARIS

27 L'Astor Westin Demeure $$$$ After a multi-million dollar renovation by Westin Hotels & Resorts, the former **Hotel Astor** has been given a new lease on life. The 135 rooms and suites, as well as the public areas, have been completely transformed by **Frédéric Méchiche,** who incorporates oak paneling, primitive trompe l'oeil paintings, and bold black-and-beige designs throughout. Rooms reflect a Regency-style elegance with modern conveniences including marble bathrooms, TV sets, CD stereos, and fax machines. Top floor rooms afford unbeatable views of the city with private terraces. ♦ 11 Rue d'Astorg (between Rues de la Ville and Roquépine). 01.53.05.05.05; fax 01.53.05.05.30. Métro: St-Augustin

Within L'Astor Westin Demeure:

Le Restaurant de l'Astor ★★★$$$
Though you'll be captivated by the comings and goings of fashionable Parisians, the cuisine is worthy of your attention too. A glass ceiling and soft yellow trompe l'oeil columns add an elegant touch to this oval-shaped dining room where the menu of chef Eric Le Cerf (a protege of the legendary Joël Robuchon) has fast become the talk of the town. Order such specialties as *tart friand de truffes aux oignons et lard fumée* (truffle, onion, and smoked bacon tart), roasted squab wrapped in linden leaves, and chestnut and truffle lobster. Desserts are tempting: Try the exceptional *crème caramélisée à la cassonade* (crème caramel with brown sugar). The wine list is limited but good. ♦ M-F lunch and dinner. Reservations recommended. 01.53.05.05.20

28 American Ambassador's Residence In the 19th century the **Hôtel de Pontalba** was owned by financier and art collector Baron Edmond de Rothschild. (When the baron died in 1934 at the age of 89, he left 3,000 drawings and 43,000 postage stamps to the **Louvre.**) Subsequently, the US government had the good taste to rent the *hôtel particulier* from Baron Maurice de Rothschild to serve as the residence of the American ambassador. The 40-room, 13-bathroom building is not open to the public, but if you are invited for dinner with the ambassador, you will see the original Oudry wood paneling and paintings by John Singer Sargent, Cézanne, and van Gogh. In one of the upstairs guest rooms is the bed where Charles Lindbergh slept after completing the first nonstop solo flight across the Atlantic on 21 May 1927. ♦ 41 Rue du Faubourg-St-Honoré (between Rues Boissy-d'Anglas and de l'Elysée). Métro: Concorde

28 British Embassy The lovely **Hôtel de Charost,** built by **Antoine Mazin** in 1723, was bought by Napoléon's sister, Pauline, who, after a tumultuous series of love affairs and marriages, became the Princess Borghese. In 1815, after Waterloo, the princess sold her **Palais Borghese** to George III of England, who turned it into his nation's embassy. Upstairs is Pauline's bed with gilded curtains descending from the talons of a Napoléonic eagle. The building is not open to the public. ♦ 39 Rue du Faubourg-St-Honoré (between Rues Boissy-d'Anglas and de l'Elysée). Métro: Concorde

28 33 Rue du Faubourg-St-Honoré Built by the architect **Grandhomme** in 1714, this house was the home of Duc Decres, who was minister of the French Navy until 1820, when a bomb hidden beneath his bed dealt him a mortal wound. For seven subsequent years, it housed the **Russian Embassy,** until it was sold to Nathaniel Rothschild. In 1918, the house was born anew as **Cercle de l'Union Interalliée,** a swank international club for business people. It is not open to the public. ♦ Between Rues Boissy-d'Anglas and de l'Elysée. Métro: Concorde

28 Japanese Embassy In 1718 **Pierre Lassurance** built this *hôtel* for Louis Blouin, confidant and premier *valet de chambre* of Louis XIV. Napoléon's sister and brother lived here, as did the king of Bavaria. It's now the Japanese ambassador's turn. ♦ 31 Rue du Faubourg-St-Honoré (between Rues Boissy-d'Anglas and de l'Elysée). Métro: Concorde

29 Georges Bernard Antiquités Satisfy that craving to magnify, measure, and modify. Bernard, co-author of a book on corkscrews, specializes in old scientific instruments. ♦ M-Sa; closed two weeks in August. 1 Rue d'Anjou (at Rue du Faubourg-St-Honoré). 01.42.65.23.83. Métro: Concorde

30 Castiglione $$$$ This 119-room hotel's high prices are in keeping with its choice location amid the splendorous boutiques. Unfortunately, a modern face-lift has left it a hostelry in search of character. There's an unremarkable restaurant on the premises. ♦ 38-40 Rue du Faubourg-St-Honoré (between Rues Boissy-d'Anglas and d'Anjou). 01.44.94.25.25; fax 01.42.65.12.27. Métro: Concorde

HERMÈS
PARIS

31 Hermès Started in 1837 as a saddle store by Thierry Hermès, *artisan d'élite,* this is perhaps the most celebrated leather-goods emporium in the world. Having outlasted the age of the horse and carriage, Hermès now furnishes the leather fittings for Lear jets. Its bags are considered necessities, not accessories, while its gloves are unsurpassed in craftsmanship. The signature scarves are huge and come in more than 200 styles, the most popular of which is the Brides de Gala; more than a half-million of these silken trifles are sold every year. ♦ M-Sa. 24 Rue du Faubourg-St-Honoré (at Rue Boissy-d'Anglas). 01.40.17.47.17. Métro: Concorde

Within Hermès:

Musée Hermès On the top floor of the store is a private museum displaying old saddles, ornamented trunks, and even Napoléon's stirrups. ♦ For admission, write in advance to the store manager (Hermès, 24 Rue de Faubourg St-Honoré, Paris 75008) or call 01.40.17.48.36

John Lobb On the second floor of **Hermès** is the Paris branch of the reputable London shoe- and bootmaker. To join the ranks of satisfied **Lobb** alumni, which include Lyndon Johnson, the Shah of Iran, Gary Cooper, and the Duke of Edinburgh, stop in to be measured heel to toe. Using the measurements, one of **Lobb**'s cobblers will fashion two wooden lasts (one for each foot) on which to model your shoes. In the nearby studio, the skins are cut and stitched, and in one month (first-time customers must wait a year), this labor will have produced a noble pair of handmade shoes sure to last at least a decade—and for a mere $2,000 per pair. ♦ M-Sa. 01.42.65.24.45

32 28 Rue Boissy-d'Anglas Le Boeuf sur le Toit, the famous avant-garde nightclub, was located here. Its 10 January 1922 inaugural party was thrown by Jean Cocteau and attended by Constantin Brancusi, Pablo Picasso, and Max Beerbohm, among others. Leading the club's orchestra that night was Vance Lowry, a black American saxophonist who was partially responsible for introducing the French to jazz and the music of George Gershwin. ♦ Between Cité Berryer and Rue de Surène. Métro: Concorde

33 Lanvin Shop here for women's scarves, perfumes, haute couture, and prêt-à-porter. ♦ M-Sa. 22 Rue du Faubourg-St-Honoré (at Rue Boissy-d'Anglas). 01.44.71.31.73. Métro: Concorde

34 Gucci A four-floor marble palazzo is filled with the trademark Gucci red and green. ♦ M-Sa. 21 Rue Royale (at Rue du Faubourg-St-Honoré). 01.42.96.83.27. Métro: Concorde

35 15 Rue du Faubourg-St-Honoré In 1804, Claude Rouget de l'Isle, composer of the *Marseillaise,* lived here, and after him, Felix, hairdresser to Empress Eugénie. The building now has both commercial and residential space. ♦ At Rue Boissy-d'Anglas. Métro: Concorde

At 15 Rue du Faubourg-St-Honoré:

Lanvin This is the place for fine men's fashion and accessories, including classic silk ties. ♦ M-Sa. 01.44.71.31.33

Within Lanvin:

Café Bleu ★★$ The cafe in the basement of the **Lanvin** boutique is a good place to fuel up with a light lunch or tea before continuing along the Faubourg St-Honoré for more power shopping. The menu is the brainchild of Gilles Epié (of **Campagne et Provence** and **Miravile** fame) and includes artichoke salad, eggs Benedict with *saumon fumé,* fresh vegetable ravioli, and club sandwiches. They serve *Le Vin des Stars* (The Wine of the Stars), a wine produced by actor Gérard Dépardieu. ♦ M-Sa lunch and tea. 01.44.71.32.32

35 Carita This lavishly decorated hair salon (whose clients have included Catherine Deneuve, Paloma Picasso, and French rocker Johnny Hallyday) has a relaxed, down-to-earth staff that sets hairstyle trends. There are separate entrances for men and women. The salon is also noted for its skin-care treatments. ♦ Tu-Sa. 11 Rue du Faubourg-St-Honoré (between Rues Royale and Boissy-d'Anglas). Men and women: 01.44.94.11.11. Métro: Concorde

36 Christofle Want to make your little one's first lost baby tooth even more precious? How about encasing it in silver? Nothing is impossible for this shop, which has provided silver-plating services for more than a century. There's also a fine selection of silverware and antique gold, as well as the stunning yellow and blue tableware Claude Monet designed for his house at Giverny. Peek into the museum at the same address. ♦ M-Sa. 9 Rue Royale (between Pl de la Concorde and Rue du Faubourg-St-Honoré). 01.49.33.43.00. Métro: Concorde

37 Lachaume The city's oldest and most exquisite florist has catered to haute couturiers and other well-heeled clientele (who can afford long-stemmed red roses in December) since 1845. For an instantaneous cure of the midwinter blues, gaze into the shop window at the gorgeous bunches of tulips and orchids. ♦ M-Sa; closed in August. 10 Rue Royale (between Pl de la Concorde and Rue St-Honoré). 01.42.60.59.74, 01.42.60.57.26. Métro: Concorde

38 Ladurée ★★★$ This turn-of-the-century *salon de thé* par excellence is posh and ultra-Parisian but not snobbish. The heavenly taste of the croissants is ample reason for taking breakfast here. Habitués recommend *financiers* (almond cakes), chocolate macaroons, *babas au rhum*, and *royals* (almond biscuits iced with chocolate or mocha frosting). Don't miss the painting of the rosy-cheeked cherub-turned-pastry chef on the downstairs ceiling. ♦ Daily breakfast, lunch, and afternoon tea. 16 Rue Royale (between Rue St-Honoré and Pl de la Madeleine). 01.42.60.21.79. Métro: Madeleine

39 La Maison du Valais ★★$$ An Alpine-style chalet, this restaurant serves *à volonté* (all you can eat) raclette (melted cheese served with potatoes, *cornichons,* and onions), delectable fondue, assortments of thinly sliced charcuterie, and cool Fendant wine. The cheerful waiters and Swiss food are heartening in winter when you fancy a ski weekend in the mountains but haven't time to escape the gray skies of Paris. ♦ M-Sa lunch and dinner. Reservations recommended, especially in winter. 20 Rue Royale (between Rue St-Honoré and Pl de la Madeleine). 01.42.60.23.75, 01.42.60.22.72. Métro: Madeleine

40 Cité Berryer The alley, formerly an open-air market, has been classified as a historic monument. ♦ Between Rues Royale and Boissy-d'Anglas. Métros: Concorde, Madeleine

41 Place de la Madeleine Around the edges of this square, the heart of upscale noshing in Paris, are specialty shops to spoil the spoiled (see the shopping map below). Amid the fumes of buses and a more-or-less perpetual rush hour, a lively flower market blossoms just east of the **Madeleine** church (open Tu-Sa; Su morning). Here, at her funeral in 1975, entertainer Josephine Baker, having already received the Légion d'Honneur and the Médaille de la Résistance, became the first American woman to be honored with a 21-gun salute. ♦ Between Rues Royale and Tronchet. Métro: Madeleine

41 Kiosque-Théâtre This kiosk sells half-price tickets to theater, dance, music hall, concert, cafe theater, and, occasionally, opera performances on the day of the event. During the first two years of operation it sold 140,600 tickets. ♦ Daily. Pl de la Madeleine (between

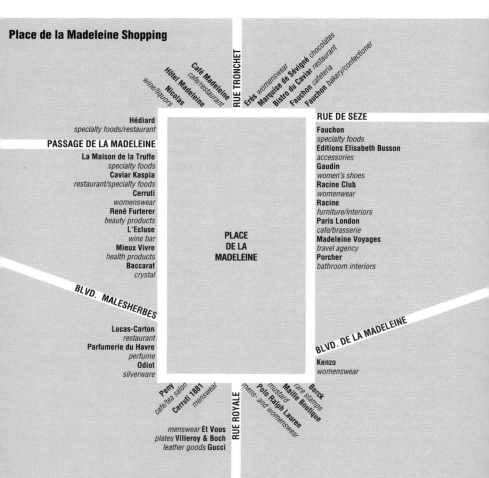

Place de la Madeleine Shopping

wine/liquors
Nicolas
Hôtel Madeleine
Café Madeleine
cafe/restaurant

RUE TRONCHET

Erés *womenswear*
Marquise de Sévigné *chocolates*
Bistro du Caviar *restaurant*
Fauchon *cafeteria*
Fauchon *bakery/confectioner*

Hédiard
specialty foods/restaurant

PASSAGE DE LA MADELEINE

La Maison de la Truffe
specialty foods
Caviar Kaspia
restaurant/specialty foods
Cerruti
womenswear
René Furterer
beauty products
L'Ecluse
wine bar
Mieux Vivre
health products
Baccarat
crystal

PLACE
DE LA
MADELEINE

RUE DE SEZE

Fauchon
specialty foods
Editions Elisabeth Busson
accessories
Gaudin
women's shoes
Racine Club
womenwear
Racine
furniture/interiors
Paris London
cafe/brasserie
Madeleine Voyages
travel agency
Porcher
bathroom interiors

BLVD. MALESHERBES

Lucas-Carton
restaurant
Parfumerie du Havre
perfume
Odiot
silverware

BLVD. DE LA MADELEINE

Kenzo
womenswear

Peny
cafe/tea salon
Cerruti 1881 *menswear*

RUE ROYALE

Polo Ralph Lauren *mens- and womenswear*
Maille *mustard*
Berck *rare stamps*
Boutique

menswear **Et Vous**
plates **Villeroy & Boch**
leather goods **Gucci**

Blvds de la Madeleine and Malesherbes). No phone. Métro: Madeleine. Also at: Châtelet–Les Halles métro station. No phone

41 Public Lavatory Even if nature isn't calling, look for a sign that reads: "Hommes et Dames W.C." It will lead you underground to an elegant 1905 facility with Art Nouveau wood paneling, stained glass, and tile built by Etablissements Porcher, now one of the largest plumbing suppliers in France. ♦ Rue Royale and Pl de la Madeleine. Métro: Madeleine

MICHAEL STORRINGS

42 La Madeleine (Eglise Ste-Marie Madeleine) The 28 monumental steps of this church rise to meet 52 immense Corinthian columns, defining an edifice (pictured above) that dominates the hub of the financial district. However, the building has always been an architectural orphan. Begun as a church in 1764 under the reign of Louis XV and modeled after a Greek temple, the structure, at various times in its turbulent past, has been slated to become a bank, parliament building, theater, stock exchange, banquet hall, and yet another temple to glorify Napoléon's army (as if the **Arc de Triomphe** and the **Invalides** were not enough). In 1837 the windowless edifice, designed by **Pierre Vignon** and **Jean-Jacques Huvé,** was selected to be the capital's first railway station but was consecrated as a church dedicated to St. Mary Magdalene five years later.

Not a single cross adorns the pediments of this church, and its rose-marble-and-gilt interior is surprisingly sensual. The imposing bronze door portraying the Ten Commandments is by Philippe Joseph Henri Lemaire, and his gigantic *Last Judgment* on the south pediment is the largest work of its kind in the world (and it contains one of the chubbiest Christs in Europe). On the north side of the church, the inscription beneath a headless statue of St. Luke reads, "On 30 May 1918, a German shell struck the church of the Madeleine and decapitated this statue." The splendid organ was played by composer Camille Saint-Saëns, and the *Funeral March* of Chopin resounded here as the composer himself was laid to rest. The grandest funeral ever accorded an American in Paris was that of Josephine Baker, held here on 15 April

1975. ♦ Pl de la Madeleine (between Blvds de la Madeleine and Malesherbes). 01.44.51.69.00. Métro: Madeleine

43 Peny ★$ The coconut cake, *croque-monsieur* (grilled ham and cheese sandwich), and yellow table umbrellas at this *salon de thé* are summertime favorites with Americans. ♦ Daily breakfast, lunch, afternoon tea, and dinner. 3 Pl de la Madeleine (between Rue Royale and Blvd Malesherbes). 01.42.65.06.75. Métro: Madeleine

44 Lucas-Carton ★★★★$$$$ The nouvelle cuisine of superstar chef Alain Senderens is better (and more expensive) than ever. In fact, this is one of the Parisian capitals of nouvelle cuisine, made even more memorable by the gorgeous Majorelle Belle Epoque maple and sycamore woodwork in the dining room. Try the delicious foie gras in steamed cabbage, duck roasted with honey and spices, ravioli filled with clams, *beignet d'ananas à la pina colada* (pineapple fritters with sauce), and bittersweet chocolate soufflé. ♦ M-F lunch and dinner; Sa dinner; closed three weeks in August and two weeks at Christmas. Reservations required. 9 Pl de la Madeleine (at Blvd Malesherbes). 01.42.65.22.90. Métro: Madeleine

45 Au Verger de la Madeleine Since 1936 this has remained one of Paris's finest family-operated *épiceries* (gourmet grocery stores). Jean-Pierre Legras, who features wines dating from 1789, will help you find an old Sauternes bottled in the year you were born, got married, or made your first trip to Paris. ♦ M-Sa. 4 Blvd Malesherbes (between Pl de la Madeleine and Rue de l'Arcade). 01.42.65.51.99. Métro: Madeleine

46 L'Ecluse ★★★$ One of a chain of six wine bars selling marvelous old Bordeaux by the glass, this spot is lively, fashionable, affordable, and ideal for people watching. ♦ Daily lunch and dinner until 1AM. 15 Pl de la Madeleine (between Blvd Malesherbes and Passage de la Madeleine). 01.42.65.34.69. Métro: Madeleine. Also at: 15 Quai des Grands-Augustins (between Pl St-Michel and Rue Gît-le-Coeur). 01.46.33.58.74. Métro: St-Michel; 64 Rue François-1er (between Rues Lincoln and Quentin-Bauchart). 01.47.20.77.09. Métro: George-V

47 Caviar Kaspia ★★★$$$ Besides purveying the finest in Russian and Iranian caviars, the chic little upstairs restaurant adorned in czarist turquoise and overlooking Place de la Madeleine offers vodka, aquavit, and blintzes languidly draped with smoked salmon. The shop downstairs sells all the makings for your own Russian dinner. ♦ Restaurant: M-Sa lunch and dinner until 1AM. Store: M-Sa 9AM-midnight. 17 Pl de la Madeleine (between Blvd Malesherbes and

Passage de la Madeleine). 01.42.65.33.52. Métro: Madeleine

48 La Maison de la Truffe ★★$$$
Brooklyn delicatessens never looked like this fancy place, which specializes in black gold (fresh truffles, in season from November through February) and any other delicacy your gourmand's heart could desire. Savour the tasty treasures at a table here or purchase them at the shop to enjoy at home. ♦ Restaurant: M-Sa lunch and dinner until 8:30 PM. Shop: M-Sa 9AM-9PM. 19 Pl de la Madeleine (at Passage de la Madeleine). 01.42.65.53.22. Métro: Madeleine

49 Hédiard This *épicerie* was founded in 1854 by Ferdinand Hédiard, who was the first to import the exotic pineapple into France. Marcel Proust once lingered here, surveying Hédiard's extraordinary selection of Asian and African delicacies: spices, oils, vinegars, 30 blends of tea, freshly roasted coffee beans, baskets of rare jams and jellies, and old rums. A 1994 renovation has turned the charming Old-World food shop into a modern souk, with a restaurant and specialty food counters on two levels around a glass-roofed market. Perhaps the grandest selection of Bordeaux wines in Paris is here. ♦ Shop: M-Sa 9:30AM-9PM. Restaurant: M-Sa breakfast, lunch, tea, and dinner. 21 Pl de la Madeleine (at Passage de la Madeleine). Shop 01.43.12.88.88, restaurant 01.43.12.88.99. Métro: Madeleine

50 Hôtel Beau Manoir $$$ Serious shoppers will appreciate this hotel's central location—down the street from the Faubourg St-Honoré and next to the gourmet food boutiques in the Place de la Madeleine. Cozily refurbished with gold and red damask walls, exposed beams, marble bathrooms, and walnut cabinetry, the 32-room hostelry is part of the French Best Western Association. There's no restaurant. Next door is its less expensive sister, the **Hôtel Lido** (4 Passage de la Madeleine, 01.42.66.27.37; fax 01.42.66.61.23). ♦ 6 Rue de l'Arcade (at Passage de la Madeleine). 01.42.66.03.07; fax 01.42.68.03.00. Métro: Madeleine

51 Chapelle Expiatoire (Expiatory Chapel)
This memorial chapel, commissioned by Louis XVIII and designed by **Pierre Fontaine,** has become a shrine for French royalists. It was erected in 1815 on the grounds of the cemetery where, among the thousands of other victims of the Revolution, Marie Antoinette, Louis XVI, and Charlotte Corday are buried. In the chapel's right apse is a statue of Louis XVI being ushered into heaven by an angel resembling Henry Essex Edgeworth, the friend who escorted the king to the guillotine. Downstairs, an altar marks the spot where Louis XVI's body was buried. ♦ W; open to groups Th by appointment. 29 Rue Pasquier (at Sq Louis-XVI). 01.42.65.35.80. Métro: St-Augustin

52 Aux Tortues Established in 1864 (long before environmentally correct consumerism), this shop sells hairbrushes for baby, chess sets, Japanese netsuke, picture frames, combs, and carved balls within balls made from tortoiseshell. Note, however, that newly purchased tortoiseshell items may not be brought into the US. ♦ M-Sa. 55 Blvd Haussmann (between Rues Tronchet and de l'Arcade). 01.42.65.56.74. Métro: Havre–Caumartin

53 Hôtel Opal $$ For the frugal traveler, here's a property with 36 doll-size chambers and modern bathrooms (but no restaurant). Located behind the **Madeleine** church, it's a handy place to stay if you love going to the ballet and shopping in the nearby stores. ♦ 19 Rue Tronchet (at Rue de Castellane). 01.42.65.77.97; fax 01.49.24.06.58. Métro: Madeleine

54 New Hôtel Roblin $$ English travelers who cross the channel for a weekend of dance at the **Opéra Garnier** and luxurious take-out food from the Place de la Madeleine find refuge in this comfortable 77-room hotel. The restaurant serves traditional French fare. ♦ 6 Rue Chauveau-Lagarde (between Pl de la Madeleine and Rue de l'Arcade). 01.44.71.20.80; fax 01.42.65.19.49. Métro: Madeleine

55 La Ferme St-Hubert ★★$$ Cheese is the focus here, and Chef Henry Voy serves the best *croque monsieur* in Paris. Other specialties include *feuilleté au roquefort* (roquefort in pastry crust), fondue, and raclette. Also on the premises is a shop selling 140 different varieties of cheese; this cheese-lover's heaven is especially known for its excellent roquefort and beaufort. ♦ M-Sa lunch and dinner. 21 Rue Vignon (between Rues de Sèze and Tronchet). 01.47.42.79.20. Métro: Madeleine

56 La Maison du Miel Run by the Gallands family since 1908, this shop is devoted entirely to honey and products containing honey, such as soap and oil. There are sample tastings and you can choose from a selection of various honeys in miniature jars. Don't pass up the *bruyère* (heather) honey. ♦ M-Sa. 24 Rue Vignon (between Rues de Sèze and Tronchet). 01.47.42.26.70. Métro: Madeleine

Restaurants/Clubs: Red   **Hotels:** Blue
Shops/ 🍴 Outdoors: Green   **Sights/Culture:** Black

57 Le Roi du Pot-au-Feu ★★$$ For some warm consolation on a frigid evening, visit this offbeat little bistro with its red-checkered tablecloths and tableside jukeboxes. The specialty is its namesake: pot-au-feu, a marrow-rich beef broth served with the meat and vegetables that gave up their substance to the stew. ♦ M-Sa lunch and dinner. 34 Rue Vignon (between Rues de Sèze and Tronchet). 01.47.42.37.10. Métro: Madeleine

58 Marquise de Sévigné ★★$ The ambience in this combination tea salon/chocolate shop is as sublime as the rich hot chocolate it serves. ♦ M-Sa breakfast, lunch, and afternoon tea. 32 Pl de la Madeleine (between Rues de Sèze and Tronchet). 01.42.65.19.47. Métro: Madeleine

59 Fauchon One look in the window tells the story. This is a supermarket for millionaires, with every exotic fruit and vegetable on earth artistically arranged in a gorgeous still life. The most famous food shop in town, it's stocked with more than 20,000 items, from Scottish salmon and chunky peanut butter to Tonganese mangoes. Customers are not allowed to handle any of the merchandise; they pay first and then are presented with their prizes at the door. Everything's expensive. ♦ M-Sa. 26 Pl de la Madeleine (at Rue de Sèze). 01.47.42.60.11. Métro: Madeleine

Within Fauchon:

Fauchon ★★$$ On-the-spot overindulgence used to mean standing at the store's self-service cafeteria across the street, but to **Fauchon** fans' delight, this casual restaurant has opened upstairs featuring a view of the illuminated **La Madeleine.** Chef Bruno Deligne's menu includes delicacies such as hot oysters and leeks with truffle sauce, and, for lighter summer fare, melon and Sauternes soup. They'll also cater your next cocktail party in Paris. ♦ M-Sa lunch and dinner. 01.47.42.60.11

60 Edouard Berck Berck is the most renowned stamp dealer in the city. ♦ M-Sa. 6 Pl de la Madeleine (between Blvd de la Madeleine and Rue Royale). 01.42.60.34.26. Métro: Madeleine

60 Boutique Maille The ideal place to stock up on mustard to suit all tastes—Champagne, Cognac, pepper, and tarragon to name a few. The shop also offers a selection of beautifully decorated ceramic jars to store your favorite condiment, flavored vinegars, and pickles. ♦ M-Sa. 6 Pl de la Madeleine (between Blvd de la Madeleine and Rue Royal). 01.40.15.06.00. Métro: Madeleine

60 4 Place de la Madeleine Alas, this is no longer the home of Durand's, the famous music publisher, where, in 1831, Liszt first met Chopin. The building now has both commercial and residential space. ♦ Between

Blvd de la Madeleine and Rue Royale. Métro: Madeleine

61 Au Nain Bleu The Paris equivalent of FAO Schwarz sells toys luxurious enough to spoil any child. ♦ M-Sa. 406-410 Rue St-Honoré (at Rue Richepance). 01.42.60.39.01. Métro: Concorde

62 Goumard Prunier ★★$$$ Fresh shellfish, ginger-grilled Brittany lobster, sea bass, and frogs' legs are a few of the specialties served here. The dining room boasts original 19th-century architectural elements that are complemented by beautiful Lalique light fixtures and sculptures. ♦ Tu-Sa lunch and dinner. Reservations recommended. 9 Rue Duphot (between Rues St-Honoré and Richepance). 01.42.60.36.07. Métro: Madeleine

63 Gaya ★★$$ Settle on one of the comfortable banquettes in this seafood bistro, owned by Jean-Claude Goumard of **Goumard Prunier** down the street, and order the delicious anchovies, marinated raw *sardines à l'escabèche*, or tuna *au piment d'Espelette* (tuna steak with peppers). ♦ M-Sa lunch and dinner. Reservations recommended. 17 Rue Duphot (between Rues St-Honoré and Richepance). 01.42.60.43.03. Métro: Madeleine. Also at: 44 Rue du Bac (between Blvd St-Germain and Rue de l'Université). 01.45.44.73.73. Métro: Rue du Bac

64 Toraya ★★$$ In Japanese, *toraya* means "tiger"; for Parisians, it denotes this elegant black-and-gray Japanese tea salon and pastry shop. Savor sweet bean noodles, *kuzukiri* (noodles made from jellied arrowroot), and energizing pots of green *ocha* (tea). ♦ M-Sa lunch and afternoon tea. 10 Rue St-Florentin (between Rues de Rivoli and St-Honoré). 01.42.60.13.00. Métro: Concorde

65 Notre-Dame-de-l'Assomption This church, built in 1676, was originally part of a convent where destitute widows and abandoned wives were given shelter; it has served as a Polish parish since 1850. The massive cupola on top has been dubbed *le sot*

dôme (the silly dome). ♦ 263 *bis* Rue St-Honoré (at Pl Maurice-Barrès). 01.42.60.07.69. Métro: Concorde

66 Cadolle Hermine Cadolle, the lady who is credited with inventing the brassiere in 1900, was the great-grandmother of Cadolle's current proprietor, Alice Cadolle. All manner of deluxe lingerie, French beachwear, and perfume is sold here. ♦ M-Sa. 14 Rue Cambon (between Rues du Mont-Thabor and St-Honoré). 01.42.60.94.94. Métro: Concorde

67 Hôtel Burgundy $$$ The last pages of *Look Homeward, Angel* sprang from the fertile imagination of Thomas Wolfe while he was here in 1928. Today it is a clean, comfortable, simply decorated hotel with 90 guest rooms and a restaurant. ♦ 8 Rue Duphot (between Rue St-Honoré and Blvd de la Madeleine). 01.42.60.34.12; fax 01.47.03.95.20. Métro: Madeleine

68 29 Rue Cambon Upon his return to Paris in November 1875, young *New York Tribune* correspondent Henry James took up residence on the third floor of what is now Chanel headquarters. This is where *The Americans,* his novel set in Paris, was written. ♦ Between Rue St-Honoré and Blvd de la Madeleine. Métros: Concorde, Madeleine

69 Demeure Castille $$$$ This comfortable 107-room hotel is decorated in the Venetian style, with marble, colorful damasks, a faux patina on the walls, and a courtyard with a fountain. Some of the rooms have views of the Chanel ateliers, where Coco Chanel created her first haute couture designs. ♦ 33-37 Rue Cambon (between Rue St-Honoré and Blvd de la Madeleine). 01.44.58.44.58; fax 01.44.58.44.00. Métro: Madeleine

Within Demeure Castille:

Il Cortile ★$$ Chef Ciro Polge prepares genuine Italian dishes, including *il salmone marinato al pepe rosa a aneto* (salmon marinated in pink peppercorns and dill), *risotto all'oro* (risotto and saffron) with truffle fondant, *scaloppa mo zia Teresa* (veal with mozzarella and fresh spinach), and, for dessert, *panna cotta frutte di bosco* (vanilla custard with wild fruit). During the week chic fashion types lunch in this Venetian-inspired dining room, which is decorated with murals and mosaics. ♦ M-Sa lunch and dinner. 01.44.58.45.67

70 Charles Jourdan Forty years ago, celebrated M. Jourdan became the first cobbler to use glue instead of nails to hold his shoes together; the result was the first truly delicate feminine footwear. The most up-to-the-minute styles are still featured at this fashionable shoe boutique. ♦ M-Sa. 5 Blvd de la Madeleine (between Rues Cambon and Duphot). 01.42.61.15.89. Métro: Madeleine

Place Vendôme Shopping

RUE DES CAPUCINES	RUE DANIELLE-CASANOVA
Emporio Armani *mens- and womenswear*	**Charvet** *mens- and womenswear*
	Comptoir sud Pacific *accessories*
Alexandre Reza *jewelry*	**Boucheron** *jewelry*
Pierre Dubail *jewelry*	**Van Cleef & Arpels** *jewelry/watches*
Hôtel Ritz	**Mauboissin** *jewelry*
Cartier *jewelry*	**Piaget** *watches*
	Robergé *jewelry*
Chanel *jewelry*	**Chaumet** *jewelry*
	Patek Philippe *watches*
Hôtel Vendôme *(under renovation)*	**Mikimoto** *jewelry*
	Repossi *jewelry*
	Giorgio Armani *mens- and womenswear*
	Gianmaria Buccellati *fine silver/jewelry*
	Galerie Alexander Butman *art gallery*
	Lhullier *florist*
	Ebel *jewelry*
	Guerlain *perfume/accessories*

(PLACE VENDOME - octagon at center)

RUE ST-HONORÉ	(RUE DE CASTIGLIONE)
chocolates **Godiva**	**Annick Goutal** *oils/perfume*
bar/restaurant **Le Lotti**	**Rhodes & Brousse** *menswear*
accessories **Ilonka**	
Weedly	
children's clothing/T-shirts	**Agry** *engraving*
watches **Le Montres**	**Carré des Feuillants** *restaurant*
Hôtel Lotti	
Dominique France *men's ties/accessories*	**Kenneth Jay Lane** *jewelry*
costume jewelry **Anémone**	**Dallas** *womenswear*
menswear **Namani**	**Léo Miller** *handbags*
optician **Meyrowitz**	**Aquascutum** *mens- and womenswear*
	Luce Brett *antiques*
	Payot *beauty products/salon*

RUE DU MONT-THABOR	
Hotel Inter-Continental	**Les Arcades** *books*
Casty *purses/jewelry*	**Parfumeria Catherine** *perfume*
	Hôtel Meurice *(back entrance)*
Cristal Vendôme *crystal*	**Swann Pharmacy**
	Jacqueline Perès *womenswear*
	Sulka *menswear*

RUE DE RIVOLI

71 Place Vendôme Like the Place de la Concorde, Place des Victoires, and other magnificent squares, this was conceived as a setting for a royal equestrian statue. The subject was Louis XIV, and the sculptor was François Girardon. In 1685, to make way for his monument, Louis bought and demolished the Duke of Vendôme's town house and the nearby Capucines convent. **Jules Hardouin-Mansart** designed gracefully formal mauve limestone facades with Corinthian pilasters and sculpted masks that were added to the square's periphery in 1715. The Sun King, a budding real estate shark, encouraged speculators to buy the lots behind the facades, then hire their own architects to fill in the blanks. During the Revolution the heads of nine victims of the guillotine were displayed here on spikes, and for a while the Place Vendôme was known as the Place des Piques (Pike Square).

On 19 June 1792 the Revolutionaries lit a huge bonfire here that incinerated bundles of genealogical documents concerning the French nobility's title deeds. Needless to say, the king's gilt statue didn't survive the mob's wrath, either; it was felled in August of the same year. Today the 440- by 420-foot octagon is characterized by an aloof opulence. It is the home of the **Hôtel Ritz** and it boasts the world's greatest concentration of banks, perfumeries, and jewelers, including **Boucheron, Van Cleef & Arpels, Cartier, Chaumet, Schiaparelli**, and **Guerlain** (see shopping map on page 211).
♦ Between Rue St-Honoré and Rues Danielle-Casanova and des Capucines. Métros: Madeleine, Opéra, Tuileries

71 Vendôme Column In place of the toppled statue of Louis XIV, Napoléon raised a 144-foot-high monument modeled on Trajan's column in Rome. Made to commemorate Napoléon's military victories in Germany, the stone column is faced with 378 spiraling sheets of bronze supplied by 1,200 cannons captured from the Austrian and Russian armies defeated at the Battle of Austerlitz in 1805. The column was originally topped with a statue of Napoléon dressed as Julius Caesar, but that was replaced by one of Henri IV in 1814. After Napoléon's defeat at Waterloo, the Bourbons commandeered the monument and mounted their own symbol, the fleur-de-lis, at the top. Along came Louis Philippe, and the fleur-de-lis was replaced with a small statue of Napoléon. But on the afternoon of 1 May 1871, the column was toppled, crashing down along Rue de la Paix and breaking into 30 pieces. This act of destruction was masterminded by the painter Gustave Courbet for aesthetic and political reasons. When the Third Republic took power, it ordered Courbet to restore the monument at his own expense. The column was thrust up again (this time topped with a replica of the original statue), and Courbet was plunged into bankruptcy.
♦ At the center of Pl Vendôme. Métros: Madeleine, Opéra, Tuileries

72 11-13 Place Vendôme This is the **Ministry of Justice** where, in 1848, the official measure for the meter was set in the facade. ♦ West side. Métros: Madeleine, Opéra, Tuileries

---

According to a poll, 53 percent of French men and women cannot use a computer and 24 percent are defeated by a CD player. Only seven percent of interviewees admitted to feeling comfortable with high technology.

72 Hôtel Ritz $$$$ Got a pooch who's hard to please? Take him to this famous hotel, where even dogs are treated like social lions. The **Ritz** has been, well, the ritziest place in Paris since 1898, when César Ritz first took it over. During that time, millionaires, Arab princes, divas, and cinema stars have stayed here. Marcel Proust used to arrive sporting lavender gloves and a variety of clothes that never seemed to fit him. Barbara Hutton loved it. Coco Chanel liked it so much she took up residence here. There are 440 employees (a third of whom have been here more than a quarter century) catering to the occupants of the hotel's 187 rooms. Sixty of these stalwarts are available for duty as private servants if your vacation just isn't a vacation without Jeeves. The prices are astronomical but, by all accounts, justified. The suites on the second floor overlooking the Place Vendôme are actually registered with the Bureau of Fine Arts. ♦ 15 Pl Vendôme (west side). 01.43.16.30.30; fax 01.43.16.36.68. Métros: Madeleine, Opéra, Tuileries

Within the Hôtel Ritz:

Ritz Espadon ★★★$$$$ The culinary reputation of the hotel's lovely garden restaurant was made from the very start by the presence of that great turn-of-the-century chef, Escoffier. He first met César Ritz when Ritz was manager of the Grand Hotel in Monte Carlo. Escoffier's celebrated recipe for foie gras in Port is still used. Latter-day creations include fillet of *St-Pierre* (John Dory) studded with olives and served with a saffron sauce, and lobster medaillons in a tarragon sauce. The wine list is nonpareil and the prices are unsurpassed. ♦ Daily lunch and dinner. Reservations recommended. 01.43.16.30.30

Ritz Bar Just off Rue Cambon is this famous little bar, which Hemingway "liberated" at the end of World War II (he was the first to arrive for a drink after the liberation of Paris). Here the legendary barman Georges served drinks to President Teddy Roosevelt, just back from an African safari. Other big-time tipplers who have imbibed here include the Prince of Wales, Greta Garbo, Noel Coward, Douglas Fairbanks, Winston Churchill, J.P. Morgan, Andrew Carnegie, F. Scott Fitzgerald, and Marlene Dietrich. It's still an English-style pub, right down to its tweedy, rubicund patrons. ♦ Daily until 1AM. 01.43.16.30.30

How to Become a French Chef (or Just Cook Like One)

How do they do it, those fabulous French chefs? Why doesn't your puff pastry have the same flake, your hollandaise sauce the same sheen, your soufflé the same, well, *souffle?* The answers to these questions and more may be found at a Parisian *école de cuisine,* where master chefs will demystify the art of French cookery.

Two schools in particular outclass the rest: The century-old **Le Cordon Bleu Ecole de Cuisine et de Pâtisserie** has a reputation that speaks for itself, while the newly established **Ritz-Escoffier Ecole de Gastronomie Française** upholds the same impeccable standards as the famous **Hôtel Ritz** from which it sprang. Both schools offer courses translated into English; choices range from cooking demonstrations and tastings to classes involving hands-on experience working under the guidance of a chef. Courses can be as short as a day or a week, or can be part of a program leading to a certificate or diploma.

Le Cordon Bleu offers gourmet sessions and workshops that last from one to five days. Courses focus on specific themes, such as French regional cuisine, bistro cuisine, bread baking, and chocolate. Also available are classes on wine, floral art, and catering, as well as instruction on more unusual topics, such as "lean cuisine," Easter eggs, Christmas chocolates, decorative sugarwork, and foie gras. There is even a course called "Sabrina's Cuisine" in memory of Audrey Hepburn, who took classes at **Le Cordon Bleu** in the film *Sabrina.*

At the **Cordon Bleu** boutique you can purchase cooking instruction videos, gourmet food items and cooking tools, and the perfect gift for amateur cooks back home—a **Cordon Bleu** chef's hat and apron.

The **Ritz-Escoffier Ecole de Gastronomie Française** is named for César Ritz, who opened the **Hôtel Ritz** in 1898, and his famous chef Auguste Escoffier. Here you can observe presentations on the preparation of seasonal dishes and pastries, or full-meal demonstrations that end with a gourmet lunch or dinner (featuring, of course, the dishes prepared during the demonstration). Classes in cheese and wine tasting also are offered, and there are week-long holiday courses featuring traditional French Christmas and New Year's dishes, several wine tastings, and flower arranging.

For information on classes and schedules contact: **Le Cordon Bleu Ecole de Cuisine et de Pâtisserie** (8 Rue Léon Delhomme, 75015 Paris, 01.53.68.22.50; fax 01.48.56.03.96) or **Ritz-Escoffier Ecole de Gastronomie Française** (15 Pl Vendôme, 75001 Paris, 01.43.16.31.43; fax 01.43.16.31.50).

Vendôme Lesser-known than the hotel's other watering hole, this bar has a terrace for drinks or tea in the summer. ◆ Daily until 1AM. 01.43.16.30.30

Ritz Health Club Where else can you work out alongside the likes of Tom Cruise, Gregory Peck, Madonna, Woody Allen, and any number of top models, politicians, and members of the *crème de la crème* of Parisian society? Staying at the **Ritz** makes you an official member, and there are flexible membership programs for others as well. Facilities include a fully equipped gymnasium, squash courts, saunas, jacuzzis, Turkish baths, spa treatments, and the largest private pool in Paris. ◆ Daily. 01.43.16.30.60.

73 **Cartier** Since 1847 this jewelry store has offered the best and the brightest in French *bijoux,* with commensurately dazzling price tags. The 17-percent tourist discount on gold, however, almost brings the pretty baubles within reach. ◆ M-Sa. 7 Pl Vendôme

(southwest corner). 01.44.55.32.50. Métros: Madeleine, Opéra, Tuileries

74 **3-5 Place Vendôme** This was formerly the **Hôtel Bristol.** From 1890 to 1910, whenever financier and art collector John Pierpont Morgan came to Paris, he would stay in the same corner suite in the old hotel, which was run by one of his father's butlers. The building is now owned by IBM Paris. ◆ At Rue de Castiglione. Métros: Madeleine, Opéra, Tuileries

75 **France et Choiseul** $$$$ Franklin and Eleanor Roosevelt stayed in this hotel on their honeymoon in 1905, during which time a clairvoyant told Franklin Roosevelt that he'd become president of either the US or the Equitable Life Insurance Company (he wasn't sure which). In 1946, after *The Heart Is a Lonely Hunter* and *Reflections in a Golden Eye* had been published in French, Carson McCullers and her husband moved here. Now the 85-room property is known for its old-

fashioned charm, modern conveniences, small rooms, and courteous staff. There's no restaurant. ♦ 239 Rue St-Honoré (between Rues de Castiglione and Cambon). 01.42.44.50.00; fax 01.42.44.50.01. Métros: Concorde, Tuileries

75 Godiva The world-renowned chocolatier takes its name from the 11th-century English noblewoman who sacrificed her modesty and rode naked through the streets of Coventry to plead with her husband, the earl, to reduce taxes on the townsfolk. If these exquisite bonbons had been available then, they might have made a better bribe. ♦ M-Sa. 237 Rue St-Honoré (at Rue de Castiglione). 01.42.60.44.64. Métros: Concorde, Tuileries

76 Hôtel Lotti $$$$ This 133-room luxury hotel is favored by British and Italian bluebloods who are drawn to the large, tastefully decorated rooms, period furniture, and impeccable service. There's a restaurant on the premises. ♦ 7 Rue de Castiglione (between Rues du Mont-Thabor and St-Honoré). 01.42.60.37.34; fax 01.40.15.93.56. Métros: Concorde, Tuileries

77 Carré des Feuillants ★★★$$$ While Nicole Dutournier minds **Au Trou Gascon**, the marvelous family restaurant in the 12th arrondissement, her husband Alain Dutournier—voted chef of the year in 1996—runs the show at the couple's second, fancier, 19th century–style restaurant near Place Vendôme. His specialty is inventive Southwestern French cuisine that includes parsley-crusted scallops with endive, fried eels with herb-and–sweet-garlic salad, wild hare with truffles, and braised veal with cèpes. For dessert try the *russe pistache* (shortbread biscuits with pistachio mousse and raspberry puree). ♦ M-F lunch and dinner; Sa dinner; closed in August. Reservations required. 14 Rue de Castiglione (between Rues du Mont-Thabor and St-Honoré). 01.42.86.82.82. Métros: Concorde, Tuileries

78 4 Rue du Mont-Thabor In the summer of 1820, still enjoying the afterglow of the triumphant reception of *Rip Van Winkle* and *The Legend of Sleepy Hollow,* 39-year-old Washington Irving moved into an apartment here. Mitigating his pleasure was Irving's powerful fear of growing old, the same problem that obsessed ol' Rip. The building is now the unremarkable **Hôtel Mont-Thabor.** ♦ Between Rues d'Alger and de Castiglione. Métro: Tuileries

79 Rue St-Honoré This ranks as one of the oldest and most historic thoroughfares in Paris. In 1622 Molière was born on this street at the corner of Rue Sauval, near Les Halles. On 6 October 1793, a tumbril traveled down Rue St-Honoré, carrying a woman whose prison-shorn hair was hidden under a frumpy bonnet. Nearby, Jacques-Louis David

sketched her as she passed, bequeathing to history a poignant image of Marie Antoinette, her hands tied behind her back, en route to the guillotine. ♦ Between Rues des Bourdonnais and Royale. Métros: Concorde, Madeleine, Tuileries, Pyramides, Palais Royal–Musée du Louvre, Louvre–Rivoli, Châtelet

79 Royal Saint-Honoré $$$$ This hotel next door to the **Tuileries Gardens** has 70 quiet rooms and a refined air. There's no restaurant. ♦ 221 Rue St-Honoré (between Rues d'Alger and de Castiglione). 01.42.60.32.79; fax 01.42.60.47.44. Métro: Tuileries

80 Chichen-Itza Fine hand-worked leather bags, briefcases, and wallets fashioned from ostrich, Madagascar crocodile, and the like are sold here. ♦ M-F 1-7PM; closed in August. 231 Rue St-Honoré (between Rues d'Alger and de Castiglione). 01.42.60.61.35. Métro: Tuileries

81 Giorgio Armani This ultra-modern designer boutique is set in the former **Hôtel du Rhin,** which became the temporary residence of Napoléon III during his 1848 presidential campaign. ♦ M-Sa. 6 Pl Vendôme (southeast corner). 01.42.61.55.09. Métros: Madeleine, Opéra, Tuileries

82 16 Place Vendôme Here Franz Anton Mesmer (1734-1815), the Austrian charlatan physician who invented mesmerism (later called hypnosis), conducted "animal magnetism" seminars wrapped in robes decorated with astrological signs. Later, in the 1930s, Obelisk Press had its office at this address. Headed by Englishman Jack Kahane, Obelisk published works that no one else would, such as Henry Miller's *Tropic of Cancer,* which appeared in 1934. It's still an office building. ♦ East side. Métros: Madeleine, Opéra, Tuileries

82 12 Place Vendôme In 1849 Frédéric Chopin, Polish composer and pianist, died here at the age of 39. It's now an office building. ♦ East side. Métros: Madeleine, Opéra, Tuileries

83 Charvet Edward VII bought his neckties and cravats here, and so can you. ♦ M-Sa; closed Monday in August. 28 Pl Vendôme (at Rue Danielle-Casanova). 01.42.60.30.70. Métro: Opéra

Ermenegildo Zegna

84 Ermenegildo Zegna The understated high fashions for men at this sophisticated shop are made with the richest of fabrics and have an appeal that's beyond snobbery. For more than a century the Zegna family has been known for making the world's finest wools, providing the best European designers with their raw materials. ◆ M-Sa. 10 Rue de la Paix (between Rues Danielle-Casanova and Daunou). 01.42.61.67.61. Métro: Opéra

ℋôtel Westminster

85 Hôtel Westminster $$$$ In the 19th century, this 101-room hotel catered to Americans such as Hamilton Fish, who was Secretary of State under Ulysses S. Grant, and the family of Henry James, who stayed here when the future novelist was 12. Today it still boasts traditional decor (wood paneling, marble fireplaces, parquet floors), a fine restaurant, and a bar (see below). ◆ 13 Rue de la Paix (between Rues des Capucines and Daunou). 01.42.61.57.46; fax 01.42.60.30.66. Métro: Opéra

Within the Hôtel Westminster:

Bar Les Chenets Frequented by a neighborhood business clientele, this bar specializes in Campari-based cocktails, which sounds misleadingly innocent. ◆ Daily 8:30AM-midnight. 01.42.61.57.46

85 Alfred Dunhill The Paris branch of a famous English company, this mahogany-paneled shop sells all manner of smoking paraphernalia. Dunhill pipes made from the best French brier, with ebony mouthpieces, are among the world's finest (and most costly). And where else will you find a thuja-wood cigar box? ◆ M-Sa. 15 Rue de la Paix (between Rues des Capucines and Daunou). 01.42.61.57.58. Métro: Opéra

86 Kitty O'Shea's The most Irish of pubs in Paris serves Guinness on tap. Businesspeople headquartered around the **Opéra** congregate here. ◆ M-Th, Su noon-1:30AM; F-Sa noon-2AM. 10 Rue des Capucines (at Rue Volney). 01.40.15.00.30. Métros: Madeleine, Opéra

87 L'Olympia Edith Piaf sang her heart out on this stage. Years later so did a group of Brits named the Beatles, who had just launched their first world tour. Playing here is still an obligatory engagement for top pop singers. ◆ 28 Blvd des Capucines (between Rues Edouard-VII and de Caumartin). 01.47.42.25.49. Métro: Madeleine

88 Musée Fragonard Get a sense of what the perfume industry is all about at this museum devoted entirely to fragrance and its history. Priceless perfume-related *objets d'art* are also on display. ◆ Admission. M-Sa. 39 Blvd des Capucines (between Rues Daunou and des Capucines). 01.42.60.37.14. Métro: Opéra

89 14 Boulevard des Capucines On 28 December 1895 the brothers Auguste and Louis Lumière, inventors of the cinematograph, projected their first public movie here in what was called the **Salon Indien.** This is now an office building. ◆ Between Rues Scribe and Edouard-VII. Métro: Opéra

89 Hôtel Scribe $$$$ Completely renovated behind its Napoléon III facade, this luxurious 227-room hotel was the Allied forces' press headquarters at the end of World War II. Correspondent John Dos Passos, who stayed here, wrote home describing Charles de Gaulle after a press conference: "He has two voices, the Sorbonne voice and the *père de famille, Henri Quatre, bonne soupe* kind of voice. There's more to him than we had been led to believe." ◆ 1 Rue Scribe (at Blvd des Capucines). 01.44.71.24.24; fax 01.42.65.39.97. Métro: Opéra

Within the Scribe:

Les Muses ★★$$$ In keeping with the hotel's grandeur, this dining room has an elegant atmosphere. Chef Philippe Pleuën offers dishes such as terrine of squab and foie gras, marinated lamb with cranberry sauce, and chicken with risotto and morels. ◆ M-F lunch and dinner. Reservations recommended. 01.44.71.24.26

Le Bar St-Laurent Business executives habitually gather around the elegant mahogany bar, sipping the Canadian whiskey cocktail of the day. ◆ Daily 9AM-2AM. 01.44.71.24.24

90 Le Grand Hôtel Inter-Continental $$$$ Designed in 1860 by **Charles Garnier,** this 514-room property is one of Europe's oldest luxury hotels. Although major renovations have stripped away some of its old-fashioned grandeur, the hotel offers such first-class perks as a sauna, tanning rooms, massage, and a gymnasium. Its proximity to the **Opéra Garnier** makes it a favorite of visiting prima ballerinas. ◆ 2 Rue Scribe (at Blvd des Capucines). 01.40.07.32.32; fax 01.42.66.12.51. Métro: Opéra

Within the Grand Hôtel Inter Continental:

La Verrière ★★$$$ Light-filled and spacious, with a glass roof and numerous plants and trees, this airy eatery serves Sunday brunch and an American-style breakfast buffet the rest of the week, as well as lunch and dinner. Specialties include turbot grilled with sage, lobster fricassee, lamb curry, and duck wings with roasted pears and sesame seeds. For dessert, try the wild strawberry and rhubarb pastry or the island fruit with coconut milk. ◆ M-Sa breakfast, lunch, and dinner; Su brunch and dinner; closed in August. 01.40.07.32.32

Bar du Grand Hôtel Tucked under the arches of the hotel is this multilevel **Opéra**-goers' watering hole. ◆ Daily 11AM-2AM. 12 Blvd des Capucines (between Pl de l'Opéra and Rue Scribe). 01.40.07.31.37

91 Place de l'Opéra Six main thoroughfares, bank headquarters, a theater district, and luxury boutiques are the spokes in this imposing hub. Back when the **Opéra** was where one scaled the social heights, the *haut monde* and *demimonde* frequented nearby beaneries such as **Café de la Paix, Café de Paris,** and **Café Riche.** ◆ At Blvd des Capucines. Métro: Opéra

91 Café de la Paix ★★$$ Looking like a scene painted by Renoir—brightly clothed patrons, green-and-white-striped umbrellas, dappled light—this lovely old cafe is classified as a historic landmark. Salvador Dalí enjoyed it, as did Harry Truman, Maurice Chevalier, Maria Callas, and General Charles de Gaulle, who ordered a take-out cold plate here on 25 August 1944—the first in liberated Paris. Tradition holds that if you sit on the terrace long enough, you will see someone you know walk by. House specialties include steak tartare and sole meunière; the cafe is also famous for its fresh shellfish from September through June. ◆ Daily lunch and dinner until 1AM. 3 Pl de l'Opéra (at Blvd des Capucines). 01.40.07.30.20. Métro: Opéra

91 Le Restaurant Opéra ★★$$$ Intimate and chic, this luscious dining spot recalls the **Opéra Garnier,** thanks to its **Charles Garnier**–inspired architectural elements. Champagne-colored table linen, Sèvres porcelain plates, and fine crystal add to the elegant ambience. Chef Le Squer's menu changes with the seasons and has included warm fillet of squab and truffle pie, vegetable ravioli in minestrone with gouda croutons, lobster stew with chestnuts, honey-roasted duckling, and rack of veal. Try the *sorbet pêche avec sauce à l'estragon* (peach with sorbet filling and tarragon sauce). The wine list is good and includes some organic varietals. ◆ M-F lunch and dinner; closed in August. Reservations recommended. 3 Pl de l'Opéra (at Blvd des Capucines). 01.40.07.30.10. Métro: Opéra

92 American Express If you did leave home without it, go no farther. Here you will find traveler's checks, a foreign exchange bank, and mail pickup. ◆ M-F; Sa for currency exchange only. 11 Rue Scribe (at Rue Auber). 01.47.77.74.75. Métro: Opéra

93 Boulevard Haussmann This drab expanse fronted with mammoth department stores becomes festive in December, when it's strung with Christmas lights. In 1784, two months after his arrival in Paris as American ambassador to France, Thomas Jefferson signed a nine-year lease on a new town house located on what is now the north side of Boulevard Haussmann. The Virginian filled it with furniture, then set about acquiring a collection of paintings, books, and engravings that would eventually adorn his beloved Monticello. History records that during his sojourn in Paris, Jefferson kept a black servant, James Hemings, whom he apprenticed to a local caterer, Combeaux, perhaps so he could take home some French culinary art along with his other acquisitions. ◆ Between Blvd des Italiens and Rue du Faubourg-St-Honoré. Métros: Richelieu–Drouot, Chausée-d'Antin, Auber (RER), Havre–Caumartin, St-Augustin, Miromesnil

❀PRINTEMPS

93 Au Printemps In the 1870s Paris introduced the world to *grands magasins* (department stores) such as **La Samaritaine** and **Bon Marché,** and the city's shopping giants have been drawing crowds ever since. Today, two outclass the rest: **Au Printemps** and **Les Galeries Lafayette** (see below), right next to each other along the Boulevard Haussmann. These are great places to get a peek at the latest in Parisian fashion as well as some indication of what it costs. Rest your feet and have a cup of tea or a slice of tart in the sixth-floor tea salon beneath **Au Printemps**'s Belle Epoque stained-glass rotunda. If possible, shop on weekday mornings, as afternoons and Saturdays in these stores can resemble a stampede at the Chicago stockyard. ◆ M-W, F-Sa; Th until 10PM. 64 Blvd Haussmann (between Rues de Caumartin and du Havre). 01.42.82.50.00. Métro: Havre–Caumartin

---

The famous Turgot Map of Paris was completed in 1739 after four years of labor by a team of artists led by Louis Bretez. Commissioned by Michel Etienne Turgot, who was in effect the mayor of Paris at the time, the extraordinary document is architecturally accurate right down to the window bays in the Louvre and the bushes in the Tuileries. The streets, however, are widened to keep them from disappearing behind the buildings.

GALERIES Lafayette

94 Les Galeries Lafayette With its
magnificent glass-and-steel dome and Art
Nouveau staircase built by the architect
Ferdinand Chanut in 1912, this 10-story
department store is classified as a historic
monument. More than 10,000 customers visit
its fashion department every day. An added
attraction is **Galeries Lafayette Gourmet:**
At sit-down counters throughout the food
department, shoppers can sample each
section's specialty, such as grilled meats near
the butcher, salads in the produce area, etc.
On the top floor there's incomparable
browsing and a marvelous vista of the Right
Bank's rooftops. ♦ M-W, F-Sa; Th until 9PM.
40 Blvd Haussmann (between Rues de la
Chaussée-d'Antin and de Mogador).
01.42.82.34.56. Métro: Chaussée-d'Antin

95 Opéra Garnier (Paris Opera) An opera
house fit for an emperor, the pièce de
résistance of Baron Haussmann's revamped
Paris, and a last hurrah of Second-Empire
opulence, this grandiose culture palace was
once the world's largest theater, with an area of
nearly three acres and a stage vast enough to
accommodate 450 performers. Designer
Charles Garnier, a 35-year-old previously
unknown architect, was selected from among a
field of 171 other competitors (including the
empress's favorite architect, **Eugène-
Emmanuel Viollet-le-Duc**).

Garnier gave the facade an unusual, ornate
look with friezes, winged horses, golden
garlands, and busts of famous composers. He
crowned his architectural extravaganza with a
copper-green cupola topped by Millet's *Apollo*
thrusting a lyre above his head. A golden bust
of the architect stands on the Rue Scribe
side of the theater. **Garnier**'s orgiastic
mishmash of styles (from Classical
to Baroque) and materials (every
possible hue of marble, from
green to red to blue) was less
than the hit he hoped it would
be. The empress, wife of
Napoléon III, is said to have
barked in disgust, "What is this
style supposed to be? It is
neither Greek nor Roman nor
Louis XIV nor Louis XV!"
Garnier diplomatically
replied: "It is Napoléon III,
Your Majesty." Second-Empire
advocates of family values were
in an uproar over the sensual
Carrier-Belleuse lamp-bearing statues

and the famous sculpted group *La Danse* by
Carpeaux.

Inside, however, the effect is eminently
upright, even majestic. Though Renoir loathed
it, you will find a night at the opera house well
worth your while, although it's the best of
classical ballet and modern dance that is
performed here now; all operas now take place
at the **Opéra Bastille.** The gold ornaments,
allegories in marble, Chagall ceilings, and the
parade of Parisian society are all good for a
gape. Horror fans will be interested to know
that the underground grotto where Leroux's
Phantom of the Opera lurked lies beneath the
Opéra's cellars, an artificial lake that provides
water for the city's fire brigade. The **Opéra
Museum** in the **West Pavilion** displays opera
and ballet memorabilia (such as the crown
Pavlova wore when dancing in *Swan Lake* and
the ballet slippers and tarot cards of Nijinsky).
♦ Admission. Box office: M-Sa. Museum: M-
Sa. Pl de l'Opéra (between Rues Halévy and
Auber). Reservations 01.44.73.13.00.
Museum 01.47.42.07.02. Métro: Opéra

Within the Opéra Garnier:

Grand Foyer and Staircase Of this
apotheosis of splendor (pictured below) Henry
James wrote: "If the world were ever reduced
to the domain of a single gorgeous potentate,
the foyer would do very well for his throne
room." The Baroque white Carrara marble
Grand Staircase, with its Algerian onyx
balustrade, is 32 feet wide at its center. At the
first landing, it divides and sweeps upward in
two flights of steps to the second-floor gallery.
The **Grand Foyer,** 175 feet long and decorated
with mirrors and allegorical paintings, is
encrusted with gilt ornamentation, and its
ceiling glows with Venetian mosaics and
colored marble from the island of Murano.
The annual **Ecole Polytechnique Ball** and
presidential galas take place here.

Grand Foyer and Staircase

MICHAEL STORRINGS

Auditorium The theater is famous for its six-ton chandelier and five tiers of loges dressed in red velvet and gold. The ceiling is adorned with Marc Chagall's 1964 masterpiece depicting Parisian scenes and images from operas ranging from *Giselle* to *The Magic Flute;* the work is as colorful as the rest of **Garnier**'s palace, yet oddly out of place. Backstage is the **Foyer de la Danse** so often painted by Edgar Degas.

96 8 Boulevard des Capucines It was at this address in 1880, the year of his death, that 61-year-old Jacques Offenbach composed his masterpiece *The Tales of Hoffmann*. It's now an office building. ♦ Between Rue de la Chaussée-d'Antin and Pl de l'Opéra. Métro: Opéra

97 Le Grand Café ★$ God bless it, one of the few Parisian bistros open 24 hours a day. It serves good seafood to boot. This haunt of Oscar Wilde is now a hangout for journalists, graveyard-shift laborers, and anyone else out walking the streets in the wee hours. ♦ Daily 24 hours. 4 Blvd des Capucines (between Rue de la Chaussée-d'Antin and Pl de l'Opéra). 01.43.12.19.00. Métro: Opéra

98 6 Rue Daunou Dr. Oliver Wendell Holmes (father of the famous jurist) knew this as the **Hotel d'Orient** and stayed here when he made a brief trip to Paris in 1886 to meet Louis Pasteur, who had just developed the vaccine for rabies. It's now the nondescript **Hôtel Daunou.** ♦ Between Ave de l'Opéra and Rue de la Paix. Métro: Opéra

99 Harry's New York Bar Opened in 1911, "Sank-Roo-Doe-Noo" (the American pronunciation of the bar's address) really came into its own two years later, when it was purchased from an American jockey by a bartender named Harry MacElhone. Here F. Scott Fitzgerald stared blearily at successive scotches and watched the plot lines of his novels take form; George Gershwin dreamed up his great fantasy *An American in Paris;* Ernest Hemingway dodged swinging fists; Gloria Swanson glowed; Noel Coward quipped; and Jean-Paul Sartre, despite himself, discovered both bourbon and hot dogs. The night before each US presidential election, the regulars around the bar are polled as to their guesses of the outcome; the legendary poll has an uncanny track record for predicting the winner. ♦ Daily until 4AM. 5 Rue Daunou (between Rues Louis-Le-Grand and de la Paix). 01.42.61.71.14. Métro: Opéra

100 Brentano's For the greatest hits in English literature, try this, one of the best and oldest English-language bookstores in Paris. ♦ M-Sa. 37 Ave de l'Opéra (between Rues Danielle-Casanova and d'Antin). 01.42.61.52.50. Métros: Opéra, Pyramides

101 Louise Delpuech A rare, immaculate self-service laundry is run by two redoubtable women inexplicably dubbed Romeo and Juliet by the neighborhood. Behind their stern scowls lurk hearts of gold. Read the hand-scrawled instructions (in English for Americans) and don't cram your machine too full. Overload and you're in big trouble with this imposing pair, and police headquarters is just across the street. ♦ Daily 8AM-9PM. 24 Pl du Marché-St-Honoré (east side, between Rues du Marché-St-Honoré and Gomboust). 01.42.61.04.49. Métro: Pyramides

101 Yakitori ★$ Try the morsels of cheese-stuffed pork, teriyaki chicken, and marinated shrimp skewered and grilled *à la Japonaise*. This restaurant is perpetually crowded, but it's worth the effort to grab a seat at the counter and watch the chefs perform. ♦ M-Sa lunch and dinner. 34 Pl du Marché-St-Honoré (east side, between Rues du Marché-St-Honoré and Gomboust). 01.42.61.03.54. Métro: Pyramides

101 Flo Prestige For those who enjoy picnicking and can afford not to bother with preparing the meal, this take-out gourmet deli offers a delectable selection of cheeses, charcuterie, salmon, salads, wines, and pastries of a quality that merits a limo for the tailgate picnic. For a setting, the nearby **Tuileries** or **Palais Royal** gardens should do just fine. ♦ Daily until 11PM. 42 Pl du Marché-St-Honoré (east side, between Rues du Marché-St-Honoré and Gomboust). 01.42.61.45.46. Métro: Pyramides

102 Tuileries $$$ Down a quiet side street, this hotel retains much of its 18th-century charm, despite having added 20th-century accoutre-ments (color TVs, minibars, and direct-dial phones) to its 26 rooms. There's no restaurant. ♦ 10 Rue St-Hyacinthe (between Rues de la Sourdière and du Marché-St-Honoré). 01.42.61.04.17; fax 01.49.27.91.56. Métros: Pyramides, Tuileries

103 Delices St. Roch ★★$ For a tasty lunch on the run, try this juice bar/quiche parlor. The quiches are filled with imaginative combinations of ingredients, such as chicken and carrot with mustard, fennel, and mushroom, and *oseille* (sorrel) and chavignol cheese. For dessert, try the red and green rhubarb pie or the coconut cream. A horde of well-heeled St-Honoré office workers and the occasional Birkenstock-shod Californian in search of freshly squeezed carrot-cucumber juice keep this place busy at lunchtime. ♦ M-F lunch until 6:30PM. 21 Rue St-Roch (between Rues St-Honoré and Gomboust). 01.42.97.50.40. Métro: Tuileries

104 Dave ★★★$$ A hideout for celebrities such as George Michael and Yves Saint Laurent, this excellent Sino-Vietnamese restaurant is named after its star-struck *maître d'*, who keeps a Polaroid collection of his most famous customers. The small dining room is decorated with deep red carpets and Chinese lamps, lending it an intimate ambience. Recommended dishes include the sweet and spicy spareribs, Vietnamese rolls served with mint, and shrimp sautéed in a spicy black bean sauce. ♦ M-F lunch and dinner; Sa-Su dinner; closed three weeks in August. 39 Rue St-Roch (between Rues St-Honoré and Gomboust). 01.42.61.49.48. Métro: Pyramides

105 St-Roch The bullet holes in this church's facade recall one of the most significant military debuts in French history. This is the site of a fierce Revolutionary skirmish that occurred on 5 October 1795, when Royalist troops took a stand on the steps of the church and were scattered by a then-unknown 27-year-old soldier named Napoléon Bonaparte. Ten days later Napoléon was appointed commander-in-chief of the home forces. An architectural mix-and-match, the structure is the city's finest Baroque church and is best known today for its splendid 1752 Rococo organ and weekly evening concerts. Built to handle the overflow from **St-Germain-l'Auxerrois**, it was originally designed by **Jacques Lemercier**, and no less a personage than Louis XIV laid its cornerstone in 1653. But it took another century to complete.

Jules Hardouin-Mansart was responsible for the oval **Lady Chapel,** and sculptor René Charpentier decorated the edifice in carved imagery. The church is dedicated to an Italian holy man who ministered to plague victims in the 14th century. Inside are memorials to the playwright Corneille, the philosopher Diderot, and Louis XIV's beloved gardener, André Le Nôtre, whose bust by Antoine Coysevox is to the left of the chancel. ♦ 296 Rue St-Honoré (at Rue St-Roch). 01.42.44.13.20. Métros: Pyramides, Tuileries

106 St-James et Albany $$$ Portions of this residential hotel date back to the reign of Louis XIV, which is appropriate, since for years its clientele was strictly old European aristocracy. It now offers 211 home-away-from-home suites, duplexes, and studios equipped with kitchenettes, so that after stocking up at the garden-floor delicatessen, guests can entertain their friends with crepes suzette and a view of the **Tuileries.** The nicest rooms are nestled in the attic beneath low-beamed ceilings. The hotel incorporates parts of the old **Noailles Mansion,** where General Lafayette married one of the Noailles daughters in 1774. ♦ 202 Rue de Rivoli (between Rues St-Roch and du 29-Juillet). 01.44.58.43.21; fax 01.44.58.43.11. Métro: Tuileries

Within St-James et Albany:

Les Noailles ★$$ Love will blossom when you stroll through the **Tuileries** with that special someone and then dine tête-à-tête in the courtyard of this elegant dining spot. Recommended dishes: *filets de lisette à la Rougail* (mackerel with tomato sauce) and *cabillaud fumé sauce vierge* (smoked cod with lemon-butter sauce). ♦ Daily lunch and dinner. 01.44.58.43.40, 01.44.58.43.21

Bar St-James ★$$ This is one of the classiest snack bars around. The lunch special, which changes daily, is always dependable and inexpensive. ♦ M-F lunch and dinner; Sa-Su dinner. 01.44.58.43.21

107 Comfort Hotel Louvre Montana $$ Clean, modern, and conveniently located near the **Tuileries** and **St-Roch** (which has marvelous evening concerts), this 25-room hotel is an isle of economy in an archipelago of extravagance. There's no restaurant. ♦ 12 Rue St-Roch (between Rues de Rivoli and St-Honoré). 01.42.60.35.10; fax 01.42.61.12.28. Métro: Tuileries

108 Hôtel Regina $$$$ Offering a splendid view of the **Tuileries Gardens,** this quiet 130-room hotel is furnished with antiques, crystal chandeliers, and a Louis XV-style elevator cage that has been retired from service and put on display in the lobby. The Belle Epoque–style restaurant serves standard French fare. ♦ 2 Pl des Pyramides (at Rue de Rivoli). 01.42.60.31.10; fax 01.42.61.12.28. Métros: Tuileries, Pyramides

109 Le Canard Enchaîné France's famous leftist satirical weekly, celebrated for its irreverent cartoons and editorials, is based here. The paper specializes in covering scandals and is usually first to the scene of the crime. ♦ 173 Rue St-Honoré (between Rues de l'Echelle and des Pyramides). 01.42.60.31.36. Métro: Palais Royal–Musée du Louvre

110 Auberge des Trois Bonheurs ★★$$ Despite the oh-so-French name, classic, elegant Chinese cuisine is what you'll find here. The chef is from Hong Kong and specializes in steamed trout, Peking duck, and jumbo shrimp *à la Cantonaise.* The pretty dining room has Chinese paintings on the walls and fresh flowers on the tables. ♦ Daily lunch and dinner. Reservations recommended. 280 Rue St-Honoré (between Rues de l'Echelle and des Pyramides). 01.42.60.43.24. Métro: Pyramides

110 Gargantua ★★$$ King Kong could leave here with a full tummy—the portions are so grand, the food (lamb curry, salmon and spinach tarts, foie gras) so delicious, the prices so reasonable. In the rear is a marble lunch counter. Pastries, charcuterie, wines, and salads are packed to go. This place is renowned for its croissants and *pain au chocolat.* ♦ Daily breakfast, lunch, and dinner. 284 Rue St-Honoré (between Rues de l'Echelle and des Pyramides). 01.42.60.52.54. Métro: Tuileries

111 Le Ruban Bleu ★★$$ The maritime decor and blue-ribbon name of this World War II–style restaurant commemorate the record transatlantic crossing by a French vessel called the *Normandie.* The menu, which changes each day, is trim and shipshape with specialties like grilled chèvre on toast, fillet of sole, and saddle of hare with fresh pasta. ♦ M-F lunch and dinner; closed in August. 29 Rue d'Argenteuil (between Rues des Pyramides and St-Roch). 01.42.61.47.53. Métro: Pyramides

112 Place André-Malraux In 1874, this square, formerly called Place du Théâtre Français, was graced by a duo of elegant but simple Davioud fountains decorated with bronze nymphs by Carrier-Belleuse and Math Moreau. ♦ Ave de l'Opéra and Rue St-Honoré. Métros: Palais Royal–Musée du Louvre, Pyramides

112 Manufacture Nationale de Sèvres (Sèvres Porcelain Factory) This showroom lies adjacent to the famous and venerable (circa 1738) Sèvres porcelain factory. An exhibition of designs ranges from Louis XVI dinner plates to an abstract lamp designed in 1984 by Japanese artist Asuka Tsu-Boi. All items sold here are tax-free. ♦ M-F. 4 Pl André-Malraux. 01.47.03.40.20. Métros: Palais Royal–Musée du Louvre, Pyramides

113 161 Rue St-Honoré On the present site of the **Moroccan Tourist Office** once stood the old **St-Honoré Gate,** where Joan of Arc was wounded in the thigh by an English archer in 1429. She was hit while measuring the depth of the moat with her lance in preparation for an assault on the city. ♦ Between Rues de Rohan and de l'Echelle. Métro: Palais Royal–Musée du Louvre

HOTEL DU LOUVRE

114 Hôtel du Louvre $$$ This modern 200-room hotel is situated beside the **Palais Royal, Tuileries,** and **Comédie Française,** and within walking distance of the **Opéra** and the **Louvre.** It offers contemporary comforts, traditional Second Empire–style decor, and a brasserie. Request the **Pissarro Suite,** from which the artist painted the Place du Théâtre-Français. ♦ Pl André-Malraux (at Rue de Rohan). 01.42.61.56.01; fax 01.44.58.38.01. Métro: Palais Royal–Musée du Louvre

114 A la Civette For more than two centuries this store has been in the forefront of tobacconists—it was the first shop in Paris to import the fine Montecristo cigar from Cuba. Shelves are cluttered with chewing tobacco, pipes, cigarillos, and stogies to delight the wheeziest connoisseur. ♦ M-Sa. 157 Rue St-Honoré (between Pl du Palais-Royal and Rue de Rohan). 01.42.96.04.99. Métro: Palais Royal–Musée du Louvre

114 Delamain The window of this wonderful old bookshop displays museum-worthy items, from 18th-century hand-bound volumes on King Clovis to modern editions of Samuel Beckett. ♦ M-Sa; closed Saturday in August. 155 Rue St-Honoré (between Pl du Palais-Royal and Rue de Rohan). 01.42.61.48.78. Métro: Palais Royal–Musée du Louvre

115 Le Louvre des Antiquaires An association of more than 240 antique shops encompasses three floors here. You'll find Art Deco prints, period perfume bottles, miniature 16th-century manuscripts, rare Japanese woodcuts, fin de siècle dolls and children's clothes, African tribal masks, and Thai Buddhas. In fact, one can find any old thing here except a bargain. Be advised that many of these dealers have their main antique shops (generally larger and less expensive) on the Left Bank, so take a card and pay them a visit when you're on the other side of the river. Also, before making a purchase, be sure you understand the complicated regulations concerning the removal of antiques from the country.

This building was formerly the **Grand Hôtel du Louvre,** where Mark Twain stayed in 1867. It was here that Twain met the tour guide Ferguson who figures in *The Innocents Abroad* (1869). ♦ Tu-Su. 2 Pl du Palais-Royal (at Rue de Rivoli). 01.42.97.27.00. Métro: Palais Royal–Musée du Louvre

116 Apothicaire Bérnard Derosne Here, two centuries ago, Count Fersen bought the invisible ink with which he penned his famous letters to Marie Antoinette. The pharmacy is still in operation, and you can still see traces of old advertisements (including one for invisible ink) between the windows on the facade. ♦ 115 Rue St-Honoré (at Rue de l'Arbre-Sec). Métro: Louvre–Rivoli

117 Maison Micro This Greek bazaar offers produce from Hellas: vats of olives and hot peppers, burlap sacks of whole grains and flour, crates of dried fruits, and barrels of *tarama.* Step inside and take a whiff of the Aegean. ♦ M afternoon; Tu-Sa. 142-144 Rue St-Honoré (between Rues du Louvre and Jean-Jacques-Rousseau). 01.42.60.53.02. Métros: Louvre–Rivoli, Palais Royal–Musée du Louvre

117 Chez Nous ★$$ The city's best jock bar and restaurant is run by Gilbert Ghiraldi, an ex-rugby player. If you manage to outmaneuver

Statue of Voltaire, Comédie Française

MICHAEL STORRINGS

the French national rugby team that huddles here, grab a table and order one of the Basque specialties. ♦ Daily lunch and dinner. 150 Rue St-Honoré (between Rues du Louvre and Jean-Jacques-Rousseau). 01.42.60.29.75. Métros: Louvre–Rivoli, Palais Royal–Musée du Louvre

118 Galerie Véro-Dodat Named after two pork butchers who were here from the start, this covered passageway was the city's first public thoroughfare to be illuminated by gas lighting. ♦ Between Rues Jean-Jacques-Rousseau and du Bouloi. Métros: Louvre–Rivoli, Palais Royal–Musée du Louvre

On Galerie Véro-Dodat:

Robert Capia This antique doll store is a favorite of Catherine Deneuve. ♦ M-Sa. 24-26 Galerie Véro-Dodat. 01.42.36.25.94

Christian Louboutin

118 Christian Louboutin The specialty of this women's shoe designer is shoes with hand-sculpted heels. The heels covered in gold leaf give you a dazzling walk. ♦ M-Sa. 19 Rue Jean-Jacques-Rousseau (at Galerie Véro-Dodat). 01.42.36.05.31. Métros: Palais Royal–Musée du Louvre, Louvre–Rivoli

119 L'Epi d'Or ★★$$ This humble 1950s Les Halles standby serves honest *pomme de ris de veau en crépine* (calf sweetbreads in crepes), salt pork and lentils, and unsophisticated Rhônes and Bordeaux. ♦ M-F lunch and dinner; Sa dinner; closed August. Reservations recommended. 25 Rue Jean-Jacques-Rousseau (between Galerie Véro-Dodat and Pl des 2-Ecus). 01.42.36.38.12. Métro: Les Halles

120 Comédie Française In 1673, while performing in his own *Le Malade Imaginaire,* the 51-year-old dramatist Molière collapsed onstage and died as the curtain came down. (Legend has it that there were several doctors in the audience who were so enraged by the play's criticism of medicine that they would not treat its dying author.) Seven years later Louis XIV founded the **Comédie Française** with the remaining members of the playwright's troupe. Today it is France's most prestigious theatrical group, residing since the end of the 18th century in this rather small Doric-style theater designed by **Victor Louis.** The company has survived the Bourbon monarchy, the Revolution, two empires, and four republics, and still plays to packed houses. After Molière, the theater's most celebrated thespian was the spirited tragic actress Sarah Bernhardt (the "Divine Sarah," born Rosine Bernard in Paris), who played roles ranging from Cleopatra to Hamlet, thereby reviving Shakespeare in France. Bernhardt was a dynamic character who was fond of saying, even in old age, "Rest? With all eternity before me?"

Today the **Comédie Française** is the bastion of French theater. It aims to keep classical theater alive while also staging works by the best modern playwrights, both French and foreign. A foyer-bar opens onto a gallery displaying busts of famous playwrights. The upstairs foyer is graced with a notable stone statue of Voltaire by Houdon (illustrated on page 222) and the leather armchair into which Molière collapsed during his last act on stage.

Additional theatrical performances may be seen at the newly opened **Comédie Française Studio Theatre** (99 Rue de Rivoli, 01.44.58.98.58) at the **Carrousel du Louvre.** Reservations are not accepted at this venue; tickets are sold one hour before each performance. ♦ Individual tours: third Su of each month at 10:15AM starting at the administration entrance on the Place Colette. Group tours: second and fourth Su of each month (must be reserved three to four months in advance). Box office: daily 11AM-6PM; a special window around the side of the building opens 45 minutes before the curtain to sell reduced-price tickets for the night's performance. 2 Rue de Richelieu (at Pl André-Malraux). 01.44.58.15.15. Métro: Palais Royal–Musée du Louvre

121 Restaurant Pierre Palais Royal ★★$$$ In the shadow of the **Comédie Française,** this restaurant offers a warm immersion in the mood of France's Massif Central region. Try veal kidneys, *St-Pierre à la rhubarbe* (John Dory with rhubarb), roast rabbit with mustard sauce, *gratin dauphinois* (potatoes au gratin), or the refined pike with chives. ♦ M-F lunch and dinner; closed in August. Reservations recommended. 10 Rue de Richelieu (between Pl André-Malraux and Passage de Richelieu). 01.42.96.09.17. Métro: Palais Royal–Musée du Louvre

121 Montpensier $$ This hotel was once the residence of a baroness who was a favorite of Louis XV, but it lacks the luxury that such a history suggests. The 42 rooms are of varying dimensions, and the room rates vary accordingly. There's no restaurant. ♦ 12 Rue de Richelieu (between Pl André-Malraux and Passage de Richelieu). 01.42.96.28.50; fax 01.42.86.02.70. Métro: Palais Royal–Musée du Louvre

121 Dynasty ★★$ This reasonably priced Chinese restaurant with pink tablecloths features a menu that's enlivened by several incendiary Vietnamese and Thai specialties. ♦ M-Sa lunch and dinner. 12 Rue de Richelieu

(between Pl André-Malraux and Passage de Richelieu). 01.42.86.06.58. Métro: Palais Royal–Musée du Louvre

MICHAEL STORRINGS

122 Palais Royal This six-acre enclave of flowering serenity is surrounded by, yet separate from, the urban bustle. Commissioned by Cardinal Richelieu and designed by his architect **Jacques Lemercier** in 1642, the mansion (pictured above) was christened **Palais Royal** when Anne of Austria temporarily lived here with her son, young Louis XIV. In 1780 the property fell into the hands of the shrewd Philippe, Duke of Orléans, who embarked on a lucrative and fancy bit of real estate speculation. He hired the architect **Victor Louis** (who built the nearby **Théâtre Français**) to design a square like Venice's Piazza San Marco, but containing a garden (700 feet by 300 feet) to be faced on three sides with elegant apartments incorporating arcades that had space for 180 shops, which the duke then sold for immense profit. (He also named the bordering streets after his three sons: Valois, Beaujolais, and Montpensier.)

Strolling through the lime-tree groves here became the fashion for French aristocrats as well as for American visitors such as Thomas Jefferson and Washington Irving. The garden's elegance soon frayed, however, when the profligate Philippe became chronically broke and began renting the galleries to magicians, wax museums, circuses, and brothels. Under his dissolute management, the palace and gardens attracted the Parisian rabble, questionable dandies, and women of easy virtue; it became a raffish, depraved enclave. (As late as 1804, historians listed the presence of 11 loan sharks, 18 gambling houses, and 17 billiard halls in the palace arcades.) Marat referred to the gardens as the "nucleus of the Revolution." It was here that Charlotte Corday bought the dagger she used to kill Marat. It was also here on 13 July 1789 that Camille Desmoulins incited his fellow Parisians to take up arms. Like the **Tuileries Palace,** the **Palais Royal** was ransacked during the revolt of 1848; a giant bonfire was kindled in the courtyard with gilt chairs, paintings, and canopies thrown from the windows by the mob. Among the furniture destroyed was the throne on which Louis Philippe first sat as king of France.

By the 20th century the luxurious apartments overlooking the gardens housed a number of famous residents. Poet and dramatist Jean Cocteau lived here, as did writer Colette. She resided at 9 Rue de Beaujolais and was often seen writing at her window overlooking the courtyard. Colette died as stylishly as she'd lived: suddenly and painlessly after drinking a glass of Champagne.

Today the buildings of the **Palais Royal** house private residences and offices that are closed to the public. However, visitors may stroll through the gardens and browse among the antiques, old books, jewelry, lead soldiers, medals, and rare stamps in the arcade's curiosity shops. The garden is embellished by the fountain where the infant Louis XIV once sailed his toy boats, and by two quite modern fountains resembling giant ball bearings. The larger court of the palace has been the focus of an aesthetic debate reminiscent of the one surrounding the **Louvre** transformation. Minister of Culture Jack Lang initiated a project (conceived by sculptor Daniel Buren) that involved the planting of 252 black-and-white striped columns, deep pools, and airport lights in the courtyard floor. In the winter of 1986 residents of the palace who objected to the scheme won a court order to halt construction on the site temporarily. The project, however, was completed the following summer. ♦ Bordered by Rues de Valois and de Montpensier, and Rues St-Honoré and des Petits-Champs. Métro: Palais Royal–Musée du Louvre

123 Le Grand Véfour ★★★★$$$$ A favorite Parisian haunt since the 1760s, this fine restaurant, part of the **Palais Royal** complex, is named after Jean Véfour, chef to Philippe, the Duke of Orléans (who voted to send his relative Louis XVI to the guillotine and later wound up there himself). Seductively and appropriately timeworn, the Louis XVI–Directoire interior is classified as a historic monument. Here Napoléon courted Joséphine, Victor Hugo romanticized, and Colette and Jean Cocteau, who lived nearby, enjoyed regular repasts. The menu offers exquisite cuisine gastronomique; favorites include fresh tomato *soupe, parmentier de queue de boeuf* (oxtail with puréed potatoes), foie gras ravioli with truffle cream, and *galette aux endives* (endive cake). Don't miss the rare cheeses and the Burgundy wines.♦ M-F lunch and dinner; closed in August. Reservations required. 17 Rue de Beaujolais (between Rues de Valois and de Montpensier). 01.42.96.56.27. Métros: Bourse, Palais Royal–Musée du Louvre

124 Bar de l'Entracte ★★$ Tucked in a corner behind the **Palais Royal,** this amusing restaurant and bar is festooned with old costumes from the theater across the street. Paper currency from all around the world flutters on the ceiling. The menu changes daily depending on what's fresh at the market; among Chef Babette's specialties are warm chèvre salad, cheese tarts, and pot-au-feu.

The wines are from the Loire Valley. On a warm summer day, enjoy a glass of cool St. Joseph on the outdoor terrace. The bar is often full of actors and journalists, who come here after performances at the **Comédie Française.** ♦ Daily lunch and dinner until 2AM; closed Sunday in winter. No credit cards accepted. 47 Rue de Montpensier (at Passage de Beaujolais). 01.42.97.57.76. Métros: Palais Royal–Musée du Louvre, Pyramides

125 Matsuri Sushi ★$$ Customers hunker around a circular bar to snag plates of raw salmon and tuna sailing by on a conveyor belt. To tally the check, waiters simply count the dishes in front of each diner. At lunch, every fifth item is free. So is home delivery throughout the day within Paris city limits. ♦ M-F lunch and dinner; Sa dinner; closed in August. 36 Rue de Richelieu (between Passages Hulot and de Beaujolais). Reservations: 01.42.61.05.73; delivery: 01.42.61.10.25. Métro: Palais Royal–Musée du Louvre

125 Les Boucholeurs ★★$$ *Boucholeurs* are the farmers who cultivate the small, finer tasting variety of mussels featured in many of the dishes served here. These particular mussels come from a *parc à huitres* (shellfish farm) near La Rochelle on the west coast, while the bankers and stockbrokers who eat them come from the nearby **Bourse.** Try the superb *mouclade Rochelaise* (small mussels in a creamy saffron and Cognac sauce) with a bottle of Fiefs Vendéen de Pissotte. Other specialties include *moules sauce au gingembre* (mussels in a ginger sauce), *moules au curry,* and haddock *poché.* Intimate and tasteful, the small blue dining room has subtle nautical details. ♦ M-F lunch and dinner; Sa dinner; closed mid-April to mid-May (or whenever the mussel season has run its course), and one week in August. Reservations recommended. 34 Rue de Richelieu (at Passage Hulot). 01.42.96.06.86. Métros: Pyramides, Palais Royal–Musée du Louvre

126 La Boutique du Bridgeur The only store in Paris catering strictly to bridge players, this boutique sells bridge tables, score pads, playing cards, and instruction manuals. If you write in advance, its affiliated bridge club might help find you a partner. ♦ M-Sa. 28 Rue de Richelieu (between Passages Potier and Hulot). 01.42.96.25.50. Métro: Palais Royal–Musée du Louvre

126 L'Incroyable Restaurant ★★$ What's incredible about this seven-table restaurant hidden on a cobbled passage are the generous portions and bargain prices. Traditional French dishes—*magret de canard* (duck fillet), carrots *râpées* (grated carrot salad), and apple tart—are served. ♦ M, Sa lunch; Tu-F, Su dinner. No credit cards accepted. 26 Rue de Richelieu or 23 Rue de Montpensier (between Passages Potier and Hulot). 01.42.96.24.64. Métro: Palais Royal–Musée du Louvre

127 Fontaine Molière The fountain, designed by **Ludovico Visconti,** was dedicated in 1773, the centennial of the playwright's death. Seurre's statue of Molière, pen in hand, is seated atop, flanked on either side by marble statues by Pradier representing light and serious comedy. ♦ Rues Molière and de Richelieu. Métro: Pyramides

127 Barrière Poquelin ★★$$ Original nouvelle cuisine is served here; menu items include steamed fish with mushrooms, salmon *unilatérale* (cooked on one side), spicy chicken, and roast game. Top off your meal with a hot apple tart. The formal dining room has red curtains reminiscent of those at the **Comédie Française** and a portrait of Molière. ♦ M-F lunch and dinner; Sa dinner; closed first three weeks of August. Reservations recommended. 17 Rue Molière (between Ave de l'Opéra and Rue Thérèse). 01.42.96.22.19. Métro: Pyramides

128 Chez Pauline ★★$$$ When tradition works this well, why change? This relaxed restaurant serves French classics such as *boeuf bourguignon, poularde de Bresse* (chicken from Bresse), creamed wild mushrooms with chives, warm foie gras salad, fricassee of sole and crayfish, game in season, and a variety of *plats du jour* such as stuffed cabbage, cassoulet with preserved goose, bacon with lentils, and calf's liver. ♦ M-F lunch and dinner; Sa dinner; closed Saturdays in summer. Reservations recommended. 5 Rue Villedo (between Rues de Richelieu and Ste-Anne). 01.42.96.20.70. Métro: Pyramides

129 Juveniles ★★$$ This lively *bistrot à vin* just down the street from the **Bibliothèque Nationale** is the brainchild of wine-lovers Mark Williamson (of **Willi's Wine Bar**) and his partner, Tim Johnston. It's a comfortable spot for noshing on tapas, rabbit pâté, chicken wings, chicken salad, and ample beef sandwiches, and afterwards enjoying a slice of the dense, flourless chocolate cake. Wash it all down with an excellent, reasonably priced Rioja. ♦ M-Sa lunch and dinner. 47 Rue de Richelieu (between Rues Villedo and des Petits-Champs). 01.42.97.46.49. Métro: Pyramides

130 Mercure Galant ★★$$$ Attractive decor, first-rate service, and specialties such as homemade duck foie gras, escargots in puff pastry, lobster gratin, and lamb marinated in spicy oil make this a perfect choice for business lunches. ♦ M-F lunch and dinner; Sa dinner. Reservations recommended. 15 Rue des Petits-Champs (between Rues Vivienne and de Richelieu). 01.42.97.53.85. Métros: Bourse, Pyramides

130 Willi's Wine Bar ★★$$ The city's most elegant wine bar bustles nonstop with journalists, lawyers, fashion designers, and the public relations crowd who come to partake of 300 French wines and changing daily specials such as grilled salmon steak, farm chicken with asparagus tips, leg of lamb, sea bass with dilled vegetables, and other classic bistro fare. The place is run by the affable Englishman Mark Williamson, who knows his Côtes-du-Rhônes. ♦ M-Sa lunch and dinner. Reservations recommended. 13 Rue des Petits-Champs (between Rues Vivienne and de Richelieu). 01.42.61.05.09. Métros: Bourse, Pyramides

130 Herboristerie du Palais-Royal Herbs, oils, and lotions for needs both medicinal and pleasurable are crammed floor to ceiling in this small shop. Every potion is designed to stimulate the senses. Michel Pierre, who has co-authored a book on salutary plants, can select just the herb to remedy your ailment. Passiflore from South America promotes relaxation, eleurocoque from Siberia increases energy, and harpagophytum from Namibia helps ease arthritis and rheumatism. ♦ M-Sa. 11 Rue des Petits-Champs (between Rues Vivienne and de Richelieu). 01.42.97.54.68. Métros: Bourse, Pyramides

Chantal Thomass
——PARIS——

131 Chantal Thomass Everything in this boutique is magically appealing, from the billowing curtains of the dressing rooms to the star-studded ceiling and the curvaceous furniture (not to mention the outfits, shoes, lingerie, and accessories for women). Thomass worked closely with interior designer Jean-Louis Ricardi to create a shop

that reflects her sensuous style. ♦ M-Sa.
1 Rue Vivienne (at Rue de Beaujolais).
01.40.15.02.40. Métros: Bourse, Pyramides

132 Galerie Colbert Like the adjoining Galerie
Vivienne (see below), this arcade has enjoyed
a stylish renaissance. The **Bibliothèque
Nationale,** which owns the passage, has
spent millions to restore the walkways, glass-
roofed rotunda, faux marble pillars, and 19th-
century bronze fixtures. The *galerie* has two
public exhibition halls featuring prints and
photos, and a small theater that hosts lunch
and evening concerts. A **Bibliothèque
Nationale** research department is also located
here. ♦ Free. Daily. Entrance on Rue des
Petits-Champs (between Rues des Petits-
Pères and Vivienne). 01.47.03.85.71. Métro:
Bourse

Adjacent to Galerie Colbert:

Galerie Vivienne From its mosaic floors to
the arching glass canopy, this gussied-up
galerie, established in 1923, is a most
fashionable arcade. Boutiques here sell
everything from high-tech jewelry and rare
books to children's masks and the best
brownies in Paris. ♦ Daily. 6 Rue Vivienne
(between Rue des Petits-Champs and Pl de la
Bourse). Métro: Bourse

Within Galerie Vivienne:

Si Tu Veux Babar, the universally loved
French elephant, comes in plush, plastic, or
posters at this old-fashioned toy store. There

are also enough paper hats and masks
available here to outfit any party of six- year-
olds. ♦ M-Sa. 68 Galerie Vivienne.
01.42.60.59.97

Jean Paul Gaultier Here's the designer
boutique of the man who brought miniskirts
to men and ice-cream-cone bras to women.
Check out the video screens—in the floor!
♦ M-Sa. 01.42.86.05.05

Legrand Filles et Fils From the back of
this Rue de la Banque *épicerie* (grocery),
Francine Legrand sells French red wines by
the case. ♦ Tu-Sa. 12 Galerie Vivienne.
01.42.60.07.12

A Priori Thé ★★$ Three expatriate
American women own this tearoom/
restaurant, whose wicker chairs and tables
with fresh-cut flowers spill into the charming
Galerie Vivienne. A creative selection of
quiches and salads is served, followed by
divine apple crumble and brownies for
dessert. The wine list is chosen by Francine
Legrand, whose wine shop (see above) is in
the same arcade. ♦ Daily lunch and afternoon
tea. 35-37 Galerie Vivienne. 01.42.97.48.75

**133 Bibliothèque Nationale (National
Library)** In 1537 a copyright act was passed
to ensure that a copy of every book published
in France would be housed in a royal library.
The result of four and a half centuries of book
and document assembly is now kept in one of
the world's greatest national libraries, in a
building whose architectural design is as
impressive as its collection.

The library came to occupy its present site in
the 17th century, when Cardinal Mazarin
merged two of his mansions, the **Hôtel
Tubeuf** and the **Hôtel Chivry.** The collection
initially included 500 pictures and art
objects owned by the cardinal himself.
When Colbert, finance minister to Louis
XIV, moved the library to his own
mansion on Rue Vivienne in 1666, the
collection numbered 200,000 volumes. In
1720, the library was combined again with
the original Mazarin collection. Today the
library's 68 miles of shelves bend under the
weight of more than nine million books,
including two Gutenberg bibles, first editions
of Rabelais, and manuscripts of works by
Proust and Hugo.

The library received its most dramatic space
in 1854, when the architect **Henri Labrouste**
was commissioned to design a reading
room within the old courtyard of the **Palais
Mazarin.** The result is the magnificent top-
lit **Salle des Imprimés** (illustrated at left),
which consists of nine square vaulted bays
supported by 16 cast-iron columns and a
network of perforated semicircular iron
arches. The room reveals a further development of ideas **Labrouste** first explored in the
design of his **Bibliothèque Ste-Geneviève,** a

Bibliothèque Nationale

MICHAEL STORRINGS

landmark building that was the first monumental public edifice to freely employ iron as both a structural and a decorative element. The reading room (admittance is for members and/or scholars only, although proof that you're an architect often works) features beautifully attenuated columns, gleaming lens-like skylights in the ceiling, and graceful curves of iron latticework. In the **Salon d'Honneur** (State Room) on the ground floor is an Houdon statue of Voltaire; the writer's heart is ensconced in the pedestal.

The library is divided into 11 departments: printed books; periodicals and newspapers; manuscripts; prints and engravings; maps and plans; medals, coins, and antiques; technical; audiovisual; arms and weapons; performing arts; and music. All are reserved for researchers and scholars; none are open to the public except for one weekend every year in October. Groups may arrange for private tours of the library by contacting **La Caisse Nationale de Monuments Historiques et Des Sites** (01.44.61.21.69) at least a month in advance.

There are several public galleries and exhibition spaces in the library. The **Musée des Médailles et Antiques** features a collection of vases, precious stones, jewelry, furniture, and other antique objets d'art. The **Galeries Mazarin** and **Mansart** and the **Photo Galerie Colbert** mount temporary exhibitions.

Some of the library's vast collection has moved to an ultra-modern building on Quai de la Gare along the Left Bank of the Seine in the east of Paris. The controversial new **Bibliothèque Nationale de France** building, designed by architect **Dominique Perrault,** will house the precious volumes in four glass towers connected by an immense public esplanade the size of the Place de la Concorde. Most of the new building is closed to the general public except for temporary exhibitions (at 11 Quai François Mauriac; métro: Quai de la Gare). ♦ Free. **Galeries Mazarin** and **Mansart:** Open for special exhibitions only. **Musée des Médailles et Antiques**: M-Su 1-6PM. **Galerie Colbert** (photographic gallery): M-Sa noon-6:30PM 58 Rue de Richelieu (between Rues des Petits-Champs and Colbert). 01.47.03.81.26. Métros: Bourse, Palais Royal–Musée du Louvre

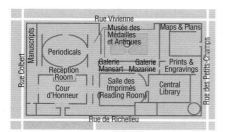

134 Café San José The Cahen family, owners of this tiny stand-up coffee bar, roast their own beans and serve the best cappuccino in town. At midday, neighborhood workers seeking a caffeine fix swarm here. ♦ M-F 7AM-7PM. 30 Rue des Petits-Champs (between Rues Chabanais and Ste-Anne). 01.42.96.69.09. Métros: Pyramides, Bourse

135 Pandora ★★$ Behind the chocolate-brown facade is a comfy little tearoom that in summer offers light lunches of cucumbers in yogurt and mint, Baltic herring, lemon tarts, and mincemeat pies. Warm winter dishes include chili con carne and chicken *tajine* (stew). ♦ M-F lunch and afternoon tea until 7PM; closed two weeks in August. 24 Passage Choiseul (between Rues des Petits-Champs and St-Augustin). 01.42.97.56.01. Métro: Quatre-Septembre

136 Issé ★★★$$$ The city's best (and most expensive) sushi bar also serves impeccable sashimi, grilled salmon, steaming miso soup, red caviar, delectably light tempura, and *chirashi,* the house specialty. ♦ M, Sa dinner; Tu-F lunch and dinner. Reservations recommended. 56 Rue Ste-Anne (at Rue Rameau). 01.42.96.67.76. Métro: Pyramides

137 Coup de Coeur ★★$$ House specialties in this small, friendly restaurant with modern decor include foie gras served with a glass of sweet Rivesaltes wine, *magret de canard* (duck fillet), roasted red mullet fillets, and a sinfully delicious chocolate dessert. ♦ M-F lunch and dinner; Sa dinner. Reservations recommended. 19 Rue St-Augustin (between Passage Choiseul and Rue Monsigny). 01.40.15.93.60. Métros: Quatre-Septembre, Pyramides

138 Restaurant Drouant ★★$$$$ At the end of each November since 1903, 10 novelists have met here to award the Prix Goncourt, France's prestigious prize for the year's best fiction. (The prize isn't much money, but fame and fortune in the form of lucrative publishing contracts follow.) The specialties of this century-old restaurant are turbot roasted in clay, Bresse chicken with onion and lemon chutney, and a chocolate and pistachio fondant. The dining room is popular with the elegant crowd from the **Opéra.** If you forget to make reservations, consider having a meal in the cafe. ♦ Daily lunch and dinner. Reservations required. 18 Rue Gaillon (at Pl Gaillon). 01.42.65.15.16. Métro: Quatre-Septembre

139 La Tour de Jade ★★$ This eatery was founded by a former minister to Indochina's Emperor Bao-Dai. Stuffed duck, lemon chicken, broiled mullet with anchovies, duck with lotus seeds, and pork balls in soy sauce are the menu highlights. The dining room has the typical Chinese-restaurant decor—dim lighting, simple furniture, and kitschy decorative items. ◆ M-Sa lunch and dinner. Reservations recommended. 20 Rue de la Michodière (between Rue de Hanovre and Blvd des Italiens). 01.47.42.07.56. Métro: Quatre-Septembre

140 5 Rue des Italiens The prestigious Parisian daily newspaper *Le Monde* is headquartered here. ◆ Between Blvd des Italiens and Rue Taitbout. Métros: Quatre-Septembre, Richelieu–Drouot

141 Au Petit Riche ★★$$ A favorite of journalists, this warm, century-old restaurant offers tasty Lyonnais sausage, roast lamb, hot apple tarts, and carafes of Bourgueil. ◆ M-Sa lunch and dinner. Reservations recommended. 25 Rue Le Peletier (at Blvd Haussmann). 01.47.70.68.68. Métro: Le Peletier

142 Hôtel Drouot The closest thing to a Sotheby's in Paris, this establishment specializes in estate sales and auctions of everything from Cartier jewels, Louis XIV furniture, and African sculpture to baskets of kitchenware and collections of rare illustrated manuscripts. On the top floor, the most valuable objets d'art are overseen by renowned auctioneers Ader Picard. Auctions take place in the afternoons starting at 2PM, but arrive early to scan the merchandise—a great experience in itself. ◆ M-Sa. 9 Rue Drouot (between Rues Rossini and de Provence). 01.48.00.20.20. Métro: Richelieu–Drouot

143 Chopin $$ At the end of the peaceful Passage Jouffroy (which is classified as a French historic monument), this modest hotel offers 36 small rooms at small rates. There's no restaurant. ◆ 46 Passage Jouffroy (between Blvd Montmartre and Rue de la Grange-Batelière). 01.47.70.58.10; fax 01.42.47.00.70. Métro: Rue Montmartre

144 Chartier ★$ This cavernous turn-of-the-century soup kitchen with pinwheel fans and surly waiters offers better theater than cuisine, but it's worth a visit nevertheless. Basic, inexpensive French food—egg salad, pâté, roast chicken—is served with rough red wine. The place is always mobbed with tourists, so get here early. ◆ Daily lunch and dinner until 9:30PM. 7 Rue du Faubourg-Montmartre (between Blvd Montmartre and Rue de la Grange-Batelière). 01.47.70.86.29. Métro: Rue Montmartre

145 Musée Grevin The city's largest wax museum is populated with distinguished paraffin personalities, including Charles de Gaulle, Catherine Deneuve, Woody Allen, and Yehudi Menuhin. Children love it. ◆ Admission. Daily 1-7PM. 10 Blvd Montmartre (between Rue du Faubourg-Montmartre and Passage Jouffroy). 01.47.70.85.05. Métro: Rue Montmartre

146 Aux Lyonnais ★★$$ Long patronized by **Bourse des Valeurs** traders in the neighborhood, this bistro's reputation is founded on classic, unadventurous cuisine. ◆ M-F lunch and dinner; Sa dinner. Reservations recommended. 32 Rue St-Marc (between Rues de Richelieu and Favart). 01.42.96.65.04. Métro: Richelieu–Drouot

147 49 Rue Vivienne On this site stood the **Salle Musard,** a concert hall where Tom Thumb, headliner for P.T. Barnum's show, performed in 1844. A new office building was under construction here at press time. ◆ Between Rue St-Marc and Blvd Montmartre. Métros: Bourse, Richelieu–Drouot

148 Passage des Panoramas Nineteenth-century American inventor Robert Fulton painted and displayed 18 panoramas, including a portrayal of the burning of Moscow, in two large cylindrical towers off Boulevard Montmartre. The French flocked to see the sagas, and, with his profits, Fulton bankrolled his steamboat and submarine schemes. ◆ Between Rue St-Marc and Blvd Montmartre. Métros: Bourse, Rue Montmartre

149 Clementine ★★$$ In this charmingly decrepit bistro, named after the owner's daughter, M. Langrenne prepares delicious and unpretentious fare. Either the homemade foie gras or the mackerel croquettes will begin the meal nicely. The entrées include rabbit in lemon mustard sauce, lamb chops with garlic, and roast chicken with chèvre. As for dessert, the dark chocolate fondant needs no further description. ◆ M-F lunch and dinner. Reservations recommended. 5 Rue St-Marc (between Rues du Faubourg-Montmartre and des Panoramas). 01.42.36.91.72. Métros: Bourse, Rue Montmartre

In 1858, a would-be assassin known as Orsini the Carbonaro threw a homemade bomb at a carriage carrying Napoléon III to an opera house. Though the emperor was unharmed, 156 bystanders were killed or injured. With this incident in mind, architect Charles Garnier added a special entrance to his design for another opera house on Rue Auber; it allowed Napoléon III's coach to be driven directly to the level of the dress circle via a double ramp into the royal box. Rumor has it that this thoughtful touch helped Garnier's design win out over those of 171 other competing architects.

150 Le Vaudeville ★★$$ This vintage 1925 brasserie was rescued from decline and obscurity by brasserie king Jean-Paul Bucher and is now packed at lunchtime by execs from the **Bourse des Valeurs** and **Club Med** headquarters, and at night by theater patrons. Specialties include andouillette, foie gras, grilled lobster, shellfish (year-round), homemade *saumon rillette* (salmon spread), and a chilled house Riesling. Dining on the sidewalk is pleasant in summer. ♦ Daily lunch and dinner until 2AM. Reservations recommended. 29 Rue Vivienne (between Rues du Quatre-Septembre and de la Bourse). 01.40.20.04.62. Métro: Bourse

151 Bourse des Valeurs (Stock Exchange) Napoléon commissioned this "Temple of Money" in 1808, and architect **Alexandre Théodore Brongniart** was inspired to adorn it with 64 Corinthian columns. The building's design is epic, and so is the chaos of brokers on the floor. Visitors are welcome to head for the spectators gallery and watch French capitalism at work. On a day of stiff trading, the excitement rivals that of European Cup soccer. Be sure to bring identification. There are two organized tours every afternoon; call for hours. ♦ Free. M-F 11AM-2PM. 4 Pl de la Bourse (between Rues Notre-Dame-des-Victoires and Vivienne). 01.49.27.14.72. Métro: Bourse

152 Pile ou Face ★★★$$$ A coin's throw from the **Bourse,** this intimate restaurant, whose name means "heads or tails," serves exquisite nouvelle cuisine without any of the pretentions that normally garnish such food. The owners raise chickens and rabbits on their farm outside Paris, and their refined tastes are exemplified in the delicious *magret de canard* (duck fillet), chicken with tarragon, rabbit in rosemary, and chocolate cake. The Cahors, Chinons, and Beaujolais are among the highlights of the wine list. This is a perfect setting for a romantic dinner. ♦ M-F lunch and dinner; closed in August. Reservations required. 52 *bis* Rue Notre-Dame-des-Victoires (at Rue Brongniart). 01.42.33.64.33. Métro: Bourse

153 Hollywood Savoy ★★$$ This trendy restaurant becomes a nightclub when the Ivy League waiters and waitresses take to the stage and belt out creditable renditions of "Stormy Monday" and other Yankee classics. ♦ M-Sa lunch and dinner.Reservations recommended.44 Rue Notre-Dame-des-Victoires (between Rues Réaumur and Brongniart). 01.42.36.16.73. Métro: Bourse

Bests

Mina Gondler
Painter/Sculptor

When roses are blooming I always go to the **Bagatelle** in the **Bois de Boulogne**—it's a haven of beauty and perfumes.

Once a week I tour the galleries of **St-Germain-des-Prés** and visit the famous bookstore **La Hune,** next to **Aux Deux Magots.** Then I meet friends at **La Palette,** the painters' cafe on the **Rue de Seine.**

Walking along the **Seine** and observing the Paris sky is always a meditation for me.

From time to time it's important to go to the **Musée Marmottan.** One can really appreciate Monet's paintings in that calm atmosphere.

In warm weather, I dine with friends in the garden of **L'Espace Restaurant,** opposite the American Embassy, or in the garden of **La Closerie des Lilas** in Montparnasse.

A concert at **Sainte-Chapelle** is a double pleasure for the spirit. You can enjoy the chapel's stained-glass windows and the excellent music at the same time.

Brian Knowlton
Editor/Columnist, *International Herald Tribune*

If Edgar Allan Poe had designed a park, it surely would look something like the **Parc des Buttes-Chaumont,** in Paris's near-northeast. It's a dark, mysterious, enchanting spot, a series of steep hills and deep ravines with a towering butte in the middle—and a lovely gazebo with one of the city's best views at its top, accessible only by crossing one of two bridges, including a suspension bridge. It is a stark contrast to Paris's mostly gentle contours. There are caves, waterfalls, bubbling brooks, and sweet-smelling pine woods. In springtime, the flowers are glorious—including one patch atop the butte, precariously close to a steep, 100-foot drop-off, which is tended by a mysterious woman occasionally seen very early in the morning. It's a wonderful place for joggers (nothing is flat in the park except the path around the pond at the base of the butte), children (take them to the popular puppet show, or let the small ones enjoy the old-fashioned crank-operated swings) gourmets (there are two good, scenically situated restaurants), and lovers (no explanation needed). The **Buttes Chaumont** métro station is closest, but you might want to stroll down the hill afterward toward the **Belleville** area—once Edith Piaf's haunt, but now the center of one of Paris's two big Chinatown areas—for a delicious and inexpensive bowl of Hong Kong–style soup.

Lionel Poilâne
CEO, Baker, Boulangerie Poilâne

Musée Bourdelle—Antoine Bourdelle's collection of works painted and sculpted in his workshop.

Restaurants:

Bofinger—For the atmosphere of Alsace and its culinary tradition.

Le Récamier—In good weather its terrace is unique.

Le Train Bleu—Spectacular decor and a unique atmosphere.

Montmartre

Rue des Épinettes
Rue Baron
Rue Lantiez
Rue Jean-Leclaire
Rue Lacaille
Rue J.-Cartier
Rue F.-Gémier
Rue Ordener
Rue Gauthey
Rue de la Jonquière
Rue Vauvenargues
Rue Championnet
Rue Sauffroy
Rue Guy-Môquet
Rue du Cap.-Lagache
Rue Marcadet
Rue des Moines
Rue Davy
Rue Lamarck
Rue Étex
Rue Coysevox
Rue Lacroix
Rue du Cap.-Madon
Rue Carpeaux
Rue Joseph-Maistre
Rue Legendre
Ave. de Clichy
Rue Fauvet
Rue Eugène-Carrière
Rue Damrémont
Rue Ganneron
Ave. de St-Ouen
Rue Touriaque
Rue Lemercier
Rue Étienne-Jodelle
52 Cimetière de Montmartre
44
43
46
50
45 Rue Lepic
47
Rue La Condamine
Rue P.-Ginier
Rue H.-Moreau
Rue Cavallotti
Rue Durantin
Rue Nollet
Rue Ganneron
Ave. de Clichy
Rue Capron
Rue Forest
51 **49** **48**
Rue J.-de-Maistre
Rue Lepic
Rue Tholozé
Rue Truffaut
Rue des Dames
Rue Biot
Rue Caulaincourt
Ave. Rachel
Rue Véron
57
Rue des Batignolles
Rue Darcet
Blvd. de Clichy
Blvd. de Clichy
Rue Lepic
56
Pl. Blanche
Blvd. de Clichy
Rue de Douai
Rue de Bruxelles
Rue Fontaine
53
Pl. de Clichy
Rue de Bruxelles
Rue de Calais
Blvd. des Batignolles
Rue de Turin
Rue d'Amsterdam
Rue de Vintimille
Rue de Clapeyron
Rue St-Petersbourg
Rue de Moscou
Rue Ballu
Rue de Berne
Rue de Bucarest
Rue de Clichy
Rue Chaptal
55
Rue de Moscou
Rue Blanche
Rue Henner
Rue de Turin
Rue Moncey
Rue La Bruyère
Rue de Liège
Rue de Liège
54
Rue Jean-Baptiste
Rue de Milan

N
km | 1/4 | 1/2
mi | 1/8 | 1/4

Montmartre

Crowned with that alabaster wedding-cake church known as **Sacré-Coeur,** Montmartre is the balcony of Paris—half dream, half nightmare. It is a tangle of contradictions: meandering country roads, seedy strip joints, early Christian sites, tourist clichés, sublime vistas, and hidden passages. The **Butte** (which is what Parisians call this sandstone height) is geographically the highest point in town (427 feet) and the traditional home of poets, singers, painters, and bohemians of all kinds.

The best day to visit Montmartre is on Tuesday, when the museums in other parts of Paris are closed, or any day when you feel like fleeing the center of the city for a few hours. Emerging from **Hector Guimard**'s Art Nouveau **Abbesses** métro station, start your tour with café au lait and brioches in one of the cafes along **Rue des Abbesses,** which is crowded with butchers, bakers, and fishmongers from the **Rue Lepic** market. Then begin the ascent to **Place du Tertre,** a 14th-century square that in summer harbors a lively crowd of street artists, outdoor restaurant waiters, and tourists. The best bets for lunch are crepes at **Le Tire Bouchon,** fish at **La Crémaillère 1900** on Place du Tertre, or the sublime *foies de volaille* (chicken livers) at **L'Assommoir.** After the obligatory pilgrimage to **Sacré-Coeur,** wind down Rue Lepic past the **Moulin de la Galette** until you see the red neon signs of the Butte's other storied temple, the **Moulin Rouge.** Come back later in the evening for the cancan show or for the cabaret at the legendary **Au Lapin Agile.** Métro service ends at 12:45AM, but you'll find a taxi just down the hill on **Rue Caulaincourt,** which is filled with revelers during the wine-festival parade held in October.

The name Montmartre has two possible origins: the "Mount of Mercury," for the Roman temple to Mercury that once stood on the Butte, or the "Mount of Martyrs," commemorating St. Denis, the first bishop of Paris, who, along with the priest Rusticus and the deacon Eleutherius, was tortured and decapitated here by the Romans in AD 250. According to the legend, St. Denis picked up his severed head and carried it from Montmartre over a hill several kilmoters away. A thousand years later, the **Basilique de St-Denis** was built on that hill. Streets in Monmartre were named for the priest and deacon, who did not join St. Denis in the headless trek.

A lesser-known local martyr is mill owner Pierre-Charles Debray, who during the Franco-Prussian War was crucified on the blades of his **Moulin de la Galette,** a windmill with a garden tavern and dance hall that a half-century later would symbolize "Gay Paree" in a painting by Renoir. Artists such as Renoir, van Gogh, Dufy, and Utrillo; poets Apollinaire, Max Jacob, and Jacques Prévert; and novelist Boris Vian, songwriter Aristide Bruant, and illustrator André Gill all worked in Montmartre. In the late 19th century, Toulouse-Lautrec sketched the cancan dancers at the **Moulin Rouge,** and in the early 1900s, Pablo Picasso, Georges Braque, and Juan Gris, working out of an abandoned piano factory nearby, gave birth to Cubism. Cabarets such as **Au Lapin Agile** further encouraged *la vie de bohème,* and the life was much romanticized by Americans in Paris. Writer John Roderigo Dos Passos, for instance, rhapsodized in 1918 that he wanted his heart "to be preserved in a pitcher of *vin de Beaujolais* in the restaurant in Place du Tertre on the summit of Montmartre."

After World War I, Paris's artistic center moved to another of the city's seven hills, Montparnasse, on the Left Bank. Its nightlife, however, remained in Montmartre and grew in notoriety. Though the neighborhood is the site of what is reputedly the oldest church sanctuary in Paris **(St-Pierre)** and was dominated in the 12th century by an abbey run by women, today the area is best known for women (and men disguised as women) plying an older, less pious profession. Painters may once have looked for portrait models among the seamstresses and dancers in **Place Pigalle**, but seamier live sex shows, porn theaters, and peep shops took over at the end of World War II. Nevertheless, the area is generally safe, even at night.

The Butte is packed on weekends, especially on the first Saturday and the first or second Sunday of October, the dates of the local annual wine-harvest festival and the vintage-car rally, respectively. You can avoid the masses by visiting on a weekday, or just come on the weekend and join in the *joie de vivre* of the crowd.

---

1 Abbesses Métro Station Named after *les abbesses*, the nuns who ran the abbey here in the Middle Ages, this métro station is the deepest in Paris—300 feet below ground level. The reason for the great depth lies in Montmartre's old gypsum mines. Gypsum, a soft stone, was burned to make the internationally famous plaster of paris used to mold, among other things, busts of George Washington and Thomas Jefferson in the US capitol. Over the years, the growing network of quarry tunnels beneath Montmartre turned the hill, geologically speaking, to Swiss cheese. In the 1840s the mines were closed, but not before 27 houses and several Parisians had disappeared into the void. The city of Paris is still filling Montmartre's cavities with high-pressure concrete. The métro platform was built at bedrock, precisely 285 steps below Place des Abbesses. Take the elevator and save your breath for the Montmartre summit.

The turn-of-the-century exterior of the station, with its green, vinelike, wrought-iron arches and amber lights, is one of the most picturesque in Paris and typifies the early Art Nouveau designs of architect **Hector Guimard.** At first, nationalistic Parisians criticized **Guimard**'s choice of German green and suggested he paint his métro stations *bleu, blanc, et rouge.* His concession to chauvinism was a ship shield (the symbol of the city of Paris) in the middle of the roof, but he stubbornly held his ground on garden green. This is one of only two **Guimard** stations that still have their original glass roofs (the other is **Porte Dauphine** near the **Bois de Boulogne**). However, the Abbesses métro entrance is not original to the Butte. For decades it stood in front of the **Hôtel de Ville** (City Hall), but when Mayor Jacques Chirac gussied up the plaza in 1977, he moved **Guimard**'s masterpiece to Montmartre. New York's Museum of Modern Art has an old *Métropolitain* sign and early **Guimard** arches similar to these. ◆ Pl des Abbesses (at Rue des Abbesses)

2 St-Jean-de-Montmartre Soon after its construction, this church, a Moorish grab bag of architectural tricks trimmed with what looks like turquoise Art Nouveau jewelry, was given the nickname "St-Jean-des-Briques" due to its redbrick facade. Looking amazingly

contemporary for a nonagenarian, the 1904 church was the first in Paris built with reinforced concrete. ◆ 19-21 Rue des Abbesses (between Rues Houdon and Germain-Pilon). 01.46.06.43.96. Métro: Abbesses

3 Hôtel Régyn's Montmartre $$ This 22-room hotel is in the heart of Montmartre, but otherwise it's nothing fancy. There's no restaurant. ◆ 18 Pl des Abbesses (at Rue des Abbesses). 01.42.54.45.21; fax 01.42.23.76.69. Métro: Abbesses

4 Le Progrès ★$ This authentic, economical neighborhood cafe and bar is patronized by Parisians rather than tourists. The simple food isn't gourmet, but it is tasty, and decent wines are poured by the pitcher. There is a daily prix-fixe lunch such as roast beef and potatoes or *rognons provençaux* (kidneys with tomatoes, olive oil, and garlic). Charcuterie and cheese are served all day. ◆ M-Sa lunch and snacks until 2AM. 1 Rue Yvonne-Le-Tac (at Rue des Trois-Frères). 01.42.51.33.33. Métro: Abbesses

La Boutique des Anges

5 La Boutique des Anges Wing your way into this shop where owners Brigitte and Patricia sell everything from heavenly-inspired CDs, jewelry, and lamps to books and paper goods—all with an angelic twist. One popular item is the personal guardian angel pin (selected to correspond with your birthdate) designed by local artisans. ◆ Daily. 2 *bis* Rue Yvonne-Le-Tac (between Rues des Trois-Frères and des Martyrs). 01.42.57.74.38. Métro: Abbesses

6 Gaspard de la Butte Annie Baron and Catherine Malaure sell their original line of colorfully patterned children's clothes in this darling little shop. You can catch a glimpse of the fabric samples and sewing machines in the backroom workshop. ◆ Daily. 10 *bis* Rue Yvonne-Le-Tac (between Rues des Trois-

Frères and des Martyrs). 01.42.55.99.40. Métro: Abbesses

7 Martyrium Just off the Street of Martyrs, where St. Denis was thought to have been decapitated, is the **Chapelle des Martyres.** In the crypt of an earlier medieval sanctuary on this site, Spaniards Ignatius Loyola and Francis Xavier founded the Jesuit order of priests on 15 August 1534. ♦ M-W, F-Su. 11 Rue Yvonne-Le-Tac (between Rues des Trois-Frères and des Martyrs). No phone. Métro: Abbesses

8 L'Abat-Jour Patrick Rossignol and Chantal Juan want people of all ages, professions, and lifestyles to feel comfortable in their cozy hair salon. No photographs of pouty models with trendy hairdos are displayed. The stylists will cut, shape, color, or perm your hair to suit you, using many products with natural ingredients. The salon's name means "the lamp shade," which refers not to any coiffure but to the business formerly located at this address, a lamp shade manufacturer. ♦ Tu-Sa. 19 Rue Yvonne-Le-Tac (between Rue des Martyrs and Pl des Abbesses). 01.42.64.39.32. Métro: Abbesses

9 Claude & Nicole ★★$ This cozy neighborhood bistro has a faithful clientele of young Montmartre residents who come for the herring fillet, ham in béchamel sauce, and *blanquette de veau* (veal with béchamel sauce and mushrooms). ♦ Tu-Sa lunch and dinner; Su lunch. 13 Rue des Trois-Frères (between Rues Yvonne-le-Tac and de la Vieuville). 01.46.06.12.48. Métro: Abbesses

10 Bonjour l'Artiste Sold here are juggling balls, batons, magic rings, trick cards, clown noses, and any other paraphernalia you might need in order to run away with the circus. ♦ M-Sa. 35 Rue des Trois-Frères (between Rue de la Vieuville and Passage des Abbesses). 01.42.51.44.53. Métro: Abbesses

---

Restaurants/Clubs: Red   Hotels: Blue
Shops/ ♥ Outdoors: Green   Sights/Culture: Black

11 Wanouchka ★$$ Eastern European immigrants swarm to this very small restaurant for classic Polish cuisine (pirogi, blintzes, Baltic herring, and borscht) prepared by chef Roman Rybicki, a veteran of the Russian Tea Room in New York. Forget the wine list and order the plum-and-lemon vodka—when in Warsaw, do as the Poles do. The dining room is formal, with traditional Polish decoration. ♦ M-Tu, Th-Sa dinner; Su lunch and dinner. Reservations recommended. 28 Rue la Vieuville (between Rue des Martyrs and Pl des Abbesses). 01.42.57.36.15. Métro: Abbesses

12 13 Place Emile-Goudeau On this site stood the famous old piano factory that art historians call the "Villa Médici of Modern Art." By the turn of the century this place had attracted poets Apollinaire and Max Jacob, and modern painters Picasso, Braque, Gris, and Modigliani. Picasso worked here for eight years, painting such works as *Les Demoiselles d'Avignon* (which is now in the collection of New York's Museum of Modern Art and is often cited as the first example of Cubism). This ramshackle building, which had but one water spigot to serve the 40 artists housed here, was sarcastically dubbed *Bateau Lavoir* after the laundry barges that used to travel along the Seine. The original structure burned in 1970, but the city of Paris built a concrete replica and now rents studios (and provides plenty of water) to the far more prosperous, though not necessarily more talented, artists of today. ♦ At Rue Ravignan. Métro: Abbesses

12 Tim Hôtel $$

Had this 60-room hotel been here 70 years ago, you might have asked neighbors Pablo Picasso or Georges Braque over for coffee and croissants. Today this member of a French budget hotel chain offers modern amenities (superior to those at most places in the same price range) but has the sterile atmosphere typical of chain hostelries. The charming location, however, makes up for the bland character. There's no restaurant. ♦ 11 Rue Ravignan (at Pl Emile-Goudeau). 01.42.55.74.79; fax 01.42.55.71.01. Métro: Abbesses

12 Fontaine de Quatre-Grâces (Four Graces Fountain) Layered in green paint, this drinking fountain and 99 other identical ones around Paris were given to the city in the 1840s by Richard Wallace, an Englishman who collected 18th-century French art and frequently lamented that it was impossible in his beloved Paris to enjoy a glass of water in a cafe without paying for it. The metal drinking cup originally attached to it disappeared in the 1950s when the city adopted sanitation standards. ♦ Rue Ravignan (at Pl Emile-Goudeau). Métro: Abbesses

12 Relais de la Butte ★$$ Not for the cholesterol conscious, the bill of fare at Nathalie Moret's casual, rustic restaurant features *fromage*. Cheese appears in every dish, including such tasty concoctions as *camembert rôti* with apples and Calvados, salmon with cantal and *vin blanc*, and beef cooked in beer with livarot (a traditional cheese from Normandy). For dessert there is a creamy *fromage blanc* with honey and almonds. ♦ Tu-F dinner; Sa-Su lunch and dinner. 12 Rue Ravignan (at Rue Trois-Frères). 01.42.23.94.64. Métro: Abbesses

13 Rue de la Mire Getting lost in the twisting streets of Montmartre can be done with the greatest of ease, except on this short pedestrian street. An 18th-century *mire* (trail marker) points due north. ♦ Between Rues Ravignon and Lepic. Métro: Abbesses

14 Le Tire Bouchon Cabaret ★★$ If you're in the mood for a little "Maple Leaf Rag" to accompany an apricot crepe or some cider *bouché*, go no farther: this *crêperie* has a jazz pianist upstairs playing the works of Fats Waller and Scott Joplin. The decor is reminiscent of an early-1960s Amsterdam jazz dive, with a vintage Coke dispenser, graffiti-scarred beams, and walls papered with posters and photos of stringy-haired musicians. ♦ Daily dinner, and afternoon and late-night snacks until 2AM. No credit cards accepted. 9 Rue Norvins (between Pl du Tertre and Rue Poulbot). 01.42.55.12.35. Métro: Abbesses

14 Au Clair de la Lune ★★$$ Alain Kerfant, a talented chef, manages to drown out this restaurant's loud decor (wall murals of **Le Moulin de la Galette** and the streets of Montmartre) with his seasonal specialties and excellent wine list. Try the wild boar and chanterelle mushrooms with a 1988 Remoissenet Meursault or, if you hit the jackpot in Deauville last weekend, splurge on a rare bottle of 1975 Château d'Yquem Sauternes to complement your *coquilles St-Jacques* in lime sauce.♦ M-Sa lunch and dinner. 9 Rue Poulbot (between Pl du Calvaire and Rue Norvins). 01.42.58.97.03. Métro: Abbesses

15 Place du Tertre Part village carnival, part operetta set, this 14th-century square (*tertre* means hillock or mound) is the hub of Montmartre, where busloads of tourists descend to pay homage to the Unknown Artist's awful landscapes and pathetic paintings of melancholy wide-eyed children. In summer (when the square sprouts parasoled restaurant tables), white-aproned waiters and hustling artists jealously guard

their territories; the daily border wars make for great theater. During the Middle Ages the abbey had a scaffold here to hang anyone who disobeyed its rules, including any vineyard owner on the Butte who refused to donate a quarter of the wine he pressed to the ladies of the cloth, *les abbesses*. The tradition of exhibiting paintings in Place du Tertre dates from the 19th century, but unfortunately the quality of art has deteriorated over the years. Located in front of **St-Pierre-de-Montmartre,** the square is hard to miss, though you may wish you had. ♦ At Rues du Mont-Cenis and Norvins. Métro: Abbesses

On Place du Tertre:

Le Clairon des Chasseurs $ In this bustling artists' cafe, where all the patrons seem to have sketchbooks under their arms and charcoal pencils behind their ears, painters gather by the window to case prospective clients in the square. The kitchen performs such improbable feats as ruining a *croque-monsieur* (grilled ham-and-cheese sandwich), and the coffee is as muddy as the canvas of **Notre-Dame** adorning the rear wall. Nevertheless, this cafe scores big points as a refuge. Ironically, the only way to escape the nagging street artists of Place du Tertre is by entering their midst; they come to this cafe strictly to take a break and won't pester you here. ♦ Daily breakfast, lunch, and dinner until 2AM. No. 3 (east side). 01.42.62.40.08

La Bohème ★$$ No-frills traditional French cuisine—*boeuf bourguignon,* au gratin potatoes, apple tarts—is served here. The dining room straddles a harshly lit cabaret stage where bored accordion and piano players boom out *chansons de Montmartre*. On weekend afternoons, this is the only music on the square. ♦ M-Sa breakfast, lunch, and dinner; Su lunch; closed in January. No. 2 (at Rue du Mont-Cenis). 01.46.06.51.69

La Mère Catherine ★$$ Founded in 1793 and, as house legend has it, commandeered in 1814 by the Russians who conquered the Montmartre villagers, this is still the oldest brasserie on Place du Tertre, and the waiters swagger as if to show it. You'll find escargots, rack of lamb, and tournedos Mère Catherine (beef filets cooked in Port and foie gras sauce) on the menu. The dining room is adorned with Belle Epoque reproduction mirrors and red-velvet benches, and piano and violin music from the 1920s accompanies your meal. There's also outdoor dining on the terrace. ◆ Daily lunch and dinner. No. 6 (between Rues du Mont-Cenis and Norvins). 01.46.06.32.69, 01.42.58.78.21

La Crémaillère 1900 ★★$$ This brasserie, with an arbored garden, fin-de-siècle decor, and Edith Piaf's greatest hits played nightly on the piano, has a healthy neighborhood following. Seafood (fresh oysters, mussels, and sole stuffed with shrimp mousse) is the strong suit. ◆ Daily lunch and dinner. No. 15 (between Rues Poulbot and Norvins). 01.46.06.58.59

16 St-Pierre-de-Montmartre An important example of early Gothic architecture, this modest, three-aisled church was begun 16 years before **Notre-Dame** and claims to be the oldest sanctuary in Paris (two other structures, **St-Germain-des-Prés** and **St-Julien-le-Pauvre**, make similar claims). What appears to be a tiny provincial church is all that remains of the original abbey, which was founded in 1134 by King Louis VI (the Fat) and his wife, Queen Adélaide, who is buried here. The church was dedicated and consecrated by Pope Eugene III in 1147. Both Dante and St. Ignatius Loyola worshiped here.

Architecturally, the church is a composite. The vaulted choir definitely dates from the 12th century (notice the walls buckling beneath the weight of more than 800 years), but archaeologists remain divided over whether the four capitaled columns incorporated in the church came from a Roman temple to Mercury or a Merovingian church (AD 500-751) on the site. The original church windows were shattered at the end of World War II by a bomb intended for a nearby bridge. New windows added in 1953 closely resemble in style the original Gothic stained glass; the three bronze west doors and the cemetery door depicting the Resurrection are by a contemporary Italian sculptor. Each Good Friday, the archbishop of Paris carries a crucifix up this "Mount of Martyrs" to **St-Pierre** as part of a stations-of-the-cross service.

The church's tiny cemetery is the smallest in Paris, with only 85 occupants, among whom are the sculptor Pigalle, the navigator Bougainville (after whom the purple flowering creeper is named), and Montmartre's first mayor, Felix Desportes. The Debray family, the original owners of the **Moulin de la Galette**, are also buried here; the family grave is easy to find—look for the miniature windmill on top. ◆ Church: daily. Cemetery: open only on All Saints' Day (1 Nov). 2 Rue du Mont-Cenis (at Rue St-Eleuthère). 01.46.06.57.63. Métro: Abbesses

MICHAEL STORRINGS

17 Basilique Sacré-Coeur Diocesan architect **Paul Abadie**'s Roman-Byzantine marble tribute, universally panned by his peers, has nevertheless become enshrined in the Tourists' Top Ten. For most people, the highlight of the church (pictured above) is not its design, but the view from its steps—or even better, from the dome (access through the north aisle) at dusk or dawn. The church was built as atonement for the massacre of some 58,000 citizens during the Franco-Prussian War, and within its mosaic-encrusted interior you can see priests praying for forgiveness for those war crimes 24 hours a day, a tradition that has been carried on since the church was consecrated more than half a century ago. Begun in 1876, **Sacré-Coeur** took decades to complete; for the first 15 years of construction, pylons were sunk below grade to stabilize the foundation over the old quarry mines. The towering campanile was added in 1904 by **Lucien Magne**; one of the world's heaviest bells, the 19-ton **Savoyarde**, hangs in the belfry.

From the north side of the dome you can see in the distance the green roof of the basilica built on the site where St. Denis finally put down his head. A trip to the **Basilique de St-Denis** is worthwhile (one métro ticket will get you there), if only to see the extraordinary collection of tombs where France buried its kings until the time of the Revolution. Most macabre are the tombs of Marie de Médicis and Henri IV, who are depicted twice in marble. On the tops of their tombs are sculptures of the two in their finest Renaissance collars and jewels; below, their skeletons are shown being eaten away by worms. (For more information, see the "Day Trips" chapter.) ◆ Admission for dome. Pl du Parvis-du-Sacré-Coeur (at Rues du Cardinal-

Guibert and Azais). 01.42.51.17.02. Métros: Abbesses, Anvers

18 Funicular The shortest, steepest métro line in Paris runs every few minutes between Place Suzanne-Valadon and the base of **Sacré-Coeur.** While fitness freaks take the stairs, the rest ride up in comfort and enjoy the view, all for the price of a normal métro ticket. ♦ Top station at Pl du Parvis-du-Sacré-Coeur; bottom station at Pl Suzanne-Valadon and Rue Foyatier. Métro: Anvers

18 Rue Foyatier The most photographed steps in Montmartre, all 266 of them, run from Rue Azais down to Place Suzanne-Valadon (named after Maurice Utrillo's mother, a talented painter in her own right). All hell breaks loose here at 4:30PM each day when an elementary school lets out and scores of screaming children with miniature leather briefcases on their backs dart across the square in search of their mothers and fathers—the local butchers, bakers, and souvenir-makers—who have come to walk them home. ♦ Between Pl Suzanne-Valadon and Rue Azais. Métro: Anvers

19 Le Gastelier ★$ The tea salon at the foot of **Sacré-Coeur** is a perfect luncheon stop before making the final ascent up the white stairs. Try a Milanese tart (spinach, tomato, and cheese) and a dish of fresh mandarin orange sorbet. Better yet, indulge in a few scoops of nougat ice cream or a plate of macaroons, and then waddle over to the **Funicular** and ride up. ♦ Tu-Su breakfast, lunch, and afternoon tea until 8PM. 1 *bis* Rue Tardieu (at Pl St-Pierre). 01.46.06.22.06. Métro: Anvers

19 A l'Angélus ★★$ The path to this nonsmoking neighborhood candy store/tea shop is well worn by schoolchildren and **Sacré-Coeur** pilgrims alike. The *fait maison* (homemade) bonbons and *angélus* (almond paste and chocolate mousse) are rich enough to sate any sweet tooth. Try the *Alesien* coffee pralines and the *orangettes,* strips of orange rind dipped into a velvety mixture of melted chocolate and almond chips. On a drizzling winter afternoon, nothing beats the hot cocoa made from melted chocolate bars. ♦ M-Tu, Th-Su. 1 Rue Tardieu (at Pl St-Pierre). 01.46.06.03.75. Métro: Anvers

20 Marché St-Pierre Paris's most celebrated discount fabric warehouse is the hub of the city's garment district. Pandemonium reigns over acres of tweed, bolts of polyester, and bins of last year's argyle socks in this five-story bazaar. Everyone comes here: students searching for cheap curtains, Punjabi women rummaging for sari silk, and New Wave couturiers stalking ersatz panther pelts. The costumes of the surly salesclerks range from three-piece suits to studded leather jackets and turquoise tights. The method in this madness? Take it from the top: fifth floor, linens and sheets; fourth floor, lace curtains and duvet covers; third floor, silks, velours, and *incroyables* (exotic odds and ends); second floor, wools and polyesters; ground floor, a bit of everything. ♦ M 1:30-6:30PM; Tu-Sa. 2 Rue Charles-Nodier (at Rue Livingstone). 01.46.06.92.25. Métro: Anvers

21 L'Eté en Pente Douce ★★$ This cafe and *salon de thé,* whose name means "summer on a soft slope," is hidden on a little square at the base of **Sacré-Coeur**'s sloping grassy park. Its outdoor terrace is a peaceful haven in this lively neighborhood. Daily specialties such as rabbit in mustard sauce are served along with your typical *salade niçoise* and your not-so-typical *filet mignon Sylvestre aux champignons* (wild boar steak with mushrooms). ♦ Daily lunch, afternoon tea, and dinner. 23 Rue Muller (at Rue Paul-Albert). 01.42.64.02.67. Métros: Château Rouge, Anvers

22 L'Ermitage Hôtel $$ Those who crave an elegant yet soothing atmosphere will delight in this small hotel, housed in a three-story 1860 residence. The warm and smiling owner, Maggie Canipel, makes each guest feel right at home. The 12 breezy rooms, each lovingly decorated by Maggie, contrast with the more somber corridors. Rooms 11 and 12 open onto a bewitching terraced garden full of chirping birds, while other rooms have splendid views of the city. Breakfast, served in each guest's room, is included in the reasonable price. There's no restaurant. ♦ No credit cards accepted. 24 Rue Lamarck (between Rues du Chevalier-de-la-Barre and Becquerel). 01.42.64.79.22; fax 01.42.64.10.33. Métro: Lamarck–Caulaincourt

23 Aux Négociants ★★$$ A favorite with locals is this simple bistro where the menu changes daily. The hearty French fare served here includes *blanquette de veau* (veal with cream sauce and mushrooms), steak tartare with *pommes de terre sautées*, and *andouillettes frites* (fried sausage of chitterlings with fries). Wines featured are from the Loire Valley. ♦ M-F lunch and dinner; Sa dinner until 10:30PM. 25 Rue Lambert (between Rues Labat and Custine). 01.46.06.15.11. Métro: Château Rouge

24 24 Rue du Mont-Cenis Composer Hector Berlioz lived with his English wife in a house on this site from 1834 to 1837. The present building was built in 1925. ♦ Between Rues Becquerel and Lamarck. Métro: Lamarck–Caulaincourt

25 Au Poulbot Gourmet ★★$$ Innovative Jean-Paul Langevin runs a simple, cozy restaurant decorated with early Montmartre photos and original Poulbot illustrations. His specialties are *foie gras de canard*, escargots with garlic cream and fresh artichokes, and a two-chocolate charlotte with pistachio sauce. ♦ M-Sa lunch and dinner; Su lunch. 39 Rue Lamarck (between Rues du Mont-Cenis and l'Abbé-Patureau). 01.46.06.86.00. Métro: Lamarck–Caulaincourt

26 Beauvilliers ★★★$$$ Its name is borrowed from Antoine Beauvilliers—*officier de bouche* to gluttonous Louis XVIII and founder of the first restaurant in Paris in 1784—but this restaurant has a style all its own. Edouard Carlier has created one of the most elegant *salons à manger* in Paris; what was once an old bakery is now three intimate Louis Philippe–style dining rooms. One room is full of bridal bouquets, the second features 18th- and 19th-century engravings of the Montmartre windmills, and the third is a portrait gallery of Beauvilliers's contemporaries painted by Louis-Léopold Boilly and the like. All three are adorned with a profusion of bouquets that seem even more numerous when reflected in the wall mirrors and lacquered ceilings. The decor is like that of a 19th-century bourgeois boudoir. Chef Jean-François Renard changes the menu weekly; memorable specialties have included lamb terrine with thyme, Brittany lobster salad, duck with passion fruit, and lemon pie in white rum for dessert. Pair your meal with a white St-Joseph wine and watch the bill climb like Rue Lepic. ♦ M dinner; Tu-Sa lunch and

dinner. Reservations required for dinner. 52 Rue Lamarck (at Rue l'Abbé-Patureau). 01.42.54.54.42. Métro: Lamarck–Caulaincourt

27 L'Auberge de la Bonne Franquette ★$$ This former van Gogh studio is now an intentionally rustic restaurant/cabaret serving escargots, *confit de canard* (duck confit), and *pâté en croûte* (pâté in a pastry crust) to Japanese, Dutch, and German bus tours. Guitarist Jacques Lescure and accordion player Jacques Vassart lead the equivalent of a nightly French hootenanny and hawk their cassettes and records at intermission. ♦ Daily lunch and dinner. Reservations recommended. 18 Rue St-Rustique (between Rues du Mont-Cenis and des Saules). 01.42.52.02.42. Métro: Abbesses

28 Musée de Montmartre Located just behind 12 Rue Cortot (whose roll call of former tenants includes Renoir, Utrillo, and Dufy), this pleasant little museum is housed in a delightful 17th-century town house called **Le Manoir de Rose de Rosimond.** The house, which is surrounded by two charming gardens, was the country residence of Rosimond, a 17th-century actor who appeared frequently in the plays of Molière and who, like Molière, died while performing *Le Malade Imaginaire.*

The museum's eclectic collection includes caricatures by Daumier and André Gill, posters and drawings by Toulouse-Lautrec, stunning Clignancourt porcelain, and the piano on which Gustave Charpentier wrote his opera *Louise* in 1900.

Though it seems outlandish in Paris to visit a museum in order to look at a bistro, an entire 19th-century bistro complete with a scalloped zinc bar is on display here. The exhibition relates the apocryphal story that the term bistro originated on the Butte, where impatient Russian soldiers used to shout at Montmartre's waiters: "*Bistraou, bistraou!*" (Russian for "Get a move on"). On Wednesday evenings, the **Art et Humour Montmartrois** meets in the museum for poetry readings and art exhibitions; lectures on local culture sponsored by the **Société du Vieux Montmartre** are held Saturday evenings. ♦ Admission. Tu-Su. 12 Rue Cortot (between Rues du Mont-Cenis and des Saules). 01.46.06.61.11. Métro: Lamarck–Caulaincourt

29 Vignes de Montmartre (Montmartre Vineyards) This is one of the last two remaining vineyards in Paris. Each year's harvest yields enough grapes for about 500 bottles of red Clos Montmartre wine. The labels are designed by Montmartre artists, and half-bottles are sold each year in the basement of the 18th arrondissement's **Mairie** (City Hall; 1 Pl Jules-Joffrin, at Rue Ordener, 01.42.52.42.00; métro: Jules

238

Joffrin). The wine is nothing special, but the harvest fete, on the first or second Saturday of October, is not to be missed. Crowds line Rue Lamarck for a celebration that feels like a combination of an academic procession, the Rose Bowl Parade, and Halloween. Participants might include baton twirlers, Auvergnat farmers in wooden clogs, and the mayor's wife, who traditionally picks the first grape. The vineyards are not open to the public, but note the plaque in front on Rue St-Vincent dedicated to Poulbot, the popular cartoonist who prevented the vineyards from being sold to high-rise developers in the 1930s. ♦ Rue des Saules (at Rue St-Vincent). Métro: Lamarck–Caulaincourt

30 La Maison Rose ★$$ Utrillo once painted a picture of this pink restaurant, and pink it has stayed—even the cutlery is rose-tinted. In the summer the tables spill onto Rue de l'Abreuvoir, and if the view doesn't make you dizzy, order foie gras with a bottle of Champagne to ensure that your head spins. Standard French fare such as escargots and smoked salmon is served, but it's not that well prepared. ♦ Daily lunch and dinner. 2 Rue de l'Abreuvoir (at Rue des Saules). 01.42.57.66.75. Métro: Lamarck–Caulaincourt

31 Au Lapin Agile The original **Cabaret des Assassins** was rechristened in 1880 when André Gill painted a rabbit with a red bow tie bounding from a copper kettle on the sign outside. The *lapin à Gill* (rabbit by Gill) became the *lapin agile* (nimble rabbit), and this famous cabaret turned into a stomping ground for intellectuals and artists who came for poetry readings and folk songs. (In 1985 the French government issued a five-franc stamp depicting Utrillo's oil painting of the cabaret.) A century later you can still grab a wooden stool, order a Kir, and sing along to those same old songs, as updated by pianist Roger Lesouad. Don't miss the 19th-century whimsy in front: a concrete fence made to look like knotty pine. No food is served. ♦ Tu-Su cabaret 9:15PM-2AM. No credit cards accepted. 22 Rue des Saules (at Rue St-Vincent). 01.46.06.85.87. Métro: Lamarck–Caulaincourt

32 Cimetière St-Vincent (St. Vincent Cemetery) Composer Arthur Honegger and painters Théophile-Alexandre Steinlen and Maurice Utrillo are buried in Paris's most intellectual cemetery. Enjoy the ivy-covered walls, a tranquil view of **Sacré-Coeur,** and (if you need to get off your feet) south-facing benches that catch the afternoon sun. The old caretaker is generally helpful but becomes cantankerous between noon and 2PM, when he is emphatically out to lunch. ♦ Daily. Rues St-Vincent and des Saules. Métro: Lamarck–Caulaincourt

33 Musée d'Art Juif (Jewish Art Museum) If your schedule can accommodate this museum's limited visiting hours, you'll be rewarded with exhibits of traditional drawings, crafts, and engravings, and a collection of scale-model synagogues. ♦ Admission. M-Th, Su 3-6PM; closed Jewish holidays and in August. 42 Rue des Saules (between Rues Caulaincourt and Francœur). 01.42.57.84.15. Métro: Lamarck–Caulaincourt

34 Le Château des Seigneurs de Clignancourt Along with **St-Pierre-de-Montmartre,** this is one of the oldest relics of this district's past. The original manor house was home to the famous porcelain manufacturer (founded in 1767) that provided Louis XVIII with plates and saucers. ♦ Regrettably, the early 16th-century house was demolished in 1861 and all that remains is its renovated turret, which now decorates the corner of a modern restaurant. ♦ Rue du Mont-Cenis (at Rue Marcadet). Métro: Jules-Joffrin

35 Mairie du 18e Arrondissement (City Hall of the 18th Arrondissement) When artist Maurice Utrillo died in 1955, he left two of his paintings to the local *mairie* (town hall)—not in payment of estate taxes as Picasso did, but simply as a gift. The paintings are displayed here; ask the *secrétariat général* on the second floor. Half bottles of wine from the **Montmartre Vineyards** are for sale in the basement. ♦ M-F. 1 Pl Jules-Joffrin (at Rue Ordener). 01.42.52.42.00. Métro: Jules-Joffrin

36 Pâtisserie de Montmartre It's tough choosing between the heavenly cherry tarts and the divine *Rose-Maries* (brioches filled with almond cream) at this pastry shop. ♦ M-Sa. 81 Rue du Mont-Cenis (between Rues Ordener and Versigny). 01.46.06.39.28. Métro: Jules-Joffrin

The Piscine Deligny, a floating swimming pool on the Seine at Quai Anatole-France and a Paris landmark since 1785, sank into the river in 1993. No one was hurt when the 165-by-50-foot pool, constructed on 12 attached barges, broke away from its supports and touched bottom. The carcass now sits on the riverbed 12 feet underwater.

Dépôts-Ventes:
Haute Couture at Bargain Prices

Ever wonder what those well-dressed Parisians do with last season's Yves Saint Laurent jacket or the Christian Lacroix party dress that just wouldn't do a second year in a row? Many of these haute-couture threads, still in perfect condition, end up in stores called *dépôts-ventes* (the name literally means "deposit-sell") and are sold for a fraction of the original price. Although *dépôts-ventes* sell merchandise of all styles and qualities, you'll find no thrift-shop fare at these elegant boutiques.

Alternatives (18 Rue du Roi-de-Sicile, between Rues Pavée and Ferdinand-Duval, 01.42.78.31.50). This shop features couture for men and women with a penchant for Japanese designers. There are labels from Matsuda, Issey Miyake, Yamamoto, and Comme des Garçons, as well as Jean Paul Gaultier, agnès b., Marithé et François Girbaud, and Thierry Mügler.

Chercheminippes (109-110-111 Rue du Cherche-Midi, between Jean-Ferrandi and Blvd du Montparnasse, 01.42.22.45.23). For men, women, and children, this boutique specializes in new designers such as Chevignon, Lolita Lempicka, Kenzo, and Bill Tornade.

Fabienne (77 *bis* Rue Boileau, between Rue Charles-Marie-Widor and Blvd Exelmans, 01.45.25.64.26). Cerruti suits, Kenzo shirts, and jackets by Gianfranco Ferré, Hugo Boss, and Armani have found their way to this *dépôt-vente* devoted to men's fashions. There's also a nice collection of Mont Blanc pens at a quarter of the usual price.

Half and Half (28 Ave des Gobelins, between Rue des Gobelins and Blvd Arago, 01.43.36.91.15). A perfect shop for the bride-to-be where silk wedding gowns are reconditioned and sold at a quarter of the original price. Designer eveningwear from Kenzo, Hermès, and Chanel is also featured.

La Marelle (21 Galerie Vivienne, off Rue Vivienne, 01.42.60.08.19). This shop has been dressing women and children for more than 20 years. Located in the elegant **Galerie Vivienne,** it carries *grandes marques* like Régina Rubens, Georges Rech, and Max Mara plus clothing by *créateurs* such as Azzedine Alaïa, Yohji Yamamoto, and Thierry Mügler. For children there are agnès b., Et Vous, Jacadi, and Bonpoint fashions.

Les Caprices de Sophie (24 Ave Mozart, between Rue Largillière and Sq Mozart, 01.45.25.63.02). An elegant boutique with a garden view, it carries Chanel, Hermès, Christian Dior, and Christian Lacroix fashions and a selection of mink coats.

Nip Shop (6 Rue Edmond-About, between Rue Guy-de-Maupassant and Blvd Emile-Augier, 01.45.04.66.19). This small, elegant boutique has a faithful and dedicated clientele, and carries ready-to-wear and famous designer fashions, including Yves Saint Laurent. There is also a fine selection of shoes, silk scarfs, and jewelry.

Rosa Troc (33 Rue Vivienne, at Rue de la Bourse, 01.42.36.91.77). Top names including Max Mara, Chantal Thomas, and Thierry Mügler can be found at this shop—and if that isn't enough, there's a beauty salon too.

37 Rue du Poteau Along this street (where Utrillo was born in 1883) lies a charming and lively neighborhood market. From behind a fog of simmering *choucroute* (sauerkraut), ruddy-faced women chant *"Chaud, chaud, Mesdames! Le boudin noir"* ("Hot, hot, ladies! Blood sausage"). Nearby, their husbands peddle pheasants and Normandy cheeses. Follow your nose to the left, up Rue Duhesme, and pass gingerly through the crowd of determined wicker-basket-toting householders who shop with the finesse and subtlety of all-American football players. The market operates every day. ♦ Between Rue Ordener and Blvd Ney; market area between Rues Ordener and Duhesme. Métro: Jules-Joffrin

38 Fromagerie de Montmartre Mme. Delbey offers nearly 50 varieties of goat cheese. ♦ Tu-Sa. 9 Rue du Poteau (between Rues Ordener and Duhesme). 01.46.06.26.03. Métro: Jules-Joffrin

39 Hôtel Damrémont $ This clean, often noisy, 36-room hotel is a 15-minute walk from **Sacré-Coeur,** but the rates border on philanthropic. There's no restaurant. ♦ 110 Rue Damrémont (at Villa Damrémont). 01.42.64.25.75; fax 01.46.06.74.64. Métro: Lamarck–Caulaincourt

40 Le Maquis ★★$$ This little bistro at the base of Avenue Junot offers light prix-fixe lunches featuring such dishes as pumpkin soup, leek quiche, and *coquilles St-Jacques.* ♦ M-Sa lunch and dinner. 69 Rue Caulaincourt (between Rue de la Fontaine-du-But and Sq Caulaincourt). 01.42.59.76.07. Métro: Lamarck–Caulaincourt

41 Square Suzanne-Buisson This unexpected little square (named after a World War II Resistance fighter) was once the backyard of the adjoining **Château des Brouillards** (Castle

Restaurants/Clubs: Red	Hotels: Blue
Shops/ Outdoors: Green	Sights/Culture: Black

of Fog), an 18th-century mansion turned dance hall. According to religious lore, St. Denis paused here to rinse his severed head. Today a statue of the forlorn-looking bishop surveys neighborhood elders playing an afternoon game of *pétanque*, a Lyonnais sand bowling game similar to boccie. The bowling alley has stone benches for spectators, and there's no better way to learn about the old Montmartre than to eavesdrop on the conversations of these tweed-capped codgers. Admission is free (as is the gossip), and the games pick up steam around mid-afternoon. ♦ Bounded by Rue Girardon, Impasse Girardon, and Pl des Quatre-Frères-Casadesus. Métro: Lamarck–Caulaincourt

42 Ciné 13 This is the best little projection room in Paris. In 1983 French filmmaker Claude Lelouch built this elegant 130-person private screening room beside his Montmartre town house. It now draws cinema glitterati such as French film's tough guy Jean-Paul Belmondo and American director Robert Altman, who comes to screen the rough cuts of his new works. While you may never get to see Altman's rushes, for a reasonable $150 an hour ($300 after 7PM), you can rent this exclusive movie theater and show home movies if you like. No popcorn is permitted, but the theater can arrange catering. Call ahead for hours and for screening and catering reservations. ♦ 1 Ave Junot (at Rue Girardon). 01.42.54.15.12. Métro: Lamarck–Caulaincourt

43 Maison Tristan Tzara In the 1920s Viennese architect **Adolf Loos,** a pioneer of the Modern movement, was the only designer whose work reflected Dadaism. It is not surprising, then, that his "architecture without qualities" should have appealed to the Romanian Dadaist poet Tristan Tzara, who brought Loos to Paris with a commission to build this house. Set into a rising embarkment, the five-story building has a rigorously symmetrical facade that is punctured by a huge double-height square terrace. The arrangement is a superb example of the Loos predilection for tensely juxtaposed, unadorned cubic forms. The interior is just as eccentrically organized. The patchwork of intersecting split-level spaces, typical of Loos's *raumplan* (room plan), provided Tzara with the sort of ironic, theatrical, and vaguely aggressive setting that befitted a Dadaist artist. This is still a private residence. ♦ 15 Ave Junot (between Rue Girardon and Villa Léandre). Métro: Lamarck–Caulaincourt

43 13 Avenue Junot This is the former residence (1879-1946) of Francisque Poulbot, the Montmartre illustrator who drew chubby little children with cowlicks. Four of his cartoon characters frolic across the tile frieze of the house. In homage to the artist,

Montmartre residents still call their children *petits poulbots;* at the corner of Norvins and Impasse du Tertre, near Place du Tertre, you will find a sign that reads: *Ralentissez. Faites attention aux petits poulbots.* (Drive slowly. Watch out for the little poulbots.) This local folk hero is also credited with saving **Montmartre Vineyards** and with founding the Fraternal Association of Wooden Billiard Players (wooden billiards is a faddish Montmartre bar game in which winning is considered immoral—the winner always pays for the drinks). The house is still a private residence. ♦ Between Rue Girardon and Villa Léandre. Métro: Lamarck–Caulaincourt

43 Hameau des Artistes Behind the gate marked *Interdit* (No Trespassing) are footpaths leading to opulent artists' studios in structures ranging from a gray cement castle to a Tuscan villa. The gate to the "Artists' Hamlet" is open during the day; be adventurous but discreet. ♦ 11 Ave Junot (between Rue Girardon and Villa Léandre). Métro: Lamarck–Caulaincourt

44 Villa Léandre Down this unexpected country lane leading off Avenue Junot is a hidden village where the eccentric little houses mirror the idiosyncrasies of the people who have inhabited them (a ballerina, two successful painters, and a few genuine hermits). It's worth a quick detour. ♦ Off Ave Junot. Métro: Lamarck–Caulaincourt

45 Rue Lepic Montmartre's meandering old quarry road is the site of an antique-car rally held on the first or second Sunday in October (for information call 01.42.52.42.00). ♦ Between Blvd de Clichy and Pl Jean-Baptiste-Clément. Métro: Blanche

46 Moulin de la Galette Painted by Renoir and many others, this windmill (and its former dance hall) is the best known of the scores of mills that once crowned Montmartre. In the 19th century, the hoi polloi of Paris journeyed here on Sunday afternoons with their sweethearts to dance, drink wine, and eat *galettes* (cakes made with flour from the mills). This windmill has a grisly history as well. During the Franco-Prussian War, Montmartre was overrun by 20,000 Prussian soldiers, some of whom crucified the heroic mill owner, Pierre-Charles Debray, on the sails of his *moulin.* It's not open to the public. ♦ 79 Rue Lepic (between Rues Girardon and Tourlaque). Métro: Lamarck–Caulaincourt

47 La Petite Galette ★$ Right across the street from **Moulin de la Galette,** this bistro provides an inexpensive post-theater stop for a steak and *tarte tatin* (apple tart). Other specialties are foie gras, escargots, and nougat ice cream with red berry sauce. ♦ Daily dinner until 2AM. 86 *bis* Rue Lepic (at Rue Tholozé). 01.42.52.99.72. Métro: Lamarck–Caulaincourt

48 54 Rue Lepic Vincent van Gogh and his brother Theo lived in this apartment building. ♦ Between Rues Abbesses and Durantin. Métro: Blanche

49 Marché Quatre Saisons Among the artisans tucked away in this alley are a woodworker, a marionette maker, and Goudji, a Russian jewelry artist who fashions his own tools for the hammer-hollowing technique that is his trademark. Goudji's contemporary designs in gold and silver have a refined primitive quality. They are exhibited in museums around the world, including the **Musée des Arts Décoratifs** (see page 179). ♦ 45 Rue Lepic (between Rues Joseph-de-Maistre and Tourlaque). Métro: Blanche

50 21 Rue Caulaincourt Innovative graphic artist Toulouse-Lautrec spent his most productive years (1886-97) at a studio in this building, just a stroll away from his favorite nocturnal haunts. ♦ 21 Rue Caulaincourt (at Rue Tourlaque). Métro: Blanche

TERRASS HOTEL

51 Terrass Hôtel $$$ Built in 1912, this is the only luxury hotel in Montmartre, with 101 rooms and a stellar panorama that takes in the **Opéra, Arc de Triomphe,** and **Eiffel Tower.** Ask to stay on the cemetery side, which in local parlance means a room with a view, unobstructed because you're overlooking the low-rise **Montmartre Cemetery.** The lobby is decorated with plaid carpets, Napoléon III–style wallpaper, and a fireplace. The restaurant serves French fare. ♦ 12-14 Rue Joseph-de-Maistre (at Rue Caulaincourt). 01.46.06.72.85; fax 01.42.52.29.11. Métro: Blanche

52 Cimetière de Montmartre (Montmartre Cemetery) A veritable academy of writers, composers, and painters, this is the final resting place of Zola, Stendhal, Dumas, Offenbach, Degas, Fragonard, and Greuze, whose eloquent headstone lauds him for having depicted "virtue, friendship, beauty, and innocence, thereby breathing soul into his paintings." Another striking memorial is the Rude bronze of a reclining Cavaignac. Composer Hector Berlioz lies between his first wife, an English actress, and his second wife, an opera singer. ♦ Daily. 20 Ave Rachel (off Blvd de Clichy). 01.43.87.64.24. Métro: Blanche

53 Place de Clichy Stop by the *Académie de Billard Clichy-Montmartre* (84 Rue de Clichy, 01.48.78.32.85), a billiards hall set in a converted 1900 stable, and then wander down Rue d'Amsterdam, past carpet shops, used-furniture stores, and homeopathic pharmacies. ♦ At Blvds de Clichy and des Batignolles, and Rue d'Amsterdam and Ave de Clichy. Métro: Place de Clichy

On Place de Clichy:

Charlot, Le Roi des Coquillages
★★$$$ If you happen to be in Montmartre during an "R" month (the months spelled with the letter R—September through April—denote prime shellfish season), stop at this Art Deco–style bistro for a no-nonsense lunch of crabs, shrimps, oysters, and the like. Menu choices include bouillabaisse, *moules à la marinière* (mussels cooked in onions with white wine), and grilled shrimp coated with sea salt. Fine wines are served, including Muscadet and Chardonnay. ♦ Daily lunch and dinner until 1AM. No. 12 (between Ave de Clichy and Rue Biot). 01.53.20.48.00

54 Androuët ★★$$$ The shop on the ground floor has been in business since 1909 and sells 30,000 pounds of cheese every month. Connoisseurs of ripened curds should settle in the cozy, softly lit restaurant upstairs and order the *dégustation du fromage* (choose from a selection of 120 cheeses), accompanied by a salad and a hearty Bordeaux. Other house specialties include *croquettes de camembert,* lobster in roquefort sauce, and Swiss cheese fondue. ♦ Tu-Sa. 41 Rue d'Amsterdam (between Rues de Londres and de Liège). Store: 01.48.74.26.90; restaurant: 01.48.74.26.93. Métro: Liège

55 A l'Annexe ★$$ This lively bistro is only a quick stroll from the glitter of Pigalle. Try the hearty *raie au beurre noir* (skate with browned butter). ♦ M-F lunch and dinner; closed in August. 15 Rue Chaptal (at Rue Henner). 01.48.74.65.52. Métro: St-Georges

56 Moulin Rouge Founded in 1889 (the year the **Eiffel Tower** was built) and still kicking after all these years, this legendary temple of the risqué proffers all the bare-breasted women, ostrich plumes, rhinestones, and multicolored lights the stage can support. The show recalls the days of the famous cancan dancers: Jane Avril, Yvette Guilbert, Valentin le Désosse, and La Goulue, who were limned by Toulouse-Lautrec. Not long ago, animal-welfare representatives stopped a number in which a performing dolphin was stealing the show. Dinner is rather expensive and nothing to write home about, so you might want to skip it and just take in the glitzy show. ◆ Cover. Dinner: daily 8PM. Show: daily 10PM, midnight. Reservations recommended for both dinner and show. 82 Blvd de Clichy (between Rue Lepic and Cité Véron). 01.46.06.00.19. Métro: Blanche

56 Cité Véron To the left of the **Moulin Rouge** is this intriguing passageway where surviving family members of French writers Jacques Prévert and Boris Vian make their homes. Along the alley you will also find the highbrow **Théâtre Ouvert** (No. 4 *bis*, 01.42.55.74.40), which features the works of contemporary French playwrights; the **Boris Vian Foundation** (No. 6 *bis*, 01.46.06.73.56), which is housed in an old hunting lodge and offers exhibitions, dance, and theater classes; and a cluttered warehouse called **Ophir Paris** (No. 8, 01.42.64.58.40). The latter is a boutique whose backroom treasure trove is camouflaged with racks of cheap Indian imports. Unfortunately, much of the best stuff (19th-century wooden carousel figures, **Moulin Rouge** stage props, and Balinese shadow puppets) collected by the owners Jacqueline and André Marcovici is not for sale. **Ophir Paris** is open weekday mornings, and afternoons and weekends by appointment. ◆ Off Blvd de Clichy. Métro: Blanche

57 Le Restaurant ★★$$ Modern, minimalist decor complements the array of original and traditional dishes served here: oyster and sorrel omelette, beef marrow tart with red wine sauce, stuffed squid *persillade* (with parsley vinaigrette), and an exquisite crème brûlée. ◆ Tu-Sa lunch and dinner; closed the second half of August. Reservations recommended. 32 Rue Véron (at Rue Audran). 01.42.23.06.22. Métro: Abbesses

58 Bruno Maître Tattooist Would you like a goldfish on your ankle? Perhaps a mermaid on your chest? Bruno, one of the more popular body artists in Paris and an officer of the artisanal Order of Artistic Merit, practices safe tattooing, using only fresh needles and disposable ink cartridges. Even if you're not ready to commit to a permanent bodily souvenir of your trip, it's fun to look in the window and imagine. ◆ M-Tu, Th-Sa. 4 Rue Germain-Pilon (between Blvd de Clichy and Rue Véron). 01.42.64.35.59. Métro: Pigalle

59 Place Pigalle Nineteenth-century sculptor Jean-Baptiste Pigalle's celebrated rendering of the Virgin Mary is displayed in **St-Sulpice Church,** but his name became synonymous with porn theaters, sex shops, and prostitutes by being associated with this square. Known as **Pig Alley** to World War II GIs who came stalking the professional wildlife, Place Pigalle has lost many of its hookers to Rue St-Denis and **Bois de Boulogne;** these days transvestites predominate. ◆ At Blvd de Clichy. Métro: Pigalle

60 Caravelle $$ This comfortable hotel has 31 air-conditioned rooms. Ask for one in back and avoid the noise of traffic and the electric-guitar store across the street. There's no restaurant. ◆ 68 Rue des Martyrs (between Ave Trudaine and Blvd de Rochechouart). 01.48.78.43.31; fax 01.40.23.98.72. Métro: Pigalle

Hôtel
CARLTON'S

61 Carlton's $$ Surprise, surprise—there's a comfortable hotel offering 103 peaceful rooms amid the strip joints and kung fu cinemas of Pigalle. There's no restaurant. ◆ 55 Blvd de Rochechouart (at Rue Lallier). 01.42.81.91.00; fax 01.42.81.97.04. Métro: Pigalle

62 L'Oriental ★★$ Moroccan specialties are served at this intimate restaurant where decor is accented with touches of marble and mirrors. Thoughtful preparation is the keyword here: Choose from among such dishes as *pastilla au poulet* (puff pastry filled with chicken, almonds, and mint), *tchakchouka* (a zesty mixture of scrambled eggs, onions, peppers, and spices), or prawn and saffron *tajine*. ◆ M-Sa lunch and dinner; closed in August. Reservations required. 76 Rue des Martyrs (between Blvd de Rochechouart and Rue d'Orsel). 01.42.64.39.80. Métro: Pigalle

63 Résidence Charles-Dullin $$ These 76 kitchen-equipped apartments, located on a tranquil square, are rented by the night or by the week. ◆ 10 Pl Charles-Dullin (at Rue des Trois-Frères). 01.42.57.14.55; fax 01.42.54.48.87. Métro: Anvers

63 Théâtre de l'Atelier When this charming theater was first built in 1822 on this cobblestoned square (named in 1957 after actor Charles Dullin), it was known for the Stefan Zweig adaptation of Ben Jonson's *Volpone* and for *L'Opéra Bouffe,* which critics called the best stage performances outside Paris (Montmartre was not yet part of the city proper). Today, under the direction of Pierre Franck, the theater is truly Parisian, and there isn't a bad red-velvet seat in the house. ◆ Box office: M-Sa 11AM-7PM. 1 Pl Charles-Dullin (at Rue d'Orsel). 01.46.06.49.24. Métro: Anvers

"The best of America drifts to Paris. It is more fun for an intelligent person to live in an intelligent country. France has the only two things toward which we drift as we grow older—intelligence and good manners."

F. Scott Fitzgerald

Additional Highlights

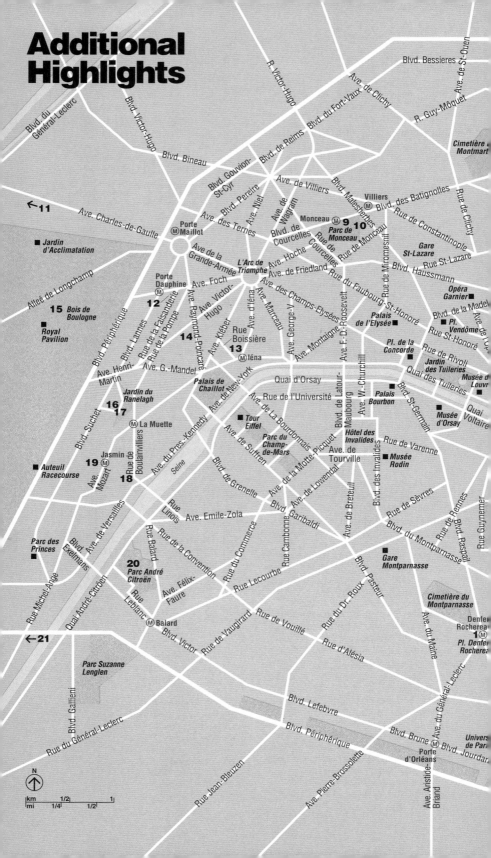

←11

■ Jardin
d'Acclimatation

■ 15 Bois de
Boulogne

■ Royal
Pavilion

Blvd. du Général-Leclerc

Blvd. Victor-Hugo

Blvd. Bineau

Ave. Charles-de-Gaulle

Allée de Longchamp

Blvd. Péripherique

Ave. Henri
Martin

Ave. de la Faisanderie
Rue de la Pompe

Rue de la Pompe

12

Blvd. Lannes

Porte
Dauphine

Ave. Foch

Ave. Victor-
Hugo

Ave. Raymond-Poincaré

Ave. G.-Mandel

14

Ave. Kléber

Rue
Boissière

13

M Iéna

Porte
M Maillot

Ave. des Ternes

Blvd. Gouvion-
St-Cyr

Blvd. Pereire

Ave. de la
Grande-Armée

L'Arc de
Triomphe

Ave. de Friedland

Ave. des Champs-Élysées

Ave. d'Iéna

Ave. Marceau

Ave. George-V

Ave. Montaigne

Ave. Hoche

Blvd. de Reims

Ave. Niel

Ave. de
Wagram

Ave. de Villiers

Blvd. Malesherbes

Blvd. de
Courcelles

Rue de
Courcelles

Rue de Monceau

Monceau
M

9

Parc de
Monceau

10

Villiers
M

Blvd. des Batignolles

Rue de Constantinople

Rue de Miromesnil

Rue du Faubourg-St-Honoré

Ave. F.-D.-Roosevelt

Palais
de l'Elysée

Blvd. du Fort-Vaux

Ave. de Clichy

R. Guy-Môquet

Cimetière
Montmart

R. Victor-Hugo

Ave. de Villiers

Blvd. Bessieres

Ave. de St-Ouen

Rue de Clichy

Gare
St-Lazare

Rue St-Lazare

Blvd. Haussmann

Opéra
Garnier

Blvd. de la Madel

■ Pl.
Vendôme

Rue St-Honoré

Pl. de la
Concorde

Jardin
des Tuileries

Quai des Tuileries

Rue de Rivoli

Musée d
Louvr

Ave. de l'Op

Blvd. St-Germain

Quai
Voltaire

Musée
d'Orsay

Palais de
Chaillot

Ave. de New-York

Quai d'Orsay

Rue de l'Université

Rue de La Bourdonnais

Blvd. de Latour-
Maubourg

Ave. W.-Churchill

Palais
Bourbon

16

17

Jardin du
Ranelagh

Blvd. Suchet

M La Muette

Ave. du Pres.-Kennedy

Rue de Boulainvilliers

■ Tour
Eiffel

Parc du
Champ-
de-Mars

Ave. de Suffren

Seine

Hôtel des
Invalides

Ave. de
Tourville

Rue de Varenne

■ Musée
Rodin

Blvd. des Invalides

Rue de Sèvres

Jasmin
M

19

Ave. Mozart

18

Rue de
Boulainvilliers

Ave. de Grenelle

Ave. de la Motte-Picquet

Ave. de Lowendal

Blvd. Garibaldi

Ave. de Breteuil

Blvd. du Montparnasse

Rue de Rennes

Blvd. Raspail

Rue Guynemer

■ Auteuil
Racecourse

Rue
Linois

Ave. Emile-Zola

Rue Cambronne

Rue du Commerce

Gare
Montparnasse

Parc des
Princes

Blvd. Exelmans

Ave. de Versailles

Rue Balard

Rue de la Convention

Rue Lecourbe

Blvd. Pasteur

20

Parc André
Citroën

Ave. Félix-
Faure

Rue
Leblanc

M Balard

Blvd. Victor

Rue de Vaugirard

Rue de Vouillé

Rue du Dr.-Roux

Rue d'Alésia

Ave. du Maine

Cimetière du
Montparnasse

Denfer
Rocherea

1 M

Pl. Denfer
Rochereau

Quai André-Citroën

Rue Michel-Ange

←21

Parc Suzanne
Lenglen

Blvd. Galliéni

Rue du Général-Leclerc

Blvd. Lefebvre

Blvd. Périphérique

Blvd. Brune

Ave. du Général-Leclerc

Blvd. Jourdar

Porte
d'Orléans

Univers
de Para

Ave. Aristide-
Briand

Ave. Pierre-Brossolette

Rue Jean-Bleuzen

N
↑

km   1/2   1
mi 1/4   1/2

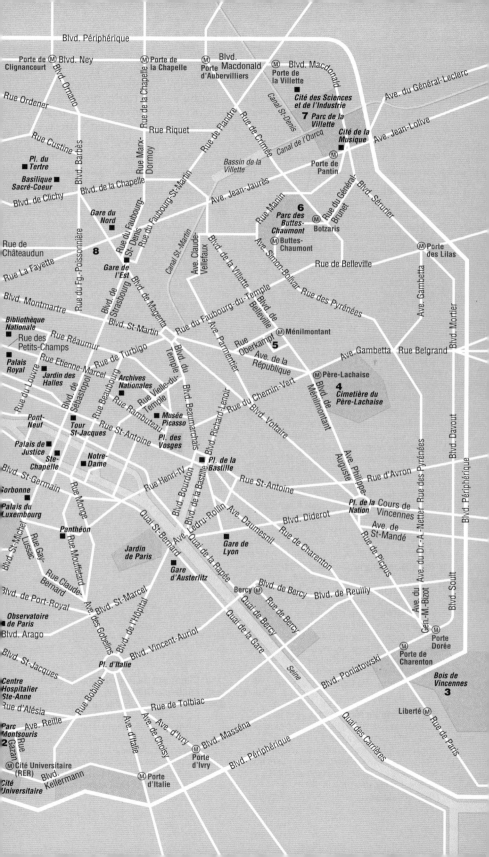

Additional Highlights

There are some wonderful spots in Paris that are not in the areas covered elsewhere in this book. This chapter features Paris's other highlights, which include something for everyone: eerie catacombs; pleasant parks, including the well-known **Monceau** and **Bois de Boulogne;** the famous **Cimetière du Père-Lachaise,** the burial place of generations of writers, musicians, and artists, from Chopin to Jim Morrison; and a variety of interesting museums, including the high-tech **La Villette** science museum, several fine art collections, and museums devoted to the lives and works of such notables as singer Edith Piaf and architect **Le Corbusier.**

1 Catacombs The catacombs began as a network of quarries that extended for miles beneath Paris. In 1785, several million skeletons were transported to these quarries from the overcrowded **Innocents Cemetery** near Les Halles. Here the skulls, femurs, and tibias of 30 generations of Parisians were stacked in a neat but rather macabre fashion. Carved near the entrance is an ominous medieval sign: "Stop. Beyond Here Is the Empire of Death." Apparently the warning deterred the occupying Nazis, because they never discovered that the secret headquarters of the French Resistance was literally under their feet. The dark reaches of the catacombs then housed radios capable of reaching London, as well as a telephone switching system handling Resistance communications for hundreds of miles around.

Today visitors can explore the catacombs and view the skeletal inhabitants as part of an hour-long tour. Bring along a flashlight and a sweater, be prepared for a lot of steps, and be sure to stay close to the group. In 1793 a Parisian took a wrong turn from his own wine cellar, got lost in the catacomb tunnels, and was not discovered until nine years later, by which time he was mummified. ♦ Admission. Tu-F 2-4PM; Sa-Su 9-11AM, 2-4PM. 1 Pl Denfert-Rochereau (at Ave du Général-Leclerc). 01.43.22.47.63. Métro: Denfert-Rochereau

2 Parc Montsouris Prior to the 19th century, this park was an abandoned granite quarry stubbled with windmills. At the turn of the century the 50-acre swath of green was a refuge for the artists and literati of nearby Montparnasse; Hemingway often came here. Today, joggers run the park's half-mile perimeter, matrons feed the swans, and brass bands play marches in the band shell. ♦ 20 Rue Gazan (between Blvd Jourdan and Ave Reille). Métro: Cité Universitaire (RER)

Within Parc Montsouris:

Le Pavillon de Montsouris ★★$$ The outdoor terrace of this Belle Epoque glass-and-iron restaurant has accommodated a great many famous customers, including Trotsky and Sartre. Not to be missed are the *purée de guacamole* and *soupe de fruits rouge.* ♦ Daily lunch and dinner. 01.45.88.38.52

3 Bois de Vincennes Only slightly smaller than the **Bois de Boulogne** to the west, this is the second principal recreation area for the city of Paris. Like the **Bois de Boulogne,** this park was a former royal hunting ground; it was given to the city by Napoléon III in 1860. The major attraction here is the **Château de Vincennes**, a stern medieval fortress that has served variously as a royal residence, prison, porcelain factory, and arsenal. The *bois* (forest) that extends to the south of the château contains the **Floral Garden; Daumesnil Lake,** where rowboats and bicycles are available for rent; the **Buddhist Center,** which boasts the largest sculpture of Buddha in Europe; and the **Zoological Park.** The zoo, with 550 mammals and more than 700 birds, provides a welcome contrast to the **Menagerie** at the **Jardin des Plantes**—here the animals live in surroundings similar to their natural habitats. In the zoo's center is a 230-foot-high artificial mountain, home to wild mountain sheep. ♦ Admission for château. Daily. Château: 01.43.4.50.00; zoological park: 01.44.75.20.10. Métros: Porte Dorée, Porte de Charenton, Vincennes (RER)

4 Cimetière du Père-Lachaise (Père-Lachaise Cemetery) Named after Louis XIV's confessor, Father La Chaise, and designed by **Alexandre Théodore Brongniart,** this is the largest and most elite cemetery in Paris. The remains of France's most famous lovers, Abélard and Héloïse, keep company with Molière, Balzac, and the painters Corot, Daumier, David, Pissarro, Modigliani, and Seurat. Also buried here are the 19th-century photographer Nadar; the city-shaping Baron

Haussmann; Jane Avril and Yvette Guilbert, two cancan dancers who modeled for Toulouse-Lautrec; Fulgence Bienvenue, who built the Paris métro; and Ferdinand de Lesseps, who designed the Suez Canal.

In remembrance of things past, a single red rose may grace the black marble slab marking Marcel Proust's grave, and singer Edith Piaf's unremarkable resting place is always surrounded with flowers. Music lovers might also search out the graves of Callas, Bizet, or Poulenc. Chopin's body is buried here (his heart is interred in Warsaw), as are the remains of Eugène Delacroix, Prosper Mérimée, and Alfred de Musset, who, like Chopin, loved George Sand, the great woman luminary of 19th-century French literature. Literati, as well as gay men and lesbians, flock to Oscar Wilde's tomb, a stylish sphinx sculpted by Sir Jacob Epstein in 1909, and leftists make the pilgrimage to the grave of Laura Marx, daughter of Karl. Sarah Bernhardt lies here, as does Jim Morrison, the Doors' lead singer who died of a drug overdose in 1971. Lovers Gertrude Stein and Alice B. Toklas are together in death as they were in life. One side of their gravestone memorializes Gertrude, the other, Alice.

This lush 108-acre sanctuary in eastern Paris is a museum of French history, but it's as much a park as a cemetery. Parisians by the hundreds come here to picnic, harvest escargots off the tombs, or neck on the benches. Chopin's tomb is used for posting love letters, and legend holds that women who kiss or rub the statue of Victor Noir, a French journalist (1848-70) killed by Pierre Bonaparte, will marry within a year. If you're lucky you may encounter Vincent de Langlade, who has spent his life studying this most famous of graveyards; he is the author of a dozen books on the necropolis. If you can't find him, pick up the detailed map available at the cemetery's entrance and set out on your own celebrity search. ♦ Daily. Blvd de Ménilmontant (between Rue du Repos and Pl Auguste-Métivier). 01.43.70.70.33. Métro: Père-Lachaise

5 Musée Edith Piaf In a tiny museum filling two rooms of a private apartment near her grave in the **Père-Lachaise Cemetery,** the renowned French chanteuse lives on through the adoration of her fans, who come to look at her dressing gown, shoes, birth certificate, autographed letters, photographs, and por-traits of her lovers. Recordings of the "little sparrow" play softly in the background and the museum's devoted curator is always present to recount the final days of the great entertainer's life. ♦ M-Th 1-6PM by appointment only. 5 Rue Crespin-du-Gast (between Passage de Ménilmontant and Rue Oberkampf). 01.43.55.52.72. Métro: Ménilmontant

6 Parc des Buttes-Chaumont If you're tired of the crowds in the **Luxembourg Gardens** (the Central Park of Paris) and need a break from the deadly symmetry of the **Tuileries,** do as the

French do. Buy some ripe brie, a baguette, and a hearty Bordeaux, and head for this urban wilderness in the northern end of Paris.

The unusual park was built in 1867 by Baron Haussmann, who also laid out the sewers and the city's grand boulevards for Napoléon III. Before Haussmann, **Buttes-Chaumont** was a city dump. In what must be the most inspired use of landfill in history, a then-new material—concrete—was used to form natural-looking cliffs, ravines, rivers, and an artificial lake. There's even a grotto and waterfall, which were restored and reopened several years ago after having been closed since World War II because of deterioration. **Buttes-Chaumont**'s island, set in the lake, is capped with a Classical colonnaded temple and commands one of the city's most striking views of Montmartre and **Sacré-Coeur.** Visitors not inclined to mountaineering may prefer sipping a *citron pressé* (lemonade) on the terrace of the **Pavillon du Lac,** which serves tea and light lunches and is located on the park's west side. ♦ Daily. Bounded by Rues de Crimée, Manin, and Botzaris. Métro: Buttes-Chaumont, Botzaris

7 Parc de la Villette The old slaughterhouse district, a 75-acre site in northeastern Paris that had been the last undeveloped space in the city, was transformed in the mid-1980s into a huge complex of buildings and parks devoted to science and technology. A series of bright-red "follies"—whimsical structures designed by architect **Bernard Tschumi**—are laid out in a grid pattern throughout the park. They serve a variety of functions, including a cafe, weathervane, a children's play area, and a belvedere. ♦ Bounded by Blvd Sérurier and Canal St-Denis, and Ave Jean-Jaurès and Blvd Macdonald. 01.40.03.75.03. Métros: Porte de Pantin, Porte de la Villette

Within Parc de la Villette:

Cité des Sciences et de l'Industrie La **Villette**'s centerpiece is an 880-foot-long, $600-million research and exhibition building designed by French architect **Adrien Fainsilber.** The gray granite, glass, and dark steel structure was built around the shell of an enormous 19th-century slaughterhouse, whose lack of central pillars created 1.5 million square feet of usable space. Exhibits are organized around general themes such as the earth and space, matter and physics, language and communication, and life on earth; many are multilingual and interactive. The most popular attraction is **La Géode,** a polished-steel sphere, 117 feet in diameter, where films are projected on a huge 180-degree screen. **La Mediathèque** houses 1,000 videodiscs, 150,000 books, and a large conference center. ♦ Admission. Tu-Su. 30 Ave Corentin-Cariou (at Blvd McDonald). 08.36.68.29.30

Restaurants/Clubs: Red	Hotels: Blue
Shops/ ♥ Outdoors: Green	Sights/Culture: Black

Cité de la Musique Opened in January 1995, this complex is **Parc de la Villette**'s newest attraction. Architect **Christian de Portzamparc's** monumental ensemble of buildings is arranged along a glass-roofed interior street and includes two concert halls, an opera house, and a museum. The schedule of high-quality programs includes dance performances, operas, and concerts of classical and contemporary music from around the world. The **Conservatoire National de Musique et de Danse** (National Conservatory of Music and Dance), where students often give free recitals, is based here, as is the **Ensemble InterContemporain,** a research and educational institution devoted to late 20th-century music. The five-story **Musée de la Musique** displays a collection of over 4,500 music-related items, including 16th-century Venetian lutes; the 19th-century instruments of Adolphe Sax, inventor of the saxophone; five Stradivarius violins; and Frank Zappa's modular E-Mu synthesizer. ◆ Admission. Box office: W-Su noon-6PM. Museum: Tu-Su. 211 Ave Jean-Jaurès (between Blvd Sérurier and Rue Adolphe-Mille). 01.44.84.45.00, 01.44.84.44.84

8 Rue de Paradis This shabby little street is the domain of the finest French and European tableware outlets. Nearly 50 shops selling porcelain, silver, earthenware, crystal, and glass are crowded along its three blocks. All the most elegant brands of tableware may be found here at prices that are 30 to 50 percent lower than in the US. ◆ Between Rues du Faubourg-St-Denis and du Faubourg-Poissonnière. Métro: Château d'Eau, Poissonnière

On Rue de Paradis:

Musée du Cristal A glittering collection of Baccarat crystal is displayed here. Some of the pieces were used by heads of state, including the Queen of Siam and King Louis Philippe. Also on view are the Baccarat glasses commissioned for Henry Ford II's yacht and Franklin Roosevelt's White House. The most dazzling pieces are the two one-ton 79-light candelabras ordered by Czar Nicholas II for his St. Petersburg palace. Baccarat crystal is sold here as well. ◆ Free; fee for group tours. M-Sa. 30 *bis* Rue de Paradis (between Rues du Faubourg St-Denis and d'Hauteville). 01.47.70.64.30

9 Parc de Monceau This small and quirky park dates from 1778, when Philippe-Egalité, the Duke of Orléans, commissioned the painter Carmontel to design a private garden on the Monceau Plain, then outside the city limits. Carmontel created a whimsical landscape full of architectural follies: a pyramid, a pagoda, a Roman temple, windmills, and artfully placed ruins. The park changed hands a few times after the Revolution, and by 1862 it had been revamped by Alphand, an engineer under Baron Haussmann. Alphand gave the landscape the picturesque, English garden– inspired elements still evident today. Of particular interest are the **Naumachie,** an oval basin with a colonnade said to have come from the unfinished mausoleum of Henri II at St-Denis, and the round **Barrière Monceau,** one of the many *barrières* (tollhouses) built along the old city wall (now destroyed) in 1784 by **Claude-Nicholas Ledoux.** Although Ledoux's commission called for 55 such tollhouses, historians are unsure how many were actually built; only four still stand. ◆ Blvd de Courcelles (between Blvd Malesherbes and Ave de Vigny); also accessible from Aves Velasquez, Ruysdaël, and Van-Dyck. Métro: Monceau

10 Musée Cernuschi A fine collection of Chinese art is housed in the former mansion of wealthy financier Henri Cernuschi. This small but exceptional museum is near the east gate of the **Parc de Monceau.** ◆ Admission. Tu-Su. 7 Ave Velasquez (between Blvd Malesherbes and Parc de Monceau). 01.45.63.50.75. Métro: Villiers

10 Musée Nissim de Camondo Around the corner from the **Musée Cernuschi,** this museum exhibits the furniture and decorative art (including several Gobelins tapestries) of the Count de Camondo, who once owned this house. ◆ Admission. W-Su. 63 Rue de Monceau (between Blvd Malesherbes and Ave Ruysdaël). 01.45.63.50.75. Métro: Villiers

11 Grande Arche de La Défense The axis that starts with the **Carrousel Arch** in front of the **Louvre** and runs westward through the **Tuileries Gardens** to the **Obelisk of Luxor,** then down the Champs-Elysées to the **Arc de Triomphe,** has been extended westward with this 300,000-ton white Carrara marble monument in the La Défense district. Designed by **Johan Otto von Spreckelsen,** who won an international competition for the commission, the arch is actually a hollow cube built on 12 pillars set 99 feet into the ground.

The building houses the **Ministry of Planning and Development,** the **Foundation for the Rights of Man,** headquarters for several cultural foundations, and private offices. Inaugurated in July 1989 as part of the 200th anniversary of the French Revolution, the building brings monumental dazzle to a sterile high-rise jungle that has become the business district of Paris. ◆ 1 Parvis de la Défense (just west of Pl de la Défense). Métro: Grande Arche de la Défense

12 Musée de la Contrefaçon (Forgeries Museum) It is not unusual to see the great ladies of Parisian society stopping by this one-room museum in the elegant 16th arrondissement to compare a new handbag or a Cartier watch to the near-perfect forgeries on display. The museum is a veritable capitalist's cabinet of curiosities, where *authentique* products are exhibited surrounded by bogus imitations from Japan, Korea, Italy, Morocco, Taiwan, and elsewhere. Note the ingenious copies of Louis Vuitton luggage, which wear counterfeit tags guaranteeing they are genuine Vuitton. A short visit here is enough to cast doubt forever on that little shop near the hotel selling Dior key chains, Omega watches, bottles of Benedictine, flacons of Chanel No. 5, and magnums of Cordon Rouge Champagne at bargain-basement prices. ♦ Admission. M-Th 2-5PM; F 9AM-noon. 16 Rue de la Faisanderie (between Rue Cothenet and Pl du Paraguay). 01.45.01.51.11. Métro: Porte Dauphine

13 Musée Guimet The finest collection of Asian art in Paris is on view here. Founded by industrialist Emile Guimet in 1879 to house his private collection of Oriental antiquities, the museum later became the **Département des Arts Asiatiques des Musées Nationaux** (National Museum of Asian Art). As such, it exhibits most of the **Louvre**'s Far East collection and has steadily expanded its holdings to include more than 50,000 works from China, Japan, India, Indochina, Afghanistan, and Tibet. At press time the museum was closed for renovations and scheduled to reopen in 1999. Until then, the only exhibition open to the public is the Buddhist collection which is housed in the annex at 19 Avenue d'Iéna. ♦ Admission. M, W-Su. 6 Pl d'Iéna (at Ave d'Iéna). 01.47.23.61.65. Métro: Iéna

14 Alain Ducasse ★★★$$$$ Joël Robuchon may have retired from the restaurant scene, but his legacy continues under the guidance of new chef-owner Alain Ducasse. The magnificent 18th-century *hôtel particulier*—one of the few Paris restaurants to be awarded three Michelin stars—features a mosaic fountain and trompe l'oeil tapestries in the three wood-paneled dining rooms. Ducasse's own renditions—freshwater crayfish with wild mushrooms, langoustine wrapped with strips of squid and served with crunchy vegetables in ginger—are outstanding. Diners with heartier appetites can feast on pig's head on a bed of salad and truffles with caramelized potatoes and bacon. All this, plus an impressive collection of wines make this quite a dining experience. ♦ M-F lunch and dinner.

Reservations recommended at least two months in advance. 59 Ave Raymond-Poincaré (between Rue St-Didier and Pl Victor-Hugo). 01.47.27.12.27. Métro: Victor Hugo

14 Le Parc $$$$ Located in the well-to-do 16th arrondissement, across the river from the **Eiffel Tower,** this aristocratic hotel is as noble and cozy as an English manor. The 120 sumptuous rooms and suites were decorated by leading British designer Nina Campbell, and the furniture was commissioned from Viscount Linley, the nephew of Her Majesty the Queen. The public areas, including the cozy lobby bar, are decorated in the style of an English gentlemen's club. The **Relais du Parc** restaurant is on the premises (see below). ♦ 55-57 Ave Raymond-Poincaré (between Rue St-Didier and Pl Victor-Hugo). 01.44.05.66.66; fax 01.44.05.66.00. Métro: Victor-Hugo

Within Le Parc:

Relais du Parc ★★★$$$ Don't despair if you can't get a reservation at **Alain Ducasse** next door—the master's touch is clearly felt at this restaurant, where having taken over the Robuchon empire, he is consulting chef. The menu tends toward the Southwest of France with dishes such as peppers stuffed with cod, tomatoes stuffed with crispy vegetables, and melon soup and John Dory with fennel. The dining room is English colonial–style and in summer you can dine beneath chestnut trees in the verdant garden courtyard. ♦ Daily breakfast, lunch, and dinner. Reservations required. 01.44.05.66.10

15 Bois de Boulogne Stretching along the western flank of Paris and occupying more than 2,200 acres, this is the city's ultimate playground. The Merovingians hunted wild boar and wolves in the *bois* (forest) in the sixth century, it was enclosed by Henri II in 1556, and in the 17th century **Jean-Baptiste Colbert** transformed the land into royal hunting grounds. After Napoléon III gave the forest to the city of Paris, Baron Haussmann remodeled the landscape; using London's Hyde Park as his guide he built many of the lakes, restaurants, racetracks, and paths that are here today. Haussmann designed the park so it would be entered from Avenue Foch, which he also designed, and which leads grandly down to the Porte Dauphine. Once in the park, you can choose from a seemingly infinite variety of activities and attractions. The most notable include the **Bagatelle** (01.40.67.97.00), a magical park with an 18th-century villa built by the then-future king, Charles X; the **Jardin d'Acclimatation** (01.40.67.90.80), an amusement park and miniature zoo; the **Auteuil** (01.42.24.47.04) and **Longchamp** (01.42.24.12.29) racecourses; the **Shakespeare Garden** (01.45.24.08.16), where the bard's works and classic French plays are performed in an open-air theater in summer; and the **Pré**

Catelan, another flower and tree garden that shelters a luxurious cafe/restaurant of the same name (see below). There are numerous sports facilities, including the **Roland Garros Stadium** (01.47.43.48.00.), where the French Open tennis tournament is held. Bicycles can be rented opposite the main entrance to the **Jardin d'Acclimatation** (at the Carrefour des Sablons) and near the **Royal Pavilion** (at the Carrefour du Bout-des-Lacs) daily May through September and on Saturdays and Sundays the rest of the year. ◆ Métros: Porte d'Auteuil, Porte Dauphine, Porte Maillot

In the Bois de Boulogne:

Pré Catelan ★★$$ Elegant and romantic, this Belle Epoque restaurant features dining on the terrace in summer. Chef Roland Durand specializes in simple dishes based on pork. The desserts, however, are more exotic: Try *lait de coco aux fruits* (coconut milk with fruits) and *pastilla au chocolat Caraïbe* (Caribbean chocolate sweets). ◆ Tu-Sa lunch and dinner; Su lunch. Route de Suresnes (at Allée de la Reine). 01.44.14.41.14. Métro: Porte Dauphine

16 Musée Marmottan The 16th arrondissement in Paris, which stretches from the **Arc de Triomphe** down between the **Bois de Boulogne** and the Seine, is a haven for the Proustian bourgeoisie. Out-of-town shoppers know this quarter as a place to buy old table linens, fine chocolates, and designer silk dresses, and others know it as the location of Omar Sharif's private gambling club. The best-kept secret of the select 16th, however, is the 19th-century Passy town house that contains this museum, which features more than a hundred original paintings, pastels, and drawings by Monet. While tour-bus loads of noisy London schoolchildren and itinerant backpackers elbow past each other in the **Musée d'Orsay** to glimpse Monet's *Wild Poppies,* this treasure trove of the artist's work from Giverny is relatively deserted.

After you take a good look at the 300 illuminated medieval manuscripts on the ground floor, skip the two floors devoted to the cold First-Empire furniture and Flemish tapestries, and head straight for the basement. Here amidst the joyous splashes and swirls of poppies, tulips, irises, and apple blossoms you'll experience the essential spirit of Monet's Giverny work. The exhibition culminates in a circular gallery with the artist's notebooks and palette in the center and 16 of his water-lily canvases on the walls. Stand in the middle of the room and pivot around to behold Monet's magical pond as it changed with the sun's daily round. (In summer you can visit the actual pond and gardens at Monet's Normandy home in Giverny. For more information, see "Day Trips" on page 256.) ◆ Admission. Tu-Su. 2 Rue Louis-Boilly (at Ave Raphaël). 01.42.24.07.02. Métro: La Muette

17 Jardin du Ranelagh Directly across Avenue Raphaël from the **Musée Marmottan** are these sumptuous English-style gardens, home to one of the last hand-cranked merry-go-rounds in Europe. The carousel is powered by a middle-aged woman with forearms rivaling those of Arnold Schwarzenegger. Children in ruffled dresses or seersucker suits hold on for dear life with one hand while wielding red sticks in the other, trying to hook the elusive brass ring. ◆ Ave Raphaël (between Ave Ingres and Blvd Suchet). Métro: La Muette

18 Castel Béranger French architect **Hector Guimard** established his reputation in 1898 as the country's premier Art Nouveau designer with this seven-story apartment building, which sits along a quiet residential street in the 16th arrondissement. Guimard's quasi-organic Expressionism is seen here in its full glory, particularly in the curvilinear details of his ironwork, faience, and carved-wood elements, which prefigure the architect's more purely sculptural métro entrances of 1900. The private building contains 36 apartments, no two alike. ◆ 14-16 Rue La Fontaine (at Hameau Béranger). Métro: Jasmin

19 Le Corbusier Foundation Charles-Edouard Jeanneret, better known as **Le Corbusier** (1887-1965), was the Swiss architect who helped revolutionize today's urban environment with his passion for cubist forms. Within Paris and its suburbs stand 15 of his modular buildings, including the apartment house in which he lived in 1933 (24 Rue Nungesser-et-Coli); a **Salvation Army** headquarters (12 Rue Cantagrel) built in 1933 of glass, brick, and exposed concrete; and the famous **Swiss Dormitory** and **Brazilian Pavilion** (constructed in 1932 and 1959, respectively) at Cité Universitaire (19-21 Blvd Jourdan). The headquarters and research library of the **Le Corbusier Foundation** are housed in **Villa Jeanneret;** the adjoining **Villa La Roche,** also designed by the architect in 1923, contains a sparse collection of Le Corbusier's own painting, sculpture, and furniture design and is open to the public. ◆ Admission. M-F; closed in August. 8-10 Sq du Docteur-Blanche (off Rue du Docteur-Blanche, between Rues Raffet and Henri-Heine). 01.42.88.41.53. Métro: Jasmin

20 Parc André Citroën When the offices of automobile manufacturer André Citroën moved outside the city in the 1980s, an expanse of land the size of 50 football fields was left free in the quiet 15th arrondissement. The city transformed half this area into public grounds, now the only park in Paris where sitting on the grass is not forbidden. Landscape designers Alan Provost and Gilles Clément have made water a dominant feature here: Shallow pools border the park, and waterfalls tumble from small stone structures. The park's north side has six small gardens, each with a different

theme and dominant color. The red garden, for example, contains cherry and apple trees.
♦ Entrance at 25 Rue Leblanc (between Rue St-Charles and Quai André-Citroën). 01.45.57.13.35. Métros: Balard, Javel

21 Jardins Albert Kahn Turn-of-the-century banker and idealist Albert Kahn envisioned a society in which there would be a cross-breeding of cultures; these enchanting gardens, in which 360 species of plants from around the world thrive in one place, are the horticultural embodiment of his sociological ideas. Here you'll find an English garden, French flower beds, a rose garden, and a meticulous Japanese garden with a wooden teahouse (where Japanese tea ceremonies are conducted two days a month in September and April; call for days and times). This Eden has been a sanctuary of meditation for such notables as Colette, Einstein, Ferdinand Foch, Edouard Herriot, and Arthur Honegger. When your stomach's needs transcend those of your spirit, go to the **Palmarium** (01.46.05.25.10), a glass-and-iron rotunda where sandwiches and pastries are served.

Kahn also had an interest in photography that was furthered by his friendship with cinematography inventor Louis Lumière. Between 1910 and 1920, Kahn sent documentary photographers all over the world to compose his *Archives de la Planète*. More than 72,000 photographs and in excess of a half-million feet of film are housed in the **Musée Albert Kahn,** on the grounds of the gardens. ♦ Admission. Tu-Su. Reservations required for tea ceremonies; call the museum. 14 Rue du Port (between Rue des Abondances and Quai du 4-Septembre), Boulogne-Billancourt. Museum 01.46.04.52.80. Métro: Boulogne–Pont de St-Cloud

From Kings to Commoners— Tennis Has Come a Long Way

The French court game *jeu de paume,* a complicated precursor of modern lawn tennis, originated when bored 13th-century French monks swatted a wad of rags around a monastery courtyard with their bare hands (*jeu de paume* literally means "game of the palm"). By the 17th century, it was played with a racket and had become the French national game: Paris alone had 250 courts. The dashing François I constructed a court in the **Louvre** as well as a floating tennis court on his 2,000-ton warship *La Grande Françoise.*

The kings and nobles who played it used lopsided rackets to send the balls ricocheting off the wall, floor, and sloping gallery roof, or sailing over a net that sagged like a hammock. Points were awarded for swatting balls through portals and striking bells in windows. It was life-size pinball, high-speed chess, and racquetball in a Gothic cathedral all wrapped into one. A player had 40 surfaces to bounce a ball off of, and the ball often traveled in excess of 120 miles per hour.

At its toughest, the royal tennis game proved to be a killer workout for overzealous sovereigns. Half a dozen kings expired from sheer exhaustion and pneumonia after ferocious *jeu de paume* matches. Another crowned casualty of the game was the affable but maladroit King Charles VIII, who keeled over shortly after a head-on collision with the lintel of the tennis-court door in his château at Amboise.

Jeu de paume became wildly popular and was repeatedly banned by nobles convinced that tennis-playing merchants and yeomen were neglecting their work and the country's defense. In spite of the prohibition, the craze raged on in hundreds of underground *tripots*—athletic speakeasies notorious for bootlegged tennis equipment, cheap wine, and reckless games of chance. (To this day, when the French gamble away their paychecks, they still curse: *"J'ai paumé."*)

In the France of Louis XIV, the game's popularity suffered as a consequence of increasingly repressive legislation and the king's indifference to the sport (he, after all, was a billiards man). Eventually *jeu de paume* courts were transformed into playhouses or public meeting places. In fact, a meeting held on 20 June 1789 in the court at **Versailles** changed the course of French history. Deputies of the Third Estate assembled there and took the historic oath that sparked the French Revolution. More than a century later, in 1907, another group of revolutionaries, the painters called Impressionists, commandeered the city's last two royal *jeu de paume* courts in the **Tuileries Gardens** and turned them into a gallery for their canvases.

Modern tennis owes a great debt to *jeu de paume.* The very name "tennis" comes from the traditional warning, *Tenez* (Take heed), which French monks shouted before each *serve*—a term added later by nobles who felt it was beneath them to start a game themselves (they ordered a servant to toss the first ball, and then they would join in).

Known as court tennis in the United States, *jeu de paume* is frequently referred to by English purists as "real tennis" or "Tennis with a capital T" to distinguish it from that slam-bang adulteration played at Flushing Meadows and Wimbledon. Although it originated in France, *jeu de paume* today is unquestionably Anglo-Saxon. Of the world's 34 courts currently in use, Britain boasts 19, the United States 9, and Australia 4. Only two courts remain in France, one in Bordeaux and one in Paris at the **Société Sportive de Jeu de Paume et de Racquets** (74 *ter* Rue Lauriston, between Rues Boissière and Copernic). To catch a glimpse of the ancient game, stop by the club in the late afternoon or evening when French and American businesspeople from the fashionable 16th arrondissement stop on their way home to play a friendly set.

Day Trips

1 Basilique de St-Denis Around AD 250, St. Denis, the first Christian evangelist to come to Paris, was beheaded by the Romans. Legend has it that he picked up his head and carried it from Montmartre several kilometers north until, finally, he fell and was buried by a peasant woman. Whatever the facts, the grave of St. Denis became a place of pilgrimage. By the 12th century, pilgrims were so numerous that many were actually trampled to death in the stampede to the saint's shrine. Abbot Suger (1081-1151) decreed that a new church, large and full of light, be constructed on the site. The result was the first Gothic edifice in the world and one of the lesser-known treasures of Paris. The basilica became the starting place for the Crusades and the burial place of three dynasties of French royalty. Badly neglected after the Revolution, the structure has been restored and is now a repository of exquisite funerary sculpture. The soaring nave glows with a rainbow of light from the stained-glass windows, illuminated most brightly on winter mornings. ◆ Admission to tombs. Take Métro line 13 to the Basilique de St-Denis stop. If traveling by car, take autoroute A1; the basilica is less than 3 km (2 miles) north of Porte de la Chapelle. 01.48.09.83.54

2 Château de Chantilly In 1671, Louis de Bourbon entertained King Louis XIV in his newly completed gardens at the Château de Chantilly in the town of Chantilly. On that occasion, Vatel, the most famous chef in France, failed to deliver the fish course on time and, rather than live with the shame, promptly took his own life. Such is the tradition of excellence here.

Rising like a mirage from a moat in the midst of a dense beech forest, the château, which now houses the **Musée Condé,** is an artful conglomeration of the best of 16th-, 18th-, and 19th-century French architecture. During the Revolution the original château, built in the early 15th century, was razed, stone by stone, by vengeful mobs. The Duc d'Aumale, who was responsible for the subsequent reconstruction in 1844, showed his fine eclectic taste in other areas as well: His art collection of medieval miniatures and French, Flemish, and Italian paintings is now on display in the **Musée Condé.** Each June the famous Prix de Diane horse race is run at a track on the edge of the palace grounds, and the **Grandes Ecuries,** Chantilly's extensive stables, are in use today as part of the **Musée**

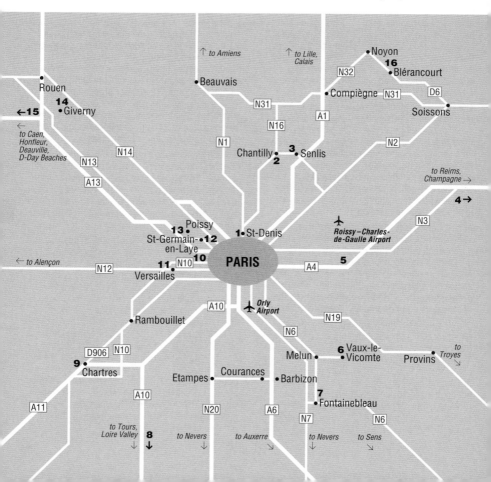

Vivant du Cheval (Living Museum of the Horse). The dressage exhibitions are great entertainment for children. ◆ Admission. M, W-Su. Trains leave from the Gare du Nord station. Paris Vision and Cityrama (see "Orientation" chapter) offer seasonal half-day trips on Sundays. If traveling by car, take highway N16 48 km (30 miles) north of Paris. Musée Condé 03.44.57.08.00, Musée Vivant du Cheval 03.44.57.40.40

3 Senlis This entire town is classified as a historical monument. It is girdled by 23-foot-high, 13-foot-thick Roman walls that are punctuated by watchtowers and pierced by massive gates. The town's cathedral is older than **Notre-Dame-de-Paris** or **Chartres** and lofts a lacy spire considered the most beautiful in France. After visiting the cathedral, tour the ruins of the royal castle, the 28 towers of the Gallo-Roman wall, and the thousand-seat Roman amphitheater just outside of town. The streets of Senlis, such as the Rue du Châtel and Rue de la Treille, are winding, stone-paved canyonways dark with history. The best bet for exploring them is to follow the small arrows that indicate a walking route through town. ◆ Take the train from the Gare du Nord station, or follow autoroute N17 or A1, 48 km (30 miles) northeast of Paris

4 Champagne The Champagne region is a realm of flowing hills dotted with vineyards, medieval stone towns, and châteaux. Its capital Reims was the coronation site of French kings, beginning with Clovis in 496. The cathedral here is stunning and definitely worth a stop. Epernay, the region's second city, is the home of Moët et Chandon, the giant among an estimated 145 Champagne producers in the region. Most of the largest producers offer tours, which usually culminate in some free sampling and (be forewarned) a persuasive sales pitch once your resistance is down. Five minutes north of Epernay are two of Champagne's best restaurants: the **Royal**

Champagne in Champillon (Rte N2051, 03.26.52.87.11) and the **Boyer** in Reims (64 Blvd Henri-Vasnier, at Ave du Général-Giraud, 03.26.82.80.80). ◆ Take a train to Reims from the Gare de l'Est, or drive east 143 km (89 miles) on autoroute A4

5 Disneyland Paris After a disappointing start, things have turned around for this all-American institution in Paris. In 1992 the 4,806-acre resort and amusement park opened in **Marne-la-Vallée** only 32 kilometers (20 miles) east of central Paris, offering a **Magic Kingdom** theme park similar to those in California, Florida, and Japan, as well as six hotels, 29 restaurants, a campground, a golf course, and office, retail, and residential space. Originally called **Euro Disneyland**, the $2.5-billion property lost $1.1 billion in its first year, but announced its first quarterly profit in the summer of 1995 and has steadily increased since then. In addition to adopting a new name, the amusement park has introduced 11 new attractions in recent years in an effort to boost attendance; among them is **Space Mountain**, a rollercoaster that reaches the speed of 47 miles per hour—20 percent faster than any other Disney ride. Like its American counterparts, the amusement park is divided into five major "lands": **Adventureland**, **Discoveryland**, **Fantasyland**, **Frontierland**, and **Main Street, USA**. And, like the US parks, there tend to be lines at the ticket windows and for the rides inside. ◆ Admission. Hours vary according to day and season; call ahead. Drive east on autoroute A4, 32 km (20 miles), or take the RER A4 train to Marne-la-Vallée/Chessy. 01.60.30.60.30

6 Vaux-le-Vicomte When Nicolas Fouquet, superintendent of finances for Louis XIV, threw a housewarming party in July 1661 to celebrate the completion of this château, he spared no expense. Molière's troupe was there to perform; the guests ate from solid-gold plates; and horses, jewels, and swords

Vaux-le-Vicomte

were the party favors. But this excess was not generous enough. Because he neglected to offer the château itself to the seethingly jealous king, Fouquet was thrown in prison on trumped-up charges. Louis then commandeered the architects and artisans who had built the château and put them to work on what was to be the royal palace at **Versailles**. Today, Fouquet's château is the largest private property in France. It's generally uncrowded and beautifully restored, and the gardens, which cover more than 125 acres, are simply stunning. ♦ Admission. Daily April through October; daily 2-5PM November through February; closed one week at Christmas. 58 km (36 miles) from Paris. Take the train to Melun, 5 km (3 miles) from the château, and take a taxi to the château (the driver may take the scenic route getting there). Or drive on autoroute N6 via Melun. If Fontainebleau is also on your must-see list, take the Paris Vision day-trip tour (see "Orientation" chapter), which includes both sites. 01.42.60.30.01

7 Château de Fontainebleau and Barbizon Newly returned from ignominious imprisonment in Spain, French King François I (who reigned from 1515 to 1547) was determined to recoup his dignity by creating a new court that would dazzle the world. He chose an old hunting lodge in the forest of Fontainebleau as its site and commanded the services of scores of Italian artists and craftsmen, who, the artist Vasari wrote, turned it into a "new Rome."

Keep in mind that the château is the size of an entire town; to tour it even casually requires at least a couple of hours. And that doesn't count a tour of the **Fontainebleau Forest**, a magnificent 96-square-mile expanse of towering trees and dramatic promontories where you can ride, climb rocks, or simply walk. At one edge of the forest is the hamlet of Barbizon, once the hub of the pre-Impressionist movement of painting. Rousseau, Millet, Daubigny, and Corot painted here, and many of their houses and studios have been lovingly restored and opened to the public. ♦ Admission. M, W-Su. Paris Vision and Cityrama (see "Orientation" chapter) offer day-trip tours. Or take the train from Gare de Lyon to the Fontainebleau station and then a bus to the palace. If driving, follow autoroute A6 or N7 66 km (41 miles) southeast of Paris. 01.60.71.50.70.

8 Loire Valley The Loire Valley would be a perfect destination for a day trip were it not for the profusion of magnificent châteaux: Two weeks spent in the valley would only begin to do it justice. Throughout the centuries French nobles have chosen to build their country houses along this calm river with lush banks. Visit as many châteaux as you can— **Chambord, Chenonceaux, Cheverny, Chinon, Loches,** and **Villandry** are particularly

beautiful. But take your time, each château warrants at least a morning of contemplation. Save your afternoons for wine-tasting. For information about this region, contact **Comités Régionaux de Tourisme, Pays de Loire Hôtel de Région** (2 Rue de la Loire, 44200 Nantes, 02.40.48.24.20) or **Centre-Val de Loire** (9 Rue St-Pierre-Lentin, 45041 Orléans Cedex, 02.38.54.95.42). ♦ 230 km (143 miles) from Paris. Take the train to Tours or Blois and from there catch a bus to Chambord or Cheverny (two buses M, W, and F). Paris Vision and Cityrama (see "Orientation" chapter) offer day tours to Cheverny, Chenonceaux, and Chaumont. If traveling by car, follow autoroute A10 to the city of Tours

9 Chartres The cathedral at Chartres must be among the most spiritual places in the world. Though the town has changed dramatically since the building of the cathedral, you can still see the signature spire cutting into the sky above the wheat fields, a sight that for medieval pilgrims meant they had reached one of five primary holy places to be visited on the path to heaven. Carved in the cathedral's celebrated portals and glowing in its stained-glass windows, Bible stories unfold with an overwhelming panoply of symbols and images. This imagery is brilliantly interpreted by Malcolm Miller—an English scholar who has devoted decades to research and writing on the cathedral—during his morning and afternoon tours. Before or after the tour, spend some time alone sitting in a pew and

Chartres Cathedral

absorb the majesty of the cathedral. The 12th- and 13th-century stained-glass windows (the finest in France) are so brilliant that in medieval times peasants believed they were made of ground-up gems. Modern science disproves this notion, but no one has explained how medieval glassmakers at Chartres created such beauty.

After touring the cathedral, stroll around the old town and along the banks of the Eure River. Or explore the area on two wheels—there are bicycles for rent at Place Pierre-Semard. If you are interested in 20th-century folk art, visit **Picassiette's House** (20 Rue du Repos, 02.37.34.10.78), an extraordinary complex of rooms, chapels, and gardens constructed entirely from broken glass by a cemetery worker; there's an admission charge. **Picassiette's House** is a 30-minute walk or a five-minute taxi ride from the cathedral and is only open a few hours a week; inquire about the schedule at the tourist office in the Place de la Cathédrale (02.37.21.50.00) before you set out. Stay overnight at **Château d'Esclimont** (02.37.31.15.15), a gorgeous 16th-century castle just 15 kilometers (9 miles) from Chartres in St-Symphorien-Le-Château. ♦ 100 km (62 miles) from Paris. Trains leave from the Gare Montparnasse; Paris Vision and Cityrama (see "Orientation" chapter) offer half-day trips. If traveling by car, take autoroute A11 or N10

10 Parc de St-Cloud For true escapists, this 1,100-acre park, lying just outside of Paris and landscaped by André Le Nôtre, is a little dream come true: a province of leafy woods that is a world apart from the urban bustle and a delight for children. For just a few francs, you can rent a tandem bicycle and take a romantic ride by the park's 17th-century fountains. ♦ By car, leave Paris from Porte Maillot and follow N185 through the Bois de Boulogne and across the Seine in the direction of Suresnes. Continue on N185 through St-Cloud and into the park. Métro: Boulogne–Pont de St-Cloud

11 Château de Versailles What can you say about the palace that has everything? On a royal whim, Louis XIV transformed a small hunting lodge bordering a marsh into the most lavish statement of monarchic privilege that has ever existed. Owing to just such excesses, the monarchy has long since fallen, but **Versailles** has not. Since 1978 the French government has spent over $19 million on the restoration of this palace, concentrating on 50 rooms in the more private family apartments. Unfortunately, the splendor can be numbing: One grand hall begins to resemble the next soon. To get the most from a visit, read up on the palace's history beforehand and reserve plenty of time for loitering. Indeed, some visitors prefer to spend the entire day just wandering in the 250 acres of gardens.

Designed by the incomparable André Le Nôtre, the gardens are too big to be crowded and too varied to bore. The air smells of damp earth and the place is as quiet as Eden, but the precise geometry and balance of the designs betray the fact that nature, along with everything else, was forced to bow before the Sun King. The famous fountains, **Grandes Eaux**, splash at 3:30PM on Sundays from May through September. The **Neptune Basin** floodlight-and-fireworks show is held four times a year; find out when—it's worth the trip. ♦ Admission to château. Château: Tu-Su; gardens: daily. Paris Vision and Cityrama (see "Orientation" chapter) offer various tours. If traveling by RER, take the C line from the Invalides or St-Michel stations and get off at the Versailles-RG station. Or take the métro to Pont-de-Sèvres and transfer to bus 171. Trains leave from Gare Montparnasse. Cars should follow autoroute N10, 24 km (15 miles) southwest of Paris. 01.30.84.76.18

12 Château de St-Germain-en-Laye For Louis XIV, this fortress in the town of St-Germain-en-Laye meant security. Born and bred in St-Germain, he later took refuge here during the popular uprising in 1648-53 known as the *Fronde*. Built in 1122 around a château that guarded the western flank of Paris, **St-Germain-en-Laye** contains an earlier version of Paris's **Sainte-Chapelle** (though it has long been without its glass), also designed by architect **Pierre de Montreuil**. Today the château also houses the **Musée des Antiquités Nationales**. The château's gardens were designed by the industrious André Le Nôtre before he was whisked away to landscape **Versailles**. In one corner of the gardens is the **Pavillon Henri IV** (21 Rue Thiers, 01.39.10.15.15), where Louis XIV was born and Alexandre Dumas wrote *The Three Musketeers*. Since 1830 this building has also been a restaurant/hotel and a good place to lunch overlooking the Seine. ♦ Admission. M, W-Su. Take the RER directly to the St-Germain-en-Laye terminal or the 158 bus from La Défense. By car, it's a 19-km (12-mile) drive west on autoroute N13. 01.34.51.53.65

13 Villa Savoye More than 70 years after its conception, this structure continues to be a striking evocation of modernist architectural purity. The last of several houses built in and around Paris in the 1920s by **Le Corbusier**, this "machine for living" synthesized many of the radical ideas the great Swiss architect espoused in his book *Vers une Architecture*. **Le Corbusier** wished to build a new type of bourgeois suburban villa, one that would reflect the precise, controlled rationalism made possible by modern technology. The result is an independent domestic mechanism separated from the landscape, which, in this case, it barely even touches. The villa is essentially an L-shaped series of rooms laid into a square tray that is elevated on slender *pilotis* (columns). As you travel on a continuous internal ramp into the building, you experience various light-filled spaces that eventually dissolve into the open air of the rooftop solarium. The strip windows, glass walls, flat roofs, cubic forms, and grid of columns were revolutionary at the time but now are familiar components of the International style that **Le Corbusier** helped establish. For more information on **Le Corbusier**, see **Le Corbusier Foundation** on page 250. ♦ Admission. M, W-Su. 82 Chemin de Villiers, Poissy. Take RER A5 to Poissy. By car, take autoroute N13; the villa is 24 km (15 miles) northwest of Paris. 01.39.65.01.06

14 Giverny Anyone who's seen the beloved Claude Monet water lily paintings knows what this place looks like. Monet's Normandy house and gardens have been well-tended and restored, looking much as they did when the Impressionist painter lived here from 1883 to 1926. After the **Académie des Beaux-Arts** moved Monet's paintings to the **Musée Marmottan** (see page 250) in Paris in 1966, **Giverny** was neglected. Grass grew in the studio and a staircase caved in. But a renovation that was begun in 1977 and funded in part by Lila Acheson Wallace has awakened its former charms. Unfortunately, this is no secret, so on weekends and in warm weather tourists swarm over the four-acre property.

Spring, when the early flowers are blooming and before the foreign tide hits France, is the best time to visit this horticultural/artistic shrine. Autumn, when you'll be able to see all the colors of the great painter's palette but with fewer distractions, is another good time. Two unexpected pleasures to be found here: Monet's collection of Japanese prints on display in the house, and the reproductions of the blue-and-yellow plates and cups designed by Monet on sale in the gift shop. ♦ Admission. Tu-Su; closed November through March. 48 km (30 miles) northwest of Paris. Trains leave from Gare St-Lazare in the direction of Rouen. Get off at Vernon, which is about four miles from Giverny, and take a bus or taxi. Citirama offers seasonal tours. Drivers should take the Normandy autoroute N13 and exit at Bonnières. 02.32.51.28.21

15 Honfleur and Deauville Normandy, with its rugged coast, is the country of camembert, Calvados, apple orchards, and brick-and-beam-crossed plaster houses topped by steep shingled gables. Honfleur is one of the coast's most solidly Norman and picturesque harbors; Samuel de Champlain departed from here in 1608 to found Québec. Don't miss the Saturday morning market bustling around the old wooden **Ste-Catherine** church. The old port section of Honfleur has many seafood eateries, and just outside of town lies **La Ferme St-Siméon** (Rue Adolphe-Marais,

14600 Honfleur, 02.31.89.23.61), one of Normandy's finest restaurants.

Farther west along the coast is Deauville, the summer playground of Europe's social elite. Known for its casinos, private mansions, racetracks, and an American film festival each fall, Deauville has a broad boardwalk and sandy stretch of beach that is a mere two-hour train ride from the center of Paris. ♦ 200 km (124 miles) from Paris. Follow the Normandy autoroute A13 and exit at Beuzeville. Trains leave frequently from Gare St-Lazare

15 D-Day Beaches Before arriving at the D-Day beaches, you pass **Dives-Sur-Mer**, the site from which William the Conqueror embarked in 1066 to vanquish England. It was an important moment in history, but farther from memory than the events of 6 June 1944. Just to the west, in Bénouville, is the **Pegasus Bridge**, the first spot taken by the Allies in **Normandy**. Farther on, the D-Day beaches begin, each with its own museum, its own monuments, and its own stories to tell. The most heartrending sight is the American cemetery at **Omaha Beach**, 16 km (10 miles) short of Pointe du Hoc, where 9,000 of the 23,000 Americans killed in the invasion are buried. Even if you have come to experience modern history and the sorrows of the victors, it is worth visiting Bayeux to see the magnificent 231-foot-long **Bayeux Tapestry** (1076) depicting William's conquests and the Norman invasion of England—a good meditation on the constancy of war. The tapestry is located in the **Centre Guillaume le Conquérant** (13 *bis* Rue de Nesmond, off Rue Larcher, 02.31.92.05.48), which is open daily. ♦ 230 km (143 miles) from Paris. Follow the Normandy autoroute A13 west via Caen and Bayeux

16 Musée National de la Coopération Franco-Américaine Created by a host of Vanderbilts and other Social Register Americans, French countesses, and expatriate Yank writers who supported France's role in World War I, the museum was built in the ruins of a 17th-century château by **Salomon de Brosse**, architect of the **Luxembourg Palace** in Paris. In 1989 it was renovated for France's bicentennial by Frenchman **Yves Lion** and Canadian **Alan Levitt**. Exhibits include hundreds of historic war photographs, war memorabilia, and a collection of graceful late 19th- and 20th-century paintings, drawings, and sculptures on loan from the **Musée d'Orsay**. Represented here are Whistler, Calder, and Childe Hassam, as well as French artists who worked in America. ♦ Admission for museum. Museum: M, W-Su; gardens: daily. Château de Blérancourt, Blérancourt. 110 km (68 miles) from Paris. By car, take autoroute A1 north and exit at Compiègne, heading in the direction of Noyon. At Noyon, continue toward Coucy-Soissons-Blérancourt. 03.23.39.69.86

History

300 BC A tribe called the Parisii lives in a small settlement known as **Lutetia** on what is the modern-day **Ile de la Cité.** These early hunters and fishermen are well organized; they circulate their own gold coins.

52 BC After a fierce resistance effort during which most of their settlement is destroyed, the Parisii are conquered by the Romans. Lutetia is rebuilt and spreads out to the left bank of the **Seine.** Roman prefects rule from a compound on the site of the **Palais de la Cité,** the place from which future French kings will rule.

AD 100 Trade and fishing are the main commercial activities of Lutetia. Boatmen play a central role in government and in the thriving economy of the young town. A coat of arms bearing the likeness of a boat and representing the Boatmen's Guild becomes the official symbol of Lutetia. A similar coat of arms remains the official seal of modern Paris.

250 St. Denis (or Dionysius) leads a Christian mission to the city and establishes a community near the Seine. Twenty years later, Denis, the first bishop of what will become Paris, is killed at **Montmartre** (Martyr's Mount . . . or Mount of Mercury).

276 Lutetia continues to grow beyond the confines of the original settlement on Ile de la Cité, but the outlying parts of the city are vulnerable to attack by barbarians. A raid destroys the left bank settlements and forces the villagers to retreat to the island, where they build a fortified wall.

300 Lutetia becomes known as Paris.

450 Attila the Hun and his armies rampage through Europe and come close to taking Paris but are turned back at **Orléans.** The prayers of a 27-year-old nun named Geneviève are credited with halting the Huns' advance on Paris. She later becomes the female patron saint of Paris.

452 King Childebert builds a church in an open pasture on the outskirts of Paris. In later centuries, the church is repeatedly destroyed by invaders and rebuilt. The final building, erected in 1163, is named **St-Germain-des-Prés** after St. Germanus, an early bishop of the city.

476 An invading tribe of Franks, under the leadership of King Clovis, captures Paris from the Gauls, marking the end of Roman rule over Paris and the founding of France. Clovis and the Franks convert to Christianity.

508 King Clovis makes Paris the capital of his kingdom of Franks, settling in the **Palais de la Cité.** Thus begins the Merovingian dynasty, which will rule until the eighth century.

751 The first of the Carolingian kings assumes the French throne. The dynasty is named for Charlemagne, who went on to rule the entire Western World as head of the Holy Roman Empire. Charlemagne subsequently makes **Aix-la-Chapelle** (Aachen) his foremost city, and Paris declines.

885 Paris in the Middle Ages is under constant attack by roaming tribes, most notably the Normans.

After decades of invasions and sieges, the Normans are defeated by Count Eudes, who is later crowned king of France.

987 Hugh Capet, a Parisian nobleman, becomes king of France and moves the throne back to Paris.

1050 King Henri I, grandson of Hugh Capet, appoints a representative called the *prévôt de Paris* (provost of Paris) to function as mayor of the city and maintain order.

1100 A marketplace in **Les Halles** appears for the first time. A permanent market is built about 80 years later and survives in the same location until 1969.

1135 The **Basilique de St-Denis** is built on the outskirts of Paris in the new Gothic style.

1163 Pope Alexander III lays the foundation stone for the cathedral of **Notre-Dame,** based on a design sketched out by Bishop Maurice de Sully. Work takes two centuries to complete.

1171 An ancient, loosely organized association of river merchants and fishermen is formally chartered as a guild by King Louis VII. The guild receives monopoly rights to river trade, and its coat of arms is adopted by Paris as the city's official seal. The guild becomes immensely powerful.

1180 King Philip II begins an extensive building program in Paris. A 30-foot-high city wall is built and, within it, the **Louvre** fortress is constructed. Streets are paved and outlying settlements are chartered as towns.

1190 King Philip II leaves Paris to lead a crusade. In his absence, he leaves the Boatmen's Guild, not the provost, in charge of Paris.

1215 The **University of Paris** is founded.

1220 The crown cedes to the Boatmen's Guild all tariff-collection rights, another sign of the growing power of the guilds. Paris is now clearly divided into three separate entities. The government is located on the Cité, the **Rive Gauche** (Left Bank) is dominated by university and academic life, and the **Rive Droite** (Right Bank) is home to most commercial activity.

1239 King Louis IX purchases sacred relics—including the crown of thorns and pieces of the cross—from the Emperor of Constantinople and later builds the Gothic **Sainte-Chapelle** (Holy Chapel) to house them.

1253 The **Sorbonne** is founded. The world-famous university begins as lodgings for a handful of theology students. It expands quickly, and by the late 13th century is headquarters for the **University of Paris** and has more than 15,000 students. (Except for a period shortly after the Revolution, it has remained open continuously to the present.)

1260 Louis IX appoints the Boatmen's Guild to administer the affairs of the city. The power of the guild is beginning to threaten that of the king.

1300 The earliest surviving house in Paris is built.

1337 As France sinks into the drawn-out campaigns of the Hundred Years' War, building and expansion in Paris come to a virtual standstill.

1348 The plague, also called the Black Death, rages throughout Europe. Paris is hit particularly hard; thousands die.

1357 Etienne Marcel, leader of the Boatmen's Guild and an early mayor of Paris, leads a revolt against the young King Charles V. The king moves the royal residence to the **Marais** district. Marcel establishes a city council at the **Place de l'Hôtel-de-Ville,** site of the present seat of Paris city government. Marcel later allies himself with the British and is subsequently killed by a mob.

1364 Restored to power after the death of Marcel, King Charles V builds a new city wall around Paris.

1370 Wary of an uprising and threats against his rule by the powerful guilds, Charles V has his provost build a fortified palace called the **Bastille.** The eight-towered palace is later converted into a prison and becomes a symbol of corruption and abuse of power.

1413 Construction begins on **Pont Notre-Dame.**

1420 English armies under Henry V capture France. John Plantagenet, Duke of Bedford, is appointed regent of France. France is under British rule.

1429 Joan of Arc leads an attack on Paris in an effort to win back and liberate the city. She is wounded in the unsuccessful siege.

1431 King Henry VI of England dispenses with the regency and has himself crowned King of France in **Notre-Dame** cathedral.

1437 Charles VII leads a counterattack against the British and succeeds in recapturing Paris.

1453 With the Hundred Years War finally over, Paris can begin rebuilding after years of neglect. Recovery is slow but steady.

1510 The **Hôtel de Cluny,** originally built in 1330 but largely destroyed during the invasions, wars, and revolutions that followed, is rebuilt. (It now houses the **Musée de Cluny**).

1527 King François I tears down most of the original structures of the **Louvre.**

1529 The prestigious **Collège de France** is founded by King François I.

1534 Ignatius Loyola and some of his followers take the vows that lead to the founding of the religious order called the Society of Jesus, whose members are known as Jesuits.

1537 A law is passed to ensure that at least one copy of every book published in France is kept in a royal library. The **Bibliothèque Nationale** (National Library) is founded.

1546 François I reestablishes Paris as the seat of royalty and commissions the building of a new Italian Renaissance palace on the grounds of the **Louvre.**

1559 Henri II dies of wounds received in a jousting tournament. His widow, Catherine de Médicis, has the **Maison des Tournelles** in the Marais demolished and commissions a new palace at the **Tuileries.**

1564 The **Palais des Tuileries** is completed. Designed by **Philibert Delorme,** it connects the two corner pavilions of the **Louvre** and takes its name from the *tuile* (tile) factories that had previously stood on the site. (It is razed in 1882-84.)

1572 Charles IX orders the assassination of 3,000 Huguenots on St. Bartholomew's Day.

1578 Work starts on the **Pont-Neuf.**

1594 Henri IV converts to Catholicism, settles in Paris, and continues building and expanding the **Louvre** and **Tuileries** palaces.

1605 Henri IV commissions a new palace in the Marais district.

1610 While waiting to move into his new palace, Henri IV is killed, becoming the only king to die within the **Louvre.**

1612 Under Louis XIII the Marais district becomes fashionable with the aristocracy.

1616 Marie de Médicis, Henri IV's widow, orders the construction of an avenue called the **Cours-la-Reine** (Queen's Way)

1627 The development of **Ile St-Louis** begins.

1631 The **Palais du Luxembourg** is built for Marie de Médicis; she never actually occupies the structure.

1632 Cardinal Richelieu commissions the **Palais Cardinal** (now the **Palais Royal**).

1635 The **Institut de France,** home of the prestigious **Académie Française,** is founded.

1666 Landscaper André Le Nôtre creates a wide, tree-lined avenue dubbed the **Grand Cours.** It is later renamed the **Avenue des Champs-Elysées.**

1672 Louis XIV transfers the court to **Versailles.** Most of the aristocracy follows.

1676 The **Hôtel des Invalides** is founded by Louis XIV to shelter several thousand veterans, most destitute.

1685 The **Place Vendôme** is built as a setting for a monument to Louis XIV. During the Revolution the monument is destroyed and the heads of victims of the guillotine are displayed on spikes, giving it the temporary name **Place des Piques** (Pike Square).

1718 The **Palais de l'Elysée** is built. Since 1873, it has been the official residence of the French president.

1728 The **Palais Bourbon** is constructed by the Duchess of Bourbon, one of Louis XIV's daughters. Today it houses the **Assemblée Nationale,** the lower house of the French Parliament.

1744 Louis XV vows to build a temple dedicated to St. Geneviève if he recovers from an illness. He does recover and builds the **Panthéon,** which later becomes a necropolis for France's distinguished atheists, among them Voltaire, Rousseau, and Hugo.

1755 Louis XV commissions a large square beside the Seine as the site for an equestrian statue of himself. The resulting 21-acre **Place de la Concorde** is the largest square in Paris.

1786 The remains of the dead from the **Cimetière des Innocents** are moved to the **Catacombs.**

1789 A mob storms the **Bastille** prison on 14 July, captures the ammunition depot, releases the half-prisoners kept there, kills the warden, and destroys the fortress. The French Revolution has begun.

1792 The **Comédie Française,** France's most prestigious theater troupe, moves into a new theater at the **Palais Royal.**

1793 A bloodthirsty mob takes over Paris and conducts a massacre of former government officials. Louis XVI is guillotined in the Place de la Concorde. During the next 13 months the Reign of Terror kills thousands, most executed at the guillotine.

1804 Napoléon crowns himself emperor in a ceremony at **Notre-Dame.**

1806 On Napoléon's orders, work commences on the **Arc de Triomphe.** The structure is not completed until 1836, well after Napoléon's downfall.

1840 Napoléon's remains are transported to **Les Invalides.**

1841 The church of **Ste-Marie Madeleine,** better known as **La Madeleine,** is consecrated.

1848 The revolutionary fervor spreading throughout Europe is especially strong in Paris. The monarchy is overthrown once and for all.

1850 Baron Haussmann begins a series of public works projects and restorations that over the next two decades completely transform Paris.

1860 The city of Paris expands its boundaries by annexing outlying villages, including Montmartre.

1870 The Franco-Prussian war brings an end to a period of growth and prosperity. The population starves during the siege of Paris and the Paris Commune is suppressed. The **Palais des Tuileries** and the **Hôtel de Ville** are virtually destroyed.

1875 The **Opéra Garnier,** also known as the **Paris Opéra,** opens. Designed by **Charles Garnier,** the opulent Second Empire structure is for a time the largest theater in the world.

1876 Work commences on the **Basilique du Sacré-Coeur** in Montmartre. Construction will take decades.

1889 Amidst considerable controversy and opposition, the **Tour Eiffel** (Eiffel Tower), designed by **Gustave Eiffel,** is built for the International Exposition. It later becomes the most widely recognized symbol of Paris.

1900 The first underground railway line in Paris (the métro) opens. The **Grand Palais, Petit Palais,** and **Pont Alexandre III** are built for the International Exposition. The city enjoys a period of commercial and artistic growth known as the Belle Epoque.

1914 During World War I, Paris is saved from a German invasion by the Battle of the Marne.

1920 Montparnasse replaces Montmartre as the center of artistic life in the city.

1937 The **Palais de Chaillot** is built for another International Exposition. The structure houses four museums, two theaters, a library, and a restaurant.

1940 In the early days of World War II, the city is bombed. But France falls quickly and occupation rather than destruction follows.

1944 Paris is liberated by the Allies. General Charles de Gaulle leads a victory parade down the Champs-Elysées.

1950 Existentialism is in full bloom and its major proponents, Jean-Paul Sartre and Albert Camus, are the intellectual stars of Europe. Paris is once again a center of intellectual fervor.

1962 The **Mémorial de la Déportation** (Deportation Memorial) opens, commemorating the thousands of French, mostly Jews, who died during the Holocaust.

1968 Student demonstrations in the **Latin Quarter** and violent labor disputes throughout the city threaten to topple the government.

1969 The market at Les Halles is moved to a suburb of Paris.

1977 Much like the **Eiffel Tower** of the last century, the **Centre Georges Pompidou** opens to a critical outcry. It quickly becomes the most popular tourist destination in Paris.

1985 The **Musée Picasso** opens and becomes an immediate hit.

1986 The **Musée d'Orsay,** a showcase for 19th-century art and culture, is unveiled.

1988 The renovation of the Les Halles district is completed.

1989 As the bicentennial of the fall of the **Bastille** is celebrated, a new addition to the **Louvre** is greeted with tremendous criticism. Designed by American architect **I.M. Pei,** the project includes a 70.5-foot glass pyramid. Again, the critics are silenced by enormous crowds of visitors.

1992 The inaugural performance is held at the new **Opéra Bastille.** The huge new opera house revitalizes the Bastille area.

1995 Socialist President François Mitterrand's 14-year term comes to an end. Conservative leader Jacques Chirac, former mayor of Paris, is elected president of the republic.

1996 President Jacques Chirac declares the banning of nuclear tests in the South Pacific. . . Writer Marguerite Duras dies at age 81. Author of more than 70 books, she is most famous for *The Lover.*

1997 After dissolution of the Assembly National by President Jacques Chirac, the Socialist Party obtained majority vote, and Lionel Jospin was named Prime Minister. Europepride 97, a Gay Rights landmark event, took place in Paris. Princess Diana Spencer is killed in a car accident.

Index

Index

Index

Hotels

The hotels listed below are grouped according to their price ratings; they are also listed in the main index. The hotel price ratings reflect the base price of a standard room for two people for one night during the peak season.

$$$$ Big Bucks ($300 and up)
$$$ Expensive ($150-$300)
$$ Reasonable ($75-$150)
$ The Price Is Right (less than $75)

$$$$